# Study Guide

(9) 339 to end
to read

363 to end

(10) 347 - 368. emotions

# STUDY GUIDE

## Richard O. Straub
University of Michigan, Dearborn

with
Focus on Vocabulary and Language
by *Cornelius Rea*
Douglas College, British Columbia

to accompany

*David G. Myers*

# Exploring Psychology
Fourth Edition

WORTH PUBLISHERS

**Study Guide**
by Richard O. Straub
to accompany
Myers: **Exploring Psychology**, Fourth Edition

Copyright © 1999, 1996, 1993, 1990 by Worth Publishers, Inc.

Printed in the United States of America

ISBN: 1–57259–676–7

Printing:  5  4  3  2

Year:  01  00  99

Cover: Alexej Jawlensky, *Kopf* / Christie's Images.

**Worth Publishers**
33 Irving Place
New York, New York 10003

# Contents

# Preface

This Study Guide is designed for use with *Exploring Psychology*, Fourth Edition, by David G. Myers. It is intended to help you to learn material in the textbook, to evaluate your understanding of that material, and then to review any problem areas. Beginning on page ix, "How to Manage Your Time Efficiently and Study More Effectively" provides detailed instructions on how to use the textbook and this Study Guide for maximum benefit. It also offers additional study suggestions based on principles of time management, effective notetaking, evaluation of exam performance, and an effective program for improving your comprehension while studying from textbooks.

The fourth edition of this Study Guide offers many useful features. Each chapter includes three review tests: In addition to the two Progress Tests that focus on facts and definitions, there is a Thinking Critically Test that evaluates your understanding of the text chapter's broader conceptual material and its application to real-world situations. This test contains 20 multiple-choice questions and an essay question. For all three review tests, the correct answers are given, followed by textbook page references (so you can easily go back and reread the material), and complete explanations not only of why the answer is correct but also of why the other choices are incorrect. Detailed guidelines for the objectives in the Study Guide are provided. These guidelines are useful for a section-by-section review of each textbook chapter and as a source of additional essay questions. In addition, each chapter includes Focus on Vocabulary and Language, written by Cornelius Rea of Douglas College, British Columbia. This section provides brief, clear explanations of some of the idioms and expressions used by David Myers that may be unfamiliar to some students. They are first listed in the relevant section of the Guided Study, then explained at the back of the chapter.

Some new features have been added to this Study Guide. As appropriate, chapters may include a Web Sighting, which is a brief Internet activity in which students are directed to one or more web sites to extend their exploration of concepts and issues discussed in the chapter. Some chapters also include a Cross-Check, which provides an engaging crossword puzzle review of chapter terms and concepts. Other chapters include fill-in-the-blank flow charts, which promote a deeper understanding of the conceptual relationships among chapter issues.

### General Internet Resources

In addition to the specific web exercises provided throughout this Study Guide, you might want to consult some web sites that provide general information about psychology-related topics. David Mahony's Psychology Internet Resource List

(PIRL) is an effort to compile all psychology-related material, including mailing lists, discussion groups, World Wide Web (WWW) sites, File Transfer Protocol (FTP) sites for downloading files from other machines, and Gopher sites for locating items on the Internet through a series of nested menus. The PIRL, now in its third edition, is available at the following WWW site: http://www.gasou.edu/psychweb/psychweb.html.

Deborah Kelley-Milburn and Michael A. Milburn's "Cyberspace: Resources for Psychologists on the Internet" (*Psychological Science*, [1995, July], Volume 6, pp. 203–211) provides another excellent resource. This feature review provides helpful information on Listservs, Usenet groups, electronic journals and newsletters, databases, grant and job information, and library catalogues.

Psych Web with host Russ Dewey, which opened April 15, 1995, also provides a good source of information. Currently available at this location are web-accessible psychology resources sorted by topic, a separate list of psychology self-help resources on the Internet, and a stereogram gallery containing public images that you can print out. The location is as follows:

http://www.gasou.edu/psychweb/psychweb.htm

Both the American Psychological Association (APA) and the American Psychological Society have Internet services. These services provide not only information about their organizations but also selected articles from their main journals, information about current research in the discipline, and links to other science-related sites on the Internet. Their locations are as follows:

APA: http://www.apa.org/   and   APS: http://psych.hanover.edu/aps/

Finally, and perhaps most important, is Psychtalk, a list for students interested in discussion topics and controversies related to psychology. Topics that have been discussed over the past few years include child abuse, the nature-nurture issue, homosexuality, and pornography. To subscribe, send a message to:

psychtalk-request@fre.fsu.umd.edu

The message should read "subscribe psychtalk (your name)."

### Acknowledgments

I would like to thank all the students and instructors who used this Study Guide in its first two editions and provided such insightful and useful suggestions. Special thanks are also due to Betty Shapiro Probert for her extraordinary editorial contributions. Most important, I want to thank my wonderful children—Jeremy, Rebecca, and Melissa—and my partner Pam, for their enduring love and patience.

Richard O. Straub
May 1998

# How to Manage Your Time Efficiently and Study More Effectively

How effectively do you study? Good study habits make the job of being a college student much easier. Many students, who *could* succeed in college, fail or drop out because they have never learned to manage their time efficiently. Even the best students can usually benefit from an in-depth evaluation of their current study habits.

There are many ways to achieve academic success, of course, but your approach may not be the most effective or efficient. Are you sacrificing your social life or your physical or mental health in order to get A's on your exams? Good study habits result in better grades *and* more time for other activities.

## Evaluate Your Current Study Habits

To improve your study habits, you must first have an accurate picture of how you currently spend your time. Begin by putting together a profile of your present living and studying habits. Answer the following questions by writing *yes* or *no* on each line.

1. Do you usually set up a schedule to budget your time for studying, recreation, and other activities?

2. Do you often put off studying until time pressures force you to cram?

3. Do other students seem to study less than you do, but get better grades?

4. Do you usually spend hours at a time studying one subject, rather than dividing that time between several subjects?

5. Do you often have trouble remembering what you have just read in a textbook?

6. Before reading a chapter in a textbook, do you skim through it and read the section headings?

7. Do you try to predict exam questions from your lecture notes and reading?

8. Do you usually attempt to paraphrase or summarize what you have just finished reading?

9. Do you find it difficult to concentrate very long when you study?

10. Do you often feel that you studied the wrong material for an exam?

Thousands of college students have participated in similar surveys. Students who are fully realizing their academic potential usually respond as follows: (1) yes, (2) no, (3) no, (4) no, (5) no, (6) yes, (7) yes, (8) yes, (9) no, (10) no.

Compare your responses to those of successful students. The greater the discrepancy, the more you could benefit from a program to improve your study habits. The questions are designed to identify areas of weakness. Once you have identified your weaknesses, you will be able to set specific goals for improvement and to implement a program for reaching them.

## Manage Your Time

Do you often feel frustrated because there isn't enough time to do all the things you must and want to do? Take heart. Even the most productive and successful people feel this way at times. But they establish priorities for their activities, and they learn to budget time for each of them. There's much in the saying "If you want something done, ask a busy person to do it." A busy person knows how to get things done.

If you don't now have a system for budgeting your time, develop one. Not only will your academic accomplishments increase, but you will actually find more time in your schedule for other activities. And you won't have to feel guilty about "taking time off," because all your obligations will be covered.

### Establish a Baseline

As a first step in preparing to budget your time, keep a diary for a few days to establish a summary, or baseline, of the time you spend in studying, socializing, working, and so on. If you are like many students, much of your "study" time is nonproductive; you may sit at your desk and leaf through a book, but the time is actually wasted. Or you may procrastinate. You are always getting ready to study, but you rarely do.

Besides revealing where you waste time, your diary will give you a realistic picture of how much time you need to allot for meals, commuting, and other fixed activities. In addition, careful records should indicate the times of the day when you are consistently most productive. A sample time-management diary is shown in Table 1.

### Plan the Term

Having established and evaluated your baseline, you are ready to devise a more efficient schedule. Buy a calendar that covers the entire school term and has ample space for each day. Using the course outlines provided by your instructors, enter the dates of all exams, term paper deadlines, and other important academic obligations. If you have any long-range personal plans (concerts, weekend trips, etc.), enter the dates on the calendar as well. Keep your calendar up to date and refer to it often. I recommend carrying it with you at all times.

### Develop a Weekly Calendar

Now that you have a general picture of the school term, develop a weekly schedule that includes all of your activities. Aim for a schedule that you can live with for the entire school term. A sample weekly schedule, incorporating the following guidelines, is shown in Table 2.

1. Enter your class times, work hours, and any other fixed obligations first. *Be thorough.* Using information from your time-management diary, allow plenty of time for such things as commuting, meals, laundry, and the like.

Table 1    Sample Time-Management Diary

| Behavior | Time Completed | Duration Hours: Minutes |
|---|---|---|
| | Monday | |
| Sleep | 7:00 | 7:30 |
| Dressing | 7:25 | :25 |
| Breakfast | 7:45 | :20 |
| Commute | 8:20 | :35 |
| Coffee | 9:00 | :40 |
| French | 10:00 | 1:00 |
| Socialize | 10:15 | :15 |
| Video game | 10:35 | :20 |
| Coffee | 11:00 | :25 |
| Psychology | 12:00 | 1:00 |
| Lunch | 12:25 | :25 |
| Study Lab | 1:00 | :35 |
| Psych. Lab | 4:00 | 3:00 |
| Work | 5:30 | 1:30 |
| Commute | 6:10 | :40 |
| Dinner | 6:45 | :35 |
| TV | 7:30 | :45 |
| Study Psych. | 10:00 | 2:30 |
| Socialize | 11:30 | 1:30 |
| Sleep | | |

Prepare a similar chart for each day of the week. When you finish an activity, note it on the chart and write down the time it was completed. Then determine its duration by subtracting the time the previous activity was finished from the newly entered time.

2. Set up a study schedule for each of your courses. The study habits survey and your time-management diary will help direct you. The following guidelines should also be useful.

(a) Establish regular study times for each course. The 4 hours needed to study one subject, for example, are most profitable when divided into shorter periods spaced over several days. If you cram your studying into one 4-hour block, what you attempt to learn in the third or fourth hour will interfere with what you studied in the first 2 hours. Newly acquired knowledge is like wet cement. It needs some time to "harden" to become memory.

(b) Alternate subjects. The type of interference just mentioned is greatest between similar topics. Set up a schedule in which you spend time on several *different* courses during each study session. Besides reducing the potential for interference, alternating subjects will help to prevent mental fatigue with one topic.

(c) Set weekly goals to determine the amount of study time you need to do well in each course. This will depend on, among other things, the difficulty of your courses and the effectiveness of your methods. Many

Table 2             Sample Weekly Schedule

| Time | Mon. | Tues. | Wed. | Thurs. | Fri. | Sat. |
|---|---|---|---|---|---|---|
| 7–8 | Dress Eat | Dress Eat | Dress Eat | Dress Eat | Dress Eat | |
| 8–9 | Psych. | Study Psych. | Psych. | Study Psych. | Psych. | Dress Eat |
| 9–10 | Eng. | Study Eng. | Eng. | Study Eng. | Eng. | Study Eng. |
| 10–11 | Study French | Free | Study French | Open Study | Study French | Study Stats. |
| 11–12 | French | Study Psych. Lab | French | Open Study | French | Study Stats. |
| 12–1 | Lunch | Lunch | Lunch | Lunch | Lunch | Lunch |
| 1–2 | Stats. | Psych. Lab | Stats. | Study or Free | Stats. | Free |
| 2–3 | Bio. | Psych. Lab | Bio. | Free | Bio. | Free |
| 3–4 | Free | Psych. | Free | Free | Free | Free |
| 4–5 | Job | Job | Job | Job | Job | Free |
| 5–6 | Job | Job | Job | Job | Job | Free |
| 6–7 | Dinner | Dinner | Dinner | Dinner | Dinner | Dinner |
| 7–8 | Study Bio. | Study Bio. | Study Bio. | Study Bio. | Free | Free |
| 8–9 | Study Eng. | Study Stats. | Study Psych. | Open Study | Open Study | Free |
| 9–10 | Open Study | Open Study | Open Study | Open Study | Free | Free |

This is a sample schedule for a student with a 16-credit load and a 10-hour-per-week part-time job. Using this chart as an illustration, make up a weekly schedule, following the guidelines outlined here.

professors recommend studying at least 1 to 2 hours for each hour in class. If your time-management diary indicates that you presently study less time than that, do not plan to jump immediately to a much higher level. Increase study time from your baseline by setting weekly goals [see (4)] that will gradually bring you up to the desired level. As an initial schedule, for example, you might set aside an amount of study time for each course that matches class time.

(d) Schedule for maximum effectiveness. Tailor your schedule to meet the demands of each course. For the course that emphasizes lecture notes, schedule time for a daily review soon after the class. This will give you a chance to revise your notes and clean up any hard-to-decipher shorthand while the material is still fresh in your mind. If you are evaluated for class participation (for example, in a language course), allow time for a review just *before* the class meets. Schedule study time for your most difficult (or least motivating) courses during hours when you are the most alert and distractions are fewest.

(e) Schedule open study time. Emergencies, additional obligations, and the like could throw off your

schedule. And you may simply need some extra time periodically for a project or for review in one of your courses. Schedule several hours each week for such purposes.

3. After you have budgeted time for studying, fill in slots for recreation, hobbies, relaxation, household errands, and the like.

4. Set specific goals. Before each study session, make a list of specific goals. The simple note "7–8 PM: study psychology" is too broad to ensure the most effective use of the time. Formulate your daily goals according to what you know you must accomplish during the term. If you have course outlines with advance assignments, set systematic daily goals that will allow you, for example, to cover fifteen chapters before the exam. And be realistic: Can you actually expect to cover a 78-page chapter in one session? Divide large tasks into smaller units; stop at the most logical resting points. When you complete a specific goal, take a 5- or 10-minute break before tackling the next goal.

5. Evaluate how successful or unsuccessful your studying has been on a daily or weekly basis. Did you

reach most of your goals? If so, reward yourself immediately. You might even make a list of five to ten rewards to choose from. If you have trouble studying regularly, you may be able to motivate yourself by making such rewards contingent on completing specific goals.

6. Finally, until you have lived with your schedule for several weeks, don't hesitate to revise it. You may need to allow more time for chemistry, for example, and less for some other course. If you are trying to study regularly for the first time and are feeling burned out, you probably have set your initial goals too high. Don't let failure cause you to despair and abandon the program. Accept your limitations and revise your schedule so that you are studying only 15 to 20 minutes more each evening than you are used to. The point is to *identify a regular schedule with which you can achieve some success.* Time management, like any skill, must be practiced to become effective.

## Techniques for Effective Study

Knowing how to put study time to best use is, of course, as important as finding a place for it in your schedule. Here are some suggestions that should enable you to increase your reading comprehension and improve your notetaking. A few study tips are included as well.

### Using SQ3R to Increase Reading Comprehension

How do you study from a textbook? If you are like many students, you simply read and reread in a *passive* manner. Studies have shown, however, that most students who simply read a textbook cannot remember more than half the material ten minutes after they have finished. Often, what is retained is the unessential material rather than the important points upon which exam questions will be based.

This Study Guide employs a program known as SQ3R (*Survey, Question, Read, Rehearse,* and *Review*) to facilitate, and allow you to assess, your comprehension of the important facts and concepts in *Exploring Psychology,* Fourth Edition, by David G. Myers.

Research has shown that students using SQ3R achieve significantly greater comprehension of textbooks than students reading in the more traditional passive manner. Once you have learned this program, you can improve your comprehension of any textbook.

**Survey**   Before you read a text chapter, determine whether the text or the study guide has an outline or list of objectives. Read this material and the summary at the end of the chapter. Next, read the textbook chapter fairly quickly, paying special attention to the major headings and subheadings. This survey will give you an idea of the chapter's contents and organization. You will then be able to divide the chapter into logical sections in order to formulate specific goals for a more careful reading of the chapter.

In this Study Guide, the *Chapter Overview* summarizes the major topics of the textbook chapter. This section also provides a few suggestions for approaching topics you may find difficult.

**Question**   You will retain material longer when you have a use for it. If you look up a word's definition in order to solve a crossword puzzle, for example, you will remember it longer than if you merely fill in the letters as a result of putting other words in. Previewing the chapter will allow you to generate important questions that the chapter will proceed to answer. These questions correspond to "mental files" into which knowledge will be sorted for easy access.

As you survey, jot down several questions for each chapter section. One simple technique is to generate questions by rephrasing a section heading. For example, the "Preoperational Thought" head could be turned into "What is preoperational thought?" Good questions will allow you to focus on the important points in the text. Examples of good questions are those that begin as follows: "List two examples of . . . ." "What is the function of . . .?" "What is the significance of . . .?" Such questions give a purpose to your reading. Similarly, you can formulate questions based on the chapter outline.

The *Guided Study* section of this Study Guide provides the types of questions you might formulate while surveying each chapter. This section is a detailed set of objectives covering the points made in the text. Guidelines for answers to these objectives are provided at the end of each chapter.

**Read**   When you have established "files" for each section of the chapter, review your first question, begin reading, and continue until you have discovered its answer. If you come to material that seems to answer an important question you don't have a file for, stop and write down the question.

Using this Study Guide, read the chapter one section at a time. First, preview the section by skimming it, noting headings and boldface items. Next, study the appropriate section objectives in the *Guided Study*. Then, as you read the chapter section, search for the answer to each objective.

Be sure to read everything. Don't skip photo or art captions, graphs, or marginal notes. In some cases, what may seem vague in reading will be made clear by a simple graph. Keep in mind that test questions are sometimes drawn from illustrations and charts.

**Rehearse**  When you have found the answer to a question, close your eyes and mentally recite the question and its answer. Then *write* the answer next to the question. It is important that you recite an answer in your own words rather than the author's. Don't rely on your short-term memory to repeat the author's words verbatim.

In responding to the objectives, pay close attention to what is called for. If you are asked to identify or list, do just that. If asked to compare, contrast, or do both, you should focus on the similarities (compare) and differences (contrast) between the concepts or theories. Answering the objectives carefully not only will help you to focus your attention on the important concepts of the text but also will provide excellent practice for essay exams.

Rehearsal is an extremely effective study technique, recommended by many learning experts. In addition to increasing reading comprehension, it is useful for review. Trying to explain something in your own words clarifies your knowledge, often by revealing aspects of your answer that are vague or incomplete. If you repeatedly rely upon "I know" in recitation, you really *may not know*.

Rehearsal has the additional advantage of simulating an exam, especially an essay exam; the same skills are required in both cases. Too often students study without ever putting the book and notes aside, which makes it easy for them to develop false confidence in their knowledge. When the material is in front of you, you may be able to *recognize* an answer, but will you be able to *recall* it later, when you take an exam that does not provide these retrieval cues?

After you have recited and written your answer, continue with your next question. Read, recite, and so on.

**Review**  When you have answered the last question on the material you have designated as a study goal, go back and review. Read over each question and your written answer to it. Your review might also include a brief written summary that integrates all of your questions and answers. This review need not take longer than a few minutes, but it is important. It will help you retain the material longer and will greatly facilitate a final review of each chapter before the exam.

In this Study Guide, the *Chapter Review* section contains fill-in and brief essay questions for you to complete after you have finished reading the text and have written answers to the objectives. The correct answers are given at the end of the chapter. Gen-

erally, your answer to a fill-in question should match exactly (as in the case of important terms, theories, or people). In some cases, the answer is not a term or name, so a word close in meaning will suffice. You should go through the *Chapter Review* several times before taking an exam, so it is a good idea to mentally fill in the answers until you are ready for a final pretest review. Textbook page references are provided with each section title, in case you need to reread any of the material.

Also provided to facilitate your review are two *Progress Tests* that include multiple-choice questions and, where appropriate, matching or true–false questions. These tests are *not* to be taken until you have read the chapter, written answers to the objectives, and completed the *Chapter Review.* Correct answers, along with explanations of why each alternative is correct or incorrect, are provided at the end of the chapter. The relevant text page numbers for each question are also given. If you miss a question, read these explanations and, if necessary, review the text pages to further understand why. The *Progress Tests* do not test every aspect of a concept, so you should treat an incorrect answer as an indication that you need to review the concept.

Following the two *Progress Tests* is a *Thinking Critically Test*, which should be taken just prior to an exam. It includes questions that test your ability to analyze, integrate, and apply the concepts in the chapter. Each *Thinking Critically Test* includes an essay question dealing with a major concept covered in the chapter. As with the *Progress Tests*, answers for the *Thinking Critically Test* are provided at the end of each chapter, along with relevant page numbers.

In most cases, the core of the chapter concludes with *Key Terms.* For chapters that contain many new technical terms, this section includes not only a list of key terms but also a crossword puzzle. *Writing Definitions* requires that you write definitions of all key terms on a separate piece of paper. *Cross-Check* reverses the process, asking you to complete a crossword puzzle by filling in the terms that apply to the definitions provided. As with the *Guided Study* objectives, it is important that these answers be written from memory, and in your own words. The *Answers* section at the end of the chapter gives a definition of each term, sometimes along with an example of its usage and/or a tip to help you remember its meaning. It also includes answers to the crossword puzzle.

Where appropriate, *Key Terms* is followed by *Summing Up*, one or two fill-in-the-blank flow charts. These charts are designed to help you integrate and apply major concepts described in the chapter.

Following the answers is a list of potentially unfamiliar idioms, words, and expressions (*Focus on Vocabulary and Language*), ordered by text page number and accompanied by definitions and examples.

This Study Guide also contains an additional section called *Web Sighting*, which describes web resources related to concepts discussed in the text chapter. In addition to serving as refreshing study break from the other sections of the Study Guide, the Web Sighting will enhance your understanding of the text material by helping you to apply it to new information. Integrating text material with this new information is an excellent way for you to learn by actively participating, rather than by merely repeating information from the text.

One final suggestion: Incorporate SQ3R into your time-management calendar. Set specific goals for completing SQ3R with each assigned chapter. Keep a record of chapters completed and reward yourself for being conscientious. Initially, it takes more time and effort to "read" using SQ3R, but with practice, the steps will become automatic. More important, you will comprehend significantly more material and retain what you have learned longer than passive readers do.

### Taking Lecture Notes

Are your class notes as useful as they might be? One way to determine their worth is to compare them with those taken by other good students. Are yours as thorough? Do they provide you with a comprehensible outline of each lecture? If not, then the following suggestions might increase the effectiveness of your notetaking.

**1.** Keep a separate notebook for each course. Use $8\frac{1}{2} \times 11$-inch pages. Consider using a ring binder, which would allow you to revise and insert notes while still preserving lecture order.

**2.** Take notes in the format of a lecture outline. Use roman numerals for major points, letters for supporting arguments, and so on. Some instructors will make this easy by delivering organized lectures and, in some cases, by outlining their lectures on the board. If a lecture is disorganized, you will probably want to reorganize your notes soon after the class.

**3.** As you take notes in class, leave a wide margin on one side of each page. After the lecture, expand or clarify any shorthand notes while the material is fresh in your mind. Use this time to write important questions in the margin next to notes that answer them.

This will facilitate later review and will allow you to anticipate similar exam questions.

## Evaluate Your Exam Performance

How often have you received a grade on an exam that did not do justice to the effort you spent preparing for the exam? This is a common experience that can leave one feeling bewildered and abused. "What do I have to do to get an A?" "The test was unfair!" "I studied the wrong material!"

The chances of this happening are greatly reduced if you have an effective time-management schedule and use the study techniques described here. But it can happen to the best-prepared student and is most likely to occur on your first exam with a new professor.

Remember that there are two main reasons for studying. One is to learn for your own general academic development. Many people believe that such knowledge is all that really matters. Of course, it is possible, though unlikely, to be an expert on a topic without achieving commensurate grades, just as one can, occasionally, earn an excellent grade without truly mastering the course material. During a job interview or in the workplace, however, your A in Cobol won't mean much if you can't actually program a computer.

In order to keep career options open after you graduate, you must know the material and maintain competitive grades. In the short run, this means performing well on exams, which is the second main objective in studying.

Probably the single best piece of advice to keep in mind when studying for exams is to *try to predict exam questions*. This means ignoring the trivia and focusing on the important questions and their answers (with your instructor's emphasis in mind).

A second point is obvious. How well you do on exams is determined by your mastery of *both* lecture and textbook material. Many students (partly because of poor time management) concentrate too much on one at the expense of the other.

To evaluate how well you are learning lecture and textbook material, analyze the questions you missed on the first exam. If your instructor does not review exams during class, you can easily do it yourself. Divide the questions into two categories: those drawn primarily from lectures and those drawn primarily from the textbook. Determine the percentage of questions you missed in each category. If your errors are evenly distributed and you are satisfied with your grade, you have no problem. If you are weaker in one area, you will need to set future goals for increasing and/or improving your study of that area.

Similarly, note the percentage of test questions drawn from each category. Although exams in most courses cover *both* lecture notes and the textbook, the relative emphasis of each may vary from instructor to instructor. While your instructors may not be entirely consistent in making up future exams, you may be able to tailor your studying for each course by placing *additional* emphasis on the appropriate area.

Exam evaluation will also point out the types of questions your instructor prefers. Does the exam consist primarily of multiple-choice, true–false, or essay questions? You may also discover that an instructor is fond of wording questions in certain ways. For example, an instructor may rely heavily on questions that require you to draw an analogy between a theory or concept and a real-world example. Evaluate both your instructor's style and how well you do with each format. Use this information to guide your future exam preparation.

Important aids, not only in studying for exams but also in determining how well prepared you are, are the *Progress* and *Thinking Critically Tests* provided in this Study Guide. If these tests don't include all of the types of questions your instructor typically writes, make up your own practice exam questions. Spend extra time testing yourself with question formats that are most difficult for you. There is no better way to evaluate your preparation for an upcoming exam than by testing yourself under the conditions most likely to be in effect during the actual test.

## A Few Practical Tips

Even the best intentions for studying sometimes fail. Some of these failures occur because students attempt to work under conditions that are simply not conducive to concentrated study. To help ensure the success of your time-management program, here are a few suggestions that should assist you in reducing the possibility of procrastination or distraction.

**1.** If you have set up a schedule for studying, make your roommate, family, and friends aware of this commitment, and ask them to honor your quiet study time. Close your door and post a "Do Not Disturb" sign.

**2.** Set up a place to study that minimizes potential distractions. Use a desk or table, not your bed or an extremely comfortable chair. Keep your desk and the walls around it free from clutter. If you need a place other than your room, find one that meets as many of the above requirements as possible—for example, in the library stacks.

**3.** Do nothing but study in this place. It should become associated with studying so that it "triggers" this activity, just as a mouth-watering aroma elicits an appetite.

**4.** Never study with the television on or with other distracting noises present. If you must have music in the background in order to mask outside noise, for example, play soft instrumental music. Don't pick vocal selections; your mind will be drawn to the lyrics.

**5.** Study by yourself. Other students can be distracting or can break the pace at which *your* learning is most efficient. In addition, there is always the possibility that group studying will become a social gathering. Reserve that for its own place in your schedule.

If you continue to have difficulty concentrating for very long, try the following suggestions.

**6.** Study your most difficult or most challenging subjects first, when you are most alert.

**7.** Start with relatively short periods of concentrated study, with breaks in between. If your attention starts to wander, get up immediately and take a break. It is better to study effectively for 15 minutes and then take a break than to fritter away 45 minutes out of an hour. Gradually increase the length of study periods, using your attention span as an indicator of successful pacing.

## Some Closing Thoughts

I hope that these suggestions help make you more successful academically, and that they enhance the quality of your college life in general. Having the necessary skills makes any job a lot easier and more pleasant. Let me repeat my warning not to attempt to make too drastic a change in your life-style immediately. Good habits require time and self-discipline to develop. Once established, they can last a lifetime.

# Study Guide

# 1

# Introduction: Thinking Critically With Psychology

## Chapter Overview

Psychology's historical development and current activities lead us to define the field as the science of behavior and mental processes. Chapter 1 discusses the development of psychology and the range of behaviors and mental processes being investigated by psychologists in each of the various specialty areas. In addition, it describes the six major perspectives from which psychologists work. This is followed by an overview of the diverse subfields in which psychologists conduct research and provide professional services.

The chapter then explains the limits of intuition and common sense in reasoning about behavior and mental processes. To counteract our human tendency toward faulty reasoning, psychologists adopt a scientific attitude that is based on healthy skepticism, open-minded humility, and critical thinking. Psychologists employ the research strategies of description, correlation, and experimentation in order to objectively describe, predict, and explain behavior.

Next, the chapter discusses several questions people often ask about psychology, including why animal research is relevant, whether laboratory experiments are ethical, whether behavior varies with culture and gender, and whether psychology's principles don't have the potential for misuse.

The chapter concludes by explaining how to get your study of psychology off on the right foot by learning (and pledging to follow!) the SQ3R study method. This study method is also discussed in the essay at the beginning of this Study Guide.

Chapter 1 should not be too difficult for you; there are not many difficult terms or theories to remember. However, the chapter does introduce a number of concepts and issues that will play an important role in later chapters. Pay particular attention to the section "How Do Psychologists Ask and Answer Questions?" Make sure you understand the method of experimentation, especially the importance of control conditions and the difference between independent and dependent variables.

NOTE: Answer guidelines for all Chapter 1 questions begin on page 16.

## Guided Study

The text chapter should be studied one section at a time. Before you read, preview each section by skimming it, noting headings and boldface items. Then read the appropriate section objectives from the following outline. Keep these objectives in mind and, as you read the chapter section, search for the information that will enable you to meet each objective. Once you have finished a section, write out answers for its objectives. Refer to the "Focus on Vocabulary and Language" on pages 24–28 for definitions of words or phrases that you do not understand.

### What Is Psychology? (pp. 2–8)

> David Myers at times uses idioms that are unfamiliar to some readers. If you do not know the meaning of any of the following words, phrases, or expressions in the context in which they appear in the text, refer to pages 24–25 for an explanation: *to remedy their woes; peekaboo; grist for psychology's mill; Magellans of the mind; unpack this definition; sift opinions and evaluate ideas; hunches; smorgasbord . . . fare; wrestled with some issues; nature-nurture tension dissolve; "red in the face"; "hot under the collar"; there is a payoff.*

1. Define *psychology* and trace its historical development.

2. Explain how psychology's different perspectives contribute to a complete view of human behavior.

3. Identify the major subfields of psychology.

## Why Do Psychology? (pp. 8–12)

> If you do not know the meaning of any of the following words, phrases, or expressions in the context in which they appear in the text, refer to pages 25–27 for an explanation: *outsmart the smartest computers; goes awry; hard-headed curiosity; leap of faith; the proof is in the pudding; auras; relegates crazy-sounding ideas to the mountain . . . , arena of competing ideas; then so much the worse for our ideas; the rat is always right; spectacles of our preconceived ideas; axe is this person grinding; gut feelings; debunked; play the tape; dresses it in jargon; after-the-fact pundits; "out of sight, out of mind"; "absence makes the heart grow fonder"; drawing the bull's eye after the arrow has struck; familiarity breeds contempt; drop a course.*

4. Discuss the attitudes that characterize scientific inquiry and explain the nature of critical thinking.

5. Identify two pitfalls in thinking that make intuition and common sense untrustworthy.

## How Do Psychologists Ask and Answer Questions? (pp. 13–28)

> If you do not know the meaning of any of the following words, phrases, or expressions in the context in which they appear in the text, refer to pages 27–28 for an explanation: *connect-the-dots-puzzle; handful of case studies; tendency to leap from unrepresentative information; numbers are numbing; anecdotes are alarming; target group; snapshot of the opinions; having affairs; flipped a coin; hot and cold streaks; laypeople; recap; voyage of discovery; wild and sometimes wacky claims.*

6. Explain the importance of theories, hypotheses, and replication in psychology.

7. Discuss the descriptive research strategies.

8. Discuss the limitations and possible pitfalls of descriptive research.

9. Describe the types of correlation and discuss why correlation enables prediction but not explanation.

10. Explain the nature and significance of illusory correlations.

11. Describe the nature and advantages of experimentation.

12. Discuss the importance of operational definitions and control techniques in research.

*Frequently Asked Questions About Psychology* (pp. 28–33)

> If you do not know the meaning of any of the following words, phrases, or expressions in the context in which they appear in the text, refer to page 28 for an explanation: *plunge in; lawn mower's engine than a Mercedes'; idle curiosity; ethics committee; values can also color "the facts"; totalitarian* Brave New World *or* 1984.

13. Discuss questions regarding the artificiality of experimentation and whether psychological principles are culture- or gender-free.

14. Explain why psychologists study animals and discuss the ethics of experimentation.

15. Describe how psychologists' values influence their work and discuss whether psychology is potentially dangerous.

*Tips for Studying Psychology* (pp. 34–36)

> If you do not know the meaning of any of the following words, phrases, or expressions from this section or the end-of-chapter Review in the context in which they appear in the text, refer to page 28 for an explanation: *spaced practice; massed practice; winnow sense from nonsense; sift reality from illusion.* (Note: the last two items are from *Reviewing Introduction.*)

**16.** Explain the SQ3R study method.

## Chapter Review

When you have finished reading the chapter, work through the material that follows to review it. Complete the sentences and answer the questions. As you proceed, evaluate your performance for each section by consulting the answers on page 10. Do not continue with the next section until you understand each answer. If you need to, review or reread the appropriate section in the textbook before continuing.

*What Is Psychology?* (pp. 2–8)

**1.** The Greek naturalist and philosopher _____ theorized about learning, memory, and other psychological phenomena.

**2.** In the 1600s, British philosopher _____ rejected the existence of _____ ideas.

**3.** In 1859, naturalist _____ explained species variation by proposing the process of _____, which works through the principle of _____ .

**4.** The first psychological laboratory was founded in 1879 by Wilhelm _____ .

**5.** The historical roots of psychology include the fields of _____ and _____ .

**6.** Some early psychologists included Ivan Pavlov, who pioneered the study of _____; the personality theorist _____; Jean Piaget, who studied _____; and _____, the author of an important 1890 psychology textbook.

**7.** In its earliest years, psychology was defined as the science of _____ life. From the 1920s into the 1960s, psychology in America was redefined as the science of _____ behavior. The author of your text defines psychology as the science of _____ and _____ processes.

**8.** In this definition, "behavior" refers to any action that we can _____ and _____, and "mental processes" refers to the internal _____ we can _____ from behavior.

**9.** As a science, psychology is less a set of findings than a way of _____ .

**10.** The controversy over the relative contributions of biology on behavior is called the _____-_____ issue.

**11.** (Table 1.1) Psychologists who study how the body and brain create emotions, memories, and sensory experiences are working within the _____ perspective.

**12.** (Table 1.1) Psychologists who study how natural selection influences behavior tendencies are working within the _____ perspective, whereas those concerned with the relative influences of genes and environment on individual differences are working within the _____ perspective.

**13.** (Table 1.1) Psychologists who study the mechanisms by which observable responses are acquired and changed are working within the _____ perspective.

**14.** (Table 1.1) The _____ perspective explores how our minds process, store, and retrieve information.

**15.** (Table 1.1) Psychologists who study how thinking and behavior vary in different situations are working within the _____-_____ perspective.

**16.** The different perspectives on the big issues _____ (contradict/complement) one another.

17. Psychologists may be involved in conducting

    _____,

    which builds psychology's knowledge base, or

    _____,

    which seeks solutions to practical problems.

18. Psychologists who study, assess, and treat troubled people are called _____ psychologists.

19. Medical doctors who provide psychotherapy and treat physical causes of psychological disorders are called _____ .

20. Worldwide, the number of psychologists has _____ (increased/decreased) since 1980. The number of women earning degrees in psychology is _____ (increasing/decreasing).

21. The first woman president of the American Psychological Association was

    _____ .

*Why Do Psychology?* (pp. 8–12)

22. The scientific approach is characterized by the attitudes of curious _____ and open-minded _____ .

23. Reasoning that examines assumptions, discerns hidden values, evaluates evidence, and assesses conclusions is called _____

    _____ .

24. The tendency to perceive an outcome that has occurred as being obvious and predictable is called the _____ .

25. Our everyday thinking is also limited by _____ in what we think we know. This stems in part from our tendency to seek information that _____ our ideas.

*How Do Psychologists Ask and Answer Questions?* (pp. 13–28)

26. An explanation using an integrated set of principles that organizes and predicts observable behaviors or events is a _____ . Testable predictions that allow a scientist to evaluate a theory are called _____ .

27. In order to prevent theoretical biases from influencing scientific observations, research must be reported precisely so that others can _____ the findings.

28. The three basic research strategies in psychology are _____ , _____ , and _____ methods.

29. The research strategy in which one or more individuals is studied in depth in order to reveal universal principles of behavior is the

    _____ .

    A potential problem with this method is that any given individual may be _____ .

30. The method in which a group of people is questioned about their attitudes or behavior is the _____ method.

31. An important factor in the validity of survey research is the _____ of questions.

32. The tendency to overestimate others' agreement with us is the _____

    _____ .

33. Surveys try to obtain a _____ sample, one that will be representative of the _____ being studied. In such a sample, every person _____ (does/does not) have a chance of being included.

34. Large, representative samples _____ (are/are not) better than small ones.

35. We are more likely to overgeneralize from select samples that are especially _____ .

36. The research strategy in which people or animals are directly observed in their natural environments is called _____

    _____ .

37. Case studies, surveys, and naturalistic observation do not explain behavior; they simply _____ it.

38. The portable buffer zone we like to maintain around our bodies is called our

    _____ .

    The size of this zone _____ (varies/does not vary) from one culture to another.

39. When changes in one factor are accompanied by changes in another, the two factors are said to be _____ , and one is thus able to _____ the other. If the factors increase or decrease together, they are

    _____  _____ .

    If, however, one decreases as the other increases, they are _____  _____ .

40. A perceived correlation that does not really exist is an _____ _____ . This error in thinking helps explain many _____ beliefs.

If your level of test anxiety goes down as your time spent studying for the exam goes up, would you say these events are positively or negatively correlated? Explain your reasoning.

_____

_____

41. Another common tendency is to perceive order in

    _____ .

42. (Thinking Critically) Basketball players and fans mistakenly believe that players are _____ (no more likely/more likely) to score after having just made the last two or three shots.

43. A common error is to assume that a correlation between two factors means that one _____ the other. To study cause-and-effect relationships, psychologists conduct _____ .

44. An experiment must involve at least two conditions: the _____ condition, in which the experimental treatment is absent, and which the experimental treatment is absent, and

the _____ condition, in which it is present.

45. Experimenters rely on _____ _____ of individuals to experimental and control groups.

46. The factor that is being manipulated in an experiment is called the _____ variable. The measurable factor that may change as a result of these manipulations is called the _____ variable.

47. Statements of procedures that specify how the _____ variable is manipulated, and how the _____ variable is measured, are called _____ _____ .

Explain at least one advantage of the experiment as a research strategy.

48. In the experiment investigating the impact of subliminal messages on self-esteem and memory, subjects in one condition received tapes without the expected message. This type of pseudotreatment, or control, is called a

    _____ .

49. In the _____ - _____ procedure, neither the subjects nor the experimenter know which condition a subject is in.

*Frequently Asked Questions About Psychology* (pp. 28–33)

50. Laboratory experiments in psychology are sometimes criticized as being _____ . However, psychologists' concern is not with the specific behaviors but with the underlying theoretical _____ .

**51.** *Culture* refers to shared _____,

_____, _____, and

_____ that one generation passes

on to the next.

**52.** Although specific attitudes and behaviors vary

across cultures, the underlying

_____ are the same. Likewise,

similarities between the _____

far outweigh differences.

**53.** (Close-Up) Humans share a common

_____ heritage and

_____ tendencies.

Give several examples of such tendencies.

**54.** (Close-Up) The vast majority of our genetic dif-

ferences are due to _____

_____ within local groups.

**55.** (Close-Up) The most important biological hall-

mark of our species is our capacity to

_____ and _____ .

**56.** Some people question whether experiments with

animals are _____ . They won-

der whether it is right to place the

_____ of humans over that of

animals.

Describe the goals of the ethical guidelines for psy-

chological research.

**57.** Psychologists' values _____

(do/do not) influence their theories, observations,

and professional advice.

*Tips for Studying Psychology* (pp. 34–36)

**58.** In order to master any subject, you must

_____ process it.

**59.** The _____ study method incor-

porates five steps: **a.** _____ ,

**b.** _____ , **c.** _____

_____ , **d.** _____ , and

**e.** _____ .

List five additional study tips identified in the text.

**a.** _____

**b.** _____

**c.** _____

**d.** _____

**e.** _____

## Web Sighting

Preparing for a career in psychology usually requires a graduate degree. To earn a doctorate in psychology (Ph.D. or Psy.D.), students complete a four- to six-year program, at the end of which they must design and conduct an original research project. Although a doctorate is required for many jobs in psychology—indeed, more than 60 percent of all psychologists hold this degree—the degree of Master of Arts (M.A.) is sufficient for others, such as teaching at some community colleges or being a school psychologist. The M.A. degree program typically requires one or two years of training beyond the undergraduate curriculum. A bachelor's degree does not prepare students to work as psychologists any more than it prepares them to work as physicians or attorneys.

An excellent, up-to-date source of information on careers in psychology (as well as psychological information of interest to the general public) is the web site maintained by the American Psychological Association. Consult the site to find answers to the following questions:

- What is the difference between a Psy.D. and a Ph.D. degree?
- What are the requirements for licensing as a psychologist?
- What can I do with a master's degree? with a doctoral degree?
- What is the best graduate program for a certain subfield of psychology or a particular region?
- Which subfields of psychology currently lead to the best opportunities for employment?

## Progress Test 1

### Multiple-Choice Questions

Circle your answers to the following questions and check them with the answers on page 18. If your answer is incorrect, read the explanation for why it is incorrect and then consult the appropriate pages of the text (in parentheses following the correct answer).

1. In its earliest days, psychology was defined as the:
   a. study of mental phenomena.
   b. study of conscious and unconscious activity.
   c. science of observable behavior.
   d. science of behavior and mental processes.

2. Who would be most likely to agree with the statement, "Psychology should investigate only behaviors that can be observed"?
   a. Wilhelm Wundt
   b. Sigmund Freud
   c. an American psychologist in the 1950s
   d. William James

3. Today, psychology is defined as the:
   a. study of mental phenomena.
   b. study of conscious and unconscious activity.
   c. study of behavior.
   d. science of behavior and mental processes.

4. Wilhelm Wundt, founder of the first psychology laboratory, was initially a(n):
   a. physiologist.
   b. philosopher.
   c. physiologist and philosopher.
   d. historian.

5. Who wrote an important 1890 psychology textbook?
   a. Wilhelm Wundt        d. William James
   b. Ivan Pavlov          e. Sigmund Freud
   c. Jean Piaget

6. Psychologists who study the degree to which genes influence our personality are working within the _____ perspective.
   a. behavioral           d. neuroscience
   b. evolutionary         e. cognitive
   c. behavior genetics

7. Which of the following exemplifies the issue of the relative importance of nature and nurture on our behavior?
   a. the issue of the relative influence of biology and experience on behavior

b. the issue of the relative influence of rewards and punishments on behavior
   c. the debate as to the relative importance of heredity and instinct in determining behavior
   d. the debate as to whether mental processes are a legitimate area of scientific study

8. Which psychological perspective emphasizes the interaction of the brain and body in behavior?
   a. neuroscience perspective
   b. cognitive perspective
   c. behavioral perspective
   d. behavior genetics perspective
   e. evolutionary perspective

9. A psychologist who explores how Asian and North American definitions of attractiveness differ is working within the _____ perspective.
   a. behavioral           c. cognitive
   b. evolutionary         d. social-cultural

10. A psychologist who conducts experiments solely intended to build psychology's knowledge base is engaged in:
    a. basic research.
    b. applied research.
    c. industrial/organizational research.
    d. clinical research.

11. Psychologists who study, assess, and treat troubled people are called:
    a. basic researchers.
    b. applied psychologists.
    c. clinical psychologists.
    d. psychiatrists.

12. After detailed study of a gunshot wound victim, a psychologist concludes that the brain region destroyed is likely to be important for memory functions. Which research strategy did the psychologist use to deduce this?
    a. the case study       c. correlation
    b. a survey             d. experimentation

13. In an experiment to determine the effects of exercise on motivation, exercise is the:
    a. control condition.
    b. intervening variable.
    c. independent variable.
    d. dependent variable.

14. In order to determine the effects of a new drug on memory, one group of subjects is given a pill that contains the drug. A second group is given a sugar pill that does not contain the drug. This second group constitutes the:

a.  random sample.      c.  control group.
b.  experimental group.   d.  test group.

15. A psychologist studies the play behavior of third-grade children by watching groups during recess at school. Which research strategy is being used?

a.  correlation
b.  case study
c.  experimentation
d.  naturalistic observation

16. To ensure exactness of the meaning of independent and dependent variables, psychologists use:

a.  control groups.
b.  random assignment.
c.  double-blind procedures.
d.  operational definitions.

17. If shoe size and IQ are negatively correlated, which of the following is true?

a.  People with large feet tend to have high IQs.
b.  People with small feet tend to have high IQs.
c.  People with small feet tend to have low IQs.
d.  IQ is unpredictable based on a person's shoe size.

18. In order, the sequence of steps in the SQ3R method is:

a.  study, query, recite, read, review
b.  survey, question, read, review, recite
c.  summarize, question, read, recite, review
d.  survey, question, read, recite, review

19. Which of the following research strategies would be best for determining whether alcohol impairs memory?

a.  case study          c.  survey
b.  naturalistic observation   d.  experiment

20. Well-done surveys measure attitudes in a representative subset, or _____ , of an entire group, or _____ .

a.  population; random sample
b.  control group; experimental group
c.  experimental group; control group
d.  random sample; population

*Matching Items*

Match each term and concept with its definition or description.

*Terms*

___  1.  psychiatry
___  2.  clinical psychology
___  3.  industrial/organizational psychology
___  4.  basic research
___  5.  applied research
___  6.  critical thinking
___  7.  placebo
___  8.  illusory correlation
___  9.  hindsight bias
___  10. false consensus effect
___  11. culture

*Definitions or Descriptions*

a.  concerned with behavior in the workplace
b.  false perception of a relationship between two variables
c.  overestimating others' agreement with us
d.  concerned with the study, assessment, and treatment of troubled people
e.  concerned with the medical treatment of psychological disorders
f.  shared ideas and behaviors passed from one generation to the next
g.  concerned with the study of practical problems
h.  "I-knew-it-all-along" phenomenon
i.  concerned with adding to psychology's knowledge base
j.  reasoning that does not blindly accept arguments
k.  chemically inert substance

## Progress Test 2

Progress Test 2 should be completed during a final chapter review. Answer the following questions after you thoroughly understand the correct answers for the Chapter Review and Progress Test 1.

### Multiple-Choice Questions

1. The first psychology laboratory was established by _____ in the year _____ .
   a. Wundt; 1879      c.  Freud; 1900
   b. James; 1890      d.  Watson; 1913

2. Who would be most likely to agree with the statement, "Psychology is the science of mental life"?
   a. Wilhelm Wundt
   b. John Watson
   c. Ivan Pavlov
   d. virtually any American psychologist during the 1960s

3. In psychology, "behavior" is best defined as:
   a. anything a person says, does, or feels.
   b. any action we can observe and record.
   c. any action, whether observable or not.
   d. anything we can infer from a person's actions.

4. In defining psychology, the text notes that psychology is most accurately described as a:
   a. way of asking and answering questions.
   b. field engaged in solving applied problems.
   c. set of findings related to behavior and mental processes.
   d. nonscientific approach to the study of mental disorders.

5. Two historical roots of psychology are the disciplines of:
   a. philosophy and chemistry.
   b. physiology and chemistry.
   c. philosophy and biology.
   d. philosophy and physics.

6. The way the mind processes, stores, and retrieves information is the primary concern of the _____ perspective.
   a. neuroscience      d.  behavioral
   b. evolutionary      e.  cognitive
   c. social-cultural

7. Which of the following individuals is also a physician?
   a. clinical psychologist
   b. experimental psychologist
   c. psychiatrist
   d. biological psychologist

8. Dr. Jones's research centers on the relationship between changes in our thinking over the life span and changes in moral reasoning. Dr. Jones is most likely a:
   a. clinical psychologist.
   b. personality psychologist.
   c. psychiatrist.
   d. developmental psychologist.

9. Which subfield is most directly concerned with studying human behavior in the workplace?
   a. clinical psychology
   b. personality psychology
   c. industrial/organizational psychology
   d. psychiatry

10. Dr. Ernst explains behavior in terms of different situations. Dr. Ernst is working within the _____ perspective.
    a. behavioral       c.  social-cultural
    b. evolutionary     d.  cognitive

11. A psychologist who studies how worker productivity might be increased by changing office layout is engaged in _____ research.
    a. applied          c.  clinical
    b. basic            d.  developmental

12. Which of the following research methods does *not* belong with the others?
    a. case study       c.  naturalistic observation
    b. survey           d.  experiment

13. In the experiment on subliminal perception, students listened for five weeks to tapes they thought would enhance their memory or self-esteem. At the end of the experiment:
    a. students who thought they had a memory tape believed their memories had improved; but, in fact, there was no improvement.
    b. self-esteem, but not memory, improved.
    c. memory, but not self-esteem, improved.
    d. both self-esteem and memory improved over the course of the experiment.

14. Which statement about the ethics of experimentation with people and animals is false?
    a. Only a small percentage of animal experiments use shock.
    b. Allegations that psychologists routinely subject animals to pain, starvation, and other inhumane conditions have been proven untrue.
    c. The American Psychological Association and the British Psychological Society have set strict guidelines for the care and treatment of human and animal subjects.

**d.** Animals are used as subjects in almost 25 percent of all psychology experiments.

15. In an experiment to determine the effects of attention on memory, memory is the:
    a. control condition.
    b. intervening variable.
    c. independent variable.
    d. dependent variable.

16. The procedure designed to ensure that the experimental and control groups do not differ in any way that might affect the experiment's results is called:
    a. variable controlling.
    b. random assignment.
    c. representative sampling.
    d. stratification.

17. Which type of research strategy would allow you to determine whether students' college grades accurately predict later income?
    a. case study
    b. naturalistic observation
    c. experimentation
    d. correlation

18. In a test of the effects of air pollution, groups of students performed a reaction-time task in a polluted or an unpolluted room. To what condition were students in the unpolluted room exposed?
    a. experimental
    b. control
    c. randomly assigned
    d. dependent

19. In order to study the effects of lighting on mood, Dr. Cooper had students fill out questionnaires in brightly lit or dimly lit rooms. In this study, the independent variable consisted of:
    a. the number of subjects assigned to each group.
    b. the students' responses to the questionnaire.
    c. the room lighting.
    d. the subject matter of the questions asked.

20. A major principle underlying the SQ3R study method is that:
    a. people learn and remember material best when they actively process it.
    b. many students overestimate their mastery of text and lecture material.
    c. study time should be spaced over time rather than crammed into one session.
    d. "overlearning" disrupts efficient retention.

*Matching Items*

Match each term with its definition or description.

*Terms*

_____ 1. hypothesis
_____ 2. theory
_____ 3. independent variable
_____ 4. dependent variable
_____ 5. experimental condition
_____ 6. control condition
_____ 7. case study
_____ 8. survey
_____ 9. replication
_____ 10. random assignment
_____ 11. experiment
_____ 12. double-blind

*Definitions or Descriptions*

a. an in-depth observational study of one person
b. the variable being manipulated in an experiment
c. the variable being measured in an experiment
d. the "treatment-absent" condition in an experiment
e. testable proposition
f. repeating an experiment to see whether the same results are obtained
g. the process in which subjects are selected by chance for different groups in an experiment
h. an explanation using an integrated set of principles that organizes and predicts observations
i. the research strategy in which the effects of one or more variables on behavior are tested
j. the "treatment-present" condition in an experiment
k. the research strategy in which a representative sample of individuals is questioned
l. experimental procedure in which neither the subject nor the experimenter knows which condition the subject is in

## Thinking Critically About Chapter 1

Answer these questions the day before an exam as a final check on your understanding of the chapter's terms and concepts.

### *Multiple-Choice Questions*

1. Psychology is defined as the "science of behavior and mental processes." Wilhelm Wundt would have omitted which of the following words from this definition?
   a. science
   b. behavior and
   c. and mental processes
   d. Wundt would have agreed with the definition as stated.

2. Jawan believes that psychologists should go back to using introspection as a research tool. This technique is based upon:
   a. survey methodology.
   b. experimentation.
   c. self-examination of mental processes.
   d. the study of observable behavior.

3. Sensations, dreams, beliefs, and feelings are:
   a. examples of behavior.
   b. examples of subjective experiences.
   c. not considered appropriate subject matter for psychology today.
   d. b. and c.

4. To say that "psychology is a science" means that:
   a. psychologists study only observable behaviors.
   b. psychologists approach the study of thoughts and actions with careful observation and rigorous analysis.
   c. psychological research should be free of value judgments.
   d. all of the above are true.

5. Dr. Waung investigates how a person's interpretation of a situation affects his or her reaction. Evidently, Dr. Waung is working within the _____ perspective.
   a. neuroscience       c. cognitive
   b. behavioral         d. social-cultural

6. Dr. Aswad is studying people's enduring inner traits. Dr. Aswad is most likely a(n):
   a. clinical psychologist.
   b. psychiatrist.
   c. personality psychologist.
   d. industrial/organizational psychologist.

7. The psychological perspective that places the *most* emphasis on how observable responses are learned is the _____ perspective.
   a. behavioral         c. behavior genetics
   b. cognitive          d. evolutionary

8. During a dinner conversation a friend says that the cognitive and behavioral perspectives are quite similar. You disagree and point out that the cognitive perspective emphasizes _____, whereas the behavioral perspective emphasizes
   _____.
   a. conscious processes; observable responses
   b. unconscious processes; conscious processes
   c. overt behaviors; covert behaviors
   d. introspection; experimentation

9. Concerning the major psychological perspectives on behavior, the text author suggests that:
   a. researchers should work within the framework of only one of the perspectives.
   b. only those perspectives that emphasize objective measurement of behavior are useful.
   c. the different perspectives often complement one another; together, they provide a fuller understanding of behavior than provided by any single perspective.
   d. psychologists should avoid all of these traditional perspectives.

10. You decide to test your belief that men drink more soft drinks than women by finding out whether more soft drinks are consumed per day in the men's dorm than in the women's dorm. Your belief is a(n) _____, and your research prediction is a(n) _____.
    a. hypothesis; theory
    b. theory; hypothesis
    c. independent variable; dependent variable
    d. dependent variable; independent variable

11. Your roommate is conducting a survey to learn how many hours the typical college student studies each day. She plans to pass out her questionnaire to the members of her sorority. You point out that her findings will be flawed because:
    a. she has not specified an independent variable.
    b. she has not specified a dependent variable.
    c. the sample will probably not be representative of the population of interest.
    d. of all the above reasons.

12. Martina believes that high doses of caffeine slow a person's reaction time. In order to test this belief, she has five friends each drink three 8-ounce cups of coffee and then measures their

reaction time on a learning task. What is wrong with Martina's research strategy?

a. No independent variable is specified.
b. No dependent variable is specified.
c. There is no control condition.
d. There is no provision for replication of the findings.

13. A researcher was interested in determining whether her students' test performance could be predicted from their proximity to the front of the classroom. So she matched her students' scores on a math test with their seating position. This study is an example of:

a. experimentation.
b. correlational research.
c. a survey.
d. naturalistic observation.

14. Your best friend criticizes psychological research for being artificial and having no relevance to behavior in real life. In defense of psychology's use of laboratory experiments you point out that:

a. psychologists make every attempt to avoid artificiality by setting up experiments that closely simulate real-world environments.
b. psychologists who conduct basic research are not concerned with the applicability of their findings to the real world.
c. most psychological research is not conducted in a laboratory environment.
d. psychologists intentionally study behavior in simplified environments in order to gain greater control over variables and to test general principles that help to explain many behaviors.

15. A professor constructs a questionnaire to determine how students at the university feel about nuclear disarmament. Which of the following techniques should be used in order to survey a random sample of the student body?

a. Every student should be sent the questionnaire.
b. Only students majoring in psychology should be asked to complete the questionnaire.
c. Only students living on campus should be asked to complete the questionnaire.
d. From an alphabetical listing of all students, every tenth (or fifteenth, e.g.) student should be asked to complete the questionnaire.

16. If eating saturated fat and the likelihood of contracting cancer are positively correlated, which of the following is true?

a. Saturated fat causes cancer.
b. People who are prone to develop cancer prefer foods containing saturated fat.
c. A separate factor links the consumption of saturated fat to cancer.
d. None of the above is necessarily true.

17. Rashad, who is participating in a psychology experiment on the effects of alcohol on perception, is truthfully told by the experimenter that he has been assigned to the "high-dose condition." What is wrong with this experiment?

a. There is no control condition.
b. Rashad's expectations concerning the effects of "high doses" of alcohol on perception may influence his performance.
c. Knowing that Rashad is in the "high-dose" condition may influence the experimenter's interpretations of Rashad's results.
d. Both b. and c. are correct.

18. A friend majoring in anthropology is critical of psychological research because it often ignores the influence of culture on thoughts and actions. You point out that:

a. there is very little evidence that cultural diversity has a significant effect on specific behaviors and attitudes.
b. most researchers assign subjects to experimental and control conditions in such a way as to fairly represent the cultural diversity of the population under study.
c. it is impossible for psychologists to control for every possible variable that might influence research participants.
d. even when specific thoughts and actions vary across cultures, as they often do, the underlying processes are much the same.

19. Which of the following procedures is an example of the use of a placebo?

a. In a test of the effects of a drug on memory, a subject is led to believe that a harmless pill actually contains an active drug.
b. A subject in an experiment is led to believe that a pill, which actually contains an active drug, is harmless.
c. Subjects in an experiment are not told which treatment condition is in effect.
d. Neither the subjects nor the experimenter know which treatment condition is in effect.

20. Your roommate announces that her schedule permits her to devote three hours to studying for an upcoming quiz. You advise her to:
   a. spend most of her time reading and rereading the text material.
   b. focus primarily on her lecture notes.
   c. space study time over several shorter sessions.
   d. cram for three hours just before the quiz.

## Essay Question

Esteban has a theory that regular exercise can improve thinking. Help him design an experiment evaluating this theory by answering questions (a) through (d). (Use the space below to list the points you want to make, and organize them. Then write the essay on a separate piece of paper.)

 a. How would you restate Esteban's theory as a testable hypothesis?

 b. What are the independent and dependent variables and how could they be manipulated, or measured?

 c. Do you need a control group? If so, why, and what should they do?

 d. How should subjects be selected and assigned to the various conditions of the experiment?

## Key Terms

### Writing Definitions

Using your own words, on a separate piece of paper write a brief definition or explanation of each of the following.

1. psychology
2. nature-nurture issue
3. basic research
4. applied research
5. clinical psychology
6. psychiatry
7. critical thinking
8. hindsight bias
9. theory
10. hypothesis
11. replication
12. case study
13. survey
14. false consensus effect
15. population
16. random sample
17. naturalistic observation
18. correlation
19. illusory correlation
20. experiment
21. experimental condition
22. control condition
23. random assignment
24. independent variable
25. dependent variable
26. operational definition
27. placebo
28. double-blind procedure
29. culture
30. SQ3R

*Cross-Check*

As you learned in Chapter 1, reviewing and overlearning of material are important to the learning process. After you have written the definitions of the key terms in this chapter, you should complete the crossword puzzle to ensure that you can reverse the process—recognize the term, given the definition.

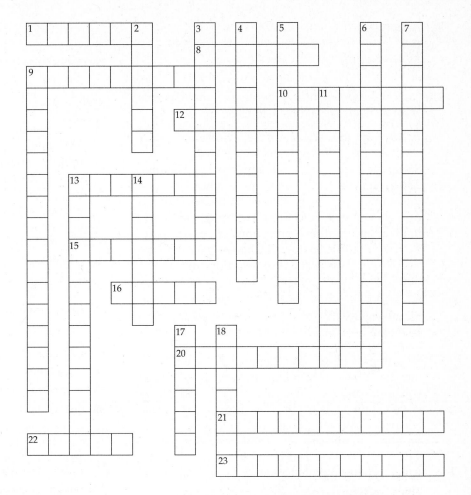

## ACROSS

1. In SQ3R, reading over your notes and the text.
8. Pioneer in the study of learning.
9. Perspective that explores how our minds process, store, and retrieve information.
10. In SQ3R, using your own words to test yourself on the material to be learned.
12. Another term for biology's influence on behavior and mental processes.
13. An inert substance or condition in an experiment.
15. The condition in an experiment in which the independent variable is withheld.
16. Pioneer in personality theory.
20. A testable proposition.
21. The variable in an experiment that is being manipulated by the investigator.
22. Type of research that seeks only to advance psychology's knowledge base.
23. Type of research that includes case studies, surveys, and naturalistic observation.

## DOWN

2. Defined psychology as the "science of observable behavior."
3. _____ definitions specify the procedures used to define independent and dependent variables.
4. Perspective concerned with the extent to which our genes and our environment influence our individual differences.

5. Research strategy that seeks to uncover predictable relationships between variables.
6. Perspective concerned with how natural selection influences our behavior.
7. The tendency to overestimate the extent to which others share our beliefs and behaviors.
9. Thinking that does not blindly accept arguments and conclusions.
11. After-the-fact belief that you would have known the outcome.
13. Medical doctors who provide psychotherapy.
14. Enduring behaviors, ideas, attitudes, and traditions shared by a large group of people and transmitted from one generation to the next.
17. An explanation using an integrated set of principles that organizes and predicts observations.
18. Type of research that aims to solve specific problems.

# ANSWERS

## Guided Study

The following guidelines provide the main points that your answers should have touched upon.

1. Psychology, the science of behavior and mental processes, is a young science with roots in many disciplines, primarily biology and philosophy. The Greek naturalist and philosopher Aristotle theorized about many contemporary psychological phenomena, including learning, memory, motivation, emotion, perception, and personality. In the mid-1800s, naturalist Charles Darwin introduced the ideas of natural selection and evolution—ideas that remain important organizing principles for psychology. Wilhelm Wundt, who founded the first psychology laboratory in 1879, was a philosopher and a physiologist. In its early years psychological research focused on inner sensations, feelings, and thoughts. From the 1920s into the 1960s, psychology in the United States was most influenced by John Watson and others who redefined it as the "science of observable behavior." In the 1960s, psychology began to recapture its interest in mental processes so that today psychology encompasses the scientific study of both overt behavior and covert thoughts and feelings.

2 Psychologists who work from a neuroscience perspective study how the body and brain create behavior and mental processes. Psychologists who work from an evolutionary perspective study how natural selection favors traits that promote the perpetuation of one's genes. Behavior geneticists study how genes and environment contribute to individual differences. The behavioral perspective emphasizes how observable behaviors are learned. The cognitive perspective explores how people process, store, and retrieve information. The social-cultural perspective calls attention to the importance of each person's social and cultural environment in shaping his or her thoughts, emotions, and behaviors. The important point is that these perspectives need not contradict one another. In fact, they usually complement one another.

3. Some psychologists conduct basic research that builds psychology's knowledge base. Biological psychologists explore the links between brain and mind, developmental psychologists study our changing abilities, and personality psychologists investigate our inner traits. Others conduct applied research to solve practical problems. Industrial/organizational psychologists, for example, study and advise on behavior in the workplace. Still others provide professional services. Clinical psychologists study, assess, and treat troubled people. Psychiatrists are physicians who treat the physical causes of psychological disorders.

4. As scientists, psychologists attempt to study thoughts and actions with an attitude of open-minded, curious skepticism. Scientists must also possess an attitude of humility, because they may have to reject their ideas in the light of new evidence. Whether applied to reading news reports or listening to a lecture, critical thinking examines assumptions, discerns hidden values, evaluates evidence, and assesses conclusions.

5. Two reliable phenomena—hindsight bias and judgmental overconfidence—make intuition and common sense untrustworthy. Hindsight bias is the tendency to perceive an outcome that has already occurred as being obvious and predictable. Overconfidence is the tendency to think we know more about an issue than we actually do, and to overestimate the accuracy of that knowledge.

6. Scientists rely on theories to explain, organize, and predict the behaviors or events under study. Good theories give direction to research by generating testable predictions, called hypotheses. Research findings are reported in the precise language of science in order to allow other scientists to replicate (repeat) them.

7. The simplest research strategy is description; examples include case studies, surveys, and naturalistic observation. In the case study one or more individuals is studied in great depth in the hope of revealing general principles underlying the behavior of all people. Surveys measure the self-reported attitudes or behaviors of a randomly selected representative sample of an entire group, or population. Naturalistic observation seeks to observe and record the behavior of organisms (including humans) in their natural environments.

8. Although descriptive research can suggest hypotheses for further study, it is limited to describing behavior and cannot reveal predictive, or cause-effect, relationships. One possible pitfall of case studies is that any given individual may be atypical, making the case misleading. Survey results may be misleading because even subtle changes in the order or wording of questions can influence responses. And the samples on which surveys are based may not be representative of the populations from which they are drawn.

9. A correlation is a statistical measure of relationship, revealing how accurately one event predicts

another. A positive correlation indicates a *direct* relationship in which two things increase or decrease together. A negative correlation indicates an *inverse* relationship in which one thing increases as the other decreases. A zero correlations means no relationship exists. A correlation between two events or behaviors means only that one event can be predicted from the other. Because two events may both be caused by some other event, a correlation between the two events does not mean that one caused the other. Correlation thus does not enable explanation.

10. A perceived correlation that does not really exist is an illusory correlation. Illusory correlations help explain superstitious beliefs; they arise from our eagerness to perceive order in events, even those that are random.

11. Conducting experiments allows psychologists to explain behaviors in terms of cause-and-effect relationships. This is because experiments allow researchers to manipulate one or more experimental factors (the independent variables) while holding all other potential independent variables constant. If a subject's behavior (the dependent variable) changes, the change can be attributed to the influence of the independent variable under study. In the typical experiment, subjects are randomly assigned to either a control condition, in which the experimental treatment is absent, or an experimental condition, in which the treatment of interest is present.

12. Operational definitions specify the procedures that manipulate the independent variable or measure the dependent variable. Such definitions prevent ambiguity by providing an exactness of meaning that allows others to replicate the study. Two control techniques involve use of a placebo and the double-blind procedure. These help ensure that any changes in the dependent variable that occur are due to the independent variable rather than to researchers' or subjects' expectations.

13. Psychologists intentionally conduct experiments on simplified behaviors in an artificial laboratory environment in order to gain control over the numerous independent and dependent variables present in more complex behaviors and the "real world." By studying simplified behaviors under controlled circumstances psychologists are able to test general principles of behavior that also operate in the real world.

For similar reasons, psychologists often apply their findings from psychological studies of people from one culture to people in general. Although attitudes and behaviors vary greatly from culture to culture, the underlying principles are much the same. Furthermore, although males and females are different in many ways, psychologically and biologically they are also overwhelmingly alike.

14. Some psychologists study animals simply to understand animal behavior. For the same reasons that psychologists investigate human behavior in simplified laboratory environments before attempting to understand more complex everyday behaviors, other psychologists attempt to learn more about human behavior by studying simpler, yet similar, behaviors in animals.

Although animals in psychological research rarely experience pain, opposition to animal experimentation raises two important issues: (1) whether it is morally right to place the well-being of humans above that of animals, and (2) what safeguards should protect the well-being of animals.

Ethical standards developed by the American Psychological Association and the British Psychological Society provide strict guidelines regarding the treatment of people and animals in psychology experiments.

15. No science, including psychology, is value-free. Psychologists' values influence their choice of research topics, their observations, and their interpretations of research findings. Psychological knowledge is a power that, like all powers, can be used for good or evil. Many psychologists conduct research aimed at solving some of the world's most serious problems, including war, prejudice, overpopulation, and crime.

16. The SQ3R study method incorporates the idea that mastery of a subject requires active processing of it. SQ3R stands for the five steps of the method: *Survey*, *Question*, *Read*, *Rehearse*, and *Review*. The text and this study guide are organized to facilitate use of the SQ3R method.

## Chapter Review

1. Aristotle
2. John Locke; inborn
3. Charles Darwin; evolution; natural selection
4. Wundt
5. biology; philosophy
6. learning; Sigmund Freud; children; William James

7. mental; observable; behavior; mental

8. observe; record; subjective experiences; infer

9. asking and answering questions

10. nature-nurture

11. neuroscience

12. evolutionary; behavior genetics

13. behavioral

14. cognitive

15. social-cultural

16. complement

17. basic research; applied research

18. clinical

19. psychiatrists

20. increased; increasing

21. Mary Whiton Calkins

22. skepticism; humility

23. critical thinking

24. hindsight bias

25. overconfidence; confirms

26. theory; hypotheses

27. replicate

28. description; correlation; experimentation

29. case study; atypical

30. survey

31. wording

32. false consensus effect

33. random; population; does

34. are

35. vivid

36. naturalistic observation

37. describe

38. personal space; varies

39. correlated; predict; positively correlated; negatively correlated

40. illusory correlation; superstitious

This is an example of a negative correlation. As one factor (time spent studying) increases, the other factor (anxiety level) decreases.

41. random events

42. more likely

43. causes; experiments

44. control; experimental

45. random assignment

46. independent; dependent

47. independent; dependent; operational definitions

Experimentation has the advantage of increasing the investigator's control of both relevant and irrelevant variables that might influence behavior. Experiments also permit the investigator to go beyond observation and description to uncover cause-and-effect relationships in behavior.

48. placebo

49. double-blind

50. artificial; principles

51. ideas; behaviors; attitudes; traditions

52. principles or processes; genders

53. biological; behavioral

Regardless of our culture or gender, we all begin to fear strangers at about 8 months of age; regard similar female features as attractive, prefer sweet tastes to sour, divide the color spectrum into similar colors, and are drawn to behaviors that protect children, for example.

54. individual variation

55. learn; adapt

56. ethical; well-being

Ethical guidelines require investigators to (1) obtain informed consent from potential subjects, (2) protect them from harm and discomfort, (3) treat information obtained from subjects confidentially, and (4) fully explain the research afterward.

57. do

58. actively

59. SQ3R; a. study; b. question; c. read; d. rehearse; e. review
   a. Distribute study time.
   b. Learn to think critically.
   c. Listen actively in class.
   d. Overlearn material.
   e. Be a smart test-taker.

## Progress Test 1

*Multiple-Choice Questions*

1. a. is the answer. (p. 3)
   b. Psychology has never been defined in terms of conscious and unconscious activity.
   c. From the 1920s into the 1960s, psychology was defined as the science of observable behavior.
   d. Psychology today is defined as the science of behavior and mental processes. In its earliest days, however, psychology focused exclusively on mental phenomena.

2. c. is the answer. (p. 3)
   a. Wilhelm Wundt, the founder of the first

psychology laboratory, used the method of introspection to study mental phenomena.

**b.** Sigmund Freud developed an influential theory of personality that focused on unconscious processes.

**d.** William James, author of a psychology textbook in 1890, was a philosopher and was more interested in mental phenomena than observable behavior.

3. **d.** is the answer. (p. 3)

**a.** In its earliest days psychology was defined as the science of mental phenomena.

**b.** Psychology has never been defined in terms of conscious and unconscious activity.

**c.** From the 1920s into the 1960s, psychology was defined as the science of behavior.

4. **c.** is the answer. (pp. 2–3)

5. **d.** is the answer (p. 3)

**a.** Wilhelm Wundt founded the first psychology laboratory.

**b.** Ivan Pavlov pioneered the study of learning.

**c.** Jean Piaget was this century's most influential observer of children.

**e.** Sigmund Freud wrote *The Interpretation of Dreams* in 1900.

6. **c.** is the answer. (pp. 5–6)

7. **a.** is the answer. Biology and experience are internal and external influences, respectively. (p. 5)

**b.** Rewards and punishments are both external influences on behavior.

**c.** Heredity and instinct are both internal influences on behavior.

**d.** The legitimacy of the study of mental processes does not relate to the internal/external issue.

8. **a.** is the answer. (pp. 5–6)

**b.** The cognitive perspective is concerned with how we process, store, and retrieve information.

**c.** The behavioral perspective studies the mechanisms by which observable responses are acquired and changed.

**d.** The behavior genetics perspective focuses on the relative contributions of genes and environment to individual differences.

**e.** The evolutionary perspective studies how natural selection favors traits that promote the perpetuation of one's genes.

9. **d.** is the answer. (pp. 5–6)

**a.** Behavioral psychologists investigate how learned behaviors are acquired. They generally do not focus on subjective opinions, such as attractiveness.

**b.** The evolutionary perspective studies how natural selection favors traits that promote the perpetuation of one's genes.

**c.** Cognitive psychologists study the mechanisms of thinking and memory, and generally do not investigate attitudes. Also, because the question specifies that the psychologist is interested in comparing two cultures, d. is the best answer.

10. **a.** is the answer. (p. 7)

**b. & c.** Applied and industrial/organizational psychologists tackle practical problems.

**d.** Clinical psychologists (and researchers) focus on treating troubled people.

11. **c.** is the answer. (p. 7)

**d.** Psychiatrists are medical doctors rather than psychologists.

12. **a.** is the answer. In a case study one subject is studied in depth. (p. 14)

**b.** In survey research a group of people are interviewed.

**c.** Correlations identify whether two factors are related.

**d.** In an experiment an investigator manipulates one variable to observe its effect on another.

13. **c.** is the answer. Exercise is the variable being manipulated in the experiment. (p. 25)

**a.** A control condition for this experiment would be a group of people not permitted to exercise.

**b.** An intervening variable is a variable other than those being manipulated that may influence behavior.

**d.** The dependent variable is the behavior measured by the experimenter, in this case, the effects of exercise.

14. **c.** is the answer. The control condition is that for which the experimental treatment (the new drug) is absent. (p. 24)

**a.** A random sample is a subset of a population in which every person has an equal chance of being selected.

**b.** The experimental condition is the group for which the experimental treatment (the new drug) is present.

**d.** "Test group" is an ambiguous term; both the experimental and control group are tested.

15. **d.** is the answer. In this case the children are being observed in their normal environment rather than in a laboratory. (p. 17)

**a.** Correlational research measures relationships between two factors. The psychologist may later want to determine whether there are correlations between the variables studied under natural conditions.

**b.** In a case study one subject is studied in depth.

**c.** This is not an experiment because the psychologist is not directly controlling the variables being studied.

**16. d.** is the answer. (p. 25)

**17. b.** is the answer. (p. 18)

**a. & c.** These answers would have been correct had the question stated that there is a *positive* correlation between shoe size and IQ. Actually, there is probably no correlation at all!

**18. d.** is the answer. (p. 34)

**19. d.** is the answer. In an experiment it would be possible to manipulate alcohol consumption and observe the effects, if any, on memory. (p. 23)

**a., b., & c.** These answers are incorrect because only by directly controlling the variables of interest can a researcher uncover cause-and-effect relationships.

**20. d.** is the answer. (pp. 15–16)

**a.** A sample is a subset of a population.

**b. & c.** Control and experimental groups are used in experimentation, not in survey research.

### Matching Items

| | | |
|---|---|---|
| **1.** e (p. 7) | **5.** g (p. 7) | **9.** h (p. 11) |
| **2.** d (p. 7) | **6.** j (p. 9) | **10.** c (p. 15) |
| **3.** a (p. 7) | **7.** k (p. 9) | **11.** f (p. 29) |
| **4.** i (p. 7) | **8.** b (p. 27) | |

## Progress Test 2

### Multiple-Choice Questions

**1. a.** is the answer. (pp. 2–3)

**2. a.** is the answer. (p. 3)

**b. & d.** John Watson, like many American psychologists at this time, believed that psychology should focus on the study of observable behavior.

**c.** Because he pioneered the study of learning, Pavlov focused on observable behavior and would certainly have *disagreed* with this statement.

**3. b.** is the answer. (p. 3)

**4. a.** is the answer. (p. 3)

**b.** Psychology is equally involved in basic research.

**c.** Psychology's knowledge base is constantly expanding.

**d.** Psychology is the *science* of behavior and mental processes.

**5. c.** is the answer. (p. 3)

**6. e.** is the answer. (pp. 5–6)

**a.** The neuroscience perspective studies the biological bases for a range of psychological phenomena.

**b.** The evolutionary perspective studies how nat-

ural selection favors traits that promote the perpetuation of one's genes.

**c.** The social-cultural perspective is concerned with variations in behavior across situations and cultures.

**d.** The behavioral perspective studies the mechanisms by which observable responses are acquired and modified in particular environments.

**7. c.** is the answer. After earning their M.D. degrees, psychiatrists specialize in the diagnosis and treatment of mental health disorders. (p. 7)

**a., b., & d.** These psychologists generally earn a Ph.D. rather than an M.D.

**8. d.** is the answer. The emphasis on change during the life span indicates that Dr. Jones is most likely a developmental psychologist. (p. 7)

**a.** Clinical psychologists study, assess, and treat people who are psychologically troubled.

**b.** Personality psychologists study our inner traits.

**c.** Psychiatrists are medical doctors.

**9. c.** is the answer. (p. 7)

**a.** Clinical psychologists study, assess, and treat people with psychological disorders.

**b. & d.** Personality psychologists and psychiatrists do not usually study people in work situations.

**10. c.** is the answer. (pp. 5–6)

**a.** Psychologists who follow the behavioral perspective emphasize observable, external influences on behavior.

**b.** The evolutionary perspective focuses on how natural selection favors traits that promote the perpetuation of one's genes.

**d.** The cognitive perspective places emphasis on conscious, rather than unconscious, processes.

**11. a.** is the answer. The research is addressing a practical issue. (p. 7)

**b.** Basic research is aimed at contributing to the base of knowledge in a given field, not at resolving particular practical problems.

**c. & d.** Clinical and developmental research would focus on issues relating to psychological disorders and life-span changes, respectively.

**12. d.** is the answer. Only experiments can reveal cause-and-effect relationships; the other methods can only *describe* relationships. (p. 23)

**13. a.** is the answer. (pp. 26–27)

**b., c., & d.** There was no actual improvement in memory or self-esteem in this experiment.

**14. d.** is the answer. Only about 7 percent of all psychological experiments involve animals. (p. 31)

**15. d.** is the answer. (p. 25)

**a.** The control condition is the comparison group, in which the experimental treatment (the treatment of interest) is absent.

**b.** Memory is a directly observed and measured dependent variable in this experiment.

**c.** Attention is the independent variable, which is being manipulated.

**16. b.** is the answer. If enough subjects are used in an experiment and they are randomly assigned to the two groups, any differences that emerge between the groups should stem from the experiment itself. (p. 24)

**a., c., & d.** None of these terms describes precautions taken in setting up groups for experimental research.

**17. d.** is the answer. Correlations show how well one factor can be predicted from another. (p. 17)

**a.** Because a case study focuses in great detail on the behavior of an individual, it's unlikely to be useful in showing whether predictions are possible.

**b.** Naturalistic observation is a method of describing, rather than predicting, behavior.

**c.** In experimental research the effects of manipulated independent variables on dependent variables are measured. It is not clear how an experiment could help determine whether IQ tests predict academic success.

**18. b.** is the answer. The control condition is the one in which the treatment—in this case, pollution—is absent. (p. 24)

**a.** Students in the polluted room would be in the experimental condition.

**c.** Presumably, all students in both conditions were randomly assigned to their groups. Random assignment is a method for establishing groups, rather than a condition.

**d.** The word *dependent* refers to a kind of variable in experiments; conditions are either experimental or control.

**19. c.** is the answer. The lighting is the factor being manipulated. (p. 25)

**a. & d.** These answers are incorrect because they involve aspects of the experiment other than the variables.

**b.** This answer is the dependent, not the independent, variable.

**20. a.** is the answer. (p. 34)

**b. & c.** Although each of these is true, SQ3R is based on the more *general* principle of active learning.

**d.** In fact, just the opposite is true.

## Matching Items

| | | |
|---|---|---|
| **1.** e (p. 13) | **5.** j (p. 24) | **9.** f (p. 13) |
| **2.** h (p. 13) | **6.** d (p. 24) | **10.** g (p. 24) |
| **3.** b (p. 25) | **7.** a (p. 14) | **11.** i (p. 23) |
| **4.** c (p. 25) | **8.** k (p. 15) | **12.** l (p. 27) |

# Thinking Critically About Chapter 1

### Multiple-Choice Questions

**1. b.** is the answer. (p. 3)

**a.** As the founder of the first psychology laboratory, Wundt certainly based his research on the scientific method.

**c.** The earliest psychologists, including Wilhelm Wundt, were concerned with the self-examination of covert thoughts, feelings, and other mental processes.

**2. c.** is the answer. (p. 3)

**3. b.** is the answer. (p. 3)

**a., c., & d.** Psychologists today study both overt *and* covert behavior.

**4. b.** is the answer. (p. 3)

**a.** Psychologists study both overt (observable) behaviors and covert thoughts and feelings.

**c.** Psychologists' values definitely *do* influence their research.

**5. c.** is the answer. (pp. 5–6)

**a.** This perspective emphasizes the influences of physiology on behavior.

**b.** This perspective emphasizes environmental influences on observable behavior.

**d.** This perspective emphasizes how behavior and thinking vary across situations and cultures.

**6. c.** is the answer. (p. 7)

**a.** Clinical psychology is concerned with the study and treatment of psychological disorders.

**b.** Psychiatry is the branch of medicine concerned with the physical diagnosis and treatment of psychological disorders.

**d.** Industrial/organizational psychologists study behavior in the workplace.

**7. a.** is the answer. (pp. 5–6)

**8. a.** is the answer. (pp. 5–6)

**b.** Neither perspective places any special emphasis on conscious or unconscious processes.

**c.** Neither perspective emphasizes covert behaviors.

**d.** Introspection was a research method used by the earliest psychologists, not those working from the cognitive perspective.

**9. c.** is the answer. (p. 6)

**a.** The text suggests just the opposite: By studying behavior from several perspectives, psychologists gain a fuller understanding.

**b. & d.** Each perspective is useful in that it calls researchers' attention to different aspects of behavior. This is equally true of those perspectives that do not emphasize objective measurement.

10. **b.** is the answer. A general belief such as this one is a theory; it helps organize, explain, and generate testable predictions (called hypotheses) such as "men drink more soft drinks than women." (p. 13)

**c. & d.** Independent and dependent variables are experimental treatments and behaviors, respectively. Beliefs and predictions may involve such variables, but are not themselves those variables.

11. **c.** is the answer. The members of one sorority are likely to share more interests, traits, and attitudes than will the members of a random sample of college students. (pp. 15–16)

**a. & b.** Unlike experiments, surveys do not specify or directly manipulate independent and dependent variables. In a sense, survey questions are independent variables, and the answers, dependent variables.

12. **c.** is the answer. In order to determine the effects of caffeine on reaction time, Martina needs to measure reaction time in a control, or comparison, group that does not receive caffeine. (p. 24)

**a.** Caffeine is the independent variable.

**b.** Reaction time is the dependent variable.

**d.** Whether or not Martina's experiment can be replicated is determined by the precision with which she reports her procedures, which is not an aspect of research strategy.

13. **b.** is the answer. (p. 17)

**a.** This is not an experiment because the researcher is not manipulating the independent variable (seating position); she is merely measuring whether variation in this factor predicts test performance.

**c.** If the study were based entirely on students' self-reported responses, this would be a survey.

**d.** This study goes beyond naturalistic observation, which merely describes behavior as it occurs, to determine if test scores can be predicted from students' seating position.

14. **d.** is the answer. (p. 29)

15. **d.** is the answer. Selecting every tenth person would probably result in a representative sample of the entire population of students at the university. (pp. 15–16)

**a.** It would be difficult, if not impossible, to survey every student on campus.

**b.** Psychology students are not representative of the entire student population.

**c.** This answer is incorrect for the same reason as b. This would constitute a biased sample.

16. **d.** is the answer. (p. 21)

**a.** Correlation does not imply causality.

**b.** Again, a positive correlation simply means that two factors tend to increase or decrease together; further relationships are not implied.

**c.** A separate factor may or may not be involved. That the two factors are correlated does not imply a separate factor. There may, for example, be a direct causal relationship between the two factors themselves.

17. **d.** is the answer. (p. 27)

**a.** The low-dose comparison group is the control group.

18. **d.** is the answer. (pp. 29–30)

**a.** In fact, just the opposite is true.

**b.** Actually, psychological experiments tend to use the most readily available subjects, often white North American college students.

**c.** Although this may be true, psychological experiments remain important because they help explain underlying processes of human behavior everywhere. Therefore, d. is a much better response than c.

19. **a.** is the answer. (p. 27)

**b.** Use of a placebo tests whether the behavior of an experimental subject, who mistakenly believes that a treatment (such as a drug) is in effect, is the same as it would be if the treatment were actually present.

**c. & d.** These are examples of "blind" and "double-blind" control procedures.

20. **c.** is the answer. (p. 35)

**a.** To be effective, study must be *active* rather than passive in nature.

**b.** Most exams are based on lecture *and* textbook material.

**d.** Cramming hinders retention.

## Essay Question

**a.** Sample hypothesis: Daily aerobic exercise for one month will improve memory.

**b.** Exercise is the independent variable. The dependent variable is memory. Exercise could be manipulated by having people in an experimental group jog for 30 minutes each day. Memory could be measured by comparing the number of words subjects recall from a test list studied before the exercise experiment begins, and again afterward.

c. A control group that does not exercise *is* needed so that any improvement in the experimental group's memory can be attributed to exercise, and not to some other factor, such as the passage of one month's time or familiarity with the memory test. The control group should engage in some nonexercise activity for the same amount of time each day that the experimental group exercises.

d. The subjects should be randomly selected from the population at large, and then randomly assigned to the experimental and control groups.

## Key Terms

### Writing Definitions

1. **Psychology** is the science of behavior and mental processes. (p. 3)

2. The **nature-nurture issue** is the controversy over the relative contributions that genes (nature) and experience (nurture) make to the development of psychological traits and behaviors. (p. 5)

3. **Basic research** is pure science that aims to increase psychology's scientific knowledge base rather than to solve practical problems. (p. 7)

4. **Applied research** is scientific study that aims to solve practical problems. (p. 7)

5. **Clinical psychology** is the branch of psychology concerned with the study, assessment, and treatment of people with psychological disorders. (p. 7)

6. **Psychiatry** is the branch of medicine concerned with the physical diagnosis and treatment of psychological disorders. (p. 7)

7. **Critical thinking** is careful reasoning that examines assumptions, discerns hidden values, evaluates evidence, and assesses conclusions. (p. 9)

8. **Hindsight bias** refers to the tendency to believe, after learning an outcome—including a psychological research finding—that one would have foreseen it. (p. 11)

9. A **theory** is an explanation using an integrated set of principles that organizes and predicts observations. (p. 13)

10. A **hypothesis** is a testable prediction, often implied by a theory; testing the hypothesis helps scientists to test the theory. (p. 13)

*Example:* In order to test his theory of why people conform, Solomon Asch formulated the testable **hypothesis** that an individual would be more likely to go along with the majority opinion of a large group than with that of a smaller group.

11. **Replication** is the process of repeating an experiment, often with different subjects and in different situations, to see whether the basic finding generalizes to other subjects and circumstances. (p. 13)

12. The **case study** is a descriptive research strategy in which one person is studied in great depth, often with the intention of revealing universal principles. (p. 14)

13. The **survey** is a descriptive research strategy in which a representative, random sample of people are questioned about their attitudes or behavior. (p. 15)

14. The **false consensus effect** is the tendency to overestimate the extent to which others share our beliefs and behaviors. (p. 15)

15. A **population** consists of all the members of a group being studied. (p. 15)

16. A **random sample** is one that is representative because every member of the population has an equal chance of being included. (p. 16)

17. **Naturalistic observation** involves observing and recording behavior in naturally occurring situations without trying to manipulate or control the situation. (p. 17)

18. **Correlation** is a statistical measure that indicates the extent to which two factors vary together and thus how well one factor can be predicted from the other. Correlations can be positive or negative. (p. 17)

*Example:* If there is a **positive correlation** between air temperature and ice cream sales, the warmer (higher) it is, the more ice cream is sold. If there is a **negative correlation** between air temperature and sales of cocoa, the cooler (lower) it is, the more cocoa is sold.

19. **Illusory correlation** is the false perception of a relationship between two events when none exists. (p. 18)

20. An **experiment** is a research strategy in which a researcher directly manipulates one or more factors (independent variables) in order to observe their effect on some behavior or mental process (the dependent variable); experiments therefore make it possible to establish cause-and-effect relationships. (p. 23)

21. The **experimental condition** of an experiment is one in which subjects are exposed to the independent variable being studied. (p. 24)

*Example:* In the study of the effects of a new drug on reaction time, subjects in the **experimental condition** would actually receive the drug being tested.

22. The **control condition** of an experiment is one in which the treatment of interest, or independent variable, is withheld so that comparison to the experimental condition can be made. (p. 24)

    *Example:* The **control condition** for an experiment testing the effects of a new drug on reaction time would be a group of subjects given a placebo (inactive drug or sugar pill) instead of the drug being tested.

23. **Random assignment** is the procedure of assigning subjects to the experimental and control conditions by chance in order to minimize preexisting differences between the groups. (p. 24)

24. The **independent variable** of an experiment is the factor being manipulated and tested by the investigator. (p. 25)

    *Example:* In the study of the effects of a new drug on reaction time, the drug is the **independent variable**.

25. The **dependent variable** of an experiment is the factor being measured by the investigator. (p. 25)

*Example:* In the study of the effects of a new drug on reaction time, the subjects' reaction time is the **dependent variable.**

26. **Operational definitions** are precise statements of the procedures (operations) used to define independent and dependent variables. (p. 25)

27. A **placebo** is an inert substance or condition that is administered as a test of whether an experimental subject, who mistakenly thinks a treatment is in effect, behaves the same as he or she would if the treatment were actually present. (p. 27)

28. A **double-blind procedure** is a control procedure in which neither the experimenter nor the research subjects are aware of which condition is in effect. It is used to prevent experimenters' and subjects' expectations from influencing the results of an experiment. (p. 27)

29. **Culture** is the enduring behaviors, ideas, attitudes, and traditions shared by a large group of people and transmitted from one generation to the next. (p. 29)

30. **SQ3R** is a method of active studying that incorporates five steps: *Survey, Question, Read, Rehearse, Review.* (p. 34)

---

## FOCUS ON VOCABULARY AND LANGUAGE

*Page 1: . . . to remedy their woes*, millions of people turn to "psychology." In order to alleviate or fix (*remedy*) their misery, anxiety, grief, pain, and suffering (*woes*), people seek help from "psychology." (Psychology is in quotes because Myers wants to point out that not everything you think of as "psychology" is part of scientific psychology.)

*Page 1:* Have you ever played *peekaboo* with a 6-month-old infant . . . ? Peekaboo is a game played in most cultures where a person hides or pretends to hide from a child and then reappears saying "PEEK-ABOO!" The important question for psychologists is why do infants all over the world react similarly to this game; what are they actually feeling, perceiving, and thinking?

*Page 1:* Such questions provide *grist for psychology's mill* . . . . The expression "*provide grist for the mill*" derives from the practice in the past where farmers brought their grain (*grist*) to the *mill* (a building with machinery for grinding grain into flour). Today the expression means that a greater volume of work (*grist*) does not present a problem; in fact it is welcomed. The amount of grain (*grist*) is analogous to the variety of questions asked, and the research conducted to answer them is like the *mill* producing flour from the grist. Thus, psychology is a science that thrives on attempting to answer a variety of questions about how we think, feel, and act through scientific methodology (research).

### What Is Psychology?

*Page 3:* This list of pioneering psychologists . . . "*Magellans of the mind*" . . . . Ferdinand Magellan (1489–1521) was a famous Portuguese navigator who made many discoveries and explored areas of the world previously unknown to his fellow Europeans. Because early psychologists made exciting discoveries and explored unknown frontiers, they are "*Magellans of the mind*."

*Page 3:* Let's *unpack* this definition. *Unpack* here means to take apart or disassemble. So psychology, defined as the science of behavior and mental processes, is broken down into overt behavior (i.e., observable events) and covert processes (i.e., events hidden within, such as thoughts, feelings, perceptions, beliefs, and so on) and is studied using the scientific or empirical method.

*Page 3:* . . . psychology aims to *sift* opinions and evaluate ideas . . . . Literally, *sift* means to separate the finer particles from the coarser ones by passing material through a sieve. Myers uses the word *sift* to explain how psychology examines or evaluates ideas, opinions, facts, and concepts and separates those that are useful and worthwhile from those that are not. (Be sure you understand the word *sift* because Myers uses it quite often.)

*Page 3:* . . . psychological science welcomes *hunches* and plausible-sounding theories. In popular usage a *hunch* is an intuitive feeling about a situation or event. Psychology can use subjective ideas to help formulate hypotheses or predictions which can then be tested empirically or scientifically.

*Page 3:* Its scientific sifting of ideas has produced a *smorgasbord* of concepts and findings, from which we can only sample the *fare.* A *smorgasbord* is a buffet meal at which a great variety of foods (*fare*) is offered. Myers is suggesting that psychology's examination and evaluation (*testing*) of ideas has produced a great variety of concepts and findings for us to sample or look at.

*Page 5:* During its short history, psychology has *wrestled* with some issues . . . . Psychology has struggled (*wrestled*) with a number of issues, particularly those of nature/nurture, stability/change, rationality/irrationality, and these issues may be perceived differently by the various perspectives in the discipline (i.e., several issues *cut across* psychology). Myers points out that these different views may be complementary or compatible rather than antagonistic or opposite.

*Page 5:* Over and over again we will see the nature-nurture *tension dissolve.* The main point is that both sides of the debate have something to offer: Each contributes to the search for the truth. Thus, the tension gets less (*dissolves*).

*Page 6:* "*Red in the face*" and "*hot under the collar*" refer to the physical changes that often accompany emotional arousal (e.g., anger). A person's face may become red due to blood rushing to it (blushing), and he or she may feel hot and perspire (*hot under the collar*). Different perspectives (neuroscience, evolutionary, behavior genetics, behavioral, cognitive, and social-cultural) view the same event (emotional change) from different points of view (see Table 1–1, p. 4). Myers points out that these different perspectives are not necessarily in opposition to each other but, rather, are complementary; that is, each helps to complete the puzzle of why the event occurs by sup-plying answers from different points of view (perspectives).

*Page 6:* But there is a *payoff:* Psychology is a *meeting ground* for different disciplines, and is thus a *perfect home* for those with *wide-ranging* interests. Myers points out that there is much diversity in the discipline of psychology (i.e., it lacks unity), but this is beneficial (a *payoff*) because it is a nice place (area) to work in (a *perfect home* ) for those who have broad or diverse (*wide-ranging*) interests. Thus, psychology is the ideal meeting place or *meeting ground* for different disciplines.

### Why Do Psychology?

*Page 8:* Although in some ways we *outsmart* the smartest computers, our *intuition* often goes *awry.* The main point is that humans are in many ways superior to computers (*we outsmart them*), but our beliefs, feelings, and perceptions (*intuition*) can often lead us astray (*awry*) or away from the truth. To be human means we can, and do, make mistakes (*to err is human*).

*Page 8:* Underlying all science is a *hard-headed curiosity. Hard-headed* here means to be practical, uncompromising, realistic, or unswayed by sentiment. All science, including psychology, is guided by this realistic desire to know (*curiosity*) about nature and life.

*Page 8:* . . . *leap of faith.* This is a belief in something in the absence of demonstrated proof. Some questions—about the existence of God or life after death, for example—cannot be answered by science and cannot be scientifically proved or disproved; if a person believes, then it is on the basis of trust and confidence alone (*leap of faith*).

*Page 8:* . . . the *proof is in the pudding.* This comes from the expression "*the proof of the pudding is in the eating.*" A *pudding* is a sweet dessert. We can test (or prove) the quality of the dessert (*pudding*) by trying it (*eating*). Likewise, many questions, even if they appear to make little sense (*crazy-sounding ideas*— p. 9), can be tested using the scientific method.

*Page 8:* . . . *auras* . . . An *aura* is a bright glow surrounding a figure or an object. Some believe that humans have auras which only certain people can see. The magician James Randi proposed a simple test of this claim, but nobody who is alleged to have this magical power (*aura-seer*) has taken the test.

*Page 9:* More often, it relegates *crazy-sounding ideas* to the *mountain* of forgotten claims. . . . The use of scientific inquiry can get rid of or dispose of (*relegate*) non-sensible concepts (*crazy-sounding ideas*) to the large stack or pile (*mountain*) of ridiculous ideas now forgotten.

*Page 9:* In the *arena* of competing ideas . . . An *arena* is an area where games, sports, and competitions take place. Myers is suggesting that in an area (*arena*) where there is a contest between ideas (competing ideas), skeptical testing can help discover the truth.

*Page 9:* . . . *then so much the worse for our ideas.* This means that we have to give up, or get rid of, our ideas if they are shown to be wrong (*so much the worse for them*). We have to be humble (i.e., have humility).

*Page 9:* "*The rat is always right.*" This early *motto* (a phrase used as a maxim or guiding principle) comes from the fact that for most of the first half of this century psychology used animals in its research (especially in the study of learning). The *rat* became a symbol of this research, and its behavior or performance in experiments demonstrated the truth. If the truth, as shown by the rat, is contrary to the prediction or hypothesis, then one has to be humble about it and try another way.

*Page 9:* We all view nature through the *spectacles* of our *preconceived ideas.* This means that what we already believe (*our preconceived ideas*) influences, and to some extent determines, what we look for and actually see or discover in nature. It's as though the type of eyeglasses (*spectacles*) we wear limits what we can see.

*Page 9:* What *axe is this person grinding?* This expression refers to having an ulterior motive or selfish reason for a behavior. Critical thinkers examine assumptions and question and evaluate statements to determine if a person reporting information has a bias or grievance (*an axe to grind*).

*Page 9:* . . . *gut feelings* . . . This refers to basic intuitive reactions or responses. Critical thinking requires determining whether a conclusion is based simply on a subjective opinion (*gut feeling*) or anecdote (a story someone tells) or on reliable scientific evidence.

*Page 10:* . . . *debunked* . . . This means to remove glamour or credibility from established ideas, persons, and traditions. Myers points out that scientific evidence and critical inquiry have indeed discredited (*debunked*) many popular presumptions.

*Page 10:* . . . one can "*play the tape*" and relive long-buried or *repressed* memories. . . . This is an example of a discredited (*debunked*) idea that hidden

(*repressed*) memories can be accurately and reliably retrieved (brought back) intact and complete in the same way that *playing a tape* on a VCR allows us to watch exactly the same show over and over again.

*Page 10:* They say psychology merely *documents* what people already know and *dresses it in jargon.* Some people criticize psychology, saying that it simply reports (*documents*) common sense, or what's obvious to everyone. Instead of stating something plainly, the critics suggest, psychology translates the information into the specialized and obscure vocabulary of the discipline (*dresses it up in jargon*). Myers makes it very clear with some good examples (pp. 10, 11) that this criticism is not justified and points out that our intuitions about reality can often be very mistaken (p. 10: intuition sometimes *blunders*).

*Page 10:* We're all *after-the-fact pundits.* A pundit is a very knowledgeable person. After the outcome of an event is known, anyone familiar with the result can claim to have foreseen it (an *after-the-fact pundit*). Myers refers to this tendency as the "I-knew-it-all-along" phenomenon or "hindsight bias."

*Page 11:* "*Out of sight, out of mind*" and "*Absence makes the heart grow fonder.*" These two sayings, or expressions, about romantic love have opposite meanings. The first one suggests that when couples are apart (*out of sight*) they are less likely to think about each other (*out of mind*) than when they are together. The second saying makes the point that being separated (*absence*) increases the feelings of love the couple shares (*makes the heart grow fonder*). People who are told that the results of a study support the first expression (*out of sight, out of mind*) see this as mere common sense. People told that the results support the second expression (*absence makes the heart grow fonder*) also say this is obviously true. There is clearly a problem here; relying on common sense can lead to opposite conclusions.

*Page 11:* How easy it is to seem *astute* when *drawing the bull's eye after the arrow has struck.* In the sport of archery the task is to shoot the arrow at the red circle in the center of the target (the *bull's eye*). If we first shoot an arrow, then draw the target so that the arrow is in the center (in the *bull's eye*), we can appear to be very accurate. Myers uses this analogy to illustrate how the hindsight bias can lead us to believe that we are shrewd (*astute*) and would have been able to predict outcomes that we have learned after-the-fact.

*Page 11:* . . . our intuition may tell us that *familiarity breeds contempt.* . . . This expression (and others) are based on many casual observations but are often wrong. For example, is it true that the better you know someone (*familiarity*), the more likely it is that you will dislike them (have *contempt*)? In fact, research shows that the opposite is probably true. (Your text, again and again, will emphasize the fact that our common sense and intuition do not always provide us with reliable evidence.)

*Page 12: . . . drop a course . . .* This means to stop going to class and to have your name removed from the class list.

### How Do Psychologists Ask and Answer Questions?

*Page 13:* G. E. Morton (1994) likens theory construction to solving a *connect-the-dots puzzle. . . .* This type of puzzle requires you to see how the various parts (*dots*) are related (*connected*) to the total picture. Likewise, a theory links (*connects*) and organizes observations and isolated facts (the *dots*) into a whole. Thus, a simpler and clearer picture emerges.

*Page 14:* Sigmund Freud constructed his theory of personality from *a handful of case studies. A handful* means a very small number. Freud published only about twelve (*a handful of* ) in-depth investigations of individuals (*case studies*).

*Page 15:* Our *tendency to leap* to conclusions from *unrepresentative* information is a common source of mistaken judgment. Our inclination (*tendency*) to decide quickly (*leap* or *jump to conclusions*) based on biased (*unrepresentative*) information frequently leads to wrong decisions.

*Page 15: Numbers are numbing . . .* and *Anecdotes are alarming. . . .* Myers is playing with words here, using *alliteration* (repeating the same initial letter in a group of words). We are often overwhelmed and our senses deadened (*numbed*) by the sometimes inappropriate use of statistics and numbers. We are also startled or frightened (*alarmed*) by the strange stories people tell (*anecdotes*).

*Page 15:* Most surveys sample a *target group.* The group of interest (*target group*) can be any group the researcher wants to talk about (*generalize to*), such as all people who smoke, or all college students, or all single mothers. It would be impossible to question or interview all the people in the group (*the population*), so a representative sample is chosen at random.

*Page 16: . . .* 1500 randomly sampled people, drawn from all areas of a country, provide a remarkably accurate *snapshot* of the opinions of a nation. A *snapshot* is a picture taken with a camera, and it captures what people are doing at a given moment in time. A good survey (1500 *randomly selected representative people*) gives an accurate picture (*snapshot*) of the opinions of the whole population of interest (the *target group*).

*Page 16: . . . having affairs . . .* Myers points out that the results of a large, nonrandom, nonrepresentative sample of married women which suggested that a large percentage (70 percent) were having sexual relations with someone other than their spouse (*having affairs or love affairs*) were not valid or reliable. A better study, using a smaller but a more representative and random sample, showed that the figure was actually closer to 10 percent. (Note: The word *affair* has other meanings. For example, in the phrase *"applying science to human affairs,"* the word *affairs* refers to human concerns or business.)

*Page 19:* If someone *flipped a coin* six times, would one of the following sequences of heads (H) or tails (T) be most likely: HHHTTT or HTTHTH or HHH-HHH? *Flipping a coin* means throwing or tossing the coin into the air and observing which side is facing up when it lands. (The side of the coin that usually has the imprint of the face of a famous person on it—e.g., the president or the queen—is called *heads* (*H*) and the other side is called *tails* (*T*). By the way, all of the above sequences are equally likely, but most people pick HTTHTH. Likewise, any series of 5 playing cards (e.g., a bridge or poker hand in a game of cards) is just as likely as any other hand.

*Page 21: . . . laypeople . . .* refers to people who do not belong to a particular profession. Both professionals and nonprofessionals (*laypeople*) mistakenly assume that correlation proves causation. It does not. Correlation means that one variable goes along with (predicts) another variable. For growing children, shoe size goes along with cognitive ability, but obviously one variable does not *cause* the other.

*Page 22:* Thinking critically: *Hot and cold streaks.* Players who have "*hot hands*" can't seem to miss. Those who have "*cold*" ones can't find the center of the hoop. In this context, *hot* and *cold* do not refer to temperature. Here, being *hot* means doing well, and doing well consistently is *having a hot streak.* Having a poor run of luck is a *cold streak.* The crucial point, however, is that our intuition about sequences of events (*streaks*) often deceives us. Random sequences often are not what we think they should be, so when we think we're doing well (*hot*), we're not.

*Page 25: Recap* is an abbreviation of *recapitulate,* which means to repeat or go over briefly, to summarize. Myers summarizes (*recaps*) the important points in each section of the chapter.

*Page 26: Scientific inquiry is a voyage of discovery toward a horizon, beyond which yet another horizon beckons.* Myers is using a metaphor here to illustrate how scientific inquiry is like a journey (*voyage*) that never really ends. Each discovery in science leads to more questions, more research, more findings, and still more questions, and so on.

*Page 26: Is there anything to these wild and sometimes wacky claims?* Absurd, bizarre, irrational, or nonsensical statements or claims are popularly called *wild* or *wacky*. The claim that subliminal tapes can improve our lives has been tested scientifically; however, numerous studies have shown that these tapes have no effect (*zilch,* p. 27). The claims are, therefore, simply ridiculous (*wild and wacky*).

### Frequently Asked Questions About Psychology

*Page 29: . . . plunge in.* In this context, *plunge in* means to move ahead quickly with the discussion. (Similarly, when you dive into a swimming pool [*plunge in*], you do so quickly.) Before going on with the discussion of psychology (*plunging in*), Myers addresses some important issues and questions.

*Page 30:* To understand how a combustion engine works, you would do better to study *a lawn mower's engine than a Mercedes'.* A *Mercedes* is a very complex luxury car, and a *lawn mower* (a machine for cutting grass in the garden) has a very simple engine. To understand the principles underlying both machines, it is easier to study the simpler one. Likewise, when trying to understand the nervous system, it is better to study a simple one (e.g., sea slugs) than a complex one (humans).

*Page 32: . . . idle curiosity. Curiosity* means an eagerness to know, and *idle curiosity* means an eagerness to know for no particular reason. The critics of animal research claim that animals are made to suffer for no worthwhile reason (*out of idle curiosity*). Myers points out that these claims are unfounded.

*Page 33: . . .* most universities today screen research proposals through an *ethics committee. . . . Ethics com-* mittees (groups of people concerned with moral behavior and acceptable standards of conduct) subject research proposals to rigorous tests (*screen them*) to ensure that they are fair and reasonable and that they do not harm the participants' well-being.

*Page 33: Values* can also *color* "the facts." Our values (what we believe is right and true) can influence (*color*) our observations, interpretations, and conclusions ("the facts").

*Page 33:* Might it [psychology] become the tool of someone seeking to create a *totalitarian Brave New World* or *1984? Brave New World* and *1984* are fictional novels about authoritarian (*totalitarian*) control of the population. (These books are well worth reading!)

### Tips for Studying Psychology

*Page 35:* One of psychology's oldest findings is that *"spaced practice"* promotes better retention than *"massed practice." Spaced practice* refers to studying over a longer period of time, say 2 hours a day over 5 days rather than 10 hours on one day (*massed practice* or cramming). Distributing your study time is much better for learning and retention than one long study period (a *blitz*).

### Reviewing Introduction: Thinking Critically With Psychology

*Page 36: . . .* helps *winnow* sense from nonsense. *Winnow* means to separate out and was originally used to describe the separation of chaff (dust, etc.) from the grains of wheat. The scientific method helps sort out, or separate (*winnow*), good ideas from bad ones.

*Page 36: . . .* a scientific approach helps us *sift* reality from illusion, taking us beyond the *horizons* of our intuition and common sense. A scientific (or empirical) attitude can separate (*sift*) what's real from what is not and take us beyond the limits of our vision and experience (*horizons*).

# 2

# *Biology and Behavior*

## Chapter Overview

Chapter 2 is concerned with the functions of the brain, its component neural systems, and their genetic blueprints, which provide the basis for all human behavior. Under the direction of the brain, the nervous and endocrine systems coordinate a variety of voluntary and involuntary behaviors and serve as the body's mechanisms for communication with the external environment.

The brain consists of the brainstem, the thalamus, the cerebellum, the limbic system, and the cerebral cortex. Knowledge of the workings of the brain has increased with recent advances in neuroscientific methods. Studies of split-brain patients have also given researchers a great deal of information about the specialized functions of the brain's right and left hemispheres.

The chapter concludes with a discussion of how psychologists use evolutionary principles to answer universal questions about human behavior and specific questions about individual differences.

Many students find the technical material in this chapter difficult to master. Not only are there many terms for you to remember, but you must also know the organization and function of the various divisions of the nervous system. Learning this material will require a great deal of rehearsal. Working the chapter review several times, drawing and labeling brain diagrams, and mentally reciting terms are all useful techniques for rehearsing this type of material.

NOTE: Answer guidelines for all Chapter 2 questions begin on page 46.

## Guided Study

The text chapter should be studied one section at a time. Before you read, preview each section by skimming it, noting headings and boldface items. Then read the appropriate section objectives from the following outline. Keep these objectives in mind and, as you read the chapter section, search for the information that will enable you to meet each objective. Once you have finished a section, write out answers for its objectives.

1. Explain why psychologists are concerned with human biology.

*Neural Communication* (pp. 40–44)

> David Myers at times uses idioms that are unfamiliar to some readers. If you do not know the meaning of any of the following words, phrases, or expressions in the context in which they appear in the text, refer to pages 58–59 for an explanation: *an ill-fated theory; wrong-headedness; happy fact of nature; building blocks; . . . like a line of dominoes falling; a sluggish 2 miles per hour to . . . a breakneck 200 or more miles; . . . rather like pushing a neuron's accelerator. . . . rather like pushing its brake; How do we distinguish a gentle touch from a firm hug; protoplasmic kisses; Roughly speaking, the neuron is democratic; runner's high; They trigger unpleasant, lingering aftereffects; Agonists work by mimicking a particular neurotransmitter; some chemicals don't have the right shape to slither through the blood-brain barrier.*

2. Explain why, at every level, our existence is both part of a larger system and a combination of smaller systems.

3. Describe the structure of a neuron and the process by which an action potential is triggered.

4. Describe how nerve cells communicate and discuss the importance of neurotransmitters for human behavior.

5. Discuss the significance of endorphins and explain how drugs influence neurotransmitters.

*The Nervous System* (pp. 44–47)

> If you do not know the meaning of any of the following words, phrases, or expressions in the context in which they appear in the text, refer to page 59 for an explanation: *Like an automatic pilot, it may be consciously overridden; yield an ever-changing wiring diagram that dwarfs a powerful computer; information highway; The knee-jerk response is one example; a headless warm body could do it.*

6. Identify the major divisions of the nervous system and their primary functions, noting how information is carried throughout the system.

7. Describe the operation of reflexes in the spinal cord.

*The Brain* (pp. 48–61)

> If you do not know the meaning of any of the following words, phrases, or expressions in the context in which they appear in the text, refer to pages 59–61 for an explanation: *we live in our heads; exceptions to the rule of thumb; This peculiar cross-wiring is but one of many surprises the brain has to offer; . . . neural traffic what London is to England's train traffic; . . . snoop on the messages . . . and on the mass action of billions; Other new windows into the brain . . . Supermanlike; snapshots of the brain's mind-making activity provide . . . divides its labor; These new brain-imaging instruments . . . are triggering a scientific revolution; a doughnut-shaped neural system; magnificent mistake; wrinkled organ, shaped rather like the meat of an oversized walnut; eyes in the back of our head; most widespread myths; What you experience as . . . the visible tip of the information-processing iceberg.*

8. Describe the functions of structures within the brainstem, as well as those of the thalamus and the cerebellum.

9. (Close-Up) Identify and explain the methods used in studying the brain.

10. Describe the functions of the structures in the limbic system.

11. Describe the structure and functions of the cerebral cortex.

12. Discuss how damage to one of several different cortical areas can impair language functioning and outline the process by which the brain directs reading aloud.

*Brain Reorganization* (pp. 62–67)

> If you do not know the meaning of any of the following words, phrases, or expressions in the context in which they appear in the text, refer to page 61 for an explanation: *"hard-wired"; one patient even managed to quip that he had a "splitting headache"; pretzel-shaped findings . . . breadstick-shaped story; the brain's press agent; look alike to the naked eye . . . harmony of the whole; dwarfs.*

13. Discuss brain plasticity and what it reveals about brain reorganization.

14. (text and Thinking Critically) Describe research on the split brain and discuss what it reveals regarding normal brain functioning.

*The Endocrine System* (pp. 67–68)

> If you do not know the meaning of any of the following words, phrases, or expressions in the context in which they appear in the text, refer to page 61 for an explanation: *kindred systems; Conducting and coordinating this whole electro-chemical orchestra is that maestro we call the brain.*

15. Discuss the functioning of the endocrine system.

*Genetics and Behavior* (pp. 69–74)

> If you do not know the meaning of any of the following words, phrases, or expressions in the context in which they appear in the text, refer to pages 61–62 for an explanation: *blueprints; tight genetic leash; mobile gene machines . . . have longings and make choices; cute stories; area of a field is more the result of its length or width.*

16. Identify the mechanisms of heredity and explain the scope of the new fields of evolutionary psychology and behavior genetics.

17. Explain why researchers use twin and adoption studies to estimate the heritability of traits.

## Chapter Review

When you have finished reading the chapter, work through the material that follows to review it. Complete the sentences and answer the questions. As you proceed, evaluate your performance for each section by consulting the answers on page 49. Do not continue with the next section until you understand each answer. If you need to, review or reread the appropriate section in the textbook before continuing.

1. In the most basic sense, every idea, mood, memory, and behavior that an individual has ever experienced is a _____ phenomenon.

2. The theory that linked our mental abilities to bumps on the skull was _____ .

3. Researchers who study the links between biology and behavior are called _____ _____ .

*Neural Communication* (pp. 40–44)

4. We are each a _____ , composed of _____ that are parts of larger _____ . Our body's neural system is built from billions of nerve cells, or _____ .

5. The extensions of a neuron that receive messages from other neurons are the _____ .

6. The extensions of a neuron that transmit information to other neurons are the _____ ; some of these extensions are insulated by a layer of fatty cells called the _____ _____ , which helps speed the neuron's impulses.

7. Identify the major parts of the neuron diagrammed below:

   a. _____     c. _____
   b. _____     d. _____

8. The neural impulse, or _____
   _____ , is a brief electrical
   charge that travels down a(n)

   _____ .

9. In order to trigger a neural impulse,
   _____ signals minus
   _____ signals must exceed a
   certain intensity, called the _____ .
   Increasing a stimulus above this level
   _____ (will/will not) increase
   the neural impulse's intensity. This phenomenon
   is called an _____ -

   _____ -_____

   response.

Outline the sequence of reactions that occur when a
neural impulse is generated and transmitted from one
neuron to another.

10. The strength of a stimulus _____
    (does/does not) affect the speed of a neural
    impulse.

11. The junction between two neurons is called a
    _____ , and the gap is called
    the _____ .

12. The chemical messengers that convey informa-
    tion across the gaps between neurons are called
    _____ . These chemicals unlock
    tiny channels on receptor sites, allowing electri-
    cally charged _____ to enter
    the neuron.

13. Neurotransmitters influence neurons either by
    _____ or
    _____ their readiness to fire.

14. A neurotransmitter that is important in muscle
    contraction is _____ . The poi-
    son _____ produces paralysis
    by blocking the activity of this neurotransmitter.

15. Naturally occurring opiatelike neurotransmitters
    that are present in the brain are called
    _____ . When the brain is
    flooded with drugs such as _____
    or _____ , it may stop producing
    these neurotransmitters.

16. Drugs that produce their effects by mimicking
    neurotransmitters are called _____ .
    Drugs that block the effects of neurotransmitters
    by occupying their _____
    _____ are called

    _____ .

17. The molecular shape of some drugs prevents
    them from passing through the

    _____ -_____

    _____ by which the brain
    fences out unwanted chemicals.

18. The tremors of _____ disease
    are due to the death of neurons that produce the
    neurotransmitter _____ . People
    with this condition can be helped to regain con-
    trol over their muscles by taking

    _____ .

*The Nervous System* (pp. 44–47)

19. Taken altogether, the neurons of the body form the _____ .

20. The brain and spinal cord comprise the _____ nervous system. The neurons that link the brain and spinal cord to the body's sense receptors, muscles, and glands form the _____ nervous system.

21. Sensory and motor axons are bundled into electrical cables called _____ .

22. Information arriving in the central nervous system from the body travels in _____ neurons. The neurons that enable internal communication within the central nervous system are called _____ .

23. The central nervous system sends instructions to the body's tissues by means of _____ neurons.

24. The division of the peripheral nervous system that transmits sensory input to the central nervous system and directs the movements of the skeletal muscles is the _____ nervous system. These movements are usually under _____ control.

25. Self-regulating responses—those of the glands and muscles of internal organs—are controlled by the _____ nervous system.

26. The body is made ready for action by the _____ division of the autonomic nervous system.

27. The _____ division of the autonomic nervous system produces relaxation.

Describe and explain the sequence of physical reactions that occur in the body as an emergency is confronted and then passes.

28. Automatic responses to stimuli, called _____ , illustrate the work of the _____ .

*The Brain* (pp. 48–61)

29. The oldest and innermost region of the brain is the _____ .

30. At the base of the brainstem, where the spinal cord enters the skull, lies the _____ , which controls _____ and _____ .

31. Nerves from each side of the brain cross over to connect with the body's opposite side in the _____ .

32. The _____ is contained inside the brainstem and helps control _____ . Electrically stimulating this area will produce an _____ animal. Lesioning this area will cause an animal to lapse into a _____ .

33. At the top of the brainstem sits the _____ , which serves as the brain's sensory switchboard.

34. (Close-Up) The oldest technique for studying the brain involves _____ of patients with brain injuries or diseases.

35. (Close-Up) Researchers have also studied brain function by producing _____ , or selectively destroyed areas of brain tissue.

36. (Close-Up) The _____ is a recording of the electrical activity of the whole brain.

37. (Close-Up) A computer-generated image of a slice of the brain based on a series of x-ray photographs taken from different angles is called a _____ .

38. (Close-Up) The technique depicting the level of activity of brain areas by measuring the brain's consumption of glucose is called the _____

(Close-Up) Briefly explain the purpose of the PET scan.

39. (Close-Up) A technique that produces clearer images of the brain by using magnetic fields and radio waves is known as _____ .
When a light is shined in a subject's eyes, the

_____

shows activity in the part of the cortex thought to control the bodily activity being studied.

40. At the rear of the brainstem lies the
_____ . It influences one type
of _____ and memory, but its major function is coordination of voluntary movement and _____ control.

41. Between the brainstem and cerebral hemispheres is the _____ system. One component of this system that processes memory is the _____ .

42. Rage or fear will result from stimulation of different regions of the _____ .

43. Below the thalamus is the _____ , which regulates bodily maintenance behaviors such as _____ ,

_____ , and _____ .
Olds and Milner discovered that this region also contains _____ centers, which animals will work hard to have stimulated. The hypothalamus also regulates behavior chemically through its influence on the _____ gland.

44. Some researchers believe that alcoholism, drug abuse, food binging, and other

_____ disorders, may stem

from a genetic _____

_____

in the pleasure systems of the brain.

45. The most complex functions of human behavior are linked to the most developed part of the brain, the _____ _____ .

46. The non-neural cells that support, protect, and nourish cortical neurons are called

_____ _____ .

47. List the four lobes of the brain.
   a. _____    c. _____
   b. _____    d. _____

48. Electrical stimulation of one side of the
_____ cortex, an arch-shaped region at the back of the _____ lobe, will produce movement on the opposite side of the body.

49. At the front of the parietal lobe lies the
_____ cortex, which, when stimulated, elicits a sensation of

_____ .

50. The more sensitive a body region, the greater the area of _____

_____ devoted to it.

Beginning with the sensory receptors in the skin, trace the course of a spinal reflex as a person reflexively jerks his or her hand away from an unexpectedly hot burner on a stove.

51. Visual information is received in the
_____ lobes, whereas auditory
information is received in the
_____ lobes.

52. Areas of the brain that don't receive sensory
information or direct movement but, rather, integrate and interpret information received by other
regions are known as _____
_____ . Approximately
_____ of the human cortex is of
this type. Such areas in the
_____ lobe are involved in recognizing faces, making judgments, and carrying
out plans, and in some aspects of personality.

53. Brain injuries may produce an impairment in language use called _____ .
Studies of people with such impairments have
shown that _____
_____ is involved in producing
speech, _____
_____ is involved in understanding speech, and the _____
_____ is involved in recoding
printed words into auditory form.

## Brain Reorganization (pp. 62–67)

54. The quality of the brain that makes it possible for
undamaged brain areas to take over the functions
of damaged regions is known as
_____ .

55. Neurons in the brain and spinal cord
_____ (will/will not) regener-
ate.

56. After age _____ , left hemisphere damage permanently disrupts language.

57. Because damage to it will impair language and
understanding, the _____
hemisphere came to be known as the
_____ hemisphere.

58. In treating several patients with severe epilepsy,
Vogel and Bogen separated the two hemispheres
of the brain by cutting the _____

_____ . When this structure is
severed, the result is referred to as a
_____ _____ .

59. In a split-brain patient, only the
_____ hemisphere will be
aware of an unseen object held in the left hand. In
this case, the person would not be able to
_____ the object. When differ-
ent words are shown in the left and right visual
fields, if the patient fixates on a point on the center line between the fields, the patient will be able
to say only the word shown on the
_____ .

Explain why a split-brain patient would be able to
read aloud the word *pencil* flashed to his or her right
visual field, but would be unable to identify a pencil
by touch using only the left hand.

## The Endocrine System (pp. 67–68)

60. The body's chemical communication network is
called the _____
_____ . This system transmits
information through chemical messengers called
_____ at a much
_____ (faster/slower) rate than
the nervous system.

61. In a moment of danger, the
_____ glands release
_____ and _____ .

62. The most influential gland is the
_____ , which, under the control of the brain area called the
_____ , helps regulate
_____ and the release of hormones by other endocrine glands.

Write a paragraph describing the feedback system
that links the nervous and endocrine systems.

*Genetics and Behavior* (pp. 69–74)

63. The master plans for development are stored within the _____ . In number, each person inherits _____ of these structures, _____ from each parent. Each is composed of a coiled chain of a molecule called _____ .

64. The biochemical units of heredity that make each of us a distinctive human being are called _____ .

65. Genetic constraints on human behavior are generally _____ (tighter/looser) than those on animal behavior.

66. Researchers who study natural selection and the adaptive nature of human behavior are called _____ .

    The principles of natural selection favor behaviors that spread one's _____ .

67. Researchers who specifically study the effects of genes on behavior are called _____ .

68. To study the power and limits of genetic influences on behavior researchers use _____ and _____ studies.

69. Twins who developed from a single egg are genetically _____ . Twins who developed from different fertilized eggs are no more genetically alike than siblings and are called _____ twins.

70. In terms of the personality traits of extraversion and neuroticism, identical twins are _____ (more/no more) alike than are fraternal twins.

71. Through research on identical twins raised apart, psychologists are able to study the influence of the _____ .

72. Studies tend to show that the personalities of adopted children _____ (do/do not) closely resemble those of their adoptive parents.

73. The proportion of variation in a trait within a group that is attributable to genes is called its _____ .

74. For _____ traits, human differences are nearly always the result of both _____ and _____ influences.

75. Genetic influences help explain individual differences in _____ , _____ , and _____ . Heritable individual differences _____ (imply/ need not imply) heritable group differences.

## WEB SIGHTING

Scientific American (**http://www.sciam.com/**), the University of Washington (**http://weber.u.washington.edu/~chudler/neurok.html**), and The Franklin Institute (**http://www.fi.edu/**) maintain three excellent web sites that provide a variety of online multimedia activities related to neurobiology. Check out the virtual tours of the nervous system. Compare the brains of nine different animal species. Read the latest research news pertaining to health, disease, and behavior genetics. Travel through time and review the history of brain science. To get started, see if you can find the answers to the following questions:

1. What is anosognosia? What clues does it offer to neuropsychologists about perception, self-awareness, and the brain?

2. How many neurons are there in the average human brain?

3. If you took all of the blood vessels of the average adult and laid them end to end, how long a line would be formed?

4. How much does the average elephant brain weigh?

5. What is the most common disease of the nervous system?

6. Who was the first neuroscientist?

7. What are the "ten rules of good brain health"?

## Progress Test 1

*Multiple-Choice Questions*

Circle your answers to the following questions and check them with the answers on page 50. If your answer is incorrect, read the explanation for why it is incorrect and then consult the appropriate pages of the text (in parentheses following the correct answer).

1. The axons of certain neurons are covered by a layer of fatty tissue that helps speed neural transmission. This tissue is:
   a. the glia.
   b. the myelin sheath.
   c. acetylcholine.
   d. an endorphin.

2. Heartbeat, digestion, and other self-regulating bodily functions are governed by the:
   a. voluntary nervous system.
   b. autonomic nervous system.
   c. sympathetic division of the autonomic nervous system.
   d. skeletal nervous system.
   e. central nervous system.

3. A strong stimulus can increase the:
   a. speed of the impulse the neuron fires.
   b. intensity of the impulse the neuron fires.
   c. number of times the neuron fires.
   d. threshold that must be reached before the neuron fires.

4. The pain of heroin withdrawal may be attributable to the fact that:
   a. under the influence of heroin the brain ceases production of endorphins.
   b. under the influence of heroin the brain ceases production of all neurotransmitters.
   c. during withdrawal the brain's production of all neurotransmitters is greatly increased.
   d. heroin destroys endorphin receptors in the brain.

5. (Close-Up) The brain research technique that involves monitoring the brain's usage of glucose is called (in abbreviated form) the:
   a. PET scan.          c. EEG.
   b. CT scan.           d. MRI.

6. Dr. Ross believes that principles of natural selection help explain why infants come to fear strangers about the time they become mobile. Dr. Ross is most likely a(n):
   a. behavior geneticist.
   b. molecular geneticist.
   c. evolutionary psychologist.
   d. molecular biologist.

7. Though there is no single "control center" for emotions, their regulation is primarily attributed to the brain region known as the:
   a. limbic system.        c. brainstem.
   b. reticular formation.   d. cerebral cortex.

8. Which is the correct sequence in the transmission of a simple reflex?
   a. sensory neuron → interneuron → sensory neuron
   b. interneuron → motor neuron → sensory neuron
   c. sensory neuron → interneuron → motor neuron
   d. interneuron → sensory neuron → motor neuron

9. Damage to _____ will usually cause a person to lose the ability to comprehend language.
   a. the angular gyrus
   b. Broca's area
   c. Wernicke's area
   d. frontal lobe association areas

10. Which of the following is typically controlled by the right hemisphere?
   a. language
   b. learned voluntary movements
   c. arithmetic reasoning
   d. perceptual tasks

11. Dr. Hernandez is studying neurotransmitter abnormalities in depressed patients. She would most likely describe herself as a:
   a. psychiatrist.
   b. clinical psychologist.
   c. psychoanalyst.
   d. biological psychologist.

12. As the brain evolved, the increasing complexity of animals' behavior was accompanied by a(n):
    a. increase in the size of the brainstem.
    b. decrease in the ratio of brain to body weight.
    c. increase in the size of the frontal lobes.
    d. increase in the amount of association area.

13. Voluntary movements, such as writing with a pencil, are directed by the:
    a. sympathetic nervous system.
    b. skeletal nervous system.
    c. parasympathetic nervous system.
    d. autonomic nervous system.

14. A neuron will generate action potentials more often when it:
    a. remains below its threshold.
    b. receives an excitatory input.
    c. receives more excitatory than inhibitory inputs.
    d. is stimulated by a neurotransmitter.
    e. is stimulated by a hormone.

15. Which is the correct sequence in the transmission of a neural impulse?
    a. axon → dendrite → cell body → synapse
    b. dendrite → axon → cell body → synapse
    c. synapse → axon → dendrite → cell body
    d. axon → synapse → cell body → dendrite
    e. dendrite → cell body → axon → synapse

16. Chemical messengers produced by endocrine glands are called:
    a. chromosomes.      c. hormones.
    b. neurotransmitters.  d. enzymes.

17. Following a head injury, a person has ongoing difficulties staying awake. Most likely, the damage occurred to the:
    a. thalamus.         c. reticular formation.
    b. corpus callosum.  d. cerebellum.

18. Based on research, which of the following seems true about the specialized functions of the right and left hemispheres?
    a. They are more clear-cut in men than in women.
    b. They are more clear-cut in women than in men.
    c. Most complex tasks emerge from the activity of one or the other hemisphere.
    d. Most complex activities emerge from the integrated activity of both hemispheres.

19. Cortical areas that are not primarily concerned with sensory, motor, or language functions are:
    a. called projection areas.
    b. called association areas.
    c. located mostly in the parietal lobe.
    d. located mostly in the temporal lobe.

20. Several studies of long-separated twins have found that these twins:
    a. have little in common, due to the different environments in which they were raised.
    b. are extremely similar, in everything from their medical histories to their personalities.
    c. have similar personalities but very different likes, dislikes, and life-styles.
    d. are no more similar than are fraternal twins reared apart.

## Matching Items

Match each structure with its corresponding function or description.

### Structures

_____   1. hypothalamus
_____   2. heritability
_____   3. fraternal
_____   4. genes
_____   5. reticular formation
_____   6. identical
_____   7. thalamus
_____   8. corpus callosum
_____   9. cerebellum
_____  10. amygdala
_____  11. medulla

### Functions or Descriptions

a. the biochemical units of heredity
b. twins that develop from a single egg
c. serves as sensory switchboard
d. contains reward centers
e. twins that develop from separate eggs
f. variation among individuals due to genes
g. helps control arousal
h. links the cerebral hemispheres
i. influences rage and fear
j. regulates breathing and heartbeat
k. enables coordinated movement

## Progress Test 2

Progress Test 2 should be completed during a final chapter review. Answer the following questions after you thoroughly understand the correct answers for the Chapter Review and Progress Test 1.

### Multiple-Choice Questions

1. The visual cortex is located in the:
   a. occipital lobe.
   b. temporal lobe.
   c. frontal lobe.
   d. parietal lobe.

2. Which of the following is typically controlled by the left hemisphere?
   a. spatial reasoning
   b. arithmetic reasoning
   c. the left side of the body
   d. perceptual skills

3. When Sandy scalded her toe in a tub of hot water, the pain message was carried to her spinal cord by the _____ nervous system.
   a. skeletal
   b. sympathetic
   c. parasympathetic
   d. central

4. Which of the following are governed by the simplest neural pathways?
   a. emotions
   b. physiological drives, such as hunger
   c. reflexes
   d. movements, such as walking
   e. balance

5. Melissa has just completed running a marathon. She is so elated that she feels little fatigue or discomfort. Her lack of pain is probably the result of the release of:
   a. ACh.
   b. endorphins.
   c. dopamine.
   d. norepinephrine.
   e. acetylcholine.

6. Parkinson's disease involves:
   a. the death of nerve cells that produce a vital neurotransmitter.
   b. impaired function in the right hemisphere only.
   c. impaired function in the left hemisphere only.
   d. excess production of the neurotransmitters dopamine and acetylcholine.

7. (Close-Up) The technique that uses magnetic fields and radio waves to produce computer images of structures within the brain is called:
   a. the EEG.
   b. a CT scan.
   c. a PET scan.
   d. MRI.

8. The myelin sheath that is on some neurons:
   a. increases the speed of neural transmission.
   b. slows neural transmission.
   c. regulates the release of neurotransmitters.
   d. does a. and c.
   e. does b. and c.

9. Each cell of the human body has a total of:
   a. 23 chromosomes.
   b. 23 genes.
   c. 46 chromosomes.
   d. 46 genes.

10. The neurotransmitter acetylcholine (ACh) is most likely to be found:
    a. at the junction between sensory neurons and muscle fibers.
    b. at the junction between motor neurons and muscle fibers.
    c. at junctions between interneurons.
    d. in all of the above locations.

11. The gland that regulates body growth is the:
    a. adrenal.
    b. thyroid.
    c. hypothalamus.
    d. pituitary.
    e. hyperthyroid.

12. Epinephrine and norepinephrine are _____ that are released by the _____ gland.
    a. neurotransmitters; pituitary
    b. hormones; pituitary
    c. neurotransmitters; adrenal
    d. hormones; adrenal
    e. hormones; thyroid

13. Jessica experienced difficulty keeping her balance after receiving a blow to the back of her head. It is likely that she injured her:
    a. medulla.
    b. thalamus.
    c. hypothalamus.
    d. cerebellum.
    e. cerebrum.

14. Moruzzi and Magoun caused a cat to lapse into a coma by severing neural connections between the cortex and the:
    a. reticular formation.
    b. hypothalamus.
    c. thalamus.
    d. cerebellum.
    e. medulla.

15. Research has found that the amount of representation in the motor cortex reflects the:
   a. size of the body parts.
   b. degree of precise control required by each of
the parts.
   c. sensitivity of the body region.
   d. area of the occipital lobe being stimulated by
the environment.

16. The effect of a drug that is an agonist is to:
   a. cause the brain to stop producing certain
neurotransmitters.
   b. mimic a particular neurotransmitter.
   c. block a particular neurotransmitter.
   d. disrupt a neuron's all-or-none firing pattern.

17. The nerve fibers that enable communication
between the right and left cerebral hemispheres
and that have been severed in split-brain patients
form a structure called the:
   a. reticular formation.    d. parietal lobes.
   b. association areas.       e. limbic system.
   c. corpus callosum.

18. Beginning at the front of the brain and working
backward then down and around, which of the
following is the correct order of the cortical
regions?
   a. occipital lobe; temporal lobe; parietal lobe;
frontal lobe
   b. temporal lobe; frontal lobe; parietal lobe;
occipital lobe

   c. frontal lobe; occipital lobe; temporal lobe;
parietal lobe
   d. frontal lobe; parietal lobe; occipital lobe; temporal lobe
   e. occipital lobe; parietal lobe; temporal lobe;
frontal lobe

19. Following a gunshot wound to his head, Jack
became more uninhibited, irritable, and profane.
It is likely that his personality change was the
result of injury to his:
   a. parietal lobe.        d. frontal lobe.
   b. temporal lobe.       e. endocrine system.
   c. occipital lobe.

20. Three-year-old Marco suffered damage to the
speech area of the brain's left hemisphere when
he fell from a swing. Research suggests that:
   a. he will never speak again.
   b. his motor abilities will improve so that he can
easily use sign language.
   c. his right hemisphere will take over much of
the language function.
   d. his earlier experience with speech will enable
him to continue speaking.

## Matching Items

Match each structure or term with its corresponding
function or description.

### Structures or Terms

_____ 1. right hemisphere
_____ 2. brainstem
_____ 3. CT scan
_____ 4. aphasia
_____ 5. EEG
_____ 6. Broca's area
_____ 7. Wernicke's area
_____ 8. limbic system
_____ 9. association areas
_____ 10. left hemisphere
_____ 11. angular gyrus

### Functions or Descriptions

a. controls speech production
b. specializes in arithmetic reasoning
c. translates writing into speech
d. specializes in spatial relations
e. a series of x-ray photographs of the brain taken
from different angles
f. language disorder
g. oldest part of the brain
h. regulates emotion
i. recording of brain waves
j. responsible for language comprehension
k. brain areas involved in higher mental functions

In the diagrams to the right, the numbers refer to brain locations that have been damaged. Match each location with its probable effect on behavior.

*Location*                     *Behavioral Effect*

_____ **1.**          **a.** vision disorder
_____ **2.**          **b.** insensitivity to touch
_____ **3.**          **c.** motor paralysis
_____ **4.**          **d.** hearing problem
_____ **5.**          **e.** lack of coordination
_____ **6.**          **f.** abnormal hunger
_____ **7.**          **g.** split brain
_____ **8.**          **h.** sleep/arousal disorder
_____ **9.**          **i.** loss of smell
                        **j.** loss of taste
                        **k.** altered personality

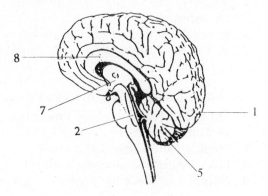

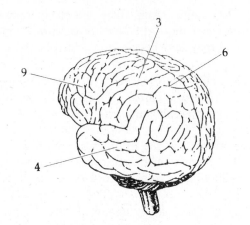

# Thinking Critically About Chapter 2

Answer these questions the day before an exam as a final check on your understanding of the chapter's terms and concepts.

*Multiple-Choice Questions*

1. A biological psychologist would be *more* likely to study:
   a. how you learn to express emotions.
   b. how to help people overcome emotional disorders.
   c. life-span changes in the expression of emotion.
   d. the chemical changes that accompany emotions.

2. The part of the human brain that is most like that of a fish is the:
   a. cortex.
   b. limbic system.
   c. brainstem.
   d. right hemisphere.
   e. corpus callosum.

3. You are able to pull your hand quickly away from hot water before pain is felt because:
   a. movement of the hand is a reflex that involves intervention of the spinal cord only.
   b. movement of the hand does not require intervention by the central nervous system.
   c. the brain reacts quickly to prevent severe injury.
   d. the autonomic division of the peripheral nervous system intervenes to speed contraction of the muscles of the hand.

4. In order to pinpoint the location of a tumor, a neurosurgeon electrically stimulated parts of the patient's sensory cortex. If the patient was conscious during the procedure, which of the following was probably experienced?
   a. "hearing" faint sounds
   b. "seeing" random visual patterns
   c. movement of the arms or legs
   d. a sense of having the skin touched

5. If Dr. Rogers wishes to conduct an experiment on the effects of stimulating the reward centers of a rat's brain, he should insert an electrode into the:
   a. thalamus.
   b. sensory cortex.
   c. hypothalamus.
   d. corpus callosum.

6. A split-brain patient has a picture of a knife flashed to her left hemisphere and that of a fork to her right hemisphere. She will be able to:
   a. identify the fork using her left hand.
   b. identify a knife using her left hand.
   c. identify a knife using either hand.
   d. identify a fork using either hand.

7. (Close-Up) Which of the following is *not* a correct description of a brain research technique?
   a. using a PET scan to examine the brain's structure
   b. using the EEG to record the brain's electrical activity
   c. using MRI to examine the brain's structure
   d. using a CT scan to examine the brain's structure

8. Following Jayshree's near-fatal car accident, her physician noticed that the pupillary reflex of her eyes was abnormal. This *may* indicate that Jayshree's _____ was damaged in the accident.
   a. occipital cortex
   b. autonomic nervous system
   c. left temporal lobe
   d. cerebellum
   e. brainstem

9. Anton is applying for a technician's job with a neurosurgeon. In trying to impress his potential employer with his knowledge of the brain, he says, "After my father's stroke I knew immediately that the blood clot had affected his left cerebral hemisphere because he no longer recognized a picture of his friend." Should Anton be hired?
   a. Yes. Anton obviously understands brain structure and function.
   b. No. The right hemisphere, not the left, specializes in picture recognition.
   c. Yes. Although blood clots never form in the left hemisphere, Anton should be rewarded for recognizing the left hemisphere's role in picture recognition.
   d. No. Blood clots never form in the left hemisphere, and the right hemisphere is more involved than the left in recognizing pictures.

10. Despite growing up in the same home environment, Karen and her brother John have personalities as different from each other as two people selected randomly from the population. Why is this so?
   a. Personality is inherited. Because Karen and John are not identical twins, it is not surprising they have very different personalities.
   b. Gender is the most important factor in personality. If Karen had a sister, the two of them would probably be much more alike.
   c. The interaction of their individual genes and nonshared experiences accounts for the common finding that children in the same family are usually very different.
   d. Their case is unusual; children in the same family usually have similar personalities.

11. Dr. Johnson briefly flashed a picture of a key in the right visual field of a split-brain patient. The patient could probably:
   a. verbally report that a key was seen.
   b. write the word *key* using the left hand.
   c. draw a picture of a key using the left hand.
   d. do none of the above.

12. In primitive vertebrate animals, the brain primarily regulates _____; in lower mammals, the brain enables _____.
   a. emotion; memory
   b. memory; emotion
   c. survival functions; emotion
   d. reproduction; emotion
   e. reproduction; memory

13. Since Malcolm has been taking a drug prescribed by his doctor, he no longer enjoys the little pleasures of life, such as eating and drinking. His doctor explains that this is because the drug:
   a. triggers release of dopamine.
   b. inhibits release of dopamine.
   c. triggers release of ACh.
   d. inhibits release of ACh.

14. A scientist from another planet wishes to study the simplest brain mechanisms underlying emotion and memory. You recommend the scientist study the:
   a. brainstem of a frog.
   b. limbic system of a dog.
   c. cortex of a monkey.
   d. cortex of a human.
   e. brainstem of a dog.

15. Which of the following was a major problem with phrenology?
    a. It was "ahead of its time" and no one believed it could be true.
    b. The brain is not neatly organized into structures that correspond to our categories of behavior.
    c. The brains of humans and animals are much less similar than the theory implied.
    d. All of the above were problems with phrenology.

16. I am a relatively slow-acting (but long-lasting) chemical messenger carried throughout the body by the bloodstream. What am I?
    a. a hormone
    b. a neurotransmitter
    c. acetylcholine
    d. dopamine

17. Your brother has been taking prescription medicine and experiencing a number of unpleasant side effects, including unusually rapid heartbeat and excessive perspiration. It is likely that the medicine is exaggerating activity in the:
    a. reticular formation.
    b. sympathetic nervous system.
    c. parasympathetic nervous system.
    d. amygdala.

18. Dr. Frankenstein made a mistake during neurosurgery on his monster. After the operation, the monster "saw" with his ears and "heard" with his eyes. It is likely that Dr. Frankenstein "rewired" neural connections in the monster's:
    a. hypothalamus.
    b. cerebellum.
    c. amygdala.
    d. thalamus.
    e. hippocampus.

19. A bodybuilder friend suddenly seems to have grown several inches in height. You suspect that your friend's growth spurt has occurred because he has been using drugs that affect the:
    a. pituitary gland.
    b. thalamus.
    c. adrenal glands.
    d. medulla.
    e. cerebellum.

20. Raccoons have much more precise control of their paws than dogs. You would expect that raccoons have more cortical space dedicated to "paw control" in the _____ of their brains.
    a. frontal lobes
    b. parietal lobes
    c. temporal lobes
    d. occipital lobes

## Essay Question

Discuss how the brainstem, limbic system, and cerebral cortex are each involved when a person plays a musical instrument. (Use the space below to list the points you want to make and organize them. Then write the essay on a separate sheet of paper.)

## Key Terms

### Writing Definitions

Using your own words, on a piece of paper write a brief definition or explanation of each of the following terms.

1. biological psychology

2. neuron

3. dendrites

4. axon

5. myelin sheath

6. action potential

7. threshold

8. synapse

9. neurotransmitters

10. acetylcholine (ACh)

11. endorphins

12. nervous system

13. central nervous system (CNS)

14. peripheral nervous system (PNS)

15. nerves

16. sensory neurons

17. interneurons

18. motor neurons

19. skeletal nervous system

20. autonomic nervous system

21. sympathetic nervous system

22. parasympathetic nervous system

23. reflex

24. brainstem

25. medulla

26. reticular formation

27. thalamus

28. lesion

29. electroencephalogram (EEG)

30. CT (computed tomography) scan

31. PET (positron emission tomography) scan

32. MRI (magnetic resonance imaging)

33. cerebellum

34. limbic system

35. amygdala

36. hypothalamus

37. cerebral cortex

38. glial cells

39. frontal lobes

40. parietal lobes

41. occipital lobes

42. temporal lobes

43. motor cortex

44. sensory cortex

45. association areas

46. aphasia

47. Broca's area

48. Wernicke's area

49. plasticity

50. corpus callosum

51. split brain

52. endocrine system

53. hormones

54. adrenal glands

55. pituitary gland

56. chromosomes

57. DNA (deoxyribonucleic acid)

58. genes

59. evolutionary psychology

60. behavior genetics

61. identical twins

62. fraternal twins

63. heritability

*Cross-Check*

As you learned in the Introduction, reviewing and overlearning of material are important to the learning process. After you have written the definitions of the key terms in this chapter, you should complete the crossword puzzle to ensure that you can reverse the process—recognize the term, given the definition.

**ACROSS**

3. Degree to which a trait's variation within a group of people can be attributed to genes.
4. Destruction of tissue.
6. Gland that secretes epinephrine.
13. Part of the brain that assists in coordination of movement.
16. "Involuntary" nervous system.
17. "Output" extension of a neuron.
19. The oldest part of the brain.
21. A series of x-rays of the brain.
23. Twins that develop from a single egg.

**DOWN**

1. Twins that develop from separate eggs.
2. Sheath surrounding some axons.
5. Part of the brain that regulates hunger, thirst, and temperature.
7. Molecule containing the genetic information that makes up the chromosomes.
8. The neurotransmitter involved in muscle contractions.
9. Part of the brain that helps regulate breathing and heartbeat.
10. Bundles of neural axons.
11. Part of the brain involved in regulating fear and rage.
12. Cortical lobe that contains the motor cortex.
14. Brain system associated with emotions.
15. Language comprehension area of the brain.
18. Cortical lobe that contains the auditory areas.
19. Person for whom area of the brain involved in motor aspects of language is named.
20. The junction between neurons.
22. Term for language difficulty.

# ANSWERS

## Guided Study

The following guidelines provide the main points that your answers should have touched upon.

1. Biological processes underlie every aspect of our behavior and mental processes. By studying the links between biology and psychology, biological psychologists achieve a greater understanding of such basic behaviors as sleep, hunger, and sex, and gain new insights into how best to treat stress, disease, depression, and other human conditions.

2. Body organs such as the stomach, heart, and brain form larger systems for digestion, circula-

tion, and information processing, which are part of an even larger system—the individual as a person, who in turn forms a part of a family, a community, and a culture. Each organ, in turn, is composed of smaller subsystems—cells—that operate biochemically.

3. Each neuron consists of a cell body, branching fibers called dendrites that receive information from other neurons, and an extension fiber called an axon through which the neuron passes information to other neurons or to muscles or glands. Some axons are insulated with a myelin sheath, which helps speed neural impulses.

   A neural impulse, or action potential, occurs if the excitatory signals minus the inhibitory signals received by the neuron on its dendrites or cell body exceeds the neuron's threshold. Then, the gates in the axon open, allowing electrically charged atoms to rush inside. This leads to the electrical chain reaction by which an electrical charge travels down the axon into junctions with other neurons and with the muscles and glands of the body.

4. When an action potential reaches the end of the axon, chemical messengers called neurotransmitters are released into the synaptic gap between the sending and receiving neuron. This junction is called a synapse. Neurotransmitter molecules bind to receptor sites on the receiving neuron and have either an excitatory or inhibitory influence on that neuron's tendency to generate its own action potential. If the receiving neuron receives more excitatory than inhibitory inputs, more neural impulses are generated.

   A particular neural pathway may use only one or two neurotransmitters, each of which may have a specific effect on behavior. Acetylcholine, for example, is the neurotransmitter at every synapse between a motor neuron and a muscle.

5. Endorphins are morphinelike neurotransmitters found in the brain that are released in response to pain and vigorous exercise. The existence of endorphins may help explain good feelings such as the "runner's high," the pain-killing effects of acupuncture, and the indifference to pain in some injured people.

   Drugs have a number of different effects on neurotransmitters. Some (agonists) mimic or block (antagonists) a particular neurotransmitter. Others interfere with the breakdown or reabsorption of the neurotransmitter. Opiate drugs, for example, may cause the brain to stop producing endorphins.

6. The central nervous system includes all the neurons in the brain and spinal cord. The peripheral nervous system, which links the central nervous system with the body's sense receptors, muscles, and glands, has two divisions: skeletal and autonomic. The skeletal nervous system controls the voluntary movements of the skeletal muscles.

   The autonomic nervous system, which influences the glands and muscles of our internal organs, also is a dual system. The sympathetic nervous system arouses the body during emergencies by accelerating heartbeat, slowing digestion, raising blood sugar, dilating arteries, and creating perspiration. When the emergency has passed, the parasympathetic nervous system relaxes the body by producing the opposite effects.

   Sensory neurons relay information from the body's tissues and sensory organs to the brain and spinal cord. Interneurons of the brain and spinal cord (the central nervous system) are involved in processing this information from the sensory neurons. The central nervous system then sends instructions to the body's tissues by means of the motor neurons.

7. Reflexes, which are automatic responses to stimuli, are governed by the simplest neural connections. In response to a painful stimulus to the fingertips, for example, a sensory neuron conveys the message to an interneuron in the spinal cord. The interneuron triggers an action potential in motor neurons that cause muscles of your arm to jerk your hand away.

8. The brainstem is the oldest and innermost region of the brain. It begins where the spinal cord enters the skull and contains the medulla and reticular formation. The medulla controls breathing and heartbeat and is the point where nerves to and from each side of the brain cross over to connect with the opposite side of the body. The reticular formation helps control arousal. The thalamus serves as the brain's sensory switchboard, routing information from sensory neurons to higher brain regions dealing with seeing, hearing, tasting, and touching. The cerebellum influences learning and memory; its most obvious function is coordinating voluntary movement.

9. The oldest method of studying the brain is by observing the effects of brain disease and injuries. More recently, electrical, chemical, or magnetic stimulation in humans and surgical lesions of brain tissue in animals have been used to study the brain. The electroencephalogram (EEG) is a recording of the brain's electrical activity from electrodes placed on its surface. Scientists also examine the brain with CT (computed tomography) scans, PET (positron emission tomography) scans, and magnetic resonance imaging (an MRI

or a functional MRI). Although the text discusses the use of scanning and imaging on the brain only, these techniques are also used to diagnose problems elsewhere in the body.

10. In the limbic system, the hippocampus processes memory. The amygdala influences aggression and fear. When this region is surgically lesioned, aggressive behavior in animals is diminished. When one region of the amygdala is electrically stimulated, a normally placid domestic animal will behave aggressively; when another area is stimulated, the animal will display signs of fear.

    The hypothalamus contains neurons that regulate hunger, thirst, body temperature, and sexual behavior; it also contains the so-called "reward centers." The hypothalamus also secretes hormones that control the pituitary gland, which influences hormone release by other glands, which the hypothalamus monitors.

11. The cerebral cortex is a thin surface layer of neural cells covering the left and right cerebral hemispheres. Each hemisphere is divided into four regions called lobes: frontal, parietal, temporal, and occipital. The frontal lobes control movement through the motor cortex and contain association areas that are involved in making plans and judgments. When specific parts of the motor cortex in the left and right hemispheres are electrically stimulated, movement is triggered in specific body parts on the opposite side of the body.

    The parietal lobes house the sensory cortex which, when electrically stimulated, triggers a sense of a particular body part having been touched. The more sensitive a body region, the greater the area of sensory cortex that is devoted to it.

    The temporal lobes receive auditory information primarily from the opposite ear, and the occipital lobes similarly receive input from the eyes.

    Approximately three-fourths of the cortex consists of uncommitted association areas that communicate with one another and with neurons of the sensory and motor areas. Association areas influence personality, recognition of faces, and many other "higher" mental abilities.

12. Damage to any one of several areas of the cortex can cause aphasia, an impaired use of language. Damage to Broca's area in the left frontal lobe disrupts speaking. Damage to Wernicke's area in the left temporal lobe disrupts language comprehension and leaves people able to speak words but in a meaningless way. Damage to the angular gyrus will disrupt the ability to read aloud.

    When you read aloud, words are registered in the visual area of the cortex and then relayed to the angular gyrus, which transforms the words into an auditory code. This code is comprehended by Wernicke's area and then sent to Broca's area, which directs the motor cortex to produce speech.

13. When a particular area of the brain is damaged, such as occurs following a stroke, other areas may in time reorganize and assume its functions (plasticity). Neurons that are near damaged ones compensate for the damage by making new neural connections to replace the damaged ones. The brains of young children, in which functions are not yet regionally fixed, exhibit the greatest plasticity. Throughout life, however, new neural connections are formed and are the brain's way of compensating for the gradual loss of neurons with age.

14. In order to control severe epileptic seizures, surgeons sometimes sever the wide band of fibers (the corpus callosum) that connects the two hemispheres of the brain.

    Sperry and Gazzaniga studied such split-brain patients, revealing that the left and right hemispheres each have special functions. In a person with an intact brain, information in the left or right side of our field of vision of both eyes projects directly to the opposite hemisphere of the brain and is quickly passed to the other hemisphere through the corpus callosum. In the split-brain patient, however, a briefly flashed image on the subject's right, for example, will be perceived only in the left hemisphere. By flashing images in this way, researchers are able to send information to either the left or right hemisphere and thereby determine its capabilities.

    These experiments demonstrate that the right hemisphere is superior to the left at recognizing pictures, perceiving differences, and expressing emotions. The left hemisphere is more logical and verbal. Despite these specialized functions, the two hemispheres work together in an integrated manner during most activities.

15. The endocrine system is a relatively slow-acting chemical communication system of glands that secrete hormones influencing growth, reproduction, metabolism, mood, and reactions to stress. For example, the adrenal glands release epinephrine (adrenaline) and norepinephrine (noradrenaline) during emergencies. These hormones provide a source of energy by increasing heart rate, blood pressure, and blood sugar. The pituitary gland, located in the base of the brain, releases hormones that influence growth and the release of hormones by other glands. It forms an elabo-

rate feedback system with the brain (the hypothalamus) in its influence on behavior.

16. When a mature egg is fertilized by a sperm, the 23 chromosomes carried in the egg pair up with the 23 chromosomes of the sperm. Each chromosome is composed of long threads of a molecule called DNA; DNA is made of thousands of genes that determine development by directing the manufacture of proteins.

Evolutionary psychologists study the adaptive nature of behavior using the principles of natural selection, which presumably favors those behaviors that contribute to the preservation of one's genes in future generations. Behavior geneticists study the extent of genetic influences on specific traits.

17. Both genes and environment influence most psychological traits. Heritability refers to the extent to which variation in a trait among individuals is due to their differing genes. Because genes and experience interact in influencing development, it is *in*correct to say that a certain trait is x percent due to genes and y percent due to experience. Because identical twins are genetically identical, the findings that they are more similar in a trait than fraternal twins or other siblings suggest that there is a substantial genetic influence on that trait. In this way, twin studies provide psychologists with a greater understanding of the role of genes in our behaviors.

Adoption studies enable psychologists to determine the relative influence of nature and nurture on development by asking whether adopted children are more like their biological parents, who contribute their genes, or their adoptive parents, who contribute a home environment.

Critics of twin studies contend that twin similarities may merely be coincidental rather than a reflection of heredity. Moreover, because adoption agencies tend to place separated twins in similar homes, critics argue that similarities in traits may reflect the impact of similar experiences rather than heredity alone.

## Chapter Review

1. biological
2. phrenology
3. biological psychologists
4. system; subsystems; systems; neurons
5. dendrites
6. axons; myelin sheath
7. a. dendrites
   b. cell body
   c. axon
   d. myelin sheath
8. action potential; axon
9. excitatory; inhibitory; threshold; will not; all-or-none

A neural impulse is generated by excitatory signals minus inhibitory signals exceeding a certain threshold. The stimuli are received through the dendrites, combined in the cell body, and electrically transmitted in an all-or-none fashion down the length of the axon. When the combined signal reaches the end of the axon, chemical messengers called neurotransmitters are released into the synaptic cleft, or gap, between two neurons. Neurotransmitter molecules bind to receptor sites on the dendrites of neighboring neurons and have either an excitatory or inhibitory influence on that neuron's tendency to generate its own neural impulse.

10. does not
11. synapse; synaptic cleft (gap)
12. neurotransmitters; atoms
13. exciting; inhibiting
14. acetylcholine (ACh); curare
15. endorphins; heroin; morphine
16. agonists; receptor sites; antagonists
17. blood-brain barrier
18. Parkinson's; dopamine; L-dopa
19. nervous system
20. central; peripheral
21. nerves
22. sensory; interneurons
23. motor
24. skeletal; voluntary
25. autonomic
26. sympathetic
27. parasympathetic

The sympathetic division of the autonomic nervous system becomes aroused in response to an emergency. The physiological changes that occur include accelerated heartbeat, elevated blood sugar, dilation of arteries, slowing of digestion, and increased perspiration to cool the body. When the emergency is over, the parasympathetic nervous system produces the opposite physical reactions.

28. reflexes; spinal cord
29. brainstem
30. medulla; breathing; heartbeat
31. brainstem

32. reticular formation; arousal; alert (awake); coma

33. thalamus

34. clinical observation

35. lesions

36. electroencephalogram (EEG)

37. CT scan

38. PET scan

By depicting the brain's consumption of radioactively labeled glucose, the PET scan allows researchers to see which brain areas are most active as a person performs various tasks. This provides additional information on the specialized functions of various regions of the brain.

39. MRI (magnetic resonance imaging); functional MRI

40. cerebellum; learning; balance

41. limbic; hippocampus

42. amygdala

43. hypothalamus; hunger, thirst, body temperature (or sex); reward; pituitary

44. addictive; reward deficiency syndrome

45. cerebral cortex

46. glial cells

47. a.  frontal lobe
    b.  parietal lobe
    c.  occipital lobe
    d.  temporal lobe

48. motor; frontal

49. sensory; touch

50. sensory cortex

From sensory receptors in the skin the message travels via sensory neurons to an interneuron in the spinal cord, which in turn activates a motor neuron. This motor neuron causes the muscles in the hand to contract, and the person jerks his or her hand away from the heat.

At the same time that the spinal reflex is initiated, other interneurons carry the message up the spinal cord to the brain, where the pain message will be processed. It reaches the thalamus, which routes it to the sensory cortex. Along the way to the thalamus, the sensory input would also reach the reticular formation, which would arouse the cerebral cortex, the hypothalamus, and the sympathetic division of the autonomic nervous system.

51. occipital; temporal

52. association areas; three-fourths; frontal

53. aphasia; Broca's area; Wernicke's area; angular gyrus

54. plasticity

55. will not

56. 5

57. left; dominant (major)

58. corpus callosum; split brain

59. right; name; right

The word *pencil* when flashed to a split-brain patient's right visual field would project only to the opposite, or left, hemisphere of the patient's brain. Because the left hemisphere contains the language control centers of the brain, the patient would be able to read the word aloud. The left hand is controlled by the right hemisphere of the brain. Because the right hemisphere would not be aware of the word, it would not be able to guide the left hand in identifying a pencil by touch.

60. endocrine system; hormones; slower

61. adrenal; epinephrine; norepinephrine

62. pituitary; hypothalamus; growth

The hypothalamus in the brain influences secretions by the pituitary. The pituitary regulates other endocrine glands, which release hormones that influence behavior. The hypothalamus monitors these changes in blood chemistry and thereby adjusts its inputs to the pituitary.

63. chromosomes; 23; one; DNA

64. genes

65. looser

66. evolutionary psychologists; genes

67. behavior geneticists

68. twin; adoption

69. identical; fraternal

70. more

71. environment

72. do not

73. heritability

74. psychological; genetic; environmental

75. height; weight, intelligence; need not imply

## Progress Test 1

### Multiple-Choice Questions

1. **b.** is the answer. (pp. 40)
   **a.** Glial cells support and nourish nerve cells.
   **c.** Acetylcholine is a neurotransmitter that triggers muscle contraction.
   **d.** Endorphins are opiatelike neurotransmitters linked to pain control and to pleasure.

2. **b.** is the answer. The autonomic nervous system controls internal functioning, including heartbeat, digestion, and glandular activity. (p. 45)
   **a.** The functions mentioned are all automatic, not voluntary, so this answer cannot be correct.
   **c.** This answer is incorrect because most organs are affected by both divisions of the autonomic nervous system.
   **d.** The skeletal nervous system transmits sensory input to the central nervous system and directs the movements of skeletal muscles.
   **e.** The central nervous system need not be involved in automatic activities.

3. **c.** is the answer. Stimulus strength can affect only the number of times a neuron fires or the number of neurons that fire. (p. 41)
   **a., b., & d.** These answers are incorrect because firing is an all-or-none response, so intensity remains the same regardless of stimulus strength. Nor can stimulus strength change the neuronal threshold or the impulse speed.

4. **a.** is the answer. Endorphins are neurotransmitters that function as natural painkillers. When the body has a supply of artificial painkillers like heroin, endorphin production stops. (pp. 42–43)
   **b.** The production of neurotransmitters other than endorphins does not cease.
   **c.** Neurotransmitter production does not increase during withdrawal.
   **d.** Heroin makes use of the same receptor sites as endorphins.

5. **a.** is the answer. The PET scan measures glucose consumption in different areas of the brain to determine their levels of activity. (p. 50)
   **b.** The CT scan is a series of x-rays taken from different angles and then analyzed by a computer to create an image representing a slice through the brain.
   **c.** The EEG is a measure of electrical activity in the brain.
   **d.** MRI uses magnetic fields and radio waves to produce computer-generated images of soft tissues of the body.

6. **c.** is the answer. (p. 69)
   **a., b., & c.** Whereas evolutionary psychologists attempt to explain universal human tendencies, these researchers investigate genetic *differences* among individuals.

7. **a.** is the answer. (p. 52)
   **b.** The reticular formation is linked to arousal.
   **c.** The brainstem governs the mechanisms of basic survival—heartbeat and breathing, for example—and has many other roles.

**d.** The cerebral cortex governs the "higher" functions of the brain.

8. **c.** is the answer. In a simple reflex, a sensory neuron carries the message that a sensory receptor has been stimulated to an interneuron in the spinal cord. The interneuron responds by activating motor neurons that will enable the appropriate response. (pp. 46–47)

9. **c.** is the answer. Wernicke's area is involved in comprehension, and aphasics with damage to Wernicke's area are unable to understand what is said to them. (p. 59)
   **a.** The angular gyrus translates printed words into speech sounds; damage would result in the inability to read aloud.
   **b.** Broca's area is involved in the physical production of speech; damage would result in the inability to speak fluently.
   **d.** The cortex's association areas are involved, among other things, in processing language; damage to these areas wouldn't specifically affect comprehension.

10. **d.** is the answer. (p. 65)
    **a.** In most persons, language is primarily a left hemisphere function.
    **b.** Learned movements are unrelated to hemispheric specialization.
    **c.** Arithmetic reasoning is generally a left hemisphere function.

11. **d.** is the answer. Biological psychologists study the links between biology (in this case, neurotransmitters) and psychology (depression, in this example). (pp. 39–40)
    **a., b., & c.** These mental health professionals are more involved in the *treatment* of troubled behavior than in research.

12. **d.** is the answer. As animals increase in complexity, there is an increase in the amount of association areas. (p. 58)
    **a.** The brainstem controls basic survival functions and is not related to the complexity of an animal's behavior.
    **b.** The ratio of body and brain weight is a poor predictor of behavior complexity.
    **c.** The frontal lobe is concerned with personality, planning, and other mental functions, but its size is unrelated to intelligence or the complexity of behavior.

13. **b.** is the answer. (p. 45)
    **a., c., & d.** The autonomic nervous system, which is divided into the sympathetic and parasympathetic divisions, is concerned with regulating basic bodily maintenance functions.

**14. c.** is the answer. (p. 41)
**a.** An action potential will occur only when the neuron's threshold is *exceeded*.
**b.** An excitatory input that does not reach the neuron's threshold will not trigger an action potential.
**d.** This answer is incorrect because some neurotransmitters inhibit a neuron's readiness to fire.
**e.** Hormones are produced by the glands of the endocrine system.

**15. e.** is the answer. A neuron receives incoming stimuli on its dendrites and cell body. These electrochemical signals are combined in the cell body, generating an impulse that travels down the axon, causing the release of neurotransmitter substances into the synaptic cleft or gap. (pp. 40–41)

**16. c.** is the answer. (p. 67)
**a.** Chromosomes are structures within the cell's nucleus, containing genetic material.
**b.** Neurotransmitters are the chemicals involved in synaptic transmission in the nervous system.
**d.** Enzymes are chemicals that facilitate various chemical reactions throughout the body but are not involved in communication within the endocrine system.

**17. c.** is the answer. The reticular formation plays an important role in arousal. (p. 49)
**a.** The thalamus relays sensory input.
**b.** The corpus callosum links the two cerebral hemispheres.
**d.** The cerebellum is involved in coordination of voluntary movement.

**18. d.** is the answer. (p. 65)

**19. b.** is the answer. Association areas interpret, integrate, and act on information from other areas of the cortex. (p. 57)

**20. b.** is the answer. (p. 71)
**a., c., & d.** Despite being raised in different environments, long-separated identical twins often have much in common, including likes, dislikes, and life-styles. This indicates the significant heritability of many traits.

*Matching Items*

1. d (p. 53)      5. g (p. 49)      9. k (p. 52)
2. f (p. 73)      6. b (p. 71)     10. i (p. 53)
3. e (p. 71)      7. c (p. 49)     11. j (p. 48)
4. a (p. 69)      8. h (p. 63)

## Progress Test 2

*Multiple-Choice Questions*

1. **a.** is the answer. The visual cortex is located at the very back of the brain. (p. 57)

2. **b.** is the answer. (p. 65)
**a., c., & d.** Spatial reasoning, perceptual skills, and the left side of the body are primarily influenced by the right hemisphere.

3. **a.** is the answer. Sensory neurons in the skeletal nervous system relay such messages. (p. 45)
**b. & c.** These divisions of the autonomic nervous system are concerned with the regulation of bodily maintenance functions such as heartbeat, digestion, and glandular activity.
**d.** The spinal cord itself is part of the central nervous system, but the message is carried to the spinal cord by the skeletal division of the peripheral nervous system.

4. **c.** is the answer. As automatic responses to stimuli, reflexes are the simplest complete units of behavior and require only simple neural pathways. (p. 46)
**a., b., & d.** Emotions, drives, and voluntary movements are all behaviors that are much more complex than reflexes and therefore involve much more complicated neural pathways.
**e.** Balance is regulated by the cerebellum.

5. **b.** is the answer. Endorphins are neurotransmitters that function as natural painkillers and are evidently involved in the "runner's high" and other situations in which discomfort or fatigue are expected but not experienced. (p. 43)
**a.** ACh is a neurotransmitter involved in muscular control.
**c.** Dopamine is a neurotransmitter involved in, among other things, motor control.
**d.** Norepinephrine is an adrenal hormone released to help us respond in moments of danger.
**e.** Acetylcholine is the complete name of ACh.

6. **a.** is the answer. Parkinson's disease causes the death of brain tissue that produces dopamine. (p. 44)
**b. & c.** This disease affects both hemispheres of the cortex.
**d.** This disease causes insufficient production of the neurotransmitters.

7. **d.** is the answer. (p. 50)
**a.** The EEG is an amplified recording of the brain's electrical activity.
**b.** The CT scan involves x-ray photographs of the brain.
**c.** The PET scan is a visual display of brain activity that detects the movement of a radioactive form of glucose as the brain performs a task.

8. **a.** is the answer. (p. 40)
**c., d., & e.** Myelin sheaths are not involved in regulating the release of neurotransmitters.

9. **c.** is the answer. (p. 69)
 **b. & d.** Each cell of the human body contains hundreds of genes.

10. **b.** is the answer. ACh is a neurotransmitter that causes the contraction of muscle fibers when stimulated by motor neurons. This function explains its location. (p. 42)
 **a. & c.** Sensory neurons and interneurons do not directly stimulate muscle fibers.

11. **d.** is the answer. The pituitary regulates body growth, and some of its secretions regulate the release of hormones from other glands. (p. 68)
 **a.** The adrenal glands are stimulated by the autonomic nervous system to release epinephrine and norepinephrine.
 **b.** The thyroid gland produces a hormone that controls the rates of various chemical reactions in the body.
 **c.** The hypothalamus regulates the pituitary but does not itself directly regulate growth.
 **e.** There is no such gland. Hyperthyroidism is a *condition* in which the thyroid gland is overactive.

12. **d.** is the answer. Also known as adrenaline and noradrenaline, epinephrine and norepinephrine are hormones released by the adrenal glands. (p. 68)

13. **d.** is the answer. The cerebellum is involved in the coordination of voluntary muscular movements. (p. 52)
 **a.** The medulla regulates breathing and heartbeat.
 **b.** The thalamus relays sensory inputs to the appropriate higher centers of the brain.
 **c.** The hypothalamus is concerned with the regulation of basic drives and emotions.
 **e.** The cerebrum is the center of all complex activities.

14. **a.** is the answer. The reticular formation controls arousal via its connections to the cortex. Thus, separating the two produces a coma. (p. 49)
 **b., c., d., & e.** None of these structures controls arousal. The hypothalamus regulates hunger, thirst, sexual behavior, and other basic drives; the thalamus is a sensory relay station; the cerebellum is involved in the coordination of voluntary movement; and the medulla controls heartbeat and breathing.

15. **b.** is the answer. (p. 56)
 **c. & d.** These refer to the sensory cortex.

16. **b.** is the answer. (p. 43)
 **a.** Abuse of certain drugs, such as heroin, may have this effect.
 **c.** This describes the effect of an antagonist.
 **d.** Drugs do not have this effect on neurons.

17. **c.** is the answer. The corpus callosum is a large band of neural fibers linking the right and left cerebral hemispheres. To sever the corpus callosum is in effect to split the brain. (p. 63)

18. **d.** is the answer. The frontal lobe is in the front of the brain. Just behind is the parietal lobe. The occipital lobe is located at the very back of the head and just below the parietal lobe. Next to the occipital lobe and toward the front of the head is the temporal lobe. (p. 55)

19. **d.** is the answer. As demonstrated in the case of Phineas Gage, injury to the frontal lobe may produce such changes in personality. (p. 59)
 **a.** Damage to the parietal lobe might disrupt functions involving the sensory cortex.
 **b.** Damage to the temporal lobe might impair hearing.
 **c.** Occipital damage might impair vision.
 **e.** The endocrine system is the body's slower chemical communication system that transmits hormones through the bloodstream from tissue to tissue.

20. **c.** is the answer. (p. 62)

*Matching Items*

1. d (p. 65)  5. i (p. 50)  9. k (p. 58)
2. g (p. 48)  6. a (p. 60)  10. b (p. 65)
3. e (p. 50)  7. j (p. 60)  11. c (p. 60)
4. f (p. 59)  8. h (p. 52)

*Brain Damage Diagram* (pp. 48–49, 52–61)

1. a  4. d  7. f
2. h  5. e  8. g
3. c  6. b  9. k

# Thinking Critically About Chapter 2

*Multiple-Choice Questions*

1. **d.** is the answer. Biological psychologists study the links between biology (chemical changes in this example) and behavior (emotions in this example). (pp. 39–40)
 **a., b., & c.** Developmental, experimental, and clinical psychologists would be more concerned with the learning of emotional expressions, the treatment of emotional disorders, and life-span changes in emotions, respectively.

2. **c.** is the answer. The brainstem is the oldest and most primitive region of the brain. It is found in lower vertebrates, such as fish, as well as in humans and other mammals. The structures mentioned in the other choices are associated with stages of brain evolution beyond that seen in the fish. (p. 48)

3.  **a.** is the answer. Since this reflex is an automatic response and involves only the spinal cord, the hand is jerked away before the brain has even received the information that causes the sensation of pain. (p. 46)

    **b.** The spinal cord, which organizes simple reflexes such as this one, is part of the central nervous system.

    **c.** The brain is not involved in directing spinal reflexes.

    **d.** The autonomic nervous system controls the glands and the muscles of the internal organs; it does not influence the skeletal muscles controlling the hand.

4.  **d.** is the answer. Stimulation of the sensory cortex elicits a sense of touch, as the experiments of Penfield demonstrated. (p. 57)

    **a., b., & c.** Hearing, seeing, or movement might be expected if the temporal, occipital, and motor regions of the cortex, respectively, were stimulated.

5.  **c.** is the answer. As Olds and Milner discovered, electrical stimulation of the hypothalamus is a highly reinforcing event, because it is the location of the animal's reward centers. The other brain regions mentioned are not associated with reward centers. (p. 53)

6.  **a.** is the answer. The left hand, controlled by the right hemisphere, would be able to identify the fork, the picture of which is flashed to the right hemisphere. (pp. 63–64)

7.  **a.** is the answer. The PET scan, which traces the brain's use of a radioactive form of glucose, measures brain *activity* in various regions. It does not reveal anything about structure. (p. 50)

    **b., c., & d.** Each of these techniques is utilized to study the structure or activity of the brain.

8.  **b.** is the answer. Simple reflexes, such as this one, are governed by activity in the autonomic nervous system. (p. 45)

    **a.** The occipital lobes process sensory messages from the eyes; they play no role in the reflexive response of the pupils to light.

    **c.** The left temporal lobe specializes in processing language.

    **d.** The cerebellum specializes in coordinating movement.

    **e.** The brainstem is the oldest and innermost region of the brain.

9.  **b.** is the answer. (p. 65)

    **a., c., & d.** The left hemisphere does not specialize in facial recognition. And blood clots can form anywhere in the brain.

10. **c.** is the answer. (p. 72)

**a.** although heredity does influence certain traits, such as outgoingness and emotional instability, it is the interaction of heredity and experience that ultimately molds personality.

**b.** There is no single "most important factor" in personality. Moreover, for the same reason two sisters or brothers often have dissimilar personalities, a sister and brother may be very much alike.

**d.** Karen and John's case is not at all unusual.

11. **a.** is the answer. The right visual field projects directly to the verbal left hemisphere. (p. 64)

    **b. & c.** The left hand is controlled by the right hemisphere, which, in this situation, would be unaware of the word since the picture has been flashed to the left hemisphere.

12. **c.** is the answer. (p. 48)

    **d. & e.** Reproduction is only one of the basic survival functions the brain regulates.

13. **b.** is the answer. (p. 54)

    **a.** By triggering release of dopamine, such a drug would probably *enhance* Malcolm's enjoyment of the pleasures of life.

    **c. & d.** ACh is the neurotransmitter at synapses between motor neurons and muscle fibers.

14. **b.** is the answer. The hippocampus of the limbic system is involved in processing memory. The amygdala of the limbic system influences fear and anger. (p. 53)

    **a. & e.** The brainstem controls vital functions such as breathing and heartbeat; it is not directly involved in either emotion or memory.

    **c. & d.** These answers are incorrect because the limbic system is an older brain structure than the cortex. Its involvement in emotions and memory is therefore more basic than that of the cortex.

15. **b.** is the answer. (p. 39)

    **a.** "Ahead of its time" implies the theory had merit, which later research clearly showed it did not. Moreover, phrenology *was* accepted as an accurate theory of brain organization by many scientists.

    **c.** Phrenology said nothing about the similarities of human and animal brains.

16. **a.** is the answer. (p. 67)

    **b., c., & d.** Acetylcholine and dopamine are fast-acting neurotransmitters released at synapses, not in the bloodstream.

17. **b.** is the answer. Sympathetic arousal produces several effects, including accelerated heartbeat and excessive perspiration. (p. 45)

    **a.** Stimulation of the reticular formation increases alertness, but would not necessarily accelerate heartbeat or cause excessive perspiration.

    **c.** Arousal of the parasympathetic nervous system would have effects opposite to those stated.

**d.** If the medication were affecting his amygdala, your brother might experience emotions such as anger or fear at illogical times.

18. **d.** is the answer. The thalamus relays sensory messages from the eyes, ears, and other receptors to the appropriate projection areas of the cortex. "Rewiring" the thalamus, theoretically, could have the effects stated in this question. (p. 49)

**a., b., c., & e.** These brain structures are not directly involved in brain processes related to sensation or perception.

19. **a.** is the answer. Hormones of the pituitary gland regulate body growth. (p. 68)

**b., d., & e.** Because they are not endocrine glands, the thalamus, medulla, and cerebellum are not influenced by hormones.

**c.** The adrenal glands produce hormones that provide energy during emergencies; they are not involved in regulating body growth.

20. **a.** is the answer. The motor cortex, which determines the precision with which various parts of the body can be moved, is located in the frontal lobes. (p. 56)

**b.** The parietal lobes contain the sensory cortex, which controls sensitivity to touch.

**c.** The temporal lobes contain the primary projection areas for hearing and, on the left side, are also involved in language use.

**d.** The occipital lobes contain the primary projection areas for vision.

### Essay Question

The brainstem contains the medulla, which controls heartbeat, breathing, and other vital life functions that keep the musician alive. It is also the crossover point, where nerves to and from each side of the brain mostly connect with the opposite side of the the body.

Atop the brainstem sits the thalamus, which routes sensory information from the musician's eyes, ears, and fingertips to the higher brain regions concerned with seeing, hearing, and touching. Through the thalamus the musician's brain receives the necessary sensory information to enable decision making regarding all aspects of playing the instrument. The thalamus also routes some of the higher brain responses to the cerebellum, which helps coordinate movements involved in playing the instrument.

Within the brainstem the reticular formation receives inputs from the thalamus and the cerebral cortex that help maintain the musician's arousal, which is important in performing before a group.

The limbic system's involvement in emotion, motivation, and memory will influence many aspects of a musical performance. The hippocampus will be involved in the formation of memories of how to play the musical instrument, as well as memories of the notes and lyrics for each song. The pleasure centers of the hypothalamus comprise the brain's reward system and will help maintain the musician's motivation for learning and playing the instrument.

The cerebral cortex will oversee all aspects of the musician's behavior. Sensory projection areas in the occipital, temporal, and parietal lobes will process messages from the musician's eyes, ears, and fingertips. The motor cortex of the frontal lobes will organize the necessary body movements. Finally, association areas in the frontal lobes and other parts of the brain will be involved in the planning and decision making inherent in playing the musical instrument.

## Key Terms

### Writing Definitions

1. **Biological psychology** is the study of the links between biology and behavior. (pp. 39–40)

2. The **neuron**, or nerve cell, is the basic building block of the nervous system. (p. 40)

3. The **dendrites** of a neuron are the bushy, branching extensions that receive messages from other nerve cells and conduct impulses toward the cell body. (p. 40)

4. The **axon** of a neuron is the extension that sends impulses to other nerve cells or to muscles or glands. (p. 40)

5. The **myelin sheath** is a layer of fatty tissue that covers many axons and helps speed neural impulses. (p. 40)

6. An **action potential** is a neural impulse generated by the movement of positively charged atoms in and out of channels in the axon's membrane. (pp. 40–41)

7. A neuron's **threshold** is the level of stimulation that must be exceeded in order for the neuron to fire, or generate an electrical impulse. (p. 41)

8. A **synapse** is the junction between the axon tip of the sending neuron and the dendrite or cell body of the receiving neuron. The tiny gap at this junction is called the synaptic cleft or gap. (p. 41)

9. **Neurotransmitters** are chemicals that are released into synaptic gaps and so *transmit neural messages* from neuron to neuron. (p. 41)

10. **Acetylcholine (ACh)** is a neurotransmitter that triggers muscle contractions. (p. 42)

11. **Endorphins** are natural, opiatelike neurotransmitters linked to pain control and to pleasure. (p. 43)

    *Memory aid:* Endorphins *end* pain.

12. The **nervous system** is the speedy, electrochemical communication system, consisting of all the nerve cells in the peripheral and central nervous systems. (p. 44)

13. The **central nervous system** consists of the brain and spinal cord; it is located at the *center*, or internal core, of the body. (p. 44)

14. The **peripheral nervous system** connects the central nervous system to the body's sense receptors, muscles, and glands; it is at the *periphery* of the body relative to the brain and spinal cord. (p. 44)

15. **Nerves** are bundles of neural axons that connect the central nervous system with muscles, glands, and sense organs. (p. 44)

16. **Sensory neurons** carry information from the sense receptors to the central nervous system for processing. (p. 44)

17. **Interneurons** are the neurons of the central nervous system that link the sensory and motor neurons in the transmission of sensory inputs and motor outputs. (p. 44)

18. **Motor neurons** carry information and instructions for action from the central nervous system to muscles and glands. (p. 44)

19. The **skeletal nervous system** is the division of the peripheral nervous system that controls voluntary movements of the skeletal muscles. (p. 45)

20. The **autonomic nervous system** is the division of the peripheral nervous system that controls the glands and the muscles of internal organs and thereby controls internal functioning; it regulates the *automatic* behaviors necessary for survival. (p. 45)

21. The **sympathetic nervous system** is the division of the autonomic nervous system that arouses the body, mobilizing its energy in stressful situations. (p. 45)

22. The **parasympathetic nervous system** is the division of the autonomic nervous system that calms the body, conserving its energy. (p. 45)

23. A **reflex** is a simple, automatic, inborn response to a sensory stimulus; it is governed by a very simple neural pathway. (p. 46)

24. The **brainstem**, the oldest and innermost region of the brain, is an extension of the spinal cord and is the central core of the brain; its structures direct automatic survival functions. (p. 48)

25. Located in the brainstem, the **medulla** controls breathing and heartbeat. (p. 48)

26. Also part of the brainstem, the **reticular formation** is a nerve network that plays an important role in controlling arousal. (p. 49)

27. Located atop the brainstem, the **thalamus** routes incoming messages to the appropriate cortical centers and transmits replies to the medulla and cerebellum. (p. 49)

28. A **lesion** is destruction of tissue; studying the consequences of lesions—both surgically produced in animals and naturally occurring—in different regions of the brain helps researchers to determine the normal functions of these regions. (p. 50)

29. An **electroencephalogram (EEG)** is an amplified recording of the waves of electrical activity of the brain. *Encephalo* comes from a Greek word meaning "related to the brain." (p. 50)

30. The **CT (computed tomography) scan** is a series of x-ray photographs of the brain taken from different positions and analyzed by computer, creating an image that represents a slice through the brain. (p. 50)

31. The **PET (positron emission tomography) scan** measures the levels of activity of different areas of the brain by tracing their consumption of a radioactive form of glucose, the brain's fuel. (p. 50)

32. **MRI (magnetic resonance imaging)** uses magnetic fields and radio waves to produce computer-generated images that show brain structures more clearly. (p. 50)

33. The **cerebellum** assists in balance and the coordination of voluntary movement. (p. 52)

34. A doughnut-shaped neural system, the **limbic system** plays an important role in the regulation of emotions and basic physiological drives. (p. 52)

    *Memory aid:* Its name comes from the Latin word *limbus*, meaning "border"; the **limbic system** is at the border of the brainstem and cerebral hemispheres.

35. The **amygdala** is part of the limbic system and is involved in regulation of the emotions of fear and rage. (p. 53)

36. Also part of the limbic system, the **hypothalamus** regulates hunger, thirst, and body temperature and contains the so-called reward centers of the brain. (p. 53)

37. The **cerebral cortex** is the thin outer covering of the cerebral hemispheres. The seat of information processing, the cortex is responsible for those complex functions that make us distinctively human. (p. 55)

*Memory aid: Cortex* in Latin means "bark." As bark covers a tree, the **cerebral cortex** is the "bark of the brain."

38. More numerous than cortical neurons, the **glial cells** of the brain guide neural connections, provide nutrients and insulating myelin, and help remove excess electrically charged atoms and neurotransmitters. (p. 55)

39. Located at the front of the brain, just behind the forehead, the **frontal lobes** are involved in speaking and muscle movements and in making plans and judgments. (p. 55)

40. Situated between the frontal and occipital lobes, the **parietal lobes** contain the sensory cortex. (p. 55)

41. Located at the back and base of the brain, the **occipital lobes** contain the visual cortex, which receives information from the eyes. (p. 55)

42. Located on the sides of the brain, the **temporal lobes** contain the auditory areas, which receive information from the ears. (p. 55)

*Memory aid:* The **temporal lobes** are located near the *temples.*

43. Located at the back of the frontal lobe, the **motor cortex** controls voluntary movement. (p. 56)

44. The **sensory cortex** is located at the front of the parietal lobes, just behind the motor cortex. It registers and processes body sensations. (p. 57)

45. Located throughout the cortex, **association areas** of the brain are involved in higher mental functions, such as learning, remembering, and abstract thinking. (p. 58)

*Memory aid:* Among their other functions, **association areas** of the cortex are involved in integrating, or *associating,* information from different areas of the brain.

46. **Aphasia** is an impairment of language as a result of damage to any of several cortical areas, including Broca's area and Wernicke's area. (p. 59)

47. **Broca's area**, located in the left frontal lobe, is involved in controlling the motor ability to produce speech. (p. 60)

48. **Wernicke's area,** located in the left temporal lobe, is involved in language comprehension. (p. 60)

49. **Plasticity** is the brain's capacity for modification, as evidenced by brain reorganization following damage (especially in children). (p. 62)

50. The **corpus callosum** is a large band of neural fibers that links the right and left cerebral hemi-spheres. Without this band of nerve fibers, the two hemispheres could not interact. (p. 63)

51. **Split brain** is a condition in which the major connections between the two cerebral hemispheres (the corpus callosum) are severed, literally resulting in a split brain. (p. 63)

52. The **endocrine system**, the body's "slower" chemical communication system, consists of glands that secrete hormones into the bloodstream. (p. 67)

53. **Hormones** are chemical messengers, mostly those manufactured by the endocrine system, that are produced in one tissue and circulate through the bloodstream to their target tissues, on which they have specific effects. (p. 67)

54. The **adrenal glands** produce epinephrine and norepinephrine, hormones that prepare the body to deal with emergencies or stress. (p. 68)

55. The **pituitary gland**, under the influence of the hypothalamus, regulates growth and controls other endocrine glands; sometimes called the "master gland." (p. 68)

56. **Chromosomes** are threadlike structures made of DNA molecules, which contain the genes. In conception, the 23 chromosomes in the egg are paired with the 23 chromosomes in the sperm. (p. 69)

57. **DNA (deoxyribonucleic acid)** is a complex molecule containing the genetic information that makes up the chromosomes. (p. 69)

58. **Genes** are the biochemical units of heredity that make up the chromosomes; they are segments of the DNA molecules capable of synthesizing a protein. (p. 69)

59. **Evolutionary psychology** is the study of the evolution of behavior using the principles of natural selection. (p. 70)

60. **Behavior genetics** is the study of genetic and environmental influences on behavior. (p. 70)

61. **Identical twins** develop from a single fertilized egg that splits in two and therefore are genetically identical. (p. 71)

62. **Fraternal twins** develop from two separate eggs fertilized by different sperm and therefore are no more genetically similar than ordinary siblings. (p. 71)

63. **Heritability** is the proportion of variation among individuals in a trait that is attributable to genetic factors. Current estimates place the heritability of intelligence at about 50 to 70 percent. (p. 73)

*Cross-Check*

**ACROSS**

3. heritability
4. lesion
6. adrenal
13. cerebellum
16. autonomic
19. brainstem
23. identical

**DOWN**

1. fraternal
2. myelin

5. hypothalamus
7. DNA
8. acetylcholine
9. medulla
10. nerves
11. amygdala
12. frontal
14. limbic
15. Wernicke's
18. temporal
19. Broca
20. synapse
22. aphasia

## FOCUS ON VOCABULARY AND LANGUAGE

*Page 39: . . . an ill-fated theory. . . .* Myers is referring to the theory that bumps or lumps on the skull could reveal our personality (*phrenology*). It was a theory destined for failure (*ill-fated*), despite its popularity during the early 1800s.

*Page 39: Despite its wrong-headedness. . . .* Even though phrenology was without any scientific merit (*wrong-headed*), it did suggest the idea that different parts of the brain influence a variety of functions and behaviors.

### Neural Communication

*Page 40:* For scientists, it is a *happy fact of nature* that the information systems of humans and other animals operate similarly. The structure and function of neurons are very similar in humans and other animals (e.g., squids and sea slugs) and this is fortunate (*a happy fact of nature*) for those researching the nervous system. Myers makes the important point about this similarity, noting that it would not be possible to tell the difference between a small piece of your brain tissue and that of a monkey.

*Page 40:* Its *building blocks* are **neurons,** or nerve cells. Building blocks are the basic or fundamental parts (e.g., bricks) that make up a structure (e.g., a house). The structure of our nervous system, or neural information system, is made up of neurons (*its building blocks*) .

*Pages 40–41: . . .* the **action potential,** is a brief electrical charge that travels down the axon, *rather like a line of dominoes falling, each one tripping the next.* Dominoes are the flat pieces used in the game of dominoes. If they are stacked side by side on end (like a shelf of books) and one end is pushed, all the

rest fall over one by one. The impulse travels down the axon in much the same way, in a series of electrochemical events.

*Page 41: . . .* the neural impulse travels at speeds ranging from a *sluggish* 2 miles per hour to, in some myelinated fibers, a *breakneck* 200 or more miles per hour. The speed of the neural impulse ranges from extremely slow (*sluggish*) to very fast (a *breakneck* speed). Compared to the speed of electricity or sophisticated electronics systems your neural impulses travel at a relatively slow pace.

*Page 41:* Some of these signals are *excitatory, rather like pushing a neuron's accelerator.* Other signals are *inhibitory, rather like pushing its brake.* Myers is making a comparison between the effect of a neuron firing and the effect of speeding up a car when accelerating (*excitatory effect*) or slowing it down by applying the brake (*inhibitory effect*).

*Page 41: How do we distinguish a gentle touch from a firm hug?* This question is concerned with how we become aware of the magnitude of a stimulus, from a soft stroke or pat (*gentle touch*) to a strong embrace (*firm hug*). The answer is that the intensity of the stimulus is a function of the number and frequency of neurons firing. A strong stimulus (*firm hug*) does not initiate (*trigger*) a more powerful or faster impulse than a weak stimulus (*gentle touch*); rather, it triggers more neurons to fire, and to fire more often.

*Page 41: . . .* these near-unions of neurons—"*protoplasmic kisses*". . . were another of nature's marvels. The reference here is to the fact that the axon terminal of one neuron is separated from the receiving neuron by a tiny space called the synaptic gap. Protoplasm is the material that constitutes all living cells, and the communication between cells is likened to a kiss between cells. The transmission between sender and receiver is via chemicals called neurotransmitters. The cells don't actually touch but send messages across the synaptic gap.

*Page 41: Roughly speaking, the neuron is democratic.* . . . What this means is that, in general (*roughly speaking*), the neuron will fire depending on whether or not there are more excitatory than inhibitory messages, just as one candidate may get elected over another depending on how many votes he or she gets in a democratic election.

*Page 43: . . . "runner's high"* . . . This refers to the feeling of emotional well-being or euphoria (*high*) following vigorous exercise such as running or jogging and is the result of the release of opiatelike substances called endorphins.

*Page 43:* They *trigger* unpleasant, *lingering aftereffects.* For suppressing the body's own neurotransmitter production, *nature charges a price.* Mood-altering drugs, such as alcohol, nicotine, heroin, and morphine, all initiate (*trigger*) disagreeable changes that persist for a long period of time (*lingering aftereffects*). When flooded with these opiates, the brain stops producing its own endorphins (i.e., they suppress production), and for the addict who stops taking the drugs the cost may be a great deal of pain and agony (*nature charges a price*).

*Page 43: Agonists* work by *mimicking* a particular neurotransmitter. . . . *Antagonists* work by *blocking* neurotransmitters. Other drugs work by *hampering* the neurotransmitter's natural breakdown or its reabsorption. An *agonist* drug molecule is enough like the neurotransmitter to imitate (*mimic*) its effects (for example, by producing a temporary euphoric feeling—a "high"). An *antagonist* drug molecule is enough like the neurotransmitter to stop (*block*) its effects but not similar enough to stimulate the receptor (for example, some toxins may cause muscle paralysis by blocking acetylcholine receptors). Other drugs work by interfering with (*hampering*) the neurotransmitter's normal breakdown or its reabsorption.

*Page 44: . . .* some *chemicals* don't have the right shape to *slither* through this [*blood-brain*] *barrier* . . . Some neurotransmitter substances (*chemicals*) such as dopamine do not work when given to patients because they can't slide or slip smoothly (*slither*) through the *blood-brain barrier* since they are the wrong shape. The *blood-brain barrier* is a system which blocks or obstructs unwanted chemicals circulating in the blood from getting into the brain (the brain *fences them out*).

## The Nervous System

*Page 45:* Like an *automatic pilot*, it may sometimes be consciously *overridden.* The autonomic nervous system automatically takes care of the operation of our internal organs much as a plane can be flown by the automatic (*or mechanical/computerized*) pilot. The system can, however, be consciously taken over (*overridden*) in the same way that the real pilot can take over flying the plane.

*Page 45:* Tens of billions of neurons, each in communication with thousands of other neurons, *yield an ever-changing wiring diagram that dwarfs a powerful computer.* The complexity of the central nervous system, which allows or makes possible (*enables*) our thinking, feeling, and behavior, is similar to the electronic circuitry (*wiring diagrams*) of the best computer, except, by comparison, the computer would appear to be extremely tiny or small (*dwarfed by*) and the brain's wiring would seem to be constantly modifying or altering itself (*ever-changing*).

*Page 46: . . . information highway.* . . . The spinal cord is similar to the freeway (*highway*), but instead of cars moving up and down, sensory and motor messages (*information*) travel between the peripheral nervous system and the brain. This information moves either up (*ascending*) or down (*descending*) bundles of nerve fibers (*tracts*).

*Page 46: The knee-jerk response is one example; a headless warm body could do it.* When the patellar tendon of a bent knee is struck, the whole leg reflexively straightens out (*the knee-jerk response*). This automatic reaction is a function of a simple spinal reflex pathway so it does not require mediation by the brain (*a headless warm* [live] *body could do it*).

## The Brain

*Page 48: . . . we live in our heads.* What this means is that you subjectively feel that the essence of your being, your mind, resides in your brain, which is inside your head. The brain in our head allows us to function psychologically as well as physically: *the mind is what the brain does.*

*Page 48:* So there are *exceptions* to the *rule of thumb* that the ratio of brain to body weight provides a clue to a species' intelligence. A *rule of thumb* is a general principle which is usually true, but there are some occasions (*exceptions*) when the maxim or guide (*rule of thumb*) is incorrect. Myers suggests that a more practical and productive approach than the brain-body weight ratio is the study of the various structures of the brain.

*Page 49: This peculiar cross-wiring is but one of many surprises the brain has to offer.* In the brainstem most nerves from the left side of the body connect to the right side of the brain and those from the right connect to the left side of the brain. This strange (*peculiar*) traverse of nerves from one side to the other (*cross-wiring*) is one of the many marvels or astonishing findings (*surprises*) about the brain.

*Page 49:* We can think of the thalamus as being to *neural traffic* what *London is to England's train traffic.* London is the relay center for trains going to all parts of the country just as Chicago is the hub or relay center for many airlines flying to different parts of the United States. Myers uses this as an analogy for the thalamus, which receives messages from sensory neurons and sends them on, or relays them (*neural traffic*) to higher brain areas.

*Page 50 (Close-Up):* We can *snoop on* the messages of individual neurons and on the *mass action* of billions. With today's technological tools it is possible to pry or spy on (*snoop on*) single nerve cells (neurons) as well as graphically depict the collective behavior (*mass action*) of millions and millions of cells.

*Page 50 (Close-Up):* Other *new windows into the brain* give us a *Supermanlike* ability to see inside the brain without *lesioning it.* Modern technological means of viewing the brain (*new windows into the brain*), such as the CT and the PET scans, provide us with a greater than normal (*Supermanlike*) ability to look inside the cortex without destroying tissue (*lesioning it*). (*Note:* Superman is a comic-book, TV, and movie character with x-ray vision which allows him to see through solid matter.)

*Page 51 (Close-Up):* Such *snapshots* of the brain's *mind-making activity* provide new insights into how and where the brain *divides its labor.* The MRI technique allows pictures (*snapshots*) to be taken of different brain areas at work (the brain *divides its labor*) while a person is carrying out various mental tasks (*mind-making activity*).

*Page 51 (Close-Up): These new brain-imaging instruments . . . are triggering a scientific revolution. Revolution,* in this context, means a complete and fundamental change. Recent technological innovations, such as the CT, PET, and MRI (*the tools*), are bringing about drastic and dramatic changes in neuroscience. Myers compares the study of the brain today to learning about world geography when the great explorer Magellan was discovering and mapping new lands and oceans.

*Page 52: . . .* a *doughnut-shaped* neural system called the **limbic system**. This system is in the shape of a ring (*doughnut-shaped*) and has three components: the **hippocampus,** which is involved in forming (*laying down*) new memories; the **amygdala,** which influences aggression and fear; and the **hypothalamus,** which regulates hunger, thirst, body temperature, and sexuality.

*Page 54: . . .* they made *a magnificent mistake.* Olds and Milner accidentally discovered (*stumbled upon*) a brain area that provides a pleasurable reward and then went on to find other similar areas which they called "*pleasure centers.*" Myers calls this a splendid and spectacular error (*a magnificent mistake*). When rats are allowed to stimulate these areas by pressing a bar (*pedal*) they seem to prefer this to any other activity and will continue at a very rapid rate (*feverish pace*) until they are too tired to go on (*until they drop from exhaustion*).

*Page 55:* Opening a human skull and exposing the brain, we would see a *wrinkled* organ, shaped rather like the *meat of an oversized walnut.* The human brain has a convoluted (*wrinkled*) surface, and the cerebral cortex is divided into two halves or hemispheres just like the two lobes of the edible portion (*the meat or seed*) in the shell of a very large (*oversized*) walnut.

*Page 57:* So, in a sense, we *do* have *eyes in the back of our head.* The reference here is to the visual cortex (or occipital lobes) which processes visual information and is located at the rear of the brain. So, in a way seeing is not just done with the eyes but also involves specialized areas at the back of the brain.

*Page 58: . . .* one of pop psychology's most widespread *myths:* that we ordinarily *use only 10 percent of our brains.* Research into the association areas of the brain showed that they don't have specific functions but rather are involved in many different operations such as interpreting, integrating, and acting on information processed by the sensory areas. The false notion (*myth*) that *we use only 10 percent of our brains* may have arisen because early researchers were unsure about the function of the association areas. Remember, we use all of our brain, all the time. Damage to the frontal lobes (association areas) would result in very serious deficits.

*Page 60: What you experience as a continuous, indivisible stream of perception is actually but the visible tip of the information-processing iceberg, most of which lies beneath the surface of your conscious awareness.* Myers is making an analogy here. Most of the important functions that allow you to see the world as a whole are not part of conscious experience, but like most of the mass of an iceberg, are below the surface and out of awareness.

### Brain Reorganization

*Page 62:* Thus, the brain may not be as *"hard-wired"* as once thought. Myers is noting a comparison that used to be made between the brain's neural networks and the fixed circuits of computer hardware. We now know that the brain is much more flexible—it is not *"hard-wired."* Myers uses the term *plastic* or *brain plasticity* to describe this malleability or adaptability.

*Page 63:* Waking from the surgery, one patient even managed to *quip* that he had a *"splitting headache."* People have had their corpus callosum severed or cut in order to control epileptic seizures. Despite such a major operation this patient managed to joke (*quip*) that he had a very bad headache (*a splitting headache*). Personality and intellectual functioning were not affected by this procedure, and you would not be able to detect anything unusual if you were having a casual conversation with a split-brain patient.

*Page 64:* The left hemisphere, which acts as *the brain's press agent*, does *mental gymnastics* to *rationalize* reactions it does not understand. In split-brain patients, if information or commands are delivered to the right hemisphere (which does not have language), then the left hemisphere, which can talk, would not be aware of what was requested. So if the patient carried out the command to do something (e.g., "walk" or "clap"), the left hemisphere will go through all kinds of contortions (*mental gymnastics*) to make up some plausible story (*rationalize*); in this way it acts to make sense of and explain behavior, much as *press agents* do for the company or person they represent.

*Page 66 (Thinking Critically):* At their worst, they distort *pretzel-shaped findings* into a *breadstick-shaped story:* Some people are left-brained, others right-brained. . . . A *pretzel* is a snack food, a piece of thinly rolled bread dough shaped like an open knot. A unique and unusual set of findings (*pretzel-shaped*) gets transformed through the process of oversimplification and distortion into something totally different (*a breadstick-shaped* [very straight] *story*). Thus, public myths, such as *"some people are left-brained, others right brained,"* develop and get more attention than the scientific facts.

*Page 67:* From looking at the two hemispheres, which *look alike* to the *naked eye*, who would suppose

that they contribute so uniquely to *the harmony of the whole?* Myers points out that research with split-brain people and normal people shows that we have unified brains with different parts that have specialized functions. Thus, if we observe the two hemispheres without optical aids (*with the naked eye*), they may appear to be the same (*look alike*); however, their differential functioning combines to produce an integrated unit (*the harmony of the whole*).

*Page 67:* Yet what is unknown still *dwarfs* what is known. This means that all that has been discovered so far is very, very small (*dwarfed*) compared to what yet remains to be discovered.

### The Endocrine System

*Page 67:* The endocrine system and nervous system are therefore *kindred* systems. These two systems are very similar and have a close relationship (*kindred systems*). The hormones of the endocrine system are chemically equivalent to neurotransmitters, but operate at a much slower speed (i.e., the endocrine messages use *the slow lane* while the nervous system *zips* [or speeds] messages from eyes to brain in a fraction of a second).

*Page 68:* Conducting and coordinating this whole *electrochemical orchestra* is that *maestro* we call the brain. Myers is comparing the functioning of the neurotransmitters and hormones to a large group of musicians (*electrochemical orchestra*) whose movements and actions are directed by the conductor or master (*maestro*), the brain.

### Genetics and Behavior

*Page 69:* . . . blueprints . . . Blueprint is an architectural term for a copy of an original diagram or plan used as a working drawing for creating the building or structure. Myers notes that the 46 chromosomes in each body cell (23 from the egg and 23 from the sperm) contain the master plan (*blueprint*) in the form of genes that ultimately makes each of us a unique human being.

*Page 69:* Everyone agrees that the tight genetic *leash* . . . is looser on humans. Just as a dog is restrained or held in check by a strap or cord (*leash*), genes generally determine the behaviors of many animals. In humans, however, genes are less influential; thus, the usually strong genetic constraints (*tight genetic leash*) operate in a less determined way (*are looser*).

*Page 70:* As *mobile gene machines*, we are predisposed by nature *to have longings and make choices* that worked for our ancestors. Evolutionary psychologists believe that behavioral tendencies that increase the probability of getting one's genes into the future have been selected for over the course of evolution. Humans who actively seek out mates and successfully procreate (*mobile gene machines*) are passing on inherited tendencies to behave in certain ways (*have longings and make choices*) because these behaviors were adaptive for our ancestors.

*Page 72:* The *cute stories* do not impress Bouchard's critics. Bouchard's investigation into the similarities between separated twins suggests that genes influence many behaviors, such as career choices, TV-watching habits, and food likes and dislikes (*cute stories*). The critics point out that any two strangers of the same sex and age would probably have many coincidental things in common if they were to spend hours comparing their behaviors and life histories.

*Page 73:* Thus, asking whether your intelligence—or your personality—is more a product of your genes or environment is like asking whether *the area of a field is more the result of its length or its width.* The area of a space, such as a soccer field or a football field, is determined by multiplying the length by the width. Obviously, you cannot find the area of the field without both length and width. Likewise, we do not become who we are without both nature and nurture. As Myers notes, for psychological characteristics, both genetic (*nature*) and environmental (*nurture*) factors are almost always involved.

# The Developing Person

## Chapter Overview

Developmental psychologists study the life cycle, from conception to death, examining how we develop physically, cognitively, and socially. Chapter 3 covers physical, cognitive, and social development over the life span and introduces three major issues in developmental psychology: (1) the relative impact of genes and experience on behavior, (2) whether development is best described as gradual and continuous or as a discontinuous sequence of stages, and (3) whether the individual's personality remains stable or changes over the life span.

Although there are not too many terms to learn in this chapter, there are a number of important research findings to remember. Pay particular attention to the stage theories of Piaget, Kohlberg, and Erikson, as well as to the discussion regarding intellectual stability during adulthood. Writing carefully prepared answers to the guided study items should be especially helpful in mastering the material in this chapter.

Note: Answer guidelines for all Chapter 3 questions begin on page 83.

## Guided Study

The text chapter should be studied one section at a time. Before you read, preview each section by skimming it, noting headings and boldface items. Then read the appropriate section objectives from the following outline. Keep these objectives in mind and, as you read the chapter section, search for the information that will enable you to meet each objective. Once you have finished a section, write out answers for its objectives.

> David Myers at times uses idioms that are unfamiliar to some readers. If you do not know the meaning of any of the following words, phrases, or expressions in the context in which they appear in the text, refer to page 95 for an explanation: . . . *journey through life from womb to tomb.*

**1.** Identify and briefly describe three major issues that pervade developmental psychology.

1) nature/nurture – How is our development influenced by our heredity (nature) and by our experience including the nurture we receive.

2) continuity/stages – change Happens. adults are different from infants

*Prenatal Development and the Newborn* (pp. 80–82)

> If you do not know the meaning of any of the following words, phrases, or expressions in the context in which they appear in the text, refer to page 95 for an explanation: *throws a master switch; tomboyish; absorbent sponge . . . stamped immediately with the smell of its mother's body.*

**2.** Describe conception and explain how sex is determined.

*The union of the sperm and the egg.*

**3.** Outline the course of prenatal development.

**4.** Discuss the possible effects of teratogens on the developing embryo and fetus.

**5.** Describe the capacities of the newborn.

**6.** Describe the brain development that occurs from infancy through childhood, including its impact on memory, and the role of experience.

**7.** Describe the roles of nature and nurture in motor development through infancy and childhood.

**8.** Discuss Piaget's view of how the mind develops and describe his cognitive stages.

**9.** Discuss current views of Piaget's theory of cognitive development.

**10.** Discuss the origins and effects of early attachment, and the roles of temperament and parenting on attachment throughout life.

### Infancy and Childhood (pp. 83–98)

> If you do not know the meaning of any of the following words, phrases, or expressions in the context in which they appear in the text, refer to pages 95–97 for an explanation: *toddler; wild growth spurt; Like pathways through a forest; wiring; fruitless; double take; bad hair day; passive receptacles; it gets high marks; cognitive milestones; pit the drawing power; windows of opportunity; gosling; footprints on the brain; parenting styles . . . lax; it bodes well.*

11. Discuss how caregiving and divorce influence attachment.

12. Discuss how parenting styles and values vary among cultures.

13. Differentiate between gender and gender identity and explain two theories of gender-typing.

### Adolescence (pp. 99–109)

> If you do not know the meaning of any of the following words, phrases, or expressions in the context in which they appear in the text, refer to page 97 for an explanation: *out of sync; intellectual summit; character—the psychological muscles for controlling impulses; moral ladder; psychosocial task; forge their identity; surfaces early; pendulum of sexual values.*

14. Identify the major physical changes that occur in adolescence.

15. Describe developments in cognitive and moral reasoning during adolescence, focusing on Kohlberg's theory and its criticisms.

16. Describe how Erikson viewed adolescence and the nature of social relationships during adolescence and explain adolescents' changing relationships with parents and peers.

17. Discuss several factors that have contributed to the increase in adolescent pregnancy.

### Adulthood (pp. 109–120)

> If you do not know the meaning of any of the following words, phrases, or expressions in the context in which they appear in the text, refer to pages 97–98 for an explanation: *quipped; P.M.F.—Post-Menstrual Freedom; mumble; levies a tax; Use it or lose it; "you can't teach an old dog new tricks"; "Pair-bonding is a trademark of the human animal"; shower one another with affection; nuzzle; look the other way; test-driving life together; empty nest syndrome.*

18. Identify the major physical changes that occur in middle adulthood and later life.

worlds" and "girl worlds." Boys who are reared in fatherless homes tend to be _____ (less strongly/no less strongly) gender-typed.

49. According to _____ _____ theory, children learn from their _____ what it means to be male or female and adjust their behavior accordingly.

50. The once-popular belief that no important changes in personality occur after childhood has given way to an understanding that development is _____.

*Adolescence* (pp. 99–109)

51. Today, sexual maturity is beginning _____ (earlier/later), and adult independence _____ (earlier/later) than in the past.

52. The "storm and stress" view of adolescence is credited to _____, one of the first American psychologists to describe adolescence.

53. Adolescence begins with the time of developing sexual maturity known as _____. A 2-year growth spurt begins in girls at about the age of _____ and in boys at about the age of _____. This growth spurt is marked by the development of the reproductive organs and external genitalia, or _____ characteristics, as well as by the development of traits such as pubic hair and enlarged breasts in females and facial hair in males. These nonreproductive traits are known as _____ _____ characteristics.

54. The first menstrual period, called _____, occurs by about age _____. In boys the first ejaculation occurs by about age _____.

55. The _____ (timing/sequence) of pubertal changes is more predictable than their _____ (timing/sequence).

56. Boys who mature _____ (early/late) tend to be more popular, self-assured, and independent. For girls, _____ (early/late) maturation can be stressful, especially when their bodies are out of sync with their _____ _____.

57. During the early teen years, reasoning is often _____, as adolescents often feel their experiences are unique.

58. Piaget's final stage of cognitive development is the stage of _____. The adolescent in this stage is capable of thinking logically about _____ as well as concrete propositions.

59. The theorist who proposed that moral thought progresses through stages is _____. These stages are divided into three basic levels: _____, _____, and _____.

60. In the preconventional stages of morality, characteristic of children, the emphasis is on obeying rules in order to avoid _____ or gain _____.

61. Conventional morality usually emerges by early _____. The emphasis is on gaining social _____ or upholding the social _____.

62. Individuals who base moral judgments on their own perceptions of basic ethical principles are said by Kohlberg to employ _____ morality.

Summarize the criticisms of Kohlberg's theory of moral development.

Complete the missing information in the following table of Erikson's stages of psychosocial development.

| Group Age | Psychosocial Stage |
|---|---|
| Infancy | *trust vs. mistrust* |
| *toddler* | Autonomy vs. shame and doubt |
| Preschooler | *Initiative vs Guilt* |
| *Elementary School* | Competence vs. inferiority |
| Adolescence | *identity vs role confusion* |
| *young adulthood* | Intimacy vs. isolation |
| Middle Adulthood | *Generativity vs stagnation* |
| *late adulthood* | Integrity vs. despair |

63. According to Erikson, the task of adolescence is to develop a clear sense of self, or *identity*. Erikson saw this development as a prerequisite for the development of *intimacy* in young adulthood.

64. Between 13 and 23 the individual's self-concept usually becomes *more* (more/less) positive.

65. Gilligan believes that females are *less* (more/less) concerned than males with establishing individualistic identities.

66. Girls play in *smaller* (smaller/larger) groups than boys. Girls' play also is less *competitive* than boys and more likely to imitate *social relationships.*

Compare the genders in terms of social connectedness.

67. Adolescence is typically a time of increasing influence from one's *peers.* and decreasing influence from *parents*.

68. Teen intercourse rates in the United States and western Europe are *higher* (higher/lower) than in *Arabian* and *Asia* countries. The increased rate of births to unmarried Canadian, British, and American women stems from two trends: (a) *decreasing birthrate + married women*; and (b) *doubling birth + unmarried women*

69. Teen use of condoms *is not* (is/is not) generally consistent.

Identify several factors that contribute to the low rate of condom usage among teens.

70. U.S. national health objectives, reflected in changing sex education, now emphasize *contraception* and *abstinence* among teens.

71. More than half of all new cases of sexually transmitted diseases occur in persons under age *25*. Teenage *girls* (boys/girls) are especially vulnerable to such diseases.

*Adulthood* (pp. 109–120)

72. During adulthood, age *is not* (is/is not) a very good predictor of people's traits.

73. The mid-twenties are the peak years for *muscular strength*, *reaction time*, *sensory keeness*, and *output*. Because they mature earlier, *women* (women/men) also peak earlier.

74. During early and middle adulthood physical vigor has less to do with _age_ than with a person's _health_ and _exercise_ habits.

75. The cessation of the menstrual cycle, known as _menopause_, occurs within a few years of _50_. This biological change results from lowered levels of the hormone _estrogen_. A woman's experience during this time depends largely on her _expectations_ and _attitude_.

76. Although men experience no equivalent to menopause, they do experience a more gradual decline in _sperm_ count, level of the hormone _testosterone_, and speed of erection and ejaculation during later life.

77. With age, the eye's pupil _shrinks_ (shrinks/enlarges) and its lens becomes _less_ (more/less) transparent. As a result, the amount of light that reaches the retina is _reduced_ (increased/reduced).

78. Although older adults are _more_ (more/less) susceptible to life-threatening ailments, they suffer from short-term ailments such as flu _less_ (more/less) often than younger adults.

79. Aging _slows_ (slows/speeds/ has no effect on) neural processing and causes a gradual loss of _brain cells_.

80. The mental erosion that results from progressive damage to the brain is called _dementia_.

81. The irreversible disorder that causes progressive brain deterioration is _Alzheimer_ disease. This disease has been linked to a deterioration of neurons that produce the neurotransmitter _acetylcholine_.

82. Studies of developmental changes in learning and memory show that during adulthood there is a decline in the ability to _recall_ (recall/recognize) new information but not in the ability to _recognize_ (recall/recognize) such information. One factor that influences memory in the elderly is the _meaningfulness_ of material.

83. A research study in which people of various ages are compared with one another is called a _cross_ - _sectional_ study. A research study in which the same people are retested over a period of years is called a _longitudinal_ study. The first kind of study found evidence of intellectual _decline_ during adulthood; the second found evidence of intellectual _stability_.

Explain why studies of intellectual decline and aging yielded conflicting results.

84. The accumulation of stored information that comes with education and experience is called _crystallized_ intelligence, which tends to _increase_ with age.

85. The ability to reason abstractly is referred to as _fluid_ intelligence, which tends to _decrease_ with age.

86. Contrary to popular opinion, job and marital dissatisfaction do not surge during the forties, thus suggesting that a midlife _crisis_ need not occur.

87. The term used to refer to the culturally preferred timing for leaving home, getting a job, marrying,

and so on is the _____ _____ . Today the timing of such life events is becoming _____ (more/less) predictable. More important than age are

_____ .

88. According to Erikson, the two basic tasks of adulthood are achieving _____ and _____ . According to Freud, the healthy adult is one who can _____ and _____ .

89. Human societies have nearly always included a relatively _____ bond between men and women. Marriage bonds are usually lasting when couples marry after age _____ and are _____ .

90. Marriages today are _____ (half/twice) as likely to end in divorce as they were in 1960. Of those who divorce, _____ percent eventually remarry. One reliable indicator of likely marital success is a large ratio of _____ to _____ interactions.

91. As children begin to absorb time and energy, satisfaction with the marriage itself _____ (increases/decreases). This is particularly true among _____ women, who shoulder most of the burden.

92. For most couples, the children's leaving home produces a feeling of greater freedom and marital satisfaction. Some, however, become distressed and feel a loss of purpose. This is called the _____ syndrome.

93. Research studies of women who are or are not employed have found that a woman's satisfaction in life depends on the _____ of her experience in her life's role.

94. According to studies, older people _____ (do/do not) report as

much happiness and satisfaction with life as younger people do.

95. According to Erikson, the final task of adulthood is to achieve a sense of _____ .

*Reflections on the Major Developmental Issues* (pp. 120–121)

96. Stage theories that have been considered include the theory of cognitive development proposed by _____ , the theory of moral development proposed by _____ , and the theory of psychosocial development proposed by _____ .

97. Although research casts doubt on the idea that life proceeds through age-linked _____ , there are spurts of _____ growth during childhood and puberty that correspond roughly to the stages proposed by _____ .

98. The first 2 years of life _____ (do/do not) provide a good basis for predicting a person's eventual traits.

99. Research on the consistency of personality shows that some traits, such as those related to _____ , are more stable than others, such as social attitudes.

# Progress Test 1

Circle your answers to the following questions and check them with the answers on page 88. If your answer is incorrect, read the explanation for why it is incorrect and then consult the appropriate pages of the text (in parentheses following the correct answer).

1. In Piaget's stage of concrete operational intelligence, the child acquires an understanding of the principle of:
   a. conservation.    c. attachment.
   b. deduction.    d. object permanence.

2. Piaget held that egocentrism is characteristic of the:
   a. sensorimotor stage.
   b. preoperational stage.
   c. concrete operational stage.
   d. formal operational stage.

3. During which stage of cognitive development do children acquire object permanence?
   a. sensorimotor    c. concrete operational
   b. preoperational  d. formal operational

4. The rooting reflex occurs when a:
   a. newborn's foot is tickled.
   b. newborn's cheek is touched.
   c. newborn hears a loud noise.
   d. newborn makes eye contact with his or her caregiver.
   e. newborn hears his or her mother's voice.

5. Harlow's studies of attachment in monkeys showed that:
   a. provision of nourishment was the single most important factor motivating attachment.
   b. a cloth mother produced the greatest attachment response.
   c. whether a cloth or wire mother was present mattered less than the presence or absence of other infants.
   d. attachment in monkeys is based on imprinting.

6. When psychologists discuss maturation, they are referring to stages of growth that are *not* influenced by:
   a. conservation.    c. nurture.
   b. nature.          d. continuity.

7. The developmental theorist who suggested that securely attached children develop an attitude of basic trust is:
   a. Piaget.    d. Freud.
   b. Harlow.    e. Erikson.
   c. Vygotsky.

8. Gender refers to:
   a. the biological and social definition of male and female.
   b. the biological definition of male and female.
   c. one's sense of being male or female.
   d. the extent to which one exhibits traditionally male or female traits.

9. The fertilized egg will develop into a boy if, at conception:
   a. the sperm contributes an X chromosome.
   b. the sperm contributes a Y chromosome.
   c. the egg contributes an X chromosome.
   d. the egg contributes a Y chromosome.

10. Research findings on infant motor development are consistent with the idea that:
    a. cognitive development lags significantly behind motor skills development.
    b. maturation of physical skills is relatively unaffected by experience.
    c. in the absence of relevant earlier learning experiences, the emergence of motor skills will be slowed.
    d. in humans the process of maturation may be significantly altered by cultural factors.

11. Which theory states that gender become a lens through which children view their experiences?
    a. social learning theory
    b. Vygotsky's sociocultural theory
    c. Piaget's theory
    d. gender schema theory

12. The hormone testosterone:
    a. is found only in females.
    b. determines the sex of the zygote.
    c. stimulates growth of the female sex organs in the fetus.
    d. stimulates growth of the male sex organs in the fetus.

13. Research studies have found that when infant rats and premature human babies are regularly touched or massaged, they:
    a. gain weight more rapidly.
    b. develop faster neurologically.
    c. have more agreeable temperaments.
    d. do a. and b.
    e. do a., b., and c.

14. According to Erikson, the central psychological challenges pertaining to adolescence, young adulthood, and middle age, respectively, are:
    a. identity formation; intimacy; generativity.
    b. intimacy; identity formation; generativity.
    c. generativity; intimacy; identity formation.
    d. intimacy; generativity; identity formation.
    e. identity formation; generativity; intimacy.

15. In preconventional morality, the person:
    a. obeys out of a sense of social duty.
    b. conforms to gain social approval.
    c. obeys to avoid punishment or to gain concrete rewards.
    d. follows the dictates of his or her conscience.

16. Which of the following is correct?
    a. Early maturation places both boys and girls at a distinct social advantage.
    b. Early-maturing girls are more popular and self-assured than girls who mature late.
    c. Early maturation places both boys and girls at a distinct social disadvantage.
    d. Early-maturing boys are more popular and self-assured than boys who mature late.

17. A person's general ability to think abstractly is called _____ intelligence. This ability generally _____ with age.
    a. fluid; increases
    b. fluid; decreases
    c. crystallized; decreases
    d. crystallized; increases

18. An elderly person who can look back on life with satisfaction and reminisce with a sense of completion has attained Erikson's stage of:
    a. generativity.
    b. intimacy.
    c. isolation.
    d. acceptance.
    e. integrity.

19. According to Piaget, the ability to think logically about abstract propositions is indicative of the stage of:
    a. preoperational thought.
    b. concrete operations.
    c. formal operations.
    d. fluid intelligence.

20. The cognitive ability that has been shown to decline during adulthood is the ability to:
    a. recall new information.
    b. recognize new information.
    c. learn meaningful new material.
    d. use judgment in dealing with daily life problems.

21. Which of the following statements concerning the effects of aging is true?
    a. Aging almost inevitably leads to dementia if the individual lives long enough.
    b. Aging increases susceptibility to short-term ailments such as the flu.
    c. Significant increases in life satisfaction are associated with aging.
    d. The aging process can be significantly affected by the individual's activity patterns.

22. Longitudinal tests:
    a. compare people of different ages.
    b. study the same people at different times.
    c. usually involve a larger sample than do cross-sectional tests.
    d. usually involve a smaller sample than do cross-sectional tests.
    e. are less informative than cross-sectional tests.

23. According to the text, some adolescents engage in unprotected sex:
    a. because they are unaware of the safe and risky times of the menstrual cycle.
    b. because their guilt about sex often results in failure to plan for and use birth control.
    c. because their use of alcohol clouds their judgment.
    d. for all of the above reasons.

24. The average age at which puberty begins is _____ in boys; in girls, it is _____ .
    a. 14; 13          c. 11; 10
    b. 13; 11          d. 10; 9

25. After puberty, the self-concept usually becomes:
    a. more positive in boys.
    b. more positive in girls.
    c. more positive in both boys and girls.
    d. more negative in both boys and girls.

*True-False Items*

Indicate whether each statement is true or false by placing *T* or *F* in the blank next to the item.

_____ 1. Most abused children later become abusive parents.

_____ 2. At birth, the brain and nervous system of a healthy child are fully developed.

_____ 3. The sequence in which children develop motor skills varies from one culture to another.

_____ 4. Recent research shows that young children are more capable and development is more continuous than Piaget believed.

_____ 5. Children of divorced parents are twice as likely to experience social, psychological, or academic problems.

_____ 6. Despite popular belief, only a small percentage of teenagers report not getting along with their parents at all.

_____ 7. During adulthood, age only moderately correlates with people's traits.

_____ 8. Children of communal cultures exhibit greater shyness toward strangers than do Western children.

_____ 9. An infant's style of attachment primarily reflects his or her temperament.

_____ 10. Compared to those who are younger, elderly people are more susceptible to short-term ailments such as flu and cold viruses.

_____ 11. The symptoms of Alzheimer's disease are simply an intensified version of normal aging.

## Progress Test 2

Progress Test 2 should be completed during a final chapter review. Answer the following questions after you thoroughly understand the correct answers for the Chapter Review and Progress Test 1.

1. Stranger anxiety develops at the same time as:
   a. the concept of conservation.
   b. egocentrism.
   c. a theory of mind.
   d. the concept of object permanence.

2. Before Piaget, people were more likely to believe that:
   a. the child's mind is a miniature model of the adult's.
   b. children think about the world in radically different ways than adults.

   c. the child's mind develops through a series of stages.
   d. children interpret their experiences in terms of their current understandings.

3. Which is the correct sequence of stages in Piaget's theory of cognitive development?
   a. sensorimotor, preoperational, concrete operational, formal operational
   b. sensorimotor, preoperational, formal operational, concrete operational
   c. preoperational, sensorimotor, concrete operational, formal operational
   d. preoperational, sensorimotor, formal operational, concrete operational
   e. sensorimotor, concrete operational, preoperational, formal operational

4. A child can be born a drug addict because:
   a. drugs used by the mother will pass into the child's bloodstream.
   b. addiction is an inherited personality trait.
   c. drugs used by the mother create genetic defects in her chromosomes.
   d. the fetus's blood has not yet developed a resistance to drugs.

5. A child whose mother drank heavily when she was pregnant is at heightened risk of:
   a. being emotionally excitable during childhood.
   b. becoming insecurely attached.
   c. being born with the physical and cognitive abnormalities of fetal alcohol syndrome.
   d. addiction to a range of drugs throughout life.

6. Which is the correct order of stages of prenatal development?
   a. zygote, fetus, embryo
   b. zygote, embryo, fetus
   c. embryo, zygote, fetus
   d. embryo, fetus, zygote
   e. fetus, embryo, zygote

7. The term *critical period* refers to:
   a. prenatal development.
   b. the initial 2 hours after a child's birth.
   c. the preoperational stage.
   d. a restricted time for learning.

8. Which of the following was *not* found by Harlow in socially deprived monkeys?
   a. They had difficulty mating.
   b. They showed extreme fear or aggression when first seeing other monkeys.
   c. They showed abnormal physical development.
   d. The females were abusive mothers.

9. Children who in infancy formed secure attachments to their parents are more likely than other children to:
   a. prefer the company of adults to that of other children.
   b. become permissive parents.
   c. show a great deal of social competence.
   d. be less achievement oriented.

10. Most people's earliest memories do not predate _____ of age.
    a. 6 months          d. 3 years
    b. 1 year            e. 4 years
    c. 2 years

11. Insecurely attached infants who are left by their mothers in an unfamiliar setting often will:
    a. hold fast to their mothers on their return.
    b. explore the new surroundings confidently.
    c. be indifferent toward their mothers on their return.
    d. display little emotion at any time.

12. Compared to those raised in Western societies, children raised in communal societies such as Japan or China:
    a. grow up with a stronger integration of the sense of family into their self-concepts.
    b. exhibit greater shyness toward strangers.
    c. exhibit greater concern for loyalty and social harmony.
    d. have all of the above characteristics.
    e. have none of the above characteristics.

13. The cross-sectional method:
    a. compares people of different ages with one another.
    b. studies the same group of people at different times.
    c. tends to paint too favorable a picture of the effects of aging on intelligence.
    d. is a more appropriate method for studying intellectual change over the life span than the longitudinal method.

14. The "social clock" refers to:
    a. an individual or society's distribution of work and leisure time.
    b. adulthood responsibilities.
    c. typical ages for starting a career, marrying, etc.
    d. age-related changes in one's circle of friends.

15. To which of Kohlberg's levels would moral reasoning based on the existence of fundamental human rights pertain?
    a. preconventional morality
    b. conventional morality
    c. postconventional morality
    d. generative morality

16. In Erikson's theory, individuals generally focus on developing _____ during adolescence and then _____ during young adulthood.
    a. identity; intimacy
    b. intimacy; identity
    c. basic trust; identity
    d. identity; basic trust

17. After menopause, most women:
    a. experience anxiety and a sense of worthlessness.
    b. lose interest in sex.
    c. secrete unusually high levels of estrogen.
    d. gain a lot of weight.
    e. feel a new sense of freedom.

18. Notable achievements in fields such as _____ are often made by younger adults in their late twenties or early thirties, when _____ intelligence is at its peak.
    a. mathematics; fluid
    b. philosophy; fluid
    c. science; crystallized
    d. literature; crystallized
    e. history; crystallized

19. After their grown children have left home, most couples experience:
    a. the distress of the "empty nest syndrome."
    b. increased strain in their marital relationship.
    c. both a. and b.
    d. greater happiness and enjoyment in their relationship.

20. Underlying Alzheimer's disease is a deterioration in neurons that produce:
    a. epinephrine.          d. acetylcholine.
    b. norepinephrine.       e. dopamine.
    c. serotonin.

21. Compared with men, women:
    a. are less likely to describe themselves as having empathy.
    b. talk less openly.
    c. are better at reading people's emotional cues.
    d. do all of the above.

22. A person's accumulation of stored information, called _____ intelligence, generally _____ with age.
    a. fluid; decreases
    b. fluid; increases
    c. crystallized; decreases
    d. crystallized; increases

23. In terms of incidence, susceptibility to short-term illnesses _____ with age and susceptibility to long-term ailments _____ with age.
    a. decreases; increases
    b. increases; decreases
    c. increases; increases
    d. decreases; decreases

24. One criticism of stage theories is that they fail to consider that development may be significantly affected by:
    a. variations in the social clock.
    b. each individual's experiences.
    c. each individual's historical and cultural setting.
    d. all of the above.

25. Research on the American family indicates that:
    a. fewer than 23 percent of unmarried adults, but nearly 40 percent of married adults, report being "very happy" with life.
    b. the divorce rate is now one-half the marriage rate.
    c. of those who divorce, 75 percent remarry.
    d. all of the above are true.

## Thinking Critically About Chapter 3

Answer these questions the day before an exam as a final check on your understanding of the chapter's terms and concepts.

*Multiple-Choice Questions*

1. Compared to when he was younger, 4-year-old Antonio is better able to empathize with his friend's feelings. This growing ability to take another's perspective indicates that Antonio is acquiring a:
    a. self-concept.      c. temperament.
    b. schema.            d. theory of mind.

2. Calvin, who is trying to impress his psychology professor with his knowledge of infant motor development, asks why some infants learn to roll over before they lift their heads from a prone position, while others develop these skills in the opposite order. What should Calvin's professor conclude from this question?
    a. Calvin clearly understands that the sequence of motor development is not the same for all infants.
    b. Calvin doesn't know what he's talking about. Although some infants reach these developmental milestones ahead of others, the order is the same for all infants.
    c. Calvin needs to be reminded that rolling over is an inherited reflex, not a learned skill.
    d. Calvin understands an important principle: motor development is unpredictable.

3. I am a rat whose cortex is lighter and thinner than my litter mates. What happened to me?
    a. You were born prematurely.
    b. You suffer from fetal alcohol syndrome.
    c. You were raised in an enriched environment.
    d. You were raised in a deprived environment.
    e. You did not imprint during the critical period.

4. Five-year-old Malcolm enjoys playing with trucks and footballs, as does his older sister. His sister evidently is:
    a. experiencing confusion in her gender identity.
    b. more strongly gender-typed.
    c. less strongly gender-typed.
    d. unable to form a coherent gender schema.

5. As a child observes, liquid is transferred from a tall, thin tube into a short, wide jar. The child is asked if there is now less liquid in order to determine if she has mastered:
    a. the schema for liquids.
    b. the concept of object permanence.
    c. the concept of conservation.
    d. the ability to reason abstractly.

6. I am 14 months old and fearful of strangers. I am in Piaget's _____ stage of cognitive development.
    a. sensorimotor       c. concrete operational
    b. preoperational     d. formal operational

7. I am 3 years old, can use language, and have trouble taking another person's perspective. I am in Piaget's _____ stage of cognitive development.
    a. sensorimotor
    b. preoperational
    c. concrete operational
    d. formal operational

8. In Piaget's theory, conservation is to egocentrism as the _____ stage is to the _____ stage.
    a. sensorimotor; formal operational
    b. formal operational; sensorimotor
    c. preoperational; sensorimotor
    d. concrete operational; preoperational

9. Four-year-old Jamail has a younger sister. When asked if he has a sister, he is likely to answer _____ ; when asked if his sister has a brother, Jamail is likely to answer _____ .
    a. yes; yes
    b. no; no
    c. yes; no
    d. no; yes

10. In a 1998 movie, a young girl finds that a gaggle of geese follow her wherever she goes because she was the first "object" they saw after they were born. This is an example of:
    a. conservation.
    b. imprinting.
    c. egocentrism.
    d. basic trust.

11. Joshua and Ann Bishop have a 13-month-old. According to Erikson, the Bishops' sensitive, loving care of their child contributes to:
    a. the child's sense of basic trust.
    b. the child's secure attachment.
    c. the child's sense of control.
    d. a. and b. only.

12. Chad, who grew up in the United States, is more likely to encourage _____ in his future children than Asian-born Hidiyaki, who is more likely to encourage _____ in his future children.
    a. obedience; independence
    b. independence; emotional closeness
    c. emotional closeness; obedience
    d. loyalty; emotional closeness

13. Thirteen-year-old Irene has no trouble defeating her 11-year-old brother at a detective game that requires following clues in order to deduce the perpetrator of a crime. How might Piaget explain Irene's superiority at the game?
    a. Being older, Irene has had more years of schooling.
    b. Girls develop intellectually at a faster rate than boys.

    c. Being an adolescent, Irene is beginning to develop abstract reasoning skills.
    d. Girls typically have more experience than boys at playing games.

14. Which of the following was *not* mentioned in the text as a criticism of Kohlberg's theory of moral development?
    a. It does not account for the fact that the development of moral reasoning is culture-specific.
    b. Postconventional morality appears mostly in educated, middle-class persons.
    c. The theory is biased against the moral reasoning of people in communal societies such as China.
    d. The theory is biased in favor of moral reasoning in men.

15. Compared with her teenage brother, 14-year-old Samantha is likely to play in groups that are:
    a. larger and less competitive.
    b. larger and more competitive.
    c. smaller and less competitive.
    d. smaller and more competitive.

16. Sixty-five-year-old Calvin cannot reason as well as he could when he was younger. More than likely, Calvin's _____ intelligence has declined.
    a. analytic
    b. crystallized
    c. fluid
    d. both b. and c.

17. Cross-sectional studies of intelligence are potentially misleading because:
    a. they are typically based on a very small and unrepresentative sample of people.
    b. retesting the same people over a period of years allows test performance to be influenced by practice.
    c. they compare people who are not only different in age, but of different eras, education levels, and affluence.
    d. of all the above reasons.

18. Which statement illustrates cognitive development during the course of adult life?
    a. Adults in their forties have better recognition memory than do adults in their seventies.
    b. Recall and recognition memory both remain strong throughout life.
    c. Recognition memory decreases sharply at midlife.
    d. Recall memory remains strong until very late in life.
    e. Adults in their forties have better recall memory than adults in their seventies.

19. Given the text discussion of life satisfaction patterns, which of the following people is likely to report the greatest life satisfaction?
    a. Billy, a 7-year-old second-grader
    b. Kathy, a 17-year-old high-school senior
    c. Alan, a 30-year-old accountant
    d. Mildred, a 70-year-old retired teacher
    e. too little information to tell

20. Which of the following statements is consistent with the current thinking of developmental psychologists?
    a. Development occurs in a series of sharply defined stages.
    b. The first two years are the most crucial in determining the individual's personality.
    c. The consistency of personality in most people tends to increase over the life span.
    d. Social and emotional style are among the characteristics that show the least stability over the life span.

21. Sam, a junior in high school, regularly attends church because his family and friends think he should. Which stage of moral reasoning is Sam in?
    a. preconventional
    b. conventional
    c. postconventional
    d. too little information to tell

22. Research on social relationships between parents and their adolescent children shows that:
    a. parental influence on children increases during adolescence.
    b. high school girls who have the most affectionate relationships with their mothers tend to enjoy the most intimate friendships with girlfriends.
    c. high school boys who have the most affectionate relationships with their fathers tend to enjoy the most intimate friendships with friends.
    d. most teens are strongly influenced by parents in matters of personal taste.
    e. parent-adolescent conflict is most common between mothers and daughters.

23. Most contemporary developmental psychologists believe that:
    a. personality is essentially formed by the end of infancy.
    b. personality continues to be formed until adolescence.

    c. the shaping of personality continues during adolescence and well beyond.
    d. adolescent development has very little impact on adult personality.

24. After a series of unfulfilling relationships, 30-year-old Carlos tells a friend that he doesn't want to marry because he is afraid of losing his freedom and independence. Erikson would say that Carlos is having difficulty with the psychosocial task of:
    a. trust versus mistrust.
    b. autonomy versus doubt.
    c. intimacy versus isolation.
    d. identity versus role confusion.
    e. generativity versus stagnation.

25. Research on the relationship between self-reported happiness and employment in American women has revealed that:
    a. women who work tend to be happier.
    b. women who do not work tend to be happier.
    c. women today are happier than in the past, whether they are working or not.
    d. the quality of a woman's experience in her various roles is more predictive of happiness than the presence or absence of a given role.

### Essay Question

Sheryl is 12 years old and in the sixth grade. Describe the developmental changes she is likely to be experiencing according to Piaget, Kohlberg, and Erikson. (Use the space below to list the points you want to make and organize them. Then write the essay on a separate sheet of paper.)

# Key Terms

## *Defining Terms*

Using your own words, on a piece of paper write a brief definition or explanation of each of the following terms.

1. developmental psychology
2. *X* chromosome
3. *Y* chromosome
4. testosterone
5. gender
6. zygote
7. embryo
8. fetus
9. teratogens
10. fetal alcohol syndrome (FAS)
11. rooting reflex
12. maturation
13. schema
14. cognition
15. sensorimotor stage
16. object permanence
17. preoperational stage
18. conservation
19. egocentrism
20. concrete operational stage
21. formal operational stage
22. stranger anxiety
23. attachment
24. critical period
25. imprinting
26. temperament
27. basic trust
28. gender identity
29. gender-typing
30. social learning theory
31. gender schema theory
32. adolescence
33. puberty
34. primary sex characteristics
35. secondary sex characteristics
36. menarche
37. identity
38. intimacy
39. menopause
40. Alzheimer's disease
41. cross-sectional study
42. longitudinal study
43. crystallized intelligence
44. fluid intelligence
45. social clock

*Cross-Check*

As you learned in Chapter 1, reviewing and overlearning of material are important to the learning process. After you have written the definitions of the key terms in this chapter, you should complete the crossword puzzle to ensure that you can reverse the process—recognize the term, given the definition.

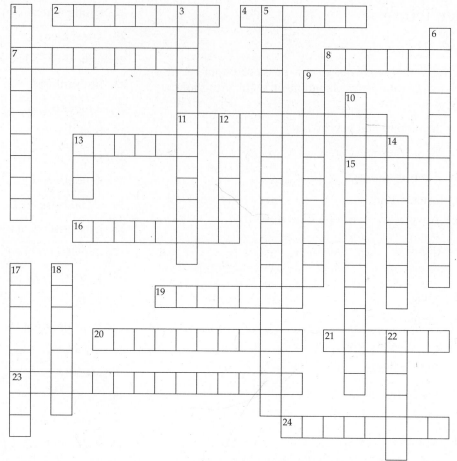

## ACROSS

2. The primary psychosocial need of young adulthood.
4. In Piaget's theory, mental concepts that help organize and interpret information.
7. The primary psychosocial need of late adulthood.
8. The second stage of prenatal development.
11. An irreversible brain disorder characterized by deterioration of neurons that produce acetylcholine.
13. In Piaget's theory, the type of mental operations that enable abstract reasoning.
15. The primary psychosocial need of infants.
16. In Piaget's theory, the type of mental operations that enable an understanding of mathematical transformations.
19. The period of sexual maturation.
20. Biological growth processes that enable orderly changes in behavior.
21. Author of an influential theory of cognitive development.
23. A study in which people of different ages are compared with one another.
24. Creator of an influential theory of moral reasoning.

## DOWN

1. Characteristics that refer to the reproductive organs and external genitalia.
3. Type of intelligence that includes one's accumulated knowledge and verbal skills.
5. The third stage of cognitive development in Piaget's theory.
6. In Kohlberg's theory, the type of morality that upholds laws and social rules simply because they are the laws and rules.
9. The primary psychosocial need of elementary school children.
10. An optimal time for exposure to certain stimuli or experiences.
12. The first stage of prenatal development.
13. Disorder suffered by an infant whose mother abused alcohol during her pregnancy (abbreviation).
14. According to Erikson, the primary psychosocial need of toddlers.
17. The first menstrual period.
18. Theorist who proposed stages of psychosocial development.
22. The biological and social definition of male and female.

# ANSWERS
## Guided Study

1. The nature/nurture issue is concerned with how much our development is influenced by heredity and how much by our experience. The continuity or stages issue concerns whether development is a gradual, continuous process or a sequence of separate stages. The stability or change issue asks whether individual traits persist over the life span or people become different persons as they age.

2. A woman's ovary releases a mature egg. The few sperm from the man that reach the egg release digestive enzymes that eat away the egg's protective covering. As soon as one sperm penetrates the egg, the egg's surface blocks out all other sperm. The egg and sperm nuclei fuse and become one.

   Sex is determined by the twenty-third pair of chromosomes, the sex chromosomes, one of which comes from each parent. The mother always contributes an X chromosome. The father's sperm contributes an X or a Y chromosome; with an X chromosome, the developing person becomes a girl; with a Y chromosome, a boy develops. The presence of a Y chromosome triggers development of the testes and the production of the principal male hormone, testosterone.

3. Prenatal development is divided into three stages: zygote (from conception to 2 weeks); embryo (2 weeks through 8 weeks); and fetus (9 weeks to birth).

   During the period of the zygote, cell division is the primary task. Within two weeks of conception the increasingly numerous cells begin to differentiate—to specialize in structure and function. At this time the zygote's outer part attaches to the mother's uterine wall, becoming the placenta. During the period of the embryo, body organs begin to form and function. By the end of the sixth month the fetus's internal organs have become sufficiently functional to allow a premature fetus a chance of survival.

4. Teratogens are damaging agents such as drugs and viruses that pass from the mother's bloodstream through the placenta into that of the embryo or fetus. Teratogens may result in a variety of physical and cognitive abnormalities in the developing child. For example, mothers who are heavy smokers often give birth to underweight infants. Mothers addicted to drugs such as heroin give birth to addicted newborns. If a mother is a heavy alcohol drinker, her infant may suffer from fetal alcohol syndrome, which involves small, misproportioned heads and brain abnormalities, which lead to mental retardation.

5. Newborns are born with a variety of reflexes that help ensure their survival. When touched on its cheek, for example, a baby will open its mouth and search for food (rooting reflex).

   The newborn's sensory capabilities facilitate social responsiveness. Newborns prefer human voices and drawings of human faces to artificial sounds and nonhuman visual patterns. Within days of birth, babies can distinguish their mother's odor and voice.

6. All the brain cells a person will ever have are present at birth. However, the neural connections that enable walking, talking, and memory are only beginning to form. This neural immaturity may explain why we have no memories of events before 3 years of age. While lasting memories may not be formed before then, infants are capable of learning simple responses.

   Sights, smells, touches, and other experiences foster the development of neural connections within the brain. Premature infants and laboratory animals who receive extra handling and a variety of experiences develop faster neurologically than those raised in deprived environments.

7. While nurture may play a role in motor development—Ugandan babies walk before age 10 months, as compared to babies with no experience—nature plays a major role. Before biological maturation creates a readiness to develop a particular skill, experience has a limited effect.

   Although the age at which infants sit, stand, walk, and control bowel and bladder varies from child to child, the sequence in which babies develop these abilities is universal.

8. Piaget believed that children actively construct their understanding of the world in radically different ways than adults. He further believed that children's minds develop through a series of stages in which they form increasingly complex schemas that organize their past experiences and provide a framework for understanding future experiences.

   In the sensorimotor stage, from birth to about 2 years, children experience their world through their senses and actions. During this stage, object permanence (and stranger anxiety) develop.

   In the preoperational stage, from about 2 to 6 or 7 years, children are able to use language but lack logical reasoning. During this stage, egocentrism develops.

   In the concrete operational stage, from about

6 or 7 to 11 years, children are able to think logically about concrete events and perform mathematical operations. Conservation also develops during this stage.

The formal operational stage, from age 12 through adulthood, is characterized by abstract and systematic reasoning, as well as by the potential for mature moral reasoning.

9. Today's researchers see development as more continuous than did Piaget. For example, object permanence, conservation, and the abilities to take another's perspective and perform mental operations unfold gradually and are not utterly absent in one stage and then suddenly present. In fact, preschoolers acquire a "theory of mind" and come to realize that others may hold false beliefs.

Researchers also believe that Piaget underestimated young children's competence. They have found rudiments of various cognitive abilities at an earlier age than Piaget supposed.

In many ways, however, Piaget's theory continues to receive support. Despite variations in the rate at which children develop, research reveals that human cognition everywhere unfolds in the basic sequence he proposed.

10. Harlow's research with monkeys reveals that attachment usually grows from body contact with parents, rather than by association with feeding. In many animals, attachment is also based on familiarity and forms during a critical period shortly after hatching or birth (a process called imprinting). Although human infants prefer faces and objects with which they are familiar, they do not have a critical period for forming attachments.

Attachment also depends on an infant's temperament, which includes inborn rudiments of personality, especially emotional excitability. The most emotionally reactive newborns tend also to be the most reactive, inhibited, and fearful 2-year-olds, shy 8-year-olds, and intense young adults. With age, these characteristics relax somewhat.

Responsive parenting is also a factor. Sensitive, responsive mothers tend to have infants who become securely attached. Insensitive, unresponsive mothers often have insecurely attached infants. Securely attached infants are less anxious and more socially competent, and these differences persist through early childhood.

11. Erik Erikson believed that infants with sensitive, loving caregivers form a lifelong attitude of basic trust—a sense that the world is predictable and reliable. Children who suffer parental neglect or abuse may form lasting scars—nightmares, de-

pression, a troubled adolescence, and a greater tendency to later abuse their own children.

The possible impact of divorce on children appears clear-cut. Even when researchers rule out other factors that may affect child development, such as parental education, race, and income, children of divorced or never-married parents are about twice as likely to experience a variety of social, psychological, or academic problems.

12. Social values vary from one culture to another. Most parents in Western societies value greater independence in their children than do parents in Asian and African cultures, who focus more on cultivating emotional closeness. Cross-cultural studies also reveal that people in Japanese and Chinese cultures exhibit greater shyness toward strangers and concern for social harmony and loyalty than do Westerners.

Researchers have found that although ethnic groups within a culture may differ in their behavior, they may be influenced by the same underlying processes. The behavior differences can result from differing inputs to the same process.

13. Gender, as noted earlier in the chapter, refers to the social definition of male or female; gender identity is our personal sense of being male or female. Gender-typing, which refers to the acquisition of a gender identity and role, has been alternatively explained by social learning theory and by gender schema theory. According to social learning theory, children acquire gender-linked behaviors by observing and imitating others and by being rewarded or punished. Gender schema theory assumes that the child's culture transmits a concept of what it means to be male or female. The child then adjusts his or her behavior to fit the concept.

14. Adolescence begins with puberty, a two-year period of rapid development that begins in girls at about age 11 and in boys at about age 13. During the growth spurt, sexual maturation occurs, as the primary sex characteristics (reproductive organs) and secondary sex characteristics (nonreproductive traits) develop dramatically.

The landmarks of puberty are the first ejaculation in boys at about age 14 and the first menstrual period, called menarche, in girls at about age 13. As in earlier life stages, the sequence of physical changes is more predictable than their timing.

15. During the early teen years, reasoning tends to be self-focused. Eventually, however, most adolescents attain Piaget's stage of formal operations

and become capable of abstract, logical thinking.

Kohlberg believed that moral reasoning builds on cognitive development and proceeds through as many as six stages. Before age 9, most children obey rules either to avoid punishment or to gain rewards (preconventional morality). By early adolescence, they develop the conventional morality of abiding by laws simply because "those are the rules." Postconventional morality, which is achieved by those who develop the abstract reasoning of formal operations, affirms people's agreed-upon rights or follows a personal code of ethics.

Critics contend that the postconventional level appears mostly in the educated middle-class of countries that value individualism. Others contend that Kohlberg's stages reflect a male bias, and that for women, moral maturity is less a matter of abstract justice than it is an ethic of caring relationships.

16. According to Erikson, the primary task of adolescence is the formation of identity. Many adolescents try out different "selves" by playing different roles in various situations until their sense of identity becomes clearer.

Once adolescents have formed a sense of who they are, said Erikson, they focus on developing close relationships. Carol Gilligan believes that females are less concerned than males with developing a sense of identity as separate individuals *before* they strive to form close relationships.

This gender difference in connectedness carries into adulthood. Women are more openly empathic than men, and have closer, more intimate relationships.

Despite popular belief, only a very small percentage of teenagers report not getting along with their parents at all. However, adolescence is a time of growing peer influence and diminishing parental influence, especially on matters of personal taste and life-style.

17. Most sexually active teenagers use contraception inconsistently, or not at all. Most teenagers are not knowledgeable about the safe and risky times of the menstrual cycle. Adolescents' guilt about sex makes it difficult for them to discuss contraception with their parents or peers and to plan birth control with their partners. Sexually active teenagers often use alcohol, which depresses brain centers that control judgment and tends to break down normal sexual restraints. Television and the other media may contribute to increased adolescent pregnancy by redefining sexual norms, which today are "Go for it *now. . . .*"

18. Muscular strength, reaction time, sensory keenness, and cardiac output all peak by the mid-twenties and begin to decline thereafter. Health and exercise habits are important factors in the rate of physical decline.

For women, menopause is the foremost biological change related to aging. Despite popular belief, menopause usually does not create psychological problems for women. Men experience a gradual decline in sperm count, testosterone level, and speed of erection and ejaculation as they get older.

Decline in the functioning of the body's disease-fighting immune system makes the elderly more susceptible to life-threatening ailments such as cancer and pneumonia. Older people suffer short-term ailments, such as colds and the flu, less often, however.

Aging also slows neural processes and results in a small, gradual loss of brain cells. Some adults experience the mental erosion of dementia that results from a series of strokes, a brain tumor, or alcoholism. A small percentage of older adults suffer Alzheimer's disease, in which acetylcholine-producing neurons degenerate.

19. Individual variation in learning ability and memory throughout adulthood makes it difficult to generalize about age-related changes in cognition. Typically, however, the ability to recall (but not to recognize) new information, particularly material that is not meaningful to the individual, declines.

Longitudinal studies of intelligence have laid to rest the myth that intelligence sharply declines with age. Whether intelligent performance on a task increases or decreases with age depends largely on the task. Tests of accumulated knowledge reveal that crystallized intelligence increases up to old age. Tests measuring one's ability to reason abstractly reveal that fluid intelligence decreases with age. These differences help explain why people in different professions produce their most notable work at different ages.

20. Some psychologists have suggested that the early forties are a time of emotional instability, when a "midlife transition," or crisis, is likely. Research has not found, however, that emotional distress of this kind peaks at any particular age.

Researchers are skeptical of stage theories of adult social development for several reasons. For one, the settings of the *social clock* prescribing "proper" ages for various life events vary from culture to culture and from era to era. Even more

68. higher; Arab; Asian; (a) a decreasing birth rate among married women; (b) a doubling of the birth rate among unmarried women.

69. is not

Among the contributing factors are *ignorance* about the safe and risky times of the menstrual cycle; *high sex guilt*, which leads to failure to use contraceptives; *minimal communication* with parents, partners, and peers about birth control; *alcohol use* that tends to cloud judgment; and *mass media norms* of unprotected promiscuity.

70. contraception; abstinence

71. 25; girls

72. is not

73. muscular strength, reaction time, sensory keenness, cardiac output; women

74. age; health and exercise

75. menopause; 50; estrogen; expectations; attitude

76. sperm; testosterone

77. shrinks; less; reduced

78. more; less

79. slows; brain cells

80. dementia

81. Alzheimer's; acetylcholine

82. recall; recognize; meaningfulness

83. cross-sectional; longitudinal; decline; stability

Because cross-sectional studies compare people not only of different ages but also of different eras, education levels, family size, and affluence, it is not surprising that such studies reveal cognitive decline with age. In contrast, longitudinal studies test one group over a span of years. However, because those who survive to the end of longitudinal studies may be the brightest and healthiest, these studies may underestimate the average decline in intelligence. Research is also complicated by the fact that certain tests measure only one type of intelligence. Tests that measure fluid intelligence reveal decline with age; tests that measure crystallized intelligence reveal just the opposite.

84. crystallized; increase

85. fluid; decrease

86. crisis (transition)

87. social clock; less; life events

88. intimacy; generativity; love; work

89. monogamous; 20; well educated

90. twice; 75; positive; negative

91. decreases; employed

92. empty nest

93. quality

94. do

95. integrity

96. Piaget; Kohlberg; Erikson

97. stages; brain; Piaget

98. do not

99. temperament

## Progress Test 1

1. **a.** is the answer. (p. 89)
   **b.** Deduction, or deductive reasoning, is a formal operational ability.
   **c.** Piaget's theory is not concerned with attachment.
   **d.** Attaining object permanence is the hallmark of preoperational thought.

2. **b.** is the answer. The preoperational child sees the world from his or her own vantage point. (p. 88)
   **a.** As immature as egocentrism is, it represents a significant cognitive advance over the sensorimotor child, who knows the world only through senses and actions. Even simple self-awareness takes a while to develop.
   **c. & d.** As children attain the operational stages, they become more able to see the world through the eyes of others.

3. **a.** is the answer. Before object permanence is attained, "out of sight" is truly "out of mind." (pp. 86–87)
   **b., c., & d.** Developments during the preoperational, concrete operational, and formal operational stages include the use of language, conservation, and abstract reasoning, respectively.

4. **b.** is the answer. The infant turns its head and begins sucking when its cheek is stroked. (p. 82)
   **a., c., & d.** These stimuli produce other reflexes in the newborn.
   **e.** The mother's voice causes the newborn to turn toward the sound; no touch is involved.

5. **b.** is the answer. (p. 91)
   **a.** When given the choice between a wire mother with a bottle and a cloth mother without, the monkeys preferred the cloth mother.
   **c.** The presence of other infants made no difference.
   **d.** Imprinting plays no role in the attachment of higher primates.

6. **c.** is the answer. Through maturation—an orderly sequence of biological growth processes that are relatively unaffected by experience—all humans develop. (p. 83)

**a.** Conservation is the cognitive awareness that objects do not change with changes in shape.

**b.** The forces of nature *are* those that direct maturation.

**d.** The continuity/stages debate has to do with whether development is a gradual and continuous process or a discontinuous, stagelike process. Those who emphasize maturation see development as occurring in stages, not continuously.

7. **e.** is the answer. Erikson proposed that development occurs in a series of stages, in the first of which the child develops an attitude of either basic trust or mistrust. (p. 94)

**a.** Piaget's theory is concerned with cognitive development.

**b.** Harlow conducted research on attachment and deprivation.

**c.** Vygotsky focused on the influence of sociocultural factors on development.

**d.** Freud's theory is concerned with personality development.

8. **a.** is the answer. (p. 80)

**b.** This refers to sex.

**c.** This is gender identity.

**d.** This is gender-typing.

9. **b.** is the answer. (p. 80)

**a.** If sperm contributes an *X* chromosome, a female will be produced.

**c.** The egg always contributes an *X* chromosome.

**d.** This statement is factually incorrect. The egg always contributes an *X* chromosome; a *Y* chromosome can be contributed only by the sperm.

10. **b.** is the answer. (p. 84)

11. **d.** is the answer. The child's schema, or gender concept, becomes the lens through which experiences are viewed. (p. 98)

**a.** Social learning theory assumes that children acquire their gender identity through observation, imitation, rewards, and punishment.

**b. & c.** These theories are not specifically concerned with the development of gender identity.

12. **d.** is the answer. (p. 80)

**a.** Testosterone is the principal *male* hormone.

**b.** The zygote's sex is determined by the twenty-third pair of chromosomes, the sex chromosomes.

13. **d.** is the answer. (p. 84)

14. **a.** is the answer. (pp. 104, 105, 116)

15. **c.** is the answer. At the preconventional level, moral reasoning centers on self-interest, whether this means obtaining rewards or avoiding punishment. (p. 102)

**a. & b.** Moral reasoning based on a sense of social duty or a desire to gain social approval is associated with the conventional level of moral development.

**d.** Reasoning based on ethical principles is characteristic of the postconventional level of moral development.

16. **d.** is the answer. Boys who show early physical maturation are generally stronger and more athletic than boys who mature late; these qualities may lead to greater popularity and self-assurance. (p. 101)

**a. & c.** Early maturation tends to be socially advantageous for boys but not for girls.

**b.** Early-maturing girls often suffer embarrassment and are objects of teasing.

17. **b.** is the answer. (p. 114)

**a.** Fluid intelligence tends to decrease with age.

**c. & d.** Crystallized intelligence refers to the accumulation of facts and general knowledge that takes place during a person's life. Crystallized intelligence generally *increases* with age.

18. **e.** is the answer. (p. 119)

**a.** Generativity is associated with middle adulthood.

**b. & c.** Intimacy and isolation are associated with young adulthood.

**d.** The term *acceptance* is not associated with Erikson's theory.

19. **c.** is the answer. Once formal operational thought has been attained, thinking is no longer limited to concrete propositions. (p. 101)

**a. & b.** Preoperational thought and concrete operational thought emerge before, and do not include, the ability to think logically about abstract propositions.

**d.** Fluid intelligence refers to abstract reasoning abilities; however, it is unrelated to Piaget's theory and stages.

20. **a.** is the answer. (p. 114)

**b., c., & d.** These cognitive abilities remain essentially unchanged as the person ages.

21. **d.** is the answer. "Use it or lose it" seems to be the rule: Often, changes in activity patterns contribute significantly to problems regarded as being part of usual aging. (p. 110)

**a.** Most elderly people do not develop dementia; even among the very old, the risk of dementia is only 40 percent.

**b.** Although the elderly are more subject to long-term ailments than younger adults, they actually suffer fewer short-term ailments.

**c.** People of all ages report equal happiness or satisfaction with life.

22. **b.** is the answer. (pp. 113–114)

**a.** This answer describes cross-sectional research.

**c. & d.** Sample size does not distinguish cross-sectional from longitudinal research.
**e.** Just the opposite is true.

23. **d.** is the answer. (pp. 107–108)

24. **b.** is the answer. (p. 100)

25. **c.** is the answer. Because the late teen years provide many new opportunities for trying out possible roles, adolescents' identities typically incorporate an increasingly positive self-concept. (p. 104)

### True-False Items

1. False.  About 30 percent of those abused later abuse their own children. (p. 94)

2. False.  Although you are born with essentially all the brain cells you will ever have, some brain processes—such as the formation of neural networks and myelination—continue to develop for many years. (p. 83)

3. False.  Although the rate at which motor skills develop varies from child to child, the *sequence* is universal. (p. 84)

4. True. (p. 87)

5. True. (p. 95)

6. True. (pp. 106)

7. True. (p. 109)

8. True. (p. 96)

9. False. Infants' attachment styles reflect both their temperaments and the responsiveness of parents and caregivers. (pp. 92–93)

10. False. In fact, just the opposite is true. (p. 111)

11. False. Alzheimer's symptoms reflect the existence of a disease, rather than normal aging processes. (p. 113)

## Progress Test 2

1. **d.** is the answer. With object permanence, a child develops schemas for familiar objects, including faces, and may become upset by a stranger who does not fit any of these schemas. (p. 91)
   **a.** The concept of conservation develops during the concrete operational stage, whereas stranger anxiety develops during the sensorimotor stage.
   **b. & c.** Egocentrism and a theory of mind both develop during the preoperational stage. This follows the sensorimotor stage, during which stranger anxiety develops.

2. **a.** is the answer. (p. 85)
   **b., c., & d.** Each of these is an understanding developed by Piaget.

3. **a.** is the answer. (p. 86)

4. **a.** is the answer. Any drug taken by the mother passes through the placenta and enters the child's bloodstream. (p. 81)
   **b.** Addiction cannot be inherited; it requires exposure to an addictive drug.
   **c.** Drugs may disrupt the mechanisms of heredity, but there is no evidence that such changes promote addiction.
   **d.** This answer is incorrect because at no age does the blood "resist" drugs.

5. **c.** is the answer. (p. 81)
   **a., b., & d.** A child's emotional temperament, attachment, and addiction have not been linked to the mother's drinking while pregnant.

6. **b.** is the answer. (p. 81)

7. **d.** is the answer. A critical period is a restricted time during which an organism must be exposed to certain influences or experiences for a particular kind of learning to occur. (p. 92)
   **a.** Critical periods refer to developmental periods after birth.
   **b.** Critical periods vary from behavior to behavior, but they are not confined to the hours following birth.
   **c.** Critical periods are not specifically associated with the preoperational period.

8. **c.** is the answer. Deprived monkeys were impaired in their social behaviors but not in their physical development. (p. 93)
   **a., b., & d.** Each of these was found in socially deprived monkeys.

9. **c.** is the answer. Thus, for example, Sroufe found that children who were securely attached at 12 to 18 months of age were, as 2- to 3-year-olds, more outgoing than other children and more enthusiastic when working on challenging tasks. (p. 94)
   **a., b., & d.** There is no indication that securely attached children prefer to be with adults, become permissive parents, or are less achievement oriented.

10. **d.** is the answer. This is because of a lack of neural connections before that age. p. 83)

11. **c.** is the answer. (p. 92)
    **a.** Insecurely attached infants often cling to their mothers when placed in a new situation; yet, when the mother returns after an absence, the infant's reaction tends to be one of indifference.
    **b.** These behaviors are characteristic of securely attached infants.
    **d.** Insecurely attached infants in unfamiliar surroundings will often exhibit a range of emotional behaviors.

12. **d.** is the answer. (p. 96)

13. **a.** is the answer. (p. 113)

   **b.** This answer describes the longitudinal research method.

   **c. & d.** Cross-sectional studies have tended to exaggerate the negative effects of aging on intellectual functioning; for this reason they may not be the most appropriate method for studying life-span development.

14. **c.** is the answer. Different societies and eras have somewhat different ideas about the age at which major life events should ideally occur. (p. 115)

15. **c.** is the answer. (p. 103)

   **a.** Preconventional morality is based on avoiding punishment and obtaining rewards.

   **b.** Conventional morality is based on gaining the approval of others and/or on following the law and social convention.

   **d.** There is no such thing as generative morality.

16. **a.** is the answer. (pp. 104–105)

   **b.** According to Erikson, identity develops before intimacy.

   **c. & d.** The formation of basic trust is the task of infancy.

17. **e.** is the answer. (p. 110)

   **a.** Most women do not experience anxiety and distress following menopause; moreover, the woman's experience will depend largely on her expectations and attitude.

   **b.** Sexual interest does not decline in post-menopausal women.

   **c.** Menopause is caused by a *reduction* in estrogen.

   **d.** This was not mentioned in the text.

18. **a.** is the answer. A mathematician's skills are likely to reflect abstract reasoning, or fluid intelligence, which declines with age. (p. 115)

   **b., d., & e.** Philosophy, literature, and history are fields in which individuals often do their most notable work later in life, after more experiential knowledge (crystallized intelligence) has accumulated.

   **c.** Scientific achievements generally reflect fluid, rather than crystallized, intelligence.

19. **d.** is the answer. (p. 118)

   **a., b., & c.** Most couples do not feel a loss of purpose or marital strain following the departure of grown children.

20. **d.** is the answer. Significantly, drugs that block the activity of the neurotransmitter acetylcholine produce Alzheimer-like symptoms. (p. 112)

   **a. & b.** Epinephrine and norepinephrine are hormones produced by glands of the endocrine system.

   **c. & e.** Serotonin and dopamine are neurotransmitters, and hence produced by neurons, but they have not been implicated in Alzheimer's disease.

21. **c.** is the answer. (p. 105)

   **a & b.** In fact, just the opposite is true.

22. **d.** is the answer. (p. 114)

   **a. & b.** Fluid intelligence, which decreases with age, refers to the ability to reason abstractly.

   **c.** Crystallized intelligence increases with age.

23. **a.** is the answer. (p. 111)

24. **d.** is the answer. (p. 115)

25. **d.** is the answer. (p. 116)

## Thinking Critically About Chapter 3

### Multiple-Choice Questions

1. **d.** is the answer. (p. 88)

2. **b.** is the answer. (p. 84)

   **a. & d.** Although the rate of motor development varies from child to child, the basic sequence is universal and, therefore, predictable.

   **c.** Rolling over and head lifting are both learned.

3. **d.** is the answer (p. 83)

   **a. & b.** Premature birth and fetal alcohol syndrome usually do not have this effect on the developing brain.

   **c.** If the question had stated "I have a heavier and thicker cortex," this answer would be correct.

   **e.** Imprinting has no effect on brain cells.

4. **c.** is the answer. Gender-typing refers to the extent to which one exhibits traditionally masculine or feminine traits and behaviors. In this example, Malcolm's sister is displaying an interest in traditionally masculine toys and activities. (p. 97)

   **a. & d.** There is no reason to believe that Malcolm's sister is either confused or unable to form a coherent gender schema.

5. **c.** is the answer. This test is designed to determine if the child understands that the quantity of liquid is conserved, despite the shift to a container that is different in shape. (pp. 87–88)

   **a.** These are general processes related to concept building.

   **b.** Object permanence is the concept that an object continues to exist even when not perceived; in this case, the water is perceived throughout the experiment.

   **d.** This experiment does not require abstract reasoning, only the ability to reason logically about the concrete.

**6. a.** is the answer. This child's age and stranger anxiety clearly place him within Piaget's sensorimotor stage. (pp. 86, 91)

**7. b.** is the answer. This child's age, ability to use language, and egocentrism clearly place her within Piaget's preoperational stage. (pp. 87–88)

**8. d.** is the answer. Conservation is a hallmark of the concrete operational stage; egocentrism is a hallmark of the preoperational stage. (pp. 87–88)

**9. c.** is the answer. Being 4 years old, Jamail would be in Piaget's preoperational stage. Preoperational thinking is egocentric, which means Jamail would find it difficult to "put himself in his sister's shoes" and perceive that she has a brother. (p. 88)

**10. b.** is the answer. (p. 92)
**a.** Conservation is the ability to realize that the amount of an object does not change even if its shape changes.
**c.** Egocentrism is the inability to take another person's perspective.
**d.** According to Erikson, basic trust is feeling that the world is safe as a result of sensitive, loving caregivers.

**11. a.** is the answer. Altough loving parents will also produce securely attached children, Erikson's theory deals with trust or mistrust. (p. 94)
**c.** Control is not a factor in this stage of Erikson's theory.

**12. b.** is the answer. Although parental values differ from one time and place to another, studies reveal that Western parents today want their children to think for themselves, while Asian and African parents place greater value on emotional closeness. (p. 96)
**d.** Both of these values are more typical of Asian than Western cultures.

**13. c.** is the answer. (p. 101)
**a., b., & d.** Piaget did not link cognitive ability to amount of schooling, gender, or differences in how boys and girls are socialized.

**14. a.** is the answer. Children in various cultures do seem to progress through Kohlberg's preconventional and conventional levels, which indicates that some aspects of the development of moral reasoning are universal. (p. 103)

**15. c.** is the answer. (p. 105)

**16. c.** is the answer. Reasoning is based on fluid intelligence. (p. 114)
**a.** There is no such thing as "analytic" intelligence.

**b.** Crystallized intelligence increases up to old age.

**17. c.** is the answer. Because several variables (education, affluence, etc.) generally distinguish the various groups in a cross-sectional study, it is impossible to rule out that one or more of these, rather than aging, is the cause of the measured intellectual decrease. (p. 113)
**a.** Small sample size and unrepresentativeness generally are not limitations of cross-sectional research.
**b.** This refers to longitudinal research.

**18. e.** is the answer. (p. 113)
**a. & c.** In tests of recognition memory, the performance of older persons shows little decline.
**b. & d.** The ability to recall material, especially meaningless material, declines with age.

**19. e.** is the answer. Research has not uncovered a tendency for people of any particular age group to report greater feelings of satisfaction or well-being. (p. 119)

**20. c.** is the answer. Although some researchers emphasize consistency and others emphasize potential for change, they all agree that consistency increases over the life span. (p. 121)
**a.** One criticism of stage theories is that development does not occur in sharply defined stages.
**b.** Research has shown that individuals' adult personalities cannot be predicted from their first two years.
**d.** Social and emotional style are two of the most stable traits.

**21. b.** is the answer. Conventional morality is based in part on a desire to gain others' approval. (p. 103)
**a.** Preconventional reasoning is based on external incentives such as gaining a reward or avoiding punishment.
**c.** Postconventional morality reflects an affirmation of agreed-upon rights or universal ethical principles.
**d.** Fear of others' disapproval is one of the bases of conventional moral reasoning.

**22. b.** is the answer. (p. 106)
**a.** In fact, just the opposite is true: Parental influence on children *decreases* during adolescence.
**d.** Teens reflect their parents' social, political, and religious views, but rely on peers for matters of personal taste.
**e.** The text does not mention this.

**23. c.** is the answer. (p. 121)

**24. c.** is the answer. Carlos' age and struggle to form

a close relationship place him squarely in this stage. (p. 105)

**a.** Trust versus mistrust is the psychosocial task of infancy.

**b.** Autonomy versus doubt is the psychosocial task of toddlerhood.

**d.** Identity versus role confusion is the psychosocial task of adolescence.

**e.** Generativity versus stagnation is the task of middle adulthood.

**25. d.** is the answer. (p. 118)

### Essay Question

Sheryl's age would place her at the threshold of Piaget's stage of formal operations. Although her thinking is probably still somewhat self-focused, Sheryl is becoming capable of abstract, logical thought. This will increasingly allow her to reason hypothetically and deductively. Because her logical thinking also enables her to detect inconsistencies in others' reasoning and between their ideals and actions, Sheryl and her parents may be having some heated debates about now.

According to Kohlberg, Sheryl is probably at the threshold of postconventional morality. When she was younger, Sheryl probably abided by rules in order to gain social approval, or simply because "rules are rules" (conventional morality). Now that she is older, Sheryl's moral reasoning will increasingly be based on her own personal code of ethics and an affirmation of people's agreed-upon rights. Because she is a woman, her morality may be more concerned with caring about relationships.

According to Erikson, psychosocial development occurs in eight stages, each of which focuses on a particular task. As an adolescent, Sheryl's psychosocial task is to develop a sense of self by testing roles, then integrating them to form a single identity. Erikson called this stage "identity versus role confusion."

## Key Terms

### Defining Terms

1. **Developmental psychology** is the branch of psychology concerned with physical, cognitive, and social change throughout the life span. (p. 79)

2. An $X$ **chromosome** is found in both males and females. At conception, the egg always contributes an $X$ sex chromosome; if the sperm also contributes an $X$ chromosome, the child will be a girl. (p. 80)

3. A $Y$ **chromosome** is found only in males. If, in addition to the $X$ chromosome contributed by the egg, the sperm contributes a $Y$ sex chromosome, the child will be a boy. (p. 80)

4. **Testosterone,** the most important male sex hormone, stimulates growth of the male sex organs in the fetus and development of the male sex characteristics during puberty. (p. 80)

   *Memory aid:* **Test**osterone is produced by the male's **test**es.

5. **Gender** is the biological and social definition of male and female. (p. 80)

6. The **zygote** (a term derived from the Greek word for "joint") is the fertilized egg, that is, the cluster of cells formed during conception by the union of sperm and egg. (p. 81)

7. The **embryo** is the developing prenatal organism from about 2 weeks through 2 months after conception. (p. 81)

8. The **fetus** is the developing prenatal human from 9 weeks after conception to birth. (p. 81)

9. **Teratogens** (literally, poisons) are any medications, drugs, viruses, or other substances that cross the mother's placenta and can harm the developing embryo or fetus. (p. 81)

10. The **fetal alcohol syndrome (FAS)** refers to the physical and cognitive abnormalities that heavy drinking by a pregnant woman may cause in the developing child. (p. 81)

11. The **rooting reflex** is the newborn's tendency, when his or her cheek is stroked, to orient toward the stimulus and begin sucking. (p. 82)

12. **Maturation** refers to the biological growth processes that enable orderly changes in behavior and are relatively uninfluenced by experience or other environmental factors. (p. 83)

    *Example*: The ability to walk depends on a certain level of neural and muscular **maturation**. For this reason, until the toddler's body is physically ready to walk, practice "walking" has little effect.

13. In Piaget's theory of cognitive development, **schemas** are mental concepts that help organize and interpret information. (p. 86)

14. **Cognition** refers to the mental processes associated with thinking, knowing, remembering, and communicating. (p. 86)

15. In Piaget's theory of cognitive stages, the **sensorimotor stage** lasts from birth to about age 2. During this stage, infants gain knowledge of the world through their senses and their motor activities. (p. 86)

16. **Object permanence,** which develops during the sensorimotor stage, is the awareness that things do not cease to exist when not perceived. (p. 86)

3. Discuss whether subliminal stimuli are sensed, and whether they are persuasive.

4. Describe the phenomenon of sensory adaptation and show how it focuses our attention on changing stimulation.

*Vision* (pp. 130–137)

> If you do not know the meaning of any of the following words, phrases, or expressions in the context in which they appear in the text, refer to pages 130–131 for an explanation: *taken-for-granted genius; This fact had scholars baffled; blind spot; Color, like all aspects of vision, . . . the theater of our brains.*

5. Explain the visual process, including the stimulus input, the structure of the eye, and the transformation of light energy.

6. Discuss how visual information is processed in parallel (through the eye's retina and the brain) and at increasingly abstract levels.

7. Discuss how both the Young-Helmholtz and the opponent-process theories contribute to our understanding of color vision.

8. Explain color constancy and discuss its significance to our understanding of vision.

*The Other Senses* (pp. 138–146)

> If you do not know the meaning of any of the following words, phrases, or expressions in the context in which they appear in the text, refer to page 131 for an explanation: *sensitive to faint sounds; A piccolo produces much shorter sound waves than does a kettledrum; earlids; If a car to the right honks. . . .; we yearn to touch—to kiss, to stroke, to snuggle; Rubbing the area around your stubbed toe; A well-trained nurse may distract needle-shy patients by chatting with them; there is more to taste than meets the tongue; you bathe your nostrils in a stream of scent-laden molecules; biological gyroscopes.*

9. Explain the auditory process, including the stimulus input, the structure and function of the ear, and how sounds are located.

10. Describe the senses of touch and pain and explain the gate-control theory of pain.

14. Explain how 3-D movies are made and describe the binocular and monocular cues in depth perception.

11. Describe taste, smell, kinesthesis, and the vestibular sense. Comment on the nature of sensory interaction.

15. Describe the perceptual constancies and show how they operate in visual illusions.

*Perceptual Organization* (pp. 146–154)

> If you do not know the meaning of any of the following words, phrases, or expressions in the context in which they appear in the text, refer to pages 131–132 for an explanation: *There is far more to perception than meets the senses; Sometimes, however, they can lead us astray; mothers then coaxed them to crawl out on the glass; The floating finger sausage; As we move, stable objects appear to move relative to us; through a paper tube.*

*Interpretation* (pp. 154–160)

> If you do not know the meaning of any of the following words, phrases, or expressions in the context in which they appear in the text, refer to page 132 for an explanation: *Ping-Pong ball; we may feel slightly disoriented and dizzy; to see is to believe . . . to believe is to see; a "monster" in Scotland's Loch Ness; from what's behind our eyes and between our ears.*

12. Discuss Gestalt psychology's contribution to our understanding of perception, including the figure-ground relationship and principles of perceptual grouping in form perception.

16. Explain the nature-nurture debate on the origins of perception.

17. Discuss research findings on sensory restriction and restored vision.

13. Discuss research on depth perception involving the use of the visual cliff.

18. Explain what the use of distorting goggles indicates regarding the adaptability of perception.

19. Discuss the effects of assumptions, expectations, schemas, and contexts on our perceptions.

### Is There Perception Without Sensation? (pp. 160–164)

> If you do not know the meaning of any of the following words, phrases, or expressions in the context in which they appear in the text, refer to pages 132–133 for an explanation: *The media overflow with reports of psychic wonders; to scoff at; uncanny; one more dashed hope; unsatisfied hunger . . . an itch.*

20. State the claims of ESP and explain why most research psychologists remain skeptical.

## Chapter Review

When you have finished reading the chapter, work through the material that follows to review it. Complete the sentences and answer the questions. As you proceed, evaluate your performance for each section by consulting the answers on page 119. Do not continue with the next section until you understand each answer. If you need to, go back and review or reread the appropriate section in the textbook before continuing.

1. The process by which we detect physical energy from the environment and encode it as neural signals is _____ . The process by which sensations are selected, organized, and interpreted is _____ .

2. Sensory analysis, which starts at the entry level and works up, is called _____-_____ _____ .

   Perceptual analysis, which works from our experience and expectations, is called

   _____-_____ .

3. The perceptual disorder in which a person has lost the ability to recognize familiar faces is

   _____ .

### Sensing the World: Some Basic Principles (pp. 126–130)

4. The study of relationships between the physical characteristics of stimuli and our psychological experience of them is _____ .

5. The _____ _____ refers to the minimum stimulation necessary for a stimulus to be detected _____ percent of the time.

6. Some weak stimuli may trigger in our sense receptors a response that is processed by the brain, even though the response doesn't cross the threshold into _____ awareness.

7. Some entrepreneurs claim that exposure to these "below threshold," or_____, stimuli can be persuasive, but their claims are probably unwarranted.

8. The minimum difference required to distinguish two stimuli 50 percent of the time is called the

   _____ .

   Another term for this value is the

_____ _____

_____ .

9. The principle that the difference threshold is not a constant amount, but a constant percentage, is known as _____

_____ . The proportion depends on the _____ .

10. After constant exposure to an unchanging stimulus, the receptor cells of our senses begin to fire less vigorously; this phenomenon is called

_____ .

Explain why sensory adaptation is beneficial.

*Vision* (pp. 130–137)

11. The visible spectrum of light is a small portion of the larger spectrum of _____ radiation.

12. The distance from one light wave peak to the next is called _____ . This value determines the wave's color, or

_____ .

13. The amount of energy in light waves, or

_____ , determined by a wave's

_____ , or height, influences

the _____ of a light.

14. Light enters the eye through the transparent

_____ , then passes through a small opening called the _____ ; the size of this opening is controlled by the colored _____ .

15. By changing its curvature, the

_____ can focus the image of

an object onto the _____ , the light-sensitive inner surface of the eye.

16. The process by which the lens changes shape to focus light is called _____ .

17. The retina's receptor cells are the

_____ and _____ .

18. The neural signals produced in the rods and cones activate the neighboring

_____ cells, then activate a network of _____ cells. The axons of ganglion cells converge to form the

_____ ,

which carries the visual information to the

_____ .

19. Where this nerve leaves the eye, there are no receptors; thus the area is called the

_____

20. It is the _____ (rods/cones) of the eye that permit the perception of color.

21. Unlike cones, in dim light the rods are

_____ (sensitive/insensitive). Adapting to a darkened room will take the retina approximately _____ minutes.

22. Hubel and Wiesel discovered that certain neurons in the _____

_____ of the brain respond only to specific features of what is viewed. They called these neurons

_____ .

23. Feature detectors in the visual cortex pass their information to higher-level brain cells in the

_____ and _____

cortex which respond to specific visual scenes. Research has shown that in monkey brains such cells specialize in responding to a specific

_____ , _____

_____ , _____ ,

or _____ .

24. The brain achieves its remarkable speed in visual perception by processing several subdivisions of a stimulus _____ (simultaneously/sequentially). This procedure, called

_____ ,

may explain why people who have suffered a stroke may lose just one aspect of vision.

25. An object appears to be red in color because it

_____ the long wavelengths of

red and because of our mental

_____ of the color.

26. According to the Young-Helmholtz trichromatic theory, the eyes have three types of color receptors: one reacts most strongly to

_____ , one to

_____ , and one to

_____ .

27. Most color-deficient people are not colorblind. They simply lack functioning

_____ - or _____ -

sensitive cones.

28. After staring at a green square for a while, you will see the color red, its _____

color, as an _____ .

29. Hering's theory of color vision is called the

_____ - _____

theory. According to this theory, after visual information leaves the receptors it is analyzed in terms of pairs of opposing colors:

_____ versus

_____ , _____

versus _____ , and

_____ versus

_____ .

Summarize the two stages of color processing.

30. The experience of color depends on the

_____ in which an object is seen.

31. In an unvarying context, a familiar object will be perceived as having consistent color, even as the light changes. This phenomenon is called

_____ .

*The Other Senses* (pp. 138–146)

32. The tendency of vision to dominate the other senses is referred to as _____

_____ .

33. The stimulus for hearing, or

_____ , is sound waves, created by the compression and expansion of

_____ _____ .

34. The amplitude of a sound wave determines the sound's_____ .

35. The pitch of a sound is derived from the

_____ of its wave.

36. Sound energy is measured in units called

_____ . The absolute threshold for hearing is arbitrarily defined as

_____ such units.

37. The ear is divided into three main parts: the

_____ ear, the

_____ ear, and the

_____ ear.

38. The outer ear channels sound waves toward the

_____ , a membrane that then vibrates.

39. The middle ear transmits the vibrations through a piston made of three small bones: the

_____ , _____ ,

and _____ .

40. In the inner ear a coiled tube called the

_____ contains the receptor cells for hearing. The fluid in this tube causes ripples in the _____

_____ , which is lined with

_____ ,

whose movement triggers impulses in adjacent nerve fibers that converge to form the auditory nerve.

41. We locate a sound by sensing differences in the

_____ and _____

with which it reaches our ears.

42. The sense of touch is a mixture of at least four senses: _____ ,

_____ , _____ ,

and _____ . Only the sense of _____ has identifiable receptors. Other skin sensations, such as tickle, itch, hot, and wetness, are _____ of the basic ones.

43. Pain is a property of the _____ as well as of the _____ .

44. A sensation of pain in an amputated leg is referred to as a _____ _____ sensation.

45. The pain system _____ (is/is not) triggered by one specific type of physical energy. The body _____ (does/does not) have specialized receptor cells for pain.

46. Melzack and Wall have proposed a theory of pain called the _____-_____ theory, which proposes that there is a neurological _____ in the _____ _____ that blocks pain signals or lets them through. It may be opened by activation of _____ (small/large) nerve fibers and closed by activation of _____ (small/large) fibers or by information from the _____ .

List some pain control techniques used in the Lamaze method of prepared childbirth.

47. The four basic taste sensations are _____ , _____ , _____ , and _____ .

48. Taste, which is a _____ sense, is enabled by the 200 or more _____ on the top and sides of the tongue. Each contains a _____ that catches food chemicals.

49. Taste receptors reproduce themselves every _____ .

50. When the sense of smell is blocked, as when we have a cold, foods do not taste the same; this illustrates the principle of _____ _____ .

51. Like taste, smell, or _____ , is a _____ sense. Unlike light, an odor _____ (can/cannot) be separated into more elemental odors.

52. The ability to identify scents peaks in _____ _____ and declines thereafter.

53. The system for sensing the position and movement of body parts is called _____ . The receptors for this sense are located in the _____ , _____ , and _____ of the body.

54. The sense that monitors the position and movement of the head and thus the body is the _____ . The receptors for this sense are located in the _____ _____ and _____ _____ of the inner ear.

*Perceptual Organization* (pp. 146–154)

55. According to the _____ school of psychology, we tend to organize a cluster of sensations into a _____ , or form. This tendency can be illustrated using a figure called a _____ cube.

56. When we view a scene, we see the central object, or _____ , as distinct from surrounding stimuli, or the _____ .

Identify the major contributions of Gestalt psychology to our understanding of perception.

57. Proximity, similarity, closure, continuity, and connectedness are examples of Gestalt rules of

_____ .

58. The principle that we organize stimuli into smooth, continuous patterns is called

_____ . The principle that we fill in gaps to create a complete, whole object is

_____ . The grouping of items that are close to each other is the principle of

_____ ; the grouping of items that look alike is the principle of

_____ . The tendency to perceive uniform or attached items as a single unit is the principle of _____ .

59. The ability to see objects in three dimensions despite their two-dimensional representations on our retinas is called _____

_____ .

60. Gibson and Walk developed the

_____

to test depth perception in infants.

Summarize the results of Gibson and Walk's studies of depth perception.

For questions 61–70, identify the depth perception cue that is defined.

61. Any cue that requires both eyes:

_____ .

62. Any cue that requires either eye alone:

_____ .

63. The greater the difference between the images received by the two eyes, the nearer the object:

_____ .

3-D movies simulate this cue by photographing each scene with _____ (how many?) cameras. This chapter's fundamental lesson is that our _____ are the constructions of our _____ .

64. The more our eyes focus inward when we view an object, the nearer the object:

_____ .

65. If two objects are presumed to be the same size, the one that casts a smaller retinal image is perceived as farther away:

_____ .

66. An object partially covered by another is seen as farther away: _____ .

67. Objects lower in the visual field are seen as nearer: _____ .

68. As we move, objects at different distances appear to move at different rates:

_____ .

69. Parallel lines appear to converge in the distance:

_____ .

70. Dimmer, or shaded, objects seem farther away:

_____ .

71. Our tendency to see objects as unchanging while the stimuli from them change in size, shape, and lightness is called _____

_____ .

72. Several illusions, including the

_____ , _____ ,

and _____ -

illusions, are explained by the interplay between perceived _____ and perceived

_____ . When distance cues are removed, these illusions are

_____ (diminished/ strengthened).

Explain how the size-distance relationship accounts for the moon illusion.

73. The brain computes an object's brightness _____ (relative to/independent of) surrounding objects. The amount of light an object reflects relative to its surroundings is called _____ _____ .

*Interpretation* (pp. 154–160)

74. The idea that knowledge comes from inborn ways of organizing sensory experiences was proposed by the philosopher _____ .

75. On the other side was the philosopher _____ who maintained that we learn to perceive the world by experiencing it.

76. Studies of cases in which vision has been restored to a person who was blind from birth show that, upon *seeing* tactilely familiar objects for the first time, the person _____ (can/cannot) recognize them.

77. Studies of sensory restriction demonstrate that visual experiences during _____ are crucial for perceptual development. Such experiences suggest that there is a _____ _____ for normal sensory and perceptual development.

78 Humans given glasses that shift or invert the visual field _____ (will/will not) adapt to the distorted perception. This is called _____ _____ .

79. A mental predisposition that influences perception is called a _____ _____ .

80. How a stimulus is perceived depends on our perceptual schemas and the _____ in which it is experienced.

81. (Psychology Applied) Psychologists who study the importance of considering perceptual principles in the design of machines, appliances, and work settings are called _____ .

*Is There Perception Without Sensation?* (pp. 160–164)

82. Perception outside the range of normal sensation is called _____ .

83. Psychologists who study ESP are called _____ .

84. The form of ESP in which people claim to be capable of reading others' minds is called _____ . A person who "senses" that a friend is in danger might claim to have the ESP ability of _____ . An ability to "see" into the future is called _____ .

85. Critics point out that a major difficulty for parapsychology is that ESP phenomena are not consistently _____ .

86. When the clairvoyance experiment conducted by Layton and Turnbull was repeated, the results of both experiments were nearly identical to what one would expect on the basis of _____ .

87. Hoping to detect faint telepathy signals, parapsychologists have used the _____ procedure to minimize distractions.

Explain why scientists are skeptical about ESP.

**WEB SIGHTINGS**

San Francisco's Exploratorium museum of science, art, and perception (**http://www.exploratorium. edu/**) maintains an excellent web site for extending your exploration of sensation and perception. Review the history of visual science. Check out the multimedia dissection of a cow's eye and see what an actual cornea, lens, and retina look like. Take an interactive, animated tour of the eye. View the world from inside the eyes of a person with a cataract. Take a sensory tour of the environment with an artist who will change the way you perceive light, shadow, and image forever. And don't stop there! Use weblinks at this site as jumping off points to dozens of other internet resources for learning more about visual information processing. To focus your tour, see if you can find the answers to the following questions.

1. Where is the aqueous humor? The ciliary body? What are the functions of these structures?

2. Why are the years 1610 and 1853 significant in the history of visual science? What is the most recent significant development in this field of research?

3. Just what is a tapetum anyway?

4. Where would you go if you needed a cow's eye?!

5. What psychophysical phenomenon does the sound of a Volvo horn blowing at 30 miles per hour demonstrate?

6. Which National Hockey League player has the fastest slapshot in the league? How does he hit a puck so that it travels so fast? How fast is your visual reaction time? Could you stop a puck traveling 100 miles per hour?

7. How could you find the sweet spot of a baseball bat? What is a sweet spot?

## Progress Test 1

### Multiple-Choice Questions

Circle your answers to the following questions and check them with the answers on page 121. If your answer is incorrect, read the explanation for why it is correct and then consult the appropriate pages of the text (in parentheses following the correct answer).

1. If you can just notice the difference between 10- and 11-pound weights, which of the following weights could you differentiate from a 100-pound weight?
   a. 101-pound weight
   b. 105-pound weight
   c. 110-pound weight
   d. There is no basis for prediction.

2. A decrease in sensory responsiveness accompanying an unchanging stimulus is called:
   a. sensory fatigue.
   b. accommodation.
   c. sensory restriction.
   d. sensory adaptation.
   e. sensory interaction.

3. The size of the pupil is controlled by the:
   a. lens.
   b. retina.
   c. cornea.
   d. iris.

4. The process by which the lens changes its curvature is:
   a. accommodation.
   b. sensory adaptation.
   c. focusing.
   d. transduction.

5. The receptor of the eye that functions best in dim light is the:
   a. iris.
   b. ganglion cell.
   c. cone.
   d. bipolar cell.
   e. rod.

6. The Young-Helmholtz theory proposes that:
   a. there are three different types of color-sensitive cones.
   b. retinal cells are excited by one color and inhibited by its complementary color.
   c. there are four different types of cones.
   d. rod, not cone, vision accounts for our ability to detect fine visual detail.

7. Frequency is to pitch as _____ is to _____ .
   a. wavelength; loudness
   b. amplitude; loudness
   c. wavelength; intensity
   d. amplitude; intensity

8. The receptors for hearing are located in:
   a. the outer ear.
   b. the middle ear.
   c. the inner ear.
   d. all parts of the ear.

9. According to the gate-control theory, a way to alleviate chronic pain would be to stimulate the _____ nerve fibers that _____ the spinal gate.
   a. small; open
   b. small; close
   c. large; open
   d. large; close

10. The brain breaks vision into separate dimensions such as color, depth, movement, and form, and works on each aspect simultaneously. This is called:
    a. feature detection.
    b. parallel processing.
    c. accommodation.
    d. opponent processing.

11. Kinesthesis involves:
    a. the bones of the middle ear.
    b. information from the muscles, tendons, and joints.
    c. membranes within the cochlea.
    d. the body's sense of balance.

12. One light may appear reddish and another greenish if they differ in:
    a. wavelength.
    b. amplitude.
    c. opponent processes.
    d. brightness.

13. Which of the following explains why a rose appears equally red in bright and dim light?
    a. the Young-Helmholtz theory
    b. the opponent-process theory
    c. feature detection
    d. color constancy

14. The historical movement associated with the statement "The whole may exceed the sum of its parts" is:
    a. parapsychology.
    b. behavioral psychology.
    c. functional psychology.
    d. Gestalt psychology.

15. Figures tend to be perceived as whole, complete objects, even if spaces or gaps exist in the representation, thus demonstrating the principle of:
    a. connectedness.         d. proximity.
    b. similarity.            e. closure.
    c. continuity.

16. The figure-ground relationship has demonstrated that:
    a. perception is largely innate.
    b. perception is simply a point-for-point representation of sensation.
    c. the same stimulus can trigger more than one perception.
    d. different people see different things when viewing a scene.

17. As we move, viewed objects cast changing shapes on our retinas, although we do not perceive the objects as changing. This is part of the phenomenon of:
    a. perceptual constancy.
    b. relative motion.
    c. linear perspective.
    d. continuity.

18. Which of the following illustrates the principle of visual capture?
    a. We tend to form first impressions of other people on the basis of appearance.
    b. Because visual processing is automatic, we can pay attention to a visual image and any other sensation at the same time.
    c. We cannot simultaneously attend to a visual image and another sensation.
    d. When there is a conflict between visual information and that from another sense, vision tends to dominate.

19. Which philosopher maintained that knowledge comes from inborn ways of organizing our sensory experiences?
    a. Locke          c. Gibson
    b. Kant           d. Walk

20. Which of the following was *not* mentioned in the text as a criticism of parapsychology?
    a. ESP effects have not been consistently reproducible.
    b. Parapsychology has suffered from a number of frauds and hoaxes.
    c. The tendency of people to recall only events that confirm their expectations accounts for much of the belief in ESP.
    d. There have been no laboratory-controlled studies of ESP.

21. _____ processing refers to how the physical characteristics of stimuli influence their interpretation.
    a. Top-down        c. Parapsychological
    b. Bottom-up       d. Human factors

22. Adults who are born blind but later have their vision restored:
    a. are almost immediately able to recognize familiar objects.
    b. typically fail to recognize familiar objects.
    c. are unable to follow moving objects with their eyes.
    d. have excellent eye-hand coordination.

23. The moon illusion occurs in part because distance cues at the horizon make the moon seem:
    a. farther away and therefore larger.
    b. closer and therefore larger.
    c. farther away and therefore smaller.
    d. closer and therefore smaller.

24. Figure is to ground as _____ is to _____.
    a. night; day
    b. top; bottom
    c. cloud; sky
    d. sensation; perception

25. In their experiment on _____, Layton and Turnbull asked students to guess the contents of a sealed envelope.
    a. telepathy        c. precognition
    b. clairvoyance     d. psychokinesis

*Matching Items*

Match each of the structures with its function or description.

*Structures*

_____ **1.** lens
_____ **2.** iris
_____ **3.** pupil
_____ **4.** rods
_____ **5.** cones
_____ **6.** middle ear
_____ **7.** inner ear
_____ **8.** large nerve fiber
_____ **9.** small nerve fiber
_____ **10.** semicircular canals
_____ **11.** sensors in joints

*Functions or Descriptions*

**a.** amplifies sounds
**b.** closes pain gate
**c.** vestibular sense
**d.** controls pupil
**e.** accommodation
**f.** opens pain gate
**g.** admits light
**h.** vision in dim light
**i.** contains basilar membrane
**j.** kinesthesis
**k.** color vision

# Progress Test 2

Progress Test 2 should be completed during a final chapter review. Answer the following questions after you thoroughly understand the correct answers for the Chapter Review and Progress Test 1.

## Multiple-Choice Questions

1. The inner ear contains receptors for:
   **a.** audition and kinesthesis.
   **b.** kinesthesis and the vestibular sense.
   **c.** audition and the vestibular sense.
   **d.** audition, kinesthesis, and the vestibular sense.

2. According to the opponent-process theory:
   **a.** there are three types of color-sensitive cones.
   **b.** the process of color vision begins in the cortex.
   **c.** neurons involved in color vision are stimulated by one color's wavelength and inhibited by another's.
   **d.** all of the above are true.

3. What enables you to feel yourself wiggling your toes even with your eyes closed?
   **a.** vestibular sense
   **b.** sense of kinesthesis
   **c.** the skin senses
   **d.** sensory interaction

4. Hubel and Wiesel discovered feature detectors in the _____ of a monkey's visual system.
   **a.** lens          **d.** cortex
   **b.** optic nerve    **e.** retina
   **c.** iris

5. Weber's law states that:
   **a.** the absolute threshold for any stimulus is a constant.
   **b.** the jnd for any stimulus is a constant.
   **c.** the absolute threshold for any stimulus is a constant percentage.
   **d.** the jnd for any stimulus is a constant percentage.

6. The principle that one sense may influence another is:
   **a.** sensory restriction.    **c.** Weber's law.
   **b.** sensory adaptation.     **d.** sensory interaction.

7. Which of the following is the correct order of the structures through which light passes after entering the eye?
   **a.** lens, pupil, cornea, retina
   **b.** pupil, cornea, lens, retina
   **c.** pupil, lens, cornea, retina
   **d.** cornea, retina, pupil, lens
   **e.** cornea, pupil, lens, retina

8. In the opponent-process theory, the three pairs of processes are:
   **a.** red-green, blue-yellow, black-white.
   **b.** red-blue, green-yellow, black-white.
   **c.** red-yellow, blue-green, black-white.
   **d.** dependent upon the individual's past experience.

9. Wavelength is to _____ as _____ is to brightness.
   **a.** hue; intensity
   **b.** intensity; hue
   **c.** frequency; amplitude
   **d.** brightness; hue

10. Concerning the evidence for subliminal stimulation, which of the following is the best answer?
    a. The brain processes some information without our awareness.
    b. Stimuli too weak to cross our thresholds for awareness may trigger a response in our sense receptors.
    c. Although we process some stimuli outside of conscious awareness, our behavior is not usually influenced by these stimuli.
    d. All of the above are true.

11. Which of the following is the most accurate description of how we process color?
    a. Throughout the visual system, color processing is divided into separate red, green, and blue systems.
    b. Red-green, blue-yellow, and black-white opponent processes operate throughout the visual system.
    c. Color processing occurs in two stages: (1) a three-color system in the retina and (2) opponent-process cells en route to the visual cortex.
    d. Color processing occurs in two stages: (1) an opponent-process system in the retina and (2) a three-color system en route to the visual cortex.

12. Given normal sensory ability, a person can hear a watch ticking in a silent room from 20 feet away. This is a description of hearing's:
    a. difference threshold.
    b. jnd.
    c. absolute threshold.
    d. subliminal stimulation.

13. The tendency to organize stimuli into smooth, uninterrupted patterns is called:
    a. closure.
    b. continuity.
    c. similarity.
    d. proximity.
    e. connectedness.

14. Which of the following is a monocular depth cue?
    a. relative size
    b. convergence
    c. retinal disparity
    d. All of the above are monocular depth cues.

15. Which of the following statements is consistent with the Gestalt theory of perception?
    a. Perception develops largely through learning.
    b. Perception is the product of heredity.
    c. The mind organizes sensations into meaningful perceptions.
    d. Perception results directly from sensation.

16. Experiments with distorted visual environments demonstrate that:
    a. adaptation rarely takes place.
    b. animals adapt readily, but humans do not.
    c. humans adapt readily, while lower animals typically do not.
    d. adaptation is possible during a critical period in infancy but not thereafter.

17. The phenomenon that refers to the ways in which an individual's expectations influence perception is called:
    a. perceptual set.
    b. retinal disparity.
    c. convergence.
    d. visual capture.

18. (Psychology Applied) Psychologists who study the importance of considering perceptual phenomena in the design of machines and work settings are called:
    a. parapsychologists.
    b. human factors psychologists.
    c. psychokineticists.
    d. Gestalt psychologists.

19. According to the philosopher _____ , we learn to perceive the world.
    a. Locke
    b. Kant
    c. Gibson
    d. Walk

20. The phenomenon of size constancy is based upon the close connection between an object's perceived _____ and its perceived _____ .
    a. size; shape
    b. size; distance
    c. size; brightness
    d. shape; distance
    e. shape; brightness

21. Which of the following statements best describes the effects of sensory restriction?
    a. It produces functional blindness when experienced for any length of time at any age.
    b. It has greater effects on humans than on animals.
    c. It has more damaging effects when experienced during infancy.
    d. It has greater effects on adults than on children.

22. Which of the following statements concerning ESP is true?
    a. Most ESP researchers are quacks.
    b. There have been a large number of reliable demonstrations of ESP.
    c. Most research psychologists are skeptical of the claims of defenders of ESP.
    d. There have been reliable laboratory demonstrations of ESP, but the results are no different from those that would occur by chance.

**23.** Each time you see your car, it projects a different image on the retinas of your eyes, yet you do not perceive it as changing. This is because of:
   **a.** perceptual set.
   **b.** retinal disparity.
   **c.** perceptual constancy.
   **d.** convergence.

**24.** Studies of the visual cliff have provided evidence that much of depth perception is:
   **a.** innate.
   **b.** learned.
   **c.** innate in lower animals, learned in humans.
   **d.** innate in humans, learned in lower animals.

●–●●–●●–●

**25.** You probably perceive the diagram above as three separate objects due to the principle of:
   **a.** proximity.          **c.** closure.
   **b.** continuity.         **d.** connectedness.

## Thinking Critically About Chapter 4

Answer these questions the day before an exam as a final check on your understanding of the chapter's terms and concepts.

### Multiple-Choice Questions

**1.** In shopping for a new stereo, you discover that you cannot differentiate between the sounds of models X and Y. The difference between X and Y is below your:
   **a.** absolute threshold.
   **b.** sensory adaptation level.
   **c.** receptor threshold.
   **d.** difference threshold.

**2.** The phantom limb sensation indicates that:
   **a.** pain is a purely sensory phenomenon.
   **b.** the central nervous system plays only a minor role in the experience of pain.
   **c.** pain involves the brain's interpretation of neural activity.
   **d.** all of the above are true.

**3.** While competing in the Olympic trials, marathoner Kirsten O'Brien suffered a stress fracture in her left leg. That she did not experience significant pain until the race was over is probably attributable to the fact that during the race:
   **a.** the pain gate in her spinal cord was closed by information coming from her brain.

   **b.** her body's production of endorphins decreased.
   **c.** an increase in the activity of small pain fibers closed the pain gate.
   **d.** a decrease in the activity of large pain fibers closed the pain gate.
   **e.** a decrease in the activity of large pain fibers opened the pain gate.

**4.** Which of the following is an example of sensory interaction?
   **a.** finding that despite its delicious aroma, a weird-looking meal tastes awful
   **b.** finding that food tastes bland when you have a bad cold
   **c.** finding it difficult to maintain your balance when you have an ear infection
   **d.** All of the above are examples.

**5.** In comparing the human eye to a camera, the film would be analogous to the eye's:
   **a.** pupil.          **c.** cornea.
   **b.** lens.           **d.** retina.

**6.** Sensation is to _____ as perception is to _____ .
   **a.** recognizing a stimulus; interpreting a stimulus
   **b.** detecting a stimulus; recognizing a stimulus
   **c.** interpreting a stimulus; detecting a stimulus
   **d.** seeing; hearing

**7.** I am a cell in the thalamus that is excited by red and inhibited by green. I am a(n):
   **a.** feature detector.     **d.** opponent-process cell.
   **b.** cone.                 **e.** rod.
   **c.** bipolar cell.

**8.** Which of the following correctly lists the order of structures through which sound travels after entering the ear?
   **a.** auditory canal, eardrum, middle ear, cochlea
   **b.** eardrum, auditory canal, middle ear, cochlea
   **c.** eardrum, middle ear, cochlea, auditory canal
   **d.** cochlea, eardrum, middle ear, auditory canal
   **e.** auditory canal, middle ear, eardrum, cochlea

**9.** Assuming that the visual systems of humans and other mammals function similarly, you would expect that the retina of a nocturnal mammal (one active only at night) would contain:
   **a.** mostly cones.
   **b.** mostly rods.
   **c.** an equal number of rods and cones.
   **d.** more bipolar cells than an animal active only during the day.

10. As the football game continued into the night, LeVar noticed that he was having difficulty distinguishing the colors of the players' uniforms. This is because the _____, which enable color vision, have a _____ absolute threshold for brightness than the available light intensity.
    a. rods; higher     c. rods; lower
    b. cones; higher     d. cones; lower

11. After staring at a very intense red stimulus for a few minutes, Carrie shifted her gaze to a beige wall and "saw" the color _____. Carrie's experience provides support for the _____ theory.
    a. green; trichromatic
    b. blue; opponent-process
    c. green; opponent-process
    d. blue; trichromatic

12. How does pain differ from other senses?
    a. It has no identifiable receptors.
    b. It has no single stimulus.
    c. It is influenced by both physical and psychological phenomena.
    d. All the above are true.

13. Tamiko hates the bitter taste of her cough syrup. Which of the following would she find most helpful in minimizing the syrup's bad taste?
    a. tasting something very sweet before taking the cough syrup
    b. keeping the syrup in her mouth for several seconds before swallowing it
    c. holding her nose while taking the cough syrup
    d. gulping the cough syrup so that it misses her tongue

14. Although carpenter Smith perceived a briefly viewed object as a screwdriver, police officer Wesson perceived the same object as a knife. This illustrates that perception is guided by:
    a. linear perspective.     d. perceptual set.
    b. shape constancy.     e. convergence.
    c. retinal disparity.

15. The fact that a white object under dim illumination appears lighter than a gray object under bright illumination is called:
    a. relative luminance.
    b. perceptual adaptation.
    c. color contrast.
    d. lightness constancy.

16. When two familiar objects of equal size cast unequal retinal images, the object that casts the smaller retinal image will be perceived as being:
    a. closer than the other object.
    b. more distant than the other object.
    c. larger than the other object.
    d. smaller than the other object.

17. If you slowly bring your finger toward your face until it eventually touches your nose, eye-muscle cues called _____ convey depth information to your brain.
    a. retinal disparity     d. proximity
    b. interposition     e. convergence
    c. continuity

18. As her friend Milo walks toward her, Noriko perceives his size as remaining constant because his perceived distance _____ at the same time that her retinal image of him _____.
    a. increases; decreases
    b. increases; increases
    c. decreases; decreases
    d. decreases; increases

19. The illusion that the St. Louis Gateway arch appears taller than it is wide (even though its height and width are equal) is based on our sensitivity to which monocular depth cue?
    a. relative size     c. relative height
    b. interposition     d. retinal disparity

20. How do we perceive a pole that partially covers a bush?
    a. as farther away
    b. as nearer
    c. as larger
    d. There is not enough information to determine the object's size or distance.

21. An artist paints a tree orchard so that the parallel rows of trees converge at the top of the canvas. Which cue has the artist used to convey distance?
    a. interposition     c. linear perspective
    b. relative size     d. relative brightness

22. Objects higher in our field of vision are perceived as _____ due to the principle of _____.
    a. nearer; relative height
    b. nearer; linear perspective
    c. farther away; relative height
    d. farther away; linear perspective

23. Which explanation of the Müller-Lyer illusion is offered by the text?

    a. The corners in our carpentered world teach us to interpret outward- or inward-pointing arrowheads at the end of a line as a cue to the line's distance from us and so to its length.
    b. The drawing's violation of linear perspective makes one line seem longer.
    c. Top-down processing of the illusion is prevented because of the stimuli's ambiguity.
    d. All of the above were offered as explanations.

24. When the traffic light changed from red to green, the drivers on both sides of Leon's vehicle pulled quickly forward, giving Leon the disorienting feeling that his car was rolling backwards. Which principle explains Leon's misperception?

    a. relative motion
    b. continuity
    c. visual capture
    d. proximity

25. While studying the road map before her trip, Colleen had no trouble following the route of the highway she planned to travel. Colleen's ability illustrates the principle of:

    a. closure.
    b. similarity.
    c. continuity.
    d. proximity.
    e. connectedness.

*Essay Question*

A dancer in a chorus line uses many sensory cues when performing. Discuss three senses that dancers rely on and explain why each is important. (Use the space below to list the points you want to make and organize them. Then write the essay on a separate sheet of paper.)

## Summing Up

Use the diagrams (pp. 114 and 115) to identify the parts of the eye and ear, then list them in the order in which they contribute to vision and hearing. Also, briefly explain the role of each structure.

**The Eye**

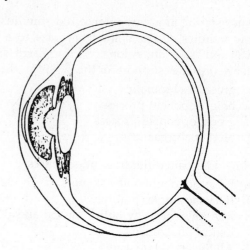

1. _____

2. _____

3. _____

4. _____

5. _____

6. _____

7. _____

**The Ear**

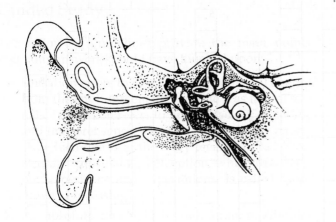

1. _____

_____

2. _____

_____

3. _____

_____

4. _____

_____

5. _____

_____

6. _____

_____

7. _____

_____

8. _____

# Key Terms

### *Writing Definitions*

Using your own words, on a piece of paper write a brief definition or explanation of each of the following terms.

1. sensation
2. perception
3. bottom-up processing
4. top-down processing
5. psychophysics
6. absolute threshold
7. subliminal
8. difference threshold (jnd)
9. Weber's law
10. sensory adaptation
11. wavelength and hue
12. intensity
13. accommodation
14. retina
15. rods and cones
16. optic nerve
17. blind spot
18. feature detectors
19. parallel processing
20. Young-Helmholtz trichromatic (three-color) theory
21. opponent-process theory
22. color constancy
23. visual capture
24. audition
25. pitch and frequency
26. middle ear
27. inner ear
28. cochlea
29. gate-control theory
30. sensory interaction
31. kinesthesis
32. vestibular sense
33. gestalt
34. figure-ground relationship
35. grouping
36. depth perception
37. visual cliff
38. binocular cue
39. monocular cue
40. retinal disparity
41. convergence
42. relative size
43. interposition
44. relative height
45. relative motion
46. linear perspective
47. relative brightness
48. perceptual constancy
49. perceptual adaptation
50. perceptual set
51. extrasensory perception (ESP)
52. parapsychology

# 5

# States of Consciousness

## Chapter Overview

Consciousness—our awareness of ourselves and our environment—can be experienced in various states. Chapter 5 examines not only waking consciousness, but also covers sleep and dreaming, daydreaming, fantasies, hypnotic states, and drug-altered states.

Most of the terminology in this chapter is introduced in the sections on Sleep and Dreams and on Drugs and Consciousness. Among the issues discussed in the chapter are why we sleep and dream, whether hypnosis is a unique state of consciousness, and possible psychological and social roots of drug use.

NOTE: Answer guidelines for all Chapter 5 questions begin on page 149.

## Guided Study

The text chapter should be studied one section at a time. Before you read, preview each section by skimming it, noting headings and boldface items. Then read the appropriate section objectives from the following outline. Keep these objectives in mind and, as you read the chapter section, search for the information that will enable you to meet each objective. Once you have finished a section, write out answers for its objectives.

### *Waking Consciousness* (pp. 169–172)

> David Myers at times uses idioms that are unfamiliar to some readers. If you do not know the meaning of any of the following words, phrases, or expressions in the context in which they appear in the text, refer to page 158 for an explanation: *a fundamental yet slippery concept; Psychology had nearly lost consciousness; attentional spotlight; draw a blank; consciousness is but the tip of the information processing iceberg.*

1. Discuss the nature of consciousness and its significance in the history of psychology.

2. Explain what is meant by selective attention and describe the different levels of information processing.

3. Discuss the nature and potential functions of day-dreams and fantasies.

7. Describe the normal content of dreams.

*Sleep and Dreams* (pp. 172–183)

> If you do not know the meaning of any of the following words, phrases, or expressions in the context in which they appear in the text, refer to pages 158–160 for an explanation: *move in concert; with a depressed body; we may fret over concerns: Does a lovers' spat signal a split?; Pulling an all-nighter; jet lag; the machine went wild . . . deep zigzags; in deep slumber; you ascend from your initial sleep dive; As the night wears on; drowsy; sleep patterns that thwart . . .; Teenagers . . . may fill this need by using home room for their first siesta and after-lunch study hall for a slumber party; riddle of sleep; deadpanned; the next-day blahs; snoozing is second only to boozing; a dream provides a psychic safety valve; cognitive machinery . . . weaves a story line.*

8. Discuss the possible functions of dreams as revealed in various theories.

*Hypnosis* (pp. 183–190)

> If you do not know the meaning of any of the following words, phrases, or expressions in the context in which they appear in the text, refer to page 160 for an explanation: *psychological truth serum; might the two views . . . be bridged?*

4. Describe the cyclical nature of sleep.

9. Define hypnosis and discuss several popular misconceptions about hypnosis.

5. Discuss the effects of sleep deprivation and describe the functions of sleep.

10. Discuss the controversy over whether hypnosis is an altered state of consciousness.

6. Identify and describe the major sleep disorders.

*Drugs and Consciousness* (pp. 191–201)

> If you do not know the meaning of any of the following words, phrases, or expressions in the context in which they appear in the text, refer to pages 160–161 for an explanation: *tipsy on one can of beer; tip more when tipsy; quicker pick-her-upper; one pays a price . . . gnawing craving for another fix; lick their addiction; crack; "acid trip"; marijuana may spell relief; being stoned.*

11. Discuss the physical and psychological effects common to all psychoactive drugs and state three common misconceptions about addiction.

12. Describe the physiological and psychological effects of depressants, stimulants, and hallucinogens.

13. Discuss the biological, psychological, and social roots of drug use.

# Chapter Review

When you have finished reading the chapter, work through the material that follows to review it. Complete the sentences and answer the questions. As you proceed, evaluate your performance for each section by consulting the answers on page 151. Do not continue with the next section until you understand each answer. If you need to, go back and review or reread the appropriate section in the textbook before continuing.

*Waking Consciousness* (pp. 169–172)

1. The study of _consciousness_ was central in the early years of psychology and in recent decades, but for quite some time it was displaced by the study of observable _behavior_ .

Define consciousness in a sentence.
_awareness of our ourselves and our environment._

2. At any moment our conscious attention is focused on only a very limited aspect of all the sensory stimuli present; this indicates that our attention is _selective_ .

3. The ability to attend selectively to one voice among many is referred to as the _cocktail party effect_ . We _can_ (can/cannot) react to stimuli that have not been consciously perceived.

4. In comparison with unconscious processing, conscious processing has a(n) _limited_ (limited/unlimited) capacity, is relatively _slow_ (fast/slow), and processes information _successively_ (simultaneously/successively).

5. Tasks that are less habitual _require_ (require/do not require) conscious attention.

6. Most people _do_ (do/do not) daydream every day. Compared to older adults, young adults spend _more_ (more/less) time daydreaming. About 4 percent of the population has such vivid fantasies and daydreams that they are referred to as _fantasy - prone_ personalities.

Explain why some psychologists consider daydreaming to be adaptive.
_help us prepare for future events by serving as mental rehearsals._

*Sleep and Dreams* (pp. 172–183)

7. The sleep-waking cycle follows a biological clock called the ___Circadian rhythm___. We may experience ___Jet lag___ if it is interrupted by travel across time zones.

8. When people are at their daily peak in circadian arousal, ___thinking___ is sharpest and ___memory___ is most accurate. In contrast to university students, who often are at their peak in the ___morning___ (morning/evening), older adults tend to peak in the ___evening___.

9. When clocks and daylight cues are absent, young adults typically adopt a ___25___-hour day.

10. The sleep cycle consists of ___4 + 1 rem___ distinct stages.

11. The rhythm of sleep cycles was discovered when Aserinsky noticed that, at periodic intervals during the night, the ___eyes___ of a sleeping child moved rapidly. This stage of sleep, during which ___dreams___ occur, is called ___rem sleep___.

12. The relatively slow brain waves of the awake but relaxed state are known as ___Alpha___ waves.

13. During stage 1 sleep, people often experience ___Hallucinations___, or sensations in the absence of sensory stimuli, or they may have a sensation of falling. These _____ sensations may later be incorporated into _____.

14. The bursts of brain-wave activity that occur during Stage 2 sleep are called ___Spindles___.

15. Large, slow brain waves are called ___delta___ waves. These begin in Stage ___3___ and predominate during Stage ___4___ sleep, and so these stages are called ___slow-wave s___

-_____ sleep. A person in these stages of sleep generally will be ___difficult___ (easy/difficult) to awaken. At the end of Stage ___4___, people may engage in sleep ___walking___.

16. Research studies comparing identical and fraternal twins ___suggest___ (suggest/do not suggest) a genetic influence on sleepwalking.

Describe the bodily changes that accompany REM sleep.

17. The genital arousal that typically occurs during REM sleep usually ___does not___ (does/does not) reflect a sexual dream.

18. During REM sleep, the motor cortex is ___active___ (active/relaxed), while the muscles are ___relaxed___ (active/relaxed). For this reason, REM is often referred to as ___paradoxical___ sleep.

19. The rapid eye movements generally signal the beginning of a ___dream___.

20. Variations on the sleep cycle repeat themselves about every ___90___ minutes. As the night progresses, Stage 4 sleep becomes ___briefer___ (longer/briefer) and REM periods become ___longer___ (longer/briefer). Approximately ___20 to 25___ percent of a night's sleep is spent in REM sleep.

21. Allowed to sleep unhindered, most people will sleep ___9 or 10___ hours a night. People who sleep less than ___7___ hours often show signs of sleep deprivation.

22. Teenagers typically need ___8 or 10___ hours of sleep but now average nearly ___2___ hours less sleep than teenagers at the turn of the century.

Describe the effects of sleep deprivation.

*sleepiness, slightly hand tremor, irritability, slowed performance.*

23. Two possible reasons for sleep are to keep us out of harm's way and to help restore body tissues, especially those of the ___*brain*___. Also, lowered body ___*temperature*___ conserves energy.

24. During sleep a growth hormone is released by the ___*pituitary*___ gland. Adults spend ___*less*___ (more/less) time in deep sleep than children and so release ___*less*___ (more/less) growth hormone.

25. Newborns spend about ___*two thirds*___ of their time asleep; adults, only about ___*one third*___.

26. Webb and Campbell found that the sleep patterns of identical twins were similar, suggesting a possible ___*genetic or hereditary*___ basis for individual differences in sleep habits.

27. A persistent difficulty in falling or staying asleep is characteristic of ___*insomnia*___. Sleeping pills and alcohol may make the problem worse since they tend to ___*reduce*___ (increase/reduce) REM sleep.

28. The sleep disorder in which a person experiences uncontrollable sleep attacks is ___*narcolepsy*___. People with this disorder may collapse directly into ___*REM*___ sleep and experience a loss of ___*muscular tension*___.

29. Individuals suffering from ___*sleep apnea*___ stop breathing while sleeping.

30. The sleep disorder characterized by extreme fright and rapid heartbeat and breathing is called ___*night terrors*___. Unlike nightmares, these episodes usually happen early in the night, during Stage ___*4*___ sleep.

31. During ___*lucid*___ dreams, the dreamer may be sufficiently aware to wonder whether he or she is, in fact, dreaming.

32. Freud referred to the actual content of a dream as its ___*manifest*___ content. Freud believed that this is a censored, symbolic version of the true meaning, or ___*latent content*___, of the dream.

33. According to Freud, most of the dreams of adults reflect ___*erotic*___ wishes and are the key to understanding inner ___*conflicts*___.

34. A second theory of dreams is that they serve an ___*information*___-processing function. Support for this theory is provided by the fact that after stressful or intense learning experiences, ___*REM*___ (REM/Stage 4) sleep tends to increase.

35. Other theories propose that dreaming serves some ___*physiological*___ function, for example, that REM sleep provides the brain with needed ___*stimulation*___. Such an explanation is supported by the fact that ___*infants*___ (infants/adults) spend the most time in REM sleep.

36. Yet other theories propose that dreams are elicited by ___*neural*___ activity originating in lower regions of the brain, such as the ___*brainstem*___.

Summarize the theory of dreaming proposed by Seligman and Yellen.

37. After being deprived of REM sleep, a person spends more time in REM sleep; this is the _____ effect.

*REM rebound*

38. REM sleep _____*does*_____ (does/does not) occur in other mammals. Animals such as fish, whose behavior is less influenced by learning, _____*do not*_____ (do/do not) dream. This finding supports the _____*information processing*_____ theory of dreaming.

*Hypnosis* (pp. 183–190)

39. The suggestion that a person forget things that occurred while he or she was under hypnosis may produce _____*posthy notic*_____ .

40. Research has shown that hypnosis _____ (does/does not) allow a person to perform dangerous feats that are impossible in the normal waking state.

41. Most people are _____ (somewhat/not at all) hypnotically suggestible.

Describe people who are the most susceptible to hypnosis.

42. The hypnotic demonstration in which a subject supposedly relives earlier experiences is referred to as _____ . Research studies show that the subjects in such demonstrations have memories that are _____ (more/no more) accurate than the memories of fully conscious persons.

43. An _____ person in a legitimate _____ can induce people—hypnotized or not—to perform some unlikely acts.

44. Hypnotherapists have helped some people alleviate headaches, asthma, or warts through the use of _____ suggestions.

45. For _____ problems such as smoking, a subject's hypnotic responsiveness _____ (does/does not) make a

difference in the effectiveness of hypnosis. As therapy for problems that are not related to will power, hypnosis _____ (is/is not) more effective in speeding recovery than techniques promoting relaxation and positive images.

46. One theory of hypnotic pain relief is that hypnosis separates, or _____ , the sensory and emotional aspects of pain. Another is that hypnotic pain relief is due to selective _____ , that is, to the person's focusing on stimuli other than pain.

47. Advocates of the _____ _____ theory argue that hypnotic phenomena are not unique to hypnosis.

Summarize the argument that hypnosis is not an altered state of consciousness.

48. Hilgard has advanced the idea that during hypnosis there is a _____ , or split, between different levels of consciousness. The existence of a separate consciousness, which is aware of what takes place during hypnosis, is expressed in the concept of the _____ .

*Drugs and Consciousness* (pp. 191–201)

49. Drugs that alter moods and perceptions are called _____ drugs.

50. Drug users who require increasing doses to experience a drug's effects have developed _____ for the drug.

51. If a person begins experiencing withdrawal symptoms after ceasing to use a drug, the person has developed a physical _____ . Regular use of a drug to relieve stress is an example of a _____ dependence.

Briefly state three common misconceptions about addiction.

52. A person who is addicted to a dysfunctional partner has been said to be _____ . This idea, however, remains controversial.

53. The three broad categories of drugs discussed in the text include _____ , which tend to slow body functions; _____ , which speed body functions; and _____ , which alter perception. These drugs all work by mimicking or affecting the activity of the brain's _____ .

54. A low dose of alcohol, which is classified as a _____ , slows the activity of the _____ nervous system.

55. Alcohol may make a person more _____ , more _____ , more _____ , or more _____ daring; on the other hand, it reduces _____ . Alcohol affects memory by interfering with the process of transferring experiences into _____-_____ memory. Also, blackouts after drinking result from alcohol's suppression of _____ .

Describe how a person's expectations can influence the behavioral effects of alcohol.

56. Tranquilizers, which are also known as _____ , have effects similar to those of alcohol.

57. Opium, morphine, and heroin all _____ (excite/depress) neural functioning. Together, these drugs are called the _____ . When they are present, the brain eventually stops producing _____ .

58. The most widely used stimulants are _____ , _____ , _____ , and _____ . Stimulants _____ (are/are not) addictive.

59. Nicotine triggers the release of _____ and _____ , which diminish appetite and boost alertness. It also stimulates the _____ to release neurotransmitters that calm _____ and reduce _____ sensitivity.

60. Cocaine and crack deplete the brain's supply of the neurotransmitters _____ , _____ , and _____ , and result in depression as the drugs' effects wear off.

61. Cocaine's psychological effects depend not only on dosage and form but also on _____ , _____ , and the _____ .

62. Hallucinogens are also referred to as _____ . Two common synthetic hallucinogens are _____ and LSD, which is chemically similar to the neurotransmitter _____ .

63. The hallucinations of LSD users are similar to the _____-_____ of those who survive a brush with death. These experiences may be the result of a deficient supply of _____ to the brain.

**64.** The active ingredient in marijuana is abbreviated
_____ . Marijuana has been
used therapeutically with those who suffer from
_____ and cancer.

Describe some of the physical and psychological
effects of marijuana.

**65.** Long-term use of marijuana may depress male

_____ _____
and _____ levels and damage
the lungs more than cigarette smoking does.
Large doses hasten the loss of _____
_____ . Because marijuana
changes _____
_____ , it may make the brain
more susceptible to _____ and
_____ addiction.

**66.** The negative aftereffects of drug use may be
explained in part by the principle that emotions
trigger _____
_____ .

**67.** Due to drug education and efforts by the media,
drug use _____ (declined/
increased) until the early 1990s.

**68.** Since then, drug use _____
(continues to decline/is on the rise). At the same
time, alcohol and tobacco use is
_____ (declining/on the rise).

**69.** Adopted individuals are more susceptible to alcoholism if they had an alcoholic
_____ (adoptive/biological)
parent. Similarly, having an alcoholic
_____ twin puts a
_____ at increased risk for
alcoholism.

Identify some of the psychological and social roots of
drug use.

**70.** Boys who at age 6 are _____ ,
_____ , and _____ ,
are more likely as teens to smoke, drink, and use
other drugs.

**71.** Among teenagers, drug use _____
(varies/is about the same) across cultural groups.

**72.** African-American high school seniors report the
_____ (highest/lowest) rates of
drug use.

**73.** State three possible channels of influence for drug
prevention and treatment programs.
a. _____
b. _____
c. _____

## Progress Test 1

*Multiple-Choice Questions*

Circle your answers to the following questions and
check them with the answers on page 153. If your
answer is incorrect, read the explanation for why it is
incorrect and then consult the appropriate pages of
the text (in parentheses following the correct answer).

**1.** As defined by the text, consciousness includes
which of the following?
a. daydreaming    c. hypnosis
b. sleeping    d. all of the above

**2.** Which of the following groups tends to daydream the most?
a. elderly men    d. middle-aged men
b. elderly women    e. young adults
c. middle-aged women

**3.** When our _____ is disrupted,
we experience jet lag.
a. daydreaming    d. Stage 4 sleep
b. REM sleep    e. Stage 1 sleep
c. circadian rhythm

4. Sleep spindles predominate during which stage of sleep?
   a. Stage 2
   b. Stage 3
   c. Stage 4
   d. REM sleep

5. During which stage of sleep does the body experience increased heart rate, rapid breathing, and genital arousal?
   a. Stage 2
   b. Stage 3
   c. Stage 4
   d. REM sleep

6. Variations of the sleep cycle last approximately _____ minutes.
   a. 30
   b. 50
   c. 75
   d. 90

7. Sleep deprivation typically leads to:
   a. disruption of muscular coordination.
   b. hallucinations and other abnormal conditions.
   c. misperceptions on monotonous tasks.
   d. all of the above.

8. One effect of sleeping pills is to:
   a. depress REM sleep.
   b. increase REM sleep.
   c. depress Stage 2 sleep.
   d. increase Stage 2 sleep.

9. Cocaine and crack produce a euphoric rush by:
   a. blocking the actions of serotonin.
   b. depressing neural activity in the brain.
   c. blocking the reabsorption of excess dopamine, norepinephrine, and serotonin.
   d. stimulating the brain's production of endorphins.
   e. preventing the body from producing endorphins.

10. Which of the following is classified as a depressant?
    a. amphetamines
    b. LSD
    c. marijuana
    d. alcohol
    e. PCP

11. The cocktail party effect refers to the:
    a. effects of random noise on a person's mood.
    b. effects of random noise on a person's perception of low pitches.
    c. ability to attend selectively to one stimulus.
    d. cumulative effect of multiple uses of a depressant drug.

12. Which of the following statements concerning hypnosis is true?
    a. People will do anything under hypnosis.
    b. Hypnosis is the same as sleeping.
    c. Hypnosis is not associated with a distinct physiological state.
    d. Hypnosis improves memory recall.

13. The fact that animals such as fish, whose behavior is less influenced by learning, do not dream provides support for the _____ theory of dreaming.
    a. manifest content
    b. physiological
    c. information-processing
    d. Seligman-Yellen
    e. latent content

14. According to Freud, dreams are:
    a. a symbolic fulfillment of erotic wishes.
    b. the result of random neural activity in the brainstem.
    c. the brain's mechanism for self-stimulation.
    d. transparent representations of the individual's conflicts.

15. Psychoactive drugs affect behavior and perception through:
    a. the power of suggestion.
    b. the placebo effect.
    c. alteration of neural activity in the brain.
    d. psychological, not physiological, influences.

16. Which of the following is *not* a common *misconception* about addiction?
    a. To overcome an addiction a person almost always needs professional therapy.
    b. Psychoactive and medicinal drugs very quickly lead to addiction.
    c. Biological factors place some individuals at increased risk for addiction.
    d. Many other repetitive, pleasure-seeking behaviors fit the drug-addiction-as-disease-needing-treatment model.

17. At its beginning, psychology focused on the study of:
    a. observable behavior.
    b. consciousness.
    c. abnormal behavior.
    d. all of the above.

18. Which of the following is *not* a theory of dreaming mentioned in the text?
    a. Dreams facilitate information processing.
    b. Dreaming stimulates the developing brain.
    c. Dreams result from random neural activity originating in the brainstem.
    d. Dreaming is an attempt to escape from social stimulation.

19. The sleep-waking cycles of people isolated without clocks or daylight typically are _____ hours in duration.
    a. 23          c. 25
    b. 24          d. 26

*Matching Items*

Match each term with its appropriate definition or description.

*Definitions or Descriptions*

____ e  1. surface meaning of dreams
____ k  2. deeper meaning of dreams
____ i  3. stage of sleep associated with delta waves
____ j  4. stage of sleep associated with muscular relaxation
____ h  5. sleep disorder in which breathing stops
____ d  6. sleep disorder occurring in Stage 4 sleep
____ b  7. depressant
____ A  8. hallucinogen
____ F  9. stimulant
____ C  10. twilight stage of sleep associated with imagery resembling hallucinations
____ g  11. disorder in which sleep attacks occur

*Terms*

a. marijuana
b. alcohol
c. Stage 1 sleep
d. night terrors
e. manifest content
f. cocaine
g. narcolepsy
h. sleep apnea
i. Stages 3 and 4 sleep
j. REM sleep
k. latent content

20. The lowest rates of drug use among high school seniors is reported by:
    a. white males.
    b. white females.
    c. black males.
    d. Latinos.

## Progress Test 2

Progress Test 2 should be completed during a final chapter review. Answer the following questions after you thoroughly understand the correct answers for the Chapter Review and Progress Test 1.

*Multiple-Choice Questions*

1. Which of the following statements regarding REM sleep is true?
    a. Adults spend more time than infants in REM sleep.
    b. REM sleep deprivation results in a REM rebound.
    c. People deprived of REM sleep adapt easily.
    d. After a stressful experience, a person's REM sleep decreases.
    e. REM sleep periods become shorter as the night progresses.

2. The hallucinatory sensations experienced by _____ users are similar to reports of _____ .
    a. amphetamine; near-death experiences
    b. LSD; near-death experiences
    c. barbiturate; divided consciousness
    d. cocaine; the phenomenon of dissociation

3. Alcohol has the most profound effect on:
   a. the transfer of experiences to long-term memory.
   b. immediate memory.
   c. previously established long-term memories.
   d. all of the above.

4. A person whose EEG shows a high proportion of alpha waves is most likely:
   a. dreaming.                d. in Stage 4 sleep.
   b. in Stage 2 sleep.        e. awake and relaxed.
   c. in Stage 3 sleep.

5. Circadian rhythms are the:
   a. brain waves that occur during Stage 4 sleep.
   b. muscular tremors that occur during opiate withdrawal.
   c. regular body cycles that occur on a daily basis.
   d. brain waves that are indicative of Stage 2 sleep.

6. A person who requires increasing amounts of a drug in order to feel its effect is said to have developed:
   a. tolerance.
   b. physical dependency.
   c. psychological dependency.
   d. resistance.
   e. withdrawal symptoms.

7. Use of which of the following drugs has been declining since the early 1990s?
   a. marijuana
   b. alcohol
   c. nicotine
   d. none of the above.

8. Which of the following is characteristic of REM sleep?
   a. genital arousal
   b. increased muscular tension
   c. night terrors
   d. slow, regular breathing
   e. alpha waves

9. Which of the following is *not* a stimulant?
   a. amphetamines      c. nicotine
   b. caffeine          d. alcohol

10. Hypnotic responsiveness is:
    a. the same in all people.
    b. generally greater in women than men.
    c. generally greater in men than women.
    d. greater when people are led to *expect* it.

11. According to Hilgard, hypnosis is:
    a. no different from a state of heightened motivation.
    b. a hoax perpetrated by frauds.
    c. the same as dreaming.
    d. a dissociation between different levels of consciousness.

12. Which of the following is a psychoactive drug?
    a. LSD
    b. sleeping pills
    c. caffeine
    d. All of the above are psychoactive drugs.

13. As a form of therapy for relieving problems such as headaches, hypnosis is:
    a. ineffective.
    b. no more effective than positive suggestions given without hypnosis.
    c. highly effective.
    d. more effective with adults than children.

14. Which of the following is usually the most powerful determinant of whether teenagers begin using drugs?
    a. family strength       c. school adjustment
    b. religiosity           d. peer influence

15. THC is the major active ingredient in:
    a. nicotine.             d. cocaine.
    b. LSD.                  e. amphetamine.
    c. marijuana.

16. Those who believe that hypnosis is a social phenomenon argue that "hypnotized" individuals are:
    a. consciously faking their behavior.
    b. merely acting out a role.
    c. underachievers striving to please the hypnotist.
    d. all of the above.

17. "Consciousness" is defined in the text as:
    a. mental life.
    b. selective attention to ongoing perceptions, thoughts, and feelings.
    c. information processing.
    d. a vague concept no longer useful to contemporary psychologists.
    e. our awareness of ourselves and our environment.

18. Which of the following is true?
    a. REM sleep tends to increase following intense learning periods.
    b. Non-REM sleep tends to increase following intense learning periods.
    c. REM-deprived people remember less presleep material than people deprived of Stage 1–4 sleep.
    d. Sleep control centers are located in the higher, association areas of the cortex, where memories are stored.

19. According to Seligman and Yellen, dreaming represents:
    a. the brain's efforts to integrate unrelated bursts of activity in the visual cortex with emotional tone provided by activity in the limbic system.
    b. a mechanism for coping with the stresses of daily life.

    c. a symbolic depiction of a person's unfulfilled wishes.
    d. an information-processing mechanism for converting the day's experiences into long-term memory.

20. How a particular psychoactive drug affects a person depends on:
    a. the dosage and form in which the drug is taken.
    b. the user's expectations and personality.
    c. the situation in which the drug is taken.
    d. all of the above.

*Matching Items*

Match each term with its appropriate definition or description.

*Definitions or Descriptions*

_e_  1. drugs that increase energy and stimulate neural activity
_c_  2. brain wave of awake, relaxed person
_g_  3. brain-wave activity during Stage 2 sleep
_i_  4. sleep stage associated with dreaming
_j_  5. drugs that reduce anxiety and depress central nervous system activity
_h_  6. natural painkiller produced by the brain
_b_  7. neurotransmitter that LSD resembles
_F_  8. our awareness of ourselves and our environment
_a_  9. theory that dreaming reflects our erotic drives
_d_  10. a split between different levels of consciousness

*Terms*

a. Freud's theory
b. serotonin
c. alpha
d. dissociation
e. amphetamines
f. consciousness
g. sleep spindle
h. endorphin
i. REM
j. barbiturates

# Thinking Critically About Chapter 5

Answer these questions the day before an exam as a final check on your understanding of the chapter's terms and concepts.

## Multiple-Choice Questions

1. A person who falls asleep in the midst of a heated argument probably suffers from:
   a. sleep apnea.
   b. narcolepsy.
   c. night terrors.
   d. insomnia.

2. Which of the following was *not* suggested by the text as an important aspect of drug prevention and treatment programs?
   a. education about the long-term costs of a drug's temporary pleasures
   b. efforts to boost people's self-esteem and purpose in life
   c. attempts to modify peer associations
   d. "scare tactics" that frighten prepubescent children into avoiding drug experimentation

3. REM sleep is referred to as "paradoxical sleep" because:
   a. studies of people deprived of REM sleep indicate that REM sleep is unnecessary.
   b. the body's muscles remain relaxed while the brain and eyes are active.
   c. it is very easy to awaken a person from REM sleep.
   d. the body's muscles are very tense while the brain is in a nearly meditative state.
   e. erection during REM sleep indicates sexual arousal.

4. An attorney wants to know if the details and accuracy of an eyewitness's memory for a crime would be improved under hypnosis. Given the results of relevant research, what should you tell the attorney?
   a. Most hypnotically retrieved memories are either false or contaminated.
   b. Hypnotically retrieved memories are usually more accurate than conscious memories.
   c. Hypnotically retrieved memories are purely the product of the subject's imagination.
   d. Hypnosis only improves memory of anxiety-provoking childhood events.

5. Dan has recently begun using an addictive, euphoria-producing drug. Which of the following will probably occur if he repeatedly uses this drug?

   a. As tolerance to the drug develops, Dan will experience increasingly pleasurable "highs."
   b. The dosage needed to produce the desired effect will decrease.
   c. After each use, he will become more and more depressed.
   d. Dependence will become less of a problem.
   e. Both b. and c. will occur.

6. Although her eyes are closed, Adele's brain is generating bursts of electrical activity in the visual cortex. It is likely that Adele is:
   a. under the influence of a depressant.
   b. under the influence of an opiate.
   c. in NREM sleep.
   d. in REM sleep.
   e. having a near-death experience.

7. Concluding his presentation on levels of information processing, Miguel states that:
   a. humans process both conscious and subconscious information in parallel.
   b. conscious processing occurs in parallel, while subconscious processing is serial.
   c. conscious processing is serial, while subconscious processing is parallel.
   d. all information processing is serial in nature.

8. Roberto is moderately intoxicated by alcohol. Which of the following changes in his behavior is likely to occur?
   a. If angered, he is more likely to become aggressive than when he is sober.
   b. He will be less self-conscious about his behavior.
   c. If sexually aroused, he will be less inhibited about engaging in sexual activity.
   d. The next day he may be unable to remember what happened while he was drinking.
   e. All of the above are likely.

9. Jill dreams that her boyfriend pushes her in front of an oncoming car. Her psychoanalyst suggests that the dream might symbolize her fear that her boyfriend is rushing her into sexual activity prematurely. The analyst is evidently attempting to interpret the _____ content of Jill's dream.
   a. manifest
   b. latent
   c. dissociated
   d. overt

10. Barry has just spent four nights as a subject in a sleep study in which he was awakened each time he entered REM sleep. Now that the experiment is over, which of the following can be expected to occur?
    a. Barry will be extremely irritable until his body has made up the lost REM sleep.
    b. Barry will sleep so deeply for several nights that dreaming will be minimal.
    c. There will be an increase in sleep Stages 1–4.
    d. There will be an increase in Barry's REM sleep.

11. Of the following individuals, who is likely to be the most hypnotically suggestible?
    a. Bill, a reality-oriented stockbroker
    b. Janice, a fantasy-prone actress
    c. Megan, a sixth-grader who has trouble focusing her attention on a task
    d. Darren, who has never been able to really "get involved" in movies or novels

12. Which of the following statements concerning alcoholism is *not* true?
    a. Adopted individuals are more susceptible to alcoholism if they had an alcoholic adoptive parent.
    b. Having an alcoholic identical twin puts a male at increased risk of becoming alcoholic.
    c. Compared to children of nonalcoholics, children of alcoholics have a higher tolerance for multiple alcoholic drinks.
    d. Researchers have bred rats that prefer alcohol to water.

13. Research studies of the effectiveness of hypnosis as a form of therapy have demonstrated that:
    a. for problems of self-control, such as smoking, hypnosis is equally effective with subjects who can be deeply hypnotized and those who cannot.
    b. posthypnotic suggestions have helped alleviate headaches, asthma, warts, and certain skin disorders.
    c. positive suggestions given without hypnosis are often as effective as hypnosis as a form of therapy.
    d. all of the above are true.

14. As a child, Jane enjoyed intense make-believe play with dolls, stuffed animals, and imaginary companions. As an adult, she spends an unusually large amount of time fantasizing. She is sometimes uncertain whether an event was real or imagined. A psychologist would most likely describe Jane as:

    a. highly suggestible.
    b. a fantasy-prone personality.
    c. a daydreamer.
    d. a dissociator.

15. A sleeping person who is hard to awaken and whose EEG shows a high proportion of delta waves is most likely:
    a. in REM sleep.
    b. in Stage 2 sleep.
    c. dreaming.
    d. in Stage 4 sleep.

16. Which of the following statements concerning marijuana is *not* true?
    a. The by-products of marijuana are cleared from the body more quickly than the by-products of alcohol.
    b. Long-term marijuana use may depress male sex hormone and sperm levels.
    c. Marijuana is not as addictive as nicotine or cocaine.
    d. Large doses of marijuana hasten the loss of brain cells.

17. Which of the following statements concerning near-death experiences is true?
    a. Fewer than 1 percent of patients who come close to dying report having them.
    b. They typically consist of fantastic, mystical imagery.
    c. They are more commonly experienced by females than by males.
    d. They are more commonly experienced by males than by females.

18. Those who consider hypnosis a social phenomenon contend that:
    a. hypnosis is an altered state of consciousness.
    b. hypnotic phenomena are unique to hypnosis.
    c. if a hypnotist eliminates the motivation for acting, hypnotized subjects become unresponsive.
    d. all of the above are true.

19. Which of the following statements concerning the roots of drug use is *not* true?
    a. Heavy users of alcohol, marijuana, and cocaine often are depressed.
    b. If an adolescent's friends use drugs, odds are that he or she will, too.
    c. Teenagers who come from happy families and do well in school seldom use drugs.
    d. It is nearly impossible to predict whether or not a particular adolescent will experiment with drugs.

in the form of imaginative play is important to social and cognitive development. Daydreams may also substitute for impulsive behavior (delinquents and drug users tend to have fewer vivid fantasies than most people).

7. circadian rhythm; jet lag

8. thinking; memory; evening; morning

9. 25

10. 5

11. eyes; dreams; REM sleep

12. alpha

13. hallucinations; hypnogogic; memories

14. sleep spindles

15. delta; 3; 4; slow-wave; difficult; 4; walking

16. suggest

During REM sleep, brain waves become as rapid as those of Stage 1 sleep, heart rate and breathing become more rapid and irregular, and genital arousal and rapid eye movements occur.

17. does not

18. active; relaxed; paradoxical

19. dream

20. 90; briefer; longer; 20 to 25

21. 9 or 10; 7

22. 8 or 9; 2

The major effect of sleep deprivation is sleepiness. Other effects include impaired creativity and concentration, diminished immunity to disease, slight hand tremors, slowed performance, irritability, and occasional misperceptions on monotonous tasks.

23. brain; temperature

24. pituitary; less; less

25. two-thirds; one-third

26. genetic or hereditary

27. insomnia; reduce

28. narcolepsy; REM; muscular tension

29. sleep apnea

30. night terrors; 4

31. lucid

32. manifest; latent content

33. erotic; conflicts

34. information; REM

35. physiological; stimulation; infants

36. neural; brainstem

Seligman and Yellen believe that dreams are the brain's attempt to integrate unrelated bursts of activity in the visual cortex, imposing meaning on mean-ingless stimuli. The emotional "tone" of the particular dream is provided by limbic system activity.

37. REM rebound

38. does; do not; information-processing

39. posthypnotic amnesia

40. does not

41. somewhat

Those who are most susceptible share with the fantasy-prone personality the capability of becoming deeply absorbed in the imaginary. They also tend to have rich fantasy lives.

42. age regression; no more

43. authoritative; context

44. posthypnotic

45. self-control; does not; is not

46. dissociates; attention

47. social influence

Although the issue is still unsettled, most studies have found that hypnosis does not produce any unique changes in physiological processes—and we would expect such changes if hypnosis is an altered state of consciousness. Nor is the behavior of hypnotized subjects fundamentally different from that of other people. Therefore, hypnosis may be mainly a social phenomenon, with hypnotized subjects acting out the role of a "good hypnotic subject."

48. dissociation; hidden observer

49. psychoactive

50. tolerance

51. dependence; psychological

The following myths about addiction are false:
  a. Taking a psychoactive drug automatically leads to addiction.
  b. One cannot overcome an addiction without professional help.
  c. The addiction-as-disease-needing-treatment model is applicable to a broad spectrum of pleasure-seeking behaviors.

52. co-dependent

53. depressants; stimulants; hallucinogens; neurotransmitters

54. depressant; sympathetic

55. aggressive; helpful; self-disclosing; sexually; self-awareness; long-term; REM sleep

Studies have found that if people believe that alcohol affects social behavior in certain ways, then, when they drink alcohol (or even mistakenly think that they have been drinking alcohol), they will behave according to their expectations.

56. barbiturates

57. depress; opiates; endorphins

58. caffeine; nicotine; amphetamines; cocaine; are

59. epinephrine; norepinephrine; central nervous system; anxiety; pain

60. dopamine; norepinephrine; serotonin

61. expectations; personality; situation

62. psychedelics; PCP; serotonin

63. near-death experiences; oxygen

64. THC; glaucoma

Like alcohol, marijuana relaxes, disinhibits, and may produce a euphoric feeling. Also like alcohol, marijuana impairs perceptual and motor skills and reaction time. Marijuana is a mild hallucinogen; it can amplify sensitivity to colors, sounds, tastes, and smells. Marijuana also interrupts memory formation.

65. sex hormone; sperm; brain cells; brain chemistry; cocaine; heroin

66. opposing emotions

67. declined

68. is on the rise; declining

69. biological; identical; male

A psychological factor in drug use is the feeling that one's life is meaningless and lacks direction. Regular users of psychoactive drugs often have experienced stress or failure and are somewhat depressed. Drug use often begins as a temporary way to relieve depression, anger, anxiety, or insomnia. A powerful social factor in drug use, especially among adolescents, is peer influence. Peers shape attitudes about drugs, provide drugs, and establish the social context for their use.

70. excitable; impulsive; fearless

71. varies

72. lowest

73. a. education about the long-term costs of a drug's temporary pleasures
    b. efforts to boost people's self-esteem and purpose in life
    c. attempts to "inoculate" youth against peer pressures

## Progress Test 1

### Multiple-Choice Questions

1. **d.** is the answer. (p. 170)

2. **e.** is the answer. (p. 171)

3. **c.** is the answer. Jet lag is experienced because, having traveled across time zones, we are awake at a time when our biological clock says, "Sleep!" This biological clock is the circadian rhythm. (p. 173)

4. **a.** is the answer. (p. 174)
   **b. & c.** Delta waves predominate during Stages 3 and 4. Stage 3 is the transition between Stages 2 and 4.
   **d.** Faster, nearly waking brain waves occur during REM sleep.

5. **d.** is the answer. (pp. 175)
   **a., b., & c.** During non-REM Stages 1–4 heart rate and breathing are slow and regular and the genitals are not aroused.

6. **d.** is the answer. (p. 176)

7. **c.** is the answer. Sleep deprivation can have serious consequences for monotonous tasks like long-distance driving. However, short, highly motivated tasks are evidently unaffected by sleep loss. (p. 178)

8. **a.** is the answer. Like alcohol, sleeping pills carry the undesirable consequence of reducing REM sleep and may make insomnia worse in the long run. (p. 179)

9. **c.** is the answer. (p. 196)
   **a.** This answer describes the effect of LSD.
   **b.** Depressants such as alcohol have this effect. Cocaine and crack are classified as stimulants.
   **d.** None of the psychoactive drugs has this effect. Opiates, however, *suppress* the brain's production of endorphins.
   **e.** Use of opiates eventually does this.

10. **d.** is the answer. Alcohol, which slows body functions and neural activity, is a depressant. (p. 193)
    **a.** Amphetamines are stimulants.
    **b., c., & e.** LSD, PCP, and marijuana are hallucinogens.

11. **c.** is the answer. An example of selective attention, the cocktail party effect, is the ability to attend to one voice among many. (pp. 170)

12. **c.** is the answer. (p. 190)
    **a.** Hypnotized subjects usually perform only acts they might perform normally.
    **b.** The brain waves of hypnotized subjects are like those seen in relaxed, awake states, not like those associated with sleeping.
    **d.** Hypnosis typically *disrupts*, or contaminates, memory.

13. **c.** is the answer. The very nature of learning is the processing of information. Since dreaming increases following intense learning periods, ani-

mals whose behavior is less influenced by learning have less need to dream. (p. 183)

14. **a.** is the answer. Freud saw dreams as psychic escape valves that discharge unacceptable feelings that are often related to erotic wishes. (pp. 181–182)

**b. & c.** These physiological theories of dreaming are not associated with Freud.

**d.** According to Freud, dreams represent the individual's conflicts and wishes but in disguised, rather than transparent, form.

15. **c.** is the answer. Such drugs work primarily at synapses, altering neural transmission. (p. 191)

**a.** What people believe will happen after taking a drug will likely have some effect on their individual reactions, but psychoactive drugs actually work by altering neural transmission.

**b.** Since a placebo is a substance without active properties, this answer is incorrect.

**d.** This answer is incorrect because the effects of psychoactive drugs on behavior, perception, and so forth have a physiological basis.

16. **c.** is the answer. This is true. Heredity, for example, influences tendencies toward alcoholism. (pp. 191–192)

17. **b.** is the answer. (p. 169)

**a.** The behaviorists' emphasis on observable behavior occurred much later in the history of psychology.

**c.** Psychology has never been primarily concerned with abnormal behavior.

18. **d.** is the answer. (pp. 181–183)

**a., b., & c.** Each of these describes a valid theory of dreaming that was mentioned in the text.

19. **c.** is the answer. (p. 173)

20. **c.** is the answer. (p. 200)

### Matching Items

| | | |
|---|---|---|
| **1.** e (p. 181) | **5.** h (p. 179) | **9.** f (p. 196) |
| **2.** k (p. 182) | **6.** d (p. 180) | **10.** c (p. 174) |
| **3.** i (p. 174) | **7.** b (p. 193) | **11.** g (p. 179) |
| **4.** j (p. 174) | **8.** a (p. 198) | |

## Progress Test 2

### Multiple-Choice Questions

1. **b.** is the answer. Following REM deprivation, people temporarily increase their amount of REM sleep, in a phenomenon known as REM rebound. (p. 183)

**a. & e.** Just the opposite is true: The amount of REM sleep is greatest in infancy, and the amount increases during the night.

**c.** Deprived of REM sleep by repeated awakenings, people return more and more quickly to the REM stages after falling back to sleep. They by no means adapt easily to the deprivations.

**d.** Just the opposite occurs: Following stressful experiences, REM sleep tends to increase.

2. **b.** is the answer. (p. 197)

3. **a.** is the answer. Alcohol disrupts the processing of experiences into long-term memory but has little effect on either immediate or previously established memories. (p. 194)

4. **e.** is the answer. (p. 174)

**a.** The brain waves of REM sleep (dream sleep) are more like those of Stage 1 sleepers.

**b.** Stage 2 is characterized by sleep spindles.

**c.** Stages 3 and 4 are characterized by slow, rolling delta waves.

5. **c.** is the answer. (p. 173)

6. **a.** is the answer. (p. 191)

**b.** Physical dependence may occur in the absence of tolerance. The hallmark of physical dependence is the presence of withdrawal symptoms when off the drug.

**c.** Psychological dependence refers to a felt, or psychological, need to use a drug, for example, a drug that relieves stress.

**d.** There is no such thing as drug "resistance."

**e.** Withdrawal symptoms occur when the drug is no longer being taken.

7. **d.** is the answer. After declining from the late 1970s to 1992, drug use has been increasing. (p. 199)

8. **a.** is the answer. (p. 175)

**b.** During REM sleep, muscular tension is low.

**c.** Night terrors are associated with Stage 4 sleep.

**d.** During REM sleep, respiration is rapid and irregular.

**e.** Alpha waves are characteristic of Stage 1 sleep.

9. **d.** is the answer. Alcohol is a depressant. (p. 193)

10. **d.** is the answer. (p. 189)

**a.** Hypnotic responsiveness varies greatly from person to person.

**b. & c.** There is no evidence of a gender difference in hypnotic responsiveness.

11. **d.** is the answer. Hilgard believes that hypnosis reflects a dissociation, or split, in consciousness, as occurs normally, only to a much greater extent. (p. 190)

12. **d.** is the answer. (pp. 193–198)

13. **b.** is the answer. (p. 188)
    **a. & c.** Hypnosis *can* be helpful in treating these problems, but it is no more effective than other forms of therapy.
    **d.** Adults are not more responsive than children to hypnosis.

14. **d.** is the answer. If adolescents' friends use drugs, the odds are that they will, too. (p. 201)
    **a., b., & c.** These are also predictors of drug use but seem to operate mainly through their effects on peer association.

15. **c.** is the answer. (p. 198)

16. **b.** is the answer. (p. 189)
    **a. & c.** There is no evidence that hypnotically responsive individuals fake their behaviors, or that they are underachievers.

17. **e.** is the answer. (p. 170)

18. **a.** is true. The fact that REM sleep tends to increase following intense learning periods has led to the theory that dreams may help sift, sort, and fix in memory the day's experiences. (p. 182)
    **b.** Non-REM sleep usually does *not* increase following intense learning periods.
    **c.** There is no evidence that REM-deprived people have poorer recall of presleep experiences than non-REM-deprived people.
    **d.** Sleep control centers are actually located in the lower centers of the brainstem, not in the association areas of the cortex.

19. **a.** is the answer. Seligman and Yellen believe that the brain's attempt to make sense of random neural activity is consistent with people's well-established tendencies to impose meaning on even meaningless stimuli. (p. 182)
    **b. & c.** These essentially Freudian explanations of the purpose of dreaming are based on the idea that a dream is a psychic safety valve that harmlessly discharges otherwise inexpressible feelings.
    **d.** This explanation of the function of dreaming is associated with the information-processing viewpoint, but not with Seligman and Yellen.

20. **d.** is the answer. (p. 197)

### Matching Items

| | | |
|---|---|---|
| **1.** e (p. 195) | **5.** j (p. 194) | **9.** a (pp. 181–182) |
| **2.** c (p. 174) | **6.** h (p. 195) | **10.** d (p. 188) |
| **3.** g (p. 174) | **7.** b (p. 197) | |
| **4.** i (p. 174) | **8.** f (p. 170) | |

## Thinking Critically About Chapter 5

### Multiple-Choice Questions

1. **b.** is the answer. Narcolepsy is characterized by uncontrollable sleep attacks. (p. 179)
   **a.** Sleep apnea is characterized by the temporary cessation of breathing while asleep.
   **c.** Night terrors are characterized by high arousal and terrified behavior, occurring during Stage 4 sleep.
   **d.** Insomnia refers to chronic difficulty in falling or staying asleep.

2. **d.** is the answer. (p. 201)

3. **b.** is the answer. Although the body is aroused internally, the messages of the activated motor cortex do not reach the muscles. (p. 175)
   **a.** Studies of REM-deprived subjects indicate just the opposite.
   **c.** It is difficult to awaken a person from REM sleep.
   **d.** Just the opposite occurs in REM sleep: The muscles are relaxed, yet the brain is aroused.
   **e.** Arousal is usually not caused by sexual dreams.

4. **a.** is the answer. Although people recall more under hypnosis, they "recall" a lot of fiction along with fact and appear unable to distinguish between the two. (p. 185)
   **b.** Hypnotically refreshed memories are usually no more accurate than conscious memories.
   **c.** Although the hypnotized subject's imagination may influence the memories retrieved, some actual memory retrieval also occurs.
   **d.** Hypnotically retrieved memories don't normally focus on anxiety-provoking events.

5. **c.** is the answer. Continued use of a drug produces a tolerance; to experience the same "high," Dan will have to use larger and larger doses. As the doses become larger, the negative aftereffects, or withdrawal symptoms, become worse. (p. 191)

6. **d.** is the answer. The rapid eye movements of REM sleep coincide with bursts of activity in the visual cortex. (p. 182)

7. **c.** is the answer. (p. 171)

8. **e.** is the answer. Alcohol reduces self-consciousness and it loosens inhibitions, making people more likely to act on their feelings of anger or sexual arousal. It also disrupts the processing of experience into long-term memory. (pp. 193–194)

**9. b.** is the answer. The analyst is evidently trying to go beyond the events in the dream and understand the dream's hidden meaning, or the dream's latent content. (p. 182)

**a.** The manifest content of a dream is its actual story line.

**c.** Dissociation refers to a split in levels of consciousness.

**d.** There is no such term. In any case, "overt" would be the same as "manifest" content.

**10. d.** is the answer. Because of the phenomenon known as REM rebound, Barry, having been deprived of REM sleep, will now increase his REM sleep. (p. 183)

**a.** Increased irritability is an effect of sleep deprivation in general, not of REM deprivation specifically.

**b.** REM rebound will cause Barry to dream more than normal.

**c.** The increase in REM sleep is necessarily accompanied by decreases in Stages 1–4 sleep.

**11. b.** is the answer. Fantasy-prone people have essentially the characteristics associated with hypnotic suggestibility: rich fantasy lives, the ability to become imaginatively absorbed, etc. The fact that Janice is an actress also suggests she possesses such traits. (p. 184)

**a.** Bill's reality orientation makes him an unlikely candidate for hypnosis.

**c.** The hypnotically suggestible are generally able to focus on tasks or on imaginative activities.

**d.** People who are hypnotically suggestible tend to become deeply engrossed in novels and movies.

**12. a.** is the answer. Adopted individuals are more susceptible to alcoholism if they had an alcoholic *biological* parent. (p. 200)

**b., c., & d.** Each of these is true, which indicates that susceptibility to alcoholism is at least partially determined by heredity.

**13. d.** is the answer. (pp. 186, 188)

**14. b.** is the answer. Although all people daydream, people with fantasy-prone personalities daydream far more and far more vividly. (p. 172)

**a.** Jane may very well also be suggestible to hypnosis; fantasy-prone personalities tend to be. The stated characteristics, however, do not necessarily indicate that she is.

**c.** The description indicates that Jane's behavior involves much more than simple daydreaming.

**d.** There is no such personality as a "dissociator." Dissociation refers to a split in consciousness that

allows some thoughts and behaviors to occur simultaneously with others.

**15. d.** is the answer. (p. 174)

**a.** REM sleep is characterized by faster, near-waking EEG waves.

**b.** Sleep spindles are typical of Stage 2 sleep.

**c.** Most dreams occur during REM sleep.

**16. a.** is the answer. THC, the active ingredient in marijuana, and its by-products linger in the body for a month or more. (p. 198)

**17. b.** is the answer. (p. 197)

**a.** Approximately 30 to 40 percent of people who have come close to death report some sort of near-death experience.

**c. & d.** The text does not indicate a gender difference in the prevalence of near-death experiences.

**18. c.** is the answer. (p. 189)

**19. d.** is the answer. As answers a., b., & c. (which are true) indicate, it *is* possible to predict whether or not an adolescent will experiment with drugs. (pp. 200–201)

**20. b.** is the answer. (p. 172)

## Essay Question

As a depressant, alcohol slows neural activity and body functions. Although low doses of alcohol may produce relaxation, with larger doses reactions slow, speech slurs, skilled performance deteriorates, and the processing of recent experiences into long-term memories is disrupted. Alcohol also reduces self-awareness and may facilitate sexual and aggressive urges the individual might otherwise resist.

Some people may be biologically vulnerable to alcoholism. This is indicated by the fact that individuals who have an alcoholic biological parent, or males who have an alcoholic identical twin, are more susceptible to alcoholism.

Stress, depression, and the feeling that life is meaningless and without direction are common feelings among heavy users of alcohol and may create a psychological vulnerability to alcoholism.

Especially for teenagers, peer group influence is strong. If an adolescent's friends use alcohol, odds are that he or she will too.

Research suggests three important channels of influence for drug prevention and treatment programs: (1) education about the long-term consequences of alcohol use; (2) efforts to boost people's self-esteem and purpose in life; and (3) attempts to counteract peer pressure that leads to experimentation with drugs.

# Key Terms

### Writing Definitions

1. The text defines **consciousness** as our awareness of ourselves and our environment. (p. 170)

2. **Selective attention** refers to the fact that at any moment our conscious awareness is focused on only a small amount of what we could be experiencing. (p. 170)

3. The **fantasy-prone personality** is one who has a vivid imagination and spends an unusual amount of time fantasizing. (p. 172)

4. A **circadian rhythm** is any cyclical biological rhythm, such as body temperature and sleep-wakefulness. (p. 173)

    *Memory aid*: In Latin, *circa* means "about" and *dies* means "day." A **circadian rhythm** is one that is about a day in duration.

5. **REM sleep** is the sleep stage in which the brain and eyes are active, the muscles are relaxed, and vivid dreaming occurs; also known as paradoxical sleep. (p. 174)

    *Memory aid*: **REM** is an acronym for rapid eye movement, the distinguishing feature of this sleep stage that led to its discovery.

6. **Alpha waves** are the relatively slow brain waves characteristic of an awake, relaxed state. (p. 174)

7. **Hallucinations** are false sensory experiences that occur without any sensory stimulus. (p. 174)

8. **Delta waves** are the larger, slow brain waves associated with deep sleep. (p. 174)

9. **Insomnia** is a sleep disorder in which the person regularly has difficulty in falling or staying asleep. (p. 179)

10. **Narcolepsy** is a sleep disorder in which the victim suffers sudden, uncontrollable sleep attacks, often characterized by entry directly into REM. (p. 179)

11. **Sleep apnea** is a sleep disorder in which the person ceases breathing while asleep, briefly arouses to gasp for air, falls back asleep, and repeats this cycle throughout the night. (p. 179)

12. A person suffering from **night terrors** experiences episodes of high arousal with apparent terror. Night terrors usually occur during Stage 4 sleep. (p. 180)

13. In Freud's theory of dreaming, the **manifest content** is the remembered story line. (p. 181)

14. In Freud's theory of dreaming, the **latent content** is the underlying but censored meaning of a dream. (p. 182)

*Memory aids for 13 and 14: Manifest* means "clearly apparent, obvious"; *latent* means "hidden, concealed." A dream's **manifest content** is that which is obvious; its **latent content** remains hidden until its symbolism is interpreted.

15. The **REM rebound** is the tendency for REM sleep to increase following deprivation. (p. 183)

16. **Hypnosis** is a social interaction in which one person (the hypnotist) suggests to another (the subject) that certain perceptions, feelings, thoughts, or behaviors will spontaneously occur. (pp. 183–184)

17. **Posthypnotic amnesia** is the condition in which, in response to the hypnotist's suggestion, subjects are unable to recall what happened while they were under hypnosis. (p. 184)

18. A **posthypnotic suggestion** is a suggestion made during a hypnosis session that is to be carried out when the subject is no longer hypnotized. (p. 186)

19. **Dissociation** is a split between different levels of consciousness, allowing a person to divide attention between two or more thoughts. (p. 188)

20. According to Hilgard, the **hidden observer** is a part of a hypnotized person's consciousness that remains aware of happenings even under hypnosis. Hilgard believes the hidden observer is an example of dissociation. (p. 188)

21. **Psychoactive drugs**—which include stimulants, depressants, and hallucinogens—are chemical substances that alter mood and perception. They work by affecting or mimicking the activity of neurotransmitters. (p. 191)

22. **Tolerance** is the diminishing of a psychoactive drug's effect that occurs with repeated use and the need for progressively larger doses in order to produce the same effect. (p. 191)

23. **Withdrawal** refers to the discomfort and distress that follow the discontinued use of addictive drugs. (p. 191)

24. **Physical dependence** is a physiological need for a drug that is indicated by the presence of withdrawal symptoms when the drug is not taken. (p. 191)

25. The psychological need to use a drug is referred to as **psychological dependence**. (p. 191)

26. **Depressants** are psychoactive drugs, such as alcohol, opiates, and barbiturates, that reduce neural activity and slow body functions. (p. 193)

27. **Stimulants** are psychoactive drugs, such as caffeine, nicotine, amphetamines, and cocaine, that excite neural activity and speed up body functions. (p. 193)

28. **Hallucinogens** are psychoactive drugs, such as LSD and marijuana, that distort perception and evoke sensory imagery in the absence of sensory input. (p. 193)

29. **Barbiturates** are depressants, sometimes used to induce sleep or reduce anxiety. (p. 194)

30. **Opiates** are depressants derived from the opium poppy, such as opium, morphine, and heroin; they reduce neural activity and relieve pain. Opiates are among the most strongly addictive of all psychoactive drugs. (p. 195)

31. **Amphetamines** are a type of stimulant and, as such, speed up body functions and neural activity. (p. 195)

32. **LSD** (*lysergic acid diethylamide*) is a powerful hallucinogen capable of producing vivid false perceptions and disorganization of thought processes. LSD produces its unpredictable effects partially because it blocks the action of the neurotransmitter serotonin. (p. 197)

33. The **near-death experience** is an altered state of consciousness that has been reported by some people who have had a close brush with death; often similar to drug-induced hallucinations. (p. 197)

34. The active ingredient in marijuana, **THC** is classified as a mild hallucinogen. (p. 198)

*Cross-Check*

| ACROSS | DOWN |
|---|---|
| 1. paradoxical | 2. age regression |
| 7. dopamine | 3. amphetamines |
| 8. nicotine | 4. opiates |
| 10. lucid dreams | 5. information processing |
| 12. LSD | 6. alcohol |
| 13. serial | 9. hidden observer |
| 14. spindle | 11. delta |
| 17. depressant | 15. dissociation |
| 18. hypnogogic | 16. alpha |
| 19. barbiturates | 17. daydream |
| 21. morning | 18. heroin |
| 22. evening | 20. THC |

## FOCUS ON VOCABULARY AND LANGUAGE

*Page 169:* To psychologists, consciousness is similarly a *fundamental* yet *slippery* concept. In science many fundamental concepts are difficult to define (e.g., life, matter, energy). Consciousness is one of the most basic (*fundamental*) ideas in psychology, yet it is an elusive and difficult concept to grasp (*a slippery concept*).

### Waking Consciousness

*Page 169:* Psychology had nearly *lost consciousness.* Myers is using a little humor here in order to illustrate the fact that changes (*swings*) have taken place during psychology's history. To "*lose consciousness*" can have two meanings in the above sentence: (1) to fall unconscious or pass out and (2) to fail to keep (lose) "consciousness" as the subject matter of psychology. Psychology started out as the study of conscious experience; then, because of problems in scientifically investigating the mind, overt behavior replaced consciousness in the 1920s. Finally, in the 1960s, psychology regained consciousness as a legitimate subject for psychologists to study.

*Page 170:* Now, suddenly, *your attentional spotlight shifts* and your *feet feel encased, your nose stubbornly intrudes on the page* before you. **Selective attention** refers to our tendency to focus on only a small part of what is possible for us to experience. If you do attend to more aspects of your experience (*your attentional spotlight shifts*), you will be surprised at the amount of stimulation you process without awareness, such as the feel of the shoes on your feet (*your feet feel encased*) and the fact that your nose actually blocks your line of vision (*your nose stubbornly intrudes on the page*).

*Page 170:* . . . *you may draw a blank* . . . This means that you achieve no result, you don't succeed. When you attend to only one voice among many (*the cocktail party effect*), you may be *unable* to say (*you may draw a blank*) what someone else was saying within hearing range of you.

*Page 171:* . . . yet *conscious awareness* is but *the tip of the information-processing iceberg.* Just as most of the mass or volume of an iceberg is below the surface of the ocean and out of sight, most mental functioning goes on without conscious awareness. Conscious awareness is a small part (*the tip of the iceberg*) of total information processing.

### Sleep and Dreams

*Page 173:* . . . limbs often *move in concert.* . . . To "*move in concert*" is to move simultaneously or in synchrony. When we dream of doing something, our arms and legs do *not* move in synchrony (*do not move in concert*) with the activity in the dream.

Page 173: Awake at 4:00 A.M., with a *depressed body,* we may *fret* over concerns: Does a *lovers' spat* signal a *split?* Our body temperature drops after we go to sleep and begins to rise again towards morning. So if we wake up in the middle of the night our temperature may be low (*depressed body*). We may start to worry (*fret*) over problems. For example, if we've had a minor disagreement or argument with a loved one (*lover's spat*), we may think this means the relationship is going to end (*signals a split*).

Page 173: *Pulling an all-nighter,* we feel *groggiest* about 4:00 A.M., but we feel a *second wind* as our normal wake-up time arrives. If we decide to stay up all night (*pull an all-nighter*), say, to finish a term paper by the deadline, we feel most mentally confused and uncoordinated (*groggiest*) around the middle of the night, but as our usual time for getting up approaches, we begin to feel renewed energy (*a second wind*).

Page 173: . . . *jet lag* . . . When we travel by plane across several time zones we may experience mental and physical fatigue (*jet lag*). Because our biological clocks naturally tend toward a 25-hour day, we may find it easier to jet west, which gives us a longer day, than to travel east.

Page 174: Before long, the machine *went wild,* tracing *deep zigzags* on the graph paper. The discovery of REM (Rapid Eye Movement) occurred accidentally. To see if an EEG (electroencephalograph) was working properly Aserinsky placed the electrodes near his 8-year-old son's eyes. Periodically during the night the machine responded vigorously (*went wild*), producing a pattern of high-frequency waves (*deep zigzags*) on the printout. These patterns were produced by rapid, jerky eye movements and accompanied by very frantic brain activity, and when awakened during one of these periods the boy said he was dreaming.

Page 175: Rather than continuing in deep *slumber,* you *ascend* from your initial *sleep dive.* During a typical night's sleep (*slumber*) you go through a number of distinct stages. If you are awake and relaxed, perhaps with your eyes closed, an EEG would show alpha waves. As you fall deeper and deeper into sleep (*sleep dive*), your brain waves continue to slow down. By Stage 4 your brain waves are long and slow (*delta waves*), but you don't stay here all night; instead, you go back up (*ascend*) through the stages into the most unique and interesting stage of all, REM (Rapid Eye Movement) sleep, where most dreams occur. Here, the brain waves resemble Stage 1 waves, but there is much more internal physiologi-

cal arousal now, and, paradoxically, your muscles are almost paralyzed.

Page 176: As the night *wears on,* variations on this sleep *cycle* repeat themselves about every 90 minutes. As the night progresses (*wears on*), the sleeper's descent and ascent through the stages (*cycles*) from Stage 1 to REM sleep occur about every 90 minutes.

Page 176: . . . *drowsy* . . . If you were deprived of sleep for a few nights, you would feel very tired and sleepy (*drowsy*).

Page 177: People today more than ever suffer from sleep patterns that *thwart* their having an energized feeling of well-being. Because of the pressures of work, school, social obligations, and so on, we often have sleep schedules that prevent (*thwart*) us from getting the amount of sleep we need. The consequence of this "sleep debt" (*accumulated insufficient sleep*) is a general lack of energy and discomfort (*malaise*), and a frequent feeling of sleepiness.

Page 177: Teenagers typically need 8 or 9 hours sleep, but they now average nearly 2 hours less sleep a night than their counterparts of 80 years ago (Holden, 1993; Maas, 1997). Many fill this need by using *home room* for their first *siesta* and after-lunch *study hall* for a *slumber party.* Today's young students often get much less sleep than they need and so, many end up using the classroom set aside for informal activities (*home room*) for a short sleep (*siesta*) and the quiet school area meant for study (*study hall*) may be occupied by whole groups of sleeping students (*slumber party*).

Page 178: These physiological discoveries are only beginning to solve the ongoing *riddle* of sleep. Recent research has shown that sleep helps us repair and restore body tissue (*recuperate*) and plays a part in physical growth. These findings are just starting to clear up the continuing puzzle (*riddle*) of sleep.

Page 178: . . . *deadpanned* . . . When someone says something funny but does not show normal emotional facial expressions, he or she is doing it in a *deadpan* manner (the person typically looks serious).

Page 179: Both [alcohol and sleeping pills] reduce REM sleep and can leave a person with *next-day blahs.* The most popular fast remedies (*quick fixes*) for insomnia are sleeping pills and alcohol. Unfortunately, they can make the problem worse (*aggravate it*) by suppressing REM sleep; the next day the person may have less energy and feel very tired (*next-day blahs*). When these "remedies" are discontinued, the insomnia may get worse.

*Page 179:* As a traffic menace, *"snoozing is second only to boozing,"* says the American Sleep Disorders Association, and those with narcolepsy are especially at risk (Aldrich, 1989). Falling asleep (*snoozing*) while driving is almost as serious a problem as drinking (*boozing*) and driving. People with **narcolepsy** suffer from occasional periods of uncontrollable sleepiness often associated with emotional arousal, and are thus in danger, and dangerous, while driving.

*Pages 181–182:* . . . He [Freud] argued that by fulfilling wishes, a dream provides a *psychic safety valve* that discharges otherwise unacceptable feelings. The story line of the dream (**manifest content**) is a disguised version of the real, but hidden, meaning of the dream (**latent content**). According to Freud, by symbolically expressing our hidden desires and exotic wishes, dreams allow us to ventilate unconscious drives that might otherwise be harmful (*acts as a psychic safety valve*). (A *safety valve* allows a system to dissipate built-up pressure and thus may prevent an explosion.) Most contemporary psychologists believe that REM sleep and dreams are important aspects of our life but very few support Freud's theory of dream interpretation.

*Page 182:* Given these visual scenes, our *cognitive machinery*, influenced by age, gender, and current concerns, *weaves a story line*. The mind (*cognitive machinery*) reacts to meaningless stimuli by imposing meaning (*it weaves a story line*). Bursts of neural activity in the visual cortex, along with activity in the emotional limbic system, occur at the same time as rapid eye movements, and so it may be that dreams arise from the mind's ceaseless attempts to make sense of these unrelated events (*it weaves a story line*).

## Hypnosis

*Page 185:* "Hypnosis is not a psychological *truth serum*," concludes researcher Kenneth Bowers (1987), "and to regard it as such has been a source of considerable *mischief*." Research shows that hypnotists can subtly influence what people recall and they may inadvertently create false memories by making suggestions and asking leading questions. Thus, hypnosis is not like a so-called *truth serum* (a drug alleged to make people tell the truth) but rather has caused a great deal of annoying—and possibly harmful—effects (*considerable mischief*).

*Page 190:* So, might the two views—social influence and divided consciousness—*be bridged?* Although there are a number of different explanations about what hypnosis really is, Myers suggests that it may

be possible to bring together some of these theories (*bridge the differences*). Thus, hypnosis may be both a part of normal aspects of social influence and our ability to have a divided (*or split*) consciousness.

## Drugs and Consciousness

*Page 191:* A person who rarely drinks alcohol might get *tipsy* on one can of beer, but an experienced drinker may not get *tipsy* until the *second six-pack*. Prolonged use of a psychoactive drug produces an ability to take more and more of the substance (*tolerance*). Thus, an infrequent user of alcohol may get somewhat intoxicated (*tipsy*) from one beer, but for a regular drinker there might be little effect until 6 or more beers have been consumed (*until the second six-pack [of beer]*).

*Page 193:* . . . as when restaurant patrons *tip more* when *tipsy*. Alcohol can increase both harmful and helpful inclinations. Thus, it often happens that restaurant clientele give a larger gratuity (*tip more*) when they are more intoxicated (*tipsy*). Whatever tendencies you have when sober will be more obvious when you are drunk.

*Page 194:* If, as commonly believed, liquor is the *quicker pick-her-upper*, the effect lies in that powerful sex organ, the mind. Alcohol (liquor) is thought by many to speed up the process of meeting members of the opposite sex and to lower sexual inhibitions. Thus, a male may believe that use of alcohol will facilitate his ability to initiate contact and get to know a female (a *quicker pick-her-upper*). Myers points out that not only alcohol is involved, but also our beliefs about its effects on sexual behavior (the effect lies partly in that *powerful sex organ, the mind*).

*Page 195:* But for pleasure *one pays a price*, which for the heroin user is the *gnawing craving* for another *fix* . . . . There is a cost (*one pays a price*) for enjoying drug-induced pleasures, and for an addict this may be a persistent inner torment (*gnawing*) and an urgent, persistent desire (*craving*) for another dose of the drug (a *fix*).

*Page 195:* Of the millions of people who try to *lick their addiction* each year, only 8 percent succeed. . . . Many people who are psychologically and/or physically dependent upon (*addicted to*) such substances as nicotine attempt to stop using the drug (*lick their addictions*). It is very difficult to cease smoking completely (*to quit or break the habit*) because nicotine withdrawal is an aversive (unpleasant) state, which is easily alleviated by smoking a cigarette.

*Page 196:* . . . *crack* . . . *Crack* is a very potent, synthetic form of cocaine which produces a feeling of euphoria (*a rush*) followed by deep depression, tiredness, and irritability (*a "crash"*).

*Page 197:* . . . *"acid trip"* . . . Taking any psychoactive drug is called a *trip* or *tripping out*. When LSD (acid) is used, it is called an *acid trip*; regular users are sometimes called *acid-heads*.

*Page 198:* . . . marijuana may *spell* relief. Although there are many reasons for not taking marijuana, it does have some therapeutic applications, such as alleviating the sick feelings that result from taking the drugs used to treat cancer (chemotherapy). Thus, it may provide (*spell*) relief for some patients.

*Page 198:* Clearly, being *stoned* is not conducive to learning. Marijuana use disrupts motor skills, perceptual abilities, memory formation, and short-term retention. Obviously, being under the influence of marijuana (*being stoned*) does not help memory and learning.

# CHAPTER 6

## Learning

### Chapter Overview

"No topic is closer to the heart of psychology than learning, a relatively permanent change in an organism's behavior due to experience." Chapter 6 covers the basic principles of three forms of learning: classical conditioning (or respondent conditioning), in which we learn associations between events; operant conditioning, in which we learn to engage in behaviors that are rewarded and to avoid behaviors that are punished; and observational learning, in which we learn by observing and imitating others.

The chapter also covers several important issues, including the generality of principles of learning, the role of cognitive processes in learning, and the ways in which learning is constrained by the biological predispositions of different species.

NOTE: Answer guidelines for all Chapter 6 questions begin on page 175.

### Guided Study

The text chapter should be studied one section at a time. Before you read, preview each section by skimming it, noting headings and boldface items. Then read the appropriate section objectives from the following outline. Keep these objectives in mind and, as you read the chapter section, search for the information that will enable you to meet each objective. Once you have finished a section, write out answers for its objectives.

1. Discuss the importance of experience in learning and describe the role of association in learning.

### Classical Conditioning (pp. 207–215)

David Myers at times uses idioms that are unfamiliar to some readers. If you do not know the meaning of any of the following words, phrases, or expressions in the context in which they appear in the text, refer to pages 184–185 for an explanation (note that some items appear in the chapter introduction): . . . *breeds hope; mugged; Japanese rancher reportedly herds cattle; For many people, the name Ivan Pavlov rings a bell; drooled; sets your mouth to watering; red-light district; breaking up . . . fire-breathing heartthrob; we stand on his shoulders; crack cocaine users; legendary significance.*

2. Describe the nature of classical conditioning and show how it demonstrates associative learning.

3. Explain the processes of acquisition, extinction, spontaneous recovery, generalization, and discrimination.

4. Discuss the importance of cognitive processes and biological constraints in classical conditioning.

5. Discuss the importance of Pavlov's work in classical conditioning and explain how Pavlov paved the way for the behaviorist position.

### Operant Conditioning (pp. 216–225)

> If you do not know the meaning of any of the following words, phrases, or expressions in the context in which they appear in the text, refer to pages 185–187 for an explanation: *to pull habits out of a rat; . . . between Bach's music and Stravinsky's; pastes gold stars; snooze button; Billy throws a tantrum; goofing off; the kick that often comes within seconds; a sale with every pitch; paid on a piecework basis; fly casters; a choppy stop-start pattern; pop quiz; loses a treat; drawbacks; hit with a couple of speeding tickets; piggy bank; stirred a hornet's nest.*

6. Describe the process of operant conditioning, including the procedure of shaping.

7. Identify the different types of reinforcers and describe the four major schedules of partial reinforcement.

8. Discuss the effects of punishment on behavior.

9. Discuss evidence of the importance of cognitive and biological processes in operant conditioning.

10. Describe some major applications of operant conditioning.

### Learning by Observation (pp. 226–228)

> If you do not know the meaning of the following phrases in the context in which they appear in the text, refer to page 187 for an explanation: *children who observed the aggressive outburst were much more likely to lash out at the doll.*

11. Describe the process of observational learning.

## Chapter Review

When you have finished reading the chapter, work through the material that follows to review it. Complete the sentences and answer the questions. As you proceed, evaluate your performance for each section by consulting the answers on page 177. Do not continue with the next section until you understand each answer. If you need to, review or reread the appropriate section in the textbook before continuing.

1.  A relatively permanent change in an organism's behavior due to experience is called _____learning_____ .

2.  During the seventeenth century, philosophers such as John Locke and David Hume argued that an important factor in learning is our tendency to _associate_ events that occur in a sequence. Even simple animals, such as the sea snail *Aplysia*, can learn simple _associations_ between stimuli. This type of learning is called _associative learning_ .

3.  The type of learning in which the organism learns to associate two stimuli is _Classical_ conditioning.

4.  The tendency of organisms to associate a response and its consequence forms the basis of _____ conditioning.

5.  Complex animals often learn behaviors merely by _____ others perform them.

### Classical Conditioning (pp. 207–215)

6.  Classical conditioning was first explored by the Russian physiologist _Ivan pavlov_ .

7.  In Pavlov's classic experiment, a tone, or

    _____ ,

    is sounded just before food, the

    _____ ,

    is placed in the animal's mouth.

8.  An animal will salivate when food is placed in its mouth. This salivation is called the _unconditional response_ .

9.  Eventually, the dogs in Pavlov's experiment would salivate on hearing the tone. This salivation is called the _CR_

_____ .

10. The initial learning of a conditioned response is called _____ . For many conditioning situations, the optimal interval between a neutral stimulus and the UCS is

_____ .

Explain why learning theorists consider classically conditioned behaviors to be biologically adaptive.

11. When the UCS is presented prior to a neutral stimulus, conditioning _____ (does/does not) occur.

12. If a CS is repeatedly presented without the UCS, _____ soon occurs; that is, the CR diminishes.

13. Following a rest, however, the CR reappears in response to the CS; this phenomenon is called

_____ .

14. Subjects often respond to a similar stimulus as they would to the original CS. This phenomenon is called _____ . Subjects can, however, also be trained not to respond to these similar stimuli. This learned ability is called

_____ .

15. Experiments by Rescorla and Wagner demonstrate that a CS must reliably _____ the UCS for an association to develop and, more generally, that _____ processes play a role in conditioning. It is as if the animal learns to _____ that the UCS will occur.

Describe two issues that have led to the rejection of Pavlov's disdain for "mentalistic" concepts.

16. The importance of cognitive processes in human conditioning is demonstrated by the failure of classical conditioning as a treatment for

_____ .

17. Garcia discovered that rats would associate _____ with taste but not with other stimuli. Garcia found that taste-aversion conditioning _____ (would/would not) occur when the delay between the CS and the UCS was more than an hour.

18. Results such as these demonstrate that the principles of learning are constrained by the _____ predispositions of each animal species and that they help each species _____ to its environment.

Explain why the study of classical conditioning is important.

19. Early in this century, psychologist _____ urged psychologists to discard references to mental concepts in favor of studying observable behavior. This view, called _____ , influenced American psychology during the first half of the century.

Describe the Watson and Rayner experiment.

*Operant Conditioning* (pp. 216–225)

20. Classical conditioning associates _____ stimuli with stimuli that elicit responses that are often _____ .

21. The reflexive responses of classical conditioning involve _____ behavior. In contrast, behavior that is more spontaneous and that is influenced by its consequences is called _____ behavior.

22. Using Thorndike's _____ _____ as a starting point, Skinner developed a behavioral technology. He designed an apparatus, called the _____ _____ , to investigate learning in animals.

23. The procedure in which a person teaches an animal to perform an intricate behavior by building up to it in small steps is called _____ . This method involves reinforcing successive _____ of the desired behavior.

24. An event that increases the frequency of a preceding response is a _____ .

25. A stimulus that strengthens a response by presenting a stimulus after a response is a _____ .

26. A stimulus that strengthens a response by reducing or removing an aversive (unpleasant) stimulus is a _____ .

27. Reinforcers, such as food and shock, that are related to basic needs and therefore do not rely on learning are called _____ . Reinforcers that must be conditioned and therefore derive their power through association are called _____ .

28. Children who are able to delay gratification tend to become _____ (more/less) socially competent and high achieving.

29. Immediate reinforcement _____ (is/is not) more effective than its alternative, _____ reinforcement.

30. The procedure involving reinforcement of each and every response is called

    _____ _____ .

    Under these conditions, learning is _____ (rapid/slow). When this type of reinforcement is discontinued, extinction is _____ (rapid/slow).

31. The procedure in which responses are only intermittently reinforced is called _____ reinforcement. Under these conditions, learning is generally _____ (faster/slower) than it is with continuous reinforcement. Behavior reinforced in this manner is _____ (very/not very) resistant to extinction.

32. When behavior is reinforced after a set number of responses, a _____ - _____ schedule is in effect.

33. Three-year-old Yusef knows that if he cries when he wants a treat, his mother will sometimes give in. When, as in this case, reinforcement occurs after an unpredictable number of responses, a

    _____ - _____

    schedule is being used.

34. Reinforcement of the first response after a set interval of time defines the

    _____ - _____

    schedule. An example of this schedule is

    _____ .

35. When the first response after varying amounts of time is reinforced, a _____ - _____ schedule is in effect.

Describe the typical patterns of response under fixed-interval, fixed-ratio, variable-interval, and variable-ratio schedules of reinforcement.

36. An aversive consequence that decreases the likelihood of the behavior that preceded it is called

    _____ .

Describe some drawbacks to the use of punishment.

37. Skinner and other behaviorists resisted the growing belief that expectations, perceptions, and other _____ processes have a valid place in the science of psychology.

38. When a well-learned route in a maze is blocked, rats sometimes choose an alternative route, acting as if they were consulting a

    _____ _____ .

39. Animals may learn from experience even when reinforcement is not available. When learning is not apparent until reinforcement has been provided, _____

    _____ is said to have occurred.

40. Operant conditioning _____ (is/is not) constrained by an animal's biological predispositions.

41. The use of teaching machines and programmed textbooks was an early application of the operant conditioning procedure of

    _____ to education. Online

    _____ systems and

    _____ software are newer examples of this application of operant principles.

42. In boosting productivity in the workplace, positive reinforcement is _____ (more/less) effective when applied to specific behaviors than when given to reward general merit and when the desired performance is

    _____ . For such behaviors, immediate reinforcement is _____ (more/no more) effective than delayed reinforcement.

*Learning by Observation* (pp. 226–228)

43. Learning by imitation is called

_____ , or _____

_____ . The psychologist best

known for research in this area is

_____ .

44. In one experiment, the child who viewed an adult
punch an inflatable doll played

_____ (more/less) aggressively

than the child who had not observed the adult.

45. Children will also model positive, or

_____ , behaviors.

46. Models are most effective when their words and

actions are _____ and when

they are perceived as _____ , as

_____ , or as

_____ .

# Progress Test 1

## Multiple-Choice Questions

Circle your answers to the following questions and
check them with the answers on page 178. If your
answer is incorrect, read the explanation for why it is
incorrect and then consult the appropriate pages of
the text (in parentheses following the correct answer).

1. Learning is best defined as:
   a. any behavior emitted by an organism without
   being elicited.
   b. a change in the behavior of an organism.
   c. a relatively permanent change in the behavior
   of an organism due to experience.
   d. behavior based on operant rather than respondent conditioning.

2. The type of learning associated with Skinner is:
   a. classical conditioning.
   b. operant conditioning.
   c. respondent conditioning.
   d. observational learning.

3. In Pavlov's original experiment with dogs, the
   meat served as a(n):
   a. CS.          c. UCS.
   b. CR.          d. UCR.

4. In Pavlov's original experiment with dogs, the
   tone was initially a(n) _____ stimulus;
   after it was paired with meat, it became a(n)
   _____ stimulus.
   a. conditioned; neutral
   b. neutral; conditioned
   c. conditioned; unconditioned
   d. unconditioned; conditioned

5. In order to obtain a reward a monkey learns to
   press a lever when a 1000-Hz tone is on but not
   when a 1200-Hz tone is on. What kind of training
   is this?
   a. extinction
   b. generalization
   c. classical conditioning
   d. spontaneous recovery
   e. discrimination

6. Which of the following statements concerning
   reinforcement is correct?
   a. Learning is most rapid with partial reinforcement, but continuous reinforcement produces
   the greatest resistance to extinction.
   b. Learning is most rapid with continuous reinforcement, but partial reinforcement produces
   the greatest resistance to extinction.
   c. Learning is fastest and resistance to extinction
   is greatest after continuous reinforcement.
   d. Learning is fastest and resistance to extinction
   is greatest following partial reinforcement.

7. Cognitive processes are:
   a. unimportant in classical and operant conditioning.
   b. important in both classical and operant conditioning.
   c. more important in classical than in operant
   conditioning.
   d. more important in operant than in classical
   conditioning.

8. The highest and most consistent rate of response
   is produced by a _____ schedule.
   a. fixed-ratio          c. fixed-interval
   b. variable-ratio       d. variable-interval

9. A response that leads to the removal of an
   unpleasant stimulus is one being:
   a. positively reinforced.
   b. negatively reinforced.
   c. punished.
   d. extinguished.

10. When a conditioned stimulus is presented without an accompanying unconditioned stimulus, _____ will soon take place.
    a. generalization
    b. discrimination
    c. extinction
    d. aversion
    e. spontaneous recovery

11. One difference between classical and operant conditioning is that:
    a. in classical conditioning the responses operate on the environment to produce rewarding or punishing stimuli.
    b. in operant conditioning the responses are triggered by preceding stimuli.
    c. in classical conditioning the responses are automatically elicited by stimuli.
    d. in operant conditioning the responses are reflexive.

12. In Garcia and Koelling's studies of taste-aversion learning, rats learned to associate:
    a. taste with electric shock.
    b. sights and sounds with sickness.
    c. taste with sickness.
    d. taste and sounds with electric shock.
    e. taste and sounds with electric shock, then sickness.

13. In Pavlov's original experiment with dogs, salivation to meat was the:
    a. CS.
    b. CR.
    c. UCS.
    d. UCR.

14. Learning by imitating others' behaviors is called _____ learning. The researcher best known for studying this type of learning is _____.
    a. secondary; Skinner
    b. observational; Bandura
    c. secondary; Pavlov
    d. observational; Watson

15. B. F. Skinner's critics argued that he dehumanized people by neglecting their:
    a. biological predispositions.
    b. personal freedom.
    c. cultural heritage.
    d. enduring personality traits.

16. Punishment is a controversial way of controlling behavior because:
    a. behavior is not forgotten and may return.
    b. punishing stimuli often create fear.
    c. punishment often increases aggressiveness.
    d. of all of the above reasons.

17. Classical conditioning experiments by Rescorla and Wagner demonstrate that an important factor in conditioning is:
    a. the subject's age.
    b. the strength of the stimuli.
    c. the predictability of an association.
    d. the similarity of stimuli.
    e. all of the above.

18. Which of the following is an example of reinforcement?
    a. presenting a positive stimulus after a response
    b. removing an unpleasant stimulus after a response
    c. being told that you have done a good job
    d. All of the above are examples.

19. Which of the following is a form of associative learning?
    a. classical conditioning
    b. operant conditioning
    c. observational learning
    d. all of the above

20. For the most rapid conditioning, a CS should be presented:
    a. about 1 second after the UCS.
    b. about one-half second before the UCS.
    c. about 15 seconds before the UCS.
    d. at the same time as the UCS.

## Matching Items

Match each definition or description with the appropriate term.

### Definitions or Descriptions

_e_  1. presentation of a desired stimulus
_h_  2. tendency for similar stimuli to evoke a CR
_F_  3. removal of an aversive stimulus
_g_  4. an innately reinforcing stimulus
_i_  5. an acquired reinforcer
_K_  6. responses are reinforced after an unpredictable amount of time
_J_  7. each and every response is reinforced
_a_  8. reinforcing closer and closer approximations of a behavior
_c_  9. the reappearance of a weakened CR
_b_ 10. presentation of an aversive stimulus
_d_ 11. learning that becomes apparent only after reinforcement is provided

### Terms

a. shaping
b. punishment
c. spontaneous recovery
d. latent learning
e. positive reinforcement
f. negative reinforcement
g. primary reinforcer
h. generalization
i. secondary reinforcer
j. continuous reinforcement
k. variable-interval schedule

## Progress Test 2

Progress Test 2 should be completed during a final chapter review. Answer the following questions after you thoroughly understand the correct answers for the Chapter Review and Progress Test 1.

### Multiple-Choice Questions

1. During extinction, the _____ is omitted; as a result, the _____ seems to disappear.
   a. UCS; UCR
   b. CS; CR
   c. UCS; CR
   d. CS; UCR

2. In Watson and Rayner's experiment, the loud noise was the _____ and the white rat was the _____ .
   a. CS; CR
   b. UCS; CS
   c. CS; UCS
   d. UCS; CR
   e. UCR; CR

3. In which of the following may classical conditioning play a role?
   a. emotional problems
   b. the body's immune response
   c. how animals adapt to the environment
   d. helping drug addicts
   e. all of the above

4. Shaping is a(n) _____ technique for _____ a behavior.
   a. operant; establishing
   b. operant; suppressing
   c. respondent; establishing
   d. respondent; suppressing

5. In Pavlov's studies of classical conditioning of a dog's salivary responses, spontaneous recovery occurred:
   a. during acquisition, when the CS was first paired with the UCS.
   b. during extinction, when the CS was first presented by itself.
   c. when the CS was reintroduced following extinction of the CR and a rest period.
   d. during discrimination training, when several conditioned stimuli were introduced.

6. For operant conditioning to be effective, when should the reinforcers be presented in relation to the desired response?
   a. immediately before
   b. immediately after
   c. at the same time as
   d. at least a half hour before
   e. in any of the above sequences

7. In distinguishing between negative reinforcers and punishment, we note that:
   a. punishment, but not negative reinforcement, involves use of an aversive stimulus.
   b. in contrast to punishment, negative reinforcement decreases the likelihood of a response by the presentation of an aversive stimulus.
   c. in contrast to punishment, negative reinforcement increases the likelihood of a response by the presentation of an aversive stimulus.
   d. in contrast to punishment, negative reinforcement increases the likelihood of a response by the termination of an aversive stimulus.

8. The "piecework," or commission, method of payment is an example of which reinforcement schedule?
   a. fixed-interval     c. fixed-ratio
   b. variable-interval  d. variable-ratio

9. Putting on your coat when it is cold outside is a behavior that is maintained by:
   a. discrimination learning.
   b. punishment.
   c. negative reinforcement.
   d. classical conditioning.
   e. positive reinforcement.

10. On a partial reinforcement schedule, reinforcement is given:
    a. in very small amounts.
    b. randomly.
    c. for successive approximations of a desired behavior.
    d. only some of the time.

11. You teach your dog to fetch the paper by giving him a cookie each time he does so. This is an example of:
    a. operant conditioning.
    b. classical conditioning.
    c. secondary reinforcement.
    d. partial reinforcement.

12. To be effective in promoting observational learning, models should be:
    a. perceived as similar to the observers.
    b. respected and admired.
    c. consistent in their actions and words.
    d. successful.
    e. any of the above.

13. A cognitive map is a(n):
    a. mental representation of one's environment.
    b. sequence of thought processes leading from one idea to another.

c. set of instructions detailing the most effective means of teaching a particular concept.
d. biological predisposition to learn a particular skill.
e. educational tool based on operant conditioning techniques.

14. After exploring a complicated maze for several days, a rat subsequently ran the maze with very few errors when food was placed in the goal box for the first time. This performance illustrates:
    a. classical conditioning.
    b. discrimination learning.
    c. observational learning.
    d. latent learning.

15. Leon's psychology instructor has scheduled an exam every third week of the term. Leon will probably study the most just before an exam and the least just after an exam. This is because the schedule of exams is reinforcing studying according to which schedule?
    a. fixed-ratio        c. fixed-interval
    b. variable-ratio     d. variable-interval

16. Operant conditioning is to _____ as classical conditioning is to _____ .
    a. Pavlov; Watson     c. Pavlov; Skinner
    b. Skinner; Bandura   d. Skinner; Pavlov

17. Teaching machines, software tutorial programs, and textbooks are applications of the operant conditioning principles of:
    a. shaping and immediate reinforcement.
    b. immediate reinforcement and punishment.
    c. shaping and primary reinforcement.
    d. continuous reinforcement and punishment.

18. Fishing is reinforced according to which schedule?
    a. fixed-interval     c. variable-interval
    b. fixed-ratio        d. variable-ratio

19. Which of the following is the best example of a secondary reinforcer?
    a. putting on a coat on a cold day
    b. relief from pain after the dentist stops drilling your teeth
    c. receiving a cool drink after washing your mother's car on a hot day
    d. receiving an approving nod from the boss for a job well done
    e. having a big meal after going without food all day

**20.** Experiments on taste-aversion learning demonstrate that:

    **a.** for the conditioning of certain stimuli, the UCS need not immediately follow the CS.

    **b.** any perceivable stimulus can become a CS.

    **c.** all animals are biologically primed to associate illness with the taste of a tainted food.

    **d.** all of the above are true.

*True-False Items*

Indicate whether each statement is true or false by placing *T* or *F* in the blank next to the item.

___F___ **1.** Operant conditioning involves behavior that is primarily reflexive.

___F___ **2.** The optimal interval between CS and UCS is about 15 seconds.

_____ **3.** Negative reinforcement decreases the likelihood that a response will recur.

_____ **4.** The learning of a new behavior proceeds most rapidly with continuous reinforcement.

_____ **5.** As a rule, variable schedules of reinforcement produce more consistent rates of responding than fixed schedules.

_____ **6.** Cognitive processes are of relatively little importance in learning.

_____ **7.** Although punishment may be effective in suppressing behavior, it can have several undesirable side effects.

___F___ **8.** All animals, including rats and birds, are biologically predisposed to associate taste cues with sickness.

_____ **9.** Whether the CS or UCS is presented first seems not to matter in terms of the ease of classical conditioning.

___T___ **10.** Spontaneous recovery refers to the tendency of extinguished behaviors to reappear suddenly.

# Thinking Critically About Chapter 6

Answer these questions the day before an exam as a final check on your understanding of the chapter's terms and concepts.

*Multiple-Choice Questions*

**1.** You always rattle the box of dog biscuits before giving your dog a treat. As you do so, your dog salivates. Rattling the box is a(n) _____CS_____ ; your dog's salivation is a(n) _____UCR_____

    **a.** CS; CR       **c.** UCS; CR

    **b.** CS; UCR     **d.** UCS; UCR

**2.** You are expecting an important letter in the mail. As the regular delivery time approaches, you glance more and more frequently out the window, searching for the letter carrier. Your behavior in this situation typifies that associated with which schedule of reinforcement?

    **a.** fixed-ratio       **c.** fixed-interval

    **b.** variable-ratio    **d.** variable-interval

**3.** Jack finally takes out the garbage in order to get his father to stop pestering him. Jack's behavior is being influenced by:

    **a.** positive reinforcement.

    **b.** negative reinforcement.

    **c.** a primary reinforcer.

    **d.** punishment.

**4.** Mrs. Ramirez often tells her children that it is important to buckle their seat belts while riding in the car, but she rarely does so herself. Her children will probably learn to:

    **a.** use their seat belts and tell others it is important to do so.

    **b.** use their seat belts but not tell others it is important to do so.

    **c.** tell others it is important to use seat belts but rarely use them themselves.

    **d.** neither tell others that seat belts are important nor use them.

**5.** A pigeon can easily be taught to flap its wings in order to avoid shock but not for food reinforcement. According to the text, this is most likely so because:

    **a.** pigeons are biologically predisposed to flap their wings in order to escape aversive events and to use their beaks to obtain food.

    **b.** shock is a more motivating stimulus for birds than food is.

    **c.** hungry animals have difficulty delaying their eating long enough to learn *any* new skill.

    **d.** of all the above reasons.

**6.** From a casino owner's viewpoint, which of the following jackpot-payout schedules would be the most desirable for reinforcing customer use of a slot machine?

    **a.** variable-ratio schedule

    **b.** fixed-ratio schedule

    **c.** variable-interval schedule

    **d.** fixed-interval schedule

7. After discovering that her usual route home was closed due to road repairs, Sharetta used her knowledge of the city and sense of direction to find an alternate route. This is an example of:
   a. latent learning.
   b. observational learning.
   c. shaping.
   d. using a cognitive map.
   e. discrimination.

For questions 8 to 11, use the following information. As a child, you were playing in the yard one day when a neighbor's cat wandered over. Your mother (who has a terrible fear of animals) screamed and snatched you into her arms. Her behavior caused you to cry. You now have a fear of cats.

8. Identify the CS.
   a. your mother's behavior    c. the cat
   b. your crying               d. your fear today

9. Identify the UCS.
   a. your mother's behavior    c. the cat
   b. your crying               d. your fear today

10. Identify the CR.
   a. your mother's behavior    c. the cat
   b. your crying               d. your fear today

11. Identify the UCR.
   a. your mother's behavior    c. the cat
   b. your crying               d. your fear today

12. The manager of a manufacturing plant wishes to use positive reinforcement to increase the productivity of workers. Which of the following procedures would probably be the most effective?
   a. Deserving employees are given a general merit bonus at the end of each fiscal year.
   b. A productivity goal that seems attainable, yet is unrealistic, is set for each employee.
   c. Employees are given immediate bonuses for specific behaviors related to productivity.
   d. Employees who fail to meet standards of productivity receive pay cuts.

13. Three-year-old Ingrid often throws a temper tantrum when she doesn't get her way. Parent training experts would recommend that her parents should:
   a. give Ingrid attention when she is behaving well.
   b. scold their child when she misbehaves.
   c. concede to their daughter's demands but only if she quiets down.
   d. do all of the above.

14. Bill once had a blue car that was in the shop more than it was out. Since then he will not even consider owning blue- or green-colored cars. Bill's aversion to green cars is an example of:
   a. discrimination.
   b. generalization.
   c. latent learning.
   d. extinction.

15. After watching coverage of the Olympics on television recently, Lynn and Susan have been staging their own "summer games." Which of the following best accounts for their behavior?
   a. classical conditioning    d. shaping
   b. observational learning    e. discrimination
   c. latent learning

16. Two groups of rats receive classical conditioning trials in which a tone and electric shock are presented. For Group 1 the electric shock always follows the tone. For Group 2 the tone and shock occur randomly. Which of the following is likely to result?
   a. The tone will become a CS for Group 1 but not for Group 2.
   b. The tone will become a CS for Group 2 but not for Group 1.
   c. The tone will become a CS for both groups.
   d. The tone will not become a CS for either group.

17. Last evening May-ling ate her first cheeseburger and french fries at an American fast-food restaurant. A few hours later she became ill. It can be expected that:
   a. May-ling will develop an aversion to the sight of a cheeseburger and french fries.
   b. May-ling will develop an aversion to the taste of a cheeseburger and french fries.
   c. May-ling will not associate her illness with the food she ate.
   d. May-ling will associate her sickness with something she experienced immediately before she became ill.

18. Reggie's mother tells him that he can watch TV after he cleans his room. Evidently, Reggie's mother is attempting to use _____ to increase room cleaning.
   a. operant conditioning
   b. secondary reinforcement
   c. positive reinforcement
   d. all of the above

19. Which of the following is an example of shaping?
   a. A dog learns to salivate at the sight of a box of dog biscuits.
   b. A new driver learns to stop at an intersection when the light changes to red.
   c. A parrot is rewarded first for making any sound, then for making a sound similar to "Laura," and then for "speaking" its owner's name.
   d. A psychology student reinforces a laboratory rat only occasionally to make its behavior more resistant to extinction.

20. Lars, a shoe salesman, is paid every two weeks, whereas Tom receives a commission for each pair of shoes he sells. Evidently, Lars is paid on a _____ schedule of reinforcement, and Tom on a _____ schedule of reinforcement.
   a. fixed-ratio; fixed-interval
   b. continuous; intermittent
   c. fixed-interval; fixed-ratio
   d. variable-interval; variable-ratio
   e. variable-ratio; variable-interval

### Essay Question

Describe the best way for a pet owner to condition her dog to roll over. (Use the space below to list the points you want to make, and organize them. Then write the essay on a separate piece of paper.)

## Key Terms

### Writing Definitions

Using your own words, on a piece of paper write a brief definition or explanation of each of the following terms.

1. learning
2. associative learning
3. classical conditioning
4. unconditioned response (UCR)
5. unconditioned stimulus (UCS)
6. conditioned response (CR)
7. conditioned stimulus (CS)
8. acquisition
9. extinction
10. spontaneous recovery
11. generalization
12. discrimination
13. behaviorism
14. operant conditioning
15. respondent behavior
16. operant behavior
17. law of effect
18. Skinner box
19. shaping
20. reinforcer
21. primary reinforcers
22. secondary reinforcers
23. continuous reinforcement
24. partial reinforcement
25. fixed-ratio schedule
26. variable-ratio schedule
27. fixed-interval schedule
28. variable-interval schedule
29. punishment
30. cognitive map
31. latent learning
32. observational learning
33. modeling
34. prosocial behavior

## Summing Up

Complete the following flow charts.

**CLASSICAL CONDITIONING**

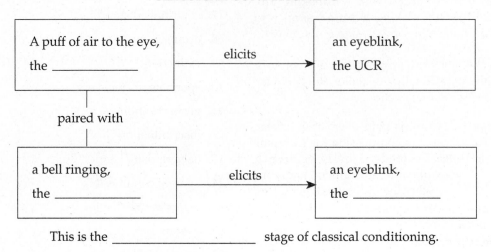

A puff of air to the eye,
the _____    →   elicits   →   an eyeblink,
the UCR

paired with

a bell ringing,
the _____   →   elicits   →   an eyeblink,
the _____

This is the _____ stage of classical conditioning.

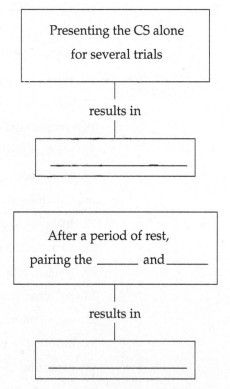

Presenting the CS alone
for several trials

results in

_____

After a period of rest,
pairing the _____ and _____

results in

_____

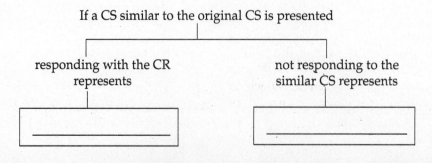

If a CS similar to the original CS is presented

responding with the CR
represents

not responding to the
similar CS represents

_____            _____

**OPERANT CONDITIONING**

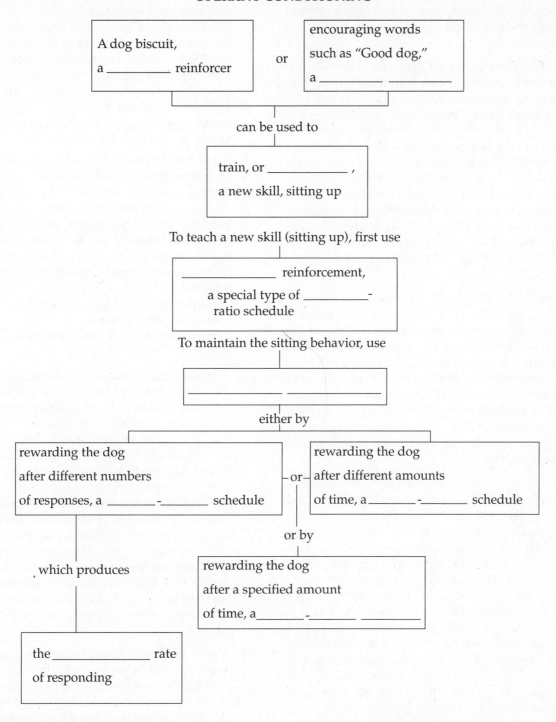

A dog biscuit,

a _____ reinforcer

or

encouraging words such as "Good dog,"

a _____ _____

can be used to

train, or _____ ,

a new skill, sitting up

To teach a new skill (sitting up), first use

_____ reinforcement,

a special type of _____-ratio schedule

To maintain the sitting behavior, use

_____ _____

either by

rewarding the dog after different numbers of responses, a _____-_____ schedule

or

rewarding the dog after different amounts of time, a _____-_____ schedule

which produces

or by

rewarding the dog after a specified amount of time, a _____-_____ _____

the _____ rate of responding

# ANSWERS

## Guided Study

The following guidelines provide the main points that your answers should have touched upon.

1. Experience is the key to learning, which is defined as a relatively permanent change in an organism's behavior due to experience. This ability to learn from experience is the foundation for adaptability—the capacity to learn new behaviors that enable humans and animals to cope with ever-changing circumstances.

As such philosophers as Aristotle, Locke, and Hume noted, our minds naturally link together events that we have experienced. This is the basis for associative learning, in which two stimuli (as in classical conditioning) or a response and a rewarding or punishing stimulus (as in operant conditioning) become linked because of their co-occurrence.

2. In associative learning, organisms learn that certain events occur together. Through classical conditioning, organisms learn to anticipate and prepare for significant events, such as the delivery of food or a painful stimulus. In other words, they learn to associate two events. Classical conditioning occurs when a neutral stimulus becomes associated with an unconditioned stimulus (UCS). By itself, the UCS will automatically trigger a reflexive, unconditioned response (UCR). If the association between the CS and UCS is predictable, conditioning will occur and the CS alone will eventually elicit a conditioned response (CR) similar to the UCR.

3. Acquisition refers to the initial stage of learning, during which the CR is established and gradually strengthened. Extinction refers to the diminishing of a CR when the CS is repeatedly presented without a UCS. Spontaneous recovery refers to the reappearance, after a period of rest, of a weakened CR. Generalization is the tendency for stimuli similar to the CS to elicit a CR. Discrimination is the ability to distinguish between an actual CS and similar stimuli that have not been associated with the UCS.

4. Pavlov and other early researchers underestimated the importance of cognitive processes and biological constraints on learning.

   Research by Rescorla and Wagner demonstrated that classical conditioning occurs best when the association between a CS and UCS is predictable. This indicates that subjects develop a cognitive expectancy, or an awareness of how likely it is that the UCS will follow the CS.

   Garcia and Koelling's studies of conditioned taste aversion demonstrated that animals are biologically primed to learn to associate certain CSs with certain UCSs. Rats, for example, develop aversions to the taste, but not the appearance, of tainted foods. In contrast, birds are biologically primed to develop aversions to the sight of tainted food. This violates the tenet that any perceivable stimulus can become a CS.

5. Pavlov's work showed that virtually all organisms can learn to adapt to their environment. It also showed how a significant internal process, such as learning, could be studied objectively. Finally, Pavlov's findings also provided a basis for the behaviorist idea that human behavior, though biologically influenced, is mainly a bunch of conditioned responses.

   The original behaviorist philosophy, as stated by John Watson, was that psychology should be an objective science that studied only observable behaviors and avoided references to all mental processes. Watson argued that by studying how organisms respond to stimuli in their environments, psychologists would eventually become able to predict and control behavior.

6. In contrast to classical conditioning, which works on automatic responses to stimuli, *operant* conditioning works on behaviors that *operate* on the environment to produce consequences that influence the future occurrence of those behaviors. Behaviors followed by favorable events (reinforcers) tend to be repeated. Behaviors followed by unpleasant stimuli (punishers) tend not to be repeated.

   Shaping is a systematic technique for establishing a new response in which successive approximations of a desired behavior are reinforced.

7. A positive reinforcer is a stimulus that strengthens a response that leads to its presentation. A negative reinforcer is an aversive stimulus that strengthens a response that leads to its removal. Primary reinforcers are innately reinforcing stimuli that satisfy biological needs. Secondary reinforcers acquire their effectiveness by being associated with primary reinforcers.

   Fixed-ratio schedules deliver reinforcement after a set number of responses. Variable-ratio schedules deliver reinforcement after an unpredictable number of responses. Fixed-interval schedules deliver reinforcement for the first response that follows a specified amount of time. Variable-interval schedules deliver reinforcement for a response that follows an unpredictable time interval.

8. A punisher is any consequence that decreases the frequency of a behavior that it follows. Although punishment may be effective in the short run, it has its drawbacks. Because punished behavior is merely suppressed rather than forgotten, it may reappear in safe settings. Punishment may also promote aggressiveness as a way of coping with problems; fear of the person who administers it; fear of the situation in which it occurs; or, when it is unpredictable, a sense that events are beyond the person's control. Because punishment does not teach positive behaviors, it is usually more effective when used in combination with positive reinforcement.

9. Latent learning is learning that occurs without reinforcement. Rats allowed to explore a maze without reinforcement nevertheless learn a cognitive map of its layout. When they later are rewarded, they immediately perform as well as rats that have been reinforced with food all along.

   Latent learning demonstrates that there is more to learning than the association of a response with a reinforcer. Cognitive processes must be taken into consideration.

   Evidence for biological processes in operant conditioning comes from studies demonstrating that animals have biologically predisposed response patterns that influence the effectiveness of operant procedures with certain behaviors.

10. Operant principles of shaping and immediate reinforcement have been applied in school settings through the use of online testing systems, interactive student software, and Internet resources. Operant principles have also helped business managers increase productivity among their employees. Operant principles also have helped people take charge of their own behavior by creating self-management programs to stop smoking, lose weight, study, or exercise.

11. Observational learning, in which people observe and imitate, or model, others' behaviors, explains how many social behaviors are acquired. Research studies have shown that children will imitate both antisocial and prosocial models. Models are most effective when their actions and words are consistent. We are most likely to imitate people we respect, those we perceive as similar to ourselves, and those we perceive as successful.

## Chapter Review

1. learning
2. associate; associations; associative learning
3. classical
4. operant
5. observing
6. Ivan Pavlov
7. conditioned stimulus; unconditioned stimulus
8. unconditioned response
9. conditioned response
10. acquisition; one-half second

Learning theorists consider classical conditioning to be adaptive because conditioned responses help organisms to prepare for good or bad events (unconditioned stimuli) that are about to occur.

11. does not
12. extinction
13. spontaneous recovery
14. generalization; discrimination
15. predict; cognitive; expect

The discounting of mental (cognitive) processes has been strongly challenged by experiments suggesting that even in animals cognition is important for learning. Second, the belief that learning principles would generalize from one response to another and from one species to another has been questioned by research indicating that conditioning principles are constrained by each organism's biological predispositions.

16. alcoholism
17. sickness; would
18. biological; adapt

Classical conditioning led to the discovery of general principles of learning that are the same for all species tested, including humans. Classical conditioning also provided an example of how complex, internal processes could be studied objectively. In addition, classical conditioning has proven to have many helpful applications to human health and well-being.

19. John Watson; behaviorism

In Watson and Rayner's experiment, classical conditioning was used to condition fear of a rat in Albert, an 11-month-old infant. When Albert touched the white rat (neutral stimulus), a loud noise (unconditioned stimulus) was sounded. After several pairings of the rat with the noise, Albert began crying at the mere sight of the rat. The rat had become a conditioned stimulus, eliciting a conditioned response of fear.

20. neutral; automatic
21. respondent; operant
22. law of effect; Skinner box
23. shaping; approximations
24. reinforcer
25. positive reinforcer
26. negative reinforcer
27. primary reinforcers; secondary reinforcers
28. more
29. is; delayed
30. continuous reinforcement; rapid; rapid
31. partial; slower; very
32. fixed-ratio
33. variable-ratio
34. fixed-interval; checking the mail as delivery time approaches

**35.** variable-interval

Following reinforcement on a fixed-interval schedule, there is a pause in responding and then an increasing rate of response as time for the next reinforcement draws near. On a fixed-ratio schedule there also is a post-reinforcement pause, followed, however, by a return to a consistent, high rate of response. Both kinds of variable schedules produce steadier rates of response, without the pauses associated with fixed schedules. In general, schedules linked to responses produce *higher* response rates and fixed schedules produce *higher* response rates than the related variable schedules.

**36.** punishment

Because punished behavior is merely suppressed, it may reappear. Punishment can lead to fear and a sense of helplessness, as well as to the association of the aversive event with the person who administers it. Punishment also often increases aggressiveness. Finally, punishment alone does not guide the organism toward more desirable behavior.

**37.** cognitive

**38.** cognitive map

**39.** latent learning

**40.** is

**41.** shaping; testing; interactive

**42.** more; achievable; more

**43.** modeling; observational learning; Bandura

**44.** more

**45.** prosocial

**46.** consistent; similar; successful; admirable

## Progress Test 1

### Multiple-Choice Questions

**1. c.** is the answer. (p. 205)
**a.** This answer is incorrect because it simply describes any behavior that is automatic rather than being triggered, or elicited, by a specific stimulus.
**b.** This answer is too general, since behaviors can change for reasons other than learning.
**d.** Respondently conditioned behavior also satisfies the criteria of our definition of learning.

**2. b.** is the answer. (p. 216)
**a. & c.** Classical conditioning is associated with Pavlov; respondent conditioning is another name for classical conditioning.
**d.** Observational learning is most closely associated with Bandura.

**3. c.** is the answer. Meat automatically triggers the response of salivation and is therefore an unconditioned stimulus. (p. 208)
**a.** A conditioned stimulus acquires its response-eliciting powers through learning. A dog does not learn to salivate to meat.
**b. & d.** Responses are behaviors elicited in the organism, in this case the dog's salivation. The meat is a stimulus.

**4. b.** is the answer. Prior to its pairing with meat (the UCS), the tone did not elicit salivation and was therefore a neutral stimulus. Afterwards, the tone elicited salivation (the CR) and was therefore a conditioned stimulus (CS). (p. 208)
**c. & d.** Unconditioned stimuli, such as meat, innately elicit responding. Pavlov's dogs had to learn to associate the tone with the food.

**5. e.** is the answer. In learning to distinguish between the conditioned stimulus and another, similar stimulus, the monkey has received training in discrimination. (pp. 210–211)
**a.** In extinction training, a stimulus and/or response is allowed to go unreinforced.
**b.** Generalization training involves responding to stimuli similar to the conditioned stimulus; here the monkey is being trained not to respond to a similar stimulus.
**c.** This cannot be classical conditioning since the monkey is acting in order to obtain a reward. Thus, this is an example of operant conditioning.
**d.** Spontaneous recovery refers to the reappearance, after a period of rest, of a weakened CR.

**6. b.** is the answer. A continuous association will naturally be easier to learn than one that occurs on only some occasions, so learning is most rapid with continuous reinforcement. Yet, once the continuous association is no longer there, as in extinction training, extinction will occur more rapidly than it would have had the organism not always experienced reinforcement. (p. 219)

**7. b.** is the answer. (pp. 211, 222)
**c. & d.** The text does not present evidence regarding the relative importance of cognitive processes in classical and operant conditioning.

**8. b.** is the answer. (p. 220)
**a.** Response rate is high with fixed-ratio schedules, but there is a pause following each reinforcement.
**c. & d.** Because reinforcement is not contingent on the rate of response, interval schedules, especially fixed-interval schedules, produce lower response rates than ratio schedules.

**9. b.** is the answer. (pp. 217–218)
**a.** Positive reinforcement involves presenting a favorable stimulus following a response.

**c.** Punishment involves presenting an unpleasant stimulus following a response.

**d.** In extinction, a previously reinforced response is no longer followed by reinforcement. In this situation, a response causes a stimulus to be terminated or removed.

10. **c.** is the answer. In this situation, the CR will decline, a phenomenon known as extinction. (p. 209)

**a.** Generalization occurs when the subject makes a CR to stimuli similar to the original CS.

**b.** Discrimination is when the subject does not make a CR to stimuli other than the original CS.

**d.** An aversion is a CR to a CS that has been associated with an unpleasant UCS, such as shock or a nausea-producing drug.

**e.** Spontaneous recovery is the reappearance, after a rest period, of a CR.

11. **c.** is the answer. (p. 216)

**a.** In *operant* conditioning the responses operate on the environment.

**b.** In *classical* conditioning responses are triggered, or elicited, by preceding stimuli.

**d.** In *classical* conditioning responses are reflexive.

12. **c.** is the answer. (p. 212)

**a., d., & e.** These studies also indicated that rats are biologically predisposed to associate visual and auditory stimuli, but not taste, with shock.

**b.** Rats are biologically predisposed to associate taste with sickness.

13. **d.** is the answer. A dog does not have to learn to salivate to food; therefore, this response is unconditioned. (p. 208)

**a. & c.** Salivation is a response, not a stimulus.

14. **b.** is the answer. (p. 226)

**a.** Skinner is best known for studies of *operant* learning. Moreover, there is no such thing as secondary learning.

**c.** Pavlov is best known for classical conditioning.

**d.** Watson is best known as an early proponent of behaviorism.

15. **b.** is the answer. (p. 223)

**a. & d.** These criticisms *have* been leveled at Skinner's theory, but not for this reason.

**c.** The very *essence* of Skinner's theory is an emphasis on external influences, such as culture, on behavior.

16. **d.** is the answer. (pp. 220–221)

17. **c.** is the answer. (p. 211)

**a., b., & d.** Rescorla and Wagner's research did not address the importance of these factors in classical conditioning.

18. **d.** is the answer. a. is an example of positive reinforcement, b. is an example of negative reinforcement, and c. is an example of secondary reinforcement. (pp. 217–218)

19. **d.** is the answer. (pp. 206–207)

20. **b.** is the answer. (p. 209)

**a.** Backward conditioning, in which the UCS precedes the CS, is ineffective.

**c.** This interval is longer than is optimum for the most rapid acquisition of a CS-UCS association.

**d.** Simultaneous presentation of CS and UCS is ineffective because it does not permit the subject to anticipate the UCS.

### Matching Items

1. e (p. 217)
2. h (p. 210)
3. f (p. 217)
4. g (p. 218)
5. i (p. 218)
6. k (p. 220)
7. j (p. 219)
8. a (p. 216)
9. c (p. 210)
10. b (p. 220)
11. d (p. 222)

## Progress Test 2

### Multiple-Choice Questions

1. **c.** is the answer. (p. 209)

2. **b.** is the answer. The loud noise automatically elicited Albert's fear and therefore functioned as a UCS. After being associated with the UCS, the white rat acquired the power to elicit fear and thus became a CS. (p. 214)

3. **e.** is the answer. (pp. 213–215)

4. **a.** is the answer. Shaping works on operant behaviors by reinforcing successive approximations to a desired goal. (p. 216)

5. **c.** is the answer. (p. 210)

**a., b., & d.** Spontaneous recovery occurs after a CR has been extinguished, and in the absence of the UCS. The situations described here all involve the continued presentation of the UCS and, therefore, the further strengthening of the CR.

6. **b.** is the answer. (p. 218)

**a., c., & d.** Reinforcement that is delayed, presented before a response, or at the same time as a response, does not increase the response's frequency of occurrence.

7. **d.** is the answer. (pp. 217, 220)

**a.** Both involve an aversive stimulus.

**b.** All reinforcers, including negative reinforcers, increase the likelihood of a response.

**c.** In negative reinforcement an aversive stimulus is withdrawn following a desirable response.

8. **c.** is the answer. Payment is given after a fixed number of pieces have been completed. (p. 219)

**a. & b.** Interval schedules reinforce according to the passage of time, not the amount of work accomplished.

**d.** Fortunately for those working on commission, the work ratio is fixed and therefore predictable.

9. **c.** is the answer. By learning to put on your coat before going outside, you have learned to reduce the aversive stimulus of the cold. (pp. 217–218)

**a.** Discrimination learning involves learning to make a response in the presence of the appropriate stimulus and not other stimuli.

**b.** Punishment is the suppression of an undesirable response by the presentation of an aversive stimulus.

**d.** Putting on a coat is a response that is willfully emitted by the person. Therefore, this is an example of operant, not classical, conditioning.

**e.** Positive reinforcement involves the *presentation* of a stimulus.

10. **d.** is the answer. (p. 219)

**a.** Partial reinforcement refers to the ratio of responses to reinforcers, not the overall quantity of reinforcement delivered.

**b.** Unlike partial reinforcement, in which the delivery of reinforcement is contingent on responding, random reinforcement is delivered independently of the subject's behavior.

**c.** This defines the technique of shaping, not partial reinforcement.

11. **a.** is the answer. You are teaching your dog by rewarding him when he produces the desired behavior. (p. 216–217)

**b.** This is not classical conditioning because the cookie is a primary reinforcer presented after the operant behavior of the dog fetching the paper.

**c.** Food is a primary reinforcer; it satisfies an innate need.

**d.** Rewarding your dog each time he fetches the paper is continuous reinforcement.

12. **e.** is the answer. (p. 227)

13. **a.** is the answer. (p. 222)

14. **d.** is the answer. The rat had learned the maze but did not display this learning until reinforcement became available. (p. 222)

**a.** Negotiating a maze is clearly operant behavior.

**b.** This example does not involve learning to distinguish between stimuli.

**c.** This is not observational learning because the rat has no one to observe!

15. **c.** is the answer. Because reinforcement (earning a good grade on the exam) is available according to the passage of time, studying is reinforced on an interval schedule. Because the interval between

exams is constant, this is an example of a fixed-interval schedule. (p. 220)

16. **d.** is the answer. (pp. 207, 216)

**a.** Pavlov and Watson are both associated with classical conditioning.

**b.** Skinner is associated with operant conditioning, and Bandura is associated with observational learning.

17. **a.** is the answer. Teaching machines and software tutorials apply operant principles such as reinforcement, immediate feedback, and shaping to the teaching of new skills. (p. 223)

**b. & d.** Computer tutorials, for example, provide immediate, and continuous, reinforcement for correct responses, but do not use aversive control procedures such as punishment.

**c.** Computer tutorials, for example, are based on feedback for correct responses; this feedback constitutes secondary, rather than primary, reinforcement.

18. **c.** is the answer. In fishing, an unpredictable amount of time passes between catches. (p. 220)

19. **d.** is the answer. An approving nod from the boss is a secondary reinforcer in that it doesn't satisfy an innate need but has become linked with desirable consequences. Cessation of cold, cessation of pain, and a drink are all primary reinforcers, which meet innate needs. (p. 218)

20. **a.** is the answer. Taste-aversion experiments demonstrate conditioning even with CS-UCS intervals as long as several hours. (p. 212)

**b.** Despite being perceivable, a visual or auditory stimulus cannot become a CS for illness in some animals, such as rats.

**c.** Some animals, such as birds, are biologically primed to associate the *appearance* of food with illness.

*True-False Items*

| | | |
|---|---|---|
| **1.** F (p. 216) | **5.** T (p. 220) | **9.** F (p. 209) |
| **2.** F (p. 209) | **6.** F (pp. 211, 222) | **10.** T (p. 210) |
| **3.** F (p. 218) | **7.** T (pp. 220–221) | |
| **4.** T (p. 219) | **8.** F (p. 212) | |

## Thinking Critically About Chapter 6

*Multiple-Choice Questions*

1. **a.** is the answer. Your dog had to learn to associate the rattling sound with the food. Rattling is therefore a conditioned, or learned, stimulus, and salivation in response to this rattling is a learned, or conditioned, response. (p. 208)

2. **c.** is the answer. Reinforcement (the letter) comes after a fixed interval, and as the likely end of the interval approaches, your behavior (glancing out the window) becomes more frequent. (p. 220)

   **a. & b.** These answers are incorrect because with ratio schedules, reinforcement is contingent upon the number of responses rather than on the passage of time.

   **d.** Assuming that the mail is delivered at about the same time each day, the interval is fixed rather than variable. Your behavior reflects this, since you glance out the window more often as the delivery time approaches.

3. **b.** is the answer. By taking out the garbage, Jack terminates an aversive stimulus—his father's nagging. (pp. 217–218)

   **a.** Positive reinforcement would involve a desirable stimulus that increases the likelihood of the response that preceded it.

   **c.** This answer would have been correct if Jack's father had rewarded Jack for taking out the garbage by providing his favorite food.

   **d.** Punishment suppresses behavior; Jack is emitting a behavior in order to obtain reinforcement.

4. **c.** is the answer. Studies indicate that when a model says one thing but does another, subjects do the same and learn not to practice what they preach. (p. 227)

5. **a.** is the answer. As in this example, conditioning must be consistent with the particular organism's biological predispositions. (p. 222)

   **b.** Some behaviors, but certainly not all, are acquired more rapidly than others when shock is used as negative reinforcement.

   **c.** Pigeons are able to acquire many new behaviors when food is used as reinforcement.

6. **a.** is the answer. Ratio schedules maintain higher rates of responding—gambling in this example—than do interval schedules. Furthermore, variable schedules are not associated with the pause in responding following reinforcement that is typical of fixed schedules. The slot machine would therefore be used more often, and more consistently, if jackpots were scheduled according to a variable-ratio schedule. (p. 220)

7. **d.** is the answer. Sharetta is guided by her mental representation of the city, or cognitive map. (p. 222)

   **a. & e.** Latent learning, or learning in the absence of reinforcement that is demonstrated when reinforcement becomes available, has no direct relevance to the example. The same is true of discrimination.

   **b.** Observational learning refers to learning from watching others.

   **c.** Shaping is the technique of reinforcing successive approximations of a desired behavior.

8. **c.** is the answer. Because the cat was associated with your mother's scream, it elicited a fear response, and is thus the CS. (p. 208)

9. **a.** is the answer. Your mother's scream and evident fear, which naturally caused you to cry, was the UCS. (p. 208)

10. **d.** is the answer. Your fear of cats is the CR. An acquired fear is always a conditioned response. (p. 208)

11. **b.** is the answer. Your crying, automatically elicited by your mother's scream and fear, was the UCR. (p. 208)

12. **c.** is the answer. (pp. 218–219)

    **a.** Positive reinforcement is most effective in boosting productivity in the workplace when specific behavior, rather than vaguely defined general merit, is rewarded. Also, immediate reinforcement is much more effective than the delayed reinforcement described in a.

    **b.** Positive reinforcement is most effective in boosting productivity when performance goals are achievable, rather than unrealistic.

    **d.** The text does not specifically discuss the use of punishment in the workplace. However, it makes the general point that although punishment may temporarily suppress unwanted behavior, it does not guide one toward more desirable behavior. Therefore, workers who receive pay cuts for poor performance may learn nothing about how to improve their productivity.

13. **a.** is the answer. By targeting and reinforcing a specific behavior, Ingrid's parents should find that their daughter's good behavior increases in frequency. (p. 221)

    **b.** Most experts believe that verbal punishment has a destructive effect on parent-child relationships.

    **c.** This would most likely *increase* Ingrid's tantrums in the future.

14. **b.** is the answer. Not only is Bill extending a learned aversion to a specific blue car to all blue cars but also to cars that are green. (p. 210)

    **a.** Whereas discrimination involves responding only to a particular stimulus, Bill is extending his aversive response to other stimuli (green cars) as well.

    **c.** Latent learning is learning that becomes apparent only after reinforcement becomes available.

**d.** Extinction occurs when a conditioned response diminishes after the CS and UCS are no longer paired.

15. **b.** is the answer. The girls are imitating behavior they have observed and admired. (p. 226)
**a.** Because these behaviors are clearly willful rather than elicited, classical conditioning plays no role.
**c.** Latent learning plays no role in this example.
**d.** Shaping is a procedure for teaching the acquisition of a new response by reinforcing successive approximations of the behavior.
**e.** Discrimination involves responding to certain stimuli but not to others. In this example, only one stimulus (the televised Olympic games) is described.

16. **a.** is the answer. Classical conditioning proceeds most effectively when the CS and UCS are reliably paired and therefore appear predictably associated. Only for Group 1 is this likely to be true. (p. 209)

17. **b.** is the answer. (p. 212)
**a., c., & d.** Taste-aversion research demonstrates that humans and some other animals, such as rats, are biologically primed to associate illness with the taste of tainted food, rather than with other cues, such as the food's appearance. Moreover, taste aversions can be acquired even when the interval between the CS and the illness is several hours.

18. **d.** is the answer. By making a more preferred activity (watching TV) contingent on a less preferred activity (room cleaning), Reggie's mother is employing the operant conditioning technique of positive reinforcement. Because TV watching is not innately reinforcing, it is a secondary reinforcer. (pp. 216–218)

19. **c.** is the answer. The parrot is reinforced for making successive approximations of a goal behavior. This defines shaping. (p. 216)
**a.** Shaping is an operant conditioning procedure; salivation at the sight of dog biscuits is a classically conditioned response.
**b.** Shaping involves the systematic reinforcement of successive approximations of a more complex behavior. In this example there is no indication that the response of stopping at the intersection involved the gradual acquisition of simpler behaviors.
**d.** This is an example of the partial reinforcement of an established response, rather than the shaping of a new response.

20. **c.** is the answer. Whereas Lars is paid (reinforced) after a fixed period of time (fixed-interval), Tom is reinforced for each sale (fixed-ratio) he makes. (p. 220)

### Essay Question

The first step in shaping an operant response, such as rolling over, is to find an effective reinforcer. Some sort of biscuit or dog treat is favored by animal trainers. This primary reinforcement should be accompanied by effusive praise (secondary reinforcement) whenever the dog makes a successful response.

Rolling over (the goal response) should be divided into a series of simple approximations, the first of which is a response, such as lying down on command, that is already in the dog's repertoire. This response should be reinforced several times. The next step is to issue a command, such as "Roll over," and withhold reinforcement until the dog (usually out of frustration) makes a closer approximation (such as rotating slightly in one direction). Following this example, the trainer should gradually require closer and closer approximations until the goal response is attained. When the new response has been established, the trainer should switch from continuous to partial reinforcement, in order to strengthen the skill.

## Key Terms

### Writing Definitions

1. **Learning** is any relatively permanent change in an organism's behavior due to experience. (p. 205)

2. In **associative learning**, organisms learn that certain events occur together. Two variations of associative learning are classical conditioning and operant conditioning. (p. 206)

3. Also know as Pavlovian conditioning, **classical conditioning** is a type of learning in which a neutral stimulus becomes capable of eliciting a conditioned response after having become associated with an unconditioned stimulus. (p. 207)

4. In classical conditioning, the **unconditioned response (UCR)** is the unlearned, naturally occurring response to the unconditioned stimulus. (p. 208)

5. In classical conditioning, the **unconditioned stimulus (UCS)** is the stimulus that naturally and automatically elicits the reflexive unconditioned response. (p. 208)

6. In classical conditioning, the **conditioned response (CR)** is the learned response to a previously neutral conditioned stimulus, which results from the acquired association between the CS and UCS. (p. 208)

7. In classical conditioning, the **conditioned stimulus (CS)** is an originally neutral stimulus that comes to elicit a CR after association with an unconditioned stimulus. (p. 208)

8. In classical conditioning, **acquisition** refers to the initial stage of conditioning in which the new response is established and gradually strengthened. In operant conditioning, it is the strengthening of a reinforced response. (pp. 209, 216)

9. In classical conditioning, **extinction** refers to the weakening of a CR when the CS is no longer followed by the UCS. In operant conditioning, extinction occurs when a response is no longer reinforced. (pp. 209, 216)

10. **Spontaneous recovery** is the reappearance of an extinguished CR after a rest period. (p. 210)

11. In classical conditioning, **generalization** refers to the tendency, once a response has been conditioned, for stimuli similar to the original CS to elicit a CR. In operant conditioning, generalization refers to responding to stimuli similar to the original one as though they signal a behavior that will be reinforced. (pp. 210, 216)

12. **Discrimination** in classical conditioning refers to the ability to distinguish the CS from similar stimuli that do not signal a UCS. In operant conditioning, responding differently to stimuli that signal a behavior will be reinforced or will not be reinforced. (pp. 210, 216)

13. **Behaviorism** is the school of thought maintaining that psychology should be an objective science, study only observable behaviors, and avoid references to mental processes. (p. 215)

    *Example*: Because he was an early advocate of the study of observable behavior, John Watson is often called the father of **behaviorism**.

14. **Operant conditioning** is a type of learning in which behavior is strengthened if followed by reinforcement or diminished if followed by punishment. (p. 216)

    *Example*: Unlike classical conditioning, which works on automatic behaviors, **operant conditioning** works on behaviors that are willfully emitted by an organism.

15. **Respondent behavior** is that which occurs as an automatic response to some stimulus. (p. 216)

    *Example*: In classical conditioning, conditioned and unconditioned responses are examples of **respondent behavior** in that they are automatic responses elicited by specific stimuli.

16. **Operant behavior** is behavior the organism emits that operates on the environment to produce reinforcing or punishing stimuli. (p. 216)

17. E. L. Thorndike proposed the **law of effect**, which states that rewarded behavior is likely to recur. (p. 216)

18. A **Skinner box** is an experimental chamber for the operant conditioning of an animal such as a pigeon or rat. The controlled environment enables the investigator to present visual or auditory stimuli, deliver reinforcement or punishment, and precisely measure simple responses such as bar presses or key pecking. (p. 216)

19. **Shaping** is the operant conditioning procedure for establishing a new response by reinforcing successive approximations of the desired behavior. (p. 216)

20. In operant conditioning, a **reinforcer** is any event that strengthens the behavior it follows. (p. 217)

21. The powers of **primary reinforcers** are inborn and do not depend on learning. (p. 218)

22. **Secondary reinforcers** are stimuli that acquire their reinforcing power through their association with a primary reinforcer. (p. 218)

23. **Continuous reinforcement** is the operant procedure of reinforcing the desired response every time it occurs. In promoting the acquisition of a new response it is best to use continuous reinforcement. (p. 219)

24. **Partial reinforcement** is the operant procedure of reinforcing a response intermittently. A response that has been partially reinforced is much more resistant to extinction than one that has been continuously reinforced. (p. 219)

25. In operant conditioning, a **fixed-ratio schedule** is one in which reinforcement is presented after a set number of responses. (p. 219)

    *Example*: Continuous reinforcement is a special kind of **fixed-ratio schedule**: Reinforcement is presented after *each* response, so the ratio of reinforcements to responses is one to one.

26. In operant conditioning, a **variable-ratio schedule** is one in which reinforcement is presented after a varying number of responses. (p. 220)

27. In operant conditioning, a **fixed-interval schedule** is one in which a response is reinforced after a specified time has elapsed. (p. 220)

28. In operant conditioning, a **variable-interval schedule** is one in which responses are reinforced after varying intervals of time. (p. 220)

29. In operant conditioning, **punishment** is the presentation of an aversive stimulus, such as shock, which decreases the behavior it follows. (p. 220)

*Memory aid*: People often confuse negative reinforcement and **punishment**. The former strengthens behavior, while the latter weakens it.

30. A **cognitive map** is a mental picture of one's environment. (p. 222)

31. **Latent learning** is learning that occurs in the
absence of reinforcement but only becomes
apparent when there is an incentive to demonstrate it. (p. 222)

32. **Observational learning** is learning by watching
and imitating the behavior of others. (p. 226)

33. **Modeling** is the process of watching and then
imitating a specific behavior and is thus an
important means through which observational
learning occurs. (p. 226)

34. The opposite of antisocial behavior, **prosocial
behavior** is positive, helpful, and constructive,
and is subject to the same principles of observational learning as is undesirable behavior, such as
aggression. (p. 227)

## Summing Up

### Classical Conditioning

The flow chart reads as follows: A puff of air to the
eye, the *UCS*, elicits an eye blink, the UCR. When the
puff of air is paired with a bell ringing, the *CS*, the CS
comes to elicit an eyeblink, the *CR*. This is the *acquisition* stage of classical conditioning. Presenting the CS
alone for several trials results in *extinction*. After a
period of rest, pairing the *CS* and *UCS* results in *spontaneous recovery*. If a CS similar to the original CS is
presented, responding with the CR represents *generalization*, not responding to the similar CS represents
*discrimination*.

### Operant Conditioning

A dog biscuit, a *primary* reinforcer, or encouraging
words such as "Good dog," the *secondary reinforcer*,
can be used to train, or *shape*, a new skill such as sitting up. To teach a new skill (sitting up), first use *continuous* reinforcement, a special type of *fixed*-ratio
schedule. To maintain the skill, use *partial reinforcement* either by rewarding the dog after different numbers of responses, a *variable-ratio* schedule (which produces the *steadiest* rate of responding) or by rewarding the dog after different amounts of time, a *variable-
interval* schedule, or by rewarding the dog after a
specified amount of time, a *fixed-interval schedule*.

---

### *FOCUS ON VOCABULARY AND LANGUAGE*

*Page 205: Learning* in all such realms *breeds hope.* The
fact that we can change and adapt as a result of
experience (*learn*) in so many different areas (*realms*)
gives rise to optimism (*breeds hope*) about our future
prospects.

*Page 206:* . . . a TV character get *mugged* . . . This
means to be attacked, (sometimes) beaten, and
robbed. The term is used here to describe how associations are formed between events, such as
between the sounds that precede an attack and the
*mugging* itself. In movies and on TV, a certain type
of music is often played before a frightening event
or scene. After a few such associations, the music
itself can elicit fear before you actually see the
frightening or scary event. This is an example of
classical conditioning.

*Page 207:* A clever Japanese *rancher* reportedly *herds*
cattle by outfitting them with electronic *pagers*,
which he calls from his portable phone. In this
example of conditioning, the cattle farmer (*rancher*)
has trained his animals to gather together and move
(*he herds them*) to the feeding station (*food trough*).
They have learned to associate the sound of the tone
(*the beep*) made by the signaling device (*electronic
pager*) with the delivery of food (classical conditioning), and they have also learned that moving fast
(*hustling*) to the trough is followed by the good feeling of satiating their hunger (operant conditioning).

### Classical Conditioning

*Page 207: For many people, the name Ivan Pavlov rings a
bell.* Myers is making a little joke here. A common
expression when hearing something familiar but
vague is to say, *"That rings a bell."* Pavlov's name is
familiar to many people, who may also be vaguely
aware that his research involved dogs and ringing
bells (classical conditioning).

*Page 208:* . . . what the dog was thinking . . . as it
*drooled.* . . . To drool means to salivate or produce
spit. When food (UCS) is placed in a dog's mouth,
the dog will automatically salivate or *drool* (UCR). If
a tone (CS) is sounded before (or precedes) the UCS
over a number of trials, then the CS alone (the tone)
will be able to elicit salivation (CR).

*Page 209 (margin note):* If the *aroma* of cake baking *sets your mouth to watering*, what is the UCS? The CS? The CR? When you bake a cake in the oven, there is a lovely smell (*aroma*) which makes you salivate or drool (*sets your mouth to watering*). This is an example of classical conditioning: The taste of the cake in your mouth is the UCS (this automatically produces saliva, the UCR), the aroma is the CS, and, because of its past associations with the UCS, it can now, by itself, elicit saliva (the CR).

*Page 209:* Moreover, the male quail developed a general liking for their cage's *red-light district*. Traditionally, a red lamp hung in the window identified the house as a brothel, and the area of town populated by many brothels became known as the *red-light district*. In Domjan's experiments with male quail a red light (CS) was used to signal the arrival of a receptive female quail (UCS), which elicited sexual arousal (UCR). Eventually, the red light (CS) alone elicited sexual arousal (CR), and the male quail appeared to develop a general liking for the cage with the red light (*the red-light district*).

*Page 210:* After *breaking up* with his *fire-breathing heartthrob*, Tirrell also experienced extinction and spontaneous recovery. He recalls that "the smell of onion breath (CS), no longer paired with the kissing (UCS), lost its ability to *shiver my timbers*." This paragraph describes the end of the relationship (*breaking up*) with his girlfriend (*heartthrob*) who loved to eat onions and thus had hot, smelly breath (*fire-breathing*). The repeated smell of onions or onion breath (CS) without the UCS (kissing) resulted in extinction of his conditioned aroused state (CR), and, consequently, the CS lost its ability to get him excited (*shiver his timbers*). He later experienced spontaneous recovery (the extinguished CR returned briefly) when he smelled onion breath once more. (The idiom "*shiver my timbers*" has no simple explanation; it is probably an old expression dating back to the days of wooden [timbered] sailing ships which would tremble or shiver in a storm.)

*Page 213:* But if we *see further* than Pavlov did, it is because we *stand on his shoulders*. This phrase is not to be taken literally; it simply means that we now know more than Pavlov did (*see further*) because we can build and expand on his great work (*stand on his shoulders*).

*Page 213:* . . . *crack cocaine users* . . . This term refers to drug addicts who use a drug that is a synthetic, but very potent, form of cocaine.

*Page 215:* . . . *legendary significance* . . . Watson and Rayner's work with Little Albert was the first investigation of how phobias or irrational fears might develop through the process of classical conditioning. Thus, the story was passed on to future generations of psychologists (it became a *legend*) and influenced their research.

### Operant Conditioning

*Page 216:* . . . *to pull habits out of a rat.* David Myers is having fun playing with the English language here. The expression "to pull rabbits out of a hat" refers to stage magicians who are able to extract rabbits from a seemingly empty hat. Can you see the way Myers has twisted this expression? Both classical and operant conditioning involve teaching new habits to various organisms, including rats. Following classical conditioning, the CS elicits a new response from the animal (i.e., the CS "*pulls a habit out of the rat*"), or the sight of the lever may elicit the habit of lever pressing (operant conditioning).

*Page 217:* With training, pigeons have even been taught to discriminate between *Bach's music and Stravinsky's*. Bach and Stravinsky were composers whose styles of musical composition were quite different. Through shaping (rewarding behaviors that are closer and closer to the target or desired response), psychologists have been able to train pigeons to discriminate (or choose) between the two musical sounds. For example, pigeons may be rewarded for pecking a disk when Bach is playing and for refraining from pecking when Stravinsky is playing. They can be trained to discriminate, or tell the difference, between the two.

*Page 217:* On a wall chart, the teacher pastes *gold stars* after the names of children scoring 100 percent on spelling tests. Teachers often use extrinsic rewards such as small, bright stickers (*gold stars*) for, say, the very best spellers in the class. Unfortunately, if only the top few students (*academic all-stars*) are recognized in this way, the rest of the students may lose motivation because, even if they improve their spelling and work very hard (but still don't get 100%), they don't get any reinforcers. Myers recommends a shaping procedure that rewards even small improvements and recognizes the child for making the effort to do better and better.

*Page 218:* When a barely awake person pushes the *snooze button*, the silencing of the annoying alarm is similarly a reinforcer. When your radio alarm goes off in the morning, you may press the switch (*snooze button*) which turns off the irritating tone for a brief period of time. The ensuing quiet period, which may allow you to go back to sleep for a while (*snooze*), and the absence of the buzzer are negative reinforcers for pushing the snooze button. (Your button-pushing behavior has been strengthened because it removed an aversive event, the alarm.)

*Page 218:* . . . *Billy throws a tantrum* . . . A child screams and shouts in an uncontrollable manner when his or her desires are blocked or thwarted. For example, a parent goes shopping and takes a child along. Once in the store the child sees some candy and asks for it. The parent says "no!" Immediately, the child starts screaming and crying (*throws a tantrum*), so the parent gives the child the candy. The child's behavior has been positively reinforced and the parent's behavior (giving in) has been strengthened by negative reinforcement.

*Page 218:* . . . *goofing off and getting a bad exam grade* . . . Students may score poorly on an exam because they were doing something unproductive, such as watching TV, instead of studying (they were *goofing off*). As a consequence, they may decide to change their behavior and work hard to avoid further exam anxiety and the unpleasant possibility of getting a low grade. The new behavior may be strengthened if it avoids the aversive consequences of anxiety (negative reinforcement); in addition, getting a good score on the exam can positively reinforce good study habits. Remember, reinforcers of either kind (positive or negative) always strengthen behavior.

*Page 219:* . . . the *kick* that often comes within seconds [after taking drugs] . . . The term *kick* as used here refers to a jolt of pleasure (not as in "to kick the ball"). Myers is making the point that behaviors such as smoking, drinking, and drug taking, in general, are followed by some immediate pleasurable consequence, which controls the behavior more than does the delayed consequence (e.g., lung cancer, memory loss, cognitive impairment, etc.).

*Page 219:* A salesperson does not make a sale with every *pitch*, nor does an *angler* get a bite with every *cast*. The *pitch* referred to here is the sales talk (*pitch*) that the salesperson uses to promote the product or service. The bite the angler (fisherman) does not get refers to the fact that throwing out the line (*casting*) does not always result in fish biting the bait. The idea is that much of our behavior is not continuously reinforced but persists, nevertheless, by being partially reinforced (you make a sale or catch a fish only once in a while despite many responses).

*Page 219:* . . . *paid on a piecework basis* . . . This refers to situations in which someone is paid for the number of items produced (and not by the hour or the week). A worker gets paid only if he or she pro-

duces, so the number of responses (i.e., the number of items produced) is reinforced on a **fixed-ratio schedule**. An example would be factory worker sewing shirts who would be paid 5 dollars for each finished shirt (*piecework*). The more shirts she makes, the more money she earns, and thus the rate of responding is usually high.

*Page 220:* . . . *fly casters* . . . A type of fishing that uses small artificial flies as bait is called fly fishing. The line is thrown out (*cast*) very frequently, because the more *fly casting* that is done the more likely it is that a fish will be caught eventually. However, because fish only occasionally and unpredictably respond to the bait, the fly caster is on a **variable-ratio schedule of reinforcement.**

*Page 220:* . . . *a choppy stop-start pattern.* When reinforcement is for the first response after a set time period (a **fixed-interval schedule**), responding is typically more frequent, as the expected time for the reinforcer gets closer, and much less frequent after the reinforcer is delivered. The pattern of responding is thus uneven (*choppy*) with the post-reinforcement pause followed by increasingly higher rates of responding as the anticipated time for reinforcement approaches (a *stop-start pattern*).

*Page 220:* . . . *pop quiz* . . . If your professor gives brief tests at unpredictable intervals (*pop quizzes*), you never know when the next exam is going to be. Thus, your best strategy would be to study on a regular basis and prepare for a test before *every* class. If you do this, your study habits will be reinforced on a **variable-interval schedule.**

*Page 220:* . . . the child who *loses a treat* after running into the street . . . Here the phrase *"loses a treat"* refers to the withholding of some pleasant consequence such as a candy bar or piece of cake (appetitive stimulus) following some unwanted behavior. This is one type of punishment; it decreases the probability of the behavior being repeated. Another example is *time out*, in which the child is put in a situation (such as in the corner) in which no reinforcement is available.

*Page 220:* . . . *drawbacks* . . . This means problems or bad consequences. One problem (*drawback*) with using punishment is that the behavior may be temporarily suppressed in the presence of the punisher but may reappear in other, safer settings. In addition, punishment may elicit aggression, create fear and apprehension, and generate avoidance behavior in those being punished. As Myers notes, punishment teaches what not to do, whereas positive reinforcement teaches what to do.

*Page 220:* The driver who is *hit with* a couple of speeding tickets. . . . The phrase *"hit with"* means issued or given, but "hit" is associated with punitive, aversive, or bad consequences. A driver who is issued (*hit with*) a speeding ticket may feel punished and, instead of changing the speeding behavior, may find ways to avoid getting tickets by using a radar detector. The point Myers is making is that punishment may not be the best way to change behavior.

*Page 223:* . . . *piggy bank* . . . This is a small container for saving money (usually coins) that is often in the shape of a pig. Children can learn to save their money by putting it in their *piggy banks*. However, as Myers points out, pigs who were trained to put big wooden coins in a large *piggy bank* soon reverted to their natural behavior of pushing the coins with their snouts (noses) despite the fact that they received no reward for doing this. This is an example of the biological constraints on learning.

*Page 223:* . . . *stirred a hornet's nest.* . . . A hornet is a large yellow and black stinging insect belonging to the wasp family. Up to 200 hornets live together in a sheltered home (*nest*); if disturbed or agitated (*stirred*), they will attack in an angry and aggressive manner. B. F. Skinner aroused a great deal of anger and hostility and was vehemently attacked by many people (*he stirred a hornet's nest*) for insisting that mental events and free will (internal events) were of little relevance as determinants of behavior compared to environmental factors such as rewards and punishments (external influences).

## Learning by Observation

*Page 226:* Compared with children not exposed to the adult model, children who observed the *aggressive outburst* were much more likely to *lash out* at the doll. Bandura's experiments on observational learning demonstrated that children who saw an adult engage in (*model*) violent behavior (an *aggressive outburst*) were more inclined to attack and beat up (*lash out at*) a Bobo doll and copy (*imitate*) the words and gestures used by the role model.

# CHAPTER 7

# *Memory*

## Chapter Overview

Chapter 7 explores human memory as a system that processes information in three steps. Encoding refers to the process of putting information into the memory system. Storage is the purely passive mechanism by which information is maintained in memory. Retrieval is the process by which information is accessed from memory through recall or recognition.

Chapter 7 also discusses the important role of meaning, imagery, and organization in encoding new memories, how memory is represented physically in the brain, and how forgetting may result from failure to encode or store information or to find appropriate retrieval cues. The final section of the chapter discusses the issue of memory construction. How "true" are our memories of events? A particularly controversial issue in this area involves children's memories of sexual abuse. As you study this chapter, try applying some of the memory and studying tips discussed in the text.

NOTE: Answer guidelines for all Chapter 7 questions begin on page 204.

## Guided Study

The text chapter should be studied one section at a time. Before you read, preview each section by skimming it, noting headings and boldface items. Then read the appropriate section objectives from the following outline. Keep these objectives in mind and, as you read the chapter section, search for the information that will enable you to meet each objective. Once you have finished a section, write out answers for its objectives.

### *The Phenomenon of Memory* (pp. 231–234)

> David Myers at times uses idioms that are unfamiliar to some readers. If you do not know the meaning of any of the following words, phrases, or expressions in the context in which they appear in the text, refer to page 212 for an explanation: . . . *mind's storehouse, the reservoir; medal winners in a memory Olympics; memory feats; tap the telephones; shine the flashlight beam of attention on.*

1. Explain memory in terms of information processing.

### *Encoding: Getting Information In* (pp. 234–241)

> If you do not know the meaning of any of the following words, phrases, or expressions in the context in which they appear in the text, refer to page 213 for an explanation: *boost; nonsense syllables; a raw script . . . finished stage production; mental snapshots; peg-word; applause for memory.*

2. Explain the process of encoding and distinguish between automatic and effortful processing.

3. Discuss the importance of rehearsal, spacing, and serial position in encoding.

4. Explain the importance of meaning, imagery, and organization in the encoding process.

5. Discuss forgetting as a form of encoding failure.

### Storage: Retaining Information (pp. 241–249)

> If you do not know the meaning of any of the following words, phrases, or expressions in the context in which they appear in the text, refer to pages 213–214 for an explanation: *flashes of lightning; Sherlock Holmes; champion memorist; memory "software"; with tongue only partially in cheek; arousal sears the events onto the brain; mirror-image writing . . . jigsaw puzzle.*

6. Distinguish between iconic and echoic memory.

7. Describe memory capacity and duration.

8. Discuss research findings on the physical basis of memory.

9. Discuss what research with amnesics reveals about memory and describe the role of the cerebellum in implicit memories.

### Retrieval: Getting Information Out (pp. 249–262)

> If you do not know the meaning of any of the following words, phrases, or expressions in the context in which they appear in the text, refer to pages 214–215 for an explanation: *recognition memory dwarfs; buoyant mood . . . rose-colored glasses; metamorphose from devils into angels; may lie poised on the tip of the tongue; mental attic; sheepishly; relit a blown-out candle; reconstruction as well as reproduction; sincerely wrong.*

10. Contrast recall, recognition, and relearning measures of memory and describe the importance of retrieval cues.

**11.** Discuss the role of interference in the process of forgetting.

**12.** Describe motivated forgetting and explain the concept of repression.

**13.** Discuss the evidence for memory's being constructive.

**14.** Explain why memory researchers are suspicious of claims of long-repressed memories "recovered" with the aid of a therapist.

**15.** Discuss whether children are reliable eyewitnesses.

*Improving Memory* (p. 263)

> If you do not know the meaning of the following word in the context in which it appears in the text, refer to page 215 for an explanation: *sprinkled.*

**16.** Discuss strategies for improving memory.

## Chapter Review

When you have finished reading the chapter, work through the material that follows to review it. Complete the sentences and answer the questions. As you proceed, evaluate your performance for each section by consulting the answers on page 205. Do not continue with the next section until you understand each term. If you need to, review or reread the appropriate section in the textbook before continuing.

**1.** Learning that persists over time indicates the existence of _____ for that learning.

*The Phenomenon of Memory* (pp. 231–234)

**2.** Memories for surprising, significant moments that are especially clear are called _____ memories.

**3.** Both human memory and computer memory can be viewed as _____-_____ systems that perform three tasks: _____, _____, and _____.

**4.** Similar to a computer's permanent storage, we maintain vast amounts of information in _____-_____ memory. From this storehouse we can retrieve a(n) _____ (limited/unlimited) amount of information into _____-_____ memory. Although we _____ (can/cannot) attend simultaneously to everything we experience, we register incoming stimuli in _____ memory.

*Encoding: Getting Information In* (pp. 234–241)

**5.** A distinction is made between encoding that does not require conscious attention and is therefore _____ and that which is _____.

Give examples of material encoded by automatic processing and by effortful processing.

6. With novel information, conscious repetition, or _____, boosts memory.

7. A pioneering researcher in verbal memory was _____. In one experiment he found that the longer he studied a list of nonsense syllables, the _____ (fewer/greater) the number of repetitions he required to relearn it later.

8. After material has been learned, additional repetition, or _____, usually will increase retention.

9. When people go around a circle reading words, their poorest memories are for the _____ (least/most) recent information heard. This phenomenon is called the _____-_____ effect.

10. Memory studies also reveal that distributed rehearsal is more effective for retention; this is called the _____.

11. The tendency to remember the first and last items in a list best is called the _____. Following a delay, first items are remembered _____ (better/less well) than last items.

12. When processing verbal information for storage, we usually encode its _____.

13. When recalling experiences, we tend to remember _____ (things as they were/what was encoded).

14. Bransford and Johnson's research suggests that it is beneficial to _____ what we read and hear into meaningful terms.

15. Memory that consists of mental pictures is based on the use of _____.

16. Your earliest memories are most likely of events that occurred when you were about _____ years old.

17. Concrete, high-imagery words tend to be remembered _____ (better/less well) than abstract, low-imagery words.

18. Memory aids are known as _____ devices. One such device involves forming associations between a familiar series of locations and to-be-remembered words; this technique is called the _____.

19. Using a jingle, such as the one that begins "one is a bun," is an example of the _____-_____ system.

20. Memory may be aided by grouping information into meaningful units called _____. An example of this technique involves forming words from the first letters of to-be-remembered words; the resulting word is called an _____.

21. In addition, material may be processed into _____, which are composed of a few broad concepts divided into lesser concepts, categories, and facts.

22. Of all the material that is sensed, much of it never actually enters the memory system. This type of "forgetting" is known as _____.

One reason for age-related memory decline is that the brain areas responsible for _____ new information are _____ (more/less) responsive in older adults.

*Storage: Retaining Information* (pp. 241–249)

23. If you are able to retrieve something from memory, you must have engaged in the process of _____.

24. Stimuli from the environment are first recorded in _____ memory.

25. George Sperling found that when people were briefly shown three rows of letters, they could recall _____ (virtually all/ about half) of them. When Sperling sounded a tone immediately after a row of letters was flashed to indicate which letters were to be recalled, the subjects were much _____ (more/less) accurate. This suggests that people have a brief photographic, or _____ , memory lasting about a few tenths of a second.

26. Sensory memory for sounds is called _____ memory. This memory fades _____ (more/less) rapidly than photographic memory, lasting for as long as _____ .

27. Peterson and Peterson found that when _____ was prevented by asking subjects to count backwards, memory for letters was gone after 12 seconds.

28. Our short-term memory capacity is about _____ chunks of information. Both children and adults have short-term recall for roughly as many words as they can _____ in _____ seconds.

29. In contrast to short-term memory—and contrary to popular belief—the capacity of permanent memory is essentially _____ .

30. Studies by Ebbinghaus and by Bahrick indicate that most forgetting occurs _____ (soon/a long time) after the material is learned.

31. Penfield's electrically stimulated patients _____ (do/do not) provide reliable evidence that our stored memories are precise and durable.

32. It is likely that forgetting occurs because new experiences _____ with our retrieval of old information and that the physical memory trace _____ with the passage of time.

33. Lashley attempted to locate memory by cutting out pieces of rats' _____ after they had learned a maze. He found that no matter where he cut, the rats _____ (remembered/forgot) the maze.

34. Gerard found that a hamster's memory remained even after its body temperature was lowered to a point where the brain's _____ activity stopped.

35. Researchers believe that memory involves a strengthening of certain neural connections, which occurs at the _____ between neurons.

36. Kandel and Schwartz have found that when learning occurs in the sea snail, the neurotransmitter _____ is released in greater amounts, making synapses more efficient.

37. After learning has occurred, a sending neuron needs _____ (more/less) prompting to fire, and the number of _____ _____ it stimulates may increase. This phenomenon, called _____-_____ , may be the neural basis for learning and memory.

38. Blocking this process with _____ , or by genetic engineering that causes the absence of an _____ , interferes with learning. Rats given a drug that enhances _____ will learn a maze _____ (faster/more slowly).

39. A blow or electrical shock to the brain _____ (will/will not) disrupt old memories and _____ (will/will not) wipe out recent experiences.

40. Alcohol impairs memory _____ (formation/retrieval) by disrupting the neurotransmitter _____ .

41. Hormones released when we are excited or under stress often make events more memorable by increasing the availability of _____ to fuel brain activity.

Drugs that block the effects of stress hormones
_____ (facilitate/disrupt) memories of emotional events.

42. The loss of memory is called _____ .
Studies of people who have lost their memory suggest that there _____ (is/is not) a single unified system of memory.

43. Although amnesics typically _____ (have/have not) lost their capacity for learning, which is called _____ memory, they _____ (are/are not) able to declare their memory, suggesting a deficit in their _____ memory systems.

44. Amnesic patients typically have suffered damage to the _____ of their limbic system. This brain structure is important in the processing and storage of _____ memories. Damage on the left side of this structure impairs _____ memory; damage on the right side impairs memory for _____ designs and locations. The cerebellum is important in the processing of _____ memories.

45. The dual explicit-implicit memory system helps explain _____ amnesia. We do not have explicit memories of our first three years because the _____ is one of the last brain structures to mature.

*Retrieval: Getting Information Out* (pp. 249–262)

46. The ability to retrieve information not in conscious awareness is called _____ .

47. Bahrick found that, 25 years after graduation, people were not able to _____ (recall/recognize) the names of their classmates but were able to _____ (recall/recognize) 90 percent of their names and their yearbook pictures.

48. If you have learned something and then forgotten it, you will probably be able to _____ it _____ (more/less) quickly than you did originally.

49. The process by which associations can lead to retrieval is called _____ .The best retrieval cues come from the associations formed at the time we _____ a memory.

50. Studies have shown that retention is best when learning and testing are done in _____ (the same/different) contexts.

Summarize the text's explanation of the déjà vu experience.

51. The type of memory in which emotions serve as retrieval cues is referred to as _____-_____ memory.

Describe the effects of mood on memory.

52. When information that is stored in memory temporarily cannot be found, _____ failure has occurred.

53. Research suggests that memories are also lost as a result of _____ , which is especially possible if we simultaneously learn similar, new material.

54. The disruptive effect of previous learning on current learning is called _____ . The disruptive effect of

learning new material on efforts to recall material previously learned is called

_____ .

55. Jenkins and Dallenbach found that if subjects went to sleep after learning, their memory for a list of nonsense syllables was

_____ (better/worse) than it was if they stayed awake.

56. In some cases, old information facilitates our learning of new information. This is called

_____ .

57. Freud proposed that motivated forgetting, or

_____ , may protect a person from painful memories. Increasing numbers of memory researchers think that motivated forgetting is _____ (less/more) common than Freud believed.

58. Research has shown that recall of an event is often influenced by past experiences and present assumptions. The workings of these influences illustrate the process of memory

_____ .

Describe what Loftus's studies have shown about the effects of misleading postevent information on eyewitness reports.

59. When witnesses to an event receive misleading information about it, they may experience a

_____

and misremember the event. Experiments by Garry, Hyman, and others demonstrate that false memories _____ (can/cannot) be created when people are induced to imagine nonexistent events.

60. Memory construction explains why memories "refreshed" under _____ are often inaccurate.

61. At the heart of many false memories is

_____ _____ , which occurs when we _____ an event to the wrong source.

62. Children _____ (are/are not) as resistant to memory suggestion as are adults. At the same time, however, children

_____ (do/do not) routinely confuse reality with fantasy.

63. Memory researchers are especially suspicious of long-repressed memories of

_____ that are "recovered" with the aid of

_____ . Such traumatic experiences usually _____ (are/are not) vividly remembered.

64. A person whose identity centers around a false but strongly believed traumatic memory is said to be suffering from the _____

_____ .

65. Memories of events that happened before age

_____ are unreliable. This phenomenon is called _____

_____ .

*Improving Memory* (p. 263)

Identify strategies for improving memory.

**WEB SIGHTING**

As noted in the text, memory researchers have become increasingly skeptical about Freud's concept of memory repression and are challenging its validity. At the same time, a rash of new court cases have involved therapeutically "recovered" memories of traumatic childhood events. After reading the chapter, you can understand how memory construction, source amnesia, and the misinformation effect contribute to this social problem.

To further your studies of these phenomena, use internet resources to see what you can learn about *recovered memory therapy (RMT)* and the *False Memory Syndrome (FMS)*. (Hint: Use your favorite search engine to locate Web sites that pertain to RMT and FMS. One that will help you get started is the Web site of the FMS Foundation, a nonprofit organization founded in 1992 to find out why FMS is spreading, try to prevent new cases of FMS, and provide assistance to all victims of FMS.)

Try to find answers to the following questions:

1. How did the False Memory Syndrome Foundation start?

2. What are "body memories"?

3. Are traumatic memories more accurate than non-traumatic memories?

4. What are the symptoms of FMS?

5. How does recovered memory therapy allegedly work?

6. What are the American Medical Association and American Psychological Association's positions regarding FMS?

## Progress Test 1

### Multiple-Choice Questions

Circle your answers to the following questions and check them with the answers on page 206. If your answer is incorrect, read the explanation for why it is incorrect and then consult the appropriate pages of the text (in parentheses following the correct answer).

1. The three steps in memory information processing are:
   a. input, processing, output.
   b. input, storage, output.
   c. input, storage, retrieval.
   d. encoding, storage, retrieval.
   e. encoding, retrieval, storage.

2. Visual sensory memory is referred to as:
   a. iconic memory.
   c. photomemory.
   b. echoic memory.
   d. semantic memory.

3. Echoic memories fade after approximately:
   a. 1 hour.
   d. 1 second.
   b. 1 minute.
   e. 3 to 4 seconds.
   c. 30 seconds.

4. Which of the following is *not* a measure of retention?
   a. recall
   c. relearning
   b. recognition
   d. retrieval

5. Our short-term memory span is approximately _____ items.
   a. 2
   c. 7
   b. 5
   d. 10

6. Memory techniques such as the method of loci, acronyms, and the peg-word system are called:
   a. consolidation devices.
   b. imagery techniques.
   c. encoding strategies.
   d. mnemonic devices.

7. One way to increase the amount of information in memory is to group it into larger, familiar units. This process is referred to as:
   a. consolidating.
   d. encoding.
   b. organization.
   e. chunking.
   c. memory construction.

8. Kandel and Schwartz have found that when learning occurs, more of the neurotransmitter _____ is released into synapses.
   a. ACh
   c. serotonin
   b. dopamine
   d. noradrenaline

9. Research on memory construction reveals that memories:
   a. are stored as exact copies of experience.
   b. reflect a person's biases and assumptions.
   c. may be chemically transferred from one organism to another.
   d. even if long term, usually decay within about five years.

10. In a study on context cues, people learned words while on land or when they were underwater. In a later test of recall, those with the best retention had:

   a. learned the words on land, that is, in the more familiar context.
   b. learned the words underwater, that is, in the more exotic context.
   c. learned the words and been tested on them in different contexts.
   d. learned the words and been tested on them in the same context.

11. People who have trouble forgetting unimportant information, such as Russian memory whiz Shereshevskii, often find it difficult to:

   a. encode new information.
   b. recall information without detailed retrieval cues.
   c. think abstractly.
   d. do all of the above.

12. The spacing effect means that:

   a. distributed study yields better retention than cramming.
   b. retention is improved when encoding and retrieval are separated by no more than 1 hour.
   c. learning causes a reduction in the size of the synaptic gap between certain neurons.
   d. delaying retrieval until memory has consolidated improves recall.

13. Studies demonstrate that learning causes permanent neural changes in the _____ between neurons.

   a. myelin            c. synapses
   b. cell bodies       d. all the above

14. In Sperling's memory experiment, subjects were shown three rows of three letters, followed immediately by a low-, medium-, or high-pitched tone. The subjects were able to report:

   a. all three rows with perfect accuracy.
   b. only the top row of letters.
   c. only the middle row of letters.
   d. any one of the three rows of letters.

15. Studies of amnesics suggest that:

   a. memory is a single, unified system.
   b. there are two distinct types of memory.
   c. there are three distinct types of memory.
   d. memory losses following brain trauma are unpredictable.
   e. brain trauma eliminates the ability to learn.

16. Memory for skills is called:

   a. explicit memory.      c. episodic memory.
   b. declarative memory.   d. implicit memory.

17. The eerie feeling of having been somewhere before is an example of:

   a. state dependency.     c. priming.
   b. encoding failure.     d. déjà vu.

18. When Gordon Bower presented subjects with words grouped by category or in random order, recall was:

   a. the same for all words.
   b. better for the categorized words.
   c. better for the random words.
   d. improved when subjects developed their own mnemonic devices.

19. Which of the following has been proposed as a neurophysiological explanation of infantile amnesia?

   a. The slow maturation of the hippocampus leaves the infant's brain unable to store images and events.
   b. The deficient supply of serotonin until about age 3 makes encoding very limited.
   c. The limited availability of association areas of the cortex until about age 3 impairs encoding and storage.
   d. All of the above explanations have been proposed.

20. Hypnotically "refreshed" memories may prove inaccurate—especially if the hypnotist asks leading questions—because of:

   a. encoding failure.
   b. state-dependent memory.
   c. proactive interference.
   d. memory construction.

*Matching Items*

Match each definition or description with the appropriate term.

*Definitions or Descriptions*

_K_ **1.** sensory memory that decays more slowly than visual sensory memory

_L_ **2.** the process by which information gets into the memory system

_I_ **3.** mental pictures that aid memory

_a_ **4.** the blocking of painful memories

____ **5.** the phenomenon in which one's mood can influence retrieval

____ **6.** memory for a list of words is affected by word order

____ **7.** "one is a bun, two is a shoe" mnemonic device

____ **8.** matching each of a series of locations with a visual representation of to-be-remembered items

_g_ **9.** new learning interferes with previous knowledge

_b_ **10.** a measure of memory

_F_ **11.** old knowledge interferes with new learning

____ **12.** misattributing the origin of an event

*Terms*

**a.** repression
**b.** relearning
**c.** serial position effect
**d.** peg-word system
**e.** method of loci
**f.** proactive interference
**g.** retroactive interference
**h.** source amnesia
**i.** imagery
**j.** mood-congruent memory
**k.** echoic memory
**l.** encoding

## Progress Test 2

Progress Test 2 should be completed during a final chapter review. Answer the following questions after you thoroughly understand the correct answers for the Chapter Review and Progress Test 1.

*Multiple-Choice Questions*

1. Which of the following best describes the typical forgetting curve?
   **a.** a steady, slow decline in retention over time
   **b.** a steady, rapid decline in retention over time
   **c.** a rapid initial decline in retention becoming stable thereafter
   **d.** a slow initial decline in retention becoming rapid thereafter

2. Jenkins and Dallenbach found that memory was better in subjects who were _____ during the retention interval, presumably because _____ was reduced.
   **a.** awake; decay
   **b.** asleep; decay
   **c.** awake; interference
   **d.** asleep; interference

3. Which of the following measures of retention is the least sensitive in triggering retrieval?
   **a.** recall          **c.** relearning
   **b.** recognition     **d.** déjà vu

4. Amnesics typically have experienced damage to the _____ of the brain.
   **a.** frontal lobes      **d.** hippocampus
   **b.** cerebellum         **e.** cortex
   **c.** thalamus

5. According to the serial position effect, when recalling a list of words you should have the greatest difficulty with those:
   **a.** at the beginning of the list.
   **b.** at the end of the list.
   **c.** at the end and in the middle of the list.
   **d.** at the beginning and end of the list.
   **e.** in the middle of the list.

6. Craik and Watkins gave subjects a list of words to be recalled. When subjects were tested after a delay, the items that were best recalled were those:
   a. at the beginning of the list.
   b. in the middle of the list.
   c. at the end of the list.
   d. at the beginning and the end of the list.

7. The cerebellum plays a critical role in _____ memory.
   a. recall          c. explicit
   b. recognition     d. implicit

8. Lashley's studies, in which rats learned a maze and then had various parts of their brains surgically removed, showed that:
   a. the memory was lost when surgery took place within 1 hour of learning.
   b. the memory was lost when surgery took place within 24 hours of learning.
   c. the memory was lost when any region of the brain was removed.
   d. the memory remained no matter which area of the brain was tampered with.

9. The disruption of memory caused by excessive consumption of alcohol provides evidence for the importance of:
   a. neurotransmitters in the formation of new memories.
   b. neurotransmitters in the retrieval of long-term memories.
   c. nutrition in normal neural functioning.
   d. all of the above.

10. *Long-term potentiation* refers to:
    a. the disruptive influence of old memories on the formation of new memories.
    b. the disruptive influence of recent memories on the retrieval of old memories.
    c. our tendency to recall experiences that are consistent with our current mood.
    d. the increased efficiency of synaptic transmission between certain neurons following learning.
    e. our increased ability to recall long-ago events as we grow older.

11. Repression is an example of:
    a. encoding failure.   c. motivated forgetting.
    b. memory decay.       d. all of the above.

12. Studies by Loftus and Palmer, in which subjects were quizzed about a film of an accident, indicate that:
    a. when quizzed immediately, subjects can recall very little, due to the stress of witnessing an accident.
    b. when questioned as little as one day later, their memory was very inaccurate.
    c. most subjects had very accurate memories as much as 6 months later.
    d. subjects' recall may easily be affected by misleading information.

13. Which of the following was *not* recommended as a strategy for improving memory?
    a. active rehearsal
    b. distributed study
    c. speed reading
    d. encoding meaningful associations
    e. use of mnemonic devices

14. The process of getting information out of memory storage is called:
    a. encoding.       c. rehearsal.
    b. retrieval.      d. storage.

15. Amnesic patients typically experience disruption of:
    a. implicit memories.   c. iconic memories.
    b. explicit memories.   d. echoic memories.

16. Information is maintained in short-term memory only briefly unless it is:
    a. encoded.        c. iconic or echoic.
    b. rehearsed.      d. retrieved.

17. In order to facilitate information processing, textbook chapters are often organized into _____
    a. mnemonic devices   c. hierarchies
    b. chunks             d. recognizable units

18. Memory researchers are suspicious of long-repressed memories of traumatic events that are "recovered" with the aid of drugs or hypnosis because:
    a. such experiences usually are vividly remembered.
    b. such memories are unreliable and easily influenced by misinformation.
    c. memories of events happening before about age 3 are especially unreliable.
    d. of all of the above reasons.

**19.** Recalling a memory through priming illustrates the operation of:

    **a.** proactive interference.
    **b.** retrieval cues.
    **c.** mnemonic devices.
    **d.** mood-congruent memory.

**20.** The misinformation effect provides evidence that memory:

    **a.** is constructed during encoding.
    **b.** is unchanging once established.
    **c.** may be reconstructed during recall according to how questions are framed.
    **d.** is highly resistant to misleading information.

### True-False Items

Indicate whether each statement is true or false by placing *T* or *F* in the blank next to the item.

    **1.** Studying that is distributed over time produces better retention than cramming.

    **2.** Generally speaking, memory for high-imagery words is better than memory for low-imagery words.

    **3.** Recall of childhood abuse through hypnosis indicates that memory is permanent, due to the reliability of such reports.

    **4.** Most people do not have memories of events that occurred before the age of 3.

    **5.** Studies by Ebbinghaus show that most forgetting takes place soon after learning.

    **6.** How real a memory feels is a good clue as to whether or not it derives from an actual experience.

    **7.** Recall of newly acquired knowledge is no better after sleeping than after being awake for the same period of time.

    **8.** Time spent in developing imagery, chunking, and associating material with what you already know is more effective than time spent repeating information again and again.

    **9.** Although repression has not been confirmed experimentally, most clinical psychologists believe that it frequently happens.

    **10.** Overlearning material by continuing to restudy it beyond mastery often disrupts recall.

## Thinking Critically About Chapter 7

Answer these questions the day before an exam as a final check on your understanding of the chapter's terms and concepts.

### Multiple-Choice Questions

**1.** Complete this analogy: Fill-in-the-blank test questions are to multiple-choice questions as:

    **a.** encoding is to storage.
    **b.** storage is to encoding.
    **c.** recognition is to recall.
    **d.** recall is to recognition.
    **e.** encoding is to recall.

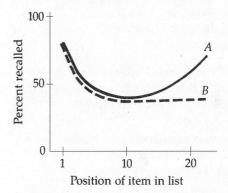

**2.** The above figure depicts the recall of a list of words under two conditions. Which of the following best describes the difference between the conditions?

    **a.** In *A*, the words were studied and retrieved in the same context; in *B*, the contexts were different.
    **b.** In *B*, the words were studied and retrieved in the same context; in *A*, the contexts were different.
    **c.** The delay between presentation of the last word and the test of recall was longer for *A* than for *B*.
    **d.** The delay between presentation of the last word and the test of recall was longer for *B* than for *A*.

**3.** When he was 7, Kip had a nightmare in which he fell from a tree. Twenty years later he mistakenly recalled falling from a tree as an actual experience. Kip's false memory is an example of:

    **a.** mood-congruent memory.
    **b.** implicit memory.
    **c.** source amnesia.
    **d.** the misinformation effect.

4. After finding her old combination lock, Janice can't remember its combination because she keeps confusing it with the combination of her new lock. She is experiencing:
   a. proactive interference.
   b. retroactive interference.
   c. encoding failure.
   d. storage failure.
   e. repression.

5. Which of the following sequences would be best to follow if you wanted to minimize interference-induced forgetting in order to improve your recall on the psychology midterm?
   a. study, eat, test
   b. study, sleep, test
   c. study, listen to music, test
   d. study, exercise, test

6. Being in a bad mood after a hard day of work, Susan could think of nothing positive in her life. This is best explained as an example of:
   a. priming.
   b. memory construction.
   c. mood-congruent memory.
   d. retrieval failure.
   e. repression.

7. In an effort to remember the name of the classmate who sat behind her in fifth grade, Martina mentally recited the names of other classmates who sat near her. Martina's effort to refresh her memory by activating related associations is an example of:
   a. priming.                c. encoding.
   b. déjà vu.                 d. relearning.

8. Walking through the halls of his high school 10 years after graduation, Tom experienced a flood of old memories. Tom's experience showed the role of:
   a. mood-congruent memory.
   b. context effects.
   c. retroactive interference.
   d. echoic memory.
   e. iconic memory.

9. The first thing Karen did when she discovered that she had misplaced her keys was to re-create in her mind the day's events. That she had little difficulty in doing so illustrates:
   a. automatic processing.
   b. effortful processing.
   c. state-dependent memory.
   d. priming.

10. Which of the following is the best example of a flashbulb memory?
    a. suddenly remembering to buy bread while standing in the checkout line at the grocery store
    b. recalling the name of someone from high school while looking at his or her yearbook snapshot
    c. remembering to make an important phone call
    d. remembering what you were doing the day Princess Diana of Wales died in a car crash.

11. When Carlos was promoted, he moved into a new office with a new phone extension. Every time he is asked for his phone number, Carlos first thinks of his old extension, illustrating the effects of:
    a. proactive interference.
    b. retroactive interference.
    c. encoding failure.
    d. storage failure.

12. Elderly Mr. Flanagan can easily recall his high school graduation, but he cannot remember the name of the president of the United States. Evidently, Mr. Flanagan's _____ memory is better than his _____ memory.
    a. implicit; explicit
    b. explicit; implicit
    c. episodic; semantic
    d. semantic; episodic

13. Although you can't recall the answer to a question on your psychology midterm, you have a clear mental image of the textbook page on which it appears. Your memory of this incidental detail illustrates:
    a. overlearning.
    b. semantic encoding.
    c. chunking.
    d. iconic memory.
    e. automatic processing.

14. At your high school reunion you cannot remember the last name of your homeroom teacher. Your failure to remember is most likely the result of:
    a. encoding failure.
    b. storage failure.
    c. retrieval failure.
    d. state-dependent memory.

15. Brenda has trouble remembering her new five-digit ZIP plus four-digit address code. What is the most likely explanation for the difficulty Brenda is having?

   a. Nine digits are at or above the upper limit of most people's short-term memory capacity.
   b. Nine digits are at or above the upper limit of most people's iconic memory capacity.
   c. The extra four digits cannot be organized into easily remembered chunks.
   d. Brenda evidently has an impaired implicit memory.

16. Lewis cannot remember the details of the torture he experienced as a prisoner of war. According to Freud, Lewis's failure to remember these painful memories is an example of:

   a. repression.
   b. retrieval failure.
   c. state-dependent memory.
   d. flashbulb memory.
   e. implicit memory.

17. Which of the following illustrates the constructive nature of memory?

   a. Janice keeps calling her new boyfriend by her old boyfriend's name.
   b. After studying all afternoon and then getting drunk in the evening, Don can't remember the material he studied.
   c. After getting some good news, elated Kareem has a flood of good memories from his younger years.
   d. Although elderly Mrs. Harvey, who has Alzheimer's disease, has many gaps in her memory, she invents sensible accounts of her activities so that her family will not worry.

18. To help him remember the order of ingredients in difficult recipes, master chef Giulio often associates them with the route he walks to work each day. Giulio is using which mnemonic technique?

   a. peg-word system     c. the method of loci
   b. acronyms            d. chunking

19. During basketball practice Jan's head was painfully elbowed. If the trauma to her brain disrupts her memory, we would expect that Jan would be most likely to forget:

   a. the name of her teammates.
   b. her telephone number.
   c. the name of the play during which she was elbowed.
   d. the details of events that happened shortly after the incident.

20. After suffering damage to the hippocampus, a person would probably:

   a. lose memory for skills such as bicycle riding.
   b. be incapable of being classically conditioned.
   c. lose the ability to store new facts.
   d. experience all of the above changes.

## Essay Question

Discuss the points of agreement among experts regarding the validity of recovered memories of child abuse. (Use the space below to jot down notes for your essay; then write the essay on a separate piece of paper.)

# Key Terms

## Writing Definitions

Using your own words, on a separate piece of paper write a brief definition or explanation of each of the following terms.

1. memory
2. flashbulb memory
3. encoding
4. storage
5. retrieval
6. long-term memory
7. short-term memory
8. sensory memory
9. automatic processing
10. effortful processing
11. rehearsal
12. spacing effect

encoding that appears to be learned. Effortful processing, or encoding that requires attention and effort, is used to encode material like telephone numbers, word lists, textbook chapters, and so on.

6. rehearsal
7. Ebbinghaus; fewer
8. overlearning
9. least; next-in-line
10. spacing effect
11. serial position effect; better
12. meaning
13. what was encoded
14. rephrase
15. imagery
16. 3 or 4
17. better
18. mnemonic; method of loci
19. peg-word
20. chunks; acronym
21. hierarchies
22. encoding failure; encoding; less
23. storage
24. sensory
25. about half; more; iconic
26. echoic; less; 3 or 4 seconds
27. rehearsal
28. 7; speak; 2
29. unlimited (limitless)
30. soon
31. do not
32. interfere; decays
33. cortexes; remembered
34. electrical
35. synapses
36. serotonin
37. less; receptor sites; long-term potentiation
38. drugs; enzyme; LTP; faster
39. will not; will
40. formation; serotonin
41. glucose; disrupt
42. amnesia; is not
43. have not; implicit; are not; explicit
44. hippocampus; explicit; verbal; visual; implicit
45. infantile; hippocampus
46. recall
47. recall; recognize
48. relearn; more

49. priming; encode
50. the same

The déjà vu experience is most likely the result of being in a context similar to one that we *have* actually been in before. If we have previously been in a similar situation, though we cannot recall what it was, the current situation may present cues that unconsciously help us to retrieve the earlier experience.

51. state-dependent

The effect of state-dependent memory is that things learned in one state are most easily recalled when we are again in the same state. Our memories are also somewhat mood-congruent. When happy, for example, we perceive things in a positive light and recall happy events; these perceptions and memories, in turn, prolong our good mood. Moods also influence how we interpret other people's behavior and how attentive we are to new information.

52. retrieval
53. interference
54. proactive interference; retroactive interference
55. better
56. positive transfer
57. repression; less
58. construction

When subjects viewed a film of a traffic accident and were quizzed a week later, misleading postevent information was found to influence recall of the event. Phrasing of questions affected answers; the word "smashed," for instance, made subjects mistakenly think they had seen broken glass.

59. misinformation effect; can
60. hypnosis
61. source amnesia; misattribute
62. are not; do not
63. traumatic events; drugs or hypnosis; are
64. false memory syndrome
65. 3; infantile amnesia

Strategies for improving memory include active and spaced rehearsal, organized encoding based on meaningful and vivid associations, use of mnemonic devices, minimizing interference, and frequent self-testing and rehearsal.

# Progress Test 1

## Multiple-Choice Questions

1. **d.** is the answer. Information must be encoded, or put into appropriate form; stored, or retained

over time; and retrieved, or located and gotten out when needed. (p. 233)

2. **a.** is the answer. Iconic memory is our fleeting memory of visual stimuli. (p. 242)
   **b.** Echoic memory is auditory sensory memory.
   **c.** There is no such thing as photomemory.
   **d.** Semantic memory is memory for meaning, not a form of sensory memory.

3. **e.** is the answer. Echoic memories last 3 to 4 seconds. (p. 242)

4. **d.** is the answer. Retrieval refers to the *process* of remembering. (p. 249)

5. **c.** is the answer. (p. 242)

6. **d.** is the answer. (p. 238)
   **a.** There is no such term as "consolidation techniques."
   **b. & c.** Imagery and encoding strategies are important in storing new memories, but *mnemonic device* is the general designation of techniques that facilitate memory, such as acronyms and the peg-word system.

7. **e.** is the answer. (p. 238)
   **a.** There is no such process of "consolidating."
   **b.** Organization *does* enhance memory but it does so through hierarchies, not grouping.
   **c.** Memory construction refers to the ways in which memories are altered by the individual's basic assumptions and experiences.
   **d.** Encoding refers to the processing of information into the memory system.

8. **c.** is the answer. Kandel and Schwartz found that when learning occurred in the sea snail, serotonin was released at certain synapses, which then became more efficient at signal transmission. (p. 245)

9. **b.** is the answer. In essence, we construct our memories, bringing them into line with our biases and assumptions, as well as with our subsequent experiences. (p. 256)
   **a.** If this were true, it would mean that memory construction does not occur. Through memory construction, memories may deviate significantly from the original experiences.
   **c.** There is no evidence that such chemical transfers occur.
   **d.** Many long-term memories are apparently unlimited in duration.

10. **d.** is the answer. In general, being in a context similar to that in which you experienced something will tend to help you recall the experience. (p. 250)
    **a. & b.** The learning environment per se—and its familiarity or exoticness—did not affect retention.

11. **c.** is the answer. (p. 240)
    **a.** Because information is remembered, it must have been encoded and placed in storage.
    **b.** The text does not suggest that S. found it more difficult to recall information without retrieval cues.

12. **a.** is the answer. (p. 235)
    **b. & d.** The text does not suggest that there is an optimal interval between encoding and retrieval.
    **c.** Learning increases the efficiency of synaptic transmission in certain neurons, but not by altering the size of the synapse.

13. **c.** is the answer. (pp. 245)

14. **d.** is the answer. When asked to recall all the letters, subjects could recall only about half; however, if immediately after the presentation they were signaled to recall a particular row, their recall was near perfect. This showed that they had a brief photographic memory—so brief that it faded in less time than it would have taken to say all nine letters. (pp. 241–242)

15. **b.** is the answer. Because amnesics lose their fact (explicit) memories but not their skill (implicit) memories or their capacity to learn, it appears that human memory can be divided into two distinct types. (pp. 246–247)
    **d.** As studies of victims of amnesia show, memory losses following damage to the hippocampus are quite predictable.

16. **d.** is the answer. (p. 247)
    **a. & b.** Explicit memory (also called declarative memory) is memory of facts and experiences that one can consciously know and declare.
    **c.** Episodic memory is explicit memory for personally experienced events.

17. **d.** is the answer. (p. 251)
    **a.** State-dependent memory is the phenomenon in which information is best retrieved when the person is in the same emotional or physiological state he or she was in when the material was learned.
    **b.** Encoding failure occurs when a person has not processed information sufficiently for it to enter the memory system.
    **c.** Priming is the process by which a memory is activated through retrieval of an associated memory.

18. **b.** is the answer. When the words were organized into categories, recall was two to three times better, indicating the benefits of hierarchical organization in memory. (p. 239)
    **d.** This study did not examine the use of mnemonic devices by subjects.

19. **a.** is the answer. We remember skills acquired in infancy, as such memories are recorded in earlier developing brain regions, but declarative memories involve the hippocampus. (p. 248)

    **b., c., & d.** There is no evidence that serotonin levels or association areas are deficient until age 3. Moreover, such proposals are unlikely, as they wouldn't explain why we remember skills learned in infancy while forgetting events experienced.

20. **d.** is the answer. It is in both encoding and retrieval that we construct our memories, and as Loftus's studies showed, leading questions affect people's memory construction. (p. 257)

    **a.** The memory encoding occurred at the time of the event in question, not during questioning by the hypnotist.

    **b.** State-dependent memory refers to the influence of one's own emotional or physiological state on encoding and retrieval, and would not apply here.

    **c.** Proactive interference is the interfering effect of prior learning on the recall of new information.

## Matching Items

1. k (p. 242)    5. j (p. 252)    9. g (p. 253)
2. l (p. 233)    6. c (p. 236)    10. b (p. 249)
3. i (p. 237)    7. d (p. 238)    11. f (p. 253)
4. a (pp. 254–255)    8. e (p. 238)    12. h (p. 257)

## Progress Test 2

### Multiple-Choice Questions

1. **c.** is the answer. As Ebbinghaus and Bahrick both showed, most of the forgetting that is going to occur happens soon after learning. (p. 243)

2. **d.** is the answer. (p. 254)

    **a. & b.** This study did not find evidence that memories fade (decay) with time.

    **c.** When one is awake, there are many *more* potential sources of memory interference than when one is asleep.

3. **a.** is the answer. A test of recall presents the fewest retrieval cues and usually produces the most limited retrieval. (p. 249)

4. **d.** is the answer. (p. 246)

5. **e.** is the answer. According to the serial position effect, items at the beginning and end of a list tend to be remembered best. (p. 236)

6. **a.** is the answer. (p. 236)

    **b.** In the serial position effect, the items in the middle of the list always show the *poorest* retention.

**c. & d.** Delayed recall erases the memory facilitation for items at the end of the list.

7. **d.** is the answer. (p. 248)

    **a, b, & c.** Recall and recognition tests of memory generally pertain to *explicit* memory of facts, which depends more on the hippocampus than on the cerebellum.

8. **d.** is the answer. Surprisingly, Lashley found that no matter where he cut, the rats had at least a partial memory of how to solve the maze. (p. 245)

    **a. & b.** Lashley's studies did not investigate the significance of the interval between learning and cortical lesioning.

9. **a.** is the answer. Alcohol disrupts memory by interfering with the neurotransmitter serotonin. (p. 246)

    **b.** The disruptive effects of alcohol are on the formation, rather than the retrieval, of memories.

    **c.** Although nutrition plays an important role in brain chemistry, the effects of alcohol are independent of nutrition.

10. **d.** is the answer. (p. 245)

11. **c.** is the answer. According to Freud, we repress painful memories to preserve our self-concepts. (pp. 254–255)

    **a. & b.** The fact that repressed memories can sometimes be retrieved suggests that they were encoded and have not decayed with time.

12. **d.** is the answer. When misled by the phrasings of questions, subjects incorrectly recalled details of the film and even "remembered" objects that weren't there. (pp. 255–256)

13. **c.** is the answer. Speed reading, which entails little active rehearsal, yields poor retention. (p. 263)

14. **b.** is the answer. (p. 233)

    **a.** Encoding is the processing of information *into* memory.

    **c.** Rehearsal is the conscious repetition of information in order to maintain it in memory.

    **d.** Storage is the maintenance of encoded material over time.

15. **b.** is the answer. Amnesics typically have suffered damage to the hippocampus, a brain structure involved in processing explicit memories for facts. (p. 247)

    **a.** Amnesics do retain implicit memories for how to do things; these are processed in the more ancient parts of the brain.

    **c. & d.** Amnesics generally do not experience impairment in their iconic and echoic sensory memories.

16. **b.** is the answer. (p. 235)

**a.** Information in short-term memory has *already* been encoded.

**c.** Iconic and echoic are types of *sensory* memory.

**d.** Retrieval is the process of getting material out of storage and into conscious, short-term memory. Thus, all material in short-term memory has either already been retrieved, or is about to be placed in storage.

17. **c.** is the answer. By breaking concepts down into subconcepts and yet smaller divisions and showing the relationships among these, hierarchies facilitate information processing. Use of main heads and subheads is an example of the organization of textbook chapters into hierarchies. (p. 239)

    **a.** Mnemonic devices are the method of loci, acronyms, and other memory *techniques* that facilitate retention.

    **b.** Chunks are organizations of knowledge into familiar, manageable units.

    **d.** Recognition is a measure of retention.

18. **d.** is the answer. (pp. 260–261)

19. **b.** is the answer. (p. 250)

    **a.** Interference *disrupts* recall.

    **c.** Mnemonic devices are memory aids which often use visual imagery.

    **d.** This is the tendency to recall experiences that are consistent with our current mood.

20. **c.** is the answer. Loftus and Palmer found that eyewitness testimony could easily be altered when questions were phrased to imply misleading information. (p. 255–256)

    **a.** Although memories *are* constructed during encoding, the misinformation effect is a retrieval, rather than an encoding, phenomenon.

    **b. & d.** In fact, just the opposite is true.

*True-False Items*

| | | | |
|---|---|---|---|
| **1.** | T (p. 263) | **6.** | F (p. 258) |
| **2.** | T (p. 237) | **7.** | F (p. 254) |
| **3.** | F (p. 260) | **8.** | T (p. 263) |
| **4.** | T (p. 248) | **9.** | T (p. 255) |
| **5.** | T (p. 243) | **10.** | F (p. 235) |

# Thinking Critically About Chapter 7

*Multiple-Choice Questions*

1. **d.** is the answer. (p. 249)

    **a., b., & e.** In order to correctly answer either type of question, the knowledge must have been encoded and stored.

    **c.** With fill-in-the-blank questions, the answer must be recalled with no retrieval cues other than the question. With multiple-choice questions, the correct answer merely has to be recognized from among several alternatives.

2. **d.** is the answer. (p. 236)

    **a. & b.** A serial position effect would presumably occur whether the study and retrieval contexts were the same or different.

    **c.** As Craik and Watkins found, when recall is delayed, only the first items in a list are recalled more accurately than the others. With immediate recall, both the first and last items are recalled more accurately.

3. **c.** is the answer. (p. 257)

    **a.** This is the tendency to recall experiences that are consistent with our current mood.

    **b.** This is memory for skills.

    **d.** Kip has confused the *source* of his memory.

4. **b.** is the answer. Retroactive interference is the disruption of something you once learned by new information. (p. 253)

    **a.** Proactive interference occurs when old information makes it difficult to correctly remember new information.

    **c. & d.** Interference produces forgetting even when the forgotten material was effectively encoded and stored. Janice's problem is at the level of retrieval.

    **e.** There is no reason to believe that Janice's old locker combination is a painful memory.

5. **b.** is the answer. (p. 254)

    **a., c., & d.** Involvement in other activities, even just eating or listening to music, is more disruptive than sleeping.

6. **c.** is the answer. Susan's memories are affected by her bad mood. (p. 252)

    **a.** Priming refers to the conscious or unconscious activation of particular associations in memory.

    **b.** Memory construction refers to changes in memory as new experiences occur.

    **d.** Although Susan's difficulty in recalling the good could be considered retrieval failure, it is caused by the mood-congruent effect, which is therefore the best explanation.

    **e.** Repression involves the suppression of *painful* memories.

7. **a.** is the answer. Priming is the conscious or unconscious activation of particular associations in memory. (p. 250)

    **b.** Déjà vu is the false impression of having previously experienced a current situation.

    **c.** That Martina is able to retrieve her former classmates' names implies that they already have been encoded.

    **d.** Relearning is a measure of retention based on how long it takes to relearn something already mastered. Martina is recalling her former classmates' names, not relearning them.

8. **b.** is the answer. Being back in the context in which the original experiences occurred triggered memories of these experiences. (p. 250)
**a.** The memories were triggered by similarity of place, not mood.
**c.** Retroactive interference would involve difficulties in retrieving old memories.
**d.** Echoic memory refers to momentary memory of auditory stimuli.
**e.** Iconic memory refers to momentary memory of visual stimuli.

9. **a.** is the answer. Time and space—and therefore sequences of events—are often automatically processed. (p. 234)
**b.** That she had *little difficulty* indicates that the processing was automatic, rather than effortful.
**c. & d.** State-dependent memory and priming have nothing to do with the automatic processing of space and time.

10. **d.** is the answer. Flashbulb memories are unusually clear memories of emotionally significant moments in life. (p. 232)

11. **a.** is the answer. Proactive interference occurs when old information makes it difficult to recall new information. (p. 253)
**b.** If Carlos were having trouble remembering the old extension, this answer would be correct.
**c. & d.** Carlos has successfully encoded and stored the extension; he's just having problems retrieving it.

12. **c.** is the answer. Episodic memory is memory for personal life experiences, such as a high school graduation; semantic memory is memory for facts, such as the name of the president. (p. 247)
**a. & b.** Implicit memories are memories for skills. Both of these examples involve explicit memory, which is memory for facts and experiences.

13. **e.** is the answer. Spatial information, such as the location of an answer (but not the actual answer) on a textbook page, is often encoded automatically. (p. 234)
**a.** This refers to the fact that, even after we learn material, additional rehearsal increases retention.
**b.** This refers to encoding information according to its meaning.
**c.** This is the memory technique of organizing material into familiar units.
**d.** This is sensory memory; your recollection is longer lasting.

14. **c.** is the answer. (p. 252)
**a. & b.** The name of your homeroom teacher, which you probably heard at least once each day

of school, was surely processed into memory (encoded) and maintained there for some time (stored).
**d.** State-dependent memory is the tendency to recall information best in the same emotional or physiological state as when it was learned. It is unlikely that a single state was associated with learning your homeroom teacher's name.

15. **a.** is the answer. Short-term memory capacity is approximately seven digits. (p. 242)
**b.** Because iconic memory lasts no more than a second or so, regardless of how much material is experienced, this cannot be the explanation for Brenda's difficulty.
**c.** The final four digits should be no more difficult to organize into chunks than the first five digits of the address code.
**d.** Memory for digits is an example of explicit, rather than implicit, memory.

16. **a.** is the answer. (pp. 254–255)
**b.** Although Lewis's difficulty in recalling these memories could be considered retrieval failure, it is caused by repression, which is therefore the *best* explanation.
**c.** This answer is incorrect because it is clear that Lewis fails to remember these experiences because they are painful memories and not because he is in a different emotional or physiological state.
**d.** Flashbulb memories are especially *vivid* memories for emotionally significant events. Lewis has no memory at all.
**e.** Implicit memories are memories of skills.

17. **d.** is the answer. (p. 256)
**a.** This is an example of proactive interference.
**b.** This is an example of the disruptive effects of depressant drugs, such as alcohol, on the formation of new memories.
**c.** This is mood-congruent memory.

18. **c.** is the answer. (p. 238)
**a.** The peg-word system involves developing associations between rhyming words in a jingle and to-be-remembered items.
**b.** Acronyms are words created from the first letters of to-be-remembered words.
**d.** Chunking is the organization of information into meaningful units, such as acronyms.

19. **c.** is the answer. Blows to the head usually disrupt the most recent experiences, such as this one, rather than long-term memories like those in choices a. and b., or new learning such as that in choice d. (p. 246)

20. **c.** is the answer. The hippocampus is involved in processing new facts for storage. (pp. 247–248)
**a., b., & d.** Studies of amnesics with hippocampal

damage show that neither classical conditioning nor skill memory are impaired, indicating that these aspects of memory are controlled by more primitive regions of the brain.

### Essay Question

Experts agree that child abuse is a real problem that can have long-term adverse effects on individuals. They also acknowledge that forgetting of isolated events, both good and bad, is an ordinary part of life. Although experts all accept the fact that recovered memories are commonplace, they warn that memories "recovered" under hypnosis or with the use of drugs are unreliable, as are memories of events before age 3. Finally, they agree that memories can be traumatic, whether real or false.

## Key Terms

1. **Memory** is the persistence of learning over time through the storage and retrieval of information. (p. 231)

2. A **flashbulb memory** is an unusually vivid memory of an emotionally important moment in one's life. (p. 232)

3. **Encoding** is the first step in memory; information is translated into some form that enables it to enter our memory system. (p. 233)

4. **Storage** is the passive process by which encoded information is maintained over time. (p. 233)

5. **Retrieval** is the process of bringing to consciousness information from memory storage. (p. 233)

6. **Long-term memory** is the relatively permanent and unlimited storehouse of the memory system into which information from short-term memory may pass. (p. 233)

7. **Short-term memory** is conscious memory, which can hold about seven items for a short time. (p. 233)

8. **Sensory memory** is the immediate, initial recording of sensory information in the memory system. (p. 234)

9. **Automatic processing** refers to our unconscious encoding of incidental information such as space, time, and frequency, and of well-learned information. (p. 234)

10. **Effortful processing** is encoding that requires attention and some degree of conscious effort. (p. 234)

11. **Rehearsal** is the conscious, effortful repetition of information that you are trying either to maintain in consciousness or to encode for storage. (p. 235)

12. The **spacing effect** is the tendency for distributed practice to yield better long-term retention than massed practice, or cramming. (p. 235)

13. The **serial position effect** is the tendency for items at the beginning and end of a list to be more easily retained than those in the middle. (p. 236)

14. **Imagery** refers to mental pictures and can be an important aid to effortful processing. (p. 237)

15. **Mnemonics** are memory aids (the method of loci, acronyms, peg-words, etc.), which often use visual imagery and organizational devices. (p. 238)

16. **Chunking** is the memory technique of organizing material into familiar, meaningful units. (p. 238)

17. **Iconic memory** is the visual sensory memory consisting of a perfect photographic memory, which lasts no more than a few tenths of a second. (p. 242)

   *Memory aid*: *Icon* means "image" or "representation." **Iconic memory** consists of brief visual images.

18. **Echoic memory** is the momentary sensory memory of auditory stimuli, lasting about 3 or 4 seconds. (p. 242)

19. **Long-term potentiation (LTP)** is an increase in a synapse's firing potential following brief, rapid stimulation. LTP is believed to be the neural basis for learning and memory. (p. 245)

20. **Amnesia** is the loss of memory. (p. 246)

21. **Implicit memories** are memories of skills, preferences, and dispositions. These memories are evidently processed, not by the hippocampus, but by a more primitive part of the brain, the cerebellum. They are also called nondeclarative memories. (p. 247)

22. **Explicit memories** are memories of facts, including names, images, and events. They are also called declarative memories. (p. 247)

23. The **hippocampus** is a neural region within the limbic system that is important in the processing of explicit memories for storage. (p. 247)

24. **Recall** is a measure of retention in which the person must remember, with few retrieval cues, information learned earlier. (p. 249)

25. **Recognition** is a measure of retention in which one need only identify, rather than recall, previously learned information. (p. 249)

26. **Relearning** is also a measure of retention in that the less time it takes to relearn information, the more that information has been retained. (p. 249)

27. **Priming** is the activation, often unconscious, of a

web of associations in memory in order to retrieve a specific memory. (p. 250)

28. **Déjà vu** is the false sense that you have already experienced a current situation. (p. 251)

29. **Mood-congruent memory** is the tendency to recall experiences that are consistent with our current mood. (p. 252)

30. **Proactive interference** is the disruptive effect of something you already have learned on your efforts to learn or recall new information. (p. 253)

31. **Retroactive interference** is the disruptive effect of something recently learned on old knowledge. (p. 253)

    *Memory aid*: *Retro* means "backward." **Retroactive interference** is "backward-acting" interference.

32. In psychoanalytic theory, **repression** is the basic defense mechanism that banishes painful and unacceptable memories from consciousness. (pp. 254–255)

33. The **misinformation effect** is the tendency of eyewitnesses of an event to incorporate misleading information about the event into their memories. (p. 256)

34. At the heart of many false memories, **source amnesia** refers to misattributing an event to the wrong source. (p. 257)

## Summing Up

### Information Processing

External events are initially recorded as sensory memory, which is either *iconic memory* (visual sensory memory) or *echoic memory* (auditory sensory memory). If we pay attention to the information, it is encoded into memory that holds a few items briefly, or *short-term* memory. To get information into storage, we must *encode* it. To get information out of storage, we must *retrieve* it. The relatively limitless, permanent memory where information is stored is *long-term* memory, which is categorized as *explicit memory* (conscious memory of facts and events) or *implicit memory* (automatic memory of skills and behaviors). Explicit memory consists of *semantic memory* (general knowledge) and *episodic memory* (life history memory). Implicit memory includes skill memory, or *skills*, and *dispositions* (or automatic reactions).

---

*FOCUS ON VOCABULARY AND LANGUAGE*

**The Phenomenon of Memory**

*Page 231:* Your memory is your mind's *storehouse*, the *reservoir* of your accumulated learning. Myers is using an analogy to help you understand the general concept of memory. Both *storehouses* and *reservoirs* are used to keep materials (water, food, etc.) until we need them. Likewise, your memory system retains most of the things you experienced (*accumulated learning*), and items can be recalled or retrieved as required.

*Page 231: . . . medal winners in a memory Olympics. . . .* People with exceptional memories are being likened or compared to top athletes in the Olympic Games. S, for example, would clearly receive the top prizes (*medals*) in any competition in which remembering vast amounts of information was being tested (*memory Olympics*).

*Page 232:* Do these memory *feats* make your own memory seem *feeble*? Myers is pointing out that although S may have demonstrated spectacular abilities in remembering all sorts of things (*memory*

*feats*), normal memory in the average person is no less astounding in many ways. Despite our occasional failures, our ordinary memory accomplishments, which we tend to take for granted, are quite remarkable (*they are far from being feeble*).

*Page 232: . . .* police caught five men trying to *tap* the telephones . . . . To *tap* a phone means to connect a device to it in order to listen in on someone's conversation. The "Watergate scandal" started with a phone tapping, and Myers makes reference throughout the chapter to John Dean's memory of all the meetings and events surrounding this famous case. (Dean was President Nixon's legal advisor.)

*Page 234:* Then we *shine the flashlight beam of attention on* certain incoming stimuli, often novel or changing stimuli that fill our on-screen, short-term memory (Figure 7.1). One model of memory suggests that we only focus on (*shine the flashlight beam of attention on*) and process one part or aspect of the total sensory input, particularly new (*novel*) or variable stimuli. We can also locate and bring back stored information from long-term memory (**LTM**) into short-term memory (**STM**).

## Encoding: Getting Information In

*Page 235:* . . . *boost* . . . One way to improve and increase the power of our memory is to use **rehearsal**. Thus, actively repeating some new information (such as a stranger's name or new terminology) will help strengthen (*boost*) our ability to remember this material. As Myers notes, it is important for effective retention to space out or distribute practice (rehearsal) over time rather than doing the repetitions all at once (massed practice or cramming).

*Page 235:* His [Ebbinghaus's] solution was to form a list of all possible *nonsense syllables* created by *sandwiching* a vowel between two consonants. In order to avoid using meaningful words with prior associations, Hermann Ebbinghaus invented three letter words that made no sense and had no meaning (*nonsense syllables*). He did this by putting a vowel (*sandwiching it*) between two consonants. His nonsense (*meaningless*) syllables were consonant (C), vowel (V), Consonant (C), or CVCs.

*Pages 236–237:* Gordon Bower and Daniel Morrow (1990) liken our minds to theater directors who, *given a raw script*, imagine a *finished stage production*. This suggests that what we remember is not an exact replica of reality. We construct some mental representation or model (*finished stage production*) from the basic sensory information (*raw script*) available to us; and so, when we recall something, it is our own version (*mental model*) that comes to mind and not the real thing.

*Page 237:* Thanks to the durability of our most vivid images, we recall our experiences with *mental snapshots* of their best or worst moments. The use of imagery or mental pictures (*snapshots*) is one way to enhance recall. We have exceptionally good memory for pictures and ideas that are encoded using visual imagery. As Myers notes, "imagery is at the heart of many memory aids" (e.g., method of loci, peg-word, etc.).

*Page 238:* For example, the *"peg-word"* system requires that you first memorize a *jingle*. A *jingle* is an easily remembered (*catchy*) succession of words that ring or resound against each other due to alliteration or rhyme and are often used in radio or TV commercials. The mnemonic (memory aid) called the *"peg-word"* method is based on memorizing a short, catchy, 10-item poem (*jingle*) that can be used to associate a new list of 10 items through visual imagery. The new items are hung on, or pegged to, the familiar items.

*Page 239:* Amidst all the *applause for memory* . . . have any voices been heard in praise of forgetting? If we could not forget, we would be like the Russian memory expert (*memory whiz*) S who was overwhelmed by the amount of useless information he had stored (*haunted by his junk heap of memories*). Thus, many people, from William James to contemporary cognitive psychologists, acknowledge the importance of forgetting.

## Storage: Retaining Information

*Page 241:* It was harder than reading by *flashes of lightning*. In his investigation of sensory storage, George Sperling showed his subjects an array of 9 letters for a very brief period (for about the length of a *flash of lightning*). He demonstrated that this was sufficient time for them to briefly view (*glimpse*) all 9 letters and that an image remained for less than half a second before fading away; he called this sensory image **iconic memory.**

*Page 242:* . . . *Sherlock Holmes* . . . Mystery writer Sir Arthur Conan Doyle's most popular character was a very intelligent and logical private detective named Sherlock Holmes. Holmes believed, as did many others, that our memory capacity was limited, much like an empty room can only hold so much furniture before it overflows. Contemporary psychologists now believe that our ability to store long-term memories is basically without any limit.

*Page 243 (caption):* Among animals, one contender for *champion memorist* would be a mere *birdbrain*—the Clark's nutcracker. . . . Clark's nutcracker is a small bird with a small brain (*birdbrain*) but a phenomenal memory (*champion memorist*) of where it buries its food. It can recall, after a period of more than 6 months, 6000 different locations of hidden food.

*Page 244:* While cognitive psychologists study our memory *"software,"* neuroscientists are gaining new insights into our memory *"hardware"* . . . . Throughout this chapter Myers uses the analogy of the computer as a model for how memory works. In attempting to understand memory, cognitive psychologists study the mind and how it works (*the computer "software"*) and neuroscientists study the physical aspect of the brain and the functioning of its neurons (*the computer "hardware"*).

*Page 245:* . . . *with tongue only partially in cheek.* When someone makes a statement that is not meant to be taken seriously, we note that it was said *with tongue in cheek.* When researchers stated that "memories are more of a spiritual than a physical reality," they were somewhat serious (*tongue only partially in cheek*).

*Page 246:* The arousal *sears* the events onto the brain. When arousal level rises because of stress so too do the levels of certain hormones. These in turn signal the brain that something important has happened and the events that triggered the arousal make an indelible impression on the brain much as a hot grill burns (*sears*) its shape on the surface of the meat placed on it.

*Page 247:* They [amnesic people] can be classically conditioned. . . . They can learn to read *mirror-image writing* or do a *jigsaw puzzle.* . . . People who have lost the ability to remember new information (*amnesics*) may nevertheless be capable of learning through association (classical conditioning) and of learning to solve problems (e.g., *jigsaw puzzles*) even if they are not aware of having done so. Myers notes that these findings suggest that memory is not a single, unified system. Amnesics can learn how to *do* something (**implicit memory**) without any knowledge of this learning (**explicit**, or **declarative, memory**).

### Retrieval: Getting Information Out

*Page 249:* The speed and vastness of our recognition memory *dwarfs* any librarian's ability to call up information. Our ability to remember can be measured by **recall** (retrieving information not in conscious awareness) or **recognition** (the ability to identify what has been previously learned). Our recognition memory is very large and works very rapidly, and it can make the librarian's capacity for retrieving information look small (*dwarfs it*).

*Pages 251–252:* If people are put in a *buoyant mood* . . . they recall the world through *rose-colored glasses.* . . . Our memories are affected by our emotional states (*moods*). Thus, if we are in a good or happy (*buoyant*) mood, we are more likely to view the total situation in a more optimistic and hopeful way (through *rose-colored glasses*). Memory of events and people is influenced by the particular mood we are in, whether it is good or bad, and we tend to remember the events accordingly.

*Page 252:* When teenagers are *down,* their world, including their parents, seems inhuman; as their mood *brightens,* their parents *metamorphose from devils into angels.* Because our memories tend to be **mood-congruent**, we are likely to explain our present emotional state by remembering events and people as being consistent (*congruent*) with how we now feel. In one study when young adolescents were in a bad mood (*down*), they viewed their parents as cruel and uncaring (inhuman); but later

when they were in a much better (*brighter*) mood, their parents were described in much nicer terms. It seemed as though their parents had undergone an amazing change in character (*metamorphose from devils to angels*), but the change was simply in the teenagers' mood. As Myers notes, "*passions [or emotions] exaggerate.*"

*Page 252:* A person's name *may lie poised on the tip of the tongue,* waiting to be retrieved. The expression "*it's on the tip of my tongue*" refers to the feeling you get when you are trying to remember something (a name, place, etc.) but can't, even though you feel you know it and can *almost* say it (*it's on the tip of your tongue*). Given an appropriate retrieval cue (for example, the first letter of the name or something it rhymes with) we can often remember the item.

*Page 253:* As you collect more and more information, your *mental attic* never fills, but it certainly gets *cluttered.* We may have an unlimited amount of space in our memory system or *mental attic* (a room at the top of a house), but with a constant flow of new information coming in, the storage can become disorganized (*cluttered*). The new information may get in the way of recalling old material (**retroactive interference**), or old material may block or disrupt recall of new information (**proactive interference**).

*Page 254:* Collectively, we *sheepishly* accepted responsibility for 89 cookies. Still, we had not come close; 160 cookies had been baked. The Myers family obviously loves chocolate chip cookies, and the story of how all 160 were devoured within 24 hours (*not a crumb was left*) is quite funny but makes an important point. Embarrassed, guilty, and feeling a little foolish (*sheepish*), they could only account for and remember eating 89. This illustrates the self-serving nature of memory and how, unknowingly, we change and revise our own histories.

*Page 255:* The words *relit a blown-out candle* in the mind . . . Just as an extinguished (*blown-out*) candle can be reignited (*relit*) with a match, the presentation of a retrieval cue may help someone recall a long forgotten memory. Although Freud proposed that we repress memories of painful experiences in the unconscious in order to protect our self-concepts and minimize anxiety, as Myers notes, most contemporary researchers believe that repression rarely, if ever, happens.

*Page 258:* Because memory is *reconstruction* as well as *reproduction,* we can't be sure whether a memory is real by how real it feels. It is difficult to determine if a memory is real simply by noting how real it feels or how confident we are about its accuracy. We not only recall and retrieve real memories (*reproduction*) but we also manufacture false memories (*reconstruction*).

*Page 258:* If memories can be *sincere*, yet so *sincerely wrong,* might children's recollections of sexual abuse err? The evidence suggests that under appropriate conditions children's memories can be reliable and accurate (*sincere*), but that they are also prone to the misinformation effect and can be misled by biased questions and suggestions; later, the children are not able to reliably separate real from false memories (*sincerely wrong*).

### Improving Memory

*Page 263: Sprinkled* throughout this chapter and summarized here for easy reference are *concrete* suggestions for improving memory. This chapter on memory has many good ideas for memory improvement scattered or interspersed (*sprinkled*) throughout it, and Myers has pulled them all together in an easy-to-understand format—the **SQ3R** (**S**urvey, **Q**uestion, **R**ead, **R**ehearse, **R**eview) method. These are real and tangible (*concrete*) ways that will help you improve your memory. Use them!!!

# Thinking, Language, and Intelligence

## Chapter Overview

Chapter 8 begins with a discussion of thinking, with emphasis on how people logically—or at times illogically—use tools such as algorithms and heuristics when making decisions and solving problems. Also discussed are several common obstacles to problem solving, including fixations that prevent us from taking a fresh perspective on a problem and our bias to seek information that confirms rather than challenges existing hypotheses. The section concludes with a discussion of how our use of intuitive heuristics can lead to faulty decision making.

The next section is concerned with language, including its development in children its existence in animals, and its relationship to thinking. Two theories of language acquisition are evaluated: Skinner's theory that language acquisition is based entirely on learning and Chomsky's theory that humans have a biological predisposition to acquire language.

The final section is concerned with how psychologists have attempted to define and measure intelligence. The historical origins of intelligence tests and several important issues concerning their use are discussed. These include the methods by which intelligence tests are constructed and whether such tests are valid and reliable. The chapter also discusses research that attempts to assess whether intelligence is a single general ability or several specific ones, and the extent of genetic and environmental influences on intelligence.

NOTE: Answer guidelines for all Chapter 8 questions begin on page 233.

## Guided Study

The text chapter should be studied one section at a time. Before you read, preview each section by skimming it, noting headings and boldface items. Then read the appropriate section objectives from the following outline. Keep these objectives in mind and, as you read the chapter section, search for the information that will enable you to meet each objective. Once you have finished a section, write out answers for its objectives.

*Thinking* (pp. 267–277)

> David Myers at times uses idioms that are unfamiliar to some readers. If you do not know the meaning of any of the following words, phrases, or expressions in the context in which they appear in the text, refer to pages 242–243 for an explanation: *kin to; birdier bird; stumbling upon one that worked; rule-of-thumb; Spying the short stick; shoot the basketball; seat of the pants; snap judgment; a broken promise; mere statistics on some world health ledger; plagues; flip-flop; fuels social conflict; filled with straw.*

1. Describe the nature, function, and formation of concepts.

2. Discuss the major problem-solving strategies and describe the nature of insight.

3. Identify obstacles to problem solving.

4. Describe the heuristics that guide decision making and explain how overconfidence, framing, and belief perseverance can affect judgment.

### Language (pp. 277–288)

> If you do not know the meaning of any of the following words, phrases, or expressions in the context in which they appear in the text, refer to page 243 for an explanation: *catapulting our species forward; read lips; a Martian scientist; grammar switches are thrown; rhapsodized; language champs . . . chumps; chicken-and-egg questions.*

5. Trace the course of language acquisition and discuss alternative theories of language development.

6. Describe the research on animal communication and discuss the controversy over whether animals have language.

7. Discuss the relationship between thought and language.

### Intelligence (pp. 289–307)

> David Myers at times uses idioms that are unfamiliar to some readers. If you do not know the meaning of any of the following words, phrases, or expressions, in the context in which they appear in the text, refer to pages 244–245 for an explanation: *controversy . . . has been more heated; dull child; out of whack; dumbfounded; island of brilliance; how to read people; clear-cut; cluster; shrunken tape measure; the pendulum of opinion . . . complete swing; virtual carbon copies of one another; bludgeoning native intelligence; dwarf; sharpest at the extremes; computer camps; Differences are not deficits.*

8. Trace the origins of intelligence tests.

9. Describe the factor-analysis approach to understanding intelligence and discuss evidence regarding intelligence as a general mental ability and/or as many specific abilities.

Describe the normal curve and explain its significance in the standardization process.

49. If a test yields consistent results, it is said to be

_____ .

50. When a test is administered more than once to the same people, the psychologist is determining its _____-_____ reliability.

51. When a person's scores for the odd- and even-numbered questions on a test are compared,

_____-_____

reliability is being assessed.

52. The Stanford-Binet and Wechsler tests have reliabilities of about _____ .

53. The degree to which a test measures or predicts what it is supposed to is referred to as the test's

_____ .

54. The degree to which a test measures the behavior it was designed to measure is referred to as the test's _____ .

55. The degree to which a test predicts future performance of a particular behavior, called the test's

_____ , is referred to as the test's _____ .

Choose a specific example and use it to illustrate and explain the concept of criterion and its relationship to predictive validity.

56. Generally speaking, the predictive validity of general aptitude tests _____ (is/is not) as high as their reliability. The predictive validity of these tests _____ (increases/diminishes) as individuals move up the educational ladder.

57. The ability to produce ideas that are both novel and valuable is called _____ . The relationship between intelligence and creativity holds only up to a certain point—an intelligence score of about _____ .

Describe five components of creativity other than intelligence.

58. (Close-Up) Individuals whose intelligence scores fall below 70 and who have difficulty adapting to life may be labeled _____

_____ . This label applies to approximately _____ percent of the population.

59. (Close-Up) Severe retardation sometimes has a physical basis, such as _____

_____ , a genetic disorder caused by an extra chromosome.

60. (Close-Up) Many children with mild retardation are integrated, or _____ , into regular classrooms.

61. The position that both heredity and environment exert some influence on intelligence is

_____ (controversial/generally accepted) among psychologists.

62. The intelligence scores of identical twins reared together are _____ (more/no more) similar than those of fraternal twins.

63. The IQ scores of fraternal twins are

_____ (more alike/no more

alike) than the IQ scores of other siblings. This provides evidence of a(n) _____ (genetic/environmental) effect because fraternal twins, being the same _____, are treated more alike.

64. Children's intelligence scores are more like those of their _____ (biological/adoptive) parents than their _____ (biological/adoptive) parents.

65. The amount of variation in a trait within a group that is attributed to genetic factors is called its _____ . For intelligence, this has been estimated at roughly _____ percent.

66. If we know a trait has perfect heritability, this knowledge _____ (does/does not) enable us to rule out environmental factors in explaining differences between groups.

67. Studies indicate that neglected children _____ (do/do not) show signs of recovery in intelligence and behavior when placed in more nurturing environments.

68. High-quality programs for disadvantaged children, such as the government-funded _____ program, produce at least short-term gains on intelligence tests.

69. Research evidence suggests that racial gaps in intelligence are due primarily to _____ (genetic/environmental) factors.

Explain why heredity may contribute to individual differences in intelligence but not necessarily contribute to group differences.

70. Group differences in intelligence scores _____ (do/do not) provide an accurate basis for judging individuals. Individual differences within a race are _____ (greater than/less than) between-race differences.

71. Although Asian students on the average score _____ (higher/lower) than North American students on math tests, this difference may be due to the fact that _____ .

72. On an infant intelligence measure (preference for looking at novel stimuli), black infants score _____ (lower than/higher than/about the same as) white infants.

73. Gender similarities in math and verbal ability are _____ (smaller/greater) than gender differences. Girls tend to outscore boys on _____ tests and in detecting _____ . Boys tend to outscore girls on tests of _____ and _____ .

74. Working from an _____ perspective, some theorists speculate that these gender differences helped our ancestors survive.

75. There is evidence that spatial abilities are enhanced by high levels of _____ during prenatal development.

76. The gender gap in math is _____ (increasing/decreasing/remaining steady), perhaps because _____ expectations for boys and girls are changing.

77. In the sense that they detect differences caused by cultural experiences, intelligence tests probably _____ (are/are not) biased.

78. Most psychologists agree that, in terms of predictive validity, the major aptitude tests _____ (are/are not) racially biased.

## WEB SIGHTING

The World Wide Web is chock full of resources related to various aspects of intelligence, including IQ testing, theories of intelligence, and animal intelligence. For example, use *Yahoo*, *WebCrawler*, or your favorite search engine to find the 30-minute Mensa intelligence-test workout. Consult an "on-line oracle" to hone your intuition. Play an interactive Web game with a cybertherapist. To get started, try to find the answers to the following questions.

1. Who is Dr. Werner Wilhelm Webowitz? How can he help you? Is he related to ELIZA?

2. Do you have a pet dog? Where is your dog's breed in the ranking of dogs for working intelligence? If you don't own a dog, can you find which breed ranks highest in working intelligence?

3. Can you find Daniel Goleman's sample emotional intelligence test? What is your EQ?

4. What is Mensa? Can you pass their test of wisdom?

## Progress Test 1

### Multiple-Choice Questions

Circle your answers to the following questions and check them with the answers on page 236. If your answer is incorrect, read the explanation for why it is incorrect and then consult the appropriate pages of the text (in parentheses following the correct answer).

1. When forming a concept, people often develop a best example, or _____ , of a category.
   a. denoter          c. prototype
   b. heuristic        d. algorithm

2. Which of the following is *not* true of babbling?
   a. It is imitation of adult speech.
   b. It is the same in all cultures.
   c. It typically occurs from about age 4 months to 1 year.
   d. Babbling increasingly comes to resemble a particular language.
   e. Deaf babies babble with gestures.

3. Whorf's linguistic relativity hypothesis states that:
   a. language is primarily a learned ability.
   b. language is partially an innate ability.
   c. the size of a person's vocabulary reflects his or her intelligence.
   d. our language shapes our thinking.

4. Failing to solve a problem that requires using an object in an unusual way illustrates the phenomenon of:
   a. heuristics.              d. belief perseverance.
   b. functional fixedness.    e. overconfidence.
   c. framing.

5. Which of the following is an example of the use of heuristics?
   a. trying every possible letter ordering when unscrambling a word
   b. considering each possible move when playing chess
   c. using the formula "area = length × width" to find the area of a rectangle
   d. playing chess using a defensive strategy that has often been successful for you

6. The chimpanzee Sultan used a short stick to pull a longer stick that was out of reach into his cage. He then used the longer stick to reach a piece of fruit. Researchers hypothesized that Sultan's discovery of the solution to his problem was the result of:
   a. trial and error.      c. functional fixedness.
   b. heuristics.           d. insight.

7. You hear that one of the Smith children is an outstanding Little League player and immediately conclude it's their one son rather than any of their four daughters. You reached your quite possibly erroneous conclusion as the result of:
   a. the confirmation bias.
   b. the availability heuristic.
   c. the representativeness heuristic.
   d. belief perseverance.

8. According to the text, language acquisition is best described as:
   a. the result of conditioning and reinforcement.
   b. a biological process of maturation.
   c. an interaction between biology and experience.
   d. a mystery of which researchers have no real understanding.

9. The linguistic relativity hypothesis is challenged by the finding that:

a. chimps can learn to communicate spontaneously by using sign language.

b. people with no word for a certain color can still perceive that color accurately.

c. the Eskimo language contains a number of words for snow, whereas English has only one.

d. infants' babbling contains many sounds that do not occur in their own language and that they therefore cannot have heard.

10. Several studies have indicated that the generic pronoun "he":

a. tends for children and adults alike to trigger images of both males and females.

b. tends for adults to trigger images of both males and females, but for children to trigger images of males.

c. tends for both children and adults to trigger images of males but not females.

d. for both children and adults triggers images of females about one-fourth of the time it is used.

11. A 6-year-old child has a mental age of 9. The child's IQ is:

a. 96.              d. 150.
b. 100.             e. 166.
c. 125.

12. Which of the following is *not* true?

a. In math grades, the average girl typically equals or surpasses the average boy.

b. The gender gap in math and science scores is increasing.

c. Women are better than men at detecting emotions.

d. Males score higher than females on tests of spatial abilities.

13. (Close-Up) Down syndrome is usually caused by:

a. an extra chromosome in the person's genetic makeup.

b. a missing chromosome in the person's genetic makeup.

c. malnutrition during the first few months of life.

d. prenatal exposure to an addictive drug.

14. Which of the following is *not* a requirement of a good test?

a. reliability          d. validity
b. standardization      e. criterion
c. reification

15. Which of the following statements is true?

a. The predictive validity of intelligence tests is not as high as their reliability.

b. The reliability of intelligence tests is not as high as their predictive validity.

c. Modern intelligence tests have extremely high predictive validity and reliability.

d. The predictive validity and reliability of most intelligence tests is very low.

16. Which of the following best describes the relationship between creativity and intelligence?

a. Creativity appears to depend on the ability to think imaginatively and has little if any relationship to intelligence.

b. Creativity is best understood as a certain kind of intelligence.

c. The more intelligent a person is, the greater his or her creativity.

d. A certain level of intelligence is necessary but not sufficient for creativity.

17. The existence of _____ reinforces the generally accepted notion that intelligence is a multidimensional quality.

a. adaptive skills       c. general intelligence
b. mental retardation    d. savant syndrome

18. Which of the following provides the strongest evidence of the role of heredity in determining intelligence?

a. The IQ scores of identical twins raised separately are very similar.

b. The intelligence scores of fraternal twins are more similar than those of ordinary siblings.

c. The intelligence scores of identical twins raised together are more similar than those of identical twins raised apart.

d. The intelligence scores of adopted children show relatively weak correlations with scores of adoptive as well as biological parents.

19. Reported racial gaps in average intelligence scores are most likely attributable to:

a. the use of biased tests of intelligence.
b. the use of unreliable tests of intelligence.
c. genetic factors.
d. environmental factors.

20. Research on the effectiveness of Head Start suggests that enrichment programs:

a. produce permanent gains in intelligence scores.

b. improve school readiness, but have no measurable impact on intelligence scores.

c. improve intelligence scores but not school readiness.

d. produce temporary gains in intelligence scores.

## Matching Items

Match each definition or description with the appropriate term.

*Terms*

_____  1. mental ability score
_____  2. *g*
_____  3. framing
_____  4. savant syndrome
_____  5. factor analysis
_____  6. aptitude test
_____  7. achievement test
_____  8. Stanford-Binet
_____  9. criterion
_____ 10. content validity
_____ 11. reliability

*Definitions or Descriptions*

a. a test designed to predict a person's ability to learn something new
b. a test designed to measure current knowledge
c. the consistency with which a test measures performance
d. the degree to which a test measures what it is designed to measure
e. Terman's revision of Binet's original intelligence test
f. the behavior that a test is designed to predict
g. an underlying, general intelligence factor
h. a person's score on an intelligence test based on performance relative to the average performance of people the same age
i. a very low intelligence score accompanied by one extraordinary skill
j. the way an issue or question is posed
k. a statistical technique that identifies related items on a test

## Progress Test 2

Progress Test 2 should be completed during a final chapter review. Answer the following questions after you thoroughly understand the correct answers for the Chapter Review and Progress Test 1.

### Multiple-Choice Questions

1. A common problem in everyday reasoning is our tendency to:
   a. accept as logical those conclusions that agree with our own opinions.
   b. accept as logical those conclusions that disagree with our own opinions.
   c. underestimate the accuracy of our knowledge.
   d. accept as logical conclusions that involve unfamiliar concepts.

2. Skinner and other behaviorists have argued that language development is the result of:
   a. imitation.          c. association.
   b. reinforcement.      d. all of the above.

3. Representativeness and availability are examples of:
   a. prototypes.          d. fixation.
   b. concepts.            e. heuristics.
   c. algorithms.

4. Assume that Congress is considering revising its approach to welfare and to this end is hearing a range of testimony. A member of Congress who uses the availability heuristic would be most likely to:
   a. want to experiment with numerous possible approaches to see which of these seems to work best.
   b. want to believe those arguments that most closely resemble his or her own views.
   c. refuse to be budged from his or her beliefs despite persuasive testimony to the contrary.
   d. base his or her ideas on the most vivid, memorable testimony given, even though many of the statistics presented run counter to this testimony.

5. If you want to be absolutely certain that you will find the solution to a problem you know *is* solvable, you should use:
   a. a heuristic.         c. insight.
   b. an algorithm.        d. trial and error.

6. Which of the following is *not* cited by Chomsky as evidence that language acquisition cannot be explained by learning alone?
   a. Children master the complicated rules of grammar with ease.

b. Children create sentences they have never heard.

c. Children make the kinds of mistakes that suggest they are attempting to apply rules of grammar.

d. Children raised in isolation from language spontaneously begin speaking words.

7. Telegraphic speech is typical of the _____ stage.

   a. babbling
   b. one-word
   c. two-word
   d. three-word

8. Researchers taught the chimpanzee Washoe and the gorilla Koko to communicate by using:

   a. various sounds.
   b. plastic symbols of various shapes and colors.
   c. sign language.
   d. all of the above.

9. Which of the following is true regarding the relationship between thinking and language?

   a. "Real" thinking requires the use of language.
   b. People sometimes think in images rather than in words.
   c. A thought that cannot be expressed in a particular language cannot occur to speakers of that language.
   d. All of the above are true.

10. The test created by Alfred Binet was designed specifically to:

    a. measure inborn intelligence in adults.
    b. measure inborn intelligence in children.
    c. predict school performance in children.
    d. identify mentally retarded children so that they could be institutionalized.
    e. do all of the above.

11. Which of the following provides the strongest evidence of environment's role in intelligence?

    a. Adopted children's intelligence scores are more like their adoptive parents' scores than their biological parents'.
    b. Children's intelligence scores are more strongly related to their mothers' scores than to their fathers'.
    c. Children moved from a deprived environment into an intellectually enriched one show gains in intellectual development.
    d. The intelligence scores of identical twins raised separately are no more alike than those of siblings.

12. If a test designed to indicate which applicants are likely to perform the best on the job fails to do so, the test has:

a. low reliability.
b. low content validity.
c. low predictive validity.
d. not been standardized.

13. Current intelligence tests compute an individual's intelligence score as the ratio:

    a. of mental age to chronological age multiplied by 100.
    b. of chronological age to mental age multiplied by 100.
    c. between the test-taker's performance and the average performance of others the same age.
    d. the test-taker's verbal intelligence score to his or her nonverbal intelligence score.

14. The concept of a g factor implies that intelligence:

    a. is a single overall ability.
    b. is several specific abilities.
    c. cannot be defined or measured.
    d. is both a. and c.
    e. is a dynamic rather than stable phenomenon.

15. Gerardeen has superb social skills, manages conflicts well, and has great empathy for her friends and co-workers. Peter Salovey and John Mayer would probably say that Gerardeen possesses a high degree of:

    a. g.
    b. social intelligence.
    c. practical intelligence.
    d. emotional intelligence.

16. In his study of children with high intelligence scores, Terman found that:

    a. the children were more emotional and less healthy than a control group.
    b. the children were ostracized by classmates.
    c. the children were healthy and well-adjusted, and did well academically.
    d. later, as adults, they nearly all achieved great vocational success.

17. High levels of male hormones during prenatal development may enhance:

    a. verbal reasoning.
    b. spatial abilities.
    c. overall intelligence.
    d. all of the above.

18. Originally, IQ was defined as:

    a. mental age divided by chronological age and multiplied by 100.
    b. chronological age divided by mental age and multiplied by 100.
    c. mental age subtracted from chronological age and multiplied by 100.
    d. chronological age subtracted from mental age and multiplied by 100.

**19.** Tests of _____ measure what an individual can do now, whereas tests of _____ predict what an individual will be able to do later.

    **a.** aptitude; achievement
    **b.** achievement; aptitude
    **c.** reliability; validity
    **d.** validity; reliability

**20.** Which of the following statements most accurately reflects the text's position regarding the relative contribution of genes and environment in determining intelligence?

    **a.** Except in cases of a neglectful early environment, each individual's basic intelligence is largely the product of heredity.
    **b.** With the exception of those with genetic disorders such as Down syndrome, intelligence is primarily the product of environmental experiences.
    **c.** Both genes and life experiences significantly influence performance on intelligence tests.
    **d.** Because intelligence tests have such low predictive validity, the question cannot be addressed until psychologists agree on a more valid test of intelligence.

### True-False Items

Indicate whether each statement is true or false by placing *T* or *F* in the blank next to the item.

    **1.** Most human problem solving involves the use of heuristics rather than reasoning that systematically considers every possible solution.

    **2.** When asked, most people underestimate the accuracy of their judgments.

    **3.** Studies have shown that even animals may sometimes have insight reactions.

    **4.** Children of all cultures babble using the same sounds.

    **5.** Thinking without using language is not possible.

    **6.** In the current version of the Stanford-Binet intelligence test, one's performance is compared only with the performance of others the same age.

    **7.** Most of the major aptitude tests have higher validity than reliability.

    **8.** The intelligence scores of adopted children are more similar to those of their adoptive parents than their biological parents.

    **9.** The consensus among psychologists is that most intelligence tests are extremely biased.

    **10.** Most psychologists agree that level of intelligence is mainly determined by heredity.

## Thinking Critically About Chapter 8

Answer these questions the day before an exam as a final check on your understanding of the chapter's terms and concepts.

### Multiple-Choice Questions

**1.** A listener hearing a recording of Japanese, Spanish, and North American children babbling would:

    **a.** not be able to tell them apart.
    **b.** be able to tell them apart if they were older than 6 months.
    **c.** be able to tell them apart if they were older than 8 to 10 months.
    **d.** be able to tell them apart at any age.

**2.** Which of the following illustrates belief perseverance?

    **a.** Your belief remains intact even in the face of evidence to the contrary.
    **b.** You refuse to listen to arguments counter to your beliefs.
    **c.** You tend to become flustered and angered when your beliefs are refuted.
    **d.** You tend to search for information that supports your beliefs.

**3.** Complete the following analogy: Rose is to flower as:

    **a.** concept is to prototype.
    **b.** prototype is to concept.
    **c.** concept is to hierarchy.
    **d.** hierarchy is to concept.

**4.** Your stand on an issue such as the use of nuclear power for electricity involves personal judgment. In such a case, one memorable occurrence can weigh more heavily than a bookful of data, thus illustrating:

    **a.** belief perseverance.
    **b.** confirmation bias.
    **c.** the representativeness heuristic.
    **d.** the availability heuristic.

5. Boris the chess master selects his next move by considering moves that would threaten his opponent's queen. His opponent, a chess-playing computer, selects its next move by considering *all* possible moves. Boris is using a(n) _____ and the computer is using a(n) _____ .
   a. algorithm; heuristic
   b. prototype; concept
   c. concept; prototype
   d. heuristic; algorithm

6. During a televised political debate, the Republican and Democratic candidates each argued that the results of a recent public opinion poll supported their party's platform regarding sexual harassment. Because both candidates saw the information as supporting their belief, it is clear that both were victims of:
   a. functional fixedness.
   b. the representativeness heuristic.
   c. insight.
   d. confirmation bias.

7. Rudy is 6 feet 6 inches tall, weighs 210 pounds, and is very muscular. If you think that Rudy is more likely to be a basketball player than a computer programmer, you are a victim of:
   a. the representativeness heuristic.
   b. the availability heuristic.
   c. framing.
   d. functional fixedness.

8. Failing to see that an article of clothing can be inflated as a life preserver is an example of:
   a. framing.
   b. the availability heuristic.
   c. the representativeness heuristic.
   d. functional fixedness.

9. Airline reservations typically decline after a highly publicized airline crash because people overestimate the incidence of such disasters. In such cases, people's decisions are being influenced by:
   a. confirmation bias.
   b. the availability heuristic.
   c. the representativeness heuristic.
   d. functional fixedness.

10. Most people tend to:
    a. accurately estimate the accuracy of their knowledge and judgments.
    b. underestimate the accuracy of their knowledge and judgments.
    c. overestimate the accuracy of their knowledge and judgments.
    d. lack confidence in their decision-making strategies.

11. In relation to ground beef, consumers respond more positively to an ad describing it as "75 percent lean" than to one referring to its "25 percent fat" content. This is an example of:
    a. the framing effect.     c. fixation.
    b. confirmation bias.       d. overconfidence.

12. Regarding the relationship between thinking and language, which of the following most accurately reflects the position taken in the text?
    a. Language determines everything about our thinking.
    b. Language determines the way we think.
    c. Thinking without language is not possible.
    d. Thinking affects our language, which then affects our thoughts.

13. Vanessa is a very creative sculptress. We would expect that Vanessa also:
    a. has an exceptionally high intelligence score.
    b. is quite introverted.
    c. has a venturesome personality and is intrinsically motivated.
    d. lacks expertise in most other skills.
    e. is more successful than other sculptors.

14. To say that the heritability of a trait is approximately 50 percent means that:
    a. genes are responsible for 50 percent of the trait in an individual, and the environment is responsible for the rest.
    b. the trait's appearance in a person will reflect approximately equal genetic contributions from both parents.
    c. of the trait's variation within a group of people, 50 percent can be attributed to heredity.
    d. all of the above are true.

15. A school psychologist found that 85 percent of those who scored above 115 on an aptitude test were "A" students and 75 percent of those who scored below 85 on the test were "D" students. The psychologist concluded that the test had high _____ validity because scores on it correlated highly with the _____ behavior.
    a. content; criterion
    b. predictive; criterion
    c. content; target
    d. predictive; target

16. Benito was born in 1937. In 1947, he scored 130 on an intelligence test. What was Benito's mental age when he took the test?
    a. 9              c. 11
    b. 10             d. 13
    e. It cannot be determined from the information provided.

17. Hiroko's math achievement score is considerably higher than that of most American students her age. Which of the following is true regarding this difference between Asian and North American students:

    a. It is a recent phenomenon.
    b. It may be due to the fact that Asian students have a longer school year.
    c. It holds only for girls.
    d. Both a. and b. are true.
    e. a., b., and c. are true.

18. Jack takes the same test of mechanical reasoning on several different days and gets virtually identical scores. This suggests that the test has:

    a. high content validity.
    b. high reliability.
    c. high predictive validity.
    d. been standardized.
    e. all of the above qualities.

19. If you compare the same trait in people of similar heredity who live in very different environments, heritability for that trait will be _____ ; heritability for the trait is most likely to be _____ among people of very different heredities who live in similar environments.

    a. low; high
    b. high; low
    c. environmental; genetic
    d. genetic; environmental

20. Don's intelligence scores were only average, but he has been enormously successful as a corporate manager. Sternberg and colleagues would probably suggest that Don's _____ intelligence exceeds his _____ intelligence.

    a. verbal; performance
    b. performance; verbal
    c. academic; practical
    d. practical; academic

*Essay Question*

You have been asked to devise a Psychology Achievement Test (PAT) that will be administered to freshmen who declare psychology as their major. What steps will you take to ensure that the PAT is a good intelligence test? (Use the space below to list the points you want to make and organize them. Then write the essay on a separate sheet of paper.)

# Key Terms

## *Writing Definitions*

Using your own words, on a piece of paper write a brief definition or explanation of each of the following terms.

1. cognition
2. concept
3. prototype
4. algorithm
5. heuristic
6. insight
7. confirmation bias
8. fixation
9. functional fixedness
10. representativeness heuristic
11. availability heuristic
12. overconfidence
13. framing
14. belief perseverance
15. language
16. babbling stage
17. one-word stage
18. two-word stage
19. telegraphic speech
20. linguistic relativity
21. intelligence
22. mental age
23. Stanford-Binet
24. intelligence quotient (IQ)
25. factor analysis
26. general intelligence ($g$)
27. savant syndrome
28. emotional intelligence
29. aptitude tests
30. achievement tests
31. Wechsler Adult Intelligence Scale—(WAIS)
32. standardization
33. normal curve (normal distribution)
34. reliability
35. validity
36. content validity
37. criterion
38. predictive validity
39. creativity
40. mental retardation
41. Down syndrome
42. heritability

*Cross-Check*

As you learned in Chapter 1, reviewing and overlearning of material are important to the learning process. After you have written the definitions of the key terms in this chapter, you should complete the crossword puzzle to ensure that you can reverse the process—recognize the term, given the definition.

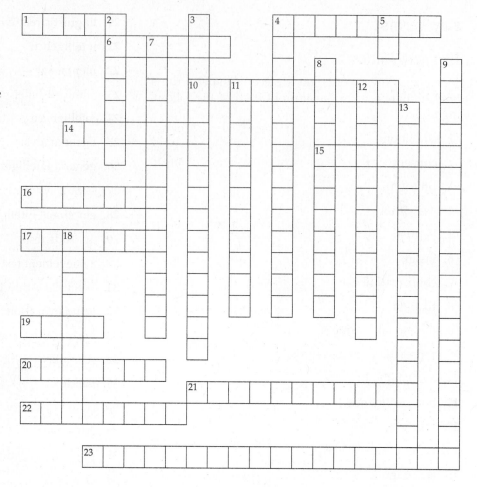

**ACROSS**

1. French educator who devised a test to predict children's learning potential.
4. An inability to approach a problem in a new way.
6. The chimpanzee taught by Allen and Beatrice Gardner to use sign language.
10. The type of fixedness in which a person can't envision a novel use for a familiar object.
14. Theorist who argues for the existence of multiple intelligences.
15. Behaviorist who explains language development with familiar learning principles.
16. Linguist who views language development as a process of maturation.
17. The stage of language development between 1 and 2 years of age.
19. The most widely used intelligence test (abbreviation).
20. A mental grouping of similar objects.
21. Type of test that measures a person's current knowledge.
22. Degree to which a test measures what it is supposed to measure.
23. An obstacle to rational thinking that may be eliminated by considering an opposing viewpoint.

**DOWN**

2. Stage of language development characterized by the use of telegraphic speech.
3. Tendency of people to search for information that confirms their preconceptions.
4. Statistical procedure that identifies clusters of items that seem to define a common ability.
5. Originally defined as the ratio of mental age to chronological age.
7. Condition in which a person of limited mental ability has one amazing skill.
8. Condition of mental retardation caused by an extra chromosome.
9. Charles Spearman's concept of *g*.
11. Bell-shaped distribution that reflects scores on aptitude tests.
12. Heuristic in which we estimate the likelihood of events based on how readily they come to mind.
13. Defined as an intelligence score below 70.
18. A critical part of social intelligence.

# ANSWERS

## Guided Study

The following guidelines provide the main points that your answers should have touched upon.

1. Concepts are mental groupings of similar objects, events, and people. Because they provide a great deal of information with minimal cognitive effort, concepts are the basic units of thinking. Most concepts are formed around a best example, or prototype, of a particular category. Concepts are often organized into hierarchies that further increase cognitive efficiency.

2. Trial and error is a haphazard strategy for solving problems, in which one solution after another is tried until success is achieved. Algorithms are methodical and logical rules for solving problems; they often are laborious and inefficient. Heuristics are based on rules of thumb. Although formally not a problem-solving strategy, a sudden flash of inspiration (insight) often helps us to solve problems. Insight has been observed in chimpanzees who are given challenging problems to solve.

3. The confirmation bias is an obstacle to problem solving in which people search for information that confirms their preconceptions. Another common obstacle to problem solving is fixation, an inability to approach a familiar problem in a new way. One example of fixation is the tendency to continue applying a particular problem-solving strategy even when it is no longer useful. Another example is functional fixedness, whereby a person is unable to perceive unusual functions for familiar objects.

4. The representativeness heuristic is the tendency to judge the likelihood of things in terms of how well they represent particular prototypes. With the availability heuristic, we base our judgments on how readily information comes to mind.

   The overconfidence phenomenon is the tendency of people to overestimate the accuracy of their knowledge and judgments. Although overconfidence may blind us to our vulnerability to error in reasoning, it has adaptive value in that it makes decision making somewhat easier.

   Framing refers to the way an issue or question is posed, which can greatly influence our perception of the issue or answer to the question. Belief perseverance is our tendency to cling to our beliefs even in the face of contrary evidence. Once beliefs are formed, it takes stronger evidence to change them than it did to create them.

5. At 4 months of age, babies enter a babbling stage in which they spontaneously utter sounds of all languages. By 1 year children enter the one-word stage. In this stage, single-syllable words are used to name things and may even be inflected to convey the meaning of an entire sentence. By age 2 most children enter the two-word stage. At this time their speech consists of telegraphic utterances containing mostly nouns and verbs, yet placed in a sensible syntactic order. Children then quickly begin uttering longer and more complex phrases and sentences.

   According to B. F. Skinner, language development can be explained according to the learning principles of association, imitation, and reinforcement. In contrast, Noam Chomsky believes that children are biologically prepared to learn language as they interact with their caregivers. Most theorists today believe that language development is the product of both hereditary and environmental influences.

6. Several attempts have been made to teach sign language and other symbolic languages to chimpanzees. Although apes have a capacity to learn a relatively large vocabulary of sign words, critics contend that much of their signing is nothing more than imitation of their trainer's signs and shows little evidence of syntax.

7. According to Whorf's linguistic relativity hypothesis, language determines the way we think. Critics of this idea claim that our language *reflects* rather than creates the way we think. Studies of the ability of vocabulary enrichment to enhance thinking reveal that it is more accurate to say that language *influences*, rather than determines, thought. Some thoughts, such as the imagery involved in art, music, and athletics, do not depend on language.

8. Modern intelligence testing began when Alfred Binet developed a test to predict children's future school performance. Binet's test was designed to compute a mental age for each child. Lewis Terman's revision of Binet's test, known as the Stanford-Binet, computed an IQ score as the ratio of mental age to chronological age. Modern intelligence tests no longer compute an intelligence quotient; instead, they produce a mental ability score based on the test-taker's performance relative to the average of others the same age.

9. Factor analysis is a statistical technique used to identify clusters of test items that measure a common ability, such as spatial or reasoning ability.

   Although psychologists agree that people have specific abilities, such as verbal or mathematical intelligence, they do not agree about the existence of an underlying general intelligence factor. People with savant syndrome, who score very low on intelligence tests but possess extraordinary specific abilities, provide support for the viewpoint that there are multiple intelligences, each independent of the others. Sternberg and others, for example, distinguish among three intelligences—academic, practical, and creative—whereas Cantor and Kihlstrom distinguish between academic and social intelligence (including emotional intelligence) and Gardner among seven different intelligences.

10. Aptitude tests, such as a college entrance exam, are intended to predict a person's ability to learn new skills. Achievement tests, such as a final exam in a college course, are intended to measure what already has been learned.

    The most widely used intelligence tests, the WAIS for adults and the WISC for children, consist of a number of subtests and yield an overall intelligence score, as well as separate verbal and performance scores.

11. Good intelligence tests have been standardized and are reliable and valid. Standardization is the process of defining meaningful scores on the test relative to a pretested group. A random group of test results should form a normal distribution.

    Reliability is the extent to which a test yields consistent results. To check a test's reliability, people are tested twice using the same or a different form of the test. If the scores correlate, the test is reliable. The Stanford-Binet, WAIS, and WISC all have high reliabilities of about +.9.

    Validity is the extent to which a test actually measures the behavior (content validity) it claims to, or predicts some criterion, such as future performance (predictive validity). The predictive validity of general aptitude tests is not as high as their reliability.

12. Creativity is the ability to produce novel and valuable ideas. Although people with high intelligence scores do well on tests of creativity, beyond an intelligence score of about 120, the correlation between intelligence scores and creativity disappears.

    Studies suggest five components to creativity other than intelligence: expertise, imaginative thinking skills, a venturesome personality, intrinsic motivation, and a creative environment.

13. Contrary to popular myth, gifted children are not frequently maladjusted. The segregation of children into gifted and nongifted educational tracks remains controversial.

Approximately 1 percent of the population have very low intelligence scores, experience difficulty adapting to the normal demands of living independently, and are labeled as mentally retarded. Severe mental retardation sometimes results from physical causes, such as Down syndrome.

14. Both genes and environment influence intelligence. Studies of twins and adopted children point to the influence of heredity. For example, the most genetically similar people have the most similar intelligence scores, and adopted children's intelligence scores are more like their biological parents' scores than their adoptive parents' scores. It is estimated that the *heritability* of intelligence is about 50 to 70 percent; that is, 50 to 70 percent of the variation in intelligence within a *group* of people can be attributed to heredity.

    Other studies that compare children reared in neglectful environments with those who have been reared in enriched environments, or in different cultures, point to the impact of environmental experiences on intelligence scores. Findings regarding Head Start and other preschool programs indicate that high-quality programs can generate short-term cognitive gains and long-term positive effects.

15. On average, there *are* group differences in intelligence scores. For example, Asian students outperform North American students on math achievement and aptitude tests, females score higher than males in math computation, and white Americans tend to score higher than African-Americans on IQ tests.

    Although heredity contributes to individual differences in intelligence, it does not necessarily contribute to group differences. Most experts believe that the intelligence score gaps between groups are the result of differences between privileged and disadvantaged groups around the world, as well as cultural differences in educational enrichment.

16. In the sense that intelligence scores are sensitive to differences caused by cultural experience, aptitude tests are certainly biased. In terms of predictive validity, however, most experts agree that the major intelligence tests are not racially biased.

    Because intelligence tests are designed to distinguish different levels of aptitude, their purpose in this sense *is* to discriminate among individuals. In another sense, however, intelligence tests reduce discrimination by reducing the use of subjective criteria in school and job placement.

## Chapter Review

1. cognition; the mental activity associated with thinking, knowing, remembering, and communicating knowledge; cognitive psychologists
2. concepts; hierarchies; are
3. prototype; male; female
4. problem solving
5. trial and error
6. algorithms
7. heuristics
8. insight; have
9. confirmation bias
10. fixation
11. functional fixedness
12. representativeness heuristic
13. availability heuristic

Using these heuristics often prevents us from processing other relevant information, and because we overlook this information, we make judgmental errors. Thus, in the text example, the representativeness heuristic leads people to overlook the fact that there are many more truck drivers than Ivy League classics professors and, as a result, to wrongly conclude that the poetry reader is more likely to be an Ivy League classics professor. Also as noted in the text, the availability heuristic leads us to incorrectly think that words beginning with *k* are more common than words having *k* as their third letter.

14. overconfidence
15. adaptive; more; easier; does
16. framing
17. belief perseverance
18. babbling; 4; do not
19. do
20. can; 10; 12; lost
21. one-word; 1
22. two-word; telegraphic
23. do
24. association; imitation; reinforcement
25. Chomsky; language acquisition device

The rate at which children acquire vocabulary and grammar is too rapid to be explained solely by learning. Children create sentences that they have never heard and, therefore, could not be imitating.

26. 1; word breaks
27. experience; do not
28. sign language

Chimps have acquired only limited vocabularies and—in contrast to children—have acquired these vocabularies only with great difficulty. Also in contrast to children, it's unclear that chimps can use syntax to express meaning. Even simpler animals, such as birds, are capable of learning behavioral sequences that some chimp researchers consider language. The signing of chimps is often nothing more than imitation of the trainer's actions. People tend to interpret such ambiguous behavior in terms of what they want to see.

29. linguistic relativity; Whorf
30. does
31. intelligence
32. can

The relationship is probably a two-way one: The linguistic relativity hypothesis suggests that language helps shape thought; that words come into the language to express new ideas indicates that thought also shapes language.

33. The mental abilities needed to select, adapt to, and shape environments.
34. Binet; mental; was not
35. Stanford-Binet; intelligence quotient

In the original formula for IQ, measured mental age is divided by chronological age and multiplied by 100. "Mental age" refers to the chronological age that most typically corresponds to a given level of performance.

36. a mental ability score; the same; 100
37. overall (general); specific
38. factor analysis; general intelligence
39. savant syndrome
40. multiple intelligences
41. academic; practical; creative; academic; social
42. emotional intelligence; perceive; express; understand; regulate

Emotionally intelligent people are self-aware. They can manage their emotions and they can delay gratification. Their empathy allows them to read others' emotions.

43. mentally demanding
44. aptitude; achievement
45. Wechsler Adult Intelligence Scale; verbal; performance
46. standardization; reliability; validity
47. standardization
48. normal

The normal curve describes the distribution of many physical phenomena and psychological attributes (including IQ scores), with most scores falling near the average and fewer and fewer near the extremes. When a test is standardized on a normal curve, individual scores are assigned according to how much they deviate above or below the distribution's average.

**49.** reliable

**50.** test-retest

**51.** split-half

**52.** +.9

**53.** validity

**54.** content validity

**55.** criterion; predictive validity

The criterion is the particular behavior that a predictive test, such as an aptitude test, is intended to predict. For example, performance in a relevant job situation would be the criterion for a test measuring managerial aptitude. The criterion determines whether a test has predictive validity. For example, the on-the-job success of those who do well on a job aptitude test would indicate the test has predictive validity.

**56.** is not; diminishes

**57.** creativity; 120

Creative people tend to have *expertise*, or a solid base of knowledge; *imaginative thinking skills*, which allow them to see things in new ways, to recognize patterns, and to make connections; *intrinsic motivation*, or the tendency to focus on the pleasure and challenge of their work; and a *venturesome personality* that tolerates ambiguity and risk and seeks new experiences. Creative people also have generally benefited from living in *creative environments*.

**58.** mentally retarded; 1

**59.** Down syndrome

**60.** mainstreamed

**61.** generally accepted

**62.** more

**63.** more alike; environmental; age

**64.** biological; adoptive

**65.** heritability; 50 to 70

**66.** does not

**67.** do

**68.** Head Start

**69.** environmental

Because of the impact of environmental factors such as education and nutrition on intelligence test performance, even if the heritability of intelligence is high within a particular group, differences in intelligence *among* groups may be environmentally caused. One group may, for example, thrive in an enriched envi-

ronment while another of the same genetic predisposition may falter in an impoverished one.

**70.** do not; greater than

**71.** higher; Asian students have a longer school year and spend more time studying math

**72.** about the same as

**73.** greater; spelling; emotions; mental rotation; math aptitude tests with a spatial component

**74.** evolutionary

**75.** male sex hormones

**76.** decreasing; social

**77.** are

**78.** are not

## Progress Test 1

*Multiple-Choice Questions*

1. **c.** is the answer. (p. 269)
   **a.** There is no such thing as a "denoter."
   **b. & d.** Heuristics and algorithms are problem-solving strategies.

2. **a.** is the answer. Babbling is not the imitation of adult speech since babbling infants produce sounds from languages they have not heard and could not be imitating. (p. 278)

3. **d.** is the answer. (p. 286)
   **a.** This is Skinner's position regarding language development.
   **b.** This is Chomsky's position regarding language development.
   **c.** The linguistic relativity hypothesis is concerned with the content of thought, not intelligence.

4. **b.** is the answer. Functional fixedness is the tendency to think of things only in terms of their usual functions. (p. 271)
   **a.** Heuristics are rule-of-thumb strategies that are based on past successes in similar situations.
   **c.** Framing refers to the way an issue is posed; this often influences our judgment.
   **d.** Belief perseverance is the tendency to cling to one's beliefs even after they have been refuted.
   **e.** Overconfidence is the tendency to think we know more than we do.

5. **d.** is the answer. Heuristics are rule-of-thumb strategies—such as playing chess defensively—that are based on past successes in similar situations. (p. 269)
   **a., b., & c.** These are all algorithms.

6. **d.** is the answer. Sultan suddenly arrived at a novel solution to his problem, thus displaying apparent insight. (pp. 269–270)

**a.** Sultan did not randomly try various strategies of reaching the fruit; he demonstrated the "light bulb" reaction that is the hallmark of insight.

**b.** Heuristics are rule-of-thumb strategies.

**c.** Functional fixedness is an impediment to problem solving. Sultan obviously solved his problem.

7. **c.** is the answer. Your conclusion is based on sex stereotypes, that is, athletic ability and participation are for you more *representative* of boys. Your conclusion is by no means necessarily right, however, especially since the Smiths have four daughters and only one son. (p. 271)

**a.** The confirmation bias is the tendency to look for information that confirms one's preconceptions.

**b.** The availability heuristic involves judging the probability of an event in terms of how readily it comes to mind.

**d.** Belief perseverance is the tendency to cling to beliefs, even when the evidence has shown that they are wrong.

8. **c.** is the answer. Children are biologically prepared to learn language as they and their caregivers interact. (p. 282)

**a.** This is Skinner's position.

**b.** No psychologist, including Chomsky, believes that language is entirely a product of biological maturation.

**d.** Although language acquisition is not completely understood, research has shed sufficient light on it to render it less than a complete mystery.

9. **b.** is the answer. The evidence that absence of a term for a color does not affect ability to perceive the color challenges the idea that language always shapes thought. (p. 286)

**a. & d.** These findings are not relevant to the linguistic relativity hypothesis, which addresses the relationship between language and thought.

**c.** This finding is in keeping with the linguistic relativity hypothesis.

10. **c.** is the answer. The generic pronoun *he* evidently tends, for both adults and children, to conjure up images of males. (p. 286)

11. **d.** is the answer. If we divide 9, the measured mental age, by 6, the chronological age, and multiply the result by 100, we obtain 150. (p. 290)

12. **b.** is the answer. As social expectations have changed, the gender gap in math and science scores is narrowing. (p. 305)

13. **a.** is the answer. (p. 297)

**b.** Down syndrome is normally caused by an extra, rather than a missing, chromosome.

**c. & d.** Down syndrome is a genetic disorder that is manifest during the earliest stages of prenatal development, well before malnutrition and exposure to drugs would produce their harmful effects on the developing fetus.

14. **c.** is the answer. Reification is a reasoning error, in which an abstract concept such as IQ is regarded as though it were real. (pp. 294–296)

15. **a.** is the answer. (p. 296)

**c. & d.** Most modern tests have high reliabilities of about +.9; their validity scores are much lower.

16. **d.** is the answer. Up to an intelligence score of about 120, there is a positive correlation between intelligence and creativity. But beyond this point the correlation disappears, indicating that factors other than intelligence are also involved. (p. 296)

**a.** The ability to think imaginatively and intelligence are *both* components of creativity.

**b.** Creativity, the capacity to produce ideas that are novel and valuable, is related to and depends in part on intelligence but cannot be considered simply a kind of intelligence.

**c.** Beyond an intelligence score of about 120 there is no correlation between intelligence scores and creativity.

17. **d.** is the answer. That people with savant syndrome excel in one area but are intellectually retarded in others suggests that there are multiple intelligences. (p. 291)

**a.** The ability to adapt defines the capacity we call intelligence.

**b.** Mental retardation is an indicator of the range of human intelligence.

**c.** A general intelligence factor was hypothesized by Spearman to underlie each specific factor of intelligent behavior, but its existence is controversial and remains to be proved.

18. **a.** is the answer. Identical twins who live apart have the same genetic makeup but different environments; if their scores are similar, this is evidence for the role of heredity. (p. 299)

**b.** Since fraternal twins are no more genetically alike than ordinary siblings, this could not provide evidence for the role of heredity.

**c.** That twins raised together have more similar scores than twins raised apart provides evidence for the role of the environment.

**d.** As both sets of correlations are weak, little evidence is provided either for or against the role of heredity.

19. **d.** is the answer. Findings from a range of studies—including studies of SAT trends, cross-cultural studies, and adoption studies—have led experts to focus on the influence of environmental factors. (pp. 303–304)

**a.** Most experts believe that in terms of predictive validity, the major tests are not racially biased.

**b.** The reliability of the major tests is actually very high.

**c.** The bulk of the evidence on which experts base their findings points to the influence of environmental factors.

20. **d.** is the answer. The benefits for intelligence scores of enrichment programs such as Head Start dissipate over time. (pp. 301–302)

**b. & c.** Enrichment programs do improve school readiness and result in measurable, but temporary, gains in intelligence scores.

### Matching Items

| | | |
|---|---|---|
| **1.** h (p. 290) | **5.** k (p. 293) | **9.** f (p. 296) |
| **2.** g (p. 291) | **6.** a (p. 293) | **10.** d (p. 296) |
| **3.** j (p. 291) | **7.** b (p. 293) | **11.** c (p.295) |
| **4.** i (p. 291) | **8.** e (p. 290) | |

## Progress Test 2

### Multiple-Choice Questions

1. **a.** is the answer. Reasoning in daily life is often distorted by our beliefs, which may lead us, for example, to accept conclusions that haven't been arrived at logically. (p. 270)

**b., c., & d.** These are just the opposite of what we tend to do.

2. **d.** is the answer. These are all basic principles of learning and, according to Skinner, explain language development. (p. 279)

3. **e.** is the answer. Both are rule-of-thumb strategies that allow us to make quick judgments. (pp. 271–272)

**a & b.** Prototypes are best examples of concepts, which are categories of objects, events, or people.

**c.** Algorithms are methodical strategies that guarantee a solution to a particular problem.

**d.** Fixation is an obstacle to problem solving in which the person tends to repeat solutions that have worked in the past and is unable to conceive of other possible solutions.

4. **d.** is the answer. If we use the availability heuristic, we base judgments on the availability of information in our memories, and more vivid information is often the most readily available. (p. 272)

**a.** This would exemplify use of the trial-and-error approach to problem solving.

**b.** This would exemplify confirmation bias.

**c.** This would exemplify belief perseverance.

5. **b.** is the answer. Because they involve the systematic examination of all possible solutions to a problem, algorithms guarantee that a solution will be found. (p. 269)

**a., c., & d.** None of these methods guarantees that a problem's solution will be found.

6. **d.** is the answer. Chomsky believes that the inborn capacity for language acquisition must be activated by exposure to language. And in fact, children raised in isolation will *not* begin to speak spontaneously. (p. 280)

7. **c.** is the answer. (p. 279)

8. **c.** is the answer. (p. 283)

9. **b.** is the answer. (p. 287)

**a.** Researchers do not make a distinction between "real" and other thinking, nor do they consider nonlinguistic thinking less valid than linguistic thinking.

**c.** As indicated by several studies cited in the text, this is not true.

10. **c.** is the answer. French compulsory education laws brought more children into the school system, and the government didn't want to rely on teachers' subjective judgments to determine which children would require special help. (p. 289)

**a. & b.** Binet's test was intended for children, and Binet specifically rejected the idea that his test measured inborn intelligence, which is an abstract capacity that cannot be quantified.

**d.** This was not a purpose of the test, which dealt with children in the school system.

11. **c.** is the answer. (p. 301)

**a., b., & d.** None of these is true.

12. **c.** is the answer. Predictive validity is the extent to which tests predict what they are intended to predict. (p. 296)

**a.** Reliability is the consistency with which a test samples the particular behavior of interest.

**b.** Content validity is the degree to which a test measures what it is designed to measure.

**d.** Standardization is the process of defining meaningful test scores based on the performance of a representative group.

13. **c.** is the answer. (p. 290)

**a.** This is William Stern's original formula for the intelligence quotient.

**b. & d.** Neither of these formulas is used to compute the score on current intelligence tests.

14. **a.** is the answer. (p. 291)

15. **d.** is the answer. (p. 292)

**a.** The concept of general intelligence pertains more to academic skills.

**b.** Although emotional intelligence *is* a key

component of social intelligence, Salovey and Mayer coined the newer term "emotional intelligence" to refer to skills such as Gerardeen's.

**c.** Practical intelligence is that which is required for everyday tasks, not all of which involve emotions.

16. **c.** is the answer. (p. 297)
**a. & b.** There was no evidence of either of these in Terman's subjects.
**d.** Vocational success in adulthood varied.

17. **b.** is the answer. (p. 305)

18. **a.** is the answer. (p. 290)

19. **b.** is the answer. (p. 293)
**c. & d.** Reliability and validity are characteristics of good tests.

20. **c.** is the answer. (p. 300)
**a. & b.** Studies of twins, family members, and adopted children point to a significant hereditary contribution to intelligence scores. These same studies, plus others comparing children reared in neglectful or enriched environments, indicate that life experiences also significantly influence test performance.

**d.** Although the issue of how intelligence should be defined is controversial, intelligence tests generally have predictive validity, especially in the early years.

### True-False Items

| | |
|---|---|
| 1. T (p. 269) | 6. T (p. 290) |
| 2. F (p. 274) | 7. F (p. 296) |
| 3. T (pp. 269–270) | 8. F (p. 300) |
| 4. T (p. 278) | 9. F (p. 307) |
| 5. F (p. 287) | 10. F (p. 300) |

## Thinking Critically About Chapter 8

### Multiple-Choice Questions

1. **a.** is the answer. (p. 278)

2. **a.** is the answer. (p. 275)
**b. & c.** These may very well occur, but they do not define belief perseverance.
**d.** This is the confirmation bias.

3. **b.** is the answer. A rose is a prototypical example of the concept *flower*. (p. 269)
**c. & d.** Hierarchies are organized clusters of concepts. In this example, there is only the single concept *flower*.

4. **d.** is the answer. The availability heuristic is the judgmental strategy that estimates the likelihood of events in terms of how readily they come to mind, and the most vivid information is often the most readily available. (p. 272)

5. **d.** is the answer. (p. 269)

6. **d.** is the answer. The confirmation bias is the tendency to search for information that confirms one's preconceptions. In this example, the politicians' preconceptions are biasing their interpretation of the survey results. (p. 270)
**a.** Functional fixedness is the inability to perceive an unusual use for a familiar object.
**b.** Insight is the sudden realization of a solution to a problem.
**c.** The representativeness heuristic refers to the tendency to judge the likelihood of things in terms of how well they fit one's prototypes.

7. **a.** is the answer. Your conclusion is based on the stereotype that muscular build is more *representative* of athletes than computer programmers. (p. 271)
**b.** The availability heuristic involves judging the probability of an event in terms of how readily it comes to mind.
**c.** Framing refers to the way an issue or question is posed.
**d.** Functional fixedness is the tendency to think of things only in terms of their usual functions.

8. **d.** is the answer. (p. 271)

9. **b.** is the answer. The publicity surrounding disasters makes such events vivid and seemingly more probable than they actually are. (p. 272)
**a.** Confirmation bias is the tendency to search for information that confirms one's preconceptions.
**c.** The representativeness heuristic operates when we judge the likelihood of things in terms of how well they represent particular prototypes. This example does not involve such a situation.
**d.** Functional fixedness operates in situations in which effective problem solving requires using an object in an unfamiliar manner.

10. **c.** is the answer. This is referred to as overconfidence. (p. 274)

11. **a.** is the answer. In this example, the way the issue is posed, or framed, has evidently influenced consumers' judgments. (p. 274)
**b.** Confirmation bias is the tendency to search for information that confirms one's preconceptions.
**c.** a fixation is an inability to approach a problem in a new way.
**d.** Overconfidence is the tendency to be more confident than correct.

12. **d.** is the answer. (p. 288)

13. **c.** is the answer. (p. 296)

**a.** Beyond an intelligence score of about 120, creativity and intelligence scores are not correlated.

**b. & d.** There is no evidence that creative people are more likely to be introverted.

**e.** This may be true, but it cannot be assumed to be a result of creativity.

14. **c.** is the answer. Heritability is a measure of the extent to which a trait's variation within a group of people can be attributed to heredity. (p. 300)

    **a. & b.** Heritability is *not* a measure of how much of an *individual's* behavior is inherited, nor of the relative contribution of genes from that person's mother and father. Further, the heritability of any trait depends on the context, or environment, in which that trait is being studied.

15. **b.** is the answer. (p. 296)

    **a., c., & d.** Content validity is the degree to which a test measures what it claims to measure. Furthermore, "target behavior" is not a term used by intelligence researchers.

16. **d.** is the answer. At the time he took the test, Benito's chronological age (CA) was 10. Knowing that IQ = 130 and CA = 10, solving the equation for mental age yields a value of 13. (p. 290)

17. **d.** is the answer. (p. 304)

    **c.** The racial gap is found in both girls and boys.

18. **b.** is the answer. (p. 295)

19. **a.** is the answer. If everyone has nearly the same heredity, then heritability—the variation in a trait attributed to heredity—must be low. If individuals within a group come from very similar environments, environmental differences cannot account for variation in a trait; heritability, therefore, must be high. (p. 300)

20. **d.** is the answer. Sternberg and colleagues distinguish among *academic* intelligence, as measured by intelligence tests; *practical* intelligence, which is involved in everyday life, such as managerial work; and *creative* intelligence. (p. 292)

    **a. & b.** Verbal and performance intelligence are both measured by standard intelligence tests such as the WAIS and would be included in Sternberg and Wagner's academic intelligence.

    **c.** Academic intelligence refers to skills assessed by intelligence tests; practical intelligence applies to skills required for everyday tasks and, often, for occupational success.

*Essay Question*

The first step in constructing the test is to create a valid set of questions that measure psychological knowledge and therefore give the test content validity. If your objective is to predict students' future achievement in psychology courses, the test questions

should be selected to measure a criterion, such as information faculty members expect all psychology majors to master before they graduate.

To enable meaningful comparisons, the test must be standardized. That is, the test should be administered to a representative sample of incoming freshmen at the time they declare psychology to be their major. From the scores of your pretested sample you will then be able to assign an average score and evaluate any individual score according to how much it deviates above or below the average.

To check your test's reliability you might retest a sample of people using the same test or another version of it. If the two scores are correlated, your test is reliable. Alternatively, you might split the test in half and determine whether scores on the two halves are correlated.

## Key Terms

1. Thinking, or **cognition**, refers to the mental activity associated with thinking, knowing, remembering, and communicating information. (pp. 267–268)

2. A **concept** is a mental grouping of similar objects, events, or people. (p. 268)

3. A **prototype** is a best example of a particular category. (p. 269)

4. An **algorithm** is a methodical, logical procedure that, while sometimes slow, guarantees success. (p. 269)

5. A **heuristic** is any problem-solving strategy based on rules of thumb. Although heuristics are more efficient than algorithms, they do not guarantee success and sometimes even impede problem solving. (p. 269)

6. **Insight** is a sudden and often novel realization of the solution to a problem. Insight contrasts with trial and error and, indeed, may often follow an unsuccessful episode of trial and error. (p. 269)

7. The **confirmation bias** is an obstacle to problem solving in which people tend to search for information that validates their preconceptions. (p. 270)

8. **Fixation** is the inability to approach a problem in a new way. (p. 270)

9. **Functional fixedness** is a type of fixation in which a person can think of things only in terms of their usual functions. (p. 271)

10. The **representativeness heuristic** is the tendency to judge the likelihood of things in terms of how well they conform to one's prototypes. (p. 271)

11. The **availability heuristic** is based on estimating the probability of certain events in terms of how readily they come to mind. (p. 272)

12. Another obstacle to problem solving, **overconfidence** refers to the tendency to overestimate the accuracy of one's beliefs and judgments. (p. 274)

13. **Framing** refers to the way an issue or question is posed. It can affect people's perception of the issue or answer to the question. (p. 274)

14. **Belief perseverance** is the tendency for people to cling to a particular belief even after the information that led to the formation of the belief is discredited. (p. 275)

15. **Language** refers to spoken, written, or gestured words and how we combine them to think and communicate meaning. (p. 277)

16. The **babbling stage** of speech development, which begins at 4 months, is characterized by the spontaneous utterance of speech sounds. During the babbling stage, children the world over sound alike. (p. 278)

17. Between 1 and 2 years of age children speak mostly in single words; they are therefore in the **one-word stage** of linguistic development. (p. 279)

18. Beginning about age 2, children are in the **two-word stage** and speak mostly in two-word sentences. (p. 279)

19. **Telegraphic speech** is the economical, telegram-like speech of children in the two-word stage. Utterances consist mostly of nouns and verbs; however, words occur in the correct order, showing that the child has learned some of the language's syntactic rules. (p. 279)

20. **Linguistic relativity** is Benjamin Whorf's hypothesis that language determines the way we think. (p. 286)

21. Many experts define **intelligence** as the mental abilities needed to select, adapt to, and shape environments. (p. 289)

22. A concept introduced by Binet, **mental age** is the chronological age that most typically corresponds to a given level of performance. (p. 289)

23. The **Stanford-Binet** is Lewis Terman's widely used revision of Binet's original intelligence test. (p. 290)

24. The **intelligence quotient**, or **IQ**, was defined originally as the ratio of mental age to chronological age multiplied by 100. Contemporary tests of intelligence assign a score of 100 to the average performance for a given age and define other scores as deviations from this average. (p. 290)

25. **Factor analysis** is a statistical procedure that identifies factors, or clusters of items, that seem to define a common ability. Using this procedure, psychologists have identified several clusters, including verbal intelligence, spatial ability, and reasoning ability factors. (p. 291)

26. **General intelligence**, or *g* factor, underlies each of the more specific intelligence clusters identified through factor analysis. (p. 291)

27. A person with **savant syndrome** has a very low intelligence score, yet possesses one exceptional ability, for example, in music or drawing. (p. 291)

28. **Emotional intelligence** is the ability to perceive, express, understand, and regulate emotions. (p. 292)

29. **Aptitude tests** are designed to predict future performance. They measure your capacity to learn new information, rather than measuring what you already know. (p. 293)

30. **Achievement tests** measure a person's current knowledge. (p. 293)

31. The **Wechsler Adult Intelligence Scale (WAIS)** is the most widely used intelligence test. It is individually administered, contains 11 subtests, and yields separate verbal and performance intelligence scores, as well as an overall intelligence score. (pp. 293–294)

32. **Standardization** is the process of defining meaningful scores on a test by pretesting a large, representative sample of people. (p. 295)

33. The **normal curve** is a bell-shaped curve that represents the distribution (frequency of occurrence) of many physical and psychological attributes. The curve is symmetrical, with most scores near the average and fewer near the extremes. (p. 295)

34. **Reliability** is the extent to which a test produces consistent results. (p. 295)

35. **Validity** is the degree to which a test measures or predicts what it is supposed to. (p. 296)

36. The **content validity** of a test is the extent to which it samples the behavior that is of interest. (p. 296)

37. A test's **criterion** is the behavior the test is designed to predict. (p. 296)

38. **Predictive validity** is the extent to which a test predicts the behavior it is designed to predict. (p. 296)

39. Most experts agree that **creativity** refers to an ability to generate novel and valuable ideas. People with high IQs may or may not be creative, which indicates that intelligence is only one component of creativity. (p. 296)

**40.** The two criteria that designate **mental retardation** are an IQ below 70 and difficulty adapting to the normal demands of independent living. (p. 297)

**41.** A common cause of severe retardation and associated physical disorders, **Down syndrome** is usually the result of an extra chromosome in the person's genetic makeup. (p. 297)

**42.** **Heritability** is the proportion of variation among individuals in a trait that is attributable to genetic factors. Current estimates place the heritability of intelligence at about 50 to 70 percent. (p. 300)

*Cross-Check*

**ACROSS**
1. Binet
4. fixation
6. Washoe
10. functional
14. Gardner
15. Skinner
16. Chomsky
17. one-word
19. WAIS
20. concept
21. achievement
22. validity
23. belief perseverance

**DOWN**
2. two-word
3. confirmation bias
4. factor analysis
5. IQ
7. savant syndrome
8. Down syndrome
9. general intelligence
11. normal curve
12. availability
13. mental retardation
18. emotional

---

## FOCUS ON VOCABULARY AND LANGUAGE

*Page 267:* . . . our species is *kin to* . . . Myers notes that we are biological creatures related to (*kin to*) other species of animals. We have exceptional abilities for innovation, learning, memory, and rational thinking; yet, at the same time we are prone to making mistakes and thinking and acting irrationally.

### Thinking

*Page 269:* For most of us, the robin is the *birdier bird* . . . We develop our ideas of how things go together (*concepts*) from definitions or by using **prototypes**. The best example (*prototype*) of a bird is a robin (*the birdier bird*) rather than a penguin or an ostrich.

*Page 269:* Thomas Edison tried thousands of light-bulb filaments before *stumbling upon one that worked*. Edison was a famous inventor and he used a **trial-and-error** method in developing the metal filament that makes the light bulb glow brightly. Using trial and error, he came upon the solution by chance (*stumbled upon one that worked*). Myers contrasts this method with following an **algorithm** (a step-by-step method which always ends with the answer and is typical of computer programs).

*Page 269:* . . . *rule-of-thumb* strategies . . . A rule of thumb is a simple guide or principle that is true in general. Rather than using the longer step-by-step procedure (an **algorithm**), we frequently use **heuristics** (*rule-of-thumb* strategies) to help us find the solution more quickly.

*Page 269: Spying* the short stick, Sultan grabbed it and tried to reach the fruit with it. Kohler's experiment with the chimpanzee Sultan showed that our closest relatives are capable of cognition. When the fruit was out of reach, Sultan noticed (*spied*) the short stick and used it to pull a longer stick into the cage, which he then used to get the fruit.

*Page 271:* Should I *shoot* the basketball or pass to the player who's *hot*?—we seldom take the time and effort to reason systematically. (Don't take this sentence literally.) For example, in a game of basketball, the player holding the ball has to decide to throw it through the hoop (*shoot the basketball*) or pass it to a player who has scored frequently (*who's hot*). We usually follow our subjective feelings (*intuitions*) rather than taking the time to use logic and reason.

*Page 271:* . . . the *seat of the pants*. When we make decisions based on subjective or intuitive reasons, rather than using logical, reflective problem-solving strategies, we are using *seat-of-the-pants* judgments. Thus, when we employ **heuristics** (quick rule-of-thumb strategies), we may make wrong (*dumb*) decisions.

*Page 272:* The **representativeness heuristic** enabled you to make a *snap* judgment. We can make quick (*snap*) judgments using a strategy that allows us to determine the probability of things by how well they appear to be typical of some prototype (*representativeness heuristic*). For example, is person A, who is intelligent, unimaginative, compulsive, and generally lifeless, more likely to (a) play jazz for a hobby or (b) play jazz for a hobby and work as an accountant? The representativeness heuristic leads most people to incorrectly pick (b) as the answer.

*Page 272:* The faster people can remember an instance of some event (*"a broken promise"*), the more they expect it to recur. We tend to use whatever information is accessible in our memories when making decisions and judgments; similarly, events or mistakes that are easiest to access (i.e., those that most readily come to mind) will most likely be used.

This is called the **availability heuristic.** So, if on one occasion, someone did not keep his or her word (*broke a promise*) about doing something, we tend to remember that event and use it in predicting future behavior. Sometimes the availability heuristic can cause errors in judgment.

*Page 273:* During those three days, more than 100,000 invisible children—*mere statistics on some world health ledger*—died of preventable starvation, diarrhea, and disease (Gore, 1992). There was worldwide media attention to the 3-day rescue of a small child trapped in a deep hole (a well) in Texas. Due to the availability heuristic we tend to remember the vivid pictures associated with the danger to one child and ignore the statistics which showed that more than 100,000 children we did not observe (*invisible*) died during the same period. They were mere numbers (*statistics*) on some world health accounting book (*ledger*).

*Page 274:* Overconfidence *plagues* decisions outside the laboratory, too. Many factors combine to produce the tendency to overestimate the accuracy of our decisions, judgments, and knowledge (**overconfidence**). In everyday life, as well as in lab experiments, our judgments are greatly afflicted (*plagued*) by overconfidence.

*Page 275:* That people's judgments *flip-flop* so dramatically is startling. Presenting the same information in two different ways can cause people to react more negatively or positively depending on how the (logically equivalent) information was **framed.** The framing effect can cause alarming and dramatic reversals (*flip-flops*) in peoples decisions and judgments. For example, a very fatty food product made by grinding meat (*ground beef*) will be seen more positively if described as "75% lean" as opposed to "25% fat," despite the fact that exactly the same information is conveyed in each case.

*Page 275: Belief perseverance* often *fuels social conflict.* Our irrationality also shows when we persist (persevere) in our views despite evidence to the contrary (*belief perseverance*). This can lead to an increase in strong feelings or passions over controversial issues (*fuels social conflict*). Myers suggests one solution for those who wish to restrain (*rein in*) the effect of belief perseverance, and that is to give serious consideration to beliefs *opposite* to your own.

*Page 276:* From this we might conclude that our heads are indeed *filled with straw.* The discussion about human irrationality might lead to the conclusion that we have ineffective and inefficient cogni-

tions (*heads filled with straw*). Myers, however, is optimistic and suggests that we can learn about our irrational propensities (tendencies) and be alert to the dangers (*raise some caution flags*) that can result in poor or foolish decisions.

## Language

*Page 277:* When the human vocal tract evolved the capacity to utter vowels, *our capacity for language exploded, catapulting our species forward.* When the physiological ability for complex vocalization evolved, the ability to communicate orally expanded exponentially (*exploded*). This new linguistic capacity propelled (*catapulted*) our species to new levels of accomplishments, enabling us to communicate from person to person and to transmit civilization's accumulated knowledge from generation to generation.

*Page 278:* Yet by 4 months of age, babies can *read lips* and *discriminate* speech sounds. When people speak, their lips move in ways that correspond to the sounds they utter. Many deaf people can understand what is being said by watching how the lips move (*lip reading*). Very young children can not only tell the difference (*discriminate*) between sounds, but can also recognize lip movements that correspond with certain sounds (*lip read*).

*Page 280:* Surely, says Chomsky, *a Martian scientist* observing children in a single-language community would conclude that language is almost entirely inborn. The famous linguist Chomsky believes that the behaviorist's views (as exemplified by Skinner) are simplistic (*naive*). He argues that language acquisition could not be simply a function of experience or learning. Instead, he contends that any unbiased observer (e.g., *an imaginary scientist from the planet Mars*) would have to arrive at the inescapable fact that our capacity for language is almost totally biologically inherited (*inborn*). The specific language you speak is a product of your environment which builds on your innate capacity for language. As Myers puts it, *"we are born with the hardware and an operating system; experience writes the software."*

*Page 281:* Chomsky would say that once the *grammar switches are thrown* during a child's developing years, mastering another grammar becomes more difficult. Chomsky likens learning a particular grammar during early childhood to turning on (*throwing*) switches that influence language acquisition. When they have been turned on for one grammar, it becomes much harder to master a second grammar.

*Page 282:* If in our use of language we humans are, as the psalmist *rhapsodized,* "little lower than God," where do other animals fit in the scheme of things? The psalmist (an author of religious or sacred songs) spoke in an extravagantly enthusiastic manner (*rhapsodized*) about human nature, and Myers notes that it is our use of human language that elevates us above nonhumans. Nevertheless, we do share a capacity for language with other animals.

*Page 283:* Were the chimps *language champs* or were the researchers *chumps*? Critics of "ape language" argue that for animals, language acquisition is painfully slow, resembles conditioned responses, does not follow syntax, and is little more than imitation. In addition, demonstrations of animal language are always subjectively interpreted by their trainers. Myers asks: Were the chimps exceptionally talented (*language champs*) or were the researchers being biased and foolish (*chumps*)? The answer is that the controversy has led to further research and progress, and a renewed appreciation of our own, as well as our closest relatives', capacity for communication and language.

*Page 285:* Thinking and language intricately intertwine. Asking which comes first is one of psychology's *chicken-and-egg* questions. "Which came first: the chicken or the egg?" Clearly, you need an egg to produce a chicken, but you also need a chicken to lay the egg. So, like this age-old conundrum (riddle), psychologists have argued over which comes first, our ideas and thoughts, or the words we use to name and verbalize them. Myers concludes that language influences (but does not determine) thought, and our thinking affects our language, which in turn affects thought.

*Intelligence*

*Page 289:* No *controversy* in psychology has been more *heated* than the question of whether there exists in each person a general intellectual capacity that can be measured and *quantified* as a number. The dispute (*controversy*) over what intelligence is, whether we possess it as we do height or eye color, and whether it can be given a precise numerical index (*quantified*) is one of the most intense and emotional (*heated*) issues in psychology.

*Page 289:* On tests, therefore, a "*dull*" child should perform as does a typical younger child, and a "*bright*" child as does a typical older child. Children develop intellectually at different rates and so Binet and Simon developed the concept of **mental age**. Children who performed below the average level of other children the same age (e.g., a 10-year-old who performed as the average 8-year-old did) would be considered retarded or slow in development

("*dull*"). Those who performed above the average (e.g., a 10-year-old who scored as the average 12-year-old did) would be considered developmentally advanced or precocious ("*bright*").

*Page 290:* Obviously, something is *out of whack*. This means that something is not right or correct. The formula for calculating IQ scores (mental age divided by chronological age and multiplied by 100) works for children but produces scores that are clearly absurd (*out of whack*) for adults.

*Page 290:* Perhaps you have known a talented artist who is *dumbfounded by* the simplest mathematical problems . . . . Researchers have used a statistical approach (factor analysis) to identify groups of test items that measure a common ability. So, someone who has a group, or cluster, of abilities in one area may be very puzzled by and completely unable to solve (*dumbfounded by*) a relatively simple problem in a different area. Spearman argued that there was a common factor (*general intelligence*, or *g*) underlying particular abilities.

*Page 291:* People with **savant syndrome**, for example, score at the low end on intelligence tests but have an *island of brilliance*—some incredible ability, as in computation, drawing, or musical memory. Some people are functionally retarded in almost every aspect except for one very specific ability (*island of brilliance*) in which they are exceptionally gifted (**savant syndrome**). Despite having very poor language skills and other cognitive dysfunctions, they may be capable of outstanding performance in computation, memory for music heard only once, drawing, etc. Some psychologists argue that this is evidence for the notion of multiple intelligences.

*Page 292: . . . how to read people . . .* People who have good practical managerial intelligence may not score high on academic ability but will be good at motivating people; assigning work to others appropriately; and knowing and understanding peoples' needs, desires, and ambitions (*knowing how to read people*). They will also be alert, astute, and wise (*shrewd*) in their approach to life in general. Other people may demonstrate different types of intelligences (for example, academic, creative, or emotional intelligence).

*Page 293:* The actual differences between *aptitude* tests and *achievement* tests are not so *clear-cut*. Some tests measure your present ability and knowledge (*achievement*), as well as predict your future capacity to learn and develop (*aptitude*). Because what you know influences what you can learn in the future, and what you are capable of learning is related to what you already know, there is no definite (*clear-*

cut) distinction between aptitude and achievement tests. It is a practical matter; a test can be used either to predict future progress or to measure your present ability and skill.

Page 295: . . . most scores tend to *cluster* around the average. Many variables that we measure (weight, height, intelligence, etc.) follow a bell-shaped curve when plotted on a frequency distribution. On intelligence tests, the average is 100; most scores (68%) are between 85 and 115, so they are gathered close together (*clustered*) near the mean (*average*).

Page 296: If you use a *shrunken tape measure* to measure people's heights, your data would have high *reliability* (consistency) but low *validity*. In order for a test to be *reliable*, the instrument should have consistent results over numerous tests. So, if you use a tape measure that is much shorter (*shrunken*) than a normal one, it will meet the *reliability* criterion because it will always give you the same result; it will not, however, be valid. To be valid it should *accurately* measure what it is supposed to measure.

Page 297: During the last two centuries, *the pendulum of opinion* about how best to care for the mentally challenged has made a *complete swing*. Over time and in different ways we have taken care of the mentally retarded—first at home, then in small residential schools, then in massive institutions (*warehouses* for keeping people), and now back to a more normal situation in which they are integrated (mainstreamed) into regular classrooms. The way we have cared has moved from one extreme to the other (*the pendulum of opinion . . . has made a complete swing*).

Page 299: Even identical twins whose parents do not dress or treat them identically are *virtual carbon copies of one another* in IQ score. Those who believe that heredity powerfully influences intelligence-test performance argue that even when parents treat their identical twins very differently, the twins are still, in essence, identical (*virtual carbon copies of one another*). Genes are more important than environment. Those who believe that the environment is more influential point out the flaws or bias in many of these studies and report evidence that supports the view that genes are less important than life experiences.

Page 301: Extreme deprivation was *bludgeoning native intelligence*. In this investigation of a destitute orphanage, Hunt (1982) found that the effect of extreme neglect was severe depression and a general mental and physical passivity (the children became "*glum lumps*"). Their inborn (*native*) intellectual capacity was taking a severe beating (*bludgeoning*) due to the physical and emotional neglect. Hunt's intervention program had dramatic results. This points to the strong influence of environment.

Page 304: Similarly, in the psychological domain, gender similarities *dwarf* gender differences, but the differences often *capture our attention*. Males and females are alike in many more ways than they are different. Although the similarities overwhelm (*dwarf*) the dissimilarities, we are more intrigued by the dissimilarities (*they capture our attention*).

Page 305: The score differences are *sharpest* at the *extremes*. Although the variability in ability is greater within the two groups, people tend to focus on the between-group male-female differences. The differences in scores between males and females on the SAT test are more noticeable (*sharpest*) at the high and low ends of the distribution (*extremes*) than in the middle. Thus, among the very highest scorers in math, the majority are likely to be male.

Page 305: . . . *computer camps* . . . Because math and science have historically been viewed as male subjects, boys have been encouraged to become involved in special science activities and computer workshops (*computer camps*), whereas girls have been urged to take an interest in English. Today, a greater and greater number of females are involved in math and science, and the male-female difference in scores in these subjects is becoming smaller and smaller (*the gender gap is narrowing*).

Page 307: *Differences are not deficits*. Individual differences in abilities exist, but need not be seen as deficiencies. Scores on an intelligence test (important but not everything) reflect only one aspect of our total array of capabilities and we should capitalize on the variety of differences whatever their origins. We should view the differences as beneficial and valuable aspects of human adaptability (*differences are not deficits*).

# 9

# *Motivation*

## Chapter Overview

Perhaps no topic is more fundamental to psychology than motivation—the study of forces that energize and direct our behavior. Chapter 9 discusses various motivational concepts and looks closely at three motives: hunger, sex, and achievement. Research on hunger points to the interplay between physiological and psychological (internal and external) factors in motivation. Sexual motivation in men and women is triggered less by physiological factors and more by external incentives. Achievement motivation, in particular, demonstrates that a drive-reduction theory is of limited usefulness in explaining human behavior: Although this motivation serves no apparent physiological need, it may be extremely forceful nonetheless.

NOTE: Answer guidelines for all Chapter 9 questions begin on page 262.

## Guided Study

The text chapter should be studied one section at a time. Before you read, preview each section by skimming it, noting headings and boldface items. Then read the appropriate section objectives from the following outline. Keep these objectives in mind and, as you read the section, search for the information that will enable you to meet each objective. Once you have finished a section, write out answers for its objectives.

*Motivational Concepts* (pp. 312–315)

> David Myers at times uses idioms that are unfamiliar to some readers. If you do not know the meaning of any of the following words, phrases, or expressions, in the context in which they appear in the text, refer to page 271 for an explanation: *truant officer; instinct-naming fad collapsed under its own weight; feedback loops; monkey around.*

1. Define motivation and discuss the three perspectives that have influenced our understanding of motivation.

2. Discuss Maslow's hierarchy of needs.

*Hunger* (pp. 315–326)

> If you do not know the meaning of any of the following words, phrases, or expressions in the context in which they appear in the text, refer to pages 271–272 for an explanation: *feasted their eyes on delectable forbidden foods; keeping tabs; miser; munching . . . M&Ms; steak . . . crackling; binge-purge; win the battle of the bulge; scarfing; thinner wallet.*

3. Discuss the basis of hunger in terms of physiology and external incentives and explain how taste preferences are determined.

4. (Close-Up) Describe the symptoms and possible causes of anorexia nervosa and bulimia nervosa.

5. Discuss the factors that contribute to obesity.

6. Explain whether genes play no role, some role, or an exclusive role in causing obesity.

*Sexual Motivation* (pp. 326–338)

> If you do not know the meaning of any of the following words, phrases, or expressions in the context in which they appear in the text, refer to pages 272–273 for an explanation: *rapid fire questions; faithful attractions . . . fatal attractions; shift it into high gear; X-rated sex films; casual hit-and-run sex; sexual come-on; sent . . . by pairing wisely; fired; neither willfully chosen nor willfully changed; swung the pendulum toward; double-edged sword, colors our thoughts and emotions.*

7. Discuss whether survey research has contributed to our understanding of sexual behavior and describe the human sexual response cycle.

8. Discuss the basis of sexual motivation in terms of both internal physiology and external incentives.

9. Identify some common sexual disorders and their possible treatment.

10. Identify gender differences in sexual attitudes and behaviors.

11. Describe research findings on the nature of sexual orientation.

12. Discuss the origins of homosexuality, including both myths and research findings.

13. Discuss the place of values in research and education about sexual behavior.

14. (Close-Up) Discuss the significance of the need to belong, including its origins and benefits.

*Achievement Motivation* (pp. 339–343)

> If you do not know the meaning of any of the following words, phrases, or expressions in the context in which they appear in the text, refer to pages 273–274 for an explanation: *daredevils . . . thrills; ring toss game; superstar achievers; avoid snuffing out . . . controlling extrinsic rewards; Different strokes for different folks; great person . . . share certain traits; exude a self-confident charisma.*

15. Describe the nature and origin of achievement motivation.

16. Distinguish between extrinsic and intrinsic motivation, focusing on their relative effectiveness in promoting achievement motivation.

17. Discuss how managers can create a motivated, productive, and satisfied work force.

# Chapter Review

When you have finished reading the chapter, work through the material that follows to review it. Complete the sentences and answer the questions. As you proceed, evaluate your performance for each section by consulting the answers on page 265. Do not continue with the next section until you understand each answer. If you need to, review or reread the appropriate section in the textbook before continuing.

1. To motivate is to _____ behavior and _____ it toward goals.

*Motivational Concepts* (pp. 312–315)

2. As a result of Darwin's influence, many behaviors were classified as rigid, biologically determined behaviors that are characteristic of a species, called _____ .

Discuss why early instinct theory failed as an explanation of human behavior.

3. The idea underlying the theory that
_____ predispose species-typical behavior remains popular.

4. According to another view of motivation, organisms may experience a deprivation, or
_____ , which creates a state of arousal, or _____ .

5. The aim of drive reduction is to maintain a constant internal state, called _____ .
Behavior is often not so much pushed by our drives as it is pulled by _____
in the environment.

6. Rather than reduce a physiological need, some motivated behaviors actually
_____ arousal. This demonstrates that human motives _____
(do/do not) always satisfy some biological need.

7. Starting from the idea that some needs take precedence over others, Maslow constructed a _____ of needs.

8. According to Maslow, the _____
needs are the most pressing, whereas the highest-order needs relate to _____ .A
criticism of Maslow's theory is that the sequence is _____ and not
_____ experienced.

*Hunger* (pp. 315–326)

9. Ancel Keys observed that men became preoccupied with thoughts of food when they underwent
_____ .

10. Cannon and Washburn's experiment using a balloon indicated that there is an association between hunger and _____
_____ .

11. When an animal has had its stomach removed, hunger _____ (does/does not) continue.

12. Increases in the hormone _____
diminish blood _____ , partly by converting it to stored fat, which causes hunger to _____ .

13. The brain area that plays a role in hunger and other bodily maintenance functions is the
_____ . Animals will begin eating when the _____
_____ is electrically stimulated.
When this region is destroyed, hunger
_____ (increases/decreases).
Animals will stop eating when the
_____
is stimulated. When this area is destroyed, animals _____ (overeat/undereat).

14. Human patients with tumors in the
_____ will eat excessively and become fat. Feedback from this area of the brain is sent to the _____
_____ , which decide behavior.

15. The weight level at which an individual's body is programmed to stay is referred to as the body's
_____ _____ .
A person whose weight goes beyond this level will tend to feel _____
(more/less) hungry than usual and expend
_____ (more/less) energy.

16. The rate of energy expenditure in maintaining basic body functions when the body is at rest is the _____
_____ . When food intake is reduced, the body compensates by
_____ (raising/lowering) this rate.

17. Some researchers believe that a person's set point can be altered by _____
_____ .

18. Rodin refers to people whose eating is more affected by food stimuli than by internal cues as _____ . Rodin found that such individuals showed a particularly marked increase in blood _____ level when confronted with the sight, smell, and sound of a steak being grilled.

19. Stress-related cravings may be due to the fact that _____ boost levels of the neurotransmitter _____ , which has calming effects.

20. Taste preferences for sweet and salty are _____ (genetic/learned). Other influences on taste include _____ and _____ .

21. (Close-Up) Eating disorders are perhaps the best example of the influence of _____ factors on eating behavior.

22. (Close-Up) The disorder in which a person becomes significantly underweight and yet feels fat is known as _____ . In terms of sex and age, this disorder tends to develop in _____ who are in their _____ .

23. (Close-Up) A more common disorder is _____ , which is characterized by repeated _____ episodes and by feelings of depression.

24. (Close-Up) The families of bulimia patients have a high incidence of _____ , _____ , and _____ . The families of anorexia patients tend to be _____ , _____ , and _____ . Eating disorders _____ (provide/do not provide) a telltale sign of childhood sexual abuse.

25. (Close-Up) Genetic factors _____ (may/do not) influence susceptibility to eating disorders. People with eating disorders may also have abnormal supplies of certain _____ that put them at risk for _____ or _____ .

26. In developing societies where people face _____ , obesity is considered a sign of _____ and _____ .

Cite some of the ways in which obesity is a threat to physical and psychological health.

27. Eating disorders are rare in countries that do not have a _____ .

28. In one experiment, job applicants were rated as less worthy of hiring when they were made to appear _____ .

29. The energy equivalent of a pound of fat is approximately _____ calories. The immediate determinant of body fat is the size and number of _____ one has. This number is, in turn, determined by several factors, including _____ .

30. The size of fat cells _____ (can/cannot) be decreased by dieting; the number of fat cells _____ (can/cannot) be decreased by dieting.

31. Fat tissue has a _____ (higher/lower) basal metabolic rate than lean tissue. The result is that fat tissue requires _____ (more/less) food energy to be maintained.

32. The body weight "thermostat" of obese people _____ (is/is not) set to maintain a higher-than-average weight. When weight drops below this setting, _____ increases and _____ decreases.

Explain why, metabolically, many obese people find it so difficult to become and stay thin.

33. Studies of adoptees and twins _____ (do/do not) provide evidence of a genetic influence on obesity.

34. Recent experiments reveal that obese mice have a defective _____ for producing the protein _____. Increased levels of this protein signal the _____ to curb _____ and increase _____. When obese mice are given injections of this protein, they become _____ (more/less) active and _____ (gain/lose) weight.

35. Obesity is _____ (more/less) common among lower-class than upper-class women and _____ (does/does not) vary from culture to culture.

36. Most obese persons who lose weight _____ (gain/do not gain) it back.

*Sexual Motivation* (pp. 326–338)

37. In the 1940s and 1950s, a biologist named _____ surveyed the sexual practices of thousands of men and women.

38. Many popular sexual surveys cannot be taken seriously because they are based on _____ samples of respondents. Recent surveys indicate that marital infidelity is _____ (more/less) common than indicated by earlier surveys.

39. The two researchers who identified a four-stage sexual response cycle are _____ and _____. In order, the stages of the cycle are the _____ phase, the _____ phase, _____, and the _____ phase.

40. During resolution, males experience a _____, during which they are incapable of another orgasm.

41. In most mammals, females are sexually receptive only during ovulation, when the hormone _____ has peaked.

42. The importance of the hormone _____ to male sexual arousal is confirmed by the fact that sexual interest declines in animals if their _____ are removed.

43. Normal hormonal fluctuations in humans have _____ (little/significant) effect on sexual motivation. In later life, frequency of intercourse _____ (increases/decreases) as sex hormone levels _____ (increase/decline).

44. The region of the brain through which hormones help trigger sexual arousal is the _____ .

45. A study by Heiman has shown that erotic stimuli _____ (are/are not) as arousing for women as for men.

Explain some of the possible harmful consequences of sexually explicit material.

46. The importance of the brain in sexual motivation is indicated by the fact that people who, because of injury, have no genital sensation _____ (do/do not) feel sexual desire.

47. Most women and men _____ (have/do not have) sexual fantasies. Compared to women's fantasies, men' sexual fantasies are more _____ .

Sexual fantasies do not indicate sexual _____ or _____ .

48. Problems that consistently impair sexual functioning are called _____ . Examples of such problems include _____

_____ , _____ ,
and _____ .
Personality disorders _____
(have/have not) been linked with most of the
problems impairing sexual functioning, and so
the usual psychotherapeutic methods
_____ (are/are not) effective.

49. Compared to females, males are
_____ (equally/more/less)
likely to initiate sexual activity.

50. Men have a _____ (higher/
lower) threshold for perceiving a woman's
friendliness as a sexual come-on. This helps
explain men's greater sexual
_____ .

51. There may be an _____
explanation of gender differences in attitudes
toward sex. This explanation is based on differences in the optimal strategy by which women
and men pass on their _____ .
According to this view, because
_____ (eggs/sperm) are much
more prevalent than _____
(eggs/sperm), males and females are selected for
different patterns of sexuality.

52. A person's sexual attraction toward members of a
particular gender is referred to as
_____ .

53. Historically, _____ (virtually
all/a slight majority) of the world's cultures have
been predominantly heterosexual.

54. Studies in Europe and the United States indicate
that approximately _____ per-
cent of men and _____ percent
of women are exclusively homosexual. This finding suggests that popular estimates of the rate of
homosexuality are _____
(high/low/accurate).

55. A person's sexual orientation _____
(does/does not) appear to be voluntarily chosen.

56. Childhood events and family relationships
_____ (are/are not) important

factors in determining a person's sexual orientation.

57. Homosexuality _____
(does/does not) involve a fear of the other gender
that leads people to direct their sexual desires
toward members of their own gender.

58. As children, most homosexuals
_____ (were/were not) sexually victimized.

59. The sons of homosexual fathers
_____ (are/are not) more likely
to become gay if they live with their fathers.

60. Homosexual people appear more often in certain
populations, including men who live in
_____ ;
_____ , _____ ,
_____ , and _____ ;
and men who have older _____ .

61. One theory proposes that people develop a
homosexual orientation if they are segregated
with _____ (their own/the
other) gender at the time their sex drive matures.
The fact that early homosexual behavior
_____ (does/does not) make
people homosexual _____
(supports/conflicts with) this theory.

62. Researcher Simon LeVay discovered a cluster of
cells in the _____ that is larger
in _____ men than in all others.
Other studies have found a section of fibers con-
necting the brain's _____ and
_____
that is larger in homosexual men than in heterosexual men.

63. Studies of twins suggest that genes probably
_____ (do/do not) play a role
in homosexuality.

64. In animals and some rare human cases, sexual
orientation has been altered by abnormal
_____ conditions during prena-
tal development. In humans, prenatal exposure to

hormone levels typical of _____ , particularly between _____ and _____ months after conception, may predispose an attraction to males.

65. Daryl Bem has theorized that genes predispose _____ that lead children to prefer sex-typical or sex-atypical activities and friends.

66. Most psychiatrists now believe that _____ (nature/nurture) plays the larger role in predisposing sexual orientation.

67. (Close-Up) From an evolutionary standpoint, social bonds in humans were very _____ for our ancestors. If those who felt this need to _____ survived and reproduced more successfully, their _____ would in time predominate.

68. (Close-Up) Much of our _____ behavior aims to increase our belonging. For most people, familiarity leads to _____ (liking/disliking).

*Achievement Motivation* (pp. 339–343)

69. The biological perspective on motivation is contradicted by the existence of many behaviors that appear to satisfy no apparent biological _____ .

70. Psychologists Murray, McClelland, and Atkinson studied achievement motivation by having people create _____ about ambiguous pictures.

71. In experiments, individuals who chose extremely difficult tasks tended to have a _____ (low/high) need for achievement.

72. The parents of highly motivated children tend to encourage their _____ and _____ and _____ them for their successes.

73. Achievement motivation has both _____ roots and _____ roots.

74. Motivation to perform a behavior for its own sake is referred to as _____ _____ . Motivation based on external rewards and punishments is called _____ . Of the two, _____ _____ appears to be more successful in fueling achievement.

75. Excessive external pressures and incentives can undermine _____ motivation.

76. The field of _____ / _____ psychology studies how managers might best motivate employees.

77. Studies have shown that rewards lower intrinsic motivation when they are used to _____ but raise it when they are used to _____ .

78. Managers who are directive, set clear standards, organize work, and focus attention on specific goals are said to employ _____ . More democratic managers who aim to build teamwork and mediate conflicts in the work force employ _____ .

79. In experiments, women tended to excel at _____ leadership, whereas men tended to excel at _____ leadership.

Give several pieces of advice offered in the text to managers who wish to motivate employees.

80. The most effective style of leadership _____ (varies/does not vary) with the situation and/or the person.

81. Effective managers _____ (rarely/often) exhibit a high degree of both task and social leadership.

## Progress Test 1

### Multiple-Choice Questions

Circle your answers to the following questions and check them with the answers on page 266. If your answer is incorrect, read the explanation for why it is incorrect and then consult the appropriate pages of the text (in parentheses following the correct answer).

1. Motivation is best understood as a state that:
   a. reduces a drive.
   b. aims at satisfying a biological need.
   c. energizes an organism to act.
   d. energizes and directs behavior.

2. Which of the following is a difference between a drive and a need?
   a. Needs are learned; drives are inherited.
   b. Needs are physiological states; drives are psychological states.
   c. Drives are generally stronger than needs.
   d. Needs are generally stronger than drives.

3. One problem with the idea of motivation as drive reduction is that:
   a. because some motivated behaviors do not seem to be based on physiological needs, they cannot be explained in terms of drive reduction.
   b. it fails to explain any human motivation.
   c. it cannot account for homeostasis.
   d. it does not explain the hunger drive.

4. Recent evidence makes a preliminary link between homosexuality and:
   a. late sexual maturation.
   b. the age of an individual's first erotic experience.
   c. atypical prenatal hormones.
   d. early problems in relationships with parents.
   e. all of the above.

5. Increases in insulin will:
   a. lower blood sugar and trigger hunger.
   b. raise blood sugar and trigger hunger.
   c. lower blood sugar and trigger satiety.
   d. raise blood sugar and trigger satiety.

6. Electrical stimulation of the lateral hypothalamus will cause an animal to:
   a. begin eating.
   b. stop eating.
   c. become obese.
   d. begin copulating.
   e. stop copulating.

7. The text suggests that a "neophobia" for unfamiliar tastes:
   a. is more common in children than in adults.
   b. protected our ancestors from potentially toxic substances.
   c. may be an early warning sign of an eating disorder.
   d. only grows stronger with repeated exposure to those tastes.
   e. does all of the above.

8. Rodin found that, in response to the sight and smell of a steak being grilled:
   a. overweight people had a greater insulin response than people of normal weight.
   b. people of normal weight had a greater insulin response than overweight people.
   c. externals had a greater insulin response than internals.
   d. internals had a greater insulin response than externals.

9. Instinct theory and drive-reduction theory both emphasize _____ factors in motivation.
   a. environmental      d. social
   b. cognitive          e. biological
   c. psychological

10. The correct order of the stages of Masters and Johnson's sexual response cycle is:
    a. plateau; excitement; orgasm; resolution.
    b. excitement; plateau; orgasm; resolution.
    c. excitement; orgasm; resolution; refractory.
    d. plateau; excitement; orgasm; refractory.
    e. excitement; orgasm; plateau; resolution.

11. In studies of obese mice, researchers have found that some mice:
    a. had a defective gene for producing leptin, a fat-detecting hormone.
    b. had abnormally high levels of insulin, a hunger-triggering hormone.
    c. could be conditioned to avoid fatty foods.
    d. had fewer-than-normal receptor sites for a fat-detecting hormone.
    e. are immune to changes in hormone levels.

12. Studies have demonstrated that meals that are high in _____ promote relaxation because they raise levels of _____ .
    a. carbohydrates; serotonin
    b. carbohydrates; cortisol
    c. protein; serotonin
    d. protein; cortisol

13. In his study of men on a semistarvation diet, Keys found that:
    a. the basal metabolic rate of the subjects increased.
    b. the subjects eventually lost interest in food.
    c. the subjects became obsessed with food.
    d. the subjects' behavior directly contradicted predictions made by Maslow's hierarchy of needs.

14. When people restrict their intake of food, as when dieting, their:
    a. metabolism increases.
    b. metabolism decreases.
    c. metabolism stays the same.
    d. insulin decreases.
    e. glucose increases.

15. (Close-Up) Bulimia involves:
    a. binging.              d. a. and b.
    b. purging.              e. a., b., and c.
    c. dramatic weight loss.

16. Castration of male rats results in:
    a. reduced testosterone and sexual interest.
    b. reduced testosterone, but no change in sexual interest.
    c. reduced estrogen and sexual interest.
    d. reduced estrogen, but no change in sexual interest.

17. Most sexual disorders are caused by:
    a. personality problems.
    b. hormone imbalances.
    c. a very restricted upbringing.
    d. none of the above.

18. It has been said that the body's major sex organ is the brain. With regard to sex education:
    a. transmission of value-free information about the wide range of sexual behaviors should be the primary focus of the educator.
    b. transmission of technical knowledge about the biological act should be the classroom focus, free from the personal values and attitudes of researchers, teachers, and students.
    c. the home, not the school, should be the focus of all instruction about reproductive behavior.
    d. people's attitudes, values, and morals cannot be separated from the biological aspects of sexuality.

19. Research on genetic influences on obesity reveals that:
    a. the body weight of adoptees correlates with that of their biological parents.
    b. the body weight of adoptees correlates with that of their adoptive parents.
    c. identical twins usually have very different body weights.
    d. the body weights of identical twin women are more similar than those of identical twin men.
    e. none of the above is true.

20. To increase employee productivity, industrial/organizational psychologists advise managers to:
    a. adopt a directive leadership style.
    b. adopt a democratic leadership style.
    c. instill competitiveness in each employee.
    d. deal with employees according to their individual motives.

## Matching Items

Match each term with its definition or description.

### Terms

_____ **1.** intrinsic motivation
_____ **2.** set point
_____ **3.** drive
_____ **4.** orgasmic disorder
_____ **5.** extrinsic motivation
_____ **6.** estrogen
_____ **7.** homeostasis
_____ **8.** sexual orientation
_____ **9.** need
_____ **10.** incentive
_____ **11.** impotence

### Definitions or Descriptions

**a.** a hormone secreted more by females than by males

**b.** the body's tendency to maintain a balanced internal state

**c.** an environmental stimulus that motivates behavior

**d.** a person's attraction to members of a particular sex

**e.** the motivation to perform a behavior for its own sake

**f.** a desire to perform a behavior due to promised rewards

**g.** an inability to have or maintain an erection

**h.** an inability to experience orgasm

**i.** an aroused state arising from some state of deprivation

**j.** a state of deprivation

**k.** the body's weight-maintenance setting

## Progress Test 2

Progress Test 2 should be completed during a final chapter review. Answer the following questions after you thoroughly understand the correct answers for the Chapter Review and Progress Test 1.

### Multiple-Choice Questions

1. Sexual motivation in women is most influenced by:
   **a.** the level of progesterone.
   **b.** the level of estrogen.
   **c.** the level of testosterone.
   **d.** the phase of the menstrual cycle.
   **e.** social and psychological factors.

2. Homeostasis refers to:
   **a.** the tendency to maintain a steady internal state.
   **b.** the tendency to seek external incentives for behavior.
   **c.** the setting of the body's "weight thermostat."
   **d.** a theory of the development of sexual orientation.

3. Which of the following tends to foster a high need for achievement?
   **a.** the frequent use of extrinsic controls on behavior

   **b.** encouraging young children to remain dependent
   **c.** the use of punishment for failures
   **d.** giving rewards that provide feedback

4. The tendency to overeat when food is plentiful:
   **a.** is a recent phenomenon that is associated with the luxury of having ample food.
   **b.** emerged in our prehistoric ancestors as an adaptive response to alternating periods of feast and famine.
   **c.** is greater in developed, than in developing, societies.
   **d.** is stronger in women than in men.

5. Although the cause of eating disorders is still unknown, explanations that have been proposed focus on all of the following *except*:
   **a.** metabolic factors.
   **b.** genetic factors.
   **c.** family background factors.
   **d.** cultural factors.

6. The brain area that when stimulated suppresses eating is the:
   **a.** lateral hypothalamus.
   **b.** ventromedial hypothalamus.
   **c.** lateral thalamus.
   **d.** ventromedial thalamus.

7. Exposure of a fetus to the hormones typical of females between ____ and ____ months after conception may predispose the developing human to become attracted to males.
   a. 1; 3
   b. 2; 5
   c. 4; 7
   d. 6; 9
   e. 9; 11

8. Which of the following statements concerning homosexuality is true?
   a. Homosexuals have abnormal hormone levels.
   b. As children, most homosexuals were molested by an adult homosexual.
   c. Homosexuals had a domineering opposite-sex parent.
   d. New research indicates that sexual orientation may be at least partly physiological.

9. Which of the following is *not* necessarily a reason that obese people have trouble losing weight?
   a. Fat tissue has a lower basal metabolic rate than lean tissue.
   b. Once a person has lost weight, it takes fewer calories to maintain his or her current weight.
   c. The tendency toward obesity may be genetically based.
   d. Obese people tend to lack willpower.

10. According to Maslow's theory:
    a. the most basic motives are based on physiological needs.
    b. needs are satisfied in a specified order.
    c. the highest motives relate to self-actualization.
    d. all of the above are true.

11. Which of the following is *inconsistent* with the drive-reduction theory of motivation?
    a. When body temperature drops below 98.6° Fahrenheit, blood vessels constrict to conserve warmth.
    b. A person is driven to seek a drink when his or her cellular water level drops below its optimum point.
    c. Monkeys will work puzzles even if not given a food reward.
    d. A person becomes hungry when body weight falls below its biological set point.
    e. None of the above is inconsistent.

12. (Close-Up) Which of the following is true concerning eating disorders?
    a. Genetic factors may influence susceptibility.
    b. Abnormal levels of certain neurotransmitters may play a role.

c. People with eating disorders are at risk for anxiety or depression.
    d. Family background is a significant factor.
    e. All of the above are true.

13. Sexual orientation refers to:
    a. a person's tendency to display behaviors typical of males or females.
    b. a person's sense of identity as a male or female.
    c. a person's enduring sexual attraction toward members of a particular gender.
    d. all of the above.

14. Which of the following is *not* an aspect of Murray's definition of achievement motivation?
    a. the desire to master skills
    b. the desire for control
    c. the desire to gain approval
    d. the desire to attain a high standard

15. The power of external stimuli in sexual motivation is illustrated in Julia Heiman's experiment, in which subjects' responses to various romantic, erotic, or neutral audio tapes were recorded. Which of the following was among the findings of her research?
    a. The women were more aroused by the romantic tape; the men were more aroused by the sexually explicit tape.
    b. The sexually experienced subjects reported greater arousal when the tape depicted a sexual encounter in which a woman is overpowered by a man and enjoys being dominated.
    c. Whereas the men's physical arousal was both obvious and consistent with their verbal reports, the women's verbal reports did not correspond very directly with their measured physical arousal.
    d. Both men and women were aroused most by the sexually explicit tape.

16. According to Masters and Johnson, the sexual response of males is most likely to differ from that of females during:
    a. the excitement phase.
    b. the plateau phase.
    c. orgasm.
    d. the resolution phase.

17. In animals, destruction of the lateral hypothalamus results in _____ , whereas destruction of the ventromedial hypothalamus results in _____ .
    a. overeating; loss of hunger
    b. loss of hunger; overeating
    c. an elevated set point; a lowered set point
    d. increased thirst; loss of thirst
    e. increased metabolic rate; weight loss

18. Why do people with a high need for achievement prefer tasks of moderate difficulty?
    a. They are afraid of failing at more difficult tasks.
    b. They want to avoid the embarrassment of failing at easy tasks.
    c. Moderately difficult tasks present an attainable goal in which success is attributable to their own skill.
    d. They have high extrinsic motivation.

19. Beginning with the most basic needs, which of the following represents the correct sequence of needs in the hierarchy described by Maslow?
    a. safety; physiological; esteem; belongingness and love; self-fulfillment
    b. safety; physiological; belongingness and love; esteem; self-fulfillment
    c. physiological; safety; esteem; belongingness and love; self-fulfillment
    d. physiological; safety; belongingness and love; esteem; self-fulfillment
    e. physiological; safety; self-fulfillment; esteem; belongingness and love

20. Which of the following is true regarding gender and sexuality?
    a. Men *and* women believe in sex between two people who like each other even if they have known each other for only a short time.
    b. Men are more likely than women to cite affection as a reason for first intercourse.
    c. Men are more likely than women to interpret warmth as a sexual come-on.
    d. Today, women are more likely than men to initiate sexual activity.

*True–False Items*

Indicate whether each statement is true or false by placing *T* or *F* in the blank next to the item.

_____ 1. When body weight rises above set point, hunger increases.

_____ 2. According to Masters and Johnson, only males experience a plateau period in the cycle of sexual arousal.

_____ 3. Testosterone affects the sexual arousal of the male only.

_____ 4. Unlike men, women tend not to be aroused by sexually explicit material.

_____ 5. All taste preferences are conditioned.

_____ 6. Most obese people who lose weight eventually gain most of it back.

_____ 7. An increase in insulin increases blood glucose levels and triggers hunger.

_____ 8. Most types of sexual disorder are associated with personality disorders.

_____ 9. Intrinsic motivation fuels achievement more than does extrinsic motivation.

_____ 10. One's sexual orientation is not voluntarily chosen.

## Thinking Critically About Chapter 9

Answer these questions the day before an exam as a final check on your understanding of the chapter's terms and concepts.

*Multiple-Choice Questions*

1. Research on obesity indicates that:
   a. pound for pound, fat tissue requires more calories to maintain than lean tissue.
   b. once fat cells are acquired they are never lost, no matter how rigorously one diets.
   c. one pound of weight is lost for every 3500-calorie reduction in diet.
   d. when weight drops below the set point, hunger and metabolism also decrease.

2. Noriko, a corporate manager in Japan, tends to give all his workers a bonus at the end of the year, regardless of their performance. He does not understand why this "reward" does not improve productivity. This is because:
   a. he does not tie performance to reward.
   b. some workers are motivated by factors other than financial reward.
   c. he may be undermining the intrinsic motivation of some workers.
   d. of all of the above reasons.

3. Mary loves hang-gliding. It would be most difficult to explain Mary's behavior according to:
   a. incentives.
   b. achievement motivation.
   c. drive-reduction theory.
   d. Maslow's hierarchy of needs.

*worth #Humber*

4. For two weeks Orlando has been on a hunger strike in order to protest his country's involvement in what he perceives as an immoral war. Orlando's willingness to starve himself in order to make a political statement conflicts with the theory of motivation advanced by:
   a. Kinsey.
   b. Murray.
   c. Keys.
   d. Masters and Johnson
   e. Maslow.

5. (Close-Up) Kathy has been undergoing treatment for bulimia. There is an above-average probability that one or more members of Kathy's family are:
   a. high-achieving.
   b. overprotective.
   c. alcoholic.
   d. all of the above.

6. (Thinking Critically) Which of the following would be the *worst* piece of advice to offer to someone trying to lose weight?
   a. "In order to treat yourself to one 'normal' meal each day, eat very little until the evening meal."
   b. "Reduce your consumption of saturated fats."
   c. "Boost your metabolism by exercising regularly."
   d. "Without increasing total caloric intake, increase the relative proportion of carbohydrates in your diet."

7. One shortcoming of the instinct theory of motivation is that:
   a. it places too much emphasis on environmental factors.
   b. it focuses only on cognitive aspects of motivation.
   c. it applies only to animal behavior.
   d. it does not explain human behaviors; it simply names them.

8. (Close-Up) Which of the following is *not* typical of both anorexia and bulimia?
   a. far more frequent occurrence in women than in men
   b. preoccupation with food and fear of being overweight
   c. weight significantly and noticeably outside normal ranges
   d. low self-esteem and feelings of depression

9. Which of the following is *not* an example of homeostasis?
   a. perspiring in order to restore normal body temperature

   b. feeling hungry and eating to restore the level of blood glucose to normal
   c. feeling hungry at the sight of an appetizing food
   d. All of the above are examples of homeostasis.

10. Two rats have escaped from their cages in the neurophysiology lab. The technician needs your help in returning them to their proper cages. One rat is grossly overweight; the other is severely underweight. You confidently state that the overweight rat goes in the "_____-lesion" cage, while the underweight rat goes in the "___-lesion" cage.
    a. hippocampus; amygdala
    b. amygdala; hippocampus
    c. lateral hypothalamus; ventromedial hypothalamus
    d. ventromedial hypothalamus; lateral hypothalamus

11. Two students are shown the same picture of a diver standing at the edge of a diving board. They each write a story describing what they see. One says the diver is concentrating on making a successful dive that will qualify her for her country's Olympic team. The other student sees the diver as balking from the intense pressure and training required to be a competitive diver. The two students probably differ in their:
    a. intrinsic motivation.
    b. extrinsic motivation.
    c. need for achievement.
    d. self-actualization.

12. Ali's parents have tried hard to minimize their son's exposure to sweet, fattening foods. If Ali has the occasion to taste sweet foods in the future, which of the following is likely?
    a. He will have a strong aversion to such foods.
    b. He will have a neutral reaction to sweet foods.
    c. He will display a preference for sweet tastes.
    d. It is impossible to predict Ali's reaction.

13. Darren, a sales clerk at a tire store, enjoys his job, not so much for the money as for its challenge and the opportunity to interact with a variety of people. The store manager asks you to recommend a strategy for increasing Darren's motivation. Which of the following is most likely to be effective?
    a. Create a competition among the salespeople so that whoever has the highest sales each week receives a bonus.
    b. Put Darren on a week-by-week employment contract, promising him continued employment only if his sales increase each week.

**c.** Leave Darren alone unless his sales drop and then threaten to fire him if his performance doesn't improve.

**d.** Involve Darren as much as possible in company decision making and use rewards to inform him of his successful performance.

14. (Close-Up) Summarizing her report on the need to belong, Rolanda states that:

**a.** "Cooperation amongst our ancestors was uncommon."

**b.** "Social bonding is not in our nature; it is a learned human trait."

**c.** "Because bonding with others increased our ancestors' success at reproduction and survival, it became part of our biological nature."

**d.** both a. and b. are true.

15. After an initial rapid weight loss, a person on a diet loses weight much more slowly. This slowdown occurs because:

**a.** most of the initial weight loss is simply water.

**b.** when a person diets, metabolism decreases.

**c.** people begin to "cheat" on their diets.

**d.** insulin levels tend to increase with reduced food intake.

16. Lucille has been sticking to a strict diet but can't seem to lose weight. What is the most likely explanation for her difficulty?

**a.** Her body has a very low set point.

**b.** Her prediet weight was near her body's set point.

**c.** Her weight problem is actually caused by an underlying eating disorder.

**d.** Lucille is an "external."

17. Randy, who has been under a lot of stress lately, has intense cravings for sugary junk foods, which tend to make him feel more relaxed. Which of the following is the most likely explanation for his craving?

**a.** Randy feels that he deserves to pamper himself with sweets because of the stress he is under.

**b.** The extra sugar gives Randy the energy he needs to cope with the demands of daily life.

**c.** Carbohydrates boost levels of serotonin, which has a calming effect.

**d.** The extra sugar tends to lower blood insulin level, which promotes relaxation.

18. A course that Janice wants very much to take is being offered by three instructors. Janice chooses the instructor with a reputation for being moderately difficult over one perceived as impossibly

difficult and another viewed as very easy. It is most likely that Janice's choice reflects her:

**a.** having a low level of intrinsic motivation.

**b.** having a low need for achievement.

**c.** having a high need for achievement.

**d.** having a high level of extrinsic motivation.

19. Nancy decided to take introductory psychology because she has always been interested in human behavior. Jack enrolled in the same course because he thought it would be easy. Nancy's behavior was motivated by _____ , Jack's by _____ .

**a.** extrinsic motivation; intrinsic motivation

**b.** intrinsic motivation; extrinsic motivation

**c.** drives; incentives

**d.** incentives; drives

20. For as long as she has been the plant manager, Juanita has welcomed input from employees and has delegated authority. Bill, in managing his department, takes a more authoritarian, iron-fisted approach. Juanita's style is one of _____ leadership, whereas Bill's is one of _____ leadership.

**a.** task; social

**b.** social; task

**c.** directive; democratic

**d.** democratic; participative

### Essay Question

Differentiate the three major theories of motivation, discuss their origins, and explain why they cannot fully account for human behavior. (Use the space below to list the points you want to make and organize them. Then write the essay on a separate sheet of paper.)

# Key Terms

*Writing Definitions*

Using your own words, write on a separate piece of paper a brief definition or explanation of each of the following terms.

1. motivation

2. instinct

3. drive-reduction theory

4. homeostasis

5. incentives

6. hierarchy of needs

7. glucose

8. set point

9. basal metabolic rate

10. anorexia nervosa

11. bulimia nervosa

12. sexual response cycle

13. refractory period

14. estrogen

15. sexual disorder

16. sexual orientation

17. achievement motivation

18. intrinsic motivation

19. extrinsic motivation

20. industrial/organizational psychology

21. task leadership

22. social leadership

*Cross-Check*

As you learned in Chapter 1, reviewing and overlearning of material are important to the learning process. After you have written the definitions of the key terms in this chapter, you should complete the crossword puzzle to ensure that you can reverse the process—recognize the term, given the definition.

### ACROSS

2. Type of motivation that reflects the desire to perform a behavior for its own sake.
5. Region of the hypothalamus that, when electrically stimulated, causes an animal to eat.
12. In Maslow's theory, human needs are organized into a
   _____ .
13. In Maslow's theory, the needs that follow physiological needs in order of priority.
14. Major energy source for the body.
16. Final stage of the sexual response cycle.
17. Group-oriented leadership.
18. Goal-oriented leadership.
19. Early researcher on sexual behavior patterns.
20. Type of motivation that reflects the desire to perform a behavior in order to obtain a reward or avoid a punishment.

### DOWN

1. Theory that explains behavior as arising from physiological needs and the states of tension they create.
3. Eating disorder characterized by repeated "binge-purge" episodes.
4. Eating disorder in which a person restricts food intake to become significantly underweight and yet still feels fat.
6. Sex hormone secreted in greater amount by females than by males.
7. Type of motivation that reflects the degree to which a person is motivated by a desire for significant accomplishment.
8. Initial stage of the sexual response cycle.

9. In Maslow's theory, the most basic types of needs.
10. The resting period after orgasm, during which a male cannot be aroused to another orgasm.
11. The body's rate of energy expenditure.
15. A positive or negative stimulus that motivates behavior.

## ANSWERS

## Guided Study

The following guidelines provide the main points that your answers should have touched upon.

1. Motivation is a need or desire that energizes behavior and directs it toward a goal. The earliest theory classified motivated behavior as instinctive and unlearned; more recently, the evolutionary perspective contends that genes predispose species-typical behavior. Drive-reduction theory argues that a physiological need—not necessarily an instinct—creates a psychological state. People are not only pushed by the need to reduce drives

but also pulled by incentives. Arousal theory emphasizes the urge for an optimum level of stimulation.

2. Maslow's hierarchy of needs expresses the idea that some needs are more fundamental than others. Maslow proposed that physiological needs, such as for food, water, and shelter, are the most basic and must be met before we are motivated to meet "higher" needs for safety, belongingness and love, self-esteem, and self-actualization. Critics of Maslow's theory contend that the proposed sequence of needs is arbitrary and not universally fixed.

3. Although stomach pangs correlate with feelings of hunger, they are not the only source. Hunger also increases when increases in insulin diminish the secretion of glucose into the bloodstream. Blood chemistry is monitored by the lateral and ventromedial areas of the hypothalamus, which therefore control body weight. Animal research shows that when the LH is electrically stimulated, hunger increases; when the LH is destroyed, hunger decreases. Stimulation of the VMH depresses hunger, while its destruction will increase hunger and trigger rapid weight gain. The body also adjusts its basal metabolic rate to maintain its weight set point.

   Our preferences for sweet and salty tastes are genetic and universal. Culture and learning also affect taste, as when people given highly salted foods or foods common only in certain societies develop preferences for these tastes. Studies by Judith Rodin indicate that, especially in "external" people, the sights and smells of food can increase hunger, in part because these stimuli trigger increases in blood levels of insulin.

4. Anorexia nervosa is a disorder in which a person becomes significantly underweight yet feels fat. The disorder usually develops in adolescent females. Anorexia patients tend to come from high-achieving and protective families.

   Bulimia nervosa is a more common disorder characterized by repeated episodes of overeating followed by vomiting or using a laxative ("binge-purge" episodes). The families of bulimia patients have a higher than usual incidence of alcoholism, obesity, and depression.

   Several factors may contribute to these eating disorders—for example, genetics or the presence of abnormal supplies of certain neurotransmitters may be implicated. Socially, a factor may be the increasingly stringent cultural standards of thinness for women. In addition, studies have demonstrated that, in Western societies such as the United States, women's self-reported ideal weights tend to be lighter than their current weights.

5. Obesity is a threat to both physical and psychological well-being. The number of fat cells in our bodies is determined by genetic predisposition, early eating patterns, and adult overeating. Fat cells may shrink in size with dieting, but they will never decrease in number. Because fat tissue has a low basal metabolic rate, it takes less food energy to maintain, and it is therefore difficult for dieters to lose weight. Because obese persons probably have a higher-than-average set-point weight, when they diet their hunger increases and metabolism decreases, making it even more difficult for them to lose weight.

6. Adoption and twin studies both provide evidence for a genetic influence on body weight. Recent animal studies reveal that obese mice may have a defective gene for producing the fat-signaling protein leptin. When obese mice are treated with leptin, they eat less, become more active, and lose weight. In obese humans, leptin receptors are insensitive to leptin. Despite these studies, genes cannot explain the fact that obesity is much more common in lower-class than in upper-class women, more common among Americans than Europeans, and more common today than at the beginning of the century.

7. Biologist Alfred Kinsey interviewed 18,000 men and women in an effort to describe human sexual behavior. Kinsey's sample, however, was not random. Other sex reports have been prepared, but because they were based on biased samples of people, they cannot be taken seriously. Better information is only now starting to become available.

   Masters and Johnson outlined four stages in the sexual response cycle. During the initial excitement phase, the genital areas become engorged with blood, causing the penis and clitoris to swell and the vagina to expand and secrete lubricant. In the plateau phase, breathing, pulse, and blood pressure rates increase along with sexual excitement. During orgasm, rhythmic genital contractions create a pleasurable feeling of sexual release. During the resolution phase, the body gradually returns to its unaroused state and males enter a refractory period during which they are incapable of another orgasm.

8. Sex hormones direct the development of male and female sex characteristics and (especially in nonhuman animals) they activate sexual behavior. In most mammals, sexual activity coincides with ovulation and peak level of estrogen in the

female. Sexual behavior in male animals is directly related to the level of testosterone in their bodies.

In humans, normal fluctuations in hormone levels have little effect on sex drive once the pubertal surge in sex hormones has occurred. In later life, however, the frequency of intercourse decreases as sex hormone levels decline.

External stimuli, such as touch and erotic material, can trigger sexual arousal in both men and women, although sexually explicit materials may lead people to devalue their partners. Our imagination—in dreams and fantasies—can also lead to arousal.

9. Sexual disorders are problems that consistently impair sexual arousal or functioning, such as premature ejaculation, the inability to have or maintain an erection (impotence), or infrequent orgasms (orgasmic disorder).

Sexual disorders do not appear to be linked to personality disorders; it is therefore not surprising that traditional psychotherapy is ineffective in treating them. Sexual disorders are most effectively treated by methods that assume that people can learn and therefore modify their sexual responses.

10. Males are more likely than females to initiate sexual activity, they are more accepting of casual sex, and they report masturbating much more often. Men also have a lower threshold for perceiving someone's warmth as a sexual come-on.

There may be an evolutionary explanation for these differences. Because sperm are much more plentiful than eggs, natural selection may have favored different mating strategies and attitudes toward sex in males and females.

11. Sexual orientation is an individual's enduring sexual attraction toward members of a particular gender. Although virtually all cultures in all times have been predominantly heterosexual, studies suggest that 3 or 4 percent of men and 1 to 2 percent of women are exclusively homosexual.

Most homosexuals report first being aware of same-gender sexual feelings around puberty, but they typically do not think of themselves as gay or lesbian until nearer their twenties. The ostracism homosexuals often face may cause them to struggle with their sexual motivation. Because sexual orientation is neither willfully chosen nor willfully changed, however, homosexual feelings generally persist.

12. There are many myths about the causes of homosexuality, including that it is linked with levels of sex hormones; as a child, being molested or seduced by an adult homosexual; having a domineering mother and an ineffectual father; or fearing or hating members of the opposite sex. Recent evidence suggests genetic influence plays a role, possibly through the inheritance of a particular gene. In animals and some exceptional human cases, sexual orientation has been altered by abnormal prenatal hormone conditions, leading some researchers to suggest that exposure to hormone levels typical of females during a critical period of brain development may predispose the individual to become attracted to males.

The consistency of genetic, prenatal, and brain research findings has caused most psychiatrists to now believe that nature more than nurture predisposes sexual orientation.

13. Most sex educators and researchers aim for objectivity and strive to keep their writings on sexuality value-free. Critics contend that the study of sex cannot, and should not, be free of values. For example, the words we use to describe sexual behavior often reflect our personal values. Second, when sexual information is separated from the context of human values, young people are sent a message that sexual behavior is merely recreational activity. Therefore, sex-related values should be discussed openly, rather than avoided.

14. (Close-Up) Humans have a need to feel connected to others in enduring, close relationships. This need boosted our ancestors' success at survival and reproduction. Today, it influences our thoughts, emotions, and much of our social nature. By conforming to group standards and striving to make favorable impressions, we shape our social behavior to increase our social acceptance and inclusion.

Children and adults who are denied others' acceptance and inclusion become withdrawn and may feel more depression, anxiety, jealousy, and loneliness.

15. As defined by Henry Murray, achievement motivation is the desire for significant accomplishment, for mastering skills or ideas, for control, and for rapidly attaining a high standard. People with a low need for achievement prefer very easy or very difficult tasks, where failure is either unlikely or unembarrassing. People with a high need for achievement prefer moderately difficult tasks, where success is attainable and attributable to their own effort.

Children with a high need for achievement often have parents who encourage their independence from an early age and praise them for their successes. Achievement motivation has both emotional and cognitive roots, as children learn to associate achievement with positive emotions and to attribute their achievements to their own competence.

16. Intrinsic motivation is the desire to perform a behavior for its own sake. Extrinsic motivation is seeking external rewards and avoiding punishments. Intrinsic motivation promotes high achievement, as does the use of extrinsic rewards that *inform* people of their successes. Extrinsic rewards that are delivered to *control* people's behaviors, however, undermine intrinsic motivation.

17. Effective managers assess workers' motives (accomplishment, recognition, affiliation, power, etc.) and adjust their managerial style accordingly. What workers value also varies from culture to culture. Regardless of the managerial style, setting clear objectives, establishing challenging goals, and providing feedback on progress motivate high productivity.

 The appropriate leadership style depends on the situation, the strengths of the manager, and his or her assumptions about employees' motives. Those who excel at task leadership are directive, goal-oriented managers who are good at keeping a group centered on its mission. Those who excel at social leadership take a more democratic approach as they promote teamwork, mediate conflicts, and support their work force. Effective managers combine goal-oriented task leadership with group-oriented social leadership, adjusting their managerial style in response to workers' motives.

## Chapter Review

1. energize; direct
2. instincts

According to instinct theory, any human behavior could be regarded as an instinct. The only evidence for each such "instinct" was the behavior used to identify it. Thus, instinct theory offered only circular explanations; it labeled behaviors but did not explain them.

3. genes
4. need; drive
5. homeostasis; incentives
6. increase; do not
7. hierarchy

8. physiological; self-actualization; arbitrary; universally
9. semistarvation
10. stomach contractions
11. does
12. insulin; glucose; increase
13. hypothalamus; lateral hypothalamus; decreases; ventromedial hypothalamus; overeat
14. hypothalamus; frontal lobes
15. set point; less; more
16. basal metabolic rate; lowering
17. slow, sustained changes in body weight
18. externals; insulin
19. carbohydrates; serotonin
20. genetic; conditioning; culture
21. psychological
22. anorexia nervosa; females; teens
23. bulimia nervosa; binge-purge
24. alcoholism; obesity; depression; competitive; high-achieving; protective; do not provide
25. may; neurotransmitters; anxiety; depression
26. famine; affluence; status

Obesity increases one's risk of diabetes, high blood pressure and heart disease, gallstones, arthritis, and certain types of cancer. It negatively affects self-image and the perceptions of others, particularly if the excess weight is seen as the fault of the individual.

27. thin-ideal for women
28. obese
29. 3500; fat cells; genetic predisposition, early childhood eating patterns, adult overeating
30. can; cannot
31. lower; less
32. is; hunger; metabolism

Obese persons have higher set-point weights than nonobese persons. During a diet, basal metabolic rate drops to defend the set-point weight. The dieter therefore finds it hard to progress beyond an initial weight loss. When the diet is concluded, the lowered basal metabolic rate continues, so that relatively small amounts of food may prove fattening. Also, some people have lower basal metabolic rates than others.

33. do
34. gene; leptin; brain; eating; activity; more; lose
35. more; does
36. gain
37. Kinsey

38. biased; less
39. Masters; Johnson; excitement; plateau; orgasm; resolution
40. refractory period
41. estrogen
42. testosterone; testes
43. little; decreases; decline
44. hypothalamus
45. are

Erotic material may lead people to devalue their partners and relationships. Material that is both sexually explicit and violent may promote violent behavior toward women.

46. do
47. have; frequent, physical, and less romantic; problems; dissatisfaction
48. sexual disorders; premature ejaculation; impotence; orgasmic disorder; have not; are not
49. more
50. lower; assertiveness
51. evolutionary; genes; sperm; eggs
52. sexual orientation
53. virtually all
54. 3 to 4; 1 to 2; high
55. does not
56. are not
57. does not
58. were not
59. are not
60. large cities; poets; writers; artists; musicians; brothers
61. their own; does not; conflicts with
62. hypothalamus; heterosexual; right; left hemispheres
63. do
64. hormone; females; 2; 5
65. temperaments
66. nature
67. adaptive; belong; genes
68. social; liking
69. need
70. stories
71. low
72. independence; praise; reward
73. emotional; cognitive
74. intrinsic motivation; extrinsic motivation; intrinsic motivation

75. intrinsic
76. industrial/organizational
77. control; inform
78. task leadership; social leadership
79. social; task

Effective managers use extrinsic rewards to *inform* employees of their successes and boost intrinsic motivation. They also adjust their managerial style to suit their employees, assessing workers' motives (accomplishment, recognition, affiliation, power), challenging them with clear objectives and specific goals, and rewarding them accordingly.

80. varies
81. often

## Progress Test 1

### Multiple-Choice Questions

1. **d.** is the answer. (p. 311)
   **a. & b.** Although motivation is often aimed at reducing drives and satisfying biological needs, this is by no means always the case, as achievement motivation illustrates.
   **c.** Motivated behavior not only is energized but also is directed at a goal.

2. **b.** is the answer. A drive is the psychological consequence of a physiological need. (p. 312)
   **a.** Needs are unlearned states of deprivation.
   **c. & d.** Since needs are physical and drives psychological, their strengths cannot be compared directly.

3. **a.** is the answer. The curiosity of a child or a scientist is an example of behavior apparently motivated by something other than a physiological need. (pp. 312–313)
   **b. & d.** Some behaviors, such as thirst and hunger, are partially explained by drive reduction.
   **c.** Drive reduction is directly based on the principle of homeostasis.

4. **c.** is the answer. (p. 335)
   **a., b., & d.** None of these is linked to homosexuality.

5. **a.** is the answer. Increases in insulin increase hunger indirectly by lowering blood sugar, or glucose. (p. 316)

6. **a.** is the answer. This area of the hypothalamus seems to elevate hunger. (p. 317)
   **b.** Stimulating the ventromedial hypothalamus has this effect.

**c.** Lesioning the ventromedial hypothalamus has this effect.

**d.** The hypothalamus is involved in sexual motivation, but not in this way.

7. **b.** is the answer. (pp. 319–320)

**a.** Neophobia for taste is typical of all age groups.

**c.** Neophobia for taste is *not* an indicator of an eating disorder.

**d.** With repeated exposure, our appreciation for a new taste typically *increases*.

8. **c.** is the answer. Externals—those whose eating is especially triggered by food stimuli—showed a greater insulin response than did internals. (p. 318)

**a. & b.** The greater insulin response occurred in people who were especially sensitive to external cues, regardless of whether they were overweight.

**d.** Blood insulin levels rose less in internal subjects.

9. **e.** is the answer. (p. 312)

10. **b.** is the answer. (pp. 327–328)

11. **a.** is the answer. (p. 322)

12. **a.** is the answer. Certain high-carbohydrate foods raise the levels of serotonin, which facilitates relaxation by increasing the amount of tryptophan reaching the brain. (p. 318)

**b.** Cortisol is a stress hormone and hence not related either to carbohydrates or to relaxation.

**c. & d.** Meals that are high in protein promote alertness.

13. **c.** is the answer. The deprived subjects focused on food almost to the exclusion of anything else. (p. 315)

**a.** In order to conserve energy, the men's basal metabolic rate actually *decreased*.

**b. & d.** Far from losing interest in food, the subjects came to care only about food—a finding consistent with Maslow's hierarchy, in which physiological needs are at the base.

14. **b.** is the answer. (p. 322)

15. **d.** is the answer. (p. 319)

16. **a.** is the answer. (p. 328)

**c. & d.** Castration of the testes, which produce testosterone, does not alter estrogen levels.

17. **d.** is the answer. (p. 331)

18. **d.** is the answer. Sex is much more than just a biological act, and its study therefore inherently involves values, attitudes, and morals, which should thus be discussed openly. (p. 338)

19. **a.** is the answer. (p. 322)

20. **d.** is the answer. As different people are motivated by different things, in order to increase motivation and thus productivity, managers are advised to learn what motivates individual employees and to challenge and reward them accordingly. (pp. 341–342)

**a. & b.** The most effective management style will depend on the situation.

**c.** This might be an effective strategy with some, but not all, employees.

*Matching Items*

| | | |
|---|---|---|
| **1.** e (p. 340) | **5.** f (p. 340) | **9.** j (p. 312) |
| **2.** k (p. 317) | **6.** a (p. 328) | **10.** c (p. 312) |
| **3.** i (p. 312) | **7.** b (p. 312) | **11.** g (p. 330) |
| **4.** h (p. 330) | **8.** d (p. 332) | |

# Progress Test 2

*Multiple-Choice Questions*

1. **e.** is the answer. In contrast to the sexual behavior of other animals, which is largely controlled by hormones, human sexual motivation is primarily influenced by social and psychological factors. (p. 328)

2. **a.** is the answer. (p. 312)

**b.** This describes extrinsic motivation.

**c.** This describes set point.

**d.** Homeostasis has nothing to do with sexual orientation.

3. **d.** is the answer. If used to inform rather than to control, rewards can increase intrinsic motivation and the need for achievement. (p. 340)

**a., b., & c.** Each of these has been shown to *discourage* the development of intrinsic motivation.

4. **a.** is the answer. (p. 320)

5. **a.** is the answer. The text does not indicate whether their metabolism is higher or lower than most. (p. 319)

**b., c., & d.** Genes, family background, and cultural influence have all been proposed as factors in eating disorders.

6. **b.** is the answer. (p. 317)

**a.** Stimulation of the lateral hypothalamus triggers eating.

**c. & d.** The thalamus is a sensory relay station; stimulation of it has no effect on eating.

7. **b.** is the answer. The time between 2 and 5 months after conception may be a critical period for the brain's neuro-hormonal control system. Exposure to abnormal hormonal conditions at other times has no effect on sexual orientation. (p. 335)

8. **d.** is the answer. Researchers have not been able to find any clear differences, psychological or otherwise, between homosexuals and heterosexuals. Thus, the basis for sexual orientation remains unknown, although recent evidence points more to a physiological basis. (p. 336)

9. **d.** is the answer. Most researchers today discount the idea that people are obese because they lack willpower. (p. 321)

10. **d.** is the answer. (p. 314)

11. **c.** is the answer. Such behavior, presumably motivated by curiosity rather than any biological need, is inconsistent with a drive-reduction theory of motivation. (pp. 312–313)
    **a., b., & d.** Each of these examples is consistent with a drive-reduction theory of motivation.

12. **e.** is the answer. (p. 319)

13. **c.** is the answer. (p. 332)

14. **c.** is the answer. (p. 339)

15. **d.** is the answer. (p. 329)

16. **d.** is the answer. During the resolution phase males experience a refractory period. (p. 328)
    **a., b., & c.** The male and female responses are very similar in each of these phases.

17. **b.** is the answer. (p. 317)
    **a. & e.** These effects are the reverse of what takes place.
    **c.** If anything, set point is lowered by destruction of the lateral hypothalamus and elevated by destruction of the ventromedial hypothalamus.
    **d.** These effects do not occur.

18. **c.** is the answer. (p. 339)

19. **d.** is the answer. (p. 314)

20. **c.** is the answer. (p. 332)

*True-False Items*

| | |
|---|---|
| **1.** F (p. 317) | **6.** T (p. 323) |
| **2.** F (p. 327) | **7.** F (p. 316) |
| **3.** F (p. 328) | **8.** F (p. 331) |
| **4.** F (p. 329) | **9.** T (p. 340) |
| **5.** F (p. 318) | **10.** T (p. 333) |

## Thinking Critically About Chapter 9

*Multiple-Choice Questions*

1. **b.** is the answer.  (p. 321)
2. **d.** is the answer. A good manager motivates workers according to their particular needs and in relation to the situation. (pp. 341–342)
3. **c.** is the answer. Drive-reduction theory maintains that behavior is motivated when a biological need creates an aroused state, driving the individual to satisfy the need. It is difficult to believe that Mary's hang-gliding is satisfying a biological need. (p. 312)
   **a., b., & d.** Mary may enjoy hang-gliding because it is a challenge that "is there" (incentive), because it satisfies a need to accomplish something challenging (achievement), or because it increases her self-esteem and sense of fulfillment in life (Maslow's hierarchy of needs).

4. **e.** is the answer. According to Maslow's theory, physiological needs, such as the need to satisfy hunger, must be satisfied before a person pursues loftier needs, such as making political statements. (p. 314)
   **a.** Kinsey and Masters and Johnson were concerned with sexual behavior.
   **b.** Murray was concerned with achievement motivation.
   **c.** Keys was concerned with hunger.

5. **c.** is the answer. (p. 319)
   **a. & b.** These are more typical of the families of anorexia patients.

6. **a.** is the answer. Dieting, including fasting, lowers the body's metabolic rate and reduces the amount of food energy needed to maintain body weight. (p. 325)
   **b., c., & d.** Each of these strategies would be a good piece of advice to a dieter.

7. **d.** is the answer. (p. 325)
   **a. & b.** Instinct theory emphasizes biological factors rather than environmental or cognitive factors.
   **c.** Instinct theory applies to both humans and other animals.

8. **c.** is the answer. Although anorexics are significantly underweight, bulimics often are not unusually thin or overweight. (p. 319)
   **a., b., & d.** Both anorexics and bulimics are more likely to be women than men, preoccupied with food, fearful of becoming overweight, and suffer from depression or low self-esteem.

9. **c.** is the answer. This is an example of salivating in response to an incentive rather than to maintain a balanced internal state. (p. 312)
   **a. & b.** Both of these are examples of behavior that maintains a balanced internal state (homeostasis).

10. **d.** is the answer. Lesions of the ventromedial hypothalamus produce overeating and rapid weight gains. Lesions of the lateral hypothalamus suppress hunger and produce weight loss. (p. 317)
    **a. & b.** The hippocampus and amygdala are not involved in regulating eating behavior.

**11. c. is the answer.** Achievement researchers regard people whose stories about ambiguous pictures express fantasies about the pursuit of goals, performing heroic acts, or feeling pride in success, as indicating achievement concerns. (p. 339)

**a., b., & d.** There is nothing in the stated information that would allow us to conclude that the students differ in their intrinsic or extrinsic orientation, or in their need to belong.

**12. c. is the answer.** Our preferences for sweet and salty tastes are genetic and universal. (p. 318)

**13. d. is the answer.** Because Darren evidently has a high intrinsic orientation, giving him feedback about his work and involving him in participative management are probably all he needs to be very satisfied with his situation. (pp. 340, 342)

**a., b., & c.** Creating competitions and using controlling, rather than informing, rewards may have the opposite effect and actually undermine Darren's intrinsic motivation.

**14. c. is the answer.** (p. 337)

**15. b. is the answer.** Following the initial weight loss, metabolism drops as the body attempts to defend its set-point weight. This drop in metabolism means that eating an amount that once produced a loss in weight may now actually result in weight gain. (p. 323)

**16. b. is the answer.** The body acts to defend its set point, or the weight to which it is predisposed. If Lucille was already near her set point, weight loss would prove difficult. (p. 317)

**a.** If the weight level to which her body is predisposed is low, weight loss upon dieting should not be difficult.

**c.** The eating disorders relate to eating behaviors and psychological factors and would not explain a difficulty with weight loss.

**d.** Externals might have greater problems losing weight, since they tend to respond to food stimuli, but this can't be the explanation in Lucille's case, since she has been sticking to her diet.

**17. c. is the answer.** Serotonin is a neurotransmitter that is elevated by the consumption of carbohydrates and has a calming effect. (p. 318)

**a. & b.** These answers do not explain the feelings of relaxation that Randy associates with eating junk food.

**d.** The consumption of sugar tends to elevate insulin level rather than lower it.

**18. c. is the answer.** Individuals with a high need for achievement tend to choose moderately difficult tasks at which they can succeed if they work at it. (p. 339)

**a & d.** That she chooses the course because it interests her implies that she is *intrinsically* motivated.

**b.** People with a low need for achievement might be more likely to prefer either the easy or the very difficult course.

**19. b. is the answer.** Wanting to do something for its own sake is intrinsic motivation; wanting to do something for a reward (in this case, presumably, a high grade) is extrinsic motivation. (p. 340)

**a.** The opposite is true. Nancy was motivated to take the course for its own sake, whereas Jack was evidently motivated by the likelihood of a reward in the form of a good grade.

**c. & d.** A good grade, such as the one Jack is expecting, is an incentive. Drives, however, are aroused states that result from physical deprivation; they are not involved in this example.

**20. b. is the answer.** (p. 342)

**a.** Bill's style is one of task leadership, whereas Juanita's is one of social leadership.

**c.** Juanita's style is participative, whereas Bill's is directive.

**d.** The term *democratic* means the same things as *participative*.

### Essay Question

Under the influence of Darwin's evolutionary theory, it became fashionable to classify all sorts of behaviors as instincts. Instinct theory fell into disfavor for several reasons. First, instincts do not explain behaviors, they merely name them. Second, to qualify as an instinct, a behavior must have a fixed and automatic pattern and occur in all people, regardless of differing cultures and experiences. Apart from a few simple reflexes, however, human behavior is not sufficiently automatic and universal to meet these criteria. Although instinct theory failed to explain human motives, the underlying assumption that genes predispose many behaviors is as strongly believed as ever.

Instinct theory was replaced by drive-reduction theory and the idea that biological needs create aroused drive states that motivate the individual to satisfy these needs and preserve homeostasis. Drive-reduction theory failed as a complete account of human motivation because many human motives do not satisfy any obvious biological need. Instead, such behaviors are motivated by environmental incentives.

Arousal theory emerged in response to evidence that some motivated behaviors *increase*, rather than decrease, arousal.

## Key Terms

*Writing Definitions*

1. **Motivation** is a need or desire that energizes and directs behavior. (p. 311)

2. An **instinct** is a complex behavior that is rigid, patterned throughout a species, and unlearned. (p. 312)

3. **Drive-reduction theory** attempts to explain behavior as arising from a physiological need that creates an aroused tension state (drive) that motivates an organism to satisfy the need. (p. 312)

4. **Homeostasis** refers to the body's tendency to maintain a balanced or constant internal state. (p. 312)

5. **Incentives** are positive or negative environmental stimuli that motivate behavior. (p. 312)

6. Maslow's **hierarchy of needs** proposes that human motives may be ranked from the basic, physiological level through higher-level needs for safety, belongingness and love, esteem, and self-actualization; and that until they are satisfied, the more basic needs are more compelling than the higher-level ones. (p. 314)

7. **Glucose**, or blood sugar, is the major source of energy for the body's tissues. Elevating the level of glucose in the body will reduce hunger. (p. 316)

8. **Set point** is an individual's regulated weight level, which is maintained by adjusting food intake and energy output. (p. 317)

9. **Basal Metabolic rate** is the rate of energy expenditure in maintaining basic body functions when the body is at rest. (p. 317)

   *Memory aid:* Basal metabolic rate is the body's **base** rate of energy expenditure.

10. **Anorexia nervosa** is an eating disorder, most common in adolescent females, in which a person restricts food intake to become significantly underweight and yet still feels fat. (p. 319)

11. **Bulimia nervosa** is an eating disorder characterized by private "binge-purge" episodes of overeating followed by vomiting or laxative use. (p. 319)

12. The **sexual response cycle** described by Masters and Johnson consists of four stages of bodily reaction: excitement, plateau, orgasm, and resolution. (p. 327)

13. The **refractory period** is a resting period after orgasm, during which a male cannot be aroused to another orgasm. (p. 328)

14. **Estrogen** is a sex hormone secreted in greater amounts by females than by males. In mammals other than humans, estrogen levels peak during ovulation and trigger sexual receptivity. (p. 328)

15. A **sexual disorder** is a problem—such as impotence, premature ejaculation, and orgasmic disorder—that consistently impairs sexual arousal or functioning. (p. 330)

16. **Sexual orientation** refers to a person's enduring attraction to members of either the same or the opposite gender. (p. 332)

17. **Achievement motivation** is the degree to which a person is motivated internally by a desire for significant accomplishment; mastery of things, people, or ideas; control; and attaining a high standard. (p. 339)

18. **Intrinsic motivation** is the desire to perform a behavior for its own sake, rather than for some external reason, and to be effective. (p. 340)

    *Memory aid: In*trinsic means *"in*ternal": A person who is **intrinsically** motivated is motivated from within.

19. **Extrinsic motivation** is the desire to perform a behavior in order to obtain a reward or avoid a punishment. (p. 340)

    *Memory aid: Ex*trinsic means *"ex*ternal": A person who is **extrinsically** motivated is motivated by some outside factor.

20. **Industrial/organizational psychology** is a subfield of psychology that studies and advises on issues related to behavior in the workplace, including employee selection, training, productivity, and morale. (p. 341)

21. **Task leadership** is goal-oriented leadership that sets standards, organizes work, and focuses attention on goals. (p. 342)

22. **Social leadership** is group-oriented leadership that builds teamwork, mediates conflict, and offers support. (p. 342)

*Cross-Check*

| ACROSS | DOWN |
|---|---|
| 2. intrinsic | 1. drive-reduction |
| 5. lateral | 3. bulimia nervosa |
| 12. hierarchy | 4. anorexia nervosa |
| 13. safety | 6. estrogen |
| 14. glucose | 7. achievement |
| 16. resolution | 8. excitement |
| 17. social | 9. physiological |
| 18. task | 10. refractory |
| 19. Kinsey | 11. metabolic rate |
| 20. extrinsic | 15. incentive |

## FOCUS ON VOCABULARY AND LANGUAGE

*Page 311:. . . truant officer . . .* A *truant* is a child who stays away from school without permission, and government officials who enforce compulsory education policy are called *truant officers*. Alfredo was forced to go to school and was spanked (*paddled*) for speaking Spanish. He decided to learn English and work hard to get good grades in school and college, and he was successful. As a well-educated college administrator, Alfredo now tries to motivate others to become aware of (*wake up to*) their own potential and ability to do well.

### Motivational Concepts

*Page 312:* Before long, *the instinct-naming fad collapsed under its own weight.* The fact that categorizing a very broad range of behaviors as instincts (*instinct-naming fad*) became very popular (*fashionable*) provides a good example of the misuse of a theory. In Darwinian theory, an **instinct** is an *unlearned* behavior that follows a fixed pattern in all members of the species. This fashion (*fad*) of naming thousands of behaviors as instincts grew so large and cumbersome that it was finally abandoned as a useful explanatory system (*collapsed under its own weight*).

*Page 312:* Both systems operate through *feedback loops.* . . . A thermostat in a house and the body's temperature-regulation system are both examples of **homeostasis**. If temperature drops, the change is detected and the information is directed (*fed*) to the system so that necessary steps are taken to bring the temperature back up to its original position. This information is then transmitted back to the system, so that there is a continuous cycle of cooling down and heating up (*feedback loop*) in an attempt to maintain a steady state. This is the basis of **drive-reduction theory**.

*Page 313:* Curiosity drives monkeys to *monkey around* trying to figure out how to unlock a latch that opens nothing, or how to open a window that allows them to see outside their room (Butler, 1954). The expression *"monkey around"* means to play or fool around (meddle) with something. Monkeys and young children have a very great need (*insatiable urge*) to explore and find out about their surroundings. **Arousal theory** suggests that we are driven to seek stimulation and increase our level of arousal to some comfortable state which is neither too high nor too low (*optimum level*).

### Hunger

*Page 315:* They talked food. They daydreamed food. They collected recipes, read cookbooks, and *feasted their eyes on delectable forbidden foods.* In this experiment, subjects were given only half their normal intake of food, and the men became lethargic (*listless*), focused all their thoughts on the topic of food, and looked longingly at (*feasted their eyes on*) pictures of delicious, but unobtainable, foods (*delectable forbidden foods*). This behavior is consistent with Maslow's theory that there is a hierarchy of needs.

*Page 316:* This suggests that the body is somehow, somewhere, *keeping tabs on* its available resources. People and other animals naturally and automatically tend to control food intake in order to keep a relatively constant body weight. This indicates that there is a mechanism, or mechanisms, which monitor (*keep tabs*) on energy fluctuations. Levels of the blood sugar glucose and brain chemicals such as the neurotransmitter serotonin may play a role in this process.

*Page 317:* . . . rather like a *miser* who runs a bit of extra money to the bank and resists taking any out. **Set point theory** suggests that two parts of the hypothalamus, the lateral hypothalamus (LH) and ventromedial hypothalamus (VMH), regulate hunger. Stimulation of the LH increases hunger, while activity in the VMH depresses hunger. If the VMH is destroyed (*lesioned*), rats tend to create and store more fat, just as a person who loves money more than anything else (*a miser*) will keep banking money and use as little of it as possible.

*Page 318:* During the first week of [summer] camp, some girls could not resist *munching* readily visible *M&Ms,* even after a full meal. People who tend to eat because tasty food is available rather than because they are hungry are called *externals*. Those girls who continued to eat (*munch*) candies (*M&Ms*), which were made available after they had eaten a complete meal, were the ones who gained the most weight by the end of 8 weeks.

*Page 318:* While blood samples were being taken, a large, juicy steak was wheeled in, *crackling* as it finished grilling. When very hungry subjects were exposed to the smell (*aroma*) and sight of an appetizing food stimulus (a tender piece of beef barbecuing on the grill [*crackling steak*] was brought into the room), externals showed the largest increase in insulin levels and associated hunger response. This shows how external stimuli (the steaks) can create psychological incentives which interact with internal physiological processes.

*Page 319:* . . . *binge-purge* . . . People who have an eating disorder called **bulimia nervosa** may have episodes of overeating (*binging*) similar to those who engage in drinking bouts (*spurts of drinking*). The bulimic person (typically females in their teens or twenties) usually follows the overeating episode (*gorging*) with self-induced vomiting and excessive laxative use (*purging*).

*Page 320:* Why do so few overweight people *win the battle of the bulge?* Most overweight people who diet do not manage to permanently lose the many pounds of fat they want to (*they do not win the battle of the bulge*). Myers discusses a number of factors: (a) the number of fat cells in the body does not decrease when you diet; (b) the tissue in fat is easier to maintain and uses less energy than other tissue; and (c) when body weight drops below the set point, your overall metabolic rate slows down. For those wanting to diet, Myers lists some useful tips (see p. 545).

*Page 322:* Being overweight is therefore *not* simply a matter of *scarfing* too many *hot fudge sundaes.* And losing weight is not simply a matter of *mind over platter.* Research has shown that being obese (*overweight*) is not a function of hungrily devouring (*scarfing*) an excessive number of desserts made from ice cream covered with chocolate sauce, fruit, whipped cream, etc. (*hot fudge sundaes*), nor is it a matter of willpower (*mind over matter*) or the ability to resist the food on your plate (*mind over platter*).

*Page 324:* For most people, however, the only long-term result is a *thinner wallet.* Most commercial weight-loss programs cost a great deal of money but, at best, only help people lose weight temporarily. For those who lose and then regain weight over and over again (*yo-yo dieting*), the end result is usually a greater weight gain each time and ultimately having less money (*thinner wallets*).

### Sexual Motivation

*Page 326:* . . . asked more than 350 *rapid fire questions.* Kinsey and Pomeroy were the first sex researchers to systematically interview a large sample of the American population. Their technique (*tactic*) involved starting with easy-to-answer questions (e.g., age, education, health, gender, etc.) and then moving on to questions that required subjects to divulge personal sexual information. These questions were asked in an aggressive interrogative style (*rapid fire questions*) and that fact, along with a nonrepresenta-

tive sample, may have biased their results.

*Page 327: Apparently faithful attractions* greatly outnumber *fatal attractions.* Recent research (based on more random representative samples) has shown that couples are more monogamous and committed to their partners (*faithful attractions*) than previous, less valid or reliable surveys have suggested. (*Fatal Attraction* is the title of a movie about a married man who has an affair with a woman who becomes obsessed with him, and this eventually leads to her death, thus the title *Fatal Attraction.*)

*Page 329:* The hormonal fuel is essential, but so are the psychological stimuli that *turn on the engine,* keep it running, and *shift it into high gear.* Myers makes an analogy between sex hormones and the fuel that propels a car. We need the hormones to be sexually motivated just as a car needs fuel to operate. In humans, however, there is a two-way interaction between the chemicals and sexuality. In addition to hormones, psychological factors are needed to initiate sexual desire (*turn on the engine*) and produce the associated behaviors (*shift it into high gear*).

*Page 330:* Viewing *X-rated sex films* similarly tends to diminish people's satisfaction with their sexual partners (Zillmann, 1989). All films are rated by a censor, and those with an *X-rating* because of their sexually explicit content are restricted to adults only. There is much debate over the influence of such films on people, and some research suggests that there may be adverse effects. For example, they may create the false impression that females enjoy rape; they may increase men's willingness to hurt women; they tend to lead both males and females to devalue their partners and their relationships; and they may reduce people's feeling of fulfillment with their lovers.

*Page 332: Casual hit-and-run sex* is most frequent among males with traditional masculine attitudes (Pleck & others, 1993). There are large gender differences in sexual values and attitudes, which are reflected in differences in male-female behaviors. Males (especially those with stereotyped views of females) tend to be nonchalant about and agreeable to having sex with someone they have just met and hardly know (*casual hit-and-run sex*).

*Page 332:* Men also have a lower threshold for perceiving someone's warmth as a *sexual come-on.* Males will typically misinterpret an affable, affectionate, friendly female's behavior (*her warmth*) as an invitation to have sex (*a sexual come-on*). Numerous studies have shown that men are more likely than women to attribute a woman's friendliness to sexual interest.

*Page 332:* In our *ancestral history*, females most often *sent their genes into the future by pairing wisely*, men *by pairing widely*. Evolutionary psychologists note that our normal desires (*natural yearnings*) help perpetuate our genes. In our evolutionary past (*ancestral history*) females accomplished this best by being selective in their choice of a mate (*pairing wisely*) and men by more promiscuous behavior (*pairing widely*). Myers points out, however, that environmental factors, such as cultural expectations, can alter how sexual behavior is expressed by both males and females (*can bend the genders*).

*Page 333:* . . . *fired* . . . To be *fired* means to lose your job (*to be laid off, let go, or sacked*). Myers suggests that one way for heterosexual people to understand how a homosexual feels in a predominantly heterosexual society is to imagine what it would be like if the situation were reversed and homosexuality was the norm. How would it feel as a heterosexual to be ostracized (*ignored*), to lose one's job (*be fired*), to be confronted by media that showed or indicated homosexuality as the societal norm.

*Page 333:* Most psychologists today view sexual orientation as neither *willfully chosen* nor *willfully changed*. Myers compares sexual orientation to handedness. You don't deliberately decide (*willfully choose*) to be right-handed or left-handed, and you can't intentionally alter (*willfully change*) your inherent inclination to use one hand over the other. Like handedness, sexual orientation is not linked to criminality nor is it associated with personality or psychological disorder.

*Page 336:* Regardless of the process, the consistency of the genetic, prenatal, and brain findings has *swung the pendulum toward* a physiological explanation. The debate over what causes different sexual orientations has continued for many years. Recent evidence from the research seems to favor (*swung the pendulum toward*) a biologically based account.

*Page 336:* To gay and lesbian activists, the new biological research is a *double-edged sword* (Diamond, 1993). The research supporting a physiological explanation of sexual orientation has both positive and negative aspects (*a double-edged sword*). On the one hand, if sexual orientation is genetically influenced, there is a basis for claiming equal civil rights, and there is no need to attribute blame. On the other hand, these findings create a nagging anxiety (*haunting possibility*) that sexual orientation may be controlled through genetic engineering or fetal abortions.

*Page 337 (Close-Up):* The need to belong *colors our thoughts and emotions*. As humans, we have a desire to be connected to others and to develop close, long-lasting relationships, and this need to belong affects the way we think and feel (*colors our thoughts and emotions*).

### Achievement Motivation

*Page 339:* Billionaires may be motivated to make ever more money . . . *daredevils* to seek ever *greater thrills*. A person who tries very hard to be successful, by being better than others at whatever task is undertaken, has a high need for achievement (**achievement motivation**). For instance, some people are high risk-takers (*daredevils*), and they frequently look for activities that produce ever higher levels of stimulation or arousal (*greater thrills*).

*Page 339:* In a *ring toss game* they often stand at an *intermediate distance* from the *stake*; this enables some successes, yet provides a suitable challenge. When faced with the task of throwing a small rubber ring onto a vertical post (*stake*) some distance away (*ring toss game*), those with a high need for achievement tend to stand neither too near nor too far away (*intermediate distance*). This makes the game somewhat difficult (*challenging*), yet ensures some correct responses which can then be attributed to skill and concentration. Those with low achievement motivation pick either a very close or a very far position from the stake.

*Pages 339–340:* These *superstar achievers* were distinguished not so much by their extraordinary *natural talent* as by their extraordinary daily discipline. Studies of people who were outstanding artists, scientists, athletes, etc. (*superstar achievers*) found that they were not different because of intelligence or innate skills (*natural talent*) but because of exceptional motivation and very high levels of self-discipline in relation to the daily pursuit of their goals.

*Page 341:* Second, *avoid snuffing out* people's sense of self-determination with an overuse of *controlling extrinsic rewards* (Deci & Ryan, 1987). **Industrial/organizational psychologists** are interested in how best to motivate people to realize their potential, and to be productive and contented workers. One thing that leaders (managers, coaches, teachers, etc.) can do is to make sure that people are intellectually challenged and that their curiosity is aroused. In addition, it is important to encourage intrinsic motivation and preclude inhibiting (*avoid snuffing out*) people's feelings of control in their lives by imposing too many externally restraining incentives (*controlling extrinsic rewards*).

*Page 342:* Different *strokes* for different *folks*, but for each a way to motivate. Good leaders change their managerial style depending on the needs of the people with whom they are working. They tend to create challenges for people who need to feel they have accomplished something, they pay attention and give praise to those who need recognition, they create a feeling of teamwork for those who have a need to belong, and they provide some competitive challenges and opportunities for success for those who value power. There are different incentives (*strokes*) for different people (*folks*), but each has the ability to motivate.

*Pages 342–343:* Because effective leadership styles vary with the situation and the person, the once-popular *"great person"* theory of leadership—that all great leaders *share certain traits—fell out of favor.* It was once believed that good management or leadership was a function of common characteristics (*shared traits*) possessed by some people (*"great persons"*). This notion is no longer popular (*it fell out of favor*), but recent research suggests that effective managers typically demonstrate high levels of *both* **task leadership** (organizing work, focusing on goals, and being directive) *and* **social leadership** (developing cooperation, settling conflicts, and being democratic).

*Page 342–343:* Effective leaders of laboratory groups, work teams, and large corporations also tend to *exude a self-confident "charisma."* . . . Competent managers who lead groups of people in an effective and productive manner typically exhibit an ability to rely on their own capacities (*exude self-confidence*), project their vision of what needs to be done, and inspire others to follow them (*"charisma"*).

# 10

# *Emotions, Stress, and Health*

## Chapter Overview

Emotions are responses of the whole individual, involving physiological arousal, expressive behaviors, and conscious experience. Chapter 10 examines these components in detail, particularly as they relate to two specific emotions: anger and happiness. In addition, the chapter discusses several theoretical controversies concerning the relationship and sequence of the components of emotion Primarily among these are whether the body's response to a stimulus causes the emotion that is felt and whether thinking is necessary to and must precede the experience of emotion.

The chapter concludes with a discussion of how emotions and responses to stress influence risk of disease. The effort to understand more fully the role of behavioral factors in maintaining health and causing illness has led to the emergence of the subfield of health psychology. A key topic in health psychology is stress: its nature, its effects on the body, and ways in which it can be managed. The final section looks at behaviors that promote good health.

NOTE: Answer guidelines for all Chapter 10 questions begin on page 291.

## Guided Study

The text chapter should be studied one section at a time. Before you read, preview each section by skimming it, noting headings and boldface items. Then read the appropriate section objectives from the following outline. Keep these objectives in mind and, as you read the section, search for the information that will enable you to meet each objective. Once you have finished a section, write out answers for its objectives.

*Introduction* and
*The Physiology of Emotion* (pp. 347–351)

> David Myers at times uses idioms that are unfamiliar to some readers. If you do not know the meaning of any of the following words, phrases, or expressions in the context in which they appear in the text, refer to pages 300–303 for an explanation: *color; rumble . . . stalking; your stomach develops butterflies; shooting free throws; clutching, sinking sensation; Pinocchio . . . telltale sign.*

1. Identify the three components of emotion and describe the physiological changes that occur during emotional arousal, including the relationship between arousal and performance.

2. Discuss the research findings on the relationship between body states and specific emotions.

3. (Thinking Critically) Discuss the effectiveness of the polygraph in detecting lies.

6. Identify some potential causes and consequences of happiness and discuss reasons for the relativity of happiness.

*Expressing Emotion* (pp. 351–356)

> If you do not know the meaning of any of the following words, phrases, or expressions in the context in which they appear in the text, refer to page 300 for an explanation: *good enough at reading; Fidgeting; Ditto; sneer; Fake a big grin.*

4. Discuss the extent to which nonverbal expressions of emotion are universally understood and describe the effects of facial expressions on emotion.

*Theories of Emotion* (pp. 364–368)

> If you do not know the meaning of any of the following words, phrases, or expressions in the context in which they appear in the text, refer to page 301 for an explanation: *lash out; Which is the chicken and which the egg?; testy; The heart is not always subject to the mind.*

7. Contrast and critique the James-Lange and Cannon-Bard theories of emotion.

8. Describe Schachter's two-factor theory of emotion and discuss evidence suggesting that some emotional reactions involve no conscious thought.

*Experiencing Emotion* (pp. 356–363)

> If you do not know the meaning of any of the following words, phrases, or expressions in the context in which they appear in the text, refer to page 301 for an explanation: *hostile outbursts; blowing off steam; sages of the ages; rush of euphoria; machines galore; lob a bombshell; passively vegetating.*

5. Identify three dimensions of emotional experience; discuss the catharsis hypothesis and identify some of the advantages and disadvantages of openly expressing anger.

*Stress and Health* (pp. 368–377)

> If you do not know the meaning of any of the following words, phrases, or expressions in the context in which they appear in the text, refer to pages 302–303 for an explanation: *tense . . . clenched teeth . . . churning stomach; slippery concept; heart rate zooms; uprooting; a cluster of crises; flow through a psychological filter; Daily Hassles; mellow and laid-back; after the honeymoon period; combat ready; headless horseman; Marital spats; ever-nice . . . bottle up; pseudoscientific hocus-pocus.*

9. Define *stress* and describe the body's response to stress.

10. Discuss research findings on the health consequences of stressful life events, as well as the factors that influence our vulnerability to stress.

11. Discuss the role of stress in coronary heart disease and contrast Type A and Type B personalities.

12. Describe how the immune system defends the body and discuss the effect of stress on the immune system.

*Promoting Health* (pp. 378–385)

> If you do not know the meaning of any of the following words, phrases, or expressions in the context in which they appear in the text, refer to pages 303 for an explanation: *run away from their troubles; "mood boost" . . . couch potatoes; stepped back . . . overblown and oversold; heartaches; open-heart therapy.*

13. Identify and discuss different strategies for coping with stress.

## Chapter Review

When you have finished reading the chapter, work through the material that follows to review it. Complete the sentences and answer the questions. As you proceed, evaluate your performance for each section by consulting the answers on page 293. Do not continue with the next section until you understand each answer. If you need to, review or reread the appropriate section in the textbook before continuing.

1. Of all the species, _____ are the most emotional.

2. Three aspects of any emotion are _____

_____ .

*The Physiology of Emotion* (pp. 347–351)

3. Describe the major physiological changes that each of the following undergoes during emotional arousal:

   a. heart: _____
   b. muscles: _____
   c. liver: _____
   d. breathing: _____
   e. digestion: _____
   f. pupils: _____
   g. blood: _____
   h. skin: _____

4. The responses of arousal are activated by the _____ division of the autonomic nervous system. In response to its signal, the _____ glands release the hormones _____ and _____ , which increase heart rate, blood pressure, and blood sugar.

5. When the need for arousal has passed, the body is calmed through activation of the _____ division.

Explain the relationship between performance and arousal.

6. The various emotions are associated with _____ (similar/different) forms of physiological arousal.

7. The emotions _____ and _____ are accompanied by differing _____ temperatures and _____ secretions.

8. The brain circuits underlying different emotions _____ (are/are not) different. For example, negative emotions are accompanied by increased activity in the _____ hemisphere, whereas positive emotions are accompanied by increased activity in the _____ hemisphere.

9. Individuals with more active _____ (right/left) _____ lobes tend to be more cheerful than those in whom this pattern of brain activity is reversed.

10. The physical accompaniments of emotion _____ (are/are not) innate and universal.

11. (Thinking Critically) The technical name for the "lie detector" is the _____.

Explain how lie detectors supposedly indicate whether a person is lying.

12. (Thinking Critically) How well the lie detector works depends on whether a person exhibits _____ while lying.

13. (Thinking Critically) Those who criticize lie detectors feel that the tests are particularly likely to err in the case of the _____ (innocent/guilty), because different _____ all register as _____ .

14. (Thinking Critically) By and large, experts _____ (agree/do not agree) that lie detector tests are highly accurate.

15. (Thinking Critically) A test that assesses a suspect's knowledge of details of a crime that only the guilty person should know is the _____ _____ _____ .

*Expressing Emotion* (pp. 351–356)

16. Emotions may be communicated in words and/or through body expressions, referred to as _____ communication.

17. Most people are especially good at interpreting nonverbal _____ . We read fear and _____ mostly from the _____ , and happiness from the _____ .

18. Introverts are _____ (better/worse) at reading others' emotions, whereas extraverts are themselves _____ (easier/harder) to read. Women are generally _____ (better/worse) than men at detecting nonverbal signs of emotion. Women are also better at conveying _____ (which emotion?), whereas men surpass women in conveying their _____ .

19. Various emotions may be linked with specific _____ .

20. Gestures have _____ (the same/different) meanings in different cultures.

21. Studies of adults indicate that in different cultures facial expressions have

_____ (the same/different) meanings. Studies of children indicate that the meaning of their facial expressions _____ (varies/does not vary) across cultures.

22. According to _____, human emotional expressions evolved because they helped our ancestors communicate before language developed. It has also been adaptive for us to _____ faces in particular _____ .

23. In cultures that encourage _____, emotional expressions are often intense and prolonged. In cultures that emphasize _____, emotions such as _____, _____, and _____ are more common than in the _____ (East/West).

24. Darwin believed that when an emotion is accompanied by an outward facial expression, the emotion is _____ (intensified/diminished).

25. In one study, students who were induced to smile _____ (found/did not find) cartoons more humorous.

26. Ekman and colleagues found that imitating emotional facial expressions resulted in _____ changes characteristic of emotional arousal.

27. Studies have found that imitating another person's facial expressions _____ (leads/does not lead) to greater empathy with that person's feelings.

### Experiencing Emotion (pp. 356–363)

28. Cross-cultural research reveals three dimensions that distinguish various emotions: _____, _____, and _____ .

29. Izard believes that there are _____ basic emotions, most of which _____ (are/are not) present in infancy.

30. Averill has found that most people become angry several times per _____ .

31. The belief that expressing pent-up emotion is adaptive is most commonly found in cultures that emphasize _____ . This is the _____ hypothesis. In cultures that emphasize _____, such as those of _____ or _____, expressions of anger are less common.

32. Psychologists have found that when anger has been provoked, retaliation may have a calming effect under certain circumstances. List the circumstances.

   a. _____
   b. _____
   c. _____

Identify some potential problems with expressing anger.

33. List two suggestions offered by experts for handling anger.

   a. _____
   b. _____

34. Happy people tend to perceive the world as _____ . They are also _____ (more/less) willing to help others. This is called the _____-_____, _____-_____ phenomenon. An individual's self-perceived happiness or satisfaction with life is called his or her _____-_____ .

35. Most people tend to _____ (underestimate/overestimate) the long-term emotional consequences of very bad news. After experiencing tragedy or dramatically positive events, people generally _____ (regain/do not regain) their previous degree of happiness.

36. Researchers have found that levels of happiness
    _____ (do/do not) mirror dif-
    ferences in standards of living. Since the 1950s,
    spendable income in the United States has more
    than doubled; personal happiness has
    _____ (increased/decreased/
    remained unchanged).

37. The idea that happiness is relative to one's recent
    experience is stated by the _____ -
    _____ principle.

38. The principle that one feels worse off than others
    is known as _____
    _____ .

39. List six factors that have been shown to be posi-
    tively correlated with feelings of happiness.

    _____   _____

    _____   _____

    _____   _____

40. List six factors that are evidently unrelated to
    happiness.

    _____   _____

    _____   _____

    _____   _____

41. When people were interrupted during their daily
    activities and asked to report their feelings, they
    reported being happier when they were engaged
    in _____
    or _____ .

42. Research studies of identical and fraternal twins
    have led to the estimate that _____
    percent of the variation in people's happiness rat-
    ings is heritable.

*Theories of Emotion* (pp. 364–368)

43. According to the James-Lange theory, emotional
    states _____ (precede/follow)
    body arousal.

Describe two problems that Walter Cannon identified
with the James-Lange theory.

44. Cannon proposed that emotional stimuli in the
    environment are routed simultaneously to the
    _____ , which results in aware-
    ness of the emotion, and to the
    _____ nervous system, which
    causes the body's reaction. Because another scien-
    tist concurrently proposed similar ideas, this the-
    ory has come to be known as the
    _____ -
    _____
    theory.

45. For victims of spinal cord injuries who have lost
    all feeling below the neck, the intensity of emo-
    tions tends to _____ . This
    result supports the _____ -
    _____ theory of emotion.

46. Most researchers _____
    (agree/disagree) with Cannon and Bard's posi-
    tion that emotions involve
    _____ as well as arousal.

47. The two-factor theory of emotion proposes that
    emotion has two components:
    _____ arousal and a
    _____ label. This theory was
    proposed by _____ .

48. Schachter and Singer found that physically
    aroused subjects told that an injection would
    cause arousal _____ (did/did
    not) become emotional in response to an accom-
    plice's aroused behavior. Physically aroused sub-
    jects not expecting arousal
    _____ (did/did not) become
    emotional in response to an accomplice's behav-
    ior.

49. Robert Zajonc believes that the feeling of emotion
    _____ (can/cannot) precede
    our cognitive labeling of that emotion.

Cite two pieces of evidence that support Zajonc's
position.

50. The researcher who disagrees with Zajonc and argues that most emotions require cognitive processing is _____ .

Express some general conclusions that can be drawn about cognition and emotion.

*Stress and Health* (pp. 368–377)

51. The process by which we appraise and bodily respond to environmental threats and challenges is called _____ .

52. In the 1920s, physiologist Walter _____ began studying the effect of stress on the body. He discovered that the hormones _____ and _____ are released into the bloodstream in response to stress. This and other bodily changes due to stress are mediated by the _____ nervous system, thus preparing the body for "_____ ."

53. After studying animals' reactions to stressors, Hans Selye identified a common bodily response to stress, which he referred to as the _____ _____ .

54. During the first phase of the GAS—the _____ reaction—the person is in a state of shock due to the sudden arousal of the _____ nervous system.

55. This is followed by the stage of _____ , in which the body's resources are mobilized to cope with the stressor.

56. If stress continues, the person enters the stage of _____ . During this stage a person is _____ (more/less) vulnerable to disease.

57. In the wake of catastrophic events, such as floods, hurricanes, and fires, there often is an increase in the rates of _____ _____ .

58. Research studies have found that people who have recently been widowed, fired, or divorced are _____ (more/no more) vulnerable to illness than other people.

59. In determining a person's response to a major life change, the actual situation is less important than the way it is _____ .

60. For most people, the most significant sources of stress are _____ _____ .

61. Negative situations are especially stressful when they are appraised as _____ .

62. People who have an _____ attitude are *less* likely than others to suffer ill health.

63. In animals and humans, sudden lack of control is followed by a drop in immune responses and a rise in the levels of _____ _____ .

64. The leading cause of death in North America is _____ _____ . List several risk factors for developing this condition: _____ _____ .

65. Friedman and Rosenman discovered that tax accountants experience an increase in blood _____ level and blood-_____ speed during tax season. This showed there was a link between coronary warning indicators and _____ .

Friedman and Rosenman, in a subsequent study, grouped people into Type A and Type B personalities. Characterize these types and indicate the difference that emerged between them over the course of this 9-year study.

66. When a person is angered, blood flow is diverted away from the internal organs, including the liver, which is responsible for removing _____ and fat from the blood. This finding may explain why _____ (Type A/Type B) persons have elevated levels of these substances in the blood.

67. The Type A characteristic that is most strongly linked with coronary heart disease is _____ _____ .

68. Depression following a heart attack or the death of a spouse _____ (increases/has no effect on) one's risk of having a heart attack or _____ . Negative emotions also explain why a large proportion of hospital patients suffer _____ or _____ disorders.

69. In _____ illnesses, physical symptoms are produced by psychological causes. Examples of such illnesses are certain forms of _____ and _____ . Such illnesses appear to be linked to _____ .

70. The body's system of fighting disease is the _____ system. This system includes two types of white blood cells, called _____ : the _____ , which fight bacterial infections, and the _____ , which form in the _____ and attack viruses, cancer cells, and foreign substances. Another immune agent, called the _____ , pursues and ingests foreign substances.

71. Responding too strongly, the immune system may attack the body's tissues and cause _____ or an _____ reaction. Or it may _____ , allowing a dormant herpes virus to erupt or _____ cells to multiply.

72. _____ (Women/Men) are the immunologically stronger gender. This makes them less susceptible to _____ , but more susceptible to _____

diseases, such as _____ and _____ _____ .

73. Stress can suppress the lymphocyte cells, resulting in a(n) _____ (increase/decrease) in disease resistance. Stress diverts energy from the _____ to the _____ and _____ , mobilizing the body for action.

Characterize the link between stress and cancer.

74. Experiments by Ader and Cohen demonstrate that the functioning of the body's immune system _____ (can/cannot) be affected by conditioning.

*Promoting Health* (pp. 378–385)

75. Sustained exercise that increases heart and lung fitness is known as _____ exercise. Experiments _____ (have/have not) been able to demonstrate conclusively that such exercise reduces anxiety and depression, and alleviates the effects of stress.

76. Exercise increases the body's production of mood-boosting neurotransmitters such as _____ , _____ , and _____ . By one estimate, moderate exercise adds _____ (how many?) years to one's life expectancy.

77. A system for recording a physiological response and providing information concerning it is called _____ . The instruments used in this system _____ (provide/do not provide) the individual with a means of controlling physiological responses.

78. Lowered blood pressure and strengthened immune defenses have been found to be

characteristic of people who regularly practice

_____ .

79. Meyer Friedman found that modifying Type A behavior in a group of heart attack survivors _____ (reduced/did not significantly reduce) the rate of recurrence of heart attacks.

80. Another buffer against the effects of stress is _____ support.

State several possible reasons for the link between health and social support.

## Progress Test 1

### Multiple-Choice Questions

Circle your answers to the following questions and check them with the answers on page 294. If your answer is incorrect, read the explanation for why it is incorrect and then consult the appropriate pages of the text (in parentheses following the correct answer).

1. Which of the following is correct regarding the relationship between arousal and performance?
   a. Generally, performance is optimal when arousal is low.
   b. Generally, performance is optimal when arousal is high.
   c. On easy tasks, performance is optimal when arousal is low.
   d. On easy tasks, performance is optimal when arousal is high.

2. Which division of the nervous system is especially involved in bringing about emotional arousal?
   a. skeletal nervous system
   b. peripheral nervous system
   c. sympathetic nervous system
   d. parasympathetic nervous system
   e. central nervous system

3. Concerning emotions and their accompanying body responses, which of the following appears to be true?
   a. Each emotion has its own body response and underlying brain circuit.
   b. All emotions involve the same body response as a result of the same underlying brain circuit.
   c. Many emotions involve similar body responses but have different underlying brain circuits.
   d. All emotions have the same underlying brain circuits but different body responses.

4. The Cannon-Bard theory of emotion states that:
   a. emotions have two ingredients: physical arousal and a cognitive label.
   b. the conscious experience of an emotion occurs at the same time as the body's physical reaction.
   c. emotional experiences are based on an awareness of the body's responses to an emotion-arousing stimulus.
   d. emotional ups and downs tend to balance in the long run.

5. The body's response to danger is triggered by the release of _____ by the _____ glands.
   a. acetylcholine; adrenal
   b. epinephrine and norepinephrine; adrenal
   c. acetylcholine; pituitary
   d. epinephrine and norepinephrine; pituitary

6. Which of the following was *not* raised as a criticism of the James-Lange theory of emotion?
   a. The body's responses are too similar to trigger the various emotions.
   b. Emotional reactions occur before the body's responses can take place.
   c. The cognitive activity of the cortex plays a role in the emotions we experience.
   d. People with spinal cord injuries at the neck typically experience less emotion.

7. In the Schachter-Singer experiment, which subjects reported feeling an emotional change in the presence of the experimenter's highly emotional confederate?
   a. those receiving epinephrine and expecting to feel physical arousal
   b. those receiving a placebo and expecting to feel physical arousal
   c. those receiving epinephrine but not expecting to feel physical arousal
   d. those receiving a placebo and not expecting to feel physical arousal

8. Research on nonverbal communication has revealed that:
   a. it is easy to hide your emotions by controlling your facial expressions.
   b. facial expressions tend to be the same the world over, while gestures vary from culture to culture.
   c. most authentic expressions last between 7 and 10 seconds.
   d. most gestures have universal meanings; facial expressions vary from culture to culture.

9. Which of the following is *not* one of the basic dimensions of emotion?
   a. duration
   b. intensity
   c. pleasantness
   d. specificity

10. Research indicates that a person is most likely to be helpful to others if he or she:
    a. is feeling guilty about something.
    b. is happy.
    c. recently received help from another person.
    d. recently offered help to another person.

11. Evidence that changes in facial expression can directly affect people's feelings and body states has convinced Robert Zajonc that:
    a. the heart is always subject to the mind.
    b. emotional reactions involve deliberate rational thinking.
    c. cognition is not necessary for emotion.
    d. the interpretation of facial expressions is a learned skill.

12. The stress hormones epinephrine and norepinephrine are released by the _____ gland in response to stimulation by the _____ branch of the nervous system.
    a. pituitary; sympathetic
    b. pituitary; parasympathetic
    c. adrenal; sympathetic
    d. adrenal; parasympathetic

13. During which stage of the general adaptation syndrome is a person especially vulnerable to disease?
    a. alarm reaction
    b. stage of resistance
    c. stage of exhaustion
    d. stage of adaptation

14. The leading cause of death in North America is:
    a. lung cancer.
    b. AIDS.
    c. coronary heart disease.
    d. alcohol-related accidents.
    e. accidents.

15. Researchers Friedman and Rosenman refer to individuals who are very time-conscious, super-motivated, verbally aggressive, and easily angered as:
    a. ulcer-prone personalities.
    b. cancer-prone personalities.
    c. Type A.
    d. Type B.

16. Genuine illnesses that are caused by stress are called _____ illnesses.
    a. psychophysiological
    b. hypochondriacal
    c. psychogenic
    d. psychotropic

17. Stress has been demonstrated to place a person at increased risk of:
    a. cancer.
    b. tuberculosis.
    c. bacterial infections.
    d. viral infections.
    e. all of the above.

18. A study in which people were asked to confide troubling feelings to an experimenter found that subjects typically:
    a. did not truthfully report feelings and events.
    b. experienced a sustained increase in blood pressure until the experiment was finished.
    c. became physiologically more relaxed after confiding their problem.
    d. denied having any problems.

19. A study demonstrated that breast cancer patients who participated in weekly group therapy:
    a. survived nearly twice as long as nonparticipants.
    b. had reduced levels of lymphocytes in their bodies.
    c. had elevated levels of cortisol and other "good" stress hormones.
    d. experienced all of the above.

20. In one study, laboratory rats drank sweetened water with a drug that causes immune suppression. After repeated pairings of the taste with the drug:
    a. the animals developed tolerance for the drug and immune responses returned to normal.
    b. sweet water alone triggered immune suppression.
    c. dependency on the drug developed and withdrawal symptoms appeared when the drug was withheld.
    d. many of the animals died.

## Matching Items

Match each definition or description with the appropriate term.

*Definitions or Descriptions*

_____ 1. the tendency to react to changes on the basis of recent experience

_____ 2. an individual's self-perceived happiness

_____ 3. emotional release

_____ 4. the tendency to evaluate our situation negatively against that of other people

_____ 5. emotions consist of physical arousal *and* a cognitive label

_____ 6. an emotion-arousing stimulus triggers cognitive and body responses simultaneously

_____ 7. the division of the nervous system that calms the body following arousal

_____ 8. the division of the nervous system that activates arousal

_____ 9. a device that measures the physiological correlates of emotion

_____ 10. the tendency of people to be helpful when they are in a good mood

_____ 11. we are sad because we cry

*Terms*

a. adaptation-level principle
b. two-factor theory
c. catharsis
d. sympathetic nervous system
e. James-Lange theory
f. polygraph
g. Cannon-Bard theory
h. parasympathetic nervous system
i. relative deprivation principle
j. feel-good, do-good phenomenon
k. subjective well-being

## Progress Test 2

Progress Test 2 should be completed during a final chapter review. Answer the following questions after you thoroughly understand the correct answers for the Chapter Review and Progress Test 1.

### Multiple-Choice Questions

1. Which of the following most accurately describes emotional arousal?
   a. Emotions prepare the body to fight or flee.
   b. Emotions are voluntary reactions to emotion-arousing stimuli.
   c. Because all emotions have the same physiological basis, emotions are primarily psychological events.
   d. Emotional arousal is always accompanied by cognition.
   e. All are accurate descriptions.

2. Schachter's two-factor theory emphasizes that emotion involves both:
   a. the sympathetic and parasympathetic divisions of the nervous system.
   b. verbal and nonverbal expression.
   c. physical arousal and a cognitive label.
   d. universal and culture-specific aspects.

3. Dermer found that students who had studied others who were worse off than themselves felt greater satisfaction with their own lives; this is the principle of:
   a. relative deprivation.   c. behavioral contrast.
   b. adaptation level.   d. opponent processes.

4. Which theory of emotion emphasizes the simultaneous experience of body response and emotional feeling?
   a. James-Lange theory   c. two-factor theory
   b. Cannon-Bard theory   d. Zajonc theory

5. Which of the following was *not* presented in the text as evidence that some emotional reactions involve no deliberate, rational thinking?
   a. Some of the neural pathways involved in emotion are separate from those involved in thinking and memory.
   b. Emotional reactions are sometimes quicker than our interpretations of a situation.
   c. People can develop an emotional preference for visual stimuli to which they have been unknowingly exposed.
   d. Arousal of the sympathetic nervous system will trigger an emotional reaction even when artificially induced by an injection of epinephrine.

6. Concerning the catharsis hypothesis, which of the following is true?
   a. Expressing anger can be temporarily calming if it does not leave one feeling guilty or anxious.
   b. The arousal that accompanies unexpressed anger never dissipates.
   c. Expressing one's anger always calms one down.
   d. Psychologists agree that under no circumstances is catharsis beneficial.

7. In an emergency situation, emotional arousal will result in:
   a. increased rate of respiration.
   b. increased blood sugar.
   c. a slowing of digestion.
   d. pupil dilation.
   e. all of the above.

8. Several studies have shown that physical arousal can intensify just about any emotion. For example, when people who have been physically aroused by exercise are insulted, they often misattribute their arousal to the insult. This finding illustrates the importance of:
   a. cognitive labels of arousal in the conscious experience of emotions.
   b. a minimum level of arousal in triggering emotional experiences.
   c. the simultaneous occurrence of physical arousal and cognitive labeling in emotional experience.
   d. all of the above.

9. (Thinking Critically) Psychologist David Lykken is opposed to the use of lie detectors because:
   a. they represent an invasion of a person's privacy and could easily be used for unethical purposes.
   b. there are often serious discrepancies among the various indicators such as perspiration and heart rate.
   c. polygraphs cannot distinguish the various possible causes of arousal.
   d. they are accurate only about 50 percent of the time.

10. Which of these factors have researchers *not* found to correlate with happiness?
    a. a satisfying marriage or close friendship
    b. high self-esteem
    c. religious faith
    d. intelligence

11. In cultures that emphasize social interdependence:
    a. emotional displays are typically intense.
    b. emotional displays are typically prolonged.
    c. negative emotions are more rarely displayed.
    d. all of the above are true.

12. In order, the sequence of stages in the general adaptation syndrome is:
    a. alarm reaction, stage of resistance, stage of exhaustion.
    b. stage of resistance, alarm reaction, stage of exhaustion.
    c. stage of exhaustion, stage of resistance, alarm reaction.
    d. alarm reaction, stage of exhaustion, stage of resistance.

13. The disease- and infection-fighting cells of the immune system are:
    a. B lymphocytes.          c. both a. and b.
    b. T lymphocytes.          d. antigens.

14. One effect of stress on the body is to:
    a. suppress the immune system.
    b. facilitate the immune system response.
    c. increase disease resistance.
    d. increase the growth of B and T lymphocytes.

15. Compared to men, women:
    a. have stronger immune systems.
    b. are less susceptible to infections.
    c. are more susceptible to self-attacking diseases such as multiple sclerosis.
    d. have none of the above characteristics.
    e. have all the characteristics described in a., b., and c.

16. Allergic reactions and arthritis are caused by:
    a. an overreactive immune system.
    b. an underreactive immune system.
    c. the presence of B lymphocytes.
    d. the presence of T lymphocytes.

17. Research on cancer patients reveals that:
    a. those who bottle up their emotions are less likely to survive than those who express them.
    b. patients' attitudes can influence their rate of recovery.
    c. participating in support groups may enhance immune responses.
    d. all of the above are true.

18. The component of Type A behavior that is the most predictive of coronary disease is:
    a. time urgency.
    d. impatience.
    b. competitiveness.
    e. anger.
    c. high motivation.

19. During biofeedback training:
    a. a subject is given sensory feedback for a subtle body response.
    b. biological functions controlled by the autonomic nervous system may come under conscious control.
    c. the accompanying relaxation is much the same as that produced by other, simpler methods of relaxation.
    d. all of the above occur.

20. Relaxation is the most effective technique for preventing:
    a. alcoholism.
    b. a stressful environment.
    c. smoking.
    d. a repeat heart attack.

### True-False Items

Indicate whether each statement is true or false by placing *T* or *F* in the blank next to the item.

_____ 1. Men are generally better than women at detecting nonverbal emotional expression.

_____ 2. When one imitates an emotional facial expression, the body may experience physiological changes characteristic of that emotion.

_____ 3. People who have lost sensation only in their lower bodies experience a considerable decrease in the intensity of their emotions.

_____ 4. Wealthy people tend to be much happier than middle-income people.

_____ 5. All emotions involve conscious thought.

_____ 6. Stressors tend to increase activity in the immune system and in this way make people more vulnerable to illness.

_____ 7. Events are most stressful when perceived as both negative and controllable.

_____ 8. Optimists cope more successfully with stressful events than do pessimists.

_____ 9. Chronic stress can lead to headaches and hypertension.

_____ 10. People with few social and community ties are more likely to die prematurely than are those with many social ties.

## Thinking Critically About Chapter 10

Answer these questions the day before an exam as a final check on your understanding of the chapter's terms and concepts.

### Multiple-Choice Questions

1. You are on your way to school to take a big exam. Suddenly, on noticing that your pulse is racing and that you are sweating, you feel nervous. With which theory of emotion is this experience most consistent?
   a. Cannon-Bard theory
   b. James-Lange theory
   c. Zajonc theory
   d. adaptation-level theory

2. When Professor Simon acquired a spacious new office, he was overjoyed. Six months later, however, he was taking the office for granted. His behavior illustrates the:
   a. relative deprivation principle.
   b. adaptation-level principle.
   c. general adaptation syndrome.
   d. optimum arousal principle.

3. After Brenda scolded her brother for forgetting to pick her up from school, the physical arousal that had accompanied her anger diminished. Which division of her nervous system mediated her physical *relaxation*?
   a. sympathetic division
   b. parasympathetic division
   c. skeletal division
   d. peripheral nervous system

4. Rana was so mad at her brother that she exploded at him when he entered her room. That she felt less angry afterward is best explained by the principle of:
   a. adaptation level.
   c. relative deprivation.
   b. general adaptation.
   d. catharsis.

5. After hitting a grand-slam home run, Mike noticed that his heart was pounding. Later that evening, after nearly having a collision while driving on the freeway, Mike again noticed that his heart was pounding. That he interpreted this reaction as fear, rather than as ecstasy, can best be explained by the:
   a. James-Lange theory.
   b. Cannon-Bard theory.
   c. two-factor theory.
   d. adaptation-level theory.

6. (Thinking Critically) As part of her job interview, Jan is asked to take a lie-detector test. Jan politely refuses and points out that:
   a. a guilty person can be found innocent by the polygraph.
   b. an innocent person can be found guilty.
   c. a liar can learn to fool a lie-detector test.
   d. these tests err one-third of the time.
   e. all of the above are true.

7. A subject in an experiment concerned with physical responses that accompany emotions reports that her mouth is dry, her heart is racing, and she feels flushed. What emotion is she experiencing?
   a. anger
   b. fear
   c. ecstasy
   d. It cannot be determined from the information given.

8. Children in New York, Nigeria, and New Zealand smile when they are happy and frown when they are sad. This suggests that:
   a. the Cannon-Bard theory is correct.
   b. some emotional expressions are learned at a very early age.
   c. the two-factor theory is correct.
   d. facial expressions of emotion are universal and biologically determined.

9. Who is the *least* likely to display negative emotions openly?
   a. Paul, a game warden in Australia
   b. Niles, a stockbroker in Belgium
   c. Deborah, a physicist in Toronto
   d. Yoko, a dentist in Japan

10. As elderly Mr. Hooper crosses the busy intersection, he stumbles and drops the packages he is carrying. Which passerby is most likely to help Mr. Hooper?
    a. Drew, who has been laid off from work for three months
    b. Leon, who is on his way to work
    c. Bonnie, who graduated from college the day before
    d. Nancy, whose father recently passed away

11. Cindy was happy with her promotion until she found out that Janice, who has the same amount of experience, receives a higher salary. Cindy's feelings are *best* explained according to the:
    a. adaptation-level phenomenon.
    b. biofeedback theory.
    c. catharsis hypothesis.
    d. principle of relative deprivation.

12. Each semester, Rhom does not start studying until just before midterms. Then he is forced to work around the clock until after final exams, which makes him sick, probably because he is in the _____ phase of the _____ .
    a. alarm; post-traumatic stress syndrome
    b. resistance; general adaptation syndrome
    c. exhaustion; general adaptation syndrome
    d. depletion; post-traumatic stress syndrome

13. Connie complains to the campus psychologist that she has too much stress in her life. The psychologist tells her that the level of stress people experience depends primarily on:
    a. how many activities they are trying to do at the same time.
    b. how they appraise the events of life.
    c. their physical hardiness.
    d. how predictable stressful events are.

14. Karen and Kyumi are taking the same course with different instructors. Karen's instructor schedules quizzes every Friday, while Kyumi's instructor gives the same number of quizzes on an unpredictable schedule. Assuming that their instructors are equally difficult, which student is probably under more stress?
    a. Karen
    b. Kyumi
    c. There should be no difference in their levels of stress.
    d. It is impossible to predict stress levels in this situation.

15. Jill is an easygoing, noncompetitive person who is happy in her job and enjoys her leisure time. She would *probably* be classified as:
    a. Type A.          c. Type C.
    b. Type B.          d. atherosclerotic.

16. A white blood cell that is formed in the thymus and that attacks cancer cells is:
    a. a macrophage.        c. a T lymphocyte.
    b. a B lymphocyte.      d. any of the above.

17. When would you expect that your immune responses would be *weakest*?
    a. during summer vacation
    b. during exam weeks
    c. just after receiving good news
    d. Immune activity would probably remain constant during these times.

18. Which of the following would be the *best* piece of advice to offer a person who is trying to minimize the adverse effects of stress on his or her health?

   a. "Avoid challenging situations that may prove stressful."
   b. "Learn to play as hard as you work."
   c. "Maintain a sense of control and a positive approach to life."
   d. "Keep your emotional responses in check by keeping your feelings to yourself."

19. Philip's physician prescribes a stress management program to help Philip control his headaches. The physician has apparently diagnosed Philip's condition as a _____ illness, rather than a physical disorder.

   a. psychogenic          c. psychophysiological
   b. hypochondriac        d. biofeedback

20. You have just transferred to a new campus and find yourself in a potentially stressful environment. According to the text, which of the following would help you cope with the stress?

   a. believing that you have some control over your environment
   b. being able to predict when stressful events will occur
   c. feeling optimistic that you will eventually adjust to your new surroundings
   d. All of the above would help.

## Essay Question

Discuss several factors that enhance a person's ability to cope with stress. (Use the space below to list the points you want to make and organize them. Then write the essay on a separate sheet of paper.)

# Key Terms

### Writing Definitions

Using your own words, on a separate piece of paper write a brief definition or explanation of each of the following terms.

1. emotion
2. polygraph
3. catharsis
4. feel-good, do-good phenomenon
5. subjective well-being
6. adaptation-level phenomenon
7. relative deprivation
8. James-Lange theory
9. Cannon-Bard theory
10. two-factor theory
11. stress
12. general adaptation syndrome (GAS)
13. coronary heart disease
14. Type A
15. Type B
16. psychophysiological illness
17. lymphocytes
18. aerobic exercise
19. biofeedback

# Summing Up

Complete the flow chart on the following page.

**THEORIES OF EMOTION**

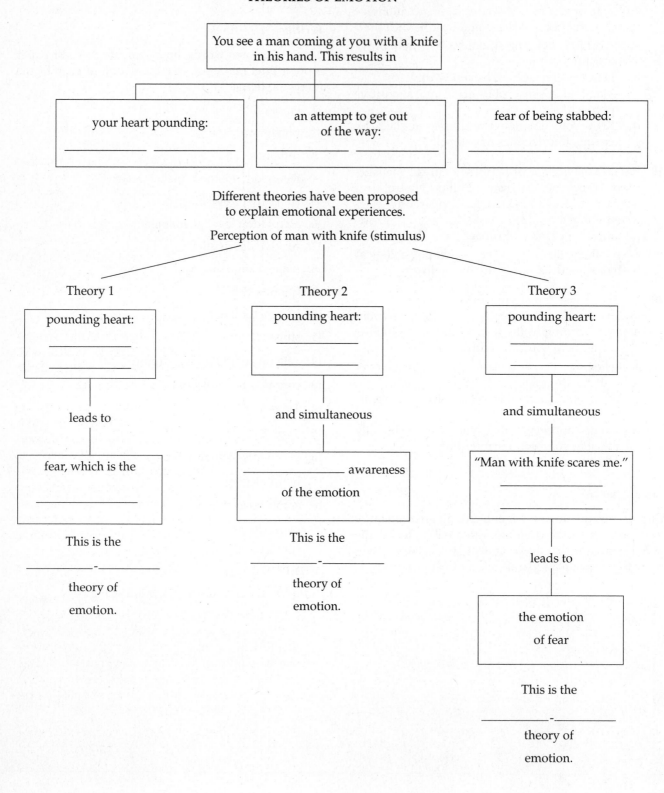

# ANSWERS

## Guided Study

The following guidelines provide the main points that your answers should have touched upon.

1. Emotions involve a mixture of physiological arousal, expressive behaviors, and conscious experience. Physiological arousal occurs when the sympathetic nervous system directs the adrenal glands to release epinephrine and norepinephrine. These hormones trigger increased heart rate, blood pressure, and blood sugar levels.

   Our performance on a task is usually best when arousal is moderate. However, the difficulty of the task affects optimum arousal level. A relatively high level of arousal is best on easy or well-learned tasks; a relatively low level of arousal is best on difficult or unrehearsed tasks.

2. The heart rate, blood pressure, and breathing patterns that accompany the different emotions often are not different. However, these emotions are accompanied by different finger temperatures and hormone secretions. Also, different brain circuits underlie different emotions. Limbic stimulation, for example, will trigger rage or terror in an animal. Negative emotions and positive emotions tend to be accompanied by greater activity in the right and left hemispheres, respectively. Infants and adults with greater activity in their left frontal lobes tend to be more cheerful than those with more active right frontal lobes.

3. (Thinking Critically) The polygraph, or lie detector, measures the physiological responses that accompany emotions. How well the polygraph works depends on whether liars become anxious and exhibit detectable physiological arousal. Critics of the use of lie detectors argue that the tests are inaccurate about one-third of the time because they can't distinguish among anxiety, irritation, and guilt. Thus, they may label the innocent guilty when a question is upsetting. The polygraph may be somewhat more effective in criminal investigations that use the guilty knowledge test, which assesses a subject's response to details of the crime known only to the police and the guilty person.

4. People differ in their abilities to detect nonverbal expressions of emotion; introverts and women are better at reading others' emotions, and extraverts are easier to read. Women express happiness best, but men are better at expressing anger. Although there are many cultural variations in the meaning of gestures, facial expressions have universal meaning. Cultures differ in how and how much they use nonverbal expressions, however. In cultures that encourage individuality, emotional displays often are more intense and prolonged than in communal cultures that value interdependence.

   Research demonstrates that facial expressions intensify emotions and also trigger physiological changes in the autonomic nervous system.

5. People place emotions along three dimensions: pleasantness, intensity, and duration. The catharsis hypothesis maintains that expressing emotion results in emotional release. Research shows that the cathartic expression of anger is most likely to reduce anger *temporarily* when it is specifically directed against the provoker, when it is justifiable, and when the provoker is not intimidating. Other studies show that openly expressing anger can have the opposite effect and amplify underlying hostility. Angry outbursts may also be habit-forming if they temporarily calm the individual.

   Anger experts recommend that the best way to handle anger is: first, bring down the level of physiological arousal by waiting; then, deal with the anger in a way that involves neither being chronically angry nor passively sulking.

6. People who are happy perceive the world as safer, make decisions more easily, rate job applicants more favorably, report greater satisfaction with their lives, and are more willing to help others. Factors that predict happiness include having high self-esteem, a close friendship or a satisfying marriage, a meaningful religious faith, being optimistic and outgoing, sleeping well, exercising, and engaging in challenging work and leisure activities.

   The effect of dramatically positive or negative events on happiness is typically temporary. Happiness is also relative to our recent experiences (adaptation-level phenomenon) and to how we compare ourselves with others (relative deprivation principle). These principles help explain why middle- and upper-income people in a given country tend to be slightly more satisfied with life than the relatively poor, even though happiness does not directly increase with affluence.

7. According to the James-Lange theory, the experience of emotion results from awareness of the physiological responses to emotion-arousing stimuli. According to the Cannon-Bard theory, an emotion-arousing stimulus is simultaneously routed to the cortex, which causes the subjective experience of emotion, and to the sympathetic nervous system, which causes the body's physiological arousal.

   In criticizing the James-Lange theory, Walter

Cannon argued that the body's responses were not sufficiently distinct to trigger the different emotions. The James-Lange theory has recently received support from evidence showing that there are physiological distinctions among the emotions and that emotions are diminished when the brain's awareness of the body's reactions is reduced. However, many researchers continue to agree with Cannon and Bard that the experience of emotion also involves cognitive activity.

8. Schachter's two-factor theory of emotion proposes that emotions have two components: physical arousal and a cognitive label. Like the James-Lange theory, the two-factor theory presumes that our experience of emotion stems from our awareness of physical arousal. Like the Cannon-Bard theory, the two-factor theory presumes that emotions are physiologically similar and require a conscious interpretation of the arousal.

Although complex emotions, such as guilt, happiness, and love, clearly arise from conscious thought, there is evidence that some simple emotional responses may not involve conscious thinking. When people repeatedly view stimuli they are not consciously aware of (subliminal stimuli), for example, they come to prefer those stimuli. Furthermore, some neural pathways involved in emotion, such as the one that links the eye to the amygdala, bypass cortical areas involved in thinking and enable an automatic emotional response.

9. Stress is the whole process by which we appraise and respond to events that threaten or challenge us. Stress triggers an outpouring of epinephrine, norepinephrine, and cortisol from nerve endings in the adrenal glands of the sympathetic nervous system. These stress hormones increase heart rate and respiration, divert blood to skeletal muscles, and release fat from the body's stores to prepare the body for "fight or flight." Hans Selye saw the body's reaction to stress as having three phases (general adaptation syndrome): the alarm reaction, in which the body's resources are mobilized; resistance, in which stress hormones flow freely to help cope with the stressor; and exhaustion, when reserves are depleted and illness is more likely.

10. Some studies have shown that stressful events, such as catastrophes, are closely followed by an increase in psychological disorders and even deaths. The level of stress we experience depends on how we appraise such events. Catastrophes, significant life changes, and daily hassles are especially stressful when they are appraised as uncontrollable and negative, and when we have a pessimistic outlook. A perceived loss of control, for example, triggers an outpouring of stress hormones.

11. Friedman and Rosenman discovered that stress triggers a variety of physical changes, such as increased cholesterol and blood-clotting speed, that may promote coronary heart disease. According to their designation, Type A people are competitive, hard-driving, impatient, verbally aggressive, and easily angered, and thus more prone to coronary disease. The most significant factor is the tendency toward the negative emotions of anger and depression. In contrast, Type B people are more relaxed and easygoing.

12. The immune system includes two types of white blood cells (lymphocytes) that defend the body by destroying foreign substances. The B lymphocytes form in the bone marrow and release antibodies that combat bacterial infections. The T lymphocytes form in the thymus and other lymphatic tissue and attack cancer cells, viruses, and foreign substances. Another immune agent, the macrophage, identifies and ingests harmful invaders.

Stress lowers the body's resistance to disease by suppressing the disease-fighting lymphocytes of the immune system. This may explain the link between stress and cancer. Animal research has shown that when the immune system is weakened by stress, tumor cells develop sooner and grow larger. Research has also shown that immune suppression can be classically conditioned. Conversely, studies of cancer patients demonstrate that reducing stress and creating a hopeful, relaxed state may improve chances of survival.

13. Stress management includes aerobic exercise, biofeedback, relaxation, and social support. Aerobic exercise can reduce stress, depression, and anxiety. Research has also shown that those who exercise regularly tend to live longer and suffer from fewer illnesses than those who don't. Exercise may produce its benefits by increasing the production of mood-boosting neurotransmitters, by strengthening the heart, and by lowering both blood pressure and the blood pressure reaction to stress.

Biofeedback systems allow people to monitor their subtle physiological responses and enjoy a calm, tranquil experience. Simple relaxation produces the same effects, however, including lowered blood pressure and strengthened immune defenses. People with strong social support systems eat better, exercise more, smoke and drink less, and have more opportunities to confide painful feelings. Research shows that such people report fewer illnesses and are less likely to die prematurely than people who lack close supportive relationships.

## Chapter Review

1. humans

2. physiological arousal, expressive behaviors, conscious experience

3. **a.** Heart rate increases.

   **b.** Muscles become tense.

   **c.** The liver pours extra sugar into the bloodstream.

   **d.** Breathing rate increases.

   **e.** Digestion slows.

   **f.** Pupils dilate.

   **g.** Blood tends to clot more rapidly.

   **h.** Skin perspires.

4. sympathetic; adrenal; epinephrine (adrenaline); norepinephrine (noradrenaline)

5. parasympathetic

Performance on a task is usually best when arousal is moderate. However, the difficulty of the task affects optimum arousal level. A relatively high level of arousal is best on easy and well-learned tasks; a relatively low level of arousal is best on difficult tasks.

6. similar

7. fear; rage; finger; hormone

8. are; right; left

9. left; frontal

10. are

11. polygraph

The polygraph measures several of the physiological responses that accompany emotion, such as changes in breathing, pulse rate, blood pressure, and perspiration. The assumption is that lying is stressful, so a person who is lying will become physiologically aroused.

12. anxiety

13. innocent; emotions; arousal

14. do not agree

15. guilty knowledge test

16. nonverbal

17. threats; anger; eyes; mouth

18. better; easier; better; happiness; anger

19. facial muscles

20. different

21. the same; does not vary

22. Darwin; interpret; contexts

23. individuality; interdependence; sympathy; respect; shame; West

24. intensified

25. found

26. physiological

27. leads

28. pleasantness; intensity; duration

29. 10; are

30. week

31. individuality; catharsis; interdependence; Tahiti; Japan

32. **a.** Retaliation must be directed against the person who provoked the anger.

    **b.** Retaliation must be justifiable.

    **c.** The target of the retaliation must not be someone who is intimidating.

One problem with expressing anger is that it breeds more anger, in part because it may trigger retaliation. Expressing anger can also magnify anger and reinforce its occurrence.

33. **a.** Wait to calm down.

    **b.** Deal with anger in a civil way that promotes reconciliation rather than retaliation.

34. safer; more; feel-good, do-good; subjective well-being

35. overestimate; regain

36. do not; remained unchanged

37. adaptation-level

38. relative deprivation

39. high self-esteem; satisfying marriage or close friendships; meaningful religious faith; optimistic outgoing personality; good sleeping habits; regular exercise

40. age; race; gender; education; parenthood; physical attractiveness

41. challenging tasks; active leisure

42. 50

43. follow

Cannon argued that the body's responses were not sufficiently distinct to trigger the different emotions and, furthermore, that physiological changes occur too slowly to trigger sudden emotion.

44. cortex; sympathetic; Cannon-Bard

45. diminish; James-Lange

46. agree; cognition

47. physiological; cognitive; Schachter

48. did not; did

49. can

First, experiments on subliminal perception indicate that although stimuli are not consciously perceived, subjects later prefer these stimuli to others they have never been exposed to. Second, there is some separation of the neural pathways involved in emotion and cognition.

**50. Lazarus**

It seems that some emotional responses—especially simple likes, dislikes, and fears—involve no conscious thinking. Other emotions are greatly affected by our interpretations and expectations.

**51. stress**

**52. Cannon; epinephrine, or adrenaline; norepinephrine, or noradrenaline; sympathetic; fight or flight**

**53. general adaptation syndrome**

**54. alarm; sympathetic**

**55. resistance**

**56. exhaustion; more**

**57. psychological disorders and stress-related health complaints**

**58. more**

**59. appraised**

**60. daily hassles**

**61. uncontrollable**

**62. optimistic**

**63. stress hormones (cortisol)**

**64. coronary heart disease; smoking, obesity, high-fat diet, physical inactivity, elevated blood pressure and cholesterol levels**

**65. cholesterol; clotting; stress**

Type A people were competitive, hard-driving, super-motivated, impatient, verbally aggressive, and easily angered. Type B people were more relaxed and easygoing. Heart attack victims over the course of the study came overwhelmingly from the Type A group.

**66. cholesterol; Type A**

**67. negative emotions, especially the anger associated with an aggressively reactive temperament**

**68. increases; stroke; mood; anxiety**

**69. psychophysiological; hypertension; headaches; stress**

**70. immune; lymphocytes; B lymphocytes; T lymphocytes; thymus; macrophage**

**71. arthritis; allergic; underreact; cancer**

**72. Women; infections; self-attacking; lupus; multiple sclerosis**

**73. decrease; immune system; brain; muscles**

Stress can affect the spread of cancer by weakening the body's defenses against malignant cells. When rodents were inoculated with tumor cells, tumors developed sooner in those that were also exposed to uncontrollable stress. Stress does not cause cancer, however; nor can relaxation prevent it. Cancer patients who remain hopeful and who share their negative emotions with others survive longer than those who keep their feelings bottled up.

**74. can**

**75. aerobic; have**

**76. norepinephrine; serotonin; endorphins; 2**

**77. biofeedback; do not provide**

**78. relaxation**

**79. reduced**

**80. social**

People with strong social ties may be healthier because they eat better, exercise more, and smoke and drink less. Close relationships also provide the opportunity to bolster self-esteem and to confide painful feelings, which may mitigate physical reactions to stressful events.

## Progress Test 1

### Multiple-Choice Questions

1. **d.** is the answer. Generally speaking, performance is optimal when arousal is moderate; for easy tasks, however, performance is optimal when arousal is high. For difficult tasks, performance is optimal when arousal is low. (p. 349)

2. **c.** is the answer. (p. 348)
   **a.** The skeletal division of the peripheral nervous system carries sensory and motor signals to and from the central nervous system.
   **b.** The peripheral nervous system is too general an answer, since it includes the sympathetic and parasympathetic divisions, as well as the skeletal division.
   **d.** The parasympathetic nervous system restores the body to its unaroused state.
   **e.** The central nervous system is involved in the labeling of emotional arousal.

3. **c.** is the answer. Although many emotions have the same general body arousal, resulting from activation of the sympathetic nervous system, they appear to be associated with different brain circuits. (p. 349)

4. **b.** is the answer. (p. 364)
   **a.** This expresses the two-factor theory.
   **c.** This expresses the James-Lange theory.
   **d.** This expresses a theory not discussed in the text, the opponent-process theory.

5. **b.** is the answer. (p. 348)

**a. & c.** Acetylcholine, a neurotransmitter involved in motor responses, is not a hormone and therefore is not secreted by a gland.

6. **d.** is the answer. The finding that people whose brains can't sense the body's responses experience considerably less emotion in fact supports the James-Lange theory, which claims that experienced emotion follows from body responses. (p. 365)

**a., b., & c.** All these statements go counter to the theory's claim that experienced emotion is essentially just an awareness of the body's response.

7. **c.** is the answer. Subjects who received epinephrine without an explanation felt arousal and experienced this arousal as whatever emotion the experimental confederate in the room with them was displaying. (pp. 365–366)

**a.** Epinephrine recipients who expected arousal attributed their arousal to the drug and reported no emotional change in reaction to the confederate's behavior.

**b. & d.** In addition to the two groups discussed in the text, the experiment involved placebo recipients; these subjects were not physically aroused and did not experience an emotional change.

8. **b.** is the answer. (pp. 353–354)

**a.** The opposite is true; relevant facial muscles are hard to control voluntarily.

**c.** Authentic facial expressions tend to fade within 4 or 5 seconds.

**d.** Facial expressions are generally universal; many gestures vary from culture to culture.

9. **d.** is the answer. (p. 356)

10. **b.** is the answer. (p. 359)

**a., c., & d.** Research studies have not found these factors to be related to altruistic behavior.

11. **c.** is the answer. (p. 367)

**a. & b.** These answers imply that cognition *always* precedes emotion.

**d.** That changes in facial expression can directly affect people's feelings and body states does not imply a learned ability to interpret facial expressions. In fact, facial expressions apparently speak a universal language, which implies that the ability to interpret them is inborn.

12. **c.** is the answer. (p. 369)

**a., b., & d.** The pituitary does not produce stress hormones nor is the parasympathetic division involved in arousal.

13. **c.** is the answer. (p. 369)

**a. & b.** During these stages the body's defensive mechanisms are at peak function.

**d.** This is not a stage of the GAS.

14. **c.** is the answer. Coronary heart disease is followed by cancer, stroke, and chronic lung disease. AIDS has not yet become one of the four leading causes of death in North America among the general population. (p. 372)

15. **c.** is the answer. (p. 372)

**a. & b.** Researchers have not identified such personality types.

**d.** Individuals who are more easygoing are labeled Type B.

16. **a.** is the answer. (p. 373)

**b.** Hypochondriacs think something is wrong with them, but nothing physical can be detected.

**c.** *Psychogenic* means "originating in the mind." One's reaction to stress is partially psychological, but this term is not used to refer to stress-related illness.

**d.** There is no such term.

17. **e.** is the answer. Because stress depresses the immune system, stressed individuals are prone to all of these conditions. (pp. 373–375)

18. **c.** is the answer. The finding that talking about grief leads to better health makes a lot of sense in light of this physiological finding. (p. 384)

**a., b., & d.** The study by Pennebaker did not find these to be true.

19. **a.** is the answer. (p. 375)

20. **b.** is the answer. (p. 376) .

### Matching Items

| | | |
|---|---|---|
| **1.** a (p. 361) | **5.** b (p. 365) | **9.** f (p. 350) |
| **2.** k (p. 359) | **6.** g (p. 364) | **10.** j (p. 359) |
| **3.** c (p. 358) | **7.** h (p. 348) | **11.** e (p. 364) |
| **4.** i (p. 362) | **8.** d (p. 348) | |

## Progress Test 2

### Multiple-Choice Questions

1. **a.** is the answer. Emotional arousal activates the sympathetic nervous system, causing the release of sugar into the blood for energy, pupil dilation, and the diverting of blood from the internal organs to the muscles, all of which help prepare the body to meet an emergency. (p. 348)

**b.** Being autonomic responses, most emotions are *involuntary* reactions.

**c.** All emotions do *not* have the same physiological basis.

**d.** Some emotions occur without cognitive awareness.

2. **c.** is the answer. According to Schachter, the two

factors in emotion are (1) body arousal and (2) conscious interpretation of the arousal. (p. 365)

3. **a.** is the answer. The principle of relative deprivation states that happiness is relative to others' attainments. This helps explain why those who are relatively well off tend to be slightly more satisfied than the relatively poor, with whom the better-off can compare themselves. (p. 362)
   **b.** Adaptation level is the tendency for our judgments to be relative to our prior experience.
   **c.** This phenomenon has nothing to do with the interpretation of emotion.
   **d.** Opponent processes are opposing emotional states that tend to balance each other.

4. **b.** is the answer. (p. 364)
   **a.** The James-Lange theory states that the experience of an emotion is an awareness of one's physical response to an emotion-arousing stimulus.
   **c.** The two-factor theory states that to experience emotion one must be physically aroused and attribute the arousal to an emotional cause.
   **d.** Zajonc proposed that we could experience emotion without cognition.

5. **d.** is the answer. As the Schachter-Singer study indicated, physical arousal is not always accompanied by an emotional reaction. Only when arousal was attributed to an emotion was it experienced as such. The results of this experiment, therefore, support the viewpoint that conscious interpretation of arousal must precede emotion. (pp. 365–366)
   **a., b., & c.** Each of these was presented as a supporting argument in the text.

6. **a.** is the answer. (p. 358)
   **b.** The opposite is true. Any emotional arousal will simmer down if you wait long enough.
   **c.** Catharsis often magnifies anger, escalates arguments, and leads to retaliation.
   **d.** When counterattack is justified and can be directed at the offender, catharsis may be helpful.

7. **e.** is the answer. (p. 348)

8. **a.** is the answer. That physical arousal can be misattributed demonstrates that it is the cognitive interpretation of arousal, rather than the intensity or specific nature of the body's arousal, that determines the conscious experience of emotions. (pp. 365–366)
   **b. & c.** The findings of these studies do not indicate that a minimum level of arousal is necessary for an emotional experience nor that applying a cognitive label must be simultaneous with the arousal.

9. **c.** is the answer. As heightened arousal may reflect feelings of anxiety or irritation rather than of guilt, the polygraph, which simply measures arousal, may easily err. (p. 350)
   **a.** Misuse and invasion of privacy are valid issues, but Lykken primarily objects to the use of lie detectors because of their inaccuracy.
   **b.** Although there are discrepancies among the various measures of arousal, this was not what Lykken objected to.
   **d.** The lie detector errs about one-third of the time.

10. **d.** is the answer. (p. 363)

11. **c.** is the answer. (p. 354)
    **a. & b.** These are true of cultures that emphasize individuality rather than interdependence.

12. **a.** is the answer. (p. 369)

13. **c.** is the answer. B lymphocytes fight bacterial infections; T lymphocytes attack cancer cells, viruses, and foreign substances. (p. 374)
    **d.** Antigens cause the production of antibodies when they are introduced into the body.

14. **a.** is the answer. A variety of studies have shown that stress depresses the immune system, increasing the risk and potential severity of many diseases. (pp. 374–375)

15. **e.** is the answer. (p. 374)

16. **a.** is the answer. (p. 374)
    **b.** An *under*reactive immune system would make an individual more susceptible to infectious diseases or the proliferation of cancer cells.
    **c. & d.** Lymphocytes are the disease- and infection-fighting white blood cells of the immune system.

17. **d.** is the answer. (p. 375)

18. **e.** is the answer. The crucial characteristic of Type A behavior seems to be a tendency to react with negative emotions, especially anger; other aspects of Type A behavior appear not to predict heart disease, and some appear to be helpful to the individual. (pp. 372–373)

19. **d.** is the answer. In biofeedback training, subjects are given sensory feedback about autonomic responses. Although biofeedback may promote relaxation, its benefits may be no greater than those produced by simpler, and less expensive, methods. (pp. 379–380)

20. **d.** is the answer. Friedman's subjects who received counseling on relaxation experienced half as many repeat heart attacks as did a control group. (p. 380)

*True-False Items*

| | |
|---|---|
| **1.** F (p. 352) | **6.** F (p. 374) |
| **2.** T (p. 355) | **7.** F (p. 371) |
| **3.** F (p. 365) | **8.** T (p. 371) |
| **4.** F (p. 361) | **9.** T (p. 373) |
| **5.** F (p. 367) | **10.** T (p. 382) |

## Thinking Critically About Chapter 10

1. **b.** is the answer. The James-Lange theory proposes that the experienced emotion is an awareness of a prior body response: Your pulse races, and so you feel nervous. (p. 364)

   **a.** According to the Cannon-Bard theory, your body's reaction would occur simultaneously with, rather than before, your experience of the emotion.

   **c.** Zajonc stated that emotion can be experienced prior to cognitive appraisal.

   **d.** The adaptation-level principle concerns our tendency to judge stimuli on the basis of recent experience.

2. **b.** is the answer. Professor Simon's judgment of his office is affected by his recent experience: When that experience was of a smaller office, his new office seemed terrific; now, however, it is commonplace. (p. 361)

   **a.** Relative deprivation is the sense that one is worse off than those with whom one compares oneself.

   **c.** This refers to Selye's description of the body's response to stress.

   **d.** This is the principle that there is an inverse relationship between the difficulty of a task and the optimum level of arousal.

3. **b.** is the answer. The parasympathetic division is involved in calming arousal. (p. 348)

   **a.** The sympathetic division is active during states of arousal and hence would not be active in the situation described.

   **c.** The skeletal division is involved in transmitting sensory information and controlling skeletal muscles; it is not involved in arousing and calming the body.

   **d.** This answer is too general, since the peripheral nervous system includes not only the parasympathetic division but also the sympathetic division and the skeletal division.

4. **d.** is the answer. In keeping with the catharsis hypothesis, Rana feels less angry after releasing her aggression. (p. 358)

   **a.** Adaptation level is our tendency to judge things relative to our experiences.

   **b.** This is Selye's name for the body's reaction to stress.

   **c.** Relative deprivation is the sense that one is worse off relative to those with whom one compares oneself.

5. **c.** is the answer. According to the two-factor theory, it is cognitive interpretation of the same general physiological arousal that distinguishes the two emotions. (p. 365)

   **a.** According to the James-Lange theory, if the same physical arousal occurred in the two instances, the same emotions should result.

   **b.** The Cannon-Bard theory argues that conscious awareness of an emotion and body reaction occur at the same time.

   **d.** Adaptation level concerns our tendency to judge things relative to our experiences.

6. **e.** is the answer. (pp. 350–351)

7. **d.** is the answer. (p. 349)

8. **d.** is the answer. (p. 354)

   **a. & c.** The Cannon-Bard and two-factor theories of emotion do not address the universality of emotional expressions.

   **b.** Even if it is true that emotional expressions are acquired at an early age, this would not necessarily account for the common facial expressions of children from around the world. If anything, the different cultural experiences of the children might lead them to express their feelings in very *different* ways.

9. **d.** is the answer. In Asian and other cultures that emphasize human connections and interdependence, negative emotional displays are rare and typically brief. (p. 354)

   **a., b., & c.** In cultures that encourage individuality, as in Western Europe, Australia, and North America, emotional displays often are intense and prolonged.

10. **c.** is the answer. People who are in a good mood are more likely to help others. Bonnie, who is probably pleased with herself following her graduation from college, is likely to be in a better mood than Drew, Leon, or Nancy. (p. 359)

11. **d.** is the answer. Cindy is unhappy with her promotion because she feels deprived relative to Janice. (p. 363)

   **a.** The adaptation-level phenomenon would predict that Cindy's raise would cause an increase in her happiness, since her most recent experience was to earn a lower salary.

   **b.** Biofeedback is a technique for reading physiological information in an effort to control bodily functions. Cindy is not trying to control her unhappiness.

**c.** The catharsis hypothesis maintains that venting one's anger may relieve aggressive urges.

12. **c.** is the answer. According to Selye's general adaptation syndrome, diseases are most likely to occur in this final stage. (p. 369)
**a. & b.** Resistance to disease is greater during the alarm and resistance phases because the body's mobilized resources are not yet depleted.
**d.** There is no such thing as the "depletion phase." Moreover, the post-traumatic stress syndrome refers to the haunting nightmares and anxiety of those who have suffered extreme stress, such as that associated with combat.

13. **b.** is the answer. (p. 370)
**a., c., & d.** Each of these is a factor in coping with stress, but it is how an event is *perceived* that determines whether it is stressful or not.

14. **b.** is the answer. Unpredictable events are more stressful than predictable events. (p. 370)

15. **b.** is the answer. (p. 372)
**a.** Type A persons are hard-driving and competitive.
**c.** There is no such thing as a "Type C" person.
**d.** Atherosclerosis refers to the blockage of the arteries that leads to coronary heart disease. Type A persons are more susceptible to atherosclerosis than Type B persons.

16. **c.** is the answer. (p. 374)
**a.** Macrophages are immune agents that search for and ingest harmful invaders.
**b.** B lymphocytes form in the bone marrow and release antibodies that fight bacterial infections.

17. **b.** is the answer. Stressful situations, such as exam weeks, decrease immune responses. (p. 374)

18. **c.** is the answer. (p. 371)
**a.** This is not realistic.
**b. & d.** These might actually *increase* the health consequences of potential stressors.

19. **c.** is the answer. (p. 373)
**a.** The text does not discuss any such thing as a "psychogenic" illness.
**b.** Hypochondriasis is the misinterpreting of normal physical sensations as symptoms of a disease.
**d.** Biofeedback is a system for recording information regarding a subtle physiological state, such as blood pressure.

20. **d.** is the answer. (pp. 371–372)

### Essay Question

When potentially stressful events occur, a person's appraisal is a major determinant of their impact. Catastrophes, significant life events, and daily hassles are especially stressful when appraised as negative, unpredictable, and uncontrollable, and when the person has a pessimistic outlook on life. Under these circumstances, stressful events may suppress immune responses and make the person more vulnerable to disease. If stressors cannot be eliminated, aerobic exercise, biofeedback, relaxation, and social support can help the person cope. Aerobic exercise can reduce stress, depression, and anxiety, perhaps by increasing production of mood-boosting neurotransmitters. During biofeedback training, people enjoy a calm, relaxing experience that can be helpful in reducing stress. Research demonstrates that people who regularly practice relaxation techniques enjoy a greater sense of tranquility and have lower blood pressure and stronger immune responses. People with strong social ties eat better, exercise more, and smoke and drink less. Social support may also help people evaluate and overcome stressful events. In addition, confiding painful feelings to others has been demonstrated to reduce the physiological responses linked to stress.

## Key Terms

### Writing Definitions

1. **Emotion** is a response of the whole organism involving three components: (1) physical arousal, (2) expressive behaviors, and (3) conscious experience. (p. 347)

2. The **polygraph**, or lie detector, is a device that measures several of the physiological responses accompanying emotion. (p. 350)

3. **Catharsis** is emotional release; according to the catharsis hypothesis, by expressing our anger, we can reduce it. (p. 358)

4. The **feel-good, do-good phenomenon** is the tendency of people to be helpful when they are in a good mood. (p. 359)

5. **Subjective well-being** refers to a person's sense of satisfaction with his or her life. (p. 359)

6. The **adaptation-level phenomenon** refers to our tendency to judge things relative to our prior experience. (p. 361)

7. The principle of **relative deprivation** is the sense that we are worse off relative to those with whom we compare ourselves. (p. 362)

8. The **James-Lange theory** states that emotional experiences are based on an awareness of the body's responses to emotion-arousing stimuli: a stimulus triggers the body's responses that in turn trigger the experienced emotion. (p. 364)

9. The **Cannon-Bard theory** states that the conscious, subjective experience of an emotion occurs at the same time as the body's physical reaction. (p. 364)

10. The **two-factor theory** of emotion proposes that emotions have two ingredients: physical arousal and a cognitive label. Thus, physical arousal is a necessary, but not a sufficient, component of emotional change. For an emotion to be experienced, arousal must be attributed to an emotional cause. (p. 365)

11. **Stress** refers to the process by which people perceive and react to stressors, or to events they perceive as threatening or challenging. (p. 369)

12. The **general adaptation syndrome (GAS)** is the three-stage sequence of bodily reaction to stress outlined by Hans Selye. (p. 369)

13. The leading cause of death in the United States today, **coronary heart disease** results from the clogging of the coronary arteries and the subsequent reduction in blood and oxygen supply to the heart muscle. (p. 372)

14. **Type A** personality is Friedman and Rosenman's term for the coronary-prone behavior pattern of competitive, hard-driving, impatient, verbally aggressive, and anger-prone people. (p. 372)

15. **Type B** personality is Friedman and Rosenman's term for the coronary-resistant behavior pattern of easygoing people. (p. 372)

16. A **psychophysiological illness** is any genuine illness such as hypertension and headaches that is apparently linked to stress rather than caused by a physical disorder. (p. 373)

*Memory aid: Psycho-* refers to mind; *physio-* refers to body; a **psychophysiological illness** is a mind-body disorder.

17. **Lymphocytes** are the two types of white blood cells of the immune system that fight bacterial infections (B lymphocytes) and viruses, cancer cells, and foreign substances in the body (T lymphocytes). (p. 374)

18. **Aerobic exercise** is any sustained activity such as running, swimming, or cycling that promotes heart and lung fitness and may help alleviate depression and anxiety. (p. 378)

19. **Biofeedback** refers to a system for electronically recording, amplifying, and feeding back information regarding a subtle physiological state. (p. 379)

*Memory aid:* A **biofeedback** device, such as a brain-wave trainer, provides auditory or visual feedback about biological responses.

## Summing Up

You see a man coming at you with a knife in his hand. This results in your heart pounding (*physiological arousal*), an attempt to get out of the way (*expressive behaviors*), and fear of being stabbed (*conscious experience*).

Different theories have been proposed to explain emotional experiences.

Perception of man with knife (stimulus): Theory 1: pounding heart (*physiological arousal*) leads to fear: the *emotion*. This is the *James-Lange* theory of emotion. Theory 2: pounding heart (*physiological arousal*) and simultaneous *subjective* awareness of emotion. This is the *Cannon-Bard* theory of emotion. Theory 3: pounding heart (*physiological arousal*) and simultaneous thought that "Man with knife scares me" (*cognitive label*) leads to the emotion of fear. This is the *two-factor* theory of emotion.

---

*FOCUS ON VOCABULARY AND LANGUAGE*

*Page 347:* No one needs to tell you that feelings add *color* to your life. . . . Without emotions we would experience a very dull and uninteresting existence; we would have no feelings of intense happiness or excitement, nor would we experience depression and sadness. Thus, emotions add a variety of interesting qualities (*color*) to our lives.

*Page 347:* . . . *rumble* of an engine and think that someone on a motorcycle is *stalking* you. Motorcycles make a vibrating, roaring sound (*rumble*), and if you believed the cyclist was pursuing or hunting you in an ominous and stealthy manner (*stalking*

*you*), you would feel frightened (*scared*); your heart rate would increase (*physiological arousal*), you would walk faster (*behavioral expression*), and you would wonder what was going on (*cognition*).

*The Physiology of Emotion*

*Page 347:* . . . *your stomach develops butterflies* . . . When you are apprehensive, fearful, and nervous, you have visceral (internal) sensations that may feel as though small flying insects (*butterflies*) are fluttering around in your stomach (*it develops butterflies*).

*Page 349:* Basketball players *shooting free throws*—a not so automatic skill—may perform slightly less well if a *packed fieldhouse* makes them *hyperaroused.*

When a basketball player is allowed (without interference) to throw the ball through the hoop (*shooting free throws*), it requires a lot of concentration because it is not a usual part of the game. If the player gets anxious and is overaroused (*hyperaroused*) because of the attention of a large crowd (*packed fieldhouse*), he is more likely to make a mistake. For easy, routine tasks a high level of arousal may be beneficial for performance.

*Page 349:* A terrified person may feel a *clutching, sinking sensation* in the chest and a *knot in the stomach.* Different emotions (anger, fear, sadness) feel different. Someone who is extremely afraid may have certain visceral (internal) reactions such as tightness in the upper abdomen (*a clutching, sinking sensation*) and a feeling of a lump (*knot*) in the stomach.

*Page 350 (Box):* Given the physical indicators of emotion, might we, like *Pinocchio*, give some *telltale sign* whenever we lie? Pinocchio is a fictional character in a children's story whose nose grows longer every time he tells a lie. The polygraph, or lie detector, does not detect lies; rather, it measures a number of physiological reactions (heart rate, blood pressure, and perspiration) (*telltale signs*) which indicate a change in emotional state. Unlike Pinocchio, there are no reliable or valid indicators of whether someone is lying or telling the truth.

### Expressing Emotion

*Page 352:* Most of us are good enough at *reading* nonverbal cues to decipher the emotions in an old *silent film.* We communicate our feelings with words (verbally) and through body language (nonverbally). Without hearing a single word, as in a movie with no sound track (*silent film*), we can discern much about someone's emotional state by observing (*reading*) his or her bodily actions and facial expressions. As Myers notes, when we look at a large group of faces, a single angry one will be extremely noticeable (*it will "pop out"*) and will be detected more quickly than a single happy one.

*Page 353: Fidgeting,* for example, may reveal *anxiety* or *boredom.* Many popular books and articles suggest what to look for in body language during interviews, business meetings, and so on. However, specific interpretations of gestures or posture cannot be made accurately or reliably. For example, restlessness, accompanied by frequent small movements (*fidgeting*), may be indicative of either disinterest (*boredom*) or extreme nervousness (*anxiety*).

*Page 354: Ditto* for the other basic expressions. There

is a great deal of consistency across cultures in the interpretation of different emotional expressions. In tests, people the world over could reliably tell which face expressed happiness; this result was found over and over again (*ditto*) for other fundamental expressions (e.g., anger, fear, sadness, and surprise).

*Page 354:* A *sneer,* for example, retains elements of an animal's *teeth-baring snarl.* Darwin believed that all humans have inherited the ability to express emotions through very similar facial expressions. Thus, a person's scornful or contemptuous grimace (*sneer*) has many aspects of the fierce growl with teeth showing (*teeth-baring snarl*) typical of dogs and other animals. Emotional expressions are one form of social communication.

*Page 355: Fake a big grin. Now scowl.* Can you feel the difference? Clearly our moods affect how we look, but Myers is inviting you to test the idea that your facial expression can affect your mood. Make a large, false smile (*fake a grin*). Next, wrinkle or furrow your brow, frown and look sullen (*scowl*). Subjects in numerous experiments felt different emotions under these conditions. Smile and inside you feel happy, scowl and you may see the world as more miserable than it is.

### Experiencing Emotion

*Page 357:* Popular books and articles on aggression sometimes advise that even *hostile outbursts* can be better than keeping anger *pent up.* The idea is that expressing your anger openly (*hostile outbursts or "venting your anger"*) provides some form of emotional release (*catharsis*) and that this is better than not expressing your feelings and holding your anger inside (*pent-up anger*). Under certain circumstances this may provide temporary relief, but the evidence also suggests that expressing anger can increase or magnify (*breed more*) anger.

*Page 358: . . . "blowing off steam" . . .* This means to openly express your anger and rage. Myers notes that doing this can increase or amplify your hostile emotions, but it may also be reinforcing because it releases some of the frustration. Consequently, the next time these feelings arise, the more likely it is that the hostile behavior (*explosive outbursts*) will be repeated.

*Page 359:* The *sages of the ages* have given us any number of *contradictory maxims.* . . . Over the centuries (*ages*) wise people (*sages*) have passed on to us a variety of principles (*maxims*) on the topic of happiness. Most of these are inconsistent and often in opposition to each other (*contradictory*). As Myers points out, to sort out (*sift*) the real predictors of happiness from the seemingly believable guesses (*plausible hunches*) requires research.

*Page 360:* Once their *rush of euphoria* wears off, state lottery winners typically find their overall happiness unchanged. We probably all dream of winning large amounts of money through gambling (*state lottery winners*) and then living happily ever after. However, once the initial feelings of excitement (*rush of euphoria*) diminish, most winners discover that they are no happier. Myers puts it succinctly ". . . there is much more to well-being than being well off (*rich*)."

*Page 360:* . . . machines *galore* . . . To have high-tech gadgets, such as VCRs, TVs, CDs, and other material possessions in plentiful supply (*galore*) does not make people happier.

*Page 361:* The findings *lob a bombshell* at modern materialism. . . . The contemporary tendency to accumulate wealth and possessions (*modern materialism*) in industrialized and affluent countries has not resulted in greater happiness. This finding challenges and destroys (*lobs a bombshell at*) the myth that riches (*affluence*) bring happiness and social well-being.

*Page 362:* Usually, they felt happier if mentally engaged by work or active leisure than if *passively vegetating*. In a study in which subjects were asked at random intervals (by use of electronic pagers) to report their present emotional state and the activities they were engaged in, they reported being happiest when busy and involved in some activity (work or leisure) that was relatively inexpensive; they were most content when totally and actively absorbed compared to when they were indifferent and mindlessly preoccupied (*passively vegetating*), such as when watching TV.

### Theories of Emotion

*Page 364:* Common sense tells most of us that we cry because we are sad, *lash out* because we are angry, *tremble* because we are afraid. The James-Lange theory states that physiological arousal precedes the experience of emotion. Thus, we cry first, then feel sad; we strike someone (*lash out*), then experience the anger; we shiver and shake (*tremble*), then feel fear. The Cannon-Bard theory proposes that physiological arousal and the experience of emotion occur at the same time but separately. One does not cause the other.

*Page 365: Which is the chicken and which the egg?* The old riddle asks, "Which came first, the chicken or the

egg?" Myers asks which comes first, our cognitions or our emotions. The two-factor theory suggests that physiological arousal has to be cognitively interpreted in order for one to experience different emotions. Stanley Schachter's research showed that the same arousal (*stirred-up state*) can be experienced as two very different emotional states (e.g., euphoria or irritation) depending on how we interpret and label it. Thus, thinking comes before feeling. (Richard Lazarus agrees with this interpretation.)

*Page 366:* . . . *testy* . . . This means to be ill-tempered or irritable. Those subjects who were physiologically aroused but did not know why were affected by ("*caught*") the apparent emotional state of the person they were with. They made different attributions about their aroused (*stirred-up*) state ("I'm happy" or "I'm feeling testy") on the basis of whether the accomplice acted in a euphoric or irritated way.

*Page 367:* The *heart* is not always subject to the *mind*. Robert Zajonc proposed that some emotional states are not preceded by cognitions. The emotions (*heart*) are not determined by our thoughts (*mind*). We can have *some* feelings, at least, without thinking first.

### Stress and Health

*Page 368:* Afterward, she notices her *tense* muscles, *clenched teeth*, and *churning stomach*. Our response to stress can be beneficial (e.g., Karl's escape from the snake) or destructive (e.g., Karen's reaction to relatively minor routine problems or *daily hassles*). Following a number of stressful events (missing her train, rush-hour pedestrian traffic, late for an appointment, etc.), she becomes aware of her physiological reaction. Her muscles feel strained and taut (*tense*), her jaws are clamped shut (*clenched teeth*), and her stomach feels upset (*churning stomach*).

*Page 368:* Stress is a *slippery concept*. The term *stress* is often used to describe a stimulus (a threatening or challenging event) or a response (fear or anxiety). Most psychologists refer to the former as a *stressor*, the latter as a *stress reaction*, and use the word *stress* to refer to the entire process of evaluating and dealing with threatening events. Thus, stress is not a simple or easily grasped (understood) construct (*it is a slippery concept*).

*Page 369:* Your heart rate *zooms*. According to Selye's general adaptation syndrome (GAS), there are three phases in our response to stress: *alarm reaction, resistance,* and *exhaustion*. During the first phase, the sympathetic nervous system responds rapidly; your heart rate quickly increases (*zooms*), blood is directed to the muscles, and you experience the weakness associated with being startled. You are now ready to fight or cope with the stressor (*resistance phase*); if the situation is not resolved soon, you will experience *exhaustion* (the third phase).

*Page 370:* . . . *uprooting* . . . Refugees and others who are forcibly made to leave their homes (*they are uprooted*) have increased rates of depression, anxiety, psychological disorders, and other stress symptoms. In most instances, the health impairments come from long-term exposure to stress.

*Page 370:* Experiencing *a cluster of crises* puts one even more at risk. Important and significant changes in our lives are other types of life-event stressors that increase the probability of health problems. If a number of these events occurs close together (*a cluster of crises*), people become more vulnerable to disease.

*Page 370:* The events of our lives *flow through a psychological filter*. Myers makes the important point that it is not so much the actual events that happen to us, but rather, it is our evaluation and appraisal of these events that determine their effect on us. Thus, it is not just your experiences, but what you think about them (*they flow through a psychological filter*) that affects your well-being.

*Page 371: Daily Hassles* Small, routine, annoying events and the little things that go wrong day by day (*daily hassles*) can have an accumulative effect on health and well-being. Some people can handle these daily hassles (*they shrug them off*) while others are severely distressed ("*driven up the wall*") by these inconveniences.

*Page 372:* Moreover, not one of the "*pure*" Type Bs —the most *mellow* and *laid-back* of their group—had suffered a *heart attack*. Researchers have identified two personality types: Type As are reactive (*easily angered*), competitive, verbally aggressive, highly motivated, always rushed, and lacking in patience; Type Bs are less easily angered (*mellow*), are easygoing (*laid-back*), patient, understanding, and noncompetitive. The most prototypical ("*pure*") Type Bs were the least likely to be afflicted by coronary heart disease (*heart attacks*).

*Page 372:* But *after the honeymoon period*, in which the finding seemed definitive and revolutionary, other researchers began asking, Is the finding reliable? The discovery of the relationship between personality type (A or B) and health and well-being aroused much interest. However, once the initial excitement abated (*after the honeymoon period*), other investiga-

tors started more detailed research and asked questions about the specific mechanisms involved in personality type and risk of disease.

*Page 372:* Further research found that reactive Type A individuals are more often "*combat ready*." Research has shown that Type As are physiologically more reactive and ready to fight (*combat ready*) than Type Bs. When stressed, their sympathetic nervous systems operate to increase the levels of cholesterol and fat in the blood; in addition, their negative (*toxic*) emotions, especially anger and depression, make them more coronary-prone.

*Page 374:* The immune system is not *a headless horseman*. The immune system does not operate as an autonomous system independent of other systems (*a headless horseman*). Instead, it works in close harmony with various brain systems and with the endocrine system, which secretes hormones. All these interact and affect each other in a very complex way.

*Page 374: Marital spats* are not good for health. Research has shown that when couples argue or fight (have *marital spats*), their negative emotions increase, and they are more likely to suffer suppression of their immune systems.

*Page 375:* What is more, *ever-nice* cancer patients who *bottle up* their negative emotions have less chance of survival than do those who verbalize their feelings. . . . Patients' attitudes can have an effect on the outcome of their disease. Those who are always trying to please others (*ever-nice*) or are constantly looking for approval and afraid to express their true feelings (*bottled-up emotions*) are more likely to die sooner compared to those who openly and honestly talk about how they feel.

*Page 376:* . . . *pseudoscientific hocus-pocus* . . . Myers makes the important point that there is a danger in publicizing reports on attitudes and their effects on diseases such as cancer because it may lead people to blame themselves for their disease. The relationship is complex, and correlation does not show cause and effect. Researchers have to distinguish the real effects of attitudes and feelings on health and well-being from those that have no scientific basis (*pseudoscientific hocus-pocus*), and that may simply reflect wishful thinking.

### Promoting Health

*Page 378:* Many of them had, quite literally, *run away from their troubles*. Many research studies have shown the beneficial effect of aerobic exercise on depression and anxiety. In one study, women who took up jogging (*running*) showed a substantial reduction in depression. As Myers humorously puts it, they had, in reality, *run away from their problems.*

*Page 379:* The *"mood boost"* is reaping dividends. Off your *duffs, couch potatoes.* Regular exercise increases longevity and cardiovascular fitness, reduces depression and anxiety, and enhances positive emotional states (*boosts our moods*). So the popular trend toward being more physically active has many benefits (*is reaping dividends*). Myers admonishes those of us who sit around, watch TV, and eat junk food (*couch potatoes*) to get off our backsides (*duffs*) and get active.

*Page 380:* After a decade of study, researchers *stepped back* to assess the results and decided the initial claims for biofeedback were *overblown and oversold* (Miller, 1985). Biofeedback became very popular in the 1970s, and the reports of its effectiveness for all kinds of problems led to much excitement. By the mid-1980s, however, when researchers took the time (*stepped back*) to evaluate the research findings objec-

tively, it became clear that these assertions were exaggerated (*overblown*) and falsely promoted (*oversold*). Simple relaxation without the use of costly equipment is just as beneficial.

*Page 382: . . . heartaches . . . Heartaches* is a term that refers to persistent mental anguish or suffering, usually resulting from the loss of a loved one or from disappointment in love. Myers points out that while close relationships and family tend to contribute to our well-being and contentment, they also can be the cause of much misery, strain, and strife (*heartaches*).

*Page 384:* Talking about our troubles can be *"open-heart therapy."* Research has shown that those with close, supportive friends and family tend to have fewer health problems and live longer. One reason for this may be that trusting relationships provide the opportunity to talk about our problems and feelings and, just as *"open-heart surgery"* can save lives, having someone to talk to can be a form of *"open-heart therapy."*

# 11

# *Personality*

## Chapter Overview

Personality refers to each individual's characteristic pattern of thinking, feeling, and acting. Chapter 11 examines four perspectives on personality. Psychoanalytic theory emphasizes the unconscious and irrational aspects of personality. Trait theory led to advances in techniques for evaluating and describing personality. Humanistic theory draws attention to the concept of self and to human potential for healthy growth. The social-cognitive perspective emphasizes the effects of our interactions with the environment. The text first describes and then evaluates the contributions and shortcomings of each perspective. In addition, within each section is a brief description of some of the techniques used by the perspective in analyzing personality.

NOTE: Answer guidelines for all Chapter 11 questions begin on page 322.

## Guided Study

The text chapter should be studied one section at a time. Before you read, preview each section by skimming it, noting headings and boldface items. Then read the appropriate section objectives from the following outline. Keep these objectives in mind, and as you read the chapter section, search for the information that will enable you to meet each objective. Once you have finished a section, write out answers for its objectives.

### *The Psychoanalytic Perspective* (pp. 390–400)

> David Myers at times uses idioms that are unfamiliar to some readers. If you do not know the meaning of any of the following words, phrases, or expressions in the context in which they appear in the text, refer to page 332 for an explanation: *ran up a bookstore debt . . . feeding his insatiable interest; mind running; glimpsed; upright . . . wantonly; biting sarcasm; twig of personality is bent; act out . . . willy-nilly; icebreaker; scientific shortcomings.*

1. Describe how Freud's search for the psychological roots of nervous disorders led to his study of the unconscious and explain psychoanalysis.

2. Describe Freud's views of personality structure.

3. Outline and describe Freud's psychosexual stages of personality development.

*The Trait Perspective* (pp. 400–406)

> If you do not know the meaning of any of the following words, phrases, or expressions in the context in which they appear in the text, refer to pages 332–333 for an explanation: *dubbed the Big Five; blind date; pundits . . . spoofing; labeling and pigeonholing.*

4. Explain Freud's view of maladaptive behavior and describe how defense mechanisms operate.

*Result from unresolved conflicts during earlier psychosexuals stages.*
*— Are the ego attempt to reduce or redirect anxiety by distorting reality.*

8. Discuss trait theories of personality and trace their history.

5. Discuss the major ideas of the neo-Freudians and today's psychodynamic theorists.

*More emphasis than freud on the role of the concious mind in determining personality, and less emphasis on sex and aggression as all consuming motivations.*
*— Agree w/ freud that much of mental is unconcious The childhood shapes personality and attachment, and we often struggle w/ inner conflicts*

9. Identify the Big Five personality factors and describe the assessment techniques associated with the trait perspective.

6. Explain how projective tests are used to assess personality and describe research findings regarding their validity and reliability.

10. Evaluate the trait perspective on personality and describe research findings regarding the consistency of behavior over time and across situations.

7. Evaluate the psychoanalytic perspective.

*The Humanistic Perspective* (pp. 406–415)

> If you do not know the meaning of any of the following words, phrases, or expressions in the context in which they appear in the text, refer to pages 333–334 for an explanation: *crippled spirits; acorn, primed for growth; negative about themselves; prowess; Lake Wobegon; pride does often go before a fall; put-downs; provides one's bearings; to save face; rugged individual; playing possum.*

11. Describe the humanistic perspective on personality and discuss the basic ideas of Maslow and Rogers.

12. Describe recent research on the way people view themselves.

13. Discuss how culture affects one's sense of self, including research findings on stigmatized groups and differences between individualist and collectivist cultures.

14. Evaluate the humanistic perspective.

*The Social-Cognitive Perspective* (pp. 415–421)

> If you do not know the meaning of any of the following words, phrases, or expressions in the context in which they appear in the text, refer to page 334 for an explanation: *touching off; leaping a hurdle; put an optimistic spin on setbacks; to bomb on the upcoming exam; scoff; suckering methods; stock spiel.*

15. Describe the social-cognitive perspective and define reciprocal determinism, giving three examples.

16. Discuss research findings on personal control.

17. Describe how social-cognitive researchers study behavior and evaluate this perspective on personality.

## Chapter Review

When you have finished reading the chapter, work through the material that follows to review it. Complete the sentences and answer the questions. As you proceed, evaluate your performance for each section by consulting the answers on page 324. Do not continue with the next section until you understand each answer. If you need to, review or reread the appropriate section in the textbook before continuing.

1. An individual's characteristic pattern of _feeling_ , _thinking_ , and _acting_ constitute that individual's _personality_ .

2. The four major perspectives on personality discussed in this chapter are the _psychoanalytic_ , _trait_ , _humanistic_ , and _social_-_cognitive_ theories.

*The Psychoanalytic Perspective* (pp. 390–400)

3. The psychoanalytic perspective on personality was proposed by ___sigmund Freud___.

4. The technique used by Freud, in which the patient relaxes and says whatever comes to mind, is called ___free association___.

5. Freud called his theory and associated techniques, whereby painful unconscious memories are exposed, ___psychoanalysis___

6. According to this theory, the mind is like an iceberg in that many of a person's thoughts, wishes, and feelings are hidden in a large ___unconscious___ region. Some of the thoughts in this region can be retrieved at will into consciousness; these thoughts are said to be ___preconcious___. Many of the memories of this region, however, are blocked, or ___repressed___, from consciousness.

7. Freud believed that a person's ___unconscious___ wishes are often reflected in his or her dreams and ___slips___ of the tongue or pen. Freud called the remembered content of dreams the ___manifest content___, which he believed to be a censored version of the dream's true ___latent content___.

8. Freud believed that all facets of personality arise from conflict between our ___biological___ impulses and the ___social___ restraints against them.

9. According to Freud, personality consists of three interacting structures: the ___id___, the ___ego___, and the ___superego___.

10. The id is a reservoir of energy that is primarily ___unconscious___ (conscious/unconscious) and operates according to the _____ principle.

11. The ego develops ___after___ (before/after) the id and consists of perceptions, thoughts, and memories that are mostly ___conscious___ (conscious/

unconscious). The ego operates according to the ___reality___ principle.

Explain why the ego is considered the "executive" of personality.

___it directs our actions as intervenes among the impulse demands of the id, and the reality of the external world, and the ideals of the superego.___

12. The personality structure that reflects moral values is the ___superego___.

13. A person with a ___weak___ (strong/weak) superego may be self-indulgent; one with an unusually ___strong___ (strong/weak) superego may be continually guilt-ridden.

14. According to Freud, personality is formed as the child passes through a series of ___psychosexual___ stages.

15. The first stage is the ___oral___ stage, which takes place during the first 18 months of life. During this stage, the id's energies are focused on behaviors such as ___sucking___.

16. The second stage is the ___anal___ stage, which lasts from about age ___18___ months to ___3___ years.

17. The third stage is the ___phallic___ stage, which lasts roughly from ages ___3___ to ___6___. During this stage the id's energies are focused on the ___genitals___. Freud also believed that during this stage children develop sexual desires for the ___opposite___ (same/opposite)-sex parent. Freud referred to these feelings as the ___oedipus complex___ in boys. Some psychoanalysts believe that girls experience a parallel ___electra complex___.

18. Freud believed that ___identification___ with the same-sex parent is the basis for ___gender identity___.

Explain how this complex of feelings is resolved through the process of identification.

19. During the next stage, sexual feelings are repressed: this phase is called the _____ *latency* _____ stage and lasts until adolescence.

20. The final stage of development is called the _____ *genital* _____ stage.

21. According to Freud, it is possible for a person's development to become blocked in any of the stages; in such an instance, the person is said to be _____ *fixated* _____.

22. The ego attempts to protect itself against anxiety through the use of _____ *defense* _____ *mechanisms* _____. The process underlying

each of these mechanisms is _____ *repression* _____.

23. Dealing with anxiety by returning to an earlier stage of development is called _____ *regression* _____.

24. When a person reacts in a manner opposite that of his or her true feelings, *reaction* *formation* is said to have occurred.

25. When a person attributes his or her own feelings to another person, _____ *projection* _____ has occurred.

26. When a person offers a false, self-justifying explanation for his or her actions, *rationalization* has occurred.

27. When impulses are directed toward an object other than the one that caused arousal, *displacement* has occurred.

28. When a person rechannels an unacceptable impulse into a socially approved activity, *sublimation* has occurred.

## Matching Items

Match each defense mechanism in the following list with the proper example of its manifestation.

### Defense Mechanisms

_e_ **1.** displacement
_d_ **2.** projection
_b_ **3.** reaction formation
_c_ **4.** rationalization
_a_ **5.** regression
_f_ **6.** sublimation

### Manifestations

_5_ **a.** nail biting or thumb sucking in an anxiety-producing situation

_3_ **b.** overzealous crusaders against "immoral behaviors," who don't want to acknowledge their own sexual desires

_4_ **c.** saying you drink "just to be sociable" when in reality you have a drinking problem

_2_ **d.** thinking someone hates you when in reality you hate that person

_1_ **e.** a child who is angry at his parents and vents this anger on the family pet, a less threatening target

_6_ **f.** a musician who channels her anger over social injustices into song writing

29. Defense mechanisms are ___unconscious___ (conscious/unconscious) processes.

30. The theorists who established their own, modified versions of psychoanalytic theory are called ___neo___-___Freudians___. These theorists typically place ___more___ (more/less) emphasis on the conscious mind than Freud did and ___less___ (more/less) emphasis on sex and aggression.

Briefly summarize how each of the following theorists departed from Freud.
a. Adler ___in prosid social rather than sexual tension of childhood.___
b. Horney ___questioned the male bias in Freud's theory such as the women have weak ego and says penis envy.___
c. Jung ___emphasized in inherited collective unconscious,___

31. More recently, some of Freud's ideas have been incorporated into ___psychodynamic___ theory. Unlike Freud, the theorists advocating this perspective do not believe that ___sex___ is the basis of personality. They do agree, however, that much of mental life is ___unconscious___, that ___childhood___ shapes personality, and that we often struggle with ___inner conflicts___.

32. Tests that provide subjects with ambiguous stimuli for interpretation are called ___projective___ tests.

33. Henry Murray introduced the personality assessment technique called the ___Thematic apperception___ Test.

34. The most widely used projective test is the ___Rorschach___, in which subjects are shown a series of ___ink blots___. Generally, these tests appear to have ___little___ (little/significant) validity and reliability.

35. Contrary to Freud's theory, research indicates that human development is ___life long___ (fixed in childhood/lifelong), children gain their gender-identity at a(n) ___earlier___ (earlier/later) age, and the presence of a same-sex parent ___is not___ (is/is not) necessary for the child to become strongly masculine or feminine. Freud's ideas about the natural superiority of men ___have___ (have/have not) been thoroughly discounted. Another Freudian idea that is no longer widely accepted is that psychological disorders are caused by ___sexual repression___.

36. Psychoanalytic theory rests on the assumption that the human mind often ___represses___ painful experiences. Many of today's researchers think that this process is much ___rarer___ (more common/rarer) than Freud believed. They also believe that when it does occur, it is a reaction to terrible ___trauma___.

37. Recent researchers primarily perceive the unconscious not as the site of instinctual urges, but as where ___information___ is processed without awareness.

Explain the views held by contemporary researchers regarding the contents of the unconscious.

38. Criticism of psychoanalysis as a scientific theory centers on the fact that it provides after-the-fact explanations and does not offer ___testable predictions___.

*The Trait Perspective* (pp. 400–406)

39. Gordon Allport developed trait theory, which defines personality in terms of people's characteristic ___behavior___ and conscious ___motives___.

**40.** Trait theorists are generally less interested in _Explaining_ individual traits than they are in _describing_ them.

**41.** The _myers - Briggs type indicator_ classifies people according to Carl Jung's personality types. Although recently criticized for its lack of predictive value, this test has been widely used in _bussiness_ and _career_ counseling.

**42.** To reduce the number of traits to a few basic ones, psychologists use the statistical procedure of _Factor Analysis_. The Eysencks think that two personality dimensions are sufficient: _extraversion - introversion_ and emotional _stability - instability_. They also contend that _extraverts_, seek stimulation because their level of _brain arousal_ is relatively low. Emotionally _stable_ (stable/unstable) people react calmly because their _autonomic nervous system_ are not as reactive as those of _unstable_ (stable/unstable) people.

**43.** Many trait theorists view personality as _____ rooted. Jerome Kagan, for example, attributes differences in children's _____ and _____ to autonomic nervous system reactivity. Research increasingly reveals that our _____ play an important role in defining our _____ and _____ style.

**44.** More recently, researchers have arrived at a cluster of five factors that seem to describe the major features of personality. List and briefly describe the Big Five.

    a. _____
    b. _____
    c. _____
    d. _____
    e. _____

**45.** Questionnaires that categorize personality traits are called _____. The most widely used of all such personality tests is the _____ _____. This test was developed by testing a large pool of items and selecting those that differentiated particular individuals; in other words, the test was _____ derived.

**46.** Human behavior is influenced both by our inner _____ and by the external _____.

**47.** To be considered a personality trait a characteristic must persist over _____ and across _____. Research on children's propensity to cheat, for example, indicates that people's behavior on different occasions is generally quite _____ (variable/consistent).

**48.** An individual's score on a personality test _____ (is/is not) very predictive of his or her behavior in any given situation.

Defend trait theory against the criticism that people seem not to have clear, consistent personalities.

## The Humanistic Perspective (pp. 406–415)

**49.** Two influential theories of humanistic psychology were proposed by _____ and _____.

**50.** According to Maslow, humans are motivated by needs that are organized into a _____. Maslow refers to the process of fulfilling one's potential as _____.

List some of the characteristics Maslow associated with those who fulfilled their potential.

**51.** According to Rogers, a person nurtures growth in a relationship by being _____, _____, and _____. People who are accepting of others offer them

_____ _____

_____ .

**52.** For both Maslow and Rogers, an important feature of personality is how an individual perceives himself or herself; this is the person's

_____ .

**53.** Since the 1940s, research on the self has greatly _____ (increased/decreased).

**54.** Hazel Markus and colleagues introduced the concept of an individual's _____

_____ to emphasize how our aspirations motivate us through specific goals.

**55.** According to the humanists, personality development hinges on our feelings of self-worth, or _____ . People who feel good about themselves are relatively _____ (dependent on/independent of) outside pressures, while people who fall short of their ideals are more prone to _____ and _____ .

**56.** People who are vulnerable to depression often feel they are falling short of their _____ . Those vulnerable to anxiety often feel they are falling short of what they _____ .

**57.** In a series of experiments, researchers found that people who were made to feel insecure were _____ (more/less) critical of other persons or tended to express heightened

_____ .

**58.** Research studies demonstrate that ethnic minori-

ties, people with disabilities, and women generally _____ (have/do not have) lower self-esteem.

**59.** Members of stigmatized groups maintain self-esteem in three ways:

a. _____ ;

b. _____ ;

c. _____ .

**60.** Research has shown that most people tend to have _____ (low/high) self-esteem.

**61.** The tendency of people to judge themselves favorably is called the _____ bias.

**62.** Responsibility for success is generally accepted _____ (more/less) readily than responsibility for failure.

**63.** Most people perceive their own behavior and traits as being _____ (above/below) average.

**64.** People who give priority to personal goals and define their identity in terms of personal attributes are members of _____ cultures. People who give priority to the goals of their groups belong to _____ cultures.

Contrast the influences of individualism and collectivism on personal identity.

**65.** Direct confrontation and blunt honesty are rare in _____ cultures. People in _____ cultures have more personal _____ ; but they also experience more _____ , more _____ , more _____ , and more _____ - _____ disease.

66. In recent decades, Western individualism has

    _____ (increased/decreased).

State three criticisms that have been made of humanistic psychology.

### The Social-Cognitive Perspective (pp. 415–421)

67. Social-cognitive theorists focus on how the individual and the _____ interact. One such theorist is _____ .

68. Social-cognitive theorists propose that personality is shaped by the mutual influence of our

    _____ , _____

    factors, and _____ factors. This

    is the principle of _____

    _____ .

Describe three different ways in which the environment and personality interact.

69. Individuals who believe that they control their own destinies are said to perceive an

    _____

    _____ .

    Individuals who believe that their fate is determined by outside forces are said to perceive an

    _____

    _____ .

70. Seligman found that exposure to inescapable punishment produced a passive resignation in behavior, which he called _____

    _____ .

71. People become happier when they are given

    _____ (more/less) control over

    what happens to them.

72. One measure of a person's feelings of effectiveness is their degree of _____ .

73. It follows from the social-cognitive perspective that the best means of predicting people's future behavior is their _____

    _____ .

Describe a criticism of the social-cognitive perspective.

(Thinking Critically) Explain several techniques used by astrologers to persuade people to accept their advice.

74. List the major contributions of each perspective to our understanding of personality.

    **a.** Psychoanalytic _____

    **b.** Trait _____

    _____

    **c.** Humanistic _____

    _____

    **d.** Social-Cognitive _____

    _____

**WEB SIGHTINGS**
Many excellent Web sites are available for exploring personality. For example, there are web pages for all the major theorists that present overviews of their understanding of personality, biographical sketches, and critical evaluations of their contributions to psychology. Other sites allow you to view samples of the major personality tests. Be careful, however. Remember to be skeptical in your inquiry and always consider the scientific credibility of the source of information you find on the web. A good way to get started is to pick several key words or phrases that are related to personality and, using *Yahoo*, *Webcrawler*, *PsychCrawler*, or your favorite search engine, try to find relevant pages. For example, try searching for "personality theory," "projective test," or "Carl Rogers." When you have exhausted this approach, access the American Psychological Association's *Frequently Asked Questions (FAQ)* page (**http://www.apa.org/science/test.html**). Then, using this site, try to find the answers to the following questions.

1. What is graphoanalysis? Can it help illuminate the mysteries of human nature?

2. Identify three scientific journals that publish theory and research articles about personality. Pick one, then find the table of contents of its most recent issue.

3. Learn as much as you can about the life of a major personality theorist.

4. Where would you find a test to measure the self-concept? Who is qualified to administer such a test? What are some of the responsibilities of those who administer personality tests?

5. What is the difference between *phrenology* and *craniology*? When were these approaches to personality popular? Are they still around?

## Progress Test 1

### Multiple-Choice Questions

Circle your answers to the following questions and check them with the answers on page 326. If your answer is incorrect, read the explanation for why it is incorrect and then consult the appropriate pages of the text (in parentheses following the correct answer).

1. The text defines *personality* as:
   a. the set of personal attitudes that characterizes a person.
   b. an individual's characteristic pattern of thinking, feeling, and acting.
   c. a predictable set of responses to environmental stimuli.
   d. an unpredictable set of responses to environmental stimuli.

2. Which of the following places the greatest emphasis on the unconscious mind?
   a. the humanistic perspective
   b. the social-cognitive perspective
   c. the trait perspective
   d. the psychoanalytic perspective

3. Which of the following is the correct order of psychosexual stages proposed by Freud?
   a. oral; anal; phallic; latency; genital
   b. anal; oral; phallic; latency; genital
   c. oral; anal; genital; latency; phallic
   d. anal; oral; genital; latency; phallic
   e. oral; phallic; anal; genital; latency

4. According to Freud, defense mechanisms are methods of reducing:
   a. anger.              c. anxiety.
   b. fear.               d. lust.

5. Collectivist cultures:
   a. give priority to the goals of their groups.
   b. value the maintenance of social harmony.
   c. foster social interdependence.
   d. are characterized by none of the above.
   e. are characterized by a., b., and c.

6. Neo-Freudians such as Adler and Horney believed that:
    a. Freud placed too great an emphasis on the conscious mind.
    **b.** Freud placed too great an emphasis on sexual and aggressive instincts.
    c. the years of childhood were more important in the formation of personality than Freud had indicated.
    d. Freud's ideas about the id, ego, and superego as personality structures were incorrect.

7. Research on locus of control indicates that internals are _____ than externals.
    a. more dependent
    b. more intelligent
    **c.** better able to cope with stress
    d. more sociable
    e. more depressed

8. Which two dimensions of personality have the Eysencks emphasized?
    **a.** extraversion-introversion and emotional stability-instability
    b. internal-external locus of control and extraversion-introversion
    c. internal-external locus of control and emotional stability-instability
    d. melancholic-phlegmatic and choleric-sanguine

9. With regard to personality, it appears that:
    a. there is little consistency of behavior from one situation to the next and little consistency of traits over the life span.
    **b.** there is little consistency of behavior from one situation to the next but significant consistency of traits over the life span.
    c. there is significant consistency of behavior from one situation to the next but little consistency of traits over the life span.
    d. there is significant consistency of behavior from one situation to the next and significant consistency of traits over the life span.

10. The humanistic perspective on personality:
    a. emphasizes the driving force of unconscious motivations in personality.
    **b.** emphasizes the growth potential of "healthy" individuals.
    c. emphasizes the importance of interaction with the environment in shaping personality.
    d. describes personality in terms of scores on various personality scales.

11. According to Rogers, three conditions are necessary to promote growth in personality. These are:
    a. honesty, sincerity, and empathy.
    b. high self-esteem, honesty, and empathy.
    c. high self-esteem, genuineness, and acceptance.
    d. high self-esteem, acceptance, and honesty.
    **e.** genuineness, acceptance, and empathy.

12. Regarding the self-serving bias, humanistic psychologists have emphasized that self-affirming thinking:
    a. is generally maladaptive to the individual because it distorts reality by overinflating self-esteem.
    **b.** is generally adaptive to the individual because it maintains self-confidence and minimizes depression.
    c. tends to prevent the individual from viewing others with compassion and understanding.
    d. tends *not* to characterize people who have experienced unconditional positive regard.

13. Which of Freud's ideas would *not* be accepted by most contemporary psychologists?
    **a.** Development is essentially fixed in childhood.
    b. Sexuality is a potent drive in humans.
    c. The mind is an iceberg with consciousness being only the tip.
    d. Repression can be the cause of forgetting.

14. Individualist cultures:
    a. value communal solidarity.
    **b.** emphasize personal achievement and identity.
    c. are less competitive than collectivist cultures.
    d. are characterized by none of the above.
    e. are characterized by a., b., and c.

15. Projective tests such as the Rorschach inkblot test have been criticized because:
    a. their scoring system is too rigid and leads to unfair labeling.
    b. they were standardized with unrepresentative samples.
    **c.** they have low reliability and low validity.
    d. it is easy for people to fake answers in order to appear healthy.

16. A major criticism of trait theory is that it:
    a. places too great an emphasis on early childhood experiences.
    **b.** overestimates the consistency of behavior in different situations.
    c. underestimates the importance of heredity in personality development.
    d. places too great an emphasis on positive traits.

**17.** For humanistic psychologists, many of our attitudes and behaviors are ultimately shaped by whether our _____ is _____ or _____ .

    **a.** ego; strong; weak

    **b.** locus of control; internal; external

    **c.** personality structure; introverted; extraverted

    **d.** self-concept; positive; negative

**18.** In studying personality, a trait theorist would *most likely*:

    **a.** use a projective test.

    **b.** observe a person in a variety of situations.

    **c.** use a personality inventory.

    **d.** use the method of free association.

**19.** Id is to ego as _____ is to _____ .

    **a.** reality principle; pleasure principle

    **b.** pleasure principle; reality principle

    **c.** conscious forces; unconscious forces

    **d.** conscience; "personality executive"

**20.** Which of the following is a major criticism of the social-cognitive perspective?

    **a.** It focuses too much on early childhood experiences.

    **b.** It focuses too little on the inner traits of a person.

    **c.** It provides descriptions but not explanations.

    **d.** It lacks appropriate assessment techniques.

## Matching Items

Match each definition or description with the appropriate term.

*Definitions or Descriptions*

  F  **1.** redirecting impulses to a less threatening object

  K  **2.** test consisting of a series of inkblots

  b  **3.** the conscious executive of personality

  L  **4.** personality inventory

  i  **5.** disguising an impulse by imputing it to another person

  d  **6.** switching an unacceptable impulse into its opposite

  a  **7.** the unconscious repository of instinctual drives

  h  **8.** a statistical technique that identifies clusters of personality traits.

  c  **9.** personality structure that corresponds to a person's conscience

  e  **10.** providing self-justifying explanations for an action

  j  **11.** a projective test consisting of a set of ambiguous pictures

  g  **12.** channeling unacceptable impulses into socially approved activities

*Terms*

  **a.** id

  **b.** ego

  **c.** superego

  **d.** reaction formation

  **e.** rationalization

  **f.** displacement

  **g.** sublimation

  **h.** factor analysis

  **i.** projection

  **j.** TAT

  **k.** Rorschach

  **l.** MMPI

# Progress Test 2

Progress Test 2 should be completed during a final chapter review. Answer the following questions after you thoroughly understand the correct answers for the Chapter Review and Progress Test 1.

## Multiple-Choice Questions

1. Which perspective on personality emphasizes the interaction between the individual and the environment in shaping personality?
   - **a.** psychoanalytic
   - **b.** trait
   - **c.** humanistic
   - **d.** social-cognitive

2. According to Freud's theory, personality arises in response to conflicts between:
   - **a.** our unacceptable urges and our tendency to become self-actualized.
   - **b.** the process of identification and the ego's defense mechanisms.
   - **c.** the collective unconscious and our individual desires.
   - **d.** our biological impulses and the social restraints against them.

3. The _____ classifies people according to Carl Jung's personality types.
   - **a.** Myers-Briggs Type Indicator
   - **b.** MMPI
   - **c.** Locus of Control Scale
   - **d.** Kagan Temperament Scale
   - **e.** TAT

4. Seligman has found that humans and animals who are exposed to aversive events they cannot escape may develop:
   - **a.** an internal locus of control.
   - **b.** a reaction formation.
   - **c.** learned helplessness.
   - **d.** neurotic anxiety.
   - **e.** displacement.

5. Research has shown that individuals who are made to feel insecure are subsequently:
   - **a.** more critical of others.
   - **b.** less critical of others.
   - **c.** more likely to display a self-serving bias.
   - **d.** less likely to display a self-serving bias.

6. An example of the self-serving bias described in the text is the tendency of people to:
   - **a.** see themselves as better than average on nearly any desirable dimension.
   - **b.** accept more responsibility for successes than failures.
   - **c.** be overly critical of other people.
   - **d.** be overly sensitive to criticism.
   - **e.** do both a. and b.

7. The Minnesota Multiphasic Personality Inventory (MMPI) is a(n):
   - **a.** projective personality test.
   - **b.** empirically derived and objective personality test.
   - **c.** personality test developed mainly to assess job applicants.
   - **d.** personality test used primarily to assess locus of control.

8. Trait theory attempts to:
   - **a.** show how development of personality is a lifelong process.
   - **b.** describe and classify people in terms of their predispositions to behave in certain ways.
   - **c.** determine which traits are most conducive to individual self-actualization.
   - **d.** explain how behavior is shaped by the interaction between traits, behavior, and the environment.

9. With which of the following statements would a social-cognitive psychologist agree?
   - **a.** People with an internal locus of control achieve more in school.
   - **b.** "Externals" are better able to cope with stress than "internals."
   - **c.** "Internals" are less independent than "externals."
   - **d.** All of the above are true.

10. Which of the following statements about self-esteem is *not* correct?
    - **a.** People with low self-esteem tend to be negative about others.
    - **b.** People with high self-esteem are less prone to drug addiction.
    - **c.** People with low self-esteem tend to be non-conformists.
    - **d.** People with high self-esteem suffer less from insomnia.
    - **e.** People with high self-esteem are more persistent at difficult tasks.

11. The Oedipus and Electra complexes have their roots in the:
    - **a.** anal stage.
    - **b.** oral stage.
    - **c.** latency stage.
    - **d.** phallic stage.
    - **e.** genital stage.

12. Which of the following is a common criticism of the humanistic perspective?

   a. Its concepts are vague and subjective.

   b. The emphasis on the self encourages selfishness in individuals.

   c. Humanism fails to appreciate the reality of evil in human behavior.

   **d. All of the above are common criticisms.**

13. In studying personality, a social-cognitive theorist would *most likely* make use of:

   a. personality inventories.

   b. projective tests.

   **c. observing behavior in different situations.**

   d. factor analyses.

14. A major difference between the psychoanalytic and trait perspectives is that:

   a. trait theory defines personality in terms of behavior; psychoanalytic theory, in terms of its underlying dynamics.

   b. trait theory describes behavior but does not attempt to explain it.

   c. psychoanalytic theory emphasizes the origins of personality in childhood sexuality.

   **d. all of the above are differences.**

15. Compared to those in collectivist cultures, people in individualist cultures:

   a. are less geographically bound to elderly parents.

   b. tend to be lonelier.

   c. are more vulnerable to stress-related disease.

   d. have all of the above characteristics.

16. The Big Five personality factors are:

   a. emotional stability, openness, introversion, sociability, locus of control.

   b. neuroticism, extraversion, openness, emotional stability, sensitivity.

   c. neuroticism, gregariousness, extraversion, impulsiveness, conscientiousness.

   d. emotional stability, extraversion, openness, agreeableness, conscientiousness.

   e. emotional stability, extraversion, openness, locus of control, sensitivity.

17. Which of the following was *not* mentioned in the text as a criticism of Freud's theory?

   a. The theory is sexist.

   b. It offers few testable hypotheses.

   c. There is no evidence of anything like an "unconscious."

   d. The theory ignores the fact that human development is lifelong.

18. According to Freud, _____ is the process by which children incorporate their parents' values into their _____.

   a. reaction formation; superegos

   b. reaction formation; egos

   c. identification; superegos

   d. identification; egos

19. Which of the following groups tends to suffer from relatively low self-esteem?

   a. women

   b. ethnic minorities

   c. disabled persons

   d. all of the above

   e. none of the above

20. In promoting personality growth, the person-centered perspective emphasizes all but:

   a. empathy.      c. genuineness.

   b. acceptance.    d. altruism.

## Matching Items

Match each term with the appropriate definition or description.

*Terms*

_____ 1. projective test
_____ 2. identification
_____ 3. collective unconscious
_____ 4. reality principle
_____ 5. psychosexual stages
_____ 6. pleasure principle
_____ 7. empirically derived test
_____ 8. reciprocal determinism
_____ 9. personality inventory
_____ 10. Oedipus complex
_____ 11. preconscious

*Definitions or Descriptions*

a. the id's demand for immediate gratification
b. a boy's sexual desires toward the opposite-sex parent
c. information that is retrievable but currently not in conscious awareness
d. stages of development proposed by Freud
e. questionnaire used to assess personality traits
f. the two-way interactions of behavior with personal and environmental factors
g. personality test that provides ambiguous stimuli
h. the repository of universal memories proposed by Jung
i. the process by which children incorporate their parents' values into their developing superegos
j. the process by which the ego seeks to gratify impulses of the id in nondestructive ways
k. developed by testing a pool of items and then selecting those that discriminate the group of interest

## Thinking Critically About Chapter 11

Answer these questions the day before an exam as a final check on your understanding of the chapter's terms and concepts.

### Multiple-Choice Questions

1. After Sheila was laid off from work, she was angry and wanted to confront her former employer. Instead, she rechanneled her feelings into a hobby and created a beautiful new piece of furniture. Freud would probably suggest that Sheila's behavior is an example of:
   a. rationalization.       d. reaction formation.
   b. regression.            e. sublimation.
   c. projection.

2. A psychoanalyst would characterize a person who is impulsive and self-indulgent as possessing a strong _____ and a weak _____ .
   a. id and ego; superego    d. id; superego
   b. id; ego and superego    e. superego; ego
   c. ego; superego

3. Because Ramona identifies with her politically conservative parents, she chose to enroll in a conservative college. After four years in this environment Ramona's politics have become even more conservative. Which perspective best accounts for the mutual influences of Ramona's upbringing, choice of school, and political viewpoint?
   a. psychoanalytic          c. humanistic
   b. trait                   d. social-cognitive

4. Jill has a biting, sarcastic manner. According to Freud, she is:
   a. projecting her anxiety onto others.
   b. fixated in the oral stage of development.
   c. fixated in the anal stage of development.
   d. displacing her anxiety onto others.

5. James attributes his failing grade in chemistry to an unfair final exam. His attitude exemplifies:
   a. internal locus of control.
   b. unconditional positive regard.
   c. the self-serving bias.
   d. reciprocal determinism.

6. Being fed up with your cultural background, you decide to move to a culture that places greater value on maintaining social harmony and family identity. To which of the following countries should you move?
   a. the United States       d. Japan
   b. Canada                  e. Great Britain
   c. Australia

7. Because you have a relatively low level of brain arousal, the Eysencks would suggest that you are a(n) _____ who would naturally seek _____ .

   a. introvert; stimulation
   b. introvert; isolation
   c. extravert; stimulation
   d. extravert; isolation

8. A psychologist at the campus mental health center administered an empirically derived personality test to diagnose an emotionally troubled student. Which test did the psychologist *most likely* administer?

   a. the MMPI
   b. the TAT
   c. the Rorschach
   d. the Locus of Control Scale

9. The personality test Teresa is taking involves her describing random patterns of dots. What type of test is she taking?

   a. an empirically derived test
   b. the MMPI
   c. a personality inventory
   d. the Myers-Briggs Type Indicator
   e. a projective test

10. Dr. Gonzalez believes that most students can be classified as "Type A" or "Type B" according to the intensities of their personalities and competitiveness. Evidently, Dr. Gonzalez is working within the _____ perspective.

    a. psychoanalytic      c. humanistic
    b. trait               d. social-cognitive

11. According to the psychoanalytic perspective, a child who frequently "slips" and calls her teacher "mom" *probably*:

    a. has some unresolved conflicts concerning her mother.
    b. is fixated in the oral stage of development.
    c. did not receive unconditional positive regard from her mother.
    d. can be classified as having a weak sense of personal control.

12. Isaiah is sober and reserved; Rashid is fun-loving and affectionate. The Eysencks would say that Isaiah _____ and Rashid _____ .

    a. has an internal locus of control; has an external locus of control
    b. has an external locus of control; has an internal locus of control

    c. is an extravert; is an introvert
    d. is an introvert; is an extravert

13. In high school Britta and Debbie were best friends. They thought they were a lot alike, as did everyone else who knew them. After high school they went on to very different colleges, careers, and life courses. Now, at their twenty-fifth reunion, they are shocked at how little they have in common. Bandura would suggest that their differences reflect the interactive effects of environment, personality, and behavior, which he refers to as:

    a. reciprocal determinism.
    b. personal control.
    c. identification.
    d. the self-serving bias.

14. For his class presentation, Bruce plans to discuss the Big Five personality factors used by people throughout the world to describe others or themselves. Which of the following is *not* a factor that Bruce will discuss?

    a. extraversion        d. conscientiousness
    b. openness            e. agreeableness
    c. independence

15. Dayna is not very consistent in showing up for class and turning in assignments when they are due. Research studies would suggest that Dayna's inconsistent behavior:

    a. indicates that she is emotionally troubled and may need professional counseling.
    b. is a sign of learned helplessness.
    c. is not necessarily unusual.
    d. probably reflects a temporary problem in another area of her life.

16. Andrew's grandfather, who has lived a rich and productive life, is a spontaneous, loving, and self-accepting person. Maslow might say that he:

    a. has an internal locus of control.
    b. is an extravert.
    c. has resolved all the conflicts of the psychosexual stages.
    d. is a self-actualizing person.

17. The school psychologist believes that having a positive self-concept is necessary before students can achieve their potential. Evidently, the school psychologist is working within the _____ perspective.

    a. psychoanalytic      c. humanistic
    b. trait               d. social-cognitive

18. Wanda wishes to instill in her children an accepting attitude toward other people. Maslow and Rogers would probably recommend that she:
    a. teach her children first to accept themselves.
    b. use discipline sparingly.
    c. be affectionate with her children only when they behave as she wishes.
    d. do all of the above.

19. Suzy bought a used, high-mileage automobile because it was all she could afford. Attempting to justify her purchase, she raves to her friends about the car's attractiveness, good acceleration, and stereo. According to Freud, Suzy is using the defense mechanism of:
    a. displacement.          c. rationalization.
    b. reaction formation.    d. projection.

20. Nadine has a relatively low level of brain arousal. The Eysencks would probably predict that she is:
    a. an extravert.          c. an unstable person.
    b. an introvert.          d. both a. and c.

## Essay Question

You are an honest, open, and responsible person. Discuss how these characteristics would be explained according to the four major perspectives on personality. (Use the space below to list points you want to make and organize them. Then write the essay on a separate piece of paper.)

# Key Terms

## Writing Definitions

Using your own words, on a separate piece of paper write a brief definition or explanation of each of the following terms.

1. personality
2. free association
3. psychoanalysis
4. unconscious
5. preconscious
6. id
7. ego
8. superego
9. psychosexual stages
10. Oedipus complex
11. identification
12. fixation
13. defense mechanisms
14. repression
15. regression
16. reaction formation
17. projection
18. rationalization
19. displacement
20. sublimation
21. collective unconscious
22. projective tests
23. Thematic Apperception Test (TAT)
24. Rorschach inkblot test
25. traits
26. personality inventory
27. Minnesota Multiphasic Personality Inventory (MMPI)
28. empirically derived test
29. self-actualization
30. unconditional positive regard
31. self-concept
32. self-esteem
33. self-serving bias
34. individualism
35. collectivism
36. reciprocal determinism
37. personal control
38. external locus of control
39. internal locus of control
40. learned helplessness

*Cross-Check*

As you learned in the Introduction, reviewing and overlearning of material are important to the learning process. After you have written the definitions of the key terms in this chapter, you should complete the crossword puzzle to ensure that you can reverse the process—recognize the term, given the definition.

**ACROSS**

5. Defense mechanism in which an impulse is shifted to an object other than the one that originally aroused the impulse.
7. A cultural emphasis on personal goals over group goals.
13. In Freud's theory, the personality system consisting of basic sexual and aggressive drives.
16. Locus of control that reflects the belief that one's fate is determined by forces not under personal control.
17. In Freud's theory, the conscious division of personality.
19. Projective test consisting of ambiguous pictures about which people are asked to make up stories.
20. Defense mechanism in which a person reverts to a less mature pattern of behavior.

**DOWN**

1. In Freud's theory, the complex developed by boys in which they are sexually attracted to their mother and resent their father.
2. People's characteristic patterns of behavior and conscious motives.
3. Type of test developed by testing many items to see which best distinguish between groups of interest.
4. A person's sense of being male or female.
6. The passive resignation a person or animal develops from repeated exposure to inescapable aversive events.
8. The ego's methods of unconsciously protecting itself against anxiety.

9. In Freud's theory, the process by which the child's superego develops and incorporates the parents' values.
10. The most widely used personality inventory.
11. In Freud's theory, the area of the unconscious containing material that is retrievable into conscious awareness.
12. The TAT and Rorschach are examples of a

    _____ _____.
14. An individual's characteristic pattern of thinking, feeling, and acting.
15. A widely used test in which people are asked to interpret ten inkblots.
18. According to Freud, _____ occurs when development becomes arrested in an immature psychosexual stage.

# ANSWERS

## Guided Study

The following guidelines provide the main points that your answers should have touched upon.

1.  While experimenting with hypnosis, Freud discovered the unconscious. He later began using free association instead of hypnosis, believing that this technique triggered a chain of thoughts leading into a patient's unconscious, thereby retrieving and releasing painful unconscious memories.

    Psychoanalysis is based on Freud's belief that below our surface consciousness is a much larger, unconscious region that contains thoughts, feelings, wishes, and memories of which we are unaware. Although some of these thoughts are held in a preconscious area and can be retrieved at will into consciousness, some unacceptable thoughts and wishes are forcibly blocked, or repressed, from consciousness. These unconscious thoughts and urges often are expressed in troubling symptoms.

2.  To Freud, personality is composed of three interacting, and often conflicting, systems: the id, ego, and superego. Operating on the pleasure principle, the unconscious id strives to satisfy basic drives to survive, reproduce, and aggress. Operating on the reality principle, the ego seeks to gratify the id's impulses in realistic and nondestructive ways. The superego, which represents the individual's internalization of the morals and values of parents and culture, forces the ego to consider not only the real but also the ideal. Because the ego must intervene among the impulsive demands of the id, the restraining demands of the superego, and those of the external world, it is the personality "executive."

3.  Freud believed that children pass through a series of psychosexual stages, during which the id's pleasure-seeking energies focus on particular erogenous zones. Between birth and 18 months (oral stage), pleasure centers on the mouth. Between 18 and 36 months (anal stage), pleasure focuses on bowel and bladder retention and elimination. Between 3 and 6 years (phallic stage), the pleasure zone shifts to the genitals and boys develop unconscious sexual desires for their mothers and the fear that their fathers will punish them (Oedipus complex). Children eventually cope with these threatening feelings by repressing them and identifying with their same-sex parent.

    Between 6 years of age and puberty (latency stage), sexual feelings are repressed and redirected. At puberty, sexual interests mature as youths begin to experience sexual feelings toward others (genital stage).

4.  According to Freud, maladaptive adult behavior results from unresolved conflicts during earlier psychosexual stages. Such unresolved conflicts may cause the person's pleasure-seeking energies to become fixated in one psychosexual stage, leading to later problem behaviors or distinctive personality characteristics.

    Defense mechanisms are the ego's attempt to reduce or redirect anxiety by distorting reality. Examples of defense mechanisms include the banishing of thoughts from consciousness (repression), retreating to behavior characteristic of an earlier stage (regression), turning threatening impulses into their opposites (reaction formation) or attributing them to others (projection), self-justification of unacceptable actions (rationalization), diverting sexual or aggressive impulses to a more acceptable object (displacement), and transforming unacceptable impulses into socially valued activities (sublimation).

5.  The neo-Freudians placed more emphasis than Freud on the role of the conscious mind in determining personality, and less emphasis on sex and aggression as all-consuming motivations. Alfred Adler and Karen Horney emphasized the importance of social rather than sexual tensions in the formation of the child's personality. Horney also countered the male bias inherent in Freud's theory. Carl Jung expanded Freud's view of the unconscious into the idea of a collective unconscious, a common reservoir of thoughts derived from the experiences of our ancestors.

    Psychodynamic theorists downplay the importance of sex in personality formation. However, they do agree with Freud that much of mental life is unconscious, that childhood shapes personality and attachment, and that we often struggle with inner conflicts.

6.  Projective tests, such as the Thematic Apperception Test and the Rorschach inkblot test, ask people to describe or tell a story about an ambiguous stimulus that has no inherent meaning. In doing so, people presumably project their own interests and conflicts and provide a sort of psychological "x-ray" of their personalities. Despite their widespread use, projective tests are considered by most researchers to be lacking in validity and reliability. For example, there is no single accepted scoring system for interpreting

the Rorschach, so two raters may not interpret a subject's responses similarly (although a new computer-aided scoring and interpretation tool is improving agreement among raters and enhancing validity). Furthermore, the test is not very successful at predicting future behavior or discriminating between groups.

7. Freud's idea that development is fixed in childhood has been contradicted by research showing that development is lifelong. It is also clear that children gain their gender identity earlier than Freud believed and become strongly feminine or masculine even without a same-sex parent present. Freud's theory of dreams, memory losses, and defense mechanisms as disguising unfulfilled or repressed urges also has been disputed, as has his idea about the natural superiority of men. Today's researchers contend that repression is actually quite rare and, contrary to Freud's views, occurs as a mental response to terrible trauma. In addition, Freud's theory has been criticized for offering after-the-fact explanations of behavior, yet failing to generate testable predictions of those behaviors. Freud's ideas concerning our limited access to all that goes on in the mind, the importance of sexuality, our attempts to defend ourselves against anxiety, and the tension between our biological impulses and our social well-being have endured, however.

8. Trait theories define personality in terms of identifiable behavior patterns and conscious motives. As compared with psychoanalytic theories, they are less concerned with explaining personality and more concerned with its description.

A popular procedure today, especially in business and career counseling, is to classify people according to Carl Jung's personality types using the Myers-Briggs Type Indicator.

The statistical technique called factor analysis is used to identify clusters of personality test items that make up basic traits. Hans and Sybil Eysenck believe that many of the personality traits researchers have identified using factor analysis can be reduced to two genetically influenced dimensions: extraversion-introversion and emotional stability-instability. They further believe that extraverts seek stimulation because their level of brain arousal is relatively low.

9. Across the world people describe others in terms roughly consistent with these five trait dimensions: emotional stability, extraversion, openness, agreeableness, and conscientiousness.

To assess traits, psychologists use trait scales that measure single traits or personality inventories that assess several traits at once. In contrast to the subjectivity of projective tests, personality inventories are scored objectively. The most widely used personality inventory is the Minnesota Multiphasic Personality Inventory (MMPI) for assessing psychological disorders. The MMPI is an empirically derived test that contains 10 clinical scales, several validity scales, and 15 content scales.

10. To be a genuine personality trait, a characteristic must persist over time and across situations. Critics of this perspective question the consistency of traits. Although people's traits do seem to persist over time, research has revealed much less consistency of specific behaviors from one situation to another. However, although people do not act with perfect consistency, their *average* behavior over *many* situations is predictable.

11. The humanistic perspective emerged as a reaction against several other perspectives on personality. In contrast to Freud's study of the negative motives of "sick" people, the humanistic psychologists have focused on the strivings of "healthy" people. Unlike the trait theorists, they view people as whole persons, rather than as collections of individual traits.

Maslow proposed that people are motivated by a hierarchy of needs and that if basic needs are fulfilled, people will strive to reach their highest potential (self-actualization). Carl Rogers agreed with much of Maslow's thinking, adding that people nurture others' actualizing tendencies by being genuine, accepting, and empathic. For both theorists a central feature of personality is a person's self-concept.

12. Research on the self documents the concept of possible selves, including people's visions of the self or selves they would like to become in motivating their behavior. Another finding is that people with high self-esteem have fewer physical problems, strive more at difficult tasks, and are happier than people with low self-esteem. One of the most firmly established findings is people's readiness to perceive themselves favorably through the self-serving bias. This bias is revealed in the willingness of people to accept responsibility for good deeds and successes more readily than for bad deeds and failures, and in the tendency of people to see themselves as better than average on nearly any desirable dimension.

13. Contrary to popular belief, and despite discrimination and lower social status, ethnic minorities, people with disabilities, and women do not suffer lower self-esteem.

Individualist cultures nurture the development of personal goals and define identity in terms of individual attributes. Collectivist cultures give priority to the goals of their groups—often the family, clan, or work group. While individualists easily move in and out of social groups, collectivists have fewer but deeper, more stable attachments to their groups and friends. Collectivist cultures also place a premium on maintaining harmony and allowing others to save face. People in individualist cultures have greater personal freedom and more privacy. But compared to collectivists, individualists also tend to be lonelier, more likely to divorce, more homicidal, and more vulnerable to stress-related diseases.

14. The ideas of humanistic psychologists have influenced counseling, education, child-rearing, and management. Critics contend, however, that the concepts of humanistic psychology are vague, subjective, and so focused on the individual that they promote self-indulgence, selfishness, and an erosion of moral restraints. Furthermore, the humanistic psychologists have been accused of being naively optimistic and unrealistic, and failing to appreciate the human capacity for evil.

15. The social-cognitive perspective applies principles of learning, cognition, and social behavior to personality and emphasizes the ways in which our personalities shape and are shaped by external events. Reciprocal determinism refers to the ways in which our personalities are influenced by the interaction of our situations, our thoughts and feelings, and our behaviors. There are many examples of reciprocal determinism. For one, different people choose different environments. For another, our personalities shape how we interpret and react to events. Finally, our personalities help create situations to which we react.

16. Whether people see themselves as controlling, or being controlled by, their environments is an important aspect of their personalities. Research reveals that people who perceive an internal locus of control achieve more in school and are more independent, less depressed, better able to delay gratification, and better able to cope with various life stresses than people who perceive an external locus of control. Seligman found that animals and people who experience uncontrollable negative events may perceive a lack of control in their lives and develop the passive resignation of learned helplessness. One measure of how helpless or effective people feel is whether they generally are optimistic or pessimistic.

17. Social-cognitive researchers study personality by exploring the effect of differing situations on peo-

ple's behavior patterns and attitudes. This perspective has increased our awareness of how social situations influence, and are influenced by, individuals. Critics contend, however, that the theory focuses so much on the situation that it ignores the importance of people's inner traits, unconscious motives, and emotions in the formation of personality.

## Chapter Review

1. thinking; feeling; acting; personality
2. psychoanalytic; trait; humanistic; social-cognitive
3. Sigmund Freud
4. free association
5. psychoanalysis
6. unconscious; preconscious; repressed
7. unconscious; slips; manifest content; latent content
8. biological; social
9. id; ego; superego
10. unconscious; pleasure
11. after; conscious; reality

The ego is considered the executive of personality because it directs our actions as it intervenes among the impulsive demands of the id, the reality of the external world, and the ideals of the superego.

12. superego
13. weak; strong
14. psychosexual
15. oral; sucking (also biting, chewing)
16. anal; 18; 3
17. phallic; 3; 6; genitals; opposite; Oedipus complex; Electra complex
18. identification; gender identity

Children eventually cope with their feelings for the opposite-sex parent by repressing them and by identifying with the rival (same-sex) parent. Through this process children incorporate many of their parents' values, thereby strengthening the superego.

19. latency
20. genital
21. fixated
22. defense mechanisms; repression
23. regression
24. reaction formation
25. projection
26. rationalization

27. displacement
28. sublimation

*Matching Items*

1. e
2. d
3. b
4. c
5. a
6. f

29. unconscious
30. neo-Freudians; more; less
   a. Adler emphasized the social, rather than the sexual, tensions of childhood.
   b. Horney questioned the male bias in Freud's theory, such as the assumptions that women have weak egos and suffer "penis envy." Like Adler, she emphasized social tensions.
   c. Jung emphasized an inherited collective unconscious.
31. psychodynamic; sex; unconscious; childhood; inner conflicts
32. projective
33. Thematic Apperception
34. Rorschach; inkblots; little
35. lifelong; earlier; is not; have; sexual repression
36. represses; rarer; trauma
37. information

Contemporary researchers contend that the unconscious involves schemas that control our perceptions, implicit memories, the priming effect of stimuli, emotions that are activated before conscious analysis, our self-concept, and stereotypes that automatically influence how we process information about ourselves and others.

38. testable predictions
39. behaviors; motives
40. explaining; describing
41. Myers-Briggs Type Indicator; business; career
42. factor analysis; extraversion-introversion; stability-instability; extraverts; brain arousal; stable; autonomic nervous systems; unstable
43. biologically; shyness; inhibition; genes; temperament; behavioral
44. a. Emotional stability: calm vs. anxious; secure vs. insecure
   b. Extraversion: sociable vs. retiring
   c. Openness: preference for variety vs. routine
   d. Agreeableness: soft-hearted vs. ruthless
   e. Conscientiousness: disciplined vs. impulsive
45. personality inventories; Minnesota Multiphasic Personality Inventory; empirically
46. traits (or dispositions); situation (or environment)
47. time; situations; variable
48. is not

At any given moment a person's behavior is powerfully influenced by the immediate situation, so that it may appear that the person does not have a consistent personality. But averaged over many situations a person's outgoingness, happiness, and carelessness, for instance, are more predictable.

49. Maslow; Rogers
50. hierarchy; self-actualization

For Maslow, such people were self-aware, self-accepting, open, spontaneous, loving, caring, secure, and problem-centered rather than self-centered.

51. genuine; accepting; empathic; unconditional positive regard
52. self-concept
53. increased
54. possible selves
55. self-esteem; independent of; anxiety; depression
56. hopes; think they ought to be
57. more; racial prejudice
58. do not have
59. a. They value the things at which they excel.
   b. They attribute problems to prejudice.
   c. They compare themselves to those in their own group.
60. high
61. self-serving
62. more
63. above
64. individualist; collectivist

Individualists identify themselves in terms of their personal convictions and values. They strive for personal control and individual achievement. Collectivists give priority to their groups and define their identity accordingly. They place a premium on maintaining harmony and allowing others to save face.

65. collectivist; individualist; freedom; loneliness; divorce; homicide; stress-related
66. increased

Humanistic psychology is criticized for being vague and subjective, for encouraging self-indulgence and selfishness, and for failing to appreciate the capacity of humans for evil.

67. environment; Bandura

**68.** behaviors; personal; environmental; reciprocal determinism

Different people choose different environments partly on the basis of their dispositions. Our personality shapes how we interpret and react to events. It also helps create the situations to which we react.

**69.** internal locus of control; external locus of control

**70.** learned helplessness

**71.** more

**72.** optimism

**73.** past behavior in similar situations

One criticism is that the theory has overemphasized situational influences to the neglect of inner traits.

Astrologers use a "stock spiel" that includes information that is generally true of almost everyone. The willingness of people to accept this type of phony information is called the "Barnum effect." A second technique used by astrologers is to "read" a person's clothing, features, reactions, etc. and build their advice from these observations.

**74. a.** The psychoanalytic perspective has drawn attention to the unconscious and irrational aspects of personality.

    **b.** The trait perspective has systematically described and measured important components of personality.

    **c.** The humanistic perspective emphasizes the healthy potential of personality and the importance of our sense of self.

    **d.** The social-cognitive perspective emphasizes that we always act in the context of situations that we help to create.

## Progress Test 1

### Multiple-Choice Questions

**1. b.** is the answer. Personality is defined as patterns of response—of thinking, feeling, and acting—that are relatively consistent across a variety of situations. (p. 389)

**2. d.** is the answer. (p. 390)
**a. & b.** Conscious processes are the focus of these perspectives.
**c.** The trait perspective focuses on the description of behaviors.

**3. a.** is the answer. (p. 392)

**4. c.** is the answer. According to Freud, defense mechanisms reduce anxiety unconsciously, by disguising one's threatening impulses. (p. 393)
**a., b., & d.** Unlike these specific emotions, anxiety need not be focused. Defense mechanisms help us cope when we are unsettled but are not sure why.

**5. e.** is the answer. (pp. 411–412)

**6. b.** is the answer. (p. 394)
**a.** According to most neo-Freudians, Freud placed too great an emphasis on the *unconscious* mind.
**c.** Freud placed great emphasis on early childhood, and the neo-Freudians basically agreed with him.
**d.** The neo-Freudians accepted Freud's ideas about the basic personality structures.

**7. c.** is the answer. (p. 417)
**a., d., & e.** In fact, just the opposite is true.
**b.** Locus of control is not related to intelligence.

**8. a.** is the answer. (p. 401)
**b. & c.** Locus of control is emphasized by the social-cognitive perspective.
**d.** This is how the ancient Greeks described personality.

**9. b.** is the answer. Studies have shown that people do not act with predictable consistency from one situation to the next. But, over a number of situations, consistent patterns emerge, and this basic consistency of traits persists over the life span. (pp. 404–405)

**10. b.** is the answer. (p. 406)
**a.** This is true of the psychoanalytic perspective.
**c.** This is true of the social-cognitive perspective.
**d.** This is true of the trait perspective.

**11. e.** is the answer. (p. 407)

**12. b.** is the answer. Humanistic psychologists emphasize that for the individual, self-affirming thinking is generally adaptive (therefore, not a.); such thinking maintains self-confidence, minimizes depression, and enables us to view others with compassion and understanding (therefore, not c.); unconditional positive regard tends to promote self-esteem and thus self-affirming thinking (therefore, not d.). (pp. 410–411)

**13. a.** is the answer. Developmental research indicates that development is lifelong. (p. 396)
**b., c., & d.** To varying degrees, research has partially supported these Freudian ideas.

**14. b.** is the answer. (p. 411)
**a. & c.** These are characteristics of collectivist cultures.

**15. c.** is the answer. As scoring is largely subjective and the tests have not been very successful in predicting behavior, their reliability and validity have been called into question. (p. 396)
**a.** This is untrue.
**b.** Unlike empirically derived personality tests, projective tests are not standardized.

**d.** Although this may be true, it was not mentioned as a criticism of projective tests.

16. **b.** is the answer. In doing so it underestimates the influence of the environment. (pp. 404–405)
**a.** The trait perspective does not emphasize early childhood experiences.
**c.** This criticism is unlikely since trait theory does not seek to explain personality development.
**d.** Trait theory does not look on traits as being "positive" or "negative."

17. **d.** is the answer. (p. 407)
**a. & c.** Personality structure is a concern of the psychoanalytic perspective.
**b.** Locus of control is a major focus of the social-cognitive perspective.

18. **c.** is the answer. (p. 402)
**a. & d.** A psychoanalytic theorist would be most likely to use a projective test or free association.
**b.** This would most likely be the approach taken by a social-cognitive theorist.

19. **b.** is the answer. In Freud's theory, the id operates according to the pleasure principle; the ego operates according to the reality principle. (p. 391)
**c.** The id is presumed to be unconscious.
**d.** The superego is, according to Freud, the equivalent of a conscience; the ego is the "personality executive."

20. **b.** is the answer. The social-cognitive theory has been accused of putting so much emphasis on the situation that inner traits are neglected. (p. 420)
**a.** Such a criticism has been made of the psychoanalytic perspective but is not relevant to the social-cognitive perspective.
**c.** Such a criticism might be more relevant to the trait perspective; the social-cognitive perspective offers an explanation in the form of reciprocal determinism.
**d.** There are assessment techniques appropriate to the theory, namely, questionnaires and observations of behavior in situations.

*Matching Items*

1. f (p. 393)
2. k (p. 396)
3. b (p. 391)
4. l (p. 402)
5. i (p. 393)
6. d (p. 393)
7. a (p. 391)
8. h (p. 401)
9. c (p. 392)
10. e (p. 393)
11. j (p. 395)
12. g (p. 394)

## Progress Test 2

*Multiple-Choice Questions*

1. **d.** is the answer. (p. 415)
**a.** This perspective emphasizes unconscious dynamics in personality.

**b.** This perspective is more concerned with *describing* than *explaining* personality.
**c.** This perspective emphasizes the healthy, self-actualizing tendencies of personality.

2. **d.** is the answer. (p. 391)
**a.** Self-actualization is a concept of the humanistic perspective.
**b.** Through identification, children *reduce* conflicting feelings as they incorporate their parents' values.
**c.** Jung, rather than Freud, proposed the concept of the collective unconscious.

3. **a.** is the answer. (p. 401)

4. **c.** is the answer. In such situations, passive resignation, called learned helplessness, develops. (p. 417)
**a.** This refers to the belief that one controls one's fate; the circumstances described lead to precisely the opposite belief.
**b.** Reaction formation is a defense mechanism in which unacceptable impulses are channeled into their opposites.
**d.** Seligman did not specify that neurotic anxiety occurs.

5. **a.** is the answer. Feelings of insecurity reduce self-esteem, and those who feel negative about themselves tend to feel negative about others as well. (p. 409)

6. **e.** is the answer. (p. 410)

7. **b.** is the answer. The MMPI was developed by selecting from many items those that differentiated between the groups of interest; hence, it was empirically derived. That it is an objective test is shown by the fact that it can be scored by computer. (pp. 402–403)
**a.** Projective tests present ambiguous stimuli for people to interpret; the MMPI is a questionnaire.
**c.** Although sometimes used to assess job applicants, the MMPI was developed to assess emotionally troubled people.
**d.** The MMPI does not focus on control but, rather, measures various aspects of personality.

8. **b.** is the answer. Trait theory attempts to describe behavior and not to develop explanations or applications. The emphasis is more on consistency than on change. (p. 400)

9. **a.** is the answer. "Internals," or those who have a sense of personal control, have been shown to achieve more in school. Relative to externals, they also cope better with stress and are more independent. (p. 417)

10. **c.** is the answer. In actuality, people with *high* self-esteem are generally more independent of pressures to conform. (pp. 408–409)

**11. d.** is the answer. (p. 392)

**12. d.** is the answer. (pp. 414–415)

**13. c.** is the answer. In keeping with their emphasis on interactions between people and situations, social-cognitive theorists would most likely make use of observations of behavior in relevant situations. (p. 420)
**a. & d.** Personality inventories and factor analyses would more likely be used by a trait theorist.
**b.** Projective tests would more likely be used by a psychologist working within the psychoanalytic perspective.

**14. d.** is the answer. Trait theory defines personality in terms of behavior and is therefore interested in describing behavior; psychoanalytic theory defines personality as dynamics underlying behavior and therefore is interested in explaining behavior in terms of these dynamics. (pp. 390–391, 400–401)

**15. d.** is the answer. (pp. 411–413)

**16. d.** is the answer. (p. 402)

**17. c.** is the answer. Although many researchers think of the unconscious as information processing without awareness rather than as a reservoir of repressed information, they agree with Freud that we do indeed have limited access to all that goes on in our minds. (p. 398)

**18. c.** is the answer. (p. 392)
**a. & b.** Reaction formation is the defense mechanism by which people transform unacceptable impulses into their opposites.
**d.** It is the superego, rather than the ego, that represents parental values.

**19. e.** is the answer. (p. 409)

**20. d.** is the answer. (p. 407)

*Matching Items*

**1.** g (p. 395)      **5.** d (p. 392)      **9.** e (p. 402)
**2.** i (p. 392)      **6.** a (p. 391)      **10.** b (p. 392)
**3.** h (p. 395)      **7.** k (p. 403)      **11.** c (p. 390)
**4.** j (pp. 391–392)  **8.** f (p. 416)

## Thinking Critically About Chapter 11

*Multiple-Choice Questions*

**1. e.** is the answer. (p. 394)
**a.** Rationalization is a defense mechanism in which a person finds self-justifying explanations to replace the real, more threatening reasons for his or her actions.
**b.** With regression, a person retreats, when faced with anxiety, to a more infantile psychosexual stage.
**c.** With this defense mechanism, people disguise their own threatening impulses by attributing them to others.
**d.** Reaction formation is the defense mechanism by which people transform unacceptable impulses into their opposites.

**2. d.** is the answer. Impulsiveness is the mark of a strong id; self-indulgence is the mark of a weak superego. Because the ego serves to mediate the demands of the id, the superego, and the outside world, its strength or weakness is judged by its decision-making ability, not by the character of the decision—so the ego is not relevant to the question asked. (pp. 391–392)

**3. d.** is the answer. The social-cognitive perspective emphasizes the reciprocal influences between people and their situations. In this example, Ramona's parents (situational factor) helped shape her political beliefs (internal factor), which influenced her choice of colleges (situational factor), and created an environment that fostered her predisposed political attitudes. (p. 416)

**4. b.** is the answer. Sarcasm is said to be an attempt to deny the passive dependence characteristic of the oral stage. (p. 393)
**a.** A person who is projecting attributes his or her own feelings to others.
**c.** Such a person might be either messy and disorganized or highly controlled and compulsively neat.
**d.** Displacement involves diverting aggressive or sexual impulses onto a more acceptable object than that which aroused them.

**5. c.** is the answer. (p. 410)
**a.** A person with an internal locus of control would be likely to *accept* responsibility for a failing grade.
**b.** Unconditional positive regard is an attitude of total acceptance directed toward others.
**d.** Reciprocal determinism refers to the mutual influences among personality, environment, and behavior.

**6. d.** is the answer. Of the countries listed, only Japan has a collectivist culture that emphasizes family identity and social harmony. (p. 411)

**7. c.** is the answer. (pp. 401–402)
**a. & b.** According to this theory, introverts have relatively *high* levels of arousal, causing them to crave solitude.
**d.** Isolation might lower arousal level even further.

8. **a.** is the answer. (p. 402)

   **b. & c.** The TAT and Rorschach are projective tests that were not empirically derived.

   **d.** A personality test that measures locus of control would not be helpful in identifying troubled behaviors.

9. **e.** is the answer. Projective tests provide ambiguous stimuli, such as random dot patterns, in an attempt to trigger in the test-taker projection of his or her personality. (p. 395)

10. **b.** is the answer. (p. 400)

    **a.** The psychoanalytic perspective emphasizes unconscious processes in personality dynamics.

    **c.** The humanistic perspective emphasizes each person's potential for healthy growth and self-actualization.

    **d.** The social-cognitive perspective emphasizes the reciprocal influences of personality and environment.

11. **a.** is the answer. Freud believed that dreams and such slips of the tongue reveal unconscious conflicts. (p. 391)

    **b.** A person fixated in the oral stage might have a sarcastic personality; this child's slip of the tongue reveals nothing about her psychosexual development.

    **c. & d.** Unconditional positive regard and personal control are not psychoanalytic concepts.

12. **d.** is the answer. (p. 401)

    **a. & b.** The traits of Isaiah and Rashid reveal nothing about their sense of personal control.

13. **a.** is the answer. Reciprocal determinism refers to the mutual influences among personal factors, environmental factors, and behavior. (p. 416)

    **b.** Personal control is one's sense of controlling, or being controlled by, the environment.

    **c.** In Freud's theory, identification is the process by which children incorporate parental values into their developing superegos.

    **d.** The self-serving bias describes our readiness to perceive ourselves favorably.

14. **c.** is the answer. (p. 402)

15. **c.** is the answer. (pp. 404–405)

16. **d.** is the answer. (p. 406)

    **a. & b.** These are concepts used by trait theorists rather than humanistic theorists such as Maslow.

    **c.** This reflects Freud's viewpoint.

17. **c.** is the answer. (p. 407)

    **a., b., & d.** The self-concept is not relevant to the psychoanalytic, trait, or social-cognitive perspectives.

18. **a.** is the answer. (p. 407)

**b.** The text does not discuss the impact of discipline on personality.

**c.** This would constitute *conditional*, rather than unconditional, positive regard and would likely cause the children to be *less* accepting of themselves and others.

19. **c.** is the answer. Suzy is trying to justify her purchase by generating (inaccurate) explanations for her behavior. (p. 393)

    **a.** Displacement is the redirecting of impulses toward an object other than the one responsible for them.

    **b.** Reaction formation is the transformation of unacceptable impulses into their opposites.

    **d.** Projection is the attribution of one's own unacceptable thoughts and feelings to others.

20. **a.** is the answer. The Eysencks believe that extraverts are predisposed to seek stimulation because their normal level of brain arousal is relatively low. (p. 401)

    **c.** Nadine's low level of brain arousal would, if anything, be related to a *stable* personality, according to the Eysencks.

## Essay Question

Since you are apparently in good psychological health, according to the psychoanalytic perspective you must have experienced a healthy childhood and successfully passed Freud's stages of psychosexual development. Freud would also say that your ego is functioning well in balancing the demands of your id with the restraining demands of your superego and reality. Freud might also say that your honest nature reflects a well-developed superego, while Jung might say it derives from a universal value found in our collective unconscious.

Trait theorists would be less concerned with explaining these specific characteristics than with describing them, determining their consistency, and classifying your personality type. Some trait theorists, such as Allport, Eysenck, and Kagan, attribute certain trait differences to biological factors such as autonomic reactivity and heredity.

According to the humanistic perspective, your open and honest nature indicates that your basic needs have been met and you are in the process of self-actualization (Maslow). Furthermore, your openness indicates that you have a healthy self-concept and were likely nurtured by genuine, accepting, and empathic caregivers (Rogers).

According to the social-cognitive perspective, your personal factors, behavior, and environmental influences interacted in shaping your personality and behaviors. The fact that you are a responsible person indicates that you perceive yourself as controlling, rather than being controlled by, your environment.

## Key Terms

### Writing Definitions

1. **Personality** is an individual's characteristic pattern of thinking, feeling, and acting. (p. 389)

2. **Free association** is the Freudian technique in which the person is encouraged to say whatever comes to mind as a means of exploring the unconscious. (p. 390)

3. In Freud's theory, **psychoanalysis** refers to the treatment of psychological disorders by seeking to expose and interpret the tensions within a patient's unconscious, using methods such as free association. (p. 390)

4. In Freud's theory, the **unconscious** is the repository of mostly unacceptable thoughts, wishes, feelings, and memories. According to contemporary psychologists, it is a level of information processing of which we are unaware. (p. 390)

5. In Freud's theory, the **preconscious** area is a region of the unconscious that contains material that is retrievable at will into conscious awareness. (p. 390)   info out

   *Example:* The Freudian notion of a **preconscious** is similar to the concept of long-term memory: Material is accessible but not currently in our awareness.

6. In Freud's theory, the **id** is the unconscious system of personality, consisting of basic sexual and aggressive drives, that supplies psychic energy to personality. (p. 390)

7. In psychoanalytic theory, the **ego** is the conscious division of personality that attempts to mediate between the demands of the id, the superego, and reality. (p. 390)

8. In Freud's theory, the **superego** is the division of personality that contains the conscience and develops by incorporating the perceived moral standards of society. (p. 392)

9. Freud's **psychosexual stages** are childhood developmental periods during which the id's pleasure-seeking energies are focused on different erogenous zones. (p. 392)

10. According to Freud, boys in the phallic stage develop a collection of feelings, known as the **Oedipus complex**, that center on sexual attraction to the mother and resentment of the father.

Some psychoanalysts believe girls have a parallel Electra complex. (p. 392)

11. In Freud's theory, **identification** is the process by which the child's superego develops and incorporates the parents' values. Freud saw identification as crucial, not only to resolution of the Oedipus complex, but also to the development of gender identity. (p. 392)

12. In Freud's theory, **fixation** occurs when development becomes arrested, due to unresolved conflicts, in an immature psychosexual stage. (p. 393)

13. In Freud's theory, **defense mechanisms** are the ego's methods of unconsciously protecting itself against anxiety by distorting reality. (p. 393)

14. The basis of all defense mechanisms, **repression** is the unconscious exclusion of anxiety-arousing thoughts, feelings, and memories from the conscious mind. Repression is an example of motivated forgetting: One "forgets" what one really does not wish to remember. (p. 393)

15. **Regression** is the defense mechanism in which a person faced with anxiety reverts to a less mature pattern of behavior. (p. 393)

16. **Reaction formation** is the defense mechanism in which the ego converts unacceptable impulses into their opposites. (p. 393)

17. In psychoanalytic theory, **projection** is the unconscious attribution of one's own unacceptable feelings, attitudes, or desires to others. (p. 393)

    *Memory aid: To project* is to thrust outward. **Projection** is an example of thrusting one's own feelings outward to another person.

18. **Rationalization** is the defense mechanism in which one devises self-justifying but incorrect reasons for one's behavior. (p. 393)

19. **Displacement** is the defense mechanism in which a sexual or aggressive impulse is shifted to a more acceptable object other than the one that originally aroused the impulse. (p. 393)

20. **Sublimation** is the defense mechanism in which one rechannels unacceptable impulses into socially approved activities. (p. 394)

21. The **collective unconscious** is Jung's concept of an inherited unconscious shared by all people and deriving from our early ancestors' universal experiences. (p. 395)

22. **Projective tests**, such as the TAT and Rorschach, present ambiguous stimuli onto which people supposedly *project* their own inner feelings. (p. 395)

23. The **Thematic Apperception Test (TAT)** is a

projective test that consists of ambiguous pictures about which people are asked to make up stories. (p. 395)

24. The **Rorschach inkblot test**, the most widely used projective test, consists of ten inkblots that people are asked to interpret. (p. 396)

25. **Traits** are people's characteristic patterns of behavior. (p. 400)

26. **Personality inventories**, associated with the trait perspective, are questionnaires used to assess personality traits. (p. 402)

27. Consisting of ten clinical scales, the **Minnesota Multiphasic Personality Inventory (MMPI)** is the most widely used personality inventory. (p. 402)

28. An **empirically derived test** is one developed by testing many items to see which best distinguish between groups of interest. (p. 403)

29. In Maslow's theory, **self-actualization** describes the process of fulfilling one's potential and becoming spontaneous, loving, creative, and self-accepting. Self-actualization is at the very top of Maslow's need hierarchy and therefore becomes active only after the more basic physical and psychological needs have been met. (p. 406)

30. **Unconditional positive regard** is, according to Rogers, an attitude of total acceptance and one of the three conditions essential to a "growth-promoting" climate. (p. 407)

31. **Self-concept** refers to one's personal awareness of "who I am." In the humanistic perspective, the self-concept is a central feature of personality; life happiness is significantly affected by whether the self-concept is positive or negative. (p. 407)

32. In humanistic psychology, **self-esteem** refers to an individual's sense of self-worth. (p. 408)

33. The **self-serving bias** is the tendency to perceive oneself favorably. (p. 410)

34. **Individualism** is a cultural emphasis on personal goals over group goals, and defining one's identity in terms of personal attributes rather than group identifications. (p. 411)

35. **Collectivism** is a cultural emphasis on the goals of one's group, and defining one's identity accordingly. (p. 411)

36. According to the social-cognitive perspective, personality is shaped through **reciprocal determinism**, or the interaction between personality and environmental factors. (p. 416)

37. **Personal control** refers to a person's sense of controlling the environment. (p. 416)

38. **External locus of control** is the perception that one's fate is determined by forces not under personal control. (p. 417)

39. **Internal locus of control** is the perception that to a great extent one controls one's own destiny. (p. 417)

40. **Learned helplessness** is the passive resignation and perceived lack of control that a person or animal develops from repeated exposure to inescapable aversive events. (p. 417)

*Cross-Check*

**ACROSS**
5. displacement
7. individualism
13. id
16. external
17. ego
19. TAT
20. regression

**DOWN**
1. Oedipus
2. trait
3. empirically derived
4. gender identity
6. learned helplessness
8. defense mechanisms
9. identification
10. MMPI
11. preconscious
12. projective test
14. personality
15. Rorschach
18. fixation

3. Describe the system used to classify psychological disorders and explain the reasons for its development.

4. Discuss the controversy surrounding the use of diagnostic labels.

### Anxiety Disorders (pp. 431–437)

> If you do not know the meaning of any of the following words, phrases, or expressions in the context in which they appear in the text, refer to page 359 for an explanation: *ringing in the ears . . . fidgeting; flashbacks and nightmares; Grooming gone wild; road tested in the Stone Age.*

5. Describe the various anxiety disorders and discuss their possible causes.

### Dissociative Disorders (pp. 437–440)

> If you do not know the meaning of any of the following words, phrases, or expressions in the context in which they appear in the text, refer to page 359 for an explanation: *a ruse; go fishing for it.*

6. Describe the nature and possible causes of dissociative disorders.

### Mood Disorders (pp. 440–449)

> If you do not know the meaning of any of the following words, phrases, or expressions in the context in which they appear in the text, refer to pages 359–360 for an explanation: *To grind to a halt; blue mood; slow motion . . . fast forward; view life through dark glasses; sour our thinking; two-way traffic; company does not love another's misery.*

7. Describe the mood disorders and discuss the alternative explanations for their occurrence.

### Schizophrenia (pp. 449–455)

> If you do not know the meaning of any of the following words, phrases, or expressions in the context in which they appear in the text, refer to page 360 for an explanation: *hodge-podge; flat affect; traffic . . . runs both ways.*

8. Describe the symptoms of schizophrenia and discuss research on the causes of schizophrenia.

### Personality Disorders (pp. 455–456)

> If you do not know the meaning of any of the following words, phrases, or expressions in the context in which they appear in the text, refer to page 360 for an explanation: *con artist; woven of biological as well as psychological strands.*

9. Describe the nature and causes of personality disorders and the specific characteristics of the antisocial personality disorder.

*Rates of Psychological Disorders* (pp. 456–457)

10. Briefly discuss the prevalence of psychological disorders.

## Chapter Review

When you have finished reading the chapter, work through the material that follows to review it. Complete the sentences and answer the questions. As you proceed, evaluate your performance for each section by consulting the answers on page 352. Do not continue with the next section until you understand each answer. If you need to, review or reread the appropriate section in the textbook before continuing.

*Perspectives on Psychological Disorders* (pp. 426–431)

1. In order to be classified as psychologically disordered, behavior must be _____ ,

_____ , _____ ,

and _____ . This definition emphasizes that standards of acceptability for behavior are _____ (constant/variable).

2. The view that psychological disorders are sicknesses is the basis of the _____ model. According to this view, psychological disorders are viewed as mental _____ ,

or _____ .

3. One of the first reformers to advocate this position and call for providing more humane living

conditions for the mentally ill was

_____ .

4. Today's psychologists recognize that all behavior arises from the interaction of _____ and _____ . To presume that a person is "mentally ill" attributes the condition solely to an _____ problem.

5. Major psychological disorders such as _____ and _____ are universal; others, such as _____ and _____ , are culture-bound. These culture-bound disorders may share an underlying _____ , such as _____ , yet differ in their _____ .

6. Most mental health workers today work from the _____ - _____ - _____ perspective, which assumes that disorders are influenced by _____ , inner _____ _____ , and _____ and circumstances.

7. The most widely used system for classifying psychological disorders is the American Psychiatric Association manual, commonly known by its abbreviation, _____ .

8. Psychological illnesses that are severely impairing, called _____ _____ , are contrasted with _____ _____ , or psychological illnesses that allow the person to function socially. In general, DSM-IV now seeks to list and _____ the disorders, rather than attempting to _____ their causes.

9. Independent diagnoses made with the current manual generally _____ (show/do not show) agreement.

10. Studies have shown that labeling has _____ (little/a significant)

effect on our interpretation of individuals and their behavior.

Outline the pros and cons of labeling psychological disorders.

*Anxiety Disorders* (pp. 431–437)

11. When a person tends to feel anxious for no apparent reason, he or she is diagnosed as suffering from a _____ _____ disorder.

12. In generalized anxiety disorder, the body reacts physiologically with the arousal of the _____ nervous system.

13. In some instances anxiety may intensify dramatically and be accompanied by trembling or dizziness; people with these symptoms are said to have _____ _____ .

14. People who fear situations in which escape or help might not be possible when panic strikes suffer from _____ .

15. When a person has an irrational fear of a specific object, activity, or situation, the diagnosis is a _____ .

16. Compared with other disorders, phobias typically appear at a(n) _____ (earlier/later) age, often in the sufferer's _____ .

17. When a person cannot control repetitive thoughts and actions, an _____ - _____ disorder is diagnosed.

18. Freud assumed that anxiety disorders are symptoms of submerged mental energy that derives from intolerable impulses that were

_____ during childhood.

19. Learning theorists, drawing on research in which rats are given unpredictable shocks, link general anxiety with _____ conditioning of _____ .

20. Some fears arise from _____ _____ , such as when a person who fears heights after a fall also comes to fear airplanes.

21. Phobias and compulsive behaviors reduce anxiety and thereby are _____ . Through _____ learning someone might also learn fear by seeing others display their own fears.

22. Humans probably _____ (are/are not) biologically prepared to develop certain fears. Compulsive acts typically are exaggerations of behaviors that contributed to our species' _____ .

23. The anxiety response probably _____ (is/is not) genetically influenced.

24. PET scans of persons with obsessive-compulsive disorder reveal excessive activity in a region of the _____ lobes. Antidepressant drugs may reduce this activity by influencing the neurotransmitter _____ .

25. (Psychology Applied) Experiencing severely threatening, uncontrollable events can produce a _____ - _____ _____ disorder, symptoms of which include _____ _____ .

*Dissociative Disorders* (pp. 437–440)

26. In dissociative disorders, _____ _____ becomes dissociated, or _____ , from painful memories, thoughts, and feelings.

27. A person who experiences a sudden loss of

memory is suffering from _____
_____ . Such memory loss is
usually for _____
(all/selective) memories.

28. When an individual not only loses memory but
also runs away, _____
_____ has occurred.

29. A person who develops two or more distinct personalities is suffering from _____
_____ disorder. Those who
accept this as a genuine disorder point to evidence that differing personalities may be associated with distinct _____ and
_____ states.

30. Nicholas Spanos has argued that such people
may merely be playing different
_____ .

Identify two pieces of evidence brought forth by
those who do not accept dissociative identity disorder
as a genuine disorder.

31. The psychoanalytic and learning perspectives
view dissociative disorders as ways of dealing
with _____ . Others view them
as a protective response to histories of
_____ .
Skeptics claim these disorders are sometimes con-
trived by _____-
_____ people, and sometimes
constructed out of the _____-
_____ interaction.

*Mood Disorders* (pp. 440–449)

32. The experience of prolonged depression with no
discernible cause is called _____
_____ disorder.

33. When a person's mood alternates between
depression and the hyperactive state of
_____ , a
_____ disorder is diagnosed.

34. Although _____ are more common, _____ is the number one
reason that people seek mental health services.

35. In between the temporary blue moods everyone
experiences and major depression is a condition
called _____
_____ , in which a person feels
down-in-the-dumps nearly every day for two
years or more.

36. The possible signs of depression include
_____
_____ .

37. Major depression occurs when its signs persist
_____
or more with no apparent cause.

38. Depressed persons usually _____
(can/cannot) recover without therapy.

39. Symptoms of mania include _____
_____ .
The bipolar disorder occurs in approximately
_____ percent of men and
women.

40. Compared with men, women are _____
(more/less) vulnerable to major depression. In
general, women are most vulnerable to
_____ (active/passive) disorders, such as _____
_____ .
Men's disorders tend to be _____
(active/passive) and include _____
_____ .
Among college students the gender difference in
depression is _____ (quite
small/much larger).

41. It usually _____ (is/is not) the
case that a depressive episode has been triggered
by a stressful event.

State the psychoanalytic explanation of depression.

Describe how depressed people differ from others in their explanations of failure and how such explanations tend to feed depression.

42. Mood disorders _____ (tend/do not tend) to run in families. Studies of _____ also reveal that genetic influences on mood disorders are _____ (weak/strong).

43. To determine which genes are involved in depression, researchers use

_____ _____ , in which they examine the _____ of both affected and unaffected family members.

44. Depression may also be caused by _____ (high/low) levels of two neurotransmitters, _____ or _____ .

45. Drugs that alleviate mania reduce _____ ; drugs that relieve depression increase _____ or _____ by blocking their _____ or their chemical _____ .

46. The brains of depressed people tend to be _____ (more/less) active, especially in an area of the _____ _____ lobe of the brain. In severely depressed patients, this brain area may also be _____ (smaller/larger) in size.

47. According to the social-cognitive perspective, depression may be linked with beliefs that are _____ . Such beliefs may arise from _____ _____ , the feeling that can arise when the individual repeatedly experiences uncontrollable, painful events.

48. Research studies suggest that depressing thoughts usually _____ (precede/follow/coincide with) a depressed mood.

49. A depressed person tends to elicit social _____ (empathy/rejection).

Outline the vicious cycle of depression.

*Schizophrenia* (pp. 449–455)

50. Schizophrenia, or "split mind," refers not to a split personality but rather to a split from _____ .

51. Three manifestations of schizophrenia are disorganized _____ , disturbed _____ , and inappropriate _____ and _____ .

52. The distorted, false beliefs of schizophrenia patients are called _____ .

53. Many psychologists attribute the disorganized thinking of schizophrenia to a breakdown in the capacity for _____ _____ .

54. The disturbed perceptions of people suffering from schizophrenia may take the form of _____ , which usually are _____ (visual/auditory).

55. Some victims of schizophrenia lapse into a zombielike state of apparent apathy, or _____ ; others, who exhibit _____ , may remain motionless for hours.

56. The term *schizophrenia* describes a _____ (single disorder/cluster of disorders).

57. *Positive symptoms* of schizophrenia include

_____

_____ .

*Negative symptoms* include

_____

_____ .

58. When schizophrenia develops slowly (called _____ schizophrenia), recovery is _____ (more/less) likely than when it develops rapidly in reaction to particular life stresses (called _____ schizophrenia).

59. The brain tissue of schizophrenia patients has been found to have an excess of receptors for the neurotransmitter _____ . Drugs that block these receptors have been found to _____ (increase/decrease) schizophrenia symptoms.

60. Brain scans have shown that many people with schizophrenia have abnormal patterns of brain _____ in the frontal lobes.

61. Enlarged, _____ -filled areas and a corresponding _____ of cerebral tissue is also characteristic of schizophrenia. Schizophrenia patients also have a smaller-than-normal _____ , which may account for their difficulty in filtering

_____ and focusing _____ .

62. Some scientists contend that the brain abnormalities of schizophrenia may be caused by a prenatal problem, such as a _____ _____ contracted by the mother. List several pieces of evidence for this theory.

63. Twin and adoptive studies _____ (support/do not support) the contention that heredity plays a role in schizophrenia.

64. The role of the prenatal environment in schizophrenia is demonstrated by the fact that identical twins who share the same _____ , and are therefore more likely to experience the same prenatal _____ , are more likely to share the disorder.

65. It appears that for schizophrenia to develop there must be both a _____ predisposition and some _____ trigger.

*Personality Disorders* (pp. 455–456)

66. Personality disorders exist when an individual has character traits that are enduring and impair

_____ .

67. An individual who seems to have no conscience, lies, steals, is generally irresponsible, and may be criminal is said to have an _____ personality. Previously, this person was labeled a _____ .

68. Studies of the children of convicted criminals suggest that there _____ (is/is not) a biological predisposition to such traits.

69. When awaiting electric shocks, antisocial persons show _____ (more/less) arousal of the autonomic nervous system than do control subjects.

70. Some studies have detected early signs of antisocial behavior in children as young as _____ . Antisocial adolescents

tended to have been _____ ,

_____ , unconcerned with

_____ _____ ,

and low in _____ .

*Rates of Psychological Disorders* (pp. 456–457)

**71.** Research reveals that approximately

_____ percent of American

adults have at some time experienced a psycho-

logical disorder and that approximately

_____ percent have an active

disorder.

**72.** The incidence of serious psychological disorders

is _____ (higher/lower) among

those below the poverty line.

**73.** In terms of age of onset, most psychological dis-

orders appear by _____

(early/middle/late) adulthood. Some, such as the

_____ _____

and _____ , appear during

childhood.

**WEB SIGHTINGS**

The National Institute of Mental Health (NIMH)
(**http://www.nimh.nih.gov/home.htm**) maintains an
excellent web site for extending your exploration of
psychological disorders. Review the major diagnostic
categories and check out the latest research findings
regarding our understanding of the causes, prevention, and treatment of specific psychological disorders. Also see the Quicktime videos and animations
produced by NIMH's Clinical Brain Disorders
Branch. Tour NIMH-funded laboratories around the
United States and peek over the shoulders of
researchers as they describe their current experiments. And don't stop there! Use web links at this site
as jumping-off points to dozens of other Internet
resources that provide information about psychological disorders. To focus your tour, see if you can find
the answers to the following questions.

1. What is the *Human Brain Project*?

2. What is the estimated total annual economic
   impact of mental disorders in the United States?
   What are some of the hidden costs of mental disorders?

3. What have NIMH researchers recently learned
   about schizophrenia using state-of-the-art brain-
   imaging techniques?

4. What are the current (and future) research priorities of NIMH?

5. What is "clozapine treatment"? For whom is it
   intended? Does it work?

## Progress Test 1

*Multiple-Choice Questions*

Circle your answers to the following questions and
check them with the answers on page 353. If your
answer is incorrect, read the explanation for why it is
incorrect and then consult the appropriate pages of
the text (in parentheses following the correct answer).

**1.** Amnesia, fugue, and multiple personality are all
   examples of _____ disorders.
   a. anxiety              c. dissociative
   b. mood                 d. personality

**2.** The criteria for classifying behavior as psychologically disordered:
   a. vary from culture to culture.
   b. vary from time to time.
   c. are characterized by both a. and b.
   d. have remained largely unchanged over the
      course of history.

3. Most mental health workers today take the view that disordered behaviors:
   a. are usually genetically triggered.
   b. are organic diseases.
   c. arise from the interaction of nature and nurture.
   d. are the product of learning.

4. The French reformer who insisted that madness was not demon possession and who called for humane treatment of patients was:
   a. Nadel.         d. Spanos.
   b. Freud.         e. Pinel.
   c. Szasz.

5. Which of the following is the most pervasive of the psychological disorders?
   a. depression
   b. schizophrenia
   c. hypochondriasis
   d. generalized anxiety disorder
   e. dissociative amnesia

6. Which of the following is *not* true concerning depression?
   a. Depression is more common in females than in males.
   b. Most depressive episodes appear not to be preceded by any particular factor or event.
   c. Most depressive episodes last less than 3 months.
   d. Most people recover from depression without professional therapy.

7. Which of the following is *not* true regarding schizophrenia?
   a. It affects men and women about equally.
   b. It occurs more frequently in the lower socioeconomic classes.
   c. It occurs more frequently in industrialized countries.
   d. It usually appears during adolescence or early adulthood.

8. Evidence of environmental effects on psychological disorders is seen in the fact that certain disorders, such as _____ , are universal, whereas others, such as _____ , are culture-bound.
   a. schizophrenia; depression
   b. depression; schizophrenia
   c. antisocial personality; neurosis
   d. depression; anorexia nervosa

9. The effect of drugs that block receptors for dopamine is to:
   a. alleviate schizophrenia symptoms.
   b. alleviate depression.

   c. increase schizophrenia symptoms.
   d. increase depression.

10. The diagnostic reliability of DSM-IV:
    a. is unknown.
    b. depends on the age of the patient.
    c. is very low.
    d. is relatively high.

11. Researchers have found that people are at increased risk for schizophrenia if their country suffers a flu epidemic during their prenatal development. This provides evidence for the idea that a(n) _____ may be a contributing factor in the development of schizophrenia.
    a. excess of norepinephrine in the frontal lobes
    b. prenatal viral infection
    c. scarcity of testosterone
    d. scarcity of dopamine

12. The DSM-IV does not use the term *neurosis* as a diagnostic category because the term:
    a. presumes to explain the causes of disorders.
    b. implies a Freudian interpretation.
    c. is medically inappropriate.
    d. implies a focus on social factors.

13. Phobias and obsessive-compulsive behaviors are classified as:
    a. anxiety disorders.
    b. mood disorders.
    c. dissociative disorders.
    d. personality disorders.

14. According to the social-cognitive perspective, a person who experiences unexpected aversive events may develop helplessness and manifest a(n):
    a. obsessive-compulsive disorder.
    b. dissociative disorder.
    c. personality disorder.
    d. mood disorder.

15. Which of the following was presented in the text as evidence of biological influences on anxiety disorders?
    a. Identical twins often develop similar phobias.
    b. PET scans of persons with obsessive-compulsive disorder reveal unusually high activity in an area of the frontal lobes.
    c. Drugs that affect the neurotransmitter serotonin may control obsessive thoughts.
    d. All of the above were presented.
    e. None of the above was presented.

16. Most of the hallucinations of schizophrenia patients involve the sense of:
    a. smell.                     c. hearing.
    b. vision.                    d. touch.

17. When expecting to be electrically shocked, people with an antisocial disorder, as compared to normal people, show:
    a. less fear and greater arousal of the autonomic nervous system.
    b. less fear and less autonomic arousal.
    c. greater fear and greater autonomic arousal.
    d. greater fear and less autonomic arousal.

18. Hearing voices would be a(n) _____ ; believing that you are Napoleon would be a(n)

    _____ .

    a. obsession; compulsion
    b. compulsion; obsession

    c. delusion; hallucination
    d. hallucination; delusion

19. In treating depression, a psychiatrist would probably prescribe a drug that would:
    a. increase levels of acetylcholine.
    b. decrease levels of dopamine.
    c. increase levels of norepinephrine.
    d. decrease levels of serotonin.

20. When schizophrenia is slow to develop, called _____ schizophrenia, recovery is _____ .
    a. reactive; unlikely       c. process; unlikely
    b. process; likely          d. reactive; likely

*Matching Items*

Match each term with the appropriate definition or description.

*Terms*

_____  1. dissociative fugue
_____  2. psychotic disorder
_____  3. mood disorders
_____  4. dissociative disorders
_____  5. neurotic disorder
_____  6. mania
_____  7. obsessive-compulsive disorder
_____  8. schizophrenia
_____  9. hallucination
_____  10. panic attack

*Definitions or Descriptions*

a. psychological disorders marked by emotional extremes
b. an extremely elevated mood
c. a false sensory experience
d. any psychological disorder that is severely debilitating and involves bizarre thinking and behavior
e. a sudden escalation of anxiety often accompanied by a sensation of choking or other physical symptoms
f. a dissociative disorder in which the person flees from home and identity
g. any psychological disorder in which the person continues to think rationally and function socially
h. disorders such as fugue, amnesia, or multiple personality
i. a group of disorders marked by disorganized thinking, disturbed perceptions, and inappropriate emotions and actions
j. a disorder characterized by repetitive thoughts and actions

# Progress Test 2

Progress Test 2 should be completed during a final chapter review. Answer the following questions after you thoroughly understand the correct answers for the Chapter Review and Progress Test 1.

## Multiple-Choice Questions

1. Which of the following is true concerning abnormal behavior?
   a. Definitions of abnormal behavior are culture-dependent.
   b. A behavior cannot be defined as abnormal unless it is considered harmful to society.
   c. Abnormal behavior can be defined as any behavior that is atypical.
   d. Definitions of abnormal behavior are based on physiological factors.

2. The psychoanalytic perspective would most likely view phobias as:
   a. conditioned fears.
   b. displaced responses to incompletely repressed impulses.
   c. biological predispositions.
   d. manifestations of self-defeating thoughts.

3. The text suggests that the disorganized thoughts of people with schizophrenia may be attributed to a breakdown in:
   a. selective attention.    d. memory retrieval.
   b. memory storage.         e. memory encoding.
   c. motivation.

4. Recent evidence links the brain abnormalities of schizophrenia to _____ during prenatal development.
   a. maternal stress
   b. a viral infection contracted
   c. abnormal levels of certain hormones
   d. the weight of the unborn child
   e. alcohol use

5. The fact that disorders such as schizophrenia are universal and influenced by heredity, whereas other disorders such as anorexia nervosa are culture-bound provides evidence for the _____ model of psychological disorders.
   a. medical           c. social-cultural
   b. bio-psycho-social  d. psychoanalytic

6. Our early ancestors commonly attributed disordered behavior to:
   a. "bad blood."      c. brain injury.
   b. evil spirits.     d. laziness.

7. In general, women are more vulnerable than men to _____ disorders such as _____.
   a. active; anxiety
   b. passive; depression
   c. active; antisocial conduct
   d. passive; alcohol abuse

8. Which of the following statements concerning the labeling of disordered behaviors is not true?
   a. Labels interfere with effective treatment of psychological disorders.
   b. Labels promote research studies of psychological disorders.
   c. Labels may create preconceptions that bias people's perceptions.
   d. Labels may influence behavior by creating self-fulfilling prophecies.

9. Nicholas Spanos considers dissociative identity disorder to be:
   a. a genuine disorder.
   b. merely role playing.
   c. a disorder that cannot be explained according to the learning perspective.
   d. both a. and c.

10. Which neurotransmitter is present in overabundant amounts during the manic phase of bipolar disorder?
    a. dopamine          c. epinephrine
    b. serotonin         d. norepinephrine

11. After falling from a ladder, Joseph is afraid of airplanes, although he has never flown. This demonstrates that some fears arise from:
    a. observational learning.
    b. reinforcement.
    c. stimulus generalization.
    d. stimulus discrimination.

12. Which of the following provides evidence that human fears have been subjected to the evolutionary process?
    a. Compulsive acts typically exaggerate behaviors that contributed to our species' survival.
    b. Most phobias focus on objects that our ancestors also feared.
    c. It is easier to condition some fears than others.
    d. All of the above provide evidence.

13. Which of the following is true of the medical model?
    a. In recent years, it has been in large part discredited.
    b. It views psychological disorders as sicknesses that are diagnosable and treatable.

c. It emphasizes the role of psychological factors in disorders over that of physiological factors.

d. It focuses on cognitive factors.

14. Psychoanalytic and learning theorists both agree that dissociative and anxiety disorders are symptoms that represent the person's attempt to deal with:

a. unconscious conflicts.

b. anxiety.

c. unfulfilled wishes.

d. unpleasant responsibilities.

15. Behavior is classified as disordered when it is:

a. atypical.          d. disturbing.

b. maladaptive.     e. all of the above.

c. unjustifiable.

16. Many psychologists dislike using DSM-IV because of its:

a. failure to emphasize observable behaviors in the diagnostic process.

b. learning theory bias.

c. medical model bias.

d. psychoanalytic bias.

e. social-cultural bias.

17. Which of the following is *not* a symptom of schizophrenia?

a. inappropriate emotions

b. disturbed perceptions

c. panic attacks

d. disorganized thinking

18. Social-cognitive theorists contend that depression is linked with:

a. negative moods.

b. maladaptive explanations of failure.

c. self-defeating beliefs.

d. all of the above.

19. According to psychoanalytic theory, memory of losses, especially in combination with internalized anger, is likely to result in:

a. learned helplessness.

b. the self-serving bias.

c. weak ego-defense mechanisms.

d. depression.

20. Among the following, which is generally accepted as a possible cause of schizophrenia?

a. an excess of endorphins in the brain

b. being a twin

c. extensive learned helplessness

d. a genetic predisposition

*Matching Items*

Match each term with the appropriate definition or description.

*Terms*

_____  1. dissociative identity disorder
_____  2. phobia
_____  3. dopamine
_____  4. dysthymic disorder
_____  5. antisocial personality
_____  6. norepinephrine
_____  7. serotonin
_____  8. bipolar disorder
_____  9. delusions
_____ 10. agoraphobia

*Definitions or Descriptions*

**a.** a neurotransmitter for which there are excess receptors in some schizophrenia patients
**b.** a neurotransmitter that is overabundant during mania and scarce during depression
**c.** an individual who seems to have no conscience
**d.** false beliefs that may accompany psychological disorders
**e.** an anxiety disorder marked by a persistent, irrational fear of a specific object or situation
**f.** a disorder formerly called multiple personality disorder
**g.** a neurotransmitter possibly linked to obsessive-compulsive behavior
**h.** a type of mood disorder
**i.** a disorder marked by chronic low energy and self-esteem
**j.** a fear of situations in which help might not be available during a panic attack

# Thinking Critically About Chapter 12

Answer these questions the day before an exam as a final check on your understanding of the chapter's terms and concepts.

*Multiple-Choice Questions*

1. Joe has an intense, irrational fear of snakes. He is suffering a(n):
   a. generalized anxiety disorder.
   b. obsessive-compulsive disorder.
   c. phobia
   d. mood disorder.
   e. bipolar disorder.

2. While mountain climbing, Jack saw his best friend killed by an avalanche. Jack himself was found months later, hundreds of miles away. On questioning, he claimed to be another person and, indeed, appeared to have no knowledge about any aspect of his former life. Most likely, Jack was suffering:
   a. a dissociative fugue.
   b. dissociative schizophrenia.
   c. dissociative identity disorder.
   d. dissociative amnesia.

3. Bob has never been able to keep a job. He's been in and out of jail for charges such as theft, sexual assault, and spousal abuse. Bob would most likely be diagnosed as having:
   a. a dissociative identity disorder.
   b. major depressive disorder.
   c. schizophrenia.
   d. an antisocial personality.

4. Julia's psychologist believes that Julia's fear of heights can be traced to a conditioned fear she developed after falling from a ladder. This explanation reflects a _____ perspective.
   a. medical           c. social-cognitive
   b. psychoanalytic    d. learning

5. Before he can study, Rashid must arrange his books, pencils, paper, and other items on his desk so that they are "just so." The campus counselor suggests that Rashid's compulsive behavior may help alleviate his anxiety about failing in school, which reinforces the compulsive actions. This explanation of obsessive-compulsive behavior is most consistent with which perspective?
   a. learning          c. humanistic
   b. psychoanalytic    d. social-cognitive

6. Sharon is continually tense, jittery, and apprehensive for no specific reason. She would probably be diagnosed as suffering a(n):
   a. phobia.
   b. major depressive disorder.
   c. obsessive-compulsive disorder.
   d. generalized anxiety disorder.

7. Jason is so preoccupied with staying clean that he showers as many as ten times each day. Jason would be diagnosed as suffering a(n):
   a. dissociative disorder.
   b. generalized anxiety disorder.
   c. personality disorder.
   d. obsessive-compulsive disorder.

8. (Close-Up) Although she escaped from war-torn Bosnia two years ago, Zheina still has haunting memories and nightmares. Because she is also severely depressed, her therapist diagnoses her condition as:
   a. dissociative identity disorder.
   b. bipolar disorder.
   c. schizophrenia.
   d. post-traumatic stress disorder.

9. Claiming that she heard a voice commanding her to warn other people that eating is harmful, Sandy attempts to convince others in a restaurant not to eat. The psychiatrist to whom she is referred finds that Sandy's thinking and speech are often fragmented and incoherent. In addition, Sandy has an unreasonable fear that someone is "out to get her" and consequently trusts no one. Her condition is most indicative of:
   a. schizophrenia.
   b. generalized anxiety disorder.
   c. a phobia.
   d. obsessive-compulsive disorder.
   e. personality disorder.

10. Irene occasionally experiences unpredictable episodes of intense dread accompanied by chest pains and a sensation of smothering. Since her symptoms have no apparent cause, they would probably be classified as indicative of:
    a. schizophrenia.
    b. dissociative fugue.
    c. post-traumatic stress disorder.
    d. panic attack.

11. To which of the following is a person *most* likely to acquire a phobia?
    a. heights
    b. being in public
    c. being dirty
    d. All of the above are equally likely.

12. Dr. Jekyll, whose second personality was Mr. Hyde, had a(n) _____ disorder.
    a. anxiety          c. mood
    b. dissociative     d. personality

13. For the past 6 months, a woman has complained of feeling isolated from others, dissatisfied with life, and discouraged about the future. This woman could be diagnosed as suffering:
    a. bipolar disorder.
    b. major depressive disorder.
    c. generalized anxiety disorder.
    d. dissociative disorder.

14. On Monday, Matt felt optimistic, energetic, and on top of the world. On Tuesday, he felt hopeless and lethargic, and thought that the future looked very grim. Matt would *most* likely be diagnosed as having:
    a. bipolar disorder.
    b. major depressive disorder.
    c. schizophrenia.
    d. dissociative disorder.

15. Connie's therapist has suggested that her depression stems from unresolved anger toward her parents. Evidently, Connie's therapist is working within the _____ perspective.
    a. learning          c. biological
    b. social-cognitive  d. psychoanalytic

16. Ken's therapist suggested that his depression is a result of his self-defeating thoughts and negative assumptions about himself, his situation, and his future. Evidently, Ken's therapist is working within the _____ perspective.
    a. learning          c. biological
    b. social-cognitive  d. psychoanalytic

17. Alicia's doctor, who thinks that Alicia's depression has a biochemical cause, prescribes a drug that:
    a. reduces norepinephrine.
    b. increases norepinephrine.
    c. reduces serotonin.
    d. increases acetylcholine.

18. Wayne's doctor attempts to help Wayne by prescribing a drug that blocks receptors for dopamine. Wayne has apparently been diagnosed with:
    a. a mood disorder.
    b. an anxiety disorder.
    c. a dissociative disorder.
    d. schizophrenia.

19. In many movies, soap operas, and novels, the hero or heroine, who is under great stress, experiences a sudden loss of memory without leaving home or establishing a new identity. This is an example of:
    a. a dissociative disorder.
    b. dissociative fugue.
    c. dissociative amnesia.
    d. an anxiety disorder.

20. Janet, whose class presentation is entitled "Current Views on the Causes of Schizophrenia," concludes her talk with the statement:
    a. "Schizophrenia is caused by intolerable stress."
    b. "Schizophrenia is inherited."
    c. "Genes may predispose some people to react to particular experiences by developing schizophrenia."
    d. "As of this date, schizophrenia is completely unpredictable and its causes are unknown."

## Essay Question

Clinical psychologists label people disordered if their behavior is (1) atypical, (2) disturbing, (3) maladaptive, and (4) unjustifiable. Demonstrate your understanding of the classification process by giving examples of behaviors that might be considered atypical, disturbing, maladaptive, or unjustifiable but, because they do not fit all four criteria, would not necessarily be labeled disordered. (Use the space below to list the points you want to make and organize them. Then write the essay on a separate piece of paper.)

## Key Terms

### Writing Definitions

Using your own words, on a separate piece of paper write a brief definition or explanation of each of the following terms.

1. psychological disorder
2. medical model
3. bio-psycho-social perspective
4. DSM-IV
5. neurotic disorders
6. psychotic disorders
7. anxiety disorders
8. generalized anxiety disorder
9. phobia
10. obsessive-compulsive disorder
11. panic disorder
12. dissociative disorders
13. dissociative amnesia
14. dissociative fugue
15. dissociative identity disorder
16. mood disorders
17. major depressive disorder
18. mania
19. bipolar disorder
20. schizophrenia
21. delusions
22. personality disorders
23. antisocial personality disorder

*Cross-Check*

As you learned in the Introduction, reviewing and overlearning of material are important to the learning process. After you have written the definitions of the key terms in this chapter, you should complete the crossword puzzle to ensure that you can reverse the process—recognize the term, given the definition.

### ACROSS

2. The "common cold" of psychological disorders.
9. Former term for disorders that, while distressing, still allow a person to think normally and function socially.
14. Selective loss of memory.
17. A euphoric, hyperactive state.
18. Category of disorders that includes major depression and bipolar disorder.
19. Mood disorder in which a person alternates between depression and mania.
20. Category of disorders that includes phobias and obsessive-compulsive disorder.

### DOWN

1. A widely used system of classifying psychological disorders.
3. Disorders that involve a separation of conscious awareness from one's previous memories, thoughts, and feelings.
4. A persistent, irrational fear of a specific object or situation.
5. False sensory experiences.
6. Biomedical research technique used to determine which genes are involved in a specific psychological disorder.
7. Perspective that assumes that genes, psychological factors, and social and cultural circumstances combine and interact to produce psychological disorders.
8. Subtype of schizophrenia in which emotion is flat or inappropriate.
10. The viewpoint that psychological disorders are illnesses.
11. Subtype of schizophrenia in which there is immobility or excessive, purposeless movement.
12. False beliefs that often are symptoms of schizophrenia.

13. Neurotransmitter for which there are excess receptors in the brains of schizophrenia patients.
15. Category of schizophrenia symptoms that includes having a toneless voice, expressionless face, and a mute or rigid body.
16. Neurotransmitter that is scarce in depression.

## ANSWERS

## Guided Study

The following guidelines provide the main points that your answers should have touched upon.

1. In order to be classified as psychologically disordered, behavior must be atypical, disturbing to others, maladaptive, and unjustifiable.
2. According to the medical perspective, psychological disorders are sicknesses that can be diagnosed on the basis of their symptoms and cured through therapy. Psychologists who work from the bio-psycho-social perspective assume that biological, sociocultural, and psychological factors combine and interact to produce psychological disorders.

3. DSM-IV groups some 230 psychological disorders into 17 major categories. Diagnostic classification is intended to describe a disorder, predict its future course, imply its appropriate treatment, and stimulate research into its causes.

4. Most clinicians believe that diagnostic labels help in describing, treating, and researching the causes of psychological disorders. Critics contend that these labels are arbitrary value judgments that create preconceptions that can bias our perceptions and interpretations. Labels can also affect people's self-images and stigmatize them in others' eyes. Finally, labels can change reality.

5. There are three types of anxiety disorders: generalized anxiety disorder, in which a person feels inexplicably tense and apprehensive; phobia, in which a person has an irrational fear of a specific object or situation; and obsessive-compulsive disorder, in which a person is troubled by repetitive thoughts or actions. An extreme form of generalized anxiety disorder is the panic disorder.

   Freud viewed an anxiety disorder as a manifestation of repressed impulses, ideas, and feelings that influence the sufferer's actions and emotions. Learning theorists link anxiety disorders with classical conditioning of fear, which may arise from stimulus generalization. Phobias and compulsive behaviors reduce anxiety by allowing the person to avoid or escape the feared situation. According to this perspective, fear may also be learned through observational learning. Biologically oriented researchers see these disorders as evolutionary adaptations or as genetic predispositions to particular fears and high anxiety. The anxiety of persons with obsessive-compulsive disorder, for example, is measurable as unusually high activity in a particular region of the frontal lobes and in a more primitive area deep within the brain.

6. In dissociative disorders, a person experiences a sudden loss of memory (dissociative amnesia) or change in identity (dissociative fugue) in response to extreme stress. Even more mysterious is the dissociative identity disorder, in which people have two or more distinct personalities; however, some skeptics believe that such persons are merely enacting a role for strategic reasons.

   Psychoanalysts view the symptoms of these disorders as defenses against anxiety. Learning theorists see them as behaviors reinforced by anxiety reduction. Some theorists see dissociative behaviors as states that serve as protective escape responses to traumatic childhood experiences.

7. There are two principal mood disorders: major depressive disorder and the bipolar disorder. Major depressive disorder, the "common cold" of psychological disorders, occurs when signs of depression last 2 weeks or more without any discernible cause. Alternating between depressive episodes and the hyperactive, wildly optimistic state of mania describes the bipolar disorder.

   According to the psychoanalytic perspective, depression occurs when significant losses evoke feelings associated with losses experienced in childhood and when unresolved anger is directed inward against the self.

   According to the biological perspective, mood disorders involve genetic predispositions and biochemical imbalances in which norepinephrine is overabundant during mania and scarce during depression. A second neurotransmitter, serotonin, is also scarce during depression. The brains of depressed people also tend to be less active and even have somewhat smaller frontal lobes.

   According to the social-cognitive perspective, depression is a vicious cycle in which stressful experiences trigger self-focused negative thinking and a self-blaming style of explaining events that hamper the way the person thinks and acts. This negative thinking and self-blaming style leads to further negative experiences.

8. Schizophrenia is a cluster of disorders in which there is a split from reality that shows itself in disorganized and delusional thinking, disturbed perceptions, and inappropriate emotions and actions. *Positive symptoms* of schizophrenia include disorganized or deluded thinking and speech as well as inappropriate emotions. *Negative symptoms* include toneless voices, expressionless faces, or mute and rigid bodies. Schizophrenia may develop gradually (chronic, or process, schizophrenia), in which case recovery is doubtful, or rapidly (acute, or reactive, schizophrenia) in response to stress, in which case recovery is much more likely.

   Some schizophrenia patients have an excess of brain receptors for dopamine. Others have abnormally low brain activity in the frontal lobes or enlarged fluid-filled areas and a corresponding shrinkage of cerebral tissue. Evidence suggests that the brain abnormalities of schizophrenia might be caused by a problem during prenatal development, such as a midpregnancy viral infection. In addition, studies of identical twins and adopted children reveal a strong genetic link to schizophrenia. Genes may predispose some people to react to particular experiences by developing a form of schizophrenia. Psychological causes of schizophrenia are difficult to pinpoint due to the variety of forms of the disorder.

**c.** The social-cognitive perspective would emphasize a person's conscious, cognitive processes, not reflexive conditioned responses.

5. **a.** is the answer. According to the learning view, compulsive behaviors are reinforced because they reduce the anxiety created by obsessive thoughts. Rashid's obsession concerns failing, and his desk-arranging compulsive behaviors apparently help him control these thoughts. (p. 434)

   **b.** The psychoanalytic perspective would view obsessive thoughts as a symbolic representation of forbidden impulses. These thoughts may prompt the person to perform compulsive acts that counter these impulses.

   **c. & d.** The text does not offer explanations of obsessive-compulsive behavior based on the humanistic or social-cognitive perspectives. Presumably, however, these explanations would emphasize growth-blocking difficulties in the person's environment (humanistic perspective) and the reciprocal influences of personality and environment (social-cognitive perspective), rather than symbolic expressions of forbidden impulses.

6. **d.** is the answer. (pp. 431–432)

   **a.** In phobias, anxiety is focused on a specific object.

   **b.** Major depressive disorder does not manifest these symptoms.

   **c.** The obsessive-compulsive disorder is characterized by repetitive and unwanted thoughts and/or actions.

7. **d.** is the answer. Jason is obsessed with cleanliness; as a result, he has developed a compulsion to shower. (p. 432)

   **a.** Dissociative disorders involve a separation of conscious awareness from previous memories and thoughts.

   **b.** Generalized anxiety disorder does not have a specific focus.

   **c.** This disorder is characterized by maladaptive character traits.

8. **d.** is the answer. (p. 435)

   **a.** There is no evidence that Zheina has *lost* either her memory or her identity, as would occur in dissociative disorders.

   **b.** Although she has symptoms of depression, Zheina does not show signs of mania, which occurs in bipolar disorder.

   **c.** Zheina shows no signs of disorganized thinking or disturbed perceptions.

9. **a.** is the answer. Because Sandy experiences hallucinations (hearing voices), delusions (fearing someone is "out to get her"), and incoherence, she would most likely be diagnosed as having schizophrenia. (pp. 449–450)

**b., c., d., & e.** These disorders are not characterized by disorganized thoughts and perceptions.

10. **d.** is the answer. (p. 432)

    **a.** Baseless physical symptoms rarely play a role in schizophrenia.

    **b.** There is no indication that she has lost her identity.

    **c.** There is no indication that she has suffered a trauma.

11. **a.** is the answer. Humans seem biologically prepared to develop a fear of heights and other dangers that our ancestors faced. (p. 436)

12. **b.** is the answer. (p. 438)

13. **b.** is the answer. The fact that this woman has had these symptoms for more than 2 weeks indicates that she is suffering from major depressive disorder. (p. 441)

14. **a.** is the answer. Matt's alternating states of the hopelessness and lethargy of depression and the energetic, optimistic state of mania are characteristic of bipolar disorder. (p. 441)

    **b.** Although he was depressed on Tuesday, Matt's manic state on Monday indicates that he is not suffering from major depressive disorder.

    **c.** Matt was depressed, not detached from reality.

    **d.** That Matt has not lost his memory or changed his identity indicates that he is not suffering from a dissociative disorder.

15. **d.** is the answer. Freud believed that the anger once felt toward parents was internalized and would produce depression. (p. 443)

    **a. & b.** The learning and social-cognitive perspectives focus on environmental experiences, conditioning, and self-defeating attitudes in explaining depression.

    **c.** The biological perspective focuses on genetic predispositions and biochemical imbalances in explaining depression.

16. **b.** is the answer. (pp. 445–447)

17. **b.** is the answer. Norepinephrine, which increases arousal and boosts mood, is scarce during depression. Drugs that relieve depression tend to increase norepinephrine. (p. 445)

    **c.** Increasing serotonin, which is sometimes scarce during depression, might relieve depression.

    **d.** This neurotransmitter is involved in motor responses but has not been linked to psychological disorders.

18. **d.** is the answer. Schizophrenia patients sometimes have an excess of receptors for dopamine. Drugs that block these receptors can therefore reduce symptoms of schizophrenia. (p. 452)

    **a., b., & c.** Dopamine receptors have not been implicated in these psychological disorders.

**19. c.** is the answer. Amnesia, which is a dissociative disorder, involves a sudden memory loss brought on by extreme stress. (p. 437)

**a.** Dissociative disorder is the *broad* category including amnesia, so this answer is not specific enough.

**b.** Fugue is a dissociative disorder in which flight from one's home and identity accompanies amnesia.

**d.** Anxiety disorders are not marked by memory loss.

**20. c.** is the answer. (p. 454)

### Essay Question

There is more to a psychological disorder than being different from other people. Gifted artists, athletes, and scientists have atypical capabilities, yet are not considered psychologically disordered. To be considered disordered, other people must find the atypical behavior disturbing. But what is disturbing in one culture may not be in another, or at another time. Homosexuality, for example, was once classified as a psychological disorder, but it is no longer. Similarly, nudity is common in some cultures and disturbing in others. Atypical and disturbing behaviors are more likely to be considered disordered when judged as maladaptive to the individual. Prolonged feelings of depression or the use of drugs to avoid dealing with problems are examples of maladaptive behaviors that may signal a psychological disorder if they become disabling. Finally, abnormal behavior is most likely to be considered disordered when others find it unjustifiable. A student loudly reciting the Greek alphabet in public, for example, who can justify his or her unusual behavior as being part of a fraternity or sorority ritual, would not be considered psychologically disordered.

## Key Terms

### Writing Definitions

1. In order to be classified as a **psychological disorder**, behavior must be atypical, disturbing, maladaptive, and unjustifiable. (p. 426)

2. The **medical model** holds that psychological disorders are illnesses that can be diagnosed, treated, and cured using traditional methods of medicine and psychiatry. (p. 428)

3. The **bio-psycho-social perspective** assumes that *bio*logical, *psycho*logical, and *socio*cultural factors combine and interact to produce psychological disorders. (p. 428)

4. **DSM-IV** is a short name for the American Psychiatric Association's *Diagnostic and Statistical Manual of Mental Disorders (Fourth Edition)*, which provides a widely used system of classifying psychological disorders. (p. 429)

5. **Neurotic disorders** is a former term for psychological disorders that, while distressing, still allow a person to think normally and function socially. The term is used mainly in contrast to *psychotic disorders*. (p. 429)

6. **Psychotic disorders** is a former term for psychological disorders that are severely debilitating and involve bizarre thoughts and behavior, and a break from reality. (p. 429)

7. **Anxiety disorders** involve distressing, persistent anxiety or maladaptive behaviors that reduce anxiety. (p. 431)

8. In the **generalized anxiety disorder**, the person is continually tense, apprehensive, and in a state of autonomic nervous system arousal for no apparent reason. (pp. 431–432)

9. A **phobia** is an anxiety disorder in which a person has a persistent, irrational fear and avoidance of a specific object or situation. (p. 432)

10. The **obsessive-compulsive disorder** is an anxiety disorder in which the person experiences uncontrollable and repetitive thoughts (obsessions) and actions (compulsions). (p. 432)

11. A **panic disorder** is an episode of intense dread accompanied by chest pain, dizziness, or choking. It is essentially an escalation of the anxiety associated with generalized anxiety disorder. (p. 432)

12. **Dissociative disorders** involve a separation of conscious awareness from one's previous memories, thoughts, and feelings. (p. 437)

*Memory aid*: To *dissociate* is to separate or pull apart. In the **dissociative disorder** a person becomes dissociated from his or her memories and identity.

13. **Dissociative amnesia** is a selective loss of memory. Amnesia may be caused by illness or head injuries, but dissociative amnesia is usually precipitated by extreme stress. (p. 437)

14. **Dissociative fugue** is a dissociative disorder in which forgetting occurs and the person physically runs away from home and identity. (p. 438)

*Memory aid*: **Fugue** and *fugitive* both derive from the same Latin root, meaning "to flee."

15. The **dissociative identity disorder** is a dissociative disorder in which a person exhibits two or more distinct and alternating personalities. (p. 438)

16. **Mood disorders** are characterized by emotional extremes. (p. 440)

17. **Major depressive disorder** is the mood disorder that occurs when a person exhibits the lethargy, feelings of worthlessness, or loss of interest in family, friends, and activities characteristic of depression for more than a 2-week period and for no discernible reason. Because of its relative frequency, depression has been called the "common cold" of psychological disorders. (p. 441)

18. **Mania** is the wildly optimistic, euphoric, hyperactive state that alternates with depression in the bipolar disorder. (p. 441)

19. The **bipolar disorder** is the mood disorder in which a person alternates between depression and the euphoria of a manic state. (p. 441)

    *Memory aid: Bipolar* means having two poles, that is, two opposite qualities. In the **bipolar disorder,** the opposing states are mania and depression.

20. **Schizophrenia** refers to the group of severe psychotic disorders whose symptoms may include disorganized and delusional thinking, inappropriate emotions and actions, and disturbed perceptions. (p. 449)

21. **Delusions** are false beliefs that often are symptoms of psychotic disorders. (p. 449)

22. **Personality disorders** are characterized by inflexible and enduring maladaptive character traits that impair social functioning. (p. 455)

23. The **antisocial personality disorder** is a personality disorder in which the person is aggressive, ruthless, and shows no sign of a conscience that would inhibit wrongdoing. (p. 455)

*Cross-Check*

**ACROSS**
2. major depressive
9. neurotic
14. amnesia
17. mania
18. mood
19. bipolar
20. anxiety

**DOWN**
1. DSM-IV
3. dissociative
4. phobia
5. hallucinations
6. linkage analysis
7. bio-psycho-social
8. disorganized
10. medical model
11. catatonia
12. delusions
13. dopamine
15. negative
16. serotonin

---

*FOCUS ON VOCABULARY AND LANGUAGE*

*Page 425:* Studying psychological disorders may therefore at times evoke an *eerie sense* of self-recognition that *illuminates* our own personality dynamics. When reading this chapter, you may sometimes experience the strange, uncanny feeling (*eerie sense*) that Myers is writing about you. On occasion we all feel, think, and behave in ways similar to disturbed people, and becoming aware of how alike we sometimes are may help shed some light on (*illuminate*) the processes underlying personality.

*Perspectives on Psychological Disorders*

*Page 426:* Where should we *draw the line* between normality and abnormality? Myers is addressing the problem of how exactly to define psychological disorders. How do we distinguish (*draw the line*) between someone who is "abnormal" and someone who is not? For psychologists and other mental-health workers a behavior will be labeled psychologically disturbed if it is judged to be atypical, disturbing, maladaptive, and unjustifiable.

*Page 427: "The devil made him do it."* Our ancestors explained strange and puzzling behavior by appealing to what they knew and believed about the nature of the world (e.g., gods, stars, demons, spirits, etc.). A person, who today would be classified as psychologically disturbed because of his or her bizarre behavior, in the past would have been considered to be possessed by evil spirits or demons (*the devil made him do it*). These types of nonscientific explanations persisted up until the last century.

*Page 429:* Thus, *the diagnostic term* provides a *handy shorthand* for describing a complex disorder. Psychology uses a classification system (DSM-IV) to describe and impose order on complicated psychological problems. When a disordered person is given a descriptive label (*diagnostic term*), it does not explain the problem, but it does provide a quick and useful means of communicating a great deal of information in abbreviated form (*a handy shorthand*).

*Page 431: Labels* can serve as *self-fulfilling prophecies.* A prophecy is a prediction about the future. When we characterize or classify (*label*) someone as a certain type of person, the very act of labeling may help bring about or create the actions described by the label (*self-fulfilling prophesy*).

## Anxiety Disorders

*Pags 432: ringing in the ears . . . edgy . . . jittery . . . racing heart , clammy hands, stomach butterflies, sleeplessness . . . furrowed brows . . . twitching eyelids . . . fidgeting.* These are all descriptions of the symptoms of generalized anxiety disorder. The person may hear high-pitched sounds (*ringing in the ears*); may be nervous and jumpy (*edgy*); start trembling (*jittery*); have increased heart rate (*racing heart*); have cold, damp, sweaty (*clammy*) hands; and feel as though winged insects are fluttering in the stomach (*stomach butterflies*). The sufferer may worry all the time, be unable to sleep (*insomnia*), and feel apprehensive, which may show in frowning (*furrowed brows*), rapidly blinking eyes (*twitching eyelids*), and quick small movements of the hands (*fidgeting*).

*Page 435 (Close-Up):* Years later, images of these events intrude as *flashbacks* and *nightmares.* Many war veterans (*vets*) and others who experienced traumatic stressful events develop post-traumatic stress disorder. Symptoms include terrifying images of the event (*flashbacks*), very frightening dreams (*nightmares*), extreme nervousness, anxiety or depression, and a tendency to become socially isolated.

*Page 436: Grooming gone wild becomes hair pulling.* The biological perspective explains our tendency to be anxious (*anxiety-prone*) in evolutionary or genetic terms. A normal behavior that once had survival value in our evolutionary past may now be distorted into compulsive action. Thus, compulsive hair pulling may be an exaggerated version of normal grooming behavior (*grooming gone wild*).

*Page 436:* The human mind was *road tested in the Stone Age.* Myers notes that the development of irrational fears (*phobias*) may have an evolutionary explanation. Just as newly designed vehicles are checked and modified as a result of driving them under normal highway traffic conditions (*they are road tested*), the human mind was changed and modified through adaptations to conditions that existed in a previous era (*road tested in the stone age*). We appear to be biologically prepared to develop some fears and not others as a result of our evolutionary heritage.

## Dissociative Disorders

*Page 438: . . . a ruse . . .* Kenneth Bianchi is a convicted psychopathic murderer who pretended to be a multiple personality in order to avoid jail or the death penalty, and his cunning ploy (*ruse*) fooled many psychologists and psychiatrists. It also raised the question of the reality of dissociative identity as a genuine disorder.

*Page 439:* Skeptics note how some therapists *go fishing for it. . . .* Those who doubt the existence of dissociative identity disorder (*skeptics*) find it strange that the number of diagnosed cases in North America has increased dramatically (*exploded*) in the last decade. (In the rest of the world it is rare or nonexistent.) In addition, the average number of personalities has multiplied (*mushroomed*) from 3 to 12 per patient. One explanation for the disorder's popularity is that many therapists expect it to be there, so they actively solicit (*go fishing for*) symptoms of dissociative identity disorder from their patients.

## Mood Disorders

*Page 441: To grind to a halt* and *ruminate,* as depressed people do, is to reassess one's life when feeling threatened. From a biological point of view, depression is a natural reaction to stress and painful events. It is like a warning signal that brings us to a complete stop (*we grind to a halt*) and allows us time to reflect on life and contemplate (*ruminate on*) the meaning of our existence.

*Page 441:* The difference between a *blue mood* after bad news and a mood disorder is like the difference between gasping for breath for a few minutes after a hard run and being chronically short of breath. We all feel depressed and sad (*we have blue moods*) in response to painful events and sometimes just to life in general. These feelings are points on a continuum; at the extreme end, and very distinct from ordinary depression, are the serious mood disorders in which the signs of chronic depression (loss of appetite, sleeplessness, tiredness, low self-esteem, and a disinterest in family, friends, and social activities) last for 2 weeks or more.

*Page 441:* If depression is living in *slow motion,* mania is *fast forward.* Bipolar disorder is characterized by mood swings. While depression slows the person down (*like living in slow motion*), the hyperactivity and heightened exuberant state (*mania*) at the other emotional extreme seems to speed the person up, similar to the images you get when you press the fast forward button on the VCR or see a "speeded-up" film.

*Page 445:* Depressed people *view life through dark glasses*. Social-cognitive theorists point out that biological factors do not operate independently of environmental influences. People who are depressed often have negative beliefs about themselves and about their present and future situations (*they view life through dark glasses*). These self-defeating beliefs can accentuate or amplify a nasty (*vicious*) cycle of interactions between chemistry, cognition, and mood.

*Page 447:* . . . even small losses can temporarily *sour* our thinking. When loyal basketball fans were depressed by their team's loss, they had a more pessimistic (*bleaker*) assessment of the outcome of future games as well as negative views of their own abilities (*the loss soured their thinking*). Depression can cause self-focused negative thinking.

*Page 448:* So, there is *two-way traffic* between depressed mood and negative thinking. The latest research shows that there is an interaction (*two-way traffic*) between depression and negative thinking. Depression tends to make people prone to self-blaming and self-focused negative thinking, and in response to painful events this style of thinking puts people at risk for becoming depressed (*they may get a bad case of the blues*).

*Page 448:* Misery may love another's company, *but company does not love another's misery*. The old saying "misery loves company" means that depressed, sad people like to be with other people. The possible social consequence of being withdrawn, self-focused, self-blaming, and complaining (*depressed*), however, is rejection by others (*company does not love another's misery*).

### Schizophrenia

*Page 450:* . . . *hodge-podge* . . . The symptoms of schizophrenia include fragmented and distorted thinking, disturbed perception, and inappropriate feelings and behaviors. Schizophrenia victims, when talking, may move rapidly from topic to topic and idea to idea so that their speech is incomprehensible (*a word salad*). This may be the result of a breakdown in selective attention, whereby an assorted mixture (*hodge-podge*) of stimuli continually distracts the person.

*Page 451:* Other victims of schizophrenia sometimes lapse into *flat affect*, a zombielike state of apparent apathy. The emotions of schizophrenia are frequently not appropriate for the situation. There may be laughter at a funeral, anger and tears for no apparent reason, or no expression of emotion whatsoever (*flat affect*), which resembles a half-dead, trancelike (*zombielike*) state of indifference (*apathy*).

*Page 454:* But as the bio-psycho-social perspective emphasizes, the *traffic* between brain biochemistry and psychological experiences *runs both ways*, so cause and effect are difficult to sort out. Neither genetic predispositions nor stressful psychological events alone cause schizophrenia. Rather, there seems to be some interaction (*the traffic runs both ways*) between the two, which makes it difficult to determine which is the causal agent.

### Personality Disorders

*Page 455:* . . . *con artist* . . . A person who has an antisocial personality is usually a male who has no conscience, who lies, steals, cheats, and is unable to keep a job or take on the normal responsibilities of family and society. When combined with high intelligence and no moral sense, the result may be a clever, smooth talking, and deceitful trickster or confidence man (*con artist*).

*Page 455:* . . . the antisocial personality disorder is *woven* of biological as well as psychological *strands*. The analogy here is between the antisocial personality and how cloth is made (*woven*). Both psychological and biological factors (*strands*) combine to produce the disorder. If the biological predispositions are fostered (*channeled*) in more positive ways, the result may be a fearless hero; alternatively, the same disposition may produce a killer or a confidence trickster (*con artist*).

# CHAPTER 13

# Therapy

## Chapter Overview

Chapter 13 discusses the major psychotherapies and biomedical therapies for maladaptive behaviors. The various psychotherapies all derive from the perspectives on personality discussed earlier, namely, the psychoanalytic, humanistic, behavioral, and cognitive perspectives. The chapter groups the therapies by perspective but also emphasizes the common threads that run through them. In evaluating the therapies, the chapter points out that, although people who are untreated often improve, those receiving psychotherapy tend to improve somewhat more, regardless of the type of therapy they receive.

The biomedical therapies discussed are drug therapies; electroconvulsive therapy; and psychosurgery, which is seldom used. By far the most important of the biomedical therapies, drug therapies are being used in the treatment of psychotic, anxiety, and mood disorders.

Because the origins of problems often lie beyond the individual, the chapter concludes with approaches that aim at preventing psychological disorders by focusing on the family or on the larger social environment as possible contributors to psychological disorders.

NOTE: Answer guidelines for all Chapter 13 questions begin on page 375.

## Guided Study

The text chapter should be studied one section at a time. Before you read, preview each section by skimming it, noting headings and boldface items. Then read the appropriate section objectives from the following outline. Keep these objectives in mind and, as you read the chapter section, search for the information that will enable you to meet each objective. Once you have finished a section, write out answers for its objectives.

### The Psychological Therapies (pp. 461–475)

> David Myers at times uses idioms that are unfamiliar to some readers. If you do not know the meaning of any of the following words, phrases, or expressions in the context in which they appear in the text, refer to pages 383–384 for an explanation: *"beating the devil" out of people; common threads; gawk; fueled . . . residue; aim to boost; knocks the props out from under you; drinks laced with a drug; aggressive and self-abusive behaviors; colors our feelings; worth his or her salt . . . nonsense-annihilating; crap!; catastrophizing.*

1. Briefly explain the current approach to therapy.

2. Discuss the aims and methods of psychoanalysis and explain the critics' concerns with this form of therapy.

3. Identify the basic themes of humanistic therapies and describe Rogers' person-centered approach.

4. Identify the basic assumptions of behavior therapy and discuss the classical conditioning therapies.

5. Describe the premise behind operant conditioning techniques and explain the critics' concerns with these techniques.

6. Identify the basic assumptions of the cognitive therapies and describe group therapy.

*Evaluating Psychotherapies* (pp. 475–482)

> If you do not know the meaning of any of the following words, phrases, or expressions in the context in which they appear in the text, refer to pages 384–385 for an explanation: *Hang in there; testimonials; ebb and flow of events; shop around; the opening volley; clear-cut; harness; empathy are hallmarks.*

7. Discuss the findings regarding the effectiveness of the psychotherapies.

8. Discuss the commonalities among the psychotherapies.

9. Discuss the role of culture and values in psychotherapy.

*The Biomedical Therapies* (pp. 482–487)

> If you do not know the meaning of any of the following words, phrases, or expressions in the context in which they appear in the text, refer to page 385 for an explanation: *cousin drugs; sluggishness, tremors, and twitches; Routinely "popping a Valium"; lift depressed people up; barbaric image.*

10. Identify the common forms of drug therapy.

11. Describe the use of electroconvulsive therapy and psychosurgery in the treatment of psychological disorders.

*Preventing Psychological Disorders* (pp. 487–488)

> If you do not know the meaning of the following expression in the context in which it appears in the text, refer to page 385 for an explanation: *upstream work.*

12. Explain the rationale and goals of preventive mental health programs.

## Chapter Review

When you have finished reading the chapter, work through the material that follows to review it. Complete the sentences and answer the questions. As you proceed, evaluate your performance for each section by consulting the answers on page 377. Do not continue with the next section until you understand each answer. If you need to, review or reread the appropriate section in the textbook before continuing.

1. Therapies are divided into two types: _____ and _____ therapies.

*The Psychological Therapies* (pp. 461–475)

2. Psychological therapy is more commonly called _____ .

3. Therapists who blend several psychotherapy techniques are said to take an _____ approach.

4. The major psychotherapies are based on four perspectives: the _____ , _____ , _____ , and _____ perspectives.

5. Freud's technique in which a client says whatever comes to mind is called _____ .

6. When, in the course of therapy, a person omits shameful or embarrassing material, _____ is occurring. Insight is facilitated by the analyst's _____ of the meaning of such omissions, of dreams, and of other information revealed during therapy sessions.

7. Freud referred to the hidden meaning of a dream as its _____ .

8. When strong feelings, similar to those experienced in other important relationships, are developed toward the therapist, _____ has occurred.

9. Humanistic therapies attempt to help people meet their potential for _____ .

List several ways that humanistic therapy differs from psychoanalysis.

**10.** The humanistic therapy based on Rogers' theory is called _____-_____ , which is described as _____ therapy because the therapist _____ (interprets/ does not interpret) the person's problems.

**11.** In order to promote growth in clients, Rogerian therapists exhibit _____ , _____ , and _____ .

**12.** Rogers' technique of restating and clarifying what a person is saying is called

_____ .

Given a nonjudgmental environment that pro-vides _____ _____ , patients are better able to accept themselves as they are and to feel val-ued and whole.

Contrast the assumptions of the behavior therapies with those of psychoanalysis and humanistic therapy.

**13.** One cluster of behavior therapies is based on the principles of _____ _____ , as developed in Pavlov's experiments. This technique, in which a new, incompatible response is substituted for a maladaptive one, is called _____ .

Two examples of this technique are

_____ and _____ .

**14.** The technique of systematic desensitization has been most fully developed by the therapist _____ . The assumption behind this technique is that one cannot simultaneously be _____ and relaxed.

**15.** The first step in systematic desensitization is the construction of a _____ of anxi-ety-arousing stimuli. The second step involves training in _____ . In the final step, the person is trained to associate the _____ state with the _____ -arousing stimuli.

**16.** In a more aggressive technique called _____ , a person is forced to confront a feared stimulus until the fear is _____ .

**17.** In helping people to overcome fears of snakes and spiders, for example, therapists sometimes combine systematic desensitization with _____ .

**18.** In aversive conditioning, the therapist attempts to substitute a _____ (positive/ negative) response for one that is currently _____ (positive/negative). In this technique, a person's unwanted behaviors become associated with _____ feelings.

**19.** Therapies that influence behavior by controlling its consequences are based on principles of _____ conditioning. One appli-cation of this form of therapy to institutional set-tings is the _____ _____ , in which desired behaviors are rewarded.

State two criticisms of "behavior modification."

**20.** Therapists who teach people new, more constructive ways of thinking are using _____ therapy.

**21.** The form of cognitive therapy that attempts to eliminate irrational thinking is

_____-

therapy. Its creator is _____ .

**22.** A technique that attempts to reverse the negative attitudes associated with depression by helping people see their irrationalities was developed by

_____ .

**23.** A form of cognitive therapy developed by Adele Rabin builds on the finding that depressed people _____ (do/do not) exhibit the self-serving bias. Studies by Martin Seligman and his colleagues demonstrate that children can be taught cognitive and social skills that help buffer them against _____ .

**24.** Treatment that combines an attack on negative thinking with efforts to modify behavior is known as _____-

_____ therapy.

List several advantages of group therapy.

**25.** The most common types of group therapy are

_____ and _____

groups for alcoholics, divorced people, and gamblers, for example.

**26.** The type of group interaction that focuses on the social context in which the individual exists is

_____ .

**27.** In this type of group, therapists focus on improving _____ within the family and helping family members to discover new ways of preventing or resolving

_____ .

*Evaluating Psychotherapies* (pp. 475–482)

**28.** In contrast to earlier times, most therapy today

_____ (is/is not) provided by psychiatrists.

**29.** A majority of psychotherapy clients express

_____ (satisfaction/dissatisfaction) with their therapy.

**30.** The debate over the effectiveness of psychotherapy began with a study by _____ ; it showed that the rate of improvement for those who received therapy _____ (was/was not) higher than the rate for those who did not.

**31.** As a rule, psychotherapy is most effective with problems that are _____ (specific/nonspecific).

**32.** Comparisons of the effectiveness of different forms of therapy reveal _____ (clear/no clear) differences.

**33.** With phobias, compulsions, and other specific behavior problems, _____ therapies have been the most effective. For depression, the _____ therapies have been the most successful.

**34.** The beneficial effect of a person's belief in treatment is called the _____

_____ .

35. Several studies found that treatment for mild problems offered by paraprofessionals _____ (is/is not) as effective as that offered by professional therapists.

36. Generally speaking, psychotherapists' personal values _____ (do/do not) influence their therapy.

## The Biomedical Therapies (pp. 482–487)

37. The most widely used biomedical treatments are the _____ therapies. Thanks to these therapies, the number of residents in mental hospitals has _____ (increased/decreased) sharply.

38. The field that studies the effects of drugs on the mind and behavior is _____ .

39. When neither the patients nor the staff are aware of which condition a given individual is in, a _____-_____ study is being conducted.

40. One effect of _____ drugs such as _____ is to help those experiencing _____ (positive/negative) symptoms of schizophrenia by decreasing their responsiveness to irrelevant stimuli; schizophrenia patients who are apathetic and withdrawn may be more effectively treated with the drug _____ . These drugs work by blocking the receptor sites for the neurotransmitter _____ .

41. Valium and Librium are classified as _____ drugs. These drugs depress activity in the _____ _____ .

42. Drugs that are prescribed to alleviate depression are called _____ drugs. The effectiveness of these drugs is due in part to a _____ effect, or the patient's hope that the drug will help them. These drugs also work by increasing levels of the neurotransmitters _____ and _____ . One example of this type of drug is _____ .

43. Equally effective in calming anxious people and energizing depressed people is _____ , which has more positive side effects than do drugs.

44. In order to stabilize the mood swings of a bipolar disorder, the drug _____ is often prescribed.

45. Drug researchers hope that the next generation of therapeutic drugs will target specific _____ that control specific _____ .

46. The therapeutic technique in which the patient receives an electric shock to the brain is referred to as _____ therapy, abbreviated as _____ .

47. ECT is most often used with patients suffering from severe _____ . One theory of how this treatment works suggests that it increases release of the neurotransmitter _____ .

48. The biomedical therapy in which a portion of brain tissue is removed or destroyed is called _____ .

49. In the 1930s, Moniz developed an operation called the _____ . In this procedure, the _____ lobe of the brain is disconnected from the rest of the brain.

50. Today, most psychosurgery has been replaced by the use of _____ or some other form of treatment.

## Preventing Psychological Disorders (pp. 487–488)

51. Unlike the psychotherapies and biomedical therapies, which focus on treatment of the _____ , psychologists who practice preventive mental health think that it is necessary to work on changing _____ conditions.

# Progress Test 1

*Multiple-Choice Questions*

Circle your answers to the following questions and check them with the answers on page 378. If your answer is incorrect, read the explanation for why it is incorrect and then consult the appropriate pages of the text (in parentheses following the correct answer).

1. Electroconvulsive therapy is most useful in the treatment of:
   a. schizophrenia.
   b. depression.
   c. personality disorders.
   d. anxiety disorders.
   e. bipolar disorder.

2. The technique in which a person is asked to report everything that comes to his or her mind is called _____ _____ ; this technique is favored by _____ therapists.
   a. active listening; cognitive
   b. spontaneous remission; humanistic
   c. free association; psychoanalytic
   d. systematic desensitization; behavior

3. Of the following categories of psychotherapy, which is known for its nondirective nature?
   a. psychoanalysis      c. behavior therapy
   b. humanistic therapy  d. cognitive therapy

4. Which of the following is *not* a common criticism of psychoanalysis?
   a. It emphasizes awareness of past feelings.
   b. It provides interpretations that are hard to disprove.
   c. It is generally a very expensive process.
   d. It gives therapists too much control over patients.

5. Which of the following types of therapy does *not* belong with the others?
   a. rational-emotive therapy
   b. family therapy
   c. self-help group
   d. support group

6. Which of the following is *not* necessarily an advantage of group therapies over individual therapies?
   a. They tend to take less time for the therapist.
   b. They tend to cost less money for the client.
   c. They are more effective.
   d. They allow the client to test new behaviors in a social context.

7. Which biomedical therapy is *most* likely to be practiced today?
   a. psychosurgery
   b. electroconvulsive therapy
   c. drug therapy
   d. counterconditioning
   e. aversive conditioning

8. The effectiveness of psychotherapy has been assessed both through clients' perspectives and through controlled research studies. What have such assessments found?
   a. Clients' perceptions and controlled studies alike strongly affirm the effectiveness of psychotherapy.
   b. Whereas clients' perceptions strongly affirm the effectiveness of psychotherapy, studies point to more modest results.
   c. Whereas studies strongly affirm the effectiveness of psychotherapy, many clients feel dissatisfied with their progress.
   d. Clients' perceptions and controlled studies paint a very mixed picture of the effectiveness of psychotherapy.

9. According to the psychoanalytic perspective, resistance during therapy indicates that a person is:
   a. repressing sensitive material.
   b. sublimating.
   c. transferring emotions linked with other relationships.
   d. doing all of the above.

10. Research studies of the effectiveness of different psychotherapies reveal that:
    a. no single type of therapy is consistently superior.
    b. behavior therapies are most effective in treating specific problems, such as phobias.
    c. cognitive therapies are most effective in treating depressed emotions.
    d. all of the above are true.

11. The antipsychotic drugs appear to produce their effects by blocking the receptor sites for:
    a. dopamine.        c. norepinephrine.
    b. epinephrine.     d. serotonin.

12. Psychologists who advocate a _____ approach to mental health contend that many psychological disorders could be prevented by changing the disturbed individual's _____ .
    a. biomedical; diet
    b. family; behavior
    c. humanistic; feelings
    d. psychoanalytic; behavior
    e. preventive; environment

13. An eclectic psychotherapist is one who:
   a. takes a nondirective approach in helping clients solve their problems.
   b. views psychological disorders as usually stemming from one cause, such as a biological abnormality.
   c. uses one particular technique, such as psychoanalysis or counterconditioning, in treating disorders.
   d. uses a variety of techniques, depending on the client and the problem.

14. The technique in which a therapist echoes and restates what a person says in a nondirective manner is called:
   a. active listening.
   b. free association.
   c. systematic desensitization.
   d. interpretation.

15. Which type of therapy is most often criticized for taking too much time?
   a. biomedical therapy
   b. behavior therapy
   c. psychoanalysis
   d. family therapy

16. The technique of systematic desensitization is based on the premise that maladaptive symptoms are:
   a. a reflection of irrational thinking.
   b. conditioned responses.
   c. expressions of unfulfilled wishes.
   d. all of the above.

17. The operant conditioning technique in which desired behaviors are rewarded with points or poker chips that can later be exchanged for various rewards is called:
   a. counterconditioning.
   b. systematic desensitization.
   c. a token economy.
   d. rational-emotive therapy.

18. One variety of _____ therapy is based on the finding that depressed people often attribute their failures to _____ .
   a. humanistic; themselves
   b. behavior; external circumstances
   c. cognitive; external circumstances
   d. cognitive; themselves

19. A person can derive benefits from psychotherapy simply by believing in it. This illustrates the importance of:
   a. spontaneous remission.
   b. the placebo effect.
   c. the transference effect.
   d. interpretation.

20. Before 1950, the main mental health providers were:
   a. psychologists.          d. the clergy.
   b. paraprofessionals.      e. social workers.
   c. psychiatrists.

## Matching Items

Match each term with the appropriate definition or description.

### Terms

_____ 1. cognitive therapy
_____ 2. behavior therapy
_____ 3. systematic desensitization
_____ 4. rational-emotive therapy
_____ 5. person-centered therapy
_____ 6. aversive conditioning
_____ 7. psychoanalysis
_____ 8. preventive mental health
_____ 9. biomedical therapy
_____ 10. counterconditioning

### Definitions or Descriptions

a. associates unwanted behavior with unpleasant experiences
b. associates a relaxed state with anxiety-arousing stimuli
c. emphasizes the social context of psychological disorders
d. attempts to eliminate irrational thinking through a confrontational approach
e. category of therapies that teach people more adaptive ways of thinking and acting
f. therapy developed by Carl Rogers
g. therapy based on Freud's theory of personality
h. treatment with psychosurgery, electroconvulsive therapy, or drugs
i. classical conditioning procedure in which new responses are conditioned to stimuli that trigger unwanted behaviors
j. category of therapies based on learning principles derived from classical and operant conditioning

## Progress Test 2

Progress Test 2 should be completed during a final chapter review. Answer the following questions after you thoroughly understand the correct answers for the Chapter Review and Progress Test 1.

### Multiple-Choice Questions

1. Carl Rogers was a _____ therapist who was the creator of _____ therapy.
   a. behavior; desensitization
   b. psychoanalytic; insight
   c. humanistic; person-centered
   d. cognitive; rational-emotive

2. Using techniques of classical conditioning to develop an association between unwanted behavior and an unpleasant experience is known as:
   a. aversive conditioning.
   b. systematic desensitization.
   c. transference.
   d. electroconvulsive therapy.
   e. a token economy.

3. Which type of psychotherapy emphasizes the individual's inherent potential for self-fulfillment?
   a. behavior therapy
   b. psychoanalysis
   c. humanistic therapy
   d. biomedical therapy

4. Teaching clients to reverse their catastrophizing beliefs about the themselves is of most direct concern to _____ therapists.
   a. cognitive
   b. behavior
   c. psychodynamic
   d. person-centered

5. Which type of psychotherapy focuses on changing unwanted behaviors rather than on discovering their underlying causes?
   a. behavior therapy
   b. cognitive therapy
   c. humanistic therapy
   d. psychoanalysis

6. The techniques of counterconditioning are based on principles of:
   a. observational learning.
   b. classical conditioning.
   c. operant conditioning.
   d. behavior modification.

7. In which of the following does the client learn to associate a relaxed state with a hierarchy of anxiety-arousing situations?
   a. rational-emotive therapy
   b. aversive conditioning
   c. counterconditioning
   d. systematic desensitization

8. Principles of operant conditioning underlie which of the following techniques?
   a. counterconditioning
   b. systematic desensitization
   c. rational-emotive therapy
   d. aversive conditioning
   e. the token economy

9. Which of the following is *not* a common criticism of behavior therapy?
   a. Clients may not develop intrinsic motivation for their new behaviors.
   b. Behavior control is unethical.
   c. Although one symptom may be eliminated, another may replace it unless the underlying problem is treated.
   d. All of the above are criticisms of behavior therapy.

10. Which type of therapy focuses on eliminating irrational thinking?
    a. psychoanalysis
    b. person-centered therapy
    c. rational-emotive therapy
    d. behavior therapy

11. Antidepressant drugs are believed to work by affecting:
    a. dopamine.
    b. lithium.
    c. norepinephrine.
    d. acetylcholine.

12. The effect of valium, librium, and alcohol on the body is to:
    a. increase the availability of the neurotransmitter serotonin.
    b. increase central nervous system activity.
    c. depress central nervous system activity.
    d. block the activity of the neurotransmitter dopamine.

13. Which of the following is the drug most commonly used to treat the bipolar disorder?
    a. Valium
    b. chlorpromazine
    c. Librium
    d. lithium

14. The most widely prescribed drugs in biomedical therapy are the:
    a. antianxiety drugs.
    b. antipsychotic drugs.
    c. antidepressant drugs.
    d. amphetamines.

15. Which form of therapy is *most* likely to be successful in treating depression?
    a. behavior therapy
    b. psychoanalysis
    c. cognitive therapy
    d. humanistic therapy

16. Although Moniz won the Nobel prize for developing the lobotomy procedure, the technique is not widely used today because:
    a. it produces a lethargic, immature personality.
    b. it is irreversible.
    c. calming drugs became available in the 1950s.
    d. of all of the above reasons.

17. Research studies comparing the effectiveness of professional therapists with paraprofessionals found that:
    a. the professionals were much more effective than the paraprofessionals.
    b. the paraprofessionals were much more effective than the professionals.
    c. except in treating depression, the paraprofessionals were about as effective as the professionals.
    d. the paraprofessionals were about as effective as the professionals.

18. Among the common ingredients of the psychotherapies is:
    a. the offer of a therapeutic relationship.
    b. the expectation among clients that the therapy will prove helpful.
    c. the chance to develop a fresh perspective on oneself and the world.
    d. all of the above.

19. Family therapy differs from other forms of psychotherapy because it focuses on:
    a. using a variety of treatment techniques.
    b. conscious rather than unconscious processes.
    c. the present instead of the past.
    d. how family tensions may cause individual problems.

**20.** One reason that aversive conditioning may only be temporarily effective is that:

    **a.** for ethical reasons, therapists cannot use sufficiently intense unconditioned stimuli to sustain classical conditioning.

    **b.** patients are often unable to become sufficiently relaxed for conditioning to take place.

    **c.** patients know that outside the therapist's office they can engage in the undesirable behavior without fear of aversive consequences.

    **d.** most conditioned responses are elicited by many nonspecific stimuli, and it is impossible to counterconditioning them all.

*Matching Items*

Match each term with the appropriate definition or description.

*Terms*

    _____ **1.** active listening
    _____ **2.** token economy
    _____ **3.** placebo effect
    _____ **4.** lobotomy
    _____ **5.** lithium
    _____ **6.** Thorazine
    _____ **7.** psychopharmacology
    _____ **8.** double-blind technique
    _____ **9.** Valium
    _____ **10.** free association

*Definitions or Descriptions*

    **a.** type of psychosurgery
    **b.** antipsychotic drug
    **c.** mood-stabilizing drug
    **d.** empathic technique used in person-centered therapy
    **e.** the beneficial effect of a person's expectation that treatment will be effective
    **f.** antianxiety drug
    **g.** technique of psychoanalytic therapy
    **h.** an operant conditioning procedure
    **i.** the study of the effects of drugs on the mind and behavior
    **j.** experimental procedure in which both the patient and staff are unaware of a patient's treatment condition

# Thinking Critically About Chapter 13

Answer these questions the day before an exam as a final check on your understanding of the chapter's terms and concepts.

*Multiple-Choice Questions*

**1.** During a session with his psychoanalyst, Jamal hesitates while describing a highly embarrassing thought. In the psychoanalytic framework, this is an example of:

    **a.** transference.    **c.** mental repression.
    **b.** insight.    **d.** resistance.

**2.** During psychoanalysis, Jane has developed strong feelings of hatred for her therapist. The analyst interprets Jane's behavior in terms of a _____ of her feelings toward her father.

    **a.** projection    **c.** regression
    **b.** resistance    **d.** transference

**3.** Given that Jim's therapist attempts to help him by offering genuineness, acceptance, and empathy, she is probably practicing:

    **a.** psychoanalysis.
    **b.** behavior therapy.
    **c.** cognitive therapy.
    **d.** person-centered therapy.

**4.** To help Sam quit smoking, his therapist blew a blast of smoke into Sam's face each time Sam inhaled. Which technique is the therapist using?

    **a.** rational-emotive therapy
    **b.** behavior modification
    **c.** systematic desensitization
    **d.** aversive conditioning

5. After Darnel dropped a pass in an important football game, he became depressed and vowed to quit the team because of his athletic incompetence. The campus psychologist challenged his illogical reasoning and pointed out that Darnel's "incompetence" had earned him an athletic scholarship. The psychologist's response was most typical of a _____ therapist.

a. behavior
b. psychoanalytic
c. person-centered
d. rational-emotive

6. Seth enters therapy to talk about some issues that have been upsetting him. The therapist prescribes some medication to help him. The therapist is most likely a:

a. psychologist.
b. psychiatrist.
c. psychiatric social worker.
d. clinical social worker.

7. In an experiment testing the effects of a new antipsychotic drug, neither Dr. Cunningham nor her patients know whether the patients are in the experimental or the control group. This is an example of the _____ technique.

a. aversive
b. within-subjects
c. double-blind
d. single-blind

8. Wilson's feelings of despair and helplessness are so severe that he frequently thinks of committing suicide. To treat Wilson, a psychiatrist would probably prescribe:

a. Prozac.
b. lithium.
c. Valium.
d. Thorazine.

9. A relative wants to know which type of therapy works best. You should tell your relative that:

a. psychotherapy does not work.
b. behavior therapy is the most effective.
c. cognitive therapy is the most effective.
d. group therapy is best for his problem.
e. no one type of therapy is consistently the most successful.

10. Leota is startled when her therapist says that she needs to focus on eliminating her problem behavior rather than gaining insight into its underlying cause. Most likely, Leota has consulted a _____ therapist.

a. behavior
b. humanistic
c. cognitive
d. psychoanalytic

11. In order to help him overcome his fear of flying, Duane's therapist has him construct a hierarchy of anxiety-triggering stimuli and then learn to associate each with a state of deep relaxation. Duane's therapist is using the technique called:

a. systematic desensitization.
b. aversive conditioning.
c. shaping.
d. free association.
e. rational-emotive therapy.

12. A patient in a hospital receives poker chips for making her bed, being punctual at meal times, and maintaining her physical appearance. The poker chips can be exchanged for privileges, such as television viewing, snacks, and magazines. This is an example of the _____ therapy technique called _____ .

a. behavior-cognitive; systematic desensitization
b. behavior; token economy
c. cognitive; token economy
d. humanistic; systematic desensitization

13. Ben is a cognitive-behavior therapist. Compared to Rachel, who is a behavior therapist, Ben is more likely to:

a. base his therapy on principles of operant conditioning.
b. base his therapy on principles of classical conditioning.
c. address clients' attitudes as well as behaviors.
d. focus on clients' unconscious urges.

14. A psychotherapist who believes that the best way to treat psychological disorders is to prevent them from developing would be most likely to view disordered behavior as:

a. maladaptive thoughts and actions.
b. expressions of unconscious conflicts.
c. conditioned responses.
d. an understandable response to stressful social conditions.

15. Linda's doctor prescribes medication that blocks the activity of dopamine in her nervous system. Evidently, Linda is probably being treated with an _____ drug.

a. antipsychotic
b. antianxiety
c. antidepressant
d. anticonvulsive

16. Abraham's doctor prescribes medication that increases the availability of norepinephrine in his nervous system. Evidently, Abraham is being treated with an _____ drug.

a. antipsychotic
b. antianxiety
c. antidepressant
d. anticonvulsive

17. In concluding her talk entitled "Psychosurgery Today," Ashley states that:

    a. "Psychosurgery is still widely used throughout the world."
    b. "Electroconvulsive therapy is the only remaining psychosurgical technique that is widely practiced."
    c. "With advances in psychopharmacology, psychosurgery has largely been abandoned."
    d. "Although lobotomies remain popular, other psychosurgical techniques have been abandoned."

18. A psychiatrist has diagnosed a patient as having bipolar disorder. It is likely that she will prescribe:

    a. an antipsychotic drug.
    b. lithium.
    c. an antianxiety drug.
    d. a drug that blocks receptor sites for serotonin.

19. Which type(s) of psychotherapy would be most likely to use the interpretation of dreams as a technique for bringing unconscious feelings into awareness?

    a. psychoanalysis
    b. behavior therapy
    c. cognitive therapy
    d. all of the above

20. Of the following therapists, who would be most likely to interpret a person's psychological problems in terms of repressed impulses?

    a. a behavior therapist
    b. a cognitive therapist
    c. a humanistic therapist
    d. a psychoanalyst

*Essay Question*

Willie has been diagnosed as suffering from major depressive disorder. Describe the treatment he might receive from a psychoanalyst, a cognitive therapist, and a biomedical therapist. (Use the space below to list points you want to make and organize them. Then write the essay on a separate sheet of paper.)

# Key Terms

## Writing Definitions

Using your own words, on a separate piece of paper write a brief definition or explanation of each of the following terms.

1. psychotherapy
2. eclectic approach
3. psychoanalysis
4. resistance
5. interpretation
6. transference
7. person-centered therapy
8. active listening
9. behavior therapy
10. counterconditioning
11. systematic desensitization
12. aversive conditioning
13. token economy
14. cognitive therapy
15. rational-emotive therapy
16. family therapy
17. psychopharmacology
18. lithium
19. electroconvulsive therapy (ECT)
20. psychosurgery
21. lobotomy

## Cross-Check

As you learned in the Introduction, reviewing and overlearning of material are important to the learning process. After you have written the definitions of the key terms in this chapter, you should complete the crossword puzzle to ensure that you can reverse the process—recognize the term, given the definition.

### ACROSS

**4.** Form of counterconditioning in which an unpleasant state becomes associated with an unwanted behavior.

**9.** Category of therapy that focuses on clients' current conscious feelings and on their taking responsibility for their own growth.

**10.** Aggressive technique for treating phobias in which the person is forced to confront a feared stimulus until the fear is extinguished.

**12.** Type of therapist who is primarily concerned with directly modifying problem behaviors.

**15.** Antidepressant drug that is used to treat bipolar disorder.

### DOWN

**1.** Category of therapy that focuses on changing the brain's functioning.

**2.** Therapeutic technique that attempts to change behavior by removing or destroying brain tissue.

**3.** Category of drugs used to treat schizophrenia.

**5.** Psychoanalytic technique in which the patient is asked to say whatever comes to mind.

**6.** Biomedical therapy often used to treat major depressive disorder.

**7.** The basic nondirective technique of person-centered therapy.

**8.** Confrontational therapy designed to eliminate irrational thinking.

**11.** Form of psychosurgery.

**13.** Approach to therapy employing a variety of perspectives.

**14.** Psychoanalysts use interpretation to promote _____ in patients.

## ANSWERS

## Guided Study

The following guidelines provide the main points that your answers should have touched upon.

1. Psychotherapy is the planned treatment of mental and emotional problems based on an emotionally charged, confiding interaction between a socially sanctioned healer and a sufferer. The various types of psychotherapy derive from psychology's major personality theories: psychoanalytic, humanistic, behavioral, and cognitive. Half of all contemporary psychotherapists take an eclectic approach, using a blend of therapies tailored to meet their clients' particular problems.

2. Psychoanalysis assumes that psychological problems are caused by repressed unconscious impulses and conflicts that develop during childhood, and so its goal is to bring these feelings into conscious awareness and help the person work through them.

Psychoanalysts may ask their patients to report everything that comes to mind (free association). Blocks in the flow of retrieval (resistance) are believed to indicate the repression of sensitive material. The analyst's interpretations of resistances aim to provide the patient with insight into their underlying meaning. Psychoanalysts interpret dreams for their latent content and for the transference of feelings from early relationships in order to expose repressed feelings.

Psychoanalysis has been criticized for offering interpretations that are impossible to prove or disprove and for being a lengthy and expensive process that only the relatively well-off can afford.

3. Humanistic therapists aim to boost self-fulfillment by helping people grow in self-awareness and self-acceptance. Unlike psychoanalysis, humanistic therapies focus on conscious thoughts as they occur in the present. Carl Rogers' nondirective person-centered therapy, which is based on the assumption that most people have within themselves the resources for growth, aims to provide an environment in which therapists exhibit genuineness, acceptance, and empathy. Humanistic therapists often use *active listening* to provide a psychological mirror that helps clients see themselves more clearly.

4. Behavior therapy applies learning principles to eliminate unwanted behavior. Counterconditioning describes classical-conditioning procedures that condition new responses to stimuli that trigger unwanted behaviors. One type of counterconditioning, systematic desensitization, is used to treat phobias, for example, by conditioning people to associate a pleasant, relaxed state with gradually increasing anxiety-provoking stimuli. Aversive conditioning is a type of counterconditioning that associates unwanted behavior (such as drinking alcohol) with unpleasant feelings (such as nausea).

5. Operant conditioning procedures are used to treat specific behavioral problems by reinforcing desired behaviors and withholding reinforcement for undesired behaviors. In institutional settings, for example, a token economy is employed to shape desired behaviors. With this procedure, patients earn tokens for exhibiting desired behavior, then exchange the accumulated tokens for various privileges.

Critics note that because "behavior modification" depends on extrinsic rewards, the appropriate behaviors may disappear when the person leaves the conditioning environment. Second, critics question whether it is ethical for a therapist to exercise so much control over a person's behavior.

6. The cognitive therapies assume that our thinking influences our feelings and that maladaptive thinking patterns can be replaced with new, more constructive ones. Rational-emotive therapy is a confrontational cognitive therapy that challenges people's illogical, self-defeating attitudes and actions. Cognitive therapy for depression helps people to discover and reform their habitually negative patterns of thinking. Cognitive-behavior therapy expands upon standard cognitive therapy to include helping people to practice their newly learned positive approach in everyday settings.

Group therapies provide a social context which allows people to discover that others have similar problems and to try out new ways of behaving. Self-help and support groups are examples of the group approach to psychotherapy. Another is family therapy, which treats individuals within their family system.

7. The effectiveness of psychotherapy depends on how it is measured. Although clients' testimonials and clinicians' perceptions strongly affirm the effectiveness of psychotherapy, controlled research studies, such as those originated by Hans Eysenck, report a similar improvement rate among treated and untreated people. More recent research reveals that although those not undergoing therapy often improve, those undergoing therapy are more likely to improve. Furthermore, although no particular type of therapy is consistently superior, certain therapies work best with certain disorders. Behavioral conditioning therapies, for example, work best with specific behavior problems. With depression, the cognitive therapies prove most successful.

8. First, because they enable people to believe that things can and will get better, psychotherapies provide hope for demoralized people. This placebo effect explains why all sorts of treatments may produce cures. Second, therapy offers people a plausible explanation of problems and alternative ways of responding. Third, therapy establishes an empathic, trusting, caring relationship between client and therapist.

9. All therapists have their own values, which may differ radically, as illustrated by Albert Ellis and Allen Bergin's widely divergent views. Because these values influence their therapy, they should be divulged to patients. Value differences may become particularly significant when a therapist from one culture meets a client from another.

10. Discoveries in psychopharmacology revolutionized the treatment of disordered people and greatly reduced the need for psychosurgery or hospitalization. Antipsychotic drugs such as Thorazine and Clozaril are used to reduce positive and negative symptoms of schizophrenia, respectively. These drugs work by blocking receptor sites for the neurotransmitter dopamine. Antianxiety drugs, such as Valium and Librium, reduce tension and anxiety by depressing central nervous system activity. Antidepressant drugs elevate mood by increasing the availability of the neurotransmitters norepinephrine and serotonin; fluoxetine (Prozac) blocks the reabsorption and removal of serotonin from synapses. The drug lithium is used to stabilize the manic-depressive mood swings of the bipolar disorder.

11. Electroconvulsive therapy (ECT), which is used by psychiatrists to treat severe depression, produces marked improvement in at least 80 percent of patients without discernible brain damage. ECT may work by increasing the release of norepinephrine, or by inducing seizures that calm neural centers in which overactivity produces depression.

  Because its effects are irreversible, psychosurgery, which removes or destroys brain tissue to change behavior, is the most drastic biomedical intervention. The best-known form, the lobotomy, was developed by Moniz in the 1930s to calm emotional and violent patients. During the 1950s, with advances in psychopharmacology, psychosurgery was largely abandoned.

12. Psychotherapists who view psychological disorders as responses to a disturbed and stressful society contend that the best approach is to prevent problems from developing by treating not only the person but also the person's social context. Accordingly, programs that help alleviate poverty, discrimination, constant criticism, unemployment, sexism, and other demoralizing situations that undermine people's sense of competence, personal control, and self-esteem are thought to be effective in reducing people's risk of psychological disorders.

## Chapter Review

1. psychological; biomedical
2. psychotherapy
3. eclectic
4. psychoanalytic; humanistic; behavioral; cognitive
5. free association

6. resistance; interpretation
7. latent content
8. transference
9. self-fulfillment

Unlike psychoanalysis, humanistic therapy is focused on the present instead of the past, on awareness of feelings as they occur rather than on achieving insights into the childhood origins of the feelings, on conscious rather than unconscious processes, on promoting growth and fulfillment instead of curing illness, and on helping clients take immediate responsibility for their feelings and actions rather than on uncovering the obstacles to doing so.

10. person-centered; nondirective; does not interpret
11. genuineness; acceptance; empathy
12. active listening; unconditional positive regard

Whereas psychoanalysis and humanistic therapies assume that problems diminish as self-awareness grows, behavior therapists doubt that self-awareness is the key. Instead of looking for the inner cause of unwanted behavior, behavior therapy applies learning principles to directly attack the unwanted behavior itself.

13. classical conditioning; counterconditioning; systematic desensitization; aversive conditioning
14. Wolpe; anxious
15. hierarchy; progressive relaxation; relaxed; anxiety
16. flooding; extinguished
17. observational learning
18. negative; positive; unpleasant
19. operant; token economy

Behavior modification is criticized because the desired behavior may stop when the rewards are stopped. Also, critics contend that one person should not be allowed to control another.

20. cognitive
21. rational-emotive; Ellis
22. Beck
23. do not; depression
24. cognitive-behavior

Group therapy saves therapists time and clients money. The social context of group therapy allows people to discover that others have similar problems and to try out new ways of behaving.

25. self-help; support
26. family therapy
27. communication; conflict
28. is not
29. satisfaction

30. Eysenck; was not
31. specific
32. no clear
33. behavior; cognitive
34. placebo effect
35. is
36. do
37. drug; decreased
38. psychopharmacology
39. double-blind
40. antipsychotic; chlorpromazine (Thorazine); positive; clozapine (Clozaril); dopamine
41. antianxiety; central nervous system
42. antidepressant; placebo; norepinephrine; serotonin; fluoxetine (Prozac)
43. aerobic exercise
44. lithium
45. receptors; symptoms
46. electroconvulsive; ECT
47. depression; norepinephrine
48. psychosurgery
49. lobotomy; frontal
50. drugs
51. individual; environmental or social

## Progress Test 1

### Multiple-Choice Questions

1. **b.** is the answer. Although no one is sure how ECT works, one possible explanation is that it increases release of norepinephrine, the neurotransmitter that elevates mood. (p. 485)

2. **c.** is the answer. (p. 462)
   **a.** Active listening is a Rogerian technique in which the therapist echoes, restates, and seeks clarification of the client's statements.
   **b.** Spontaneous remission, which is not mentioned in the text, refers to improvement without treatment.
   **d.** Systematic desensitization is a process in which a person is conditioned to associate a relaxed state with anxiety-triggering stimuli.

3. **b.** is the answer. (p. 464)

4. **d.** is the answer. This is not among the criticisms commonly made of psychoanalysis. (It would more likely be made of behavior therapies.) (p. 463)

5. **a.** is the answer. This is a variety of cognitive therapy. (p. 471)

**b., c., & d.** Each of these is a type of group therapy.

6. **c.** is the answer. Outcome research of the relative effectiveness of different therapies reveals no clear winner; the other factors mentioned are advantages of group therapies. (p. 479)

7. **c.** is the answer. (p. 482)
   **a.** The fact that its effects are irreversible makes psychosurgery a drastic procedure, and with advances in psychopharmacology, psychosurgery was largely abandoned.
   **b.** ECT is still widely used as a treatment of major depression, but in general it is not used as frequently as drug therapy.
   **d. & e.** Counterconditioning and aversive conditioning are not biomedical therapies.

8. **b.** is the answer. Clients' testimonials regarding psychotherapy are generally very positive. The research, in contrast, seems to show that therapy is only *somewhat* effective. (pp. 476, 477–478)

9. **a.** is the answer. (p. 463)
   **b.** Sublimation occurs when a person finds a socially acceptable outlet for unacceptable urges.
   **c.** This occurs when a patient redirects to a psychoanalyst emotions from another relationship.

10. **d.** is the answer. (p. 478–479)

11. **a.** is the answer. By occupying receptor sites for dopamine, these drugs block its activity and reduce its production. (p. 483)

12. **e.** is the answer. (p. 487)

13. **d.** is the answer. Today, half of all psychotherapists describe themselves as eclectic—as using a blend of therapies. (p. 462)
    **a.** An eclectic therapist may use a nondirective approach with certain behaviors; however, a more directive approach might be chosen for other clients and problems.
    **b.** In fact, just the opposite is true. Eclectic therapists generally view disorders as stemming from many influences.
    **c.** Eclectic therapists, in contrast to this example, use a combination of treatments.

14. **a.** is the answer. (p. 465)

15. **c.** is the answer. (p. 463)

16. **b.** is the answer. (p. 467)
    **a.** This reflects a cognitive perspective.
    **c.** This reflects a psychoanalytic perspective.

17. **c.** is the answer. (p. 470)
    **a. & b.** Counterconditioning is the replacement of an undesired response with a desired one by means of aversive conditioning or systematic desensitization.

**d.** Rational-emotive therapy is a cognitive approach that challenges people's self-defeating attitudes.

**18. d.** is the answer. (p. 473)

**19. b.** is the answer. (p. 480)

**a.** Spontaneous remission refers to improvement without any treatment.

**c.** Transference is the psychoanalytic phenomenon in which a client transfers feelings from other relationships onto his or her analyst.

**d.** Interpretation is the psychoanalytic procedure through which the analyst helps the client become aware of resistances and understand their meaning.

**20. c.** is the answer. (p. 475)

### Matching Items

| | | |
|---|---|---|
| **1.** e (p. 470) | **5.** f (p. 464) | **9.** h (p. 482) |
| **2.** j (p. 466) | **6.** a (p. 469) | **10.** i (p. 467) |
| **3.** b (p. 467) | **7.** g (p. 462) | |
| **4.** d (p. 471) | **8.** c (p. 487) | |

## Progress Test 2

### Multiple-Choice Questions

**1. c.** is the answer. (p. 464)

**a.** This answer would be a correct description of Joseph Wolpe.

**b.** There is no such thing as insight therapy.

**d.** This answer would be a correct description of Albert Ellis.

**2. a.** is the answer. (p. 469)

**b.** In systematic desensitization, a hierarchy of anxiety-provoking stimuli is gradually associated with a relaxed state.

**c.** Transference refers to a patient's transferring of feelings from other relationships onto his or her psychoanalyst.

**d.** Electroconvulsive therapy is a biomedical shock treatment.

**e.** A token economy is based on operant conditioning techniques.

**3. c.** is the answer. (p. 464)

**a.** Behavior therapy focuses on behavior, not self-awareness.

**b.** Psychoanalysis focuses on bringing repressed feelings into awareness.

**d.** Biomedical therapy focuses on physical treatment through drugs, ECT, or psychosurgery.

**4. a.** is the answer. (p. 472)

**b.** Behavior therapy focuses on behavior, not cognition.

**c.** Psychodynamic therapists try to understand patients' current symptoms by exploring their childhood experiences.

**d.** Person-centered therapists generally take a nondirective approach in working with clients.

**5. a.** is the answer. For behavior therapy, the problem behaviors *are* the problems. (p. 466)

**b.** Cognitive therapy teaches people to think and act in more adaptive ways.

**c.** Humanistic therapy promotes growth and self-fulfillment by providing an empathic, genuine, and accepting environment.

**d.** Psychoanalytic therapy focuses on uncovering and interpreting repressed feelings.

**e.** Family therapy focuses on the individual's relation to others.

**6. b.** is the answer. Counterconditioning techniques involve taking an established CS, which triggers an undesirable CR, and pairing it with a new UCS in order to condition a new, and more adaptive, CR. (p. 467)

**a.** As indicated by the name, counterconditioning techniques are a form of conditioning; they do not involve learning by observation.

**c. & d.** The principles of operant conditioning are the basis of behavior modification, which, in contrast to counterconditioning techniques, involves use of reinforcement.

**7. d.** is the answer. (p. 467)

**a.** This is a confrontational therapy, which is aimed at teaching people to think and act in more adaptive ways.

**b.** Aversive conditioning is a form of counterconditioning in which unwanted behavior is associated with unpleasant feelings.

**c.** Counterconditioning is a general term, including not only systematic desensitization, in which a hierarchy of fears is desensitized, but also other techniques, such as aversive conditioning.

**8. e.** is the answer. (p. 470)

**a., b., & d.** These techniques are based on classical conditioning.

**c.** This is a type of cognitive therapy.

**9. d.** is the answer. (p. 470)

**10. c.** is the answer. (p. 471)

**a.** Psychoanalysis focuses on bringing repressed feelings into awareness, so irrational thinking is not a concern.

**b.** In this humanistic therapy, the therapist facilitates the client's growth by offering a genuine, accepting, and empathic environment.

**d.** Behavior therapy concentrates on modifying the actual symptoms of psychological problems.

**11. c.** is the answer. (p. 484)

12. **c.** is the answer. (p. 484)

13. **d.** is the answer. Lithium works as a mood stabilizer. (p. 485)
    **a. & c.** Valium and Librium are antianxiety drugs.
    **b.** Chlorpromazine is an antipsychotic drug.

14. **a.** is the answer. Antianxiety drugs are among the most heavily prescribed of all drugs. (p. 484)

15. **c.** is the answer. (p. 470)
    **a.** Behavior therapy is most likely to be successful in treating specific behavior problems, such as phobias.
    **b. & d.** The text does not single out particular disorders for which these therapies tend to be most effective.

16. **d.** is the answer. (p. 487)

17. **d.** is the answer. Even when dealing with seriously depressed adults, the paraprofessionals were as effective as the professionals. (p. 481)

18. **d.** is the answer. (pp. 480–481)

19. **d.** is the answer. (p. 474)
    **a.** This is true of most forms of psychotherapy.
    **b. & c.** This is true of humanistic, cognitive, and behavior therapies.

20. **c.** is the answer. Although aversive conditioning may work in the short run, the person's ability to discriminate between the situation in which the aversive conditioning occurs and other situations can limit the treatment's effectiveness. (p. 469)
    **a., b., & d.** These were not offered in the text as limitations of the effectiveness of aversive conditioning.

## Matching Items

| | | |
|---|---|---|
| **1.** d (p. 465) | **5.** c (p. 485) | **9.** f (p. 484) |
| **2.** h (p. 470) | **6.** b (p. 483) | **10.** g (p. 462) |
| **3.** e (p. 480) | **7.** i (p. 482) | |
| **4.** a (p. 486) | **8.** j (p. 483) | |

# Thinking Critically About Chapter 13

## Multiple-Choice Questions

1. **d.** is the answer. Resistances are blocks in the flow of free association that hint at underlying anxiety. (p. 463)
   **a.** In transference, a patient redirects feelings from other relationships to his or her analyst.
   **b.** The goal of psychoanalysis is for patients to gain insight into their feelings.
   **c.** Although such hesitation may well involve material that has been repressed, the hesitation itself is a resistance.

2. **d.** is the answer. In transference, the patient develops feelings toward the therapist that were experienced in important early relationships but were repressed. (p. 463)
   **a.** Projection is a defense mechanism in which a person imputes his or her own feelings to someone else.
   **b.** Resistances are blocks in the flow of free association that indicate repressed material.
   **c.** Regression is a defense mechanism in which a person retreats to an earlier form of behavior.

3. **d.** is the answer. According to Rogers' person-centered therapy, the therapist must exhibit genuineness, acceptance, and empathy if the client is to move toward self-fulfillment. (p. 464)
   **a.** Psychoanalysts are much more directive in providing interpretations of clients' problems than are humanistic therapists.
   **b.** Behavior therapists focus on modifying the behavioral symptoms of psychological problems.
   **c.** Cognitive therapists teach people to think and act in new, more adaptive ways.

4. **d.** is the answer. Aversive conditioning is the classical conditioning technique in which a positive response is replaced by a negative response. (In this example, the UCS is the blast of smoke, the CS is the taste of the cigarette as it is inhaled, and the intended CR is aversion to cigarettes.) (p. 469)
   **a.** Rational-emotive therapy is a confrontational cognitive therapy.
   **b.** Behavior modification applies the principles of operant conditioning and thus, in contrast to the example, uses reinforcement.
   **c.** Systematic desensitization is used to help people overcome specific anxieties.

5. **d.** is the answer. Because the psychologist is challenging Darnel's illogical, self-defeating attitude, this response is most typical of rational-emotive therapy. (p. 471)
   **a.** Behavior therapists focus on modifying the behavioral symptoms of psychological problems.
   **b.** Psychoanalysts focus on helping patients gain insight into previously repressed feelings.
   **c.** Person-centered therapists attempt to facilitate clients' growth by offering a genuine, accepting, empathic environment.

6. **b.** is the answer. Psychiatrists are physicians who specialize in treating psychological disorders. As doctors they can prescribe medications. (p. 477)
   **a., c., & d.** These professionals cannot prescribe drugs.

7. **c.** is the answer. (p. 483)

**a.** This is a classical conditioning technique in which an unpleasant state is associated with an unwanted behavior.

**b.** In this design, which is not mentioned in the text, there is only a single research group.

**d.** This answer would be correct if the experimenter, but not the subjects, knew which condition was in effect.

8. **a.** is the answer. (p. 484)
   **b.** Lithium is used to treat bipolar disorder.
   **c.** Valium is an antianxiety drug.
   **d.** Thorazine is an antipsychotic drug.

9. **e.** is the answer. (p. 479)
   **a.** Psychotherapy has proven "somewhat effective" and more cost-effective than physician care for psychological disorders.
   **b. & c.** Behavior and cognitive therapies are effective in treating specific behavior problems and depression, respectively, but not necessarily in treating other problems.
   **d.** The text does not specify which problems are best treated with group therapy.

10. **a.** is the answer. (p. 466)
    **b. & c.** These types of therapists are more concerned with promoting self-fulfillment (humanistic) and healthy patterns of thinking (cognitive) than with correcting specific problem behaviors.
    **d.** Psychoanalysts see the behavior merely as a symptom and focus their treatment on its presumed underlying cause.

11. **a.** is the answer. (p. 467)
    **b.** Aversive conditioning associates unpleasant states with unwanted behaviors.
    **c.** Shaping is an operant conditioning technique in which successive approximations of a desired behavior are reinforced.
    **d.** Free association is a psychoanalytic technique in which a patient says whatever comes to mind.
    **e.** Rational-emotive therapy is a confrontational cognitive therapy.

12. **b.** is the answer. (p. 470)

13. **c.** is the answer. (p. 473)
    **a. & b.** Behavior therapists make extensive use of techniques based on both operant and classical conditioning.
    **d.** Neither behavior therapists nor cognitive-behavior therapists focus on clients' unconscious urges.

14. **d.** is the answer. (p. 487)
    **a.** This would be the perspective of a cognitive-behavior therapist.
    **b.** This would be the perspective of a psychoanalyst or Gestalt therapist.

**c.** This would be the perspective of a behavior therapist.

15. **a.** is the answer. (p. 483)

16. **c.** is the answer. (p. 484)

17. **c.** is the answer. (p. 487)

18. **b.** is the answer. (p. 485)

19. **a.** is the answer. (p. 462)
    **c.** Cognitive therapists avoid reference to unconscious feelings and would therefore be uninterested in interpreting dreams.

20. **d.** is the answer. A key aim of psychoanalysis is to unearth and understand repressed impulses. (p. 462)
    **a., b., & c.** Behavior and cognitive therapists avoid concepts such as "repression" and "unconscious"; behavior and humanistic therapists focus on the present rather than the past.

### Essay Question

Psychoanalysts assume that psychological problems such as depression are caused by unresolved, repressed, and unconscious impulses and conflicts from childhood. A psychoanalyst would probably attempt to bring these repressed feelings into Willie's conscious awareness and help him gain insight into them. He or she would likely try to interpret Willie's resistance during free association, the latent content of his dreams, and any emotional feelings he might transfer to the analyst.

Cognitive therapists assume that a person's emotional reactions are influenced by the person's thoughts in response to the event in question. A cognitive therapist would probably try to teach Willie new and more constructive ways of thinking in order to reverse his catastrophizing beliefs about himself, his situation, and his future.

Biomedical therapists attempt to treat disorders by altering the functioning of the patient's brain. A biomedical therapist would probably prescribe an antidepressant drug such as fluoxetine to increase the availability of norepinephrine and serotonin in Willie's nervous system. If Willie's depression is especially severe, a *psychiatrist* might treat it with several sessions of electroconvulsive therapy.

## Key Terms

### Writing Definitions

1. **Psychotherapy** is an emotionally charged, confiding interaction between a trained therapist and someone who suffers from psychological difficulties. (p. 461)

2. With an **eclectic approach**, therapists are not locked into one form of psychotherapy, but draw on whatever combination seems best suited to a client's needs. (p. 462)

3. **Psychoanalysis**, the therapy developed by Freud, attempts to give clients self-insight by bringing into awareness and interpreting previously repressed feelings. (p. 462)

   *Example*: The tools of the **psychoanalyst** include free association, the analysis of dreams and transferences, and the interpretation of repressed impulses.

4. **Resistance** is the psychoanalytic term for the blocking from consciousness of anxiety-provoking memories. Hesitation during free association may reflect resistance. (p. 463)

5. **Interpretation** is the psychoanalytic term for the analyst's helping the client to understand resistances and other aspects of behavior, so that the client may gain deeper insights. (p. 463)

6. **Transference** is the psychoanalytic term for a patient's redirecting to the analyst emotions from other relationships. (p. 463)

7. **Person-centered therapy** is a humanistic therapy developed by Rogers, in which growth and self-awareness are facilitated in an environment that offers genuineness, acceptance, and empathy. (p. 464)

8. **Active listening** is a nondirective technique of person-centered therapy, in which the listener echoes, restates, clarifies, but does not interpret, clients' remarks. (p. 465)

9. **Behavior therapy** is therapy that applies principles of operant or classical conditioning to the elimination of problem behaviors. (p. 466)

10. **Counterconditioning** is a category of behavior therapy in which new responses are classically conditioned to stimuli that elicit unwanted behaviors. (p. 467)

11. **Systematic desensitization** is a type of counterconditioning in which a state of relaxation is classically conditioned to a hierarchy of gradually increasing anxiety-provoking stimuli. (p. 467)

    *Memory aid*: This is a form of counterconditioning in which sensitive, anxiety-triggering stimuli are *desensitized* in a progressive, or **systematic**, fashion.

12. **Aversive conditioning** is a form of counterconditioning in which an unpleasant state becomes associated with an unwanted behavior. (p. 469)

13. A **token economy** is an operant conditioning procedure in which desirable behaviors are promoted in people by rewarding them with tokens, or secondary reinforcers, which can be exchanged for privileges or treats. For the most part, token economies are used in hospitals, schools, and other institutional settings. (p. 470)

14. **Cognitive therapy** focuses on teaching people new and more adaptive ways of thinking and acting. The therapy is based on the idea that our feelings and responses to events are strongly influenced by our thinking, or cognition. (p. 470)

15. **Rational-emotive therapy** is a confrontational cognitive therapy that maintains that irrational thinking is the cause of many psychological problems. (p. 471)

16. **Family therapy** views problem behavior as partially engendered by the client's family system and environment. Therapy therefore focuses on relationships and problems among the various members of the family. (p. 474)

17. **Psychopharmacology** is the study of the effects of drugs on mind and behavior. (p. 482)

    *Memory aid*: Pharmacology is the science of the uses and effects of drugs. *Psycho*pharmacology is the science that studies the psychological effects of drugs.

18. **Lithium** is an antidepressant drug that is commonly used to stabilize the manic-depressive mood swings of the bipolar disorder. (p. 485)

19. In **electroconvulsive therapy (ECT)**, a biomedical therapy often used to treat major depressive disorder, electric shock is passed through the brain. ECT may work by increasing the availability of norepinephrine, the neurotransmitter that elevates mood. (p. 485)

20. **Psychosurgery** is a biomedical therapy that attempts to change behavior by removing or destroying brain tissue. Since drug therapy became widely available in the 1950s, psychosurgery has been infrequently used. (p. 486)

21. Once used to control violent patients, the **lobotomy** is a form of psychosurgery in which the nerves linking the emotion centers of the brain to the frontal lobes are severed. (p. 486)

*Cross-Check*

**ACROSS**

4. aversive
9. humanistic
10. flooding
12. behavior
15. lithium

**DOWN**

1. biomedical
2. psychosurgery
3. antipsychotic
5. free association
6. electroconvulsive
7. active listening
8. rational-emotive
11. lobotomy
13. eclectic
14. insight

---

## FOCUS ON VOCABULARY AND LANGUAGE

### The Psychological Therapies

*Page 461:* . . . *"beating the devil" out of people* . . . Myers notes that we have dealt with people suffering from psychological problems with many different odd and strange techniques (*a bewildering variety of methods*), including cutting holes in the skull, piercing veins or attaching leeches to remove blood from the body (*bleeding*), and striking or whipping people in order to force demons out of the body (*"beating the devil" out of people*). This history shows how puzzling (*mystifying*) and difficult to cure (*intractable*) these disorders have been.

*Page 461:* Each technique is distinctive, but there are *common threads.* The most common forms of psychological therapy (**psychotherapy**) are based on the four major perspectives in psychology: psychoanalytic, humanistic, behavioral, and cognitive. While each type of therapy is unique (*distinctive*), the effectiveness of all may derive from similar underlying factors (*common threads*). About fifty percent of psychotherapists claim that they use a combination (*blend*) of techniques (an **eclectic approach**).

*Page 462 (caption):* Visitors paid to *gawk* at the *patients* as if they were viewing zoo animals. In the past, mentally disordered people (*patients*) were confined to hospitals (*insane asylums*) and were often treated badly. For instance, some hospitals raised money by selling tickets to the public who could come and stare (*gawk*) at the inmates (*patients*), much as we do today when we visit the zoo and look at the captive animals.

*Page 462:* . . . psychoanalysis assumes that many psychological problems are *fueled* by childhood's *residue* of supposedly *repressed impulses and conflicts.* Freud's psychoanalytic techniques are used by many therapists; their fundamental tenet (*assumption*) is that mental disorders are created and kept in existence (*fueled*) by hidden (*repressed*) childhood

urges and opposing psychic forces (*conflicts*). Psychoanalysis attempts to restore the patient to mental health by bringing these submerged (*buried*) feelings into conscious awareness where they can be examined and dealt with (*worked through*). As Myers puts it, psychoanalysis digs up (*unearths*) the past in the hopes of uncovering (*unmasking*) the present.

*Page 464:* Not surprisingly, then, humanistic therapists *aim to boost* self-fulfillment by helping people grow in self-awareness and self-acceptance. The most popular humanistic technique is Carl Rogers' nondirective person-centered therapy. The goal is to increase (*the aim is to boost*) the client's feelings of accomplishment and achievement (self-actualization) by providing nonthreatening opportunities for living in the present, for becoming less critical of one's self, and for becoming more self-aware.

*Page 465: "And that just really knocks the props out from under you."* In Carl Rogers' therapy sessions, he attempts to be genuine, accepting, and empathic; he also mirrors (*reflects*) back to the client in different words the feelings that were expressed. The client said he had been told that he was no good, and Rogers reflects the feelings he detects by saying that it must seem that the client's self-worth had been undermined (*knocked the props out from under you*).

*Page 469:* In treating *an alcoholic,* aversion therapists offer appealing drinks *laced* with a drug that produces *severe nausea.* Behavior therapists, focusing on observable behaviors, use a number of techniques based on well established learning principles. Two counterconditioning techniques based on classical conditioning are *systematic desensitization* and *aversive conditioning.* In aversive therapy, people who regularly drink too much (*alcoholics*) are given enticing alcoholic beverages which are infused (*laced*) with a substance that induces sickness (*severe nausea*). Alcohol should now be a potent conditioned stimulus that elicits unpleasant feelings; as a result, the alcoholic should want to avoid these drinks.

Research shows some limited success with this approach.

*Page 469:* The combination of positive reinforcement of desired behaviors and the ignoring or punishing of *aggressive and self-abusive* behaviors *worked wonders.* Another type of behavior therapy is based on operant conditioning principles and involves voluntary behavior followed by pleasant or unpleasant consequences. Socially withdrawn autistic children, treated to an intensive 2-year program of positive reinforcement for desired behaviors and punishment for violent and self-injurious (*aggressive and self-abusive*) behaviors, responded extremely well (*it worked wonders for them*).

*Page 470:* The **cognitive therapies** assume that our thinking *colors* our feelings. . . . The underlying assumption of the cognitive approach to therapy is that thoughts precede and influence (*color*) our feelings. If certain destructive patterns of thinking are learned, then it must be possible to unlearn them and replace them with more constructive ways of viewing what happens to us.

*Page 471:* They can be easily elicited and demolished by any scientist *worth his or her salt;* and the rational-emotive therapist is exactly that: an exposing and *nonsense-annihilating* scientist. Albert Ellis's rational-emotive therapy is based on the belief that our faulty and illogical cognitions are the cause of much of our unhappiness. These often hidden (*covert*) thoughts or hypotheses about ourselves and others can be brought out (*elicited*) by any competent professional (*worth his or her salt*); the rational-emotive therapist exposes and destroys (*annihilates* or *"makes mincemeat of"*) these illogical and irrational (*nonsensical*) ideas.

*Page 471:* . . . *crap!* . . . *turd?* Ellis uses a very confrontational style with his clients and does not refrain from using obscenities to challenge their illogical thinking. In the excerpt from a therapy session, Ellis uses several such expletives. *Crap* means excrement and is commonly used to refer to anything worthless, objectionable, or ridiculous; a *turd* is a piece of excrement and in common usage refers to a contemptible person.

*Page 472:* . . . *catastrophizing* . . . Aaron Beck, another cognitive therapist, agrees with Ellis that the way to help depressed people feel better is to turn around (*reverse*) their negative, distorted thinking, which tends to transform ordinary events into disasters (*catastrophizing*). The goal is to get them to think about their lives in more positive terms (*get them to take off the dark glasses*).

*Evaluating Psychotherapies*

*Page 475:* "*Hang in there* until you find [a psychotherapist] *who fills the bill.*" Each year in the United States about 15 percent of the population seek help for psychological and addictive disorders. Many people, including advice columnist Ann Landers, recommend that troubled people get professional help and that they persevere (*hang in there*) in finding the right therapist to meet their needs (*who fills the bill*).

*Page 476:* If clients' *testimonials* were the only yardstick, we could strongly affirm the effectiveness of psychotherapy. The question of whether or not psychotherapy is effective is a very complex issue. If the only measure (*yardstick*) was what clients said about their therapy (*testimonials*), then the conclusion would have to be that psychotherapy works. (A very high percentage of people surveyed about their experiences with mental health professionals claim they were satisfied.) Myers points out that such testimonials can be misleading and invalid.

*Page 476:* When, with the normal *ebb and flow* of events, the crisis passes, people may attribute their improvement to the therapy. Because of some serious traumatic events (*crises*) in their lives, people may end up seeing a therapist; after many sessions they may feel much better. During the ordinary course (*ebb and flow*) of events, however, the crisis is likely to have passed; thus, their present feelings of well-being may have little to do with the psychotherapy.

*Page 477 (Close-Up):* If you are looking for a therapist, you may wish to *shop around* by having a preliminary consultation with two or three therapists. Myers lists some of the most frequent signs (*common trouble signals*) which may indicate that a person needs professional psychological help. He also recommends contacting a number of different therapists (*shopping around*) to find out about their credentials, their approach to treatment, how much they charge, and how they would treat your particular problem.

*Page 478:* In psychology, *the opening volley* in what became a spirited debate over such research was *fired* by British psychologist Hans Eysenck (1952). Eysenck was one of the first psychologists to criticize psychotherapy (*he fired the opening volley*), starting a major battle between those who believed in the effectiveness of therapy and those who were skeptical. Much controlled research has been done since then.

*Page 479:* In general, therapy is most effective when the problem is *clear-cut* (Singer, 1981). Psychotherapy tends to work best when the disturbances are well-defined (*clear-cut*) and explicitly stated or understood. For example, those who suffer from irrational fears (*phobias*), are timid or shy (*unassertive*), or have a psychologically caused sexual disorder respond better to therapy than those who suffer from *schizophrenia* or who want a total personality change.

*Page 480:* Each therapy, in its individual way, may *harness* the client's own healing powers. Research has shown that actual therapy is better than no treatment, but that placebo-treated people improve significantly. This suggests that therapies work in part because they offer hope; each different type of therapy may be effective to the extent that it capitalizes on and uses (*harnesses*) the clients' ability for self-healing.

*Page 481:* Indeed, some believe that warmth and *empathy* are *hallmarks* of healers everywhere, whether psychiatrists, witch doctors, or shamans (Torrey, 1986). In general, therapies are approximately the same in effectiveness, but that does not mean that all therapists are equal in this respect. Fundamental qualities (*hallmarks*) of effective therapists are an ability to understand other peoples' experiences (*empathy*) and a capacity to show genuine concern and care (*warmth*). In addition, good listening skills, a reassuring manner, and concern for gaining (*earning*) the client's respect and trust help in the therapeutic process.

### The Biomedical Therapies

*Page 483:* Researchers are testing possible *cousin* drugs that would offer the same benefits without the blood problem. A relatively new antipsychotic drug, clozapine, is one of the most effective treatments for schizophrenia. It does, however, have a toxic effect on white blood cells in 1 or 2 percent of patients, so scientists are now testing closely related (*cousin*) drugs that are equally effective but appear to be without the poisonous side effects.

*Page 484:* Antipsychotics such as Thorazine are powerful drugs that can produce *sluggishness, tremors, and twitches* similar to those of Parkinson's disease, which is marked by too little dopamine (Kaplan & Saddock, 1989). Because of the serious side effects of some antipsychotic drugs—tiredness and apathy (*sluggishness*), shaking limbs (*tremors*), and sudden involuntary spasms (*twitches*)—therapists have to be

very careful (*they have to tread a fine line*) in selecting the dose that will relieve the symptoms but will not produce the side effects.

*Page 484:* Routinely "*popping a Valium*" at the first sign of tension can produce psychological dependence on the drug. The most popular antianxiety drugs (Valium and Librium) are central nervous system depressants, and they reduce tension without causing too much drowsiness. As a consequence, they are prescribed for a variety of problems, including minor emotional stresses. If a person regularly takes an antianxiety drug (routinely "*pops a Valium*") whenever there is the slightest feeling of anxiety, the result can be psychological dependence on the drug. Withdrawal symptoms for heavy users include increased anxiety and an inability to sleep (*insomnia*).

*Page 484:* As the antianxiety drugs calm anxious people down, the antidepressants sometimes *lift depressed people up*. Antidepressants work by either increasing the availability of the neurotransmitters norepinephrine or serotonin, blocking their reabsorption, or by inhibiting an enzyme that breaks them down. Thus, they tend to make depressed people feel more alive and aroused (*they lift them up*).

*Page 485:* ECT therefore gained a *barbaric* image that lingers to the present. Electroconvulsive therapy (ECT) has proven quite effective and is used mainly for chronically depressed people who have not responded to drug therapy. In 1938, when ECT was first introduced, wide-awake patients were strapped to a table to prevent them from hurting themselves during the convulsions and were shocked (*jolted*) with 100 volts of electricity to the brain. Although the procedure is different today, these inhumane (*barbaric*) images tend to remain in people's minds. As Myers notes, ECT is credited with saving many from suicide, but its *Frankensteinlike* image continues. (Dr. Frankenstein is a fictional character who created a monster from the body parts of dead people.)

### Preventing Psychological Disorders

*Page 487:* Preventive mental health is *upstream work*. Some psychologists believe that prevention is better than cure, and they support programs that help relieve and stop poverty, racism, discrimination, and other disempowering or demoralizing situations. The attempt to prevent psychological disorders by getting rid of conditions that may cause them is extremely difficult (*upstream work*).

# 14

# Social Psychology

## Chapter Overview

Chapter 14 demonstrates the powerful influences of social situations on the behavior of individuals. Central to this topic are research studies on attitudes and actions, conformity, compliance, and group and cultural influences. The social principles that emerge help us to understand how individuals are influenced by advertising, political candidates, and the various groups to which they belong. Although social influences are powerful, it is important to remember the significant role of individuals in choosing and creating the social situations that influence them.

The chapter also discusses how people relate to one another, from the negative—developing prejudice, behaving aggressively, and provoking conflict—to the positive—being attracted to people who are nearby and/or similar and behaving altruistically.

The chapter concludes with a discussion of techniques that have been shown to promote conflict resolution.

Although there is some terminology for you to learn in this chapter, your primary task is to absorb the findings of the many research studies discussed. The chapter headings, which organize the findings, should prove especially useful to you here. In addition, you might, for each main topic (conformity, group influence, aggression, etc.), ask yourself the question, "What situational factors promote this phenomenon?" The research findings can then form the basis for your answers.

NOTE: Answer guidelines for all Chapter 14 questions begin on page 402.

## Guided Study

The text chapter should be studied one section at a time. Before you read, preview each section by skimming it, noting headings and boldface items. Then read the appropriate section objectives from the following outline. Keep these objectives in mind and, as you read the chapter section, search for the information that will enable you to meet each objective. Once you have finished a section, write out answers for its objectives.

*Social Thinking* (pp. 491–496)

> David Myers at times uses idioms that are unfamiliar to some readers. If you do not know the meaning of any of the following words, phrases, or expressions in the context in which they appear in the text, refer to page 413 for an explanation: *tart-tongued remark; freeloaders; folks often talk and act a different game; brainwashed; chicken-and-egg spiral; heartening implications.*

1. Discuss attribution theory, focusing on the fundamental attribution error, and describe some possible effects of attribution.

2. Define *attitude* and identify the conditions under which attitudes predict behavior.

3. Describe how actions influence attitudes and explain how cognitive dissonance theory accounts for this phenomenon.

7. Describe group polarization and show how it can be a source of groupthink.

8. Discuss how personal control and social control interact in guiding behavior and explain how a minority can influence the majority.

## Social Influence (pp. 496–509)

> If you do not know the meaning of any of the following words, phrases, or expressions in the context in which they appear in the text, refer to pages 413–415 for an explanation: *canned laughter; open-minded; draw slips from a hat; draw back; kindness and obedience on a collision course; zap; devilish villains; tug-of-war; one-way flight to annihilation; waffles; norms also grease the social machinery; norms often bemuse or befuddle; men initiate dates . . . pick up the check; In the flick of an apron.*

9. Discuss the influence of culture and gender roles on behavior.

4. Describe the results of Asch's experiments on conformity and distinguish between normative and informational social influence.

## Social Relations (pp. 509–533)

> If you do not know the meaning of any of the following words, phrases, or expressions in the context in which they appear in the text, refer to pages 415–416 for an explanation: *horsing around; with the toss of a coin; handy emotional outlet; Ferdinand; skyrocketed; she melts; an outlet for bottled-up impulses; diabolical images; familiarity breeds fondness; beauty is only skin deep; E.T. was as ugly as Darth Vader; opposites retract; revved up; bystanders turns people away from the path that leads to helping; blasé; sneaky, smart-alecky stinkers; down the tension ladder to a safer rung.*

5. Summarize the findings from Milgram's obedience studies.

6. Discuss how the presence of others may produce social facilitation, social loafing, or deindividuation.

10. Describe the roles of social inequalities, ingroup bias, and scapegoating in prejudice.

**11.** Discuss the cognitive roots of prejudice.

**12.** Describe the impact of biology, aversive events, and learning experiences on aggressive behavior.

**13.** Discuss the effects of television violence and pornographic films on viewers.

**14.** Identify factors that fuel conflict and discuss effective ways of resolving such conflict.

**15.** Identify the determinants of social attraction and distinguish between passionate and companionate love.

**16.** Describe and explain the bystander effect.

**17.** Discuss how social exchange theory and social norms explain altruism.

## Chapter Review

When you have finished reading the chapter, work through the material that follows to review it. Complete the sentences and answer the questions. As you proceed, evaluate your performance for each section by consulting the answers on page 405. Do not continue with the next section until you understand each answer. If you need to, review or reread the appropriate section in the textbook before continuing.

**1.** Psychologists who study how we think about, influence, and relate to one another are called

_____ _____ .

*Social Thinking* (pp. 491–496)

**2.** Heider's theory of how we explain others' behavior is the _____ theory. According to this theory, we attribute behavior either to an internal cause, which is called a

_____ _____ ,

or to an external cause, which is called a

_____ .

**3.** Most people tend to _____ (overestimate/underestimate) the extent to which people's actions are influenced by social situations because their _____ is focused on the person. This tendency is called the

_____ _____

_____. When a person is explaining his or her *own* behavior, this tendency is _____ (stronger/weaker). When observers view the world from others' perspectives, attributions are _____ (the same/reversed).

Give an example of the practical consequences of attributions.

4. Beliefs and feelings that predispose our responses are called _____.

5. The many research studies on attitudes and actions conducted during the 1960s _____ (challenged/supported) the common assumption that our actions are guided by our attitudes.

List three conditions under which our attitudes do predict our actions. Give examples.

6. Many research studies demonstrate that our attitudes are strongly influenced by our _____. One example of this is the tendency for people who agree to a small request to comply later with a larger one. This is the _____-_____-_____ phenomenon.

7. A set of behaviors expected of someone in a given social position is called a _____.

8. Taking on a set of behaviors, or acting in a certain way, generally _____ (changes/does not change) people's attitudes.

9. According to _____ theory, thoughts and feelings change because people are motivated to justify actions that would otherwise seem hypocritical. This theory was proposed by _____.

10. Dissonance theory predicts that people induced (without coercion) to behave contrary to their true attitudes will be motivated to reduce the resulting _____ by changing their _____.

*Social Influence* (pp. 496–509)

11. The term that refers to the tendency to adjust one's behavior to coincide with an assumed group standard is _____.

12. The psychologist who first studied the effects of group pressure on conformity is _____.

13. In this study, when the opinion of other group members was contradicted by objective evidence, subjects _____ (were/were not) willing to conform to the group opinion.

14. One reason that people comply with social pressure is to gain approval or avoid rejection; this is called _____.

Understood rules for accepted and expected behavior are called _____.

15. Another reason people comply is that they have genuinely been influenced by what they have learned from others; this type of influence is called _____.

16. Conformity rates tend to be lower in _____ (individualist/collectivist) cultures.

17. The classic social psychology studies of obedience were conducted by _____.

When ordered by the experimenter to electrically shock the "learner," the majority of subjects (the "teachers") in these studies _____ (complied/refused).

List the conditions under which obedience was highest in Milgram's studies.

18. In getting people to administer increasingly larger shocks, Milgram was in effect applying the

_____-_____-

_____-_____

technique.

19. The tendency to perform a task better when other people are present is called _____

_____ . In general, people become aroused in the presence of others, and arousal enhances the correct response on a(n) _____ (easy/difficult) task. Later research revealed that arousal strengthens the response that is most _____ in a given situation.

20. Researchers have found that the reactions of people in crowded situations are often _____ (lessened/amplified).

21. Ingham found that people worked _____ (harder/less hard) in a team tug-of-war than they had in an individual contest. This phenomenon has been called

_____ _____ .

22. The feeling of anonymity and loss of restraint that an individual may develop when in a group is called _____ .

23. Over time, the initial differences between groups usually _____ (increase/decrease). The enhancement of each group's prevailing tendency is called

_____ .

24. When the desire for group harmony overrides realistic thinking in individuals, the phenomenon known as _____ has occurred.

25. In considering the power of social influence, we cannot overlook the interaction of

_____ _____

(the power of the situation) and

_____ _____

(the power of the individual).

26. A minority opinion will have the most success in swaying the majority if it takes a stance that is _____ (unswerving/flexible).

27. The enduring behaviors, ideas, attitudes, and traditions of a group of people defines its

_____ .

28. All cultural groups _____ (do/do not) evolve their own social norms.

29. The buffer zone that people maintain around their bodies is called _____

_____ . Culture _____ (does/does not) influence personal space.

Identify several cultural differences in personal space, expressiveness, and pace of life.

30. A set of expectations regarding how a female or male should act is called a _____

_____ .

31. Evolution may predispose men to

_____ and women to

_____ skills in order to serve the species' reproductive goals. Gender roles

_____ (are/are not) rigidly fixed by evolution because they vary across _____ and over

**32.** In the United States, gender roles _____ (have/have not) changed dramatically since the 1960s.

*Social Relations* (pp. 509–533)

**33.** Prejudice is an _____ and usually _____ attitude toward a group that involves overgeneralized beliefs known as _____ .

**34.** Based on what Americans say today, racial and gender attitudes _____ (have changed dramatically/have not changed very much) over the last half century.

**35.** Worldwide, two-thirds of children without basic schooling are _____ (boys/girls).

**36.** For those with money, power, and prestige, prejudice often serves as a means of _____ social inequalities.

**37.** In the phenomenon called the _____ prophecy, discrimination increases prejudice through the reactions it provokes in its _____ . Equally damaging is the tendency of people to _____ victims for their plight.

**38.** Prejudice is also fostered by the _____ , a tendency to favor groups to which one belongs.

**39.** That prejudice derives from attempts to blame others for one's frustration is proposed by the _____ theory.

**40.** Research suggests that prejudice may also derive from _____ , the process by which we attempt to simplify our world by classifying people into groups. One by-product of this process is that people tend to _____ the similarity of those within a group.

**41.** Another factor that fosters the formation of group stereotypes and prejudice is the tendency to _____ from vivid or memorable cases.

**42.** The belief that people get what they deserve— that the good are rewarded and the bad pun-

ished—is expressed in the _____-_____ phenomenon. This phenomenon is based in part on _____ _____ , the tendency to believe that one would have foreseen how something turned out.

**43.** Aggressive behavior is defined by the text as _____ _____ .

**44.** Freud believed that people have a self-destructive _____ that is manifest as aggression when it is _____ toward others. Today most psychologists _____ (do/do not) consider human aggression to be instinctive.

**45.** In humans, aggressiveness _____ (varies/does not vary) greatly from culture to culture.

**46.** That there are genetic influences on aggression can be shown by the fact that many species of animals have been _____ for aggressiveness.

**47.** Twin studies suggest that genes _____ (do/do not) influence human aggression.

**48.** In humans and animals, aggression is activated and inhibited by _____ systems, such as those in the _____ _____ , which are in turn influenced by _____ and other substances in the blood.

**49.** The aggressive behavior of animals can be manipulated by altering the levels of the hormone _____ . When this level is _____ (increased/decreased), aggressive tendencies are reduced.

**50.** One drug that unleashes aggressive responses to provocation is _____ .

**51.** According to the _____-_____ principle, inability to achieve a goal leads to anger, which may generate aggression.

**52.** Aggressive behavior can be learned through direct _____ , as shown by the fact that people use aggression where they've found it pays, and through _____ of others.

53. Crime rates are higher in countries in which there is a large disparity between those who are _____ and those who are _____ . High violence rates also are typical of cultures and families in which there is minimal _____ _____ .

54. Violence on television appears to promote aggressive behavior as a result of four factors: the excitement of television causes _____ ; seeing violence triggers _____ related to violence; TV violence erodes viewers' _____ ; and viewers tend to _____ behaviors they have seen.

55. The incidence of reported rape in the United States has _____ (increased/ decreased) dramatically over the past 30 years. Most rapes _____ (are/are not) reported.

56. Studies of pornography and aggression _____ (generally/do not generally) show a relationship between availability of pornography and the incidence of sexual aggression.

Comment on the impression of women that pornography frequently conveys and the effects this impression has on attitudes and behavior.

57. Most men _____ (are/are not) sexually aroused when viewing rape depictions. Convicted rapists _____ (are/ are not) sexually aroused by the same depictions.

Summarize the findings of the Zillmann and Bryant study on the effects of pornography on attitudes toward rape.

58. Experiments have shown that it is not eroticism but depictions of _____ _____ that most directly affect men's acceptance and performance of aggression against women.

59. A perceived incompatibility of actions, goals, or ideas is called _____ . This perception can take place between individuals, _____ , or _____ .

60. Two destructive social processes that contribute to conflict are _____ _____ and _____ perceptions.

61. When the "non-zero-sum game" is played, most people fall into the social trap by mistrusting the other player and pursuing their own _____ .

62. The diabolical images people in conflict form of each other are called _____ - _____ perceptions.

63. Several psychological tendencies foster biased perceptions. First, leaders, like other people, tend to accept credit for good deeds but not blame for bad deeds, a phenomenon called the _____ .

Second, conflicting parties tend to attribute the other's actions to a negative disposition, an example of the _____ .

Preconceived attitudes, or _____ , also contribute to the problem, as does the _____ that often emerges within a group as the members' attitudes become _____ .

64. A prerequisite for, and perhaps the most powerful predictor of, attraction is _____ .

65. When people are repeatedly exposed to unfamiliar stimuli, their liking of the stimuli _____ (increases/decreases). This phenomenon is the _____ _____ effect. Robert Zajonc contends that this phenomenon was _____ for our ancestors, for whom the unfamiliar was often _____ . One implication of this is that _____ against those who are culturally different may be an _____ emotional response.

66. Our first impression of another person is most influenced by the person's _____ .

67. In a sentence, list several of the characteristics that physically attractive people are judged to possess: _____ _____ .

68. A person's attractiveness _____ (is/is not) strongly related to his or her self-esteem.

69. Cross-cultural research reveals that men judge women as more attractive if they have a _____ appearance, whereas women judge men who appear _____ , _____ , and _____ as more attractive.

State how evolutionary psychologists explain this gender difference.

70. Relationships in which the partners are very similar are _____ (more/less) likely to last.

71. Compared with strangers, friends and couples are more likely to be similar in terms of _____ _____ .

Explain what a reward theory of attraction is and how it can account for the three predictors of liking—proximity, attractiveness, and similarity.

72. Hatfield has distinguished two types of love: _____ love and _____ love.

73. According to the two-factor theory, emotions have two components: physical _____ and a _____ label.

74. When college men were placed in an aroused state, their feelings toward an attractive woman _____ (were/were not) more positive than those of men who had not been aroused.

75. Companionate love is promoted by _____ —mutual sharing and giving by both partners. Another key ingredient of loving relationships is the revealing of intimate aspects of ourselves through _____ .

76. An unselfish regard for the welfare of others is called _____ .

77. According to Darley and Latané, people will help only if a three-stage decision-making process is completed: Bystanders must first _____ the incident, then _____ it as an emergency, and finally _____ _____ for helping.

78. When people who overheard a seizure victim calling for help thought others were hearing the same plea, they were _____ (more/less) likely to go to his aid than when they thought no one else was aware of the emergency.

79. In a series of staged accidents, Latané and Darley found that a bystander was _____

(more/less) likely to help if other bystanders were present. This phenomenon has been called the _____ .

Identify the circumstances in which a person is most likely to offer help during an emergency.

80. The idea that social behavior aims to maximize rewards and minimize costs is proposed by

_____

theory.

81. One rule of social behavior tells us to return help to those who have helped us; this is the

_____ norm. Another tells us to help those who need our help; this is the

_____

norm.

82. Conflict resolution is most likely in situations characterized by _____ ,

_____ , and _____ .

83. In most situations, establishing contact between two conflicting groups _____ (is/is not) sufficient to resolve conflict.

84. In Sherif's study, two conflicting groups of campers were able to resolve their conflicts by working together on projects in which they shared _____ goals.

85. When conflicts arise, a third-party _____ may facilitate communication and promote understanding.

86. Osgood has advanced a strategy of conciliation called GRIT, which stands for

_____ and _____

_____ in _____-

_____ . The key to this method is each side's offering of a small

_____ gesture in order to increase mutual trust and cooperation.

## Progress Test 1

### Multiple-Choice Questions

Circle your answers to the following questions and check them with the answers on page 407. If your answer is incorrect, read the explanation for why it is incorrect and then consult the appropriate pages of the text (in parentheses following the correct answer).

1. In his study of obedience, Stanley Milgram found that the majority of subjects:
   a. refused to shock the learner even once.
   b. complied with the experiment until the "learner" first indicated pain.
   c. complied with the experiment until the "learner" began screaming in agony.
   d. complied with all the demands of the experiment.

2. According to cognitive dissonance theory, dissonance is most likely to occur when:
   a. a person's behavior is not based on strongly held attitudes.
   b. two people have conflicting attitudes and find themselves in disagreement.
   c. an individual does something that is personally disagreeable.
   d. an individual is coerced into doing something that he or she does not want to do.

3. Which of the following statements is true?
   a. Groups are almost never swayed by minority opinions.
   b. Group polarization is most likely to occur when group members frequently disagree with one another.
   c. Groupthink provides the consensus needed for effective decision making.
   d. A group that is like-minded will probably not change its opinions through discussion.

4. Conformity increased under which of the following conditions in Asch's studies of conformity?
   a. The group had three or more people.
   b. The group had high status.
   c. Individuals were made to feel insecure.
   d. The group was unanimous.
   e. All of the above increased conformity.

5. Social traps are situations in which:
   a. conflicting parties realize that they have shared goals, the attainment of which requires their mutual cooperation.
   b. conflicting parties have similar, and generally negative, views of one another.

c. conflicting parties each pursue their self-interests and become caught in mutually destructive behavior.

d. two conflicting groups meet face-to-face in an effort to resolve their differences.

6. The phenomenon in which individuals lose their identity and relinquish normal restraints when they are part of a group is called:

a. groupthink.
b. cognitive dissonance.
c. empathy.
d. deindividuation.

7. Subjects in Asch's line-judgment experiment conformed to the group standard when their judgments were observed by others but not when they were made in private. This tendency to conform in public demonstrates:

a. social facilitation.
b. overjustification.
c. informational social influence.
d. normative social influence.

8. In Milgram's obedience studies, subjects were *less* likely to follow the experimenter's orders when:

a. they heard the "learner" cry out in pain.
b. they merely administered the test while someone else delivered the shocks.
c. the "learner" was an older person or mentioned having some physical problem.
d. they saw another subject disobey instructions.

9. *Aggression* is defined as behavior that:

a. hurts another person.
b. is intended to hurt another person.
c. is hostile, passionate, and produces physical injury.
d. has all of the above characteristics.

10. Which of the following is true about aggression?

a. It varies too much to be instinctive in humans.
b. It is just one instinct among many.
c. It is instinctive but shaped by learning.
d. It is the most important human instinct.

11. Research studies have found a positive correlation between aggressive tendencies in animals and levels of the hormone:

a. estrogen.
b. adrenaline.
c. noradrenaline.
d. testosterone.
e. epinephrine.

12. Research studies have indicated that the tendency of viewers to misperceive normal sexuality, devalue their partners, and trivialize rape is:

a. increased by exposure to pornography.
b. not changed after exposure to pornography.

c. decreased in men by exposure to pornography.
d. decreased in both men and women by exposure to pornography.

13. Increasing the number of people that are present during an emergency tends to:

a. increase the likelihood that people will cooperate in rendering assistance.
b. decrease the empathy that people feel for the victim.
c. increase the role that social norms governing helping will play.
d. decrease the likelihood that anyone will help.

14. Which of the following was *not* mentioned in the text discussion of the roots of prejudice?

a. people's tendency to overestimate the similarity of people within groups
b. people's tendency to assume that exceptional, or especially memorable, individuals are unlike the majority of members of a group
c. people's tendency to assume that the world is just and that people get what they deserve
d. people's tendency to discriminate against those they view as "outsiders"

15. The mere exposure effect demonstrates that:

a. familiarity breeds contempt.
b. opposites attract.
c. birds of a feather flock together.
d. familiarity breeds fondness.

16. In one experiment, college men were physically aroused and then introduced to an attractive woman. Compared to men who had not been aroused, these men reported:

a. more positive feelings toward the woman.
b. more negative feelings toward the woman.
c. more ambiguous feelings about the woman.
d. feeling that the woman was "out of their league" in terms of attractiveness.
e. greater interest in the woman's attractiveness and less on her intelligence and personality.

17. The deep affection that is felt in long-lasting relationships is called _____ love; this feeling is fostered in relationships in which _____ .

a. passionate; there is equity between the partners
b. passionate; traditional roles are maintained
c. companionate; there is equity between the partners
d. companionate; traditional roles are maintained

18. Which of the following is associated with an increased tendency on the part of a bystander to offer help in an emergency situation?
    a. being in a good mood
    b. having recently needed help and not received it
    c. observing someone as he or she refuses to offer help
    d. being a female

19. The belief that those who suffer deserve their fate is expressed in the:
    a. just-world phenomenon.
    b. phenomenon of ingroup bias.
    c. fundamental attribution error.
    d. mirror-image perception principle.

20. According to social exchange theory, a person's tendency toward altruistic behavior is based on:
    a. a determination of the relatedness of those who will be affected.
    b. a cost-benefit analysis of any action.
    c. social norms.
    d. all of the above.

## Matching Items

Match each term with the appropriate definition or description.

**Terms**

_____  1. social facilitation
_____  2. social loafing
_____  3. culture
_____  4. norms
_____  5. role
_____  6. normative social influence
_____  7. informational social influence
_____  8. group polarization
_____  9. stereotype
_____ 10. attribution
_____ 11. altruism
_____ 12. mere exposure effect

**Definitions or Descriptions**

a. a causal explanation for someone's behavior
b. a generalized belief about a group of people
c. people work less hard in a group
d. performance is improved by an audience
e. a set of social expectations for a position
f. the effect of social approval or disapproval
g. rules for acceptable behavior
h. group discussion enhances prevailing tendencies
i. the effect of accepting others' opinions about something
j. unselfish regard for others
k. attitudes and traditions shared by a group
l. the increased liking of a stimulus that results from repeated exposure to it

# Progress Test 2

Progress Test 2 should be completed during a final chapter review. Answer the following questions after you thoroughly understand the correct answers for the Chapter Review and Progress Test 1.

## Multiple-Choice Questions

1. Which theorist argued that aggression was a manifestation of a person's "death instinct" redirected toward another person?
   a. Milgram
   b. Freud
   c. Lorenz
   d. Janis
   e. Asch

2. Regarding cultural diversity, which of the following is *not* true?
   a. Culture influences emotional expressiveness.
   b. Culture influences personal space.
   c. Culture does not have a strong influence on how strictly social roles are defined.
   d. All cultures evolve their own norms.

3. Regarding the influence of alcohol and testosterone on aggressive behavior, which of the following is true?
   a. Consumption of alcohol increases aggressive behavior; injections of testosterone reduce aggressive behavior.
   b. Consumption of alcohol reduces aggressive behavior; injections of testosterone increase aggressive behavior.
   c. Consumption of alcohol and injections of testosterone both promote aggressive behavior.
   d. Consumption of alcohol and injections of testosterone both reduce aggressive behavior.

4. Most people prefer mirror-image photographs of their faces. This is best explained by:
   a. the principle of equity.
   b. the principle of self-disclosure.
   c. the mere exposure effect.
   d. mirror-image perceptions.
   e. deindividuation.

5. Research studies have shown that frequent exposure to sexually explicit films:
   a. may promote increased acceptance of promiscuity.
   b. diminishes the attitude that rape is a serious crime.
   c. may lead individuals to devalue their partners.
   d. may produce all of the above effects.

6. Research studies indicate that in an emergency situation the presence of others often:
   a. prevents people from even noticing the situation.
   b. prevents people from interpreting an unusual event as an emergency.
   c. prevents people from assuming responsibility for assisting.
   d. leads to all of the above.

7. Two neighboring nations are each stockpiling weapons. Each sees its neighbor's actions as an act of aggression and its own actions as self-defense. Evidently, these nations are victims of:
   a. the self-fulfilling prophecy.
   b. groupthink.
   c. the self-serving bias.
   d. the fundamental attribution error.

8. Which of the following factors is the *most* powerful predictor of friendship?
   a. similarity in age
   b. common racial and religious background
   c. similarity in physical attractiveness
   d. physical proximity

9. Most researchers agree that:
   a. television violence leads to aggressive behavior.
   b. although there is a correlation between television watching and aggressiveness, it's impossible to establish causation.
   c. paradoxically, watching excessive television violence ultimately diminishes an individual's aggressive tendencies.
   d. television violence is too unreal to promote aggression in viewers.

10. When subjects in an experiment were told that a woman to whom they would be speaking had been instructed to act in a friendly or unfriendly way, most of them subsequently attributed her behavior to:
    a. the situation.
    b. the situation *and* her personal disposition.
    c. her personal disposition.
    d. their own skill or lack of skill in a social situation.

11. Which of the following is true?
    a. Attitudes and actions rarely correspond.
    b. Attitudes predict behavior about half the time.
    c. Attitudes are excellent predictors of behavior.
    d. Attitudes predict behavior under certain conditions.

12. People with power and status may become prejudiced because:
    a. they tend to justify the social inequalities
       between themselves and others.
    b. those with less status and power tend to
       resent them.
    c. those with less status and power appear less
       capable.
    d. they feel proud and are boastful of their
       achievements.

13. Which of the following most accurately states the
effects of crowding on behavior?
    a. Crowding makes people irritable.
    b. Crowding sometimes intensifies people's
       reactions.
    c. Crowding promotes altruistic behavior.
    d. Crowding usually weakens the intensity of
       people's reactions.

14. Research has found that for a minority to succeed
in swaying a majority, the minority must:
    a. make up a sizable portion of the group.
    b. express its position as consistently as possible.
    c. express its position in the most extreme terms
       possible.
    d. be able to convince a key leader of the majori-
       ty.

15. Which of the following conclusions did Milgram
derive from his studies of obedience?
    a. Even ordinary people, without any particular
       hostility, can become agents in a destructive
       process.
    b. Most people are able, under the proper cir-
       cumstances, to suppress their natural aggres-
       siveness.
    c. The need to be accepted by others is a power-
       ful motivating force.
    d. All of the above conclusions were reached.

16. Which of the following best summarizes the relative importance of personal control and social
control of our behavior?
    a. Situational influences on behavior generally
       are much greater than personal influences.
    b. Situational influences on behavior generally
       are slightly greater than personal influences.
    c. Personal influences on behavior generally are
       much greater than situational influences.
    d. Situational and personal influences interact in
       determining our behavior.

17. Which of the following best describes how GRIT
works?
    a. The fact that two sides in a conflict have great

respect for the other's strengths prevents further escalation of the problem.
    b. The two sides engage in a series of reciprocat-
       ed conciliatory acts.
    c. The two sides agree to have their differences
       settled by a neutral, third-party mediator.
    d. The two sides engage in cooperation in those
       areas in which shared goals are possible.

18. Which of the following is important in promoting
conformity in individuals?
    a. whether an individual's behavior will be
       observed by others in the group
    b. whether the individual is male or female
    c. the size of the room in which a group is meet-
       ing
    d. the age of the members in a group
    e. whether the individual is of a higher status
       than other group members

19. Which theory describes how we explain others'
behavior as being due to internal dispositions or
external situations?
    a. social exchange theory
    b. reward theory
    c. two-factor theory
    d. attribution theory

20. Which of the following is most likely to promote
groupthink?
    a. The group's leader fails to take a firm stance
       on an issue.
    b. A minority faction holds to its position.
    c. The group consults with various experts.
    d. Group polarization is evident.

*True–False Items*

Indicate whether each statement is true or false by
placing *T* or *F* in the blank next to the item.

_____    1. When explaining another's behavior,
               we tend to underestimate situational
               influences.
_____    2. When explaining our own behavior, we
               tend to underestimate situational influ-
               ences.
_____    3. An individual is more likely to conform
               when the rest of the group is unani-
               mous.
_____    4. The tendency of people to conform is
               influenced by the culture in which they
               were socialized.
_____    5. A bystander is more likely to offer help
               in an emergency if other bystanders are
               present.

_____ 6. Counter-attitudinal behavior (acting contrary to our beliefs) often leads to attitude change.

_____ 7. Human aggression is instinctual.

_____ 8. Group polarization tends to prevent groupthink from occurring.

_____ 9. Crowded conditions usually subdue people's reactions.

_____ 10. When individuals lose their sense of identity in a group, they often become more uninhibited.

# Thinking Critically About Chapter 14

Answer these questions the day before an exam as a final check on your understanding of the chapter's terms and concepts.

## Multiple-Choice Questions

1. After waiting in line for an hour to buy concert tickets, Teresa is told that the concert is sold out. In her anger she pounds her fist on the ticket counter, frightening the clerk. Teresa's behavior is best explained by:
   a. evolutionary psychology.
   b. the reciprocity norm.
   c. social exchange theory.
   d. the frustration-aggression principle.

2. Before she gave a class presentation favoring gun control legislation, Wanda opposed it. Her present attitude favoring such legislation can best be explained by:
   a. attribution theory.
   b. cognitive dissonance theory.
   c. social exchange theory.
   d. evolutionary psychology.
   e. two-factor theory.

3. Which of the following would most likely be subject to social facilitation?
   a. proofreading a page for spelling errors
   b. typing a letter with accuracy
   c. playing a difficult piece on a musical instrument
   d. giving a speech
   e. running quickly around a track

4. Jane and Sandy were best friends as freshmen. Jane joined a sorority; Sandy didn't. By the end of their senior year, they found that they had less in common with each other than with the other members of their respective circles of friends. Which of the following phenomena most likely explains their feelings?
   a. group polarization
   b. groupthink
   c. deindividuation
   d. social facilitation

5. Which of the following strategies would be *most* likely to foster positive feelings between two conflicting groups?
   a. Take steps to reduce the likelihood of social traps.
   b. Separate the groups so that tensions diminish.
   c. Have one representative from each group visit the other and field questions.
   d. Increase the amount of contact between the two conflicting groups.
   e. Have the groups work on a superordinate goal.

6. José is the one student member on the college board of trustees. At the board's first meeting, José wants to disagree with the others on several issues but in each case decides to say nothing. Studies on conformity suggest all except one of the following are factors in José's not speaking up. Which one is *not* a factor?
   a. The board is a large group.
   b. The board is prestigious and most of its members are well known.
   c. The board members are already aware that José and the student body disagree with them on these issues.
   d. Because this is the first meeting José has attended, he feels insecure and not fully competent.

7. Given the tendency of people to categorize information according to preformed schemas, which of the following stereotypes would Juan, a 65-year-old political liberal and fitness enthusiast, be most likely to have?
   a. "People who exercise regularly are very extraverted."
   b. "All political liberals are advocates of a reduced defense budget."
   c. "Young people today have no sense of responsibility."
   d. "Older people are lazy."

8. Ever since their cabin lost the camp softball competition, the campers have become increasingly hostile toward one camper in their cabin, blaming her for every problem in the cabin. This behavior is best explained in terms of:
   a. the ingroup bias.
   b. prejudice.
   c. the scapegoat theory.
   d. the reciprocity norm.
   e. mirror-image perceptions.

9. Maria recently heard a speech calling for a ban on aerosol sprays that endanger the earth's ozone layer. Maria's subsequent decision to stop using aerosol sprays is an example of:
   a. informational social influence.
   b. normative social influence.
   c. deindividuation.
   d. social facilitation.

10. Mr. and Mrs. Samuels are constantly fighting, and each perceives the other as hard-headed and insensitive. Their conflict is being fueled by:
    a. self-disclosure.
    b. stereotypes.
    c. a social trap.
    d. mirror-image perceptions.

11. Which of the following situations should produce the *greatest* cognitive dissonance?
    a. A soldier is forced to carry out orders he finds disagreeable.
    b. A student who loves animals has to dissect a cat in order to pass biology.
    c. As part of an experiment, a subject is directed to deliver electric shocks to another person.
    d. A student volunteers to debate an issue, taking the side he personally disagrees with.

12. Professor Washington's students did very poorly on the last exam. The tendency to make the fundamental attribution error might lead her to conclude that the class did poorly because:
    a. the test was unfair.
    b. not enough time was given for students to complete the test.
    c. students were distracted by some social function on campus.
    d. students were unmotivated.

13. Students at State University are convinced that their school is better than any other; this most directly illustrates:
    a. an ingroup bias.
    b. prejudice and discrimination.
    c. the scapegoat effect.
    d. the just-world phenomenon.
    e. mirror-image perceptions.

14. After Sandy helped Jack move into his new apartment, Jack felt obligated to help Sandy when she moved. Jack's sense of responsibility can best be explained by:
    a. evolutionary psychology.
    b. two-factor theory.
    c. the social responsibility norm.
    d. the reciprocity norm.

15. Ahmed and Monique are on a blind date. Which of the following will probably be *most* influential in determining whether they like each other?
    a. their personalities
    b. their beliefs
    c. their social skills
    d. their physical attractiveness

16. Opening her mail, Joan discovers a romantic greeting card from her boyfriend. According to the two-factor theory, she is likely to feel the most intense romantic feelings if, prior to reading the card, she has just:
    a. completed her daily run.
    b. finished reading a chapter in her psychology textbook.
    c. awakened from a nap.
    d. finished eating lunch.
    e. been listening to a tape of love songs.

17. Driving home from work, Althea saw a car run off the road and burst into flames. Althea stopped her car, ran to the burning vehicle, and managed to pull the elderly driver to safety before the car exploded. Althea's behavior can best be explained by:
    a. the social responsibility norm.
    b. the reciprocity norm.
    c. two-factor theory.
    d. reward theory.

18. Having read the chapter, which of the following is best borne out by research on attraction?
    a. Birds of a feather flock together.
    b. Opposites attract.
    c. Familiarity breeds contempt.
    d. Absence makes the heart grow fonder.

19. George's discriminatory behavior toward minorities often provokes anger in his victims, which only serves to increase George's prejudice. George's behavior is an example of the:
    a. blame-the-victim dynamic.
    b. self-fulfilling prophecy.
    c. just-world phenomenon.
    d. scapegoat phenomenon.

20. Which of the following is an example of the foot-in-the-door phenomenon?
    a. To persuade a customer to buy a product a store owner offers a small gift.
    b. After agreeing to wear a small "Enforce Recycling" lapel pin, a woman agrees to collect signatures on a petition to make recycling required by law.

**c.** After offering to sell a car at a ridiculously low price, a car salesperson is forced to tell the customer the car will cost $1000 more.

**d.** All of the above are examples.

### Essay Question

The Panhellenic Council on your campus has asked you to make a presentation on the topic "Social Psychology" to all freshmen who have signed up to "rush" a fraternity or sorority. In a fit of cynicism following your rejection last year by a prestigious fraternity or sorority, you decide to speak on the negative influences of groups on the behavior of individuals. What will you discuss? (Use the space below to list the points you want to make and organize them. Then write the essay on a separate sheet of paper.)

## Key Terms

### Writing Definitions

Using your own words, on a separate piece of paper write a brief definition or explanation of each of the following terms.

1. social psychology
2. attribution theory
3. fundamental attribution error
4. attitudes
5. foot-in-the-door phenomenon
6. role
7. cognitive dissonance theory
8. conformity
9. normative social influence
10. norms
11. informational social influence
12. social facilitation
13. social loafing
14. deindividuation
15. group polarization
16. groupthink
17. culture
18. personal space
19. gender role
20. prejudice
21. stereotype
22. ingroup bias
23. scapegoat theory
24. just-world phenomenon
25. aggression
26. frustration-aggression principle
27. conflict
28. social trap
29. mere exposure effect
30. passionate love
31. companionate love
32. equity
33. self-disclosure
34. altruism
35. bystander effect
36. social exchange theory
37. superordinate goals
38. GRIT

*Cross-Check*

As you learned in the Introduction, reviewing and overlearning of material are important to the learning process. After you have written the definitions of the key terms in this chapter, you should complete the crossword puzzle to ensure that you can reverse the process—recognize the term, given the definition.

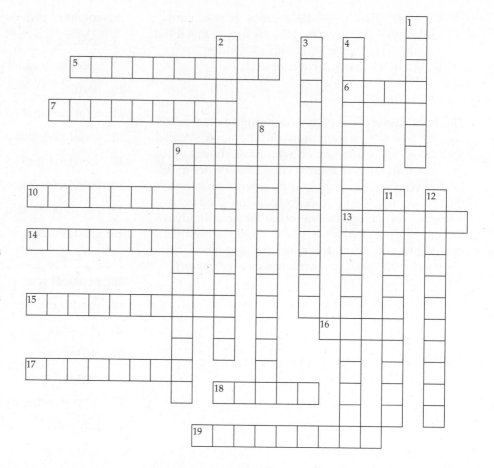

### ACROSS

5. A generalized belief about a group of people.
6. A strategy of conflict resolution in which both groups make conciliatory gestures. (abbrev.)
7. Theory that proposes that prejudice provides an outlet for anger by finding someone to blame.
9. The tendency to change one's attitudes to coincide with those held by a group.
10. An unselfish regard for the welfare of others.
13. Mutual giving and receiving in a relationship.
14. Type of love that refers to an aroused state of intense positive absorption in another person.
15. A culturally prescribed set of behaviors for males and females.
16. A set of expectations about the behavior of someone in a particular situation.
17. Perceived incompatibility between individuals or groups.
18. Rules for accepted and expected behavior.
19. Personal beliefs and feelings that influence our behavior.

### DOWN

1. Traditions shared by a group and passed down from one generation to the next.
2. A person's tendency not to offer help to someone if others are present.
3. Type of social influence that results when one goes along with a group when one is unsure of what to do.
4. Psychological discomfort we experience when two of our thoughts conflict.
8. Phenomenon whereby people who agree to a small request are more likely to comply later with a larger request.

9. Type of love in which there is a deep, enduring attachment.
11. Our tendency to underestimate situational influences and overestimate dispositional influences upon the behavior of others is the _____ attribution error.
12. A causal explanation of a given behavior.

## ANSWERS

## Guided Study

The following guidelines provide the main points that your answers should have touched upon.

1. According to attribution theory, people explain others' behavior as being due either to their dispositions or to their situations. Because people have enduring personality traits, we tend to overestimate the influence of personality and underestimate the impact of situational influences, particularly when explaining others' behavior. This is called the *fundamental attribution error*. When explaining our own behavior, or when we take another's perspective, we are less likely to make this type of error. Our attributions, of course, have important practical consequences. For

example, there are political implications to the question of whether people's behavior is attributed to social conditions or to their own choices, abilities, and shortcomings.

2. An attitude is a belief and feeling that predisposes our reactions to objects, people, and events. Our attitudes are most likely to guide our actions when outside influences on what we say and do are minimal, when the attitude is specifically relevant to the behavior, and when we are aware of our attitudes.

3. Studies of the foot-in-the-door phenomenon and role playing demonstrate that our actions can influence our attitudes. The foot-in-the-door phenomenon is the tendency for people who agree to a small request to comply later with a larger one. Similarly, people who play a role tend to adjust their attitudes to coincide with behavior enacted while playing the role. The theory of cognitive dissonance maintains that when our thoughts and behaviors don't coincide, we experience tension. To relieve this tension, we bring our attitudes into line with our actions.

4. Suggestibility studies conducted by Solomon Asch demonstrate that a unanimous group makes us unsure about our behavior or thinking, and so we are more likely to conform to the group standard, even if it is incorrect. Conformity is promoted when people feel incompetent or insecure, when they are in groups of three or more, when the group is unanimous and of high status and attractiveness, when no prior commitment has been made, when behavior will be observed, and when people have been socialized in a culture that encourages respect for social standards. We conform to gain social approval (normative social influence) or because the group provides valuable information (informational social influence).

5. Subjects in Milgram's experiments were ordered to teach a list of word pairs to another person by punishing the learner's wrong answers with electric shocks. Obedience was highest when the experimenter was nearby and was perceived as a legitimate authority supported by a prestigious institution, when the victim was depersonalized or at a distance, and when there was no role model for defiance.

6. Social facilitation occurs when tasks are simple or well-learned but not when they are difficult or unfamiliar. When observed by others, people become aroused. Arousal *facilitates* the most likely response—the correct one on an easy task, an incorrect one on a difficult task. Social loafing occurs when people who work anonymously as part of a group exert less effort than those individually accountable for performance. Deindividuation occurs when group participation makes individuals feel aroused, anonymous, and less self-conscious. The uninhibited and impulsive behavior of mobs may occur as a result of this phenomenon.

7. Group polarization refers to the enhancement of a group's prevailing tendencies that occurs when like-minded members discuss issues and attitudes. The unrealistic group decision making called groupthink occurs when the desire for group harmony outweighs the desire for realistic thinking. It is fed by overconfidence, conformity, self-justification, and group polarization. Groupthink can be prevented when the leader welcomes dissenting opinions and invites criticism.

8. The power of the situation (social control) and of the individual (personal control) interact in two significant ways. First, when feeling pressured, people may react by doing the opposite. Second, people often choose or help create the situations that influence their behavior. Their expectations may cause them to act in ways that trigger the expected results. In this way, expectations may be self-fulfilling.

   The impact of a minority in swaying the majority opinion illustrates the power of personal control. Research reveals that a minority that unswervingly holds to its position is more likely to be successful in swaying the majority than a minority that waffles.

9. We live in a global multicultural village and need to understand how our cultures and gender roles influence us. A culture is the enduring traditions, behaviors, ideas, and attitudes shared by a large group of people and passed from one generation to the next. All cultural groups evolve their own norms for acceptable and expected behavior. Because of differing norms, personal space, expressiveness, and pace of life, for example, misunderstandings are commonplace.

   Gender roles vary over time as well as across cultures. In industrialized societies, for example, gender roles vary—in North America, men are doctors and dentists; in Russia, women are usually the doctors. In the United States, gender roles have shifted, with a large increase in women's employment.

10. Prejudice is an unjustifiable and usually negative attitude toward a group. People who have money, power, and prestige may become prejudiced toward those less fortunate in order to rationalize social inequalities. The reactions provoked in

victims of discrimination may further increase prejudice. The tendencies to favor one's own group (ingroup bias) and to blame victims for their plight may also lead to prejudice. According to the scapegoat theory, when people are frustrated or angry, blaming another individual or group may provide an outlet for their anger.

11. Stereotyped beliefs emerge as a result of our tendency to cognitively simplify the world. One way to do this is by categorizing people into groups and then overestimating the similarity of people within groups other than our own. Group stereotypes are also influenced by vivid but exceptional cases involving individuals from other groups, because they are more readily available to memory. Another cognitive root of prejudice is the just-world phenomenon, the idea that good is rewarded and evil is punished, so those who are successful are good and those who suffer are bad. Hindsight bias also fosters prejudice, as people blame victims for "getting what they deserved."

12. Biology influences aggression at three levels—the genetic, the neural, and the biochemical. Studies of human twins and selective breeding in animals reveal that genes influence aggression. Electrical stimulation and injuries to certain regions of the limbic system, such as the amygdala, suggest that animal and human brains have neural systems that control aggressive behavior (although no one spot in the brain actually controls aggression). Studies of animal aggression and violent criminals demonstrate that aggressive tendencies increase with low levels of the neurotransmitter serotonin and high blood levels of the hormone testosterone (although the reverse is also true).

   A variety of psychological factors influence aggression. The frustration-aggression principle indicates that pain, insults, excessive heat, and other aversive stimuli can evoke hostility. Learning also plays a role in aggression. Aggressive reactions are more likely in situations in which experience has taught the individual that aggression will be rewarded. Furthermore, children who observe aggressive models often imitate their behavior.

13. Correlational and experimental studies reveal a link between children's viewing of violent television programs and their later aggressiveness as teenagers and young adults. Experts maintain that the effects of viewing violent programs stem from a combination of factors, including arousal by the violent excitement, the strengthening of violence-related ideas, the erosion of inhibitions, and imitation.

   Research indicates that depictions of sexual violence portray women as enjoying being the victims of sexual aggression, and this perception increases the acceptance of coercion in sexual relationships. Repeated viewing of pornographic films can also lead viewers to trivialize rape and devalue their partners.

14. Conflict is a seeming incompatibility of actions, goals, or ideas among individuals, groups, or nations. Conflict is fostered by social traps in which conflicting parties get caught up in mutually destructive behavior by pursuing their own self-interests. Another factor that fuels conflict is the tendency for those in conflict to form diabolical images of each other (mirror-image perceptions). The psychological roots of distorted perceptions include the self-serving bias, the fundamental attribution error, stereotyping, group polarization, and groupthink.

   Conflict resolution is most likely in situations characterized by cooperation, communication, and conciliation. Studies by Sherif and others demonstrate that cooperation between groups in the pursuit of superordinate goals is more effective than mere contact between conflicting groups in reducing differences. Communication between conflicting groups can be facilitated by a third-party mediator when conflicts are so intense that civil discussion between the groups is not possible. When cooperation and communication are impossible between conflicting groups, Osgood's "Graduated and Reciprocated Initiatives in Tension-Reduction" (GRIT) may help reduce hostilities. GRIT promotes trust and cooperation between groups by having each group initiate one or more small, conciliatory acts.

15. Studies of attraction indicate that proximity is the most powerful predictor of friendship, in part because being repeatedly exposed to any person or thing tends to increase our liking for it (mere exposure effect). Experiments also reveal that physical appearance is the most powerful factor in the first impression a person triggers. Although many aspects of attractiveness vary with place and time, some may be universal. Once relationships are formed, similarity of attitudes, beliefs, interests, and other characteristics increases attraction between people.

   Passionate love is an intense state of physical arousal triggered by another person, usually at the beginning of a relationship, that is cognitively labeled as love. Companionate love is the steadier, deeply felt attachment that emerges as love matures. Companionate love is fostered by feelings of equity between the partners in a relationship, and the acceptability of self-disclosures.

16. The bystander effect states that a bystander is less likely to give aid if other bystanders are present. Darley and Latané maintain that bystanders will help only if they notice the incident, interpret it as an emergency, and assume responsibility for helping. At each step in this decision-making process the presence of other bystanders makes it less likely that a helping decision will be made. Further research reveals that bystanders are most likely to help when they have seen someone else being helpful, when they are not in a hurry, when the victim appears similar to them and deserving of assistance, when they are in a small town or rural area, when they feel guilty, when they are focused on others and not preoccupied, and when they are in a good mood.

17. The social exchange theory maintains that self-interest underlies all human interactions, including altruism, so that our constant goal is to maximize rewards and minimize costs. This theory helps explain why people often help those whose approval they seek or who can reciprocate favors in the future.

    People are also sensitive to social norms that promote helping. The reciprocity norm, for example, dictates that we should help those who have helped us. The social responsibility norm is the expectation that we should help those who need our help.

## Chapter Review

1. social psychologists

2. attribution; dispositional attribution; situational attribution

3. underestimate; attention; fundamental attribution error; weaker; reversed

Our attributions—to individuals' dispositions or to situations—have important practical consequences. A hurtful remark from an acquaintance, for example, is more likely to be forgiven if it is attributed to a temporary situation than to a mean disposition.

4. attitudes

5. challenged

Attitudes predict actions when other influences on the attitudes and actions are minimized, when the attitude is specifically relevant to the behavior, and when we are especially aware of our attitudes. Thus, our attitudes are more likely to predict behavior when we are not attempting to adjust our behavior to please others, when we are in familiar situations in which we don't have to stop and think about our attitudes, and when the attitude pertains to a specific behavior, such as purchasing a product or casting a vote.

6. actions or behavior; foot-in-the-door

7. role

8. changes

9. cognitive dissonance; Festinger

10. dissonance; attitudes

11. conformity

12. Asch

13. were

14. normative social influence; norms

15. informational social influence

16. individualist

17. Milgram; complied

Obedience was highest when the person giving the orders was close at hand and was perceived to be a legitimate authority figure, when the authority figure was supported by a prestigious institution, when the victim was depersonalized, and when there were no role models for defiance.

18. foot-in-the-door

19. social facilitation; easy; likely

20. amplified

21. less hard; social loafing

22. deindividuation

23. increase; group polarization

24. groupthink

25. social control; personal control

26. unswerving

27. culture

28. do

29. personal space; does

Most Americans, the British, and Scandinavians prefer more personal space than do Latin Americans, Arabs, and the French. Cultural differences in expressiveness and the pace of life often create misunderstandings. For example, people with northern European roots may perceive people from Mediterranean cultures as warm and charming but inefficient and time wasting, whereas Mediterraneans may see the northern Europeans as efficient but emotionally cold.

30. gender role

31. assertiveness; interpersonal; are not; cultures; time

32. have

33. unjustifiable; negative; stereotypes

34. have changed dramatically

35. girls

36. justifying

37. self-fulfilling; victims; blame

38. ingroup bias

39. scapegoat

40. categorization; overestimate

41. overgeneralize

42. just-world; hindsight bias

43. any physical or verbal behavior intended to hurt or destroy

44. death instinct; displaced; do not

45. varies

46. bred

47. do

48. neural; limbic system (or the amygdala); hormones

49. testosterone; decreased

50. alcohol

51. frustration-aggression

52. rewards; observation (or imitation)

53. rich; poor; father care

54. arousal; ideas; inhibitions; imitate

55. increased; are not

56. generally

Pornography tends to portray women as enjoying being the victims of sexual aggression, and this perception increases the acceptance of coercion in sexual relationships.

57. are not; are

The Zillmann and Bryant study found that after viewing sexually explicit films for several weeks, undergraduates were more likely to recommend a lighter prison sentence for a convicted rapist than were subjects who viewed nonerotic films.

58. sexual violence

59. conflict; groups; nations

60. social traps; distorted

61. self-interests

62. mirror-image

63. self-serving bias; fundamental attribution error; stereotypes; groupthink; polarized

64. proximity

65. increases; mere exposure; adaptive; dangerous; prejudice; automatic

66. appearance

67. Attractive people are perceived as happier, more sensitive, more successful, and more socially skilled.

68. is not

69. youthful; mature; dominant; affluent

According to evolutionary psychology, this gender difference evolved because men drawn to healthy, fertile-appearing women and women drawn to men who appear able to provide support and protection stood a better chance of sending their genes into the future.

70. more

71. attitudes, beliefs, interests, religion, race, education, intelligence, smoking behavior, economic status, age

Reward theories of attraction say that we are attracted to, and continue relationships with, those people whose behavior provides us with more benefits than costs. Proximity makes it easy to enjoy the benefits of friendship at little cost, attractiveness is pleasing, and similarity is reinforcing to us.

72. passionate; companionate

73. arousal; cognitive

74. were

75. equity; self-disclosure

76. altruism

77. notice; interpret; assume responsibility

78. less

79. less; bystander effect

People are most likely to help someone when they have just observed someone else being helpful; when they are not in a hurry; when the victim appears to need and deserve help; when they are in some way similar to the victim; when in a small town; when feeling guilty; when not preoccupied; and when in a good mood.

80. social exchange

81. reciprocity; social responsibility

82. cooperation; communication; conciliation

83. is not

84. superordinate

85. mediator

86. Graduated; Reciprocated Initiatives; Tension-Reduction; conciliatory

# Progress Test 1

## Multiple-Choice Questions

1. **d.** is the answer. In Milgram's initial experiments, 63 percent of the subjects fully complied with the experiment. (p. 499)

2. **c.** is the answer. Cognitive dissonance is the tension we feel when we are aware of a discrepancy between our thoughts and actions, as would occur when we do something we find distasteful. (p. 495)
   **a.** Dissonance requires strongly held attitudes, which must be perceived as not fitting behavior.
   **b.** Dissonance is a personal cognitive process.
   **d.** In such a situation the person is less likely to experience dissonance, since the action can be attributed to "having no choice."

3. **d.** is the answer. In such groups, discussion usually strengthens prevailing opinion; this phenomenon is known as group polarization. (pp. 504–505)
   **a.** Minority opinions, especially if consistently and firmly stated, can sway the majority in a group.
   **b.** Group polarization, or the strengthening of a group's prevailing tendencies, is most likely in groups where members agree.
   **c.** When groupthink occurs, there is so much consensus that decision making becomes less effective.

4. **e.** is the answer. (p. 497)

5. **c.** is the answer. Social traps foster conflict in that two parties, by pursuing their self-interests, create a result that neither group wants. (p. 520)
   **a.** As Sherif's studies demonstrated, the possession of shared or superordinate goals tends to reduce conflict between groups.
   **b.** This is an example of mirror-image perceptions, which, along with social traps, foster conflict.
   **d.** Face-to-face confrontations between conflicting parties generally do not reduce conflict, nor are they social traps.

6. **d.** is the answer. (p. 504)
   **a.** Groupthink refers to the mode of thinking that occurs when the desire for group harmony overrides realistic and critical thinking.
   **b.** Cognitive dissonance refers to the discomfort we feel when two thoughts (which include the knowledge of our *behavior*) are inconsistent.
   **c.** Empathy is feeling what another person feels.

7. **d.** is the answer. Normative social influence refers to influence on behavior that comes from a desire to look good to others. Subjects who were observed conformed because they didn't want to look like oddballs. (p. 498)
   **a.** Social facilitation involves performing tasks better or faster in the presence of others.
   **b.** Overjustification occurs when a person is rewarded for doing something that is already enjoyable.
   **c.** Informational social influence is the tendency of individuals to accept the opinions of others, especially in situations where they themselves are unsure.

8. **d.** is the answer. Role models for defiance reduce levels of obedience. (p. 500)
   **a. & c.** These did not result in diminished obedience.
   **b.** This "depersonalization" of the victim resulted in increased obedience.

9. **b.** is the answer. Aggression is any behavior, physical or verbal, that is intended to hurt or destroy. (p. 513)
   **a.** A person may accidentally be hurt in a nonaggressive incident; aggression does not necessarily prove hurtful.
   **c.** Verbal behavior, which does not result in physical injury, may also be aggressive. Moreover, acts of aggression may be cool and calculated, rather than hostile and passionate.

10. **a.** is the answer. The very wide variations in aggressiveness from culture to culture indicate that aggression cannot be considered an instinct, or unlearned, universal characteristic of the species. (p. 513)

11. **d.** is the answer. (p. 514)

12. **a.** is the answer. (pp. 518–519)

13. **d.** is the answer. This phenomenon is known as the bystander effect. (p. 528)
    **a.** This answer is incorrect because individuals are less likely to render assistance at all if others are present.
    **b.** Although people are less likely to assume responsibility for helping, this does not mean that they are less empathic.
    **c.** This answer is incorrect because norms such as the social responsibility norm encourage helping others, yet people are less likely to help with others around.

14. **b.** is the answer. In fact, people tend to overgeneralize from vivid cases, rather than assume that they are unusual. (pp. 511–513)
    **a., c., & d.** Each of these is an example of a cognitive (a. & c.) or a social (d.) root of prejudice.

15. **d.** is the answer. Being repeatedly exposed to

novel stimuli increases our liking for them. (p. 523)

**a.** For the most part, the opposite is true.

**b. & c.** The mere exposure effect concerns our tendency to develop likings on the basis, not of similarities or differences, but simply of familiarity, or repeated exposure.

16. **a.** is the answer. This result supports the two-factor theory of emotion and passionate attraction, according to which arousal from any source can facilitate an emotion, depending on how we label the arousal. (p. 526)

17. **c.** is the answer. Deep affection is typical of companionate love, rather than passionate love, and is promoted by equity, whereas traditional roles may be characterized by the dominance of one sex. (p. 528)

18. **a.** is the answer. (p. 529)

**b. & c.** These factors would most likely decrease a person's altruistic tendencies.

**d.** There is no evidence that one sex is more altruistic than the other.

19. **a.** is the answer. (p. 513)

**b.** Ingroup bias is the tendency of people to favor their own group.

**c.** The fundamental attribution error is the tendency of people to underestimate situational influences when observing the behavior of other people.

**d.** The mirror-image perception principle is the tendency of conflicting parties to form similar, diabolical images of each other.

20. **b.** is the answer. (p. 530)

**a.** This is a tenet of evolutionary psychology.

**c.** Social exchange theory focuses on costs and benefits, rather than on norms.

### Matching Items

| | | |
|---|---|---|
| **1.** d (p. 503) | **5.** e (p. 495) | **9.** b (p. 509) |
| **2.** c (p. 503) | **6.** f (p. 498) | **10.** a (p. 491) |
| **3.** k (p. 506) | **7.** i (p. 498) | **11.** j (p. 528) |
| **4.** g (p. 498) | **8.** h (p. 504) | **12.** l (p. 523) |

## Progress Test 2

### Multiple-Choice Questions

1. **b.** is the answer. (p. 513)

**a.** Milgram conducted studies of obedience.

**c.** Lorenz, too, was an instinct theorist, but only Freud argued the existence of a "death instinct."

**d.** Janis studied the process that led to groupthink.

**e.** Asch studied conformity.

2. **c.** is the answer. Culture *does* have a strong influence on how rigidly social roles are defined. (p. 507)

3. **c.** is the answer. (p. 514)

4. **c.** is the answer. The mere exposure effect refers to our tendency to like what we're used to, and we're used to seeing mirror images of ourselves. (p. 523)

**a.** Equity refers to equality in giving and taking between the partners in a relationship.

**b.** Self-disclosure is the sharing of intimate feelings with a partner in a loving relationship.

**d.** Although people prefer mirror images of their faces, mirror-image perceptions are often held by parties in conflict. Each party views itself favorably and the other negatively.

**e.** Deindividuation involves a loss of self-awareness.

5. **d.** is the answer. (pp. 518–519)

6. **d.** is the answer. (pp. 528–529)

7. **d.** is the answer. In this case, each nation has mistakenly attributed the other's action to a *dispositional* trait, whereas its own action is viewed as a *situational* response. (p. 491)

8. **d.** is the answer. Because it provides people with an opportunity to meet, proximity is the most powerful predictor of friendship, even though, once a friendship is established, the other factors mentioned become more important. (p. 523)

9. **a.** is the answer. (pp. 517–518)

**b.** Although some researchers take this view, the consensus, as expressed by the National Institute of Mental Health, is that violence on television does lead to aggressive behavior.

**c. & d.** Most viewers would maintain the opposite.

10. **c.** is the answer. In this example of the fundamental attribution error, even when given the situational explanation for the woman's behavior, students ignored it and attributed her behavior to her personal disposition. (pp. 491–492)

11. **d.** is the answer. Our attitudes are more likely to guide our actions when other influences are minimal, when there's a specific connection between the two, and when we're keenly aware of our beliefs. The presence of other people would more likely be an outside factor that would lessen the likelihood of actions being guided by attitude. (pp. 493–494)

**12. a.** is the answer. Such justifications arise as a way to preserve inequalities. The just-world phenomenon presumes that people get what they deserve. According to this view, someone who has less must deserve less. (p. 513)

**13. b.** is the answer. (p. 503)
**a. & c.** Crowding may amplify irritability or altruistic tendencies that are already present. Crowding does not, however, produce these reactions as a general effect.
**d.** In fact, just the opposite is true. Crowding often intensifies people's reactions.

**14. b.** is the answer. (p. 506)
**a.** Even if they made up a sizable portion of the group, although still a minority, their numbers would not be as important as their consistency.
**c. & d.** These aspects of minority influence were not discussed in the text; even so, they are not likely to help a minority sway a majority.

**15. a.** is the answer. (p. 501)

**16. d.** is the answer. The text emphasizes the ways in which personal and social controls interact in influencing behavior. It does not suggest that one factor is more influential than the other. (p. 506)

**17. b.** is the answer. (p. 532)
**a.** GRIT is a technique for reducing conflict through a series of conciliatory gestures, not for maintaining the status quo.
**c. & d.** These measures may help reduce conflict but they are not aspects of GRIT.

**18. a.** is the answer. As Solomon Asch's experiments demonstrated, individuals are more likely to conform when they are being observed by others in the group. The other factors were not discussed in the text and probably would not promote conformity. (p. 497)

**19. d.** is the answer. (p. 491)

**20. d.** is the answer. Group polarization, or the enhancement of a group's prevailing attitudes, promotes groupthink, which leads to the disintegration of critical thinking. (pp. 504–505)
**a.** Groupthink is more likely when a leader highly favors an idea, which may make members reluctant to disagree.
**b.** A strong minority faction would probably have the opposite effect: It would diminish group harmony while promoting critical thinking.
**c.** Consulting experts would discourage groupthink by exposing the group to other opinions.

*True-False Items*

**1.** T (p. 491)     **6.** T (p. 495)
**2.** F (p. 492)     **7.** F (p. 513)
**3.** T (p. 498)     **8.** F (pp. 504–505)
**4.** T (p. 498)     **9.** F (p. 503)
**5.** F (pp. 528–529)     **10.** T (p. 504)

## Thinking Critically About Chapter 14

**1. d.** is the answer. According to the frustration-aggression principle, the blocking of an attempt to achieve some goal—in Teresa's case, buying concert tickets—creates anger and can generate aggression. (p. 515)
**a.** Evolutionary psychology maintains that aggressive behavior is a genetically based drive. Teresa's behavior clearly was a reaction to a specific situation.
**b.** The reciprocity norm—that we should return help to those who have helped us—would not engender Teresa's angry reaction.
**c.** Social exchange theory views behavior as an exchange process in which people try to maximize the benefits of their behavior by minimizing the costs. Teresa's behavior likely brought her few benefits while exacting some costs, including potential injury, embarrassment, and retaliation by the clerk.

**2. b.** is the answer. Dissonance theory focuses on what happens when our actions contradict our attitudes. (p. 495)
**a.** Attribution theory holds that we give causal explanations for others' behavior, often by crediting either the situation or people's dispositions.
**c.** Social exchange theory maintains that social behaviors maximize benefits and minimize costs. It is not clear in this example whether Wanda perceives such costs and benefits.
**d. & e.** These are not theories of social influence.

**3. e.** is the answer. Social facilitation, or better performance in the presence of others, occurs for easy tasks but not for more difficult ones. For tasks such as proofreading, typing, playing an instrument, or giving a speech, the arousal resulting from the presence of others can lead to mistakes. (p. 503)

**4. a.** is the answer. Group polarization means that the tendencies within a group—and therefore the differences among groups—grow stronger over time. Thus, because the differences between the sorority and nonsorority students have increased, Jane and Sandy are likely to have little in common. (p. 504)

**b.** Groupthink is the tendency for realistic decision making to disintegrate when the desire for group harmony is strong.

**c.** Deindividuation is the loss of self-consciousness and restraint that sometimes occurs when one is part of a group.

**d.** Social facilitation refers to improved performance of a task in the presence of others.

5. **e.** is the answer. Sherif found that hostility between two groups could be dispelled by giving the groups superordinate, or shared, goals. (p. 531)

**a.** Although reducing the likelihood of social traps might reduce mutually destructive behavior, it would not lead to positive feelings between the groups.

**b.** Such segregation would likely increase ingroup bias and group polarization, resulting in further group conflict.

**c.** This might help, or it might increase hostilities; it would not be as helpful a strategy as communication through an outside mediator or, as in e., cooperation toward a superordinate goal.

**d.** Contact by itself is not likely to reduce conflict.

6. **c.** is the answer. Prior commitment to an opposing view generally tends to work against conformity. In contrast, large group size, prestigiousness of a group, and an individual's feelings of incompetence and insecurity all strengthen the tendency to conform. (p. 498)

7. **c.** is the answer. People tend to overestimate the similarity of people within groups other than their own. Thus, Juan is not likely to form stereotypes of fitness enthusiasts (a.), political liberals (b.), or older adults (d.), because these are groups to which he belongs. (p. 512)

8. **c.** is the answer. According to the scapegoat theory, when things go wrong, people look for someone on whom to take out their anger and frustration. (p. 511)

**a.** These campers are venting their frustration on a member of their *own* cabin group (although this is not always the case with scapegoats).

**b.** Prejudice refers to an unjustifiable and usually negative attitude toward another group.

**d.** The reciprocity norm, which refers to our tendency to help those who have helped us, was not discussed as a root of prejudice.

**e.** Mirror-image perceptions involve our percep-

tions of groups other than our own, not of members of our ingroup.

9. **a.** is the answer. As illustrated by Maria's decision to stop buying aerosol products, informational social influence occurs when people have genuinely been influenced by what they have learned from others. (p. 498)

**b.** Had Maria's behavior been motivated by the desire to avoid rejection or to gain social approval (which we have no reason to suspect is the case), it would have been an example of normative social influence.

**c.** Deindividuation refers to the sense of anonymity a person may feel as part of a group.

**d.** Social facilitation is the improvement in performance of well-learned tasks that may result when one is observed by others.

10. **d.** is the answer. The couple's similar, and presumably distorted, feelings toward each other fuel their conflict. (p. 521)

**a.** Self-disclosure, or the sharing of intimate feelings, fosters love.

**b.** Stereotypes are overgeneralized ideas about groups.

**c.** Social traps are situations in which conflicting parties engage in mutually destructive behavior while pursuing their own self-interests.

11. **d.** is the answer. In this situation, the counterattitudinal behavior is performed voluntarily and cannot be attributed to the demands of the situation. (p. 495)

**a., b., & c.** In all of these situations, the counterattitudinal behaviors should not arouse much dissonance because they can be attributed to the demands of the situation.

12. **d.** is the answer. The fundamental attribution error refers to the tendency to underestimate situational influences in favor of this type of dispositional attribution when explaining the behavior of other people. (p. 491)

**a., b., & c.** These are situational attributions.

13. **a.** is the answer. (p. 511)

**b.** Prejudices are unjustifiable and usually negative attitudes toward other groups. They may result from an ingroup bias, but they are probably not why students favor their own university.

**c.** Scapegoats are individuals or groups toward which prejudice is directed as an outlet for the anger of frustrated individuals or groups.

**d.** The just-world phenomenon is the tendency for people to believe others "get what they deserve."

**e.** Mirror-image perception refers to the tendency of conflicting parties to form similar, diabolical images of each other.

14. **d.** is the answer. (p. 530)

**a.** Evolutionary psychology is not discussed in terms of altruism, but it would maintain that altruistic actions are predisposed by our genes.

**b.** The two-factor theory holds that emotions consist of physical arousal and an appropriate cognitive label.

**c.** The social responsibility norm refers to the social attitude that we should help those who need our help.

15. **d.** is the answer. Hundreds of experiments indicate that first impressions are most influenced by physical appearance. (p. 524)

16. **a.** is the answer. According to the two-factor theory, physical arousal can intensify whatever emotion is currently felt. Only in the situation described in a. is Joan likely to be physically aroused. (p. 526)

17. **a.** is the answer. (p. 530)

**b.** The reciprocity norm mandates that we help those who have helped us.

**c.** The two-factor theory of emotion, which assumes that emotions are based on physical arousal and a cognitive label, makes no predictions regarding altruism.

**d.** The reward theory, which states that social behavior is maintained by rewards, would explain Althea's altruism as being due to her having previously been rewarded for similar altruistic actions.

18. **a.** is the answer. Friends and couples are much more likely than randomly paired people to be similar in views, interests, and a range of other factors. (p. 526)

**b.** The opposite is true.

**c.** The mere exposure effect demonstrates that familiarity tends to breed fondness.

**d.** This is unlikely, given the positive effects of proximity and intimacy.

19. **b.** is the answer. By eliciting reactions in others that fuel his prejudice, George is fulfilling his expectation, or "prophecy," regarding members of a particular minority. (p. 511)

20. **b.** is the answer. In the foot-in-the-door phenomenon, compliance with a small initial request, such as wearing a lapel pin, later is followed by compliance with a much larger request, such as collecting petition signatures. (p. 494)

### Essay Question

Your discussion might focus on some of the following topics: normative social influence; conformity, which includes suggestibility; obedience; group polarization; and groupthink.

As a member of any group with established social norms, individuals will often act in ways that enable them to avoid rejection or gain social approval. Thus, a fraternity or sorority pledge would probably be very suggestible and likely to eventually conform to the attitudes and norms projected by the group—or be rejected socially. In extreme cases of pledge hazing, acute social pressures may lead to atypical and antisocial individual behaviors—for example, on the part of pledges complying with the demands of senior members of the fraternity or sorority. Over time, meetings and discussions will probably enhance the group's prevailing attitudes (group polarization). This may lead to the unrealistic and irrational decision making that is groupthink. The potentially negative consequences of groupthink depend on the issues being discussed, but may include a variety of socially destructive behaviors.

## Key Terms

### Writing Definitions

1. **Social psychology** is the scientific study of how we think about, influence, and relate to one another. (p. 491)

2. **Attribution theory** deals with our causal explanations of behavior. We attribute behavior to the individual's disposition or to the situation. (p. 491)

3. The **fundamental attribution error** is our tendency to underestimate the impact of situations and to overestimate the impact of personal dispositions upon the behavior of others. (p. 491)

4. **Attitudes** are personal beliefs and feelings that may predispose a person to respond in particular ways to objects, people, and events. (p. 493)

5. The **foot-in-the-door phenomenon** is the tendency for people who agree to a small request to comply later with a larger request. (p. 494)

6. A **role** is a set of expectations about the behavior of someone in a particular social position. (p. 495)

7. **Cognitive dissonance theory** refers to the theory that we act to reduce the psychological discomfort we experience when our behavior conflicts with what we think and feel, or more generally, when two of our thoughts conflict. This is frequently accomplished by changing our attitude rather than our behavior. (p. 495)

*Memory aid*: *Dissonance* means "lack of harmony." **Cognitive dissonance** occurs when two thoughts, or cognitions, are at variance with one another.

8. **Conformity** is the tendency to change one's thinking or behavior to coincide with a group standard. (p. 497)

9. **Normative social influence** refers to the pressure on individuals to conform in order to avoid rejection or to gain social approval. (p. 498)

   *Memory aid*: *Normative* means "based on a norm, or pattern, regarded as typical for a specific group." **Normative social influence** is the pressure groups exert on the individual to behave in ways acceptable to the group standard.

10. **Norms** are understood social prescriptions, or rules, for accepted and expected behavior. (p. 498)

11. **Informational social influence** results when one goes along with a group when one is unsure or lacks information. (p. 498)

12. **Social facilitation** is the improvement in performance of simple or well-learned tasks that occurs when other people are present. (p. 503)

13. **Social loafing** is the tendency for individual effort to be diminished when one is part of a group working toward a common goal. (p. 503)

14. **Deindividuation** refers to the loss of self-awareness and self-restraint that sometimes occurs in group situations that foster arousal and anonymity. (p. 5042)

    *Memory aid*: As a prefix, *de-* indicates reversal or undoing. To **de**individuate is to undo one's individuality.

15. **Group polarization** refers to the enhancement of a group's prevailing tendencies through discussion, which often has the effect of accentuating the group's differences from other groups. (p. 504)

    *Memory aid*: To *polarize* is to "cause thinking to concentrate about two poles, or contrasting positions."

16. **Groupthink** refers to the unrealistic thought processes and decision making that occur within groups when the desire for group harmony becomes paramount. (p. 505)

    *Example*: The psychological tendencies of self-justification, conformity, and group polarization foster the development of the "team spirit" mentality known as **groupthink**.

17. A **culture** is the enduring behaviors, ideas, attitudes, and traditions shared by a large group of people and transmitted from one generation to the next. (p. 506)

18. **Personal space** refers to the buffer zone, or mobile territory, that people like to maintain around their bodies. (p. 507)

19. A **gender role** is a culturally prescribed set of behaviors for males and females. (p. 507)

20. **Prejudice** is an unjustifiable and usually negative attitude toward a group and its members. (p. 509)

21. A **stereotype** is a generalized (often overgeneralized) belief about a group of people. (p. 509)

22. The **ingroup bias** is the tendency to favor one's own group. (p. 511)

23. The **scapegoat theory** proposes that prejudice provides an outlet for anger by finding someone to blame. (p. 511)

24. The **just-world phenomenon** is a manifestation of the commonly held belief that good is rewarded and evil is punished. The logic is indisputable: "If I am rewarded, I must be good." (p. 513)

25. **Aggression** is any physical or verbal behavior intended to hurt or destroy. (p. 513)

26. The **frustration-aggression principle** states that aggression is triggered when people become angry because their efforts to achieve a goal have been blocked. (p. 515)

27. **Conflict** is a perceived incompatibility of actions, goals, or ideas between individuals or groups. (p. 520)

28. A **social trap** is a situation in which conflicting parties become caught up in mutually harmful behavior as they pursue their perceived best interests. (p. 520)

29. The **mere exposure effect** refers to the fact that repeated exposure to an unfamiliar stimulus increases our liking of it. (p. 523)

30. **Passionate love** refers to an aroused state of intense positive absorption in another person, especially at the beginning of a relationship. (p. 526)

31. **Companionate love** refers to a deep, enduring, affectionate attachment. (p. 527)

32. **Equity** refers to the condition in which there is mutual giving and receiving between the partners in a relationship. (p. 528)

33. **Self-disclosure** refers to a person's sharing intimate feelings with another. (p. 528)

34. **Altruism** is unselfish regard for the welfare of others. (p. 528)

35. The **bystander effect** is the tendency of a person to be less likely to offer help to someone if there are other people present. (p. 529)

36. **Social exchange theory** states that our social behavior revolves around exchanges, in which we try to minimize our costs and maximize our benefits. (p. 530)

37. **Superordinate goals** are mutual goals that require the cooperation of individuals or groups otherwise in conflict. (p. 531)

38. **GRIT** (Graduated and Reciprocated Initiatives in Tension-Reduction) is a strategy of conflict resolution based on the defusing effect that conciliatory gestures can have on parties in conflict. (p. 532)

*Cross-Check*

**ACROSS**
- 5. stereotype
- 6. GRIT
- 7. scapegoat
- 9. conformity
- 10. altruism
- 13. equity
- 14. passionate
- 15. gender role
- 16. role
- 17. conflict
- 18. norms
- 19. attitudes

**DOWN**
- 1. culture
- 2. bystander effect
- 3. informational
- 4. cognitive dissonance
- 8. foot-in-the-door
- 9. companionate
- 11. fundamental
- 12. attribution

## FOCUS ON VOCABULARY AND LANGUAGE

### Social Thinking

*Page 492:* Happily married couples attribute *their spouse's tart-tongued remark* to a temporary situation ("She must have had a bad day at work"). How we make attributions can have serious consequences. Couples who think that their partner's sarcastic or unkind comment (*tart-tongued remark*) was due to a cruel personality (*mean disposition*) are more likely to be dissatisfied with their marriages than couples who believe that the same remark was simply a result of some situational influence, such as a stressful day at work.

*Page 492:* . . . *freeloaders*. This refers to people who voluntarily live off other people. Those who believe that people are poor and/or unemployed because of personal dispositions tend to underestimate the influence of situational variables. Thus, they might call someone on welfare a *freeloader* rather than simply a victim of circumstances.

*Page 493:* Moreover, studies of people's attitudes and behaviors regarding cheating, religion, and racial minorities revealed that *folks often talk and act a different game*. Social psychologists were surprised to find that what people think, feel, or believe (*attitudes*) is not always reflected in their behaviors (*folks often talk and act a different game*). This apparent inconsistency led to further studies which showed that attitudes correlate with behavior (a) when the influence of others is negligible, (b) when the behavior and the attitude are specific rather than general, and (c) when we are made conscious or mindful of our beliefs and feelings.

*Page 494:* . . . *"brainwashed"* . . . This refers to a person's beliefs, values, and attitudes being changed by relentless indoctrination and mental torture. One component of this mind-changing process (*"thought-control"*) involves use of the **foot-in-the-door phenomenon**, whereby a person is first coerced into agreeing to a small request, then to complying with much greater requests. People's attitudes often change to be consistent with their new behavior.

*Page 494:* This *chicken-and-egg spiral* of actions feeding attitudes feeding actions enables behavior to escalate. Whether used for good or for bad, the foot-in-the-door strategy involves starting with small requests (*trifling demands*), then slowly increasing the level of demand. The new behavior will be followed by a change in attitude which, in turn, will make the behavior more likely and that will then lead to more change in belief, etc. (*the chicken-and-egg spiral*).

*Page 496:* The attitudes-follow-behavior principle has some *heartening implications*. When our attitudes and behaviors are inconsistent, we feel a certain amount of tension (**cognitive dissonance**), which makes us want to do something to reduce this uncomfortable state. Thus, if we are feeling depressed (*down in the dumps*) and we behave in a more outgoing manner, talk in a more positive way, and *act* as though we are happy, we may, in fact, start feeling much better. As Myers notes, the feelings-follow-actions notion has positive ramifications (*heartening implications*).

### Social Influence

*Page 497:* Laughter, even *canned laughter*, can be *infectious*. Many TV and radio comedy shows do not have live audiences. Instead, they play recorded soundtracks of people laughing (*canned laughter*) at the appropriate moments; the laughter can be very contagious (*infectious*) for listeners, making them laugh heartily, too. This is a form of suggestibility.

*Page 498:* When influence supports what we approve, we applaud those who are *"open-minded"* and *"sensitive"* enough to be *"responsive."* We can be influenced by others because they provide useful knowledge (**informational influence**) or because we want them to view us favorably and not ignore us (**normative influence**). Conformity that is consistent with what we believe is true will be seen in a positive light (the conformists are *"open-minded,"* etc.), and conformity that is not will be viewed negatively (*"submissive conformity"*).

*Page 499:* You and another person *draw slips from a hat* to see who will be the "teacher" (which your slip says) and who will be the "learner." In Milgram's famous obedience experiments participants were deceived into believing they were randomly assigned to one of two conditions ("teacher" or "learner") by picking a piece of paper out of a container (*drawing slips from a hat*). All the subjects were actually "teachers" and were asked to "shock" the "learners" whenever they made mistakes on a memory task. A majority of the participants complied with the experimenter's request.

*Page 499:* You *draw back* when you hear these pleas, but the experimenter *prods* you: "Please continue—the experiment requires that you continue." If you were a particpant ("teacher") in Milgram's experiment, you would be pressured (*prodded*) by the research assistant to carry on with the experiment even though you may show great reluctance (*you draw back*) after hearing the "learner's" cries of distress at being "shocked."

*Page 501:* With *kindness and obedience on a collision course*, obedience usually won. Milgram's research on obedience showed that social factors that foster conformity are powerful enough to make almost anyone behave in ways inconsistent with our beliefs. When subjects were in a conflict over (*torn between*) whether to refuse to harm an individual or to follow orders (*kindness and obedience were on a collision course*), they usually did what they were asked to do.

*Page 501:* Milgram entrapped his subjects not by asking them first to *zap* "learners" with enough electricity to make their hair stand on end. Milgram used the foot-in-the-door tactic to get his subjects to comply with his requests to shock (*zap*) the "learners" with larger and larger voltages. He started with a small amount (*a little tickle*) of electricity; after obtaining compliance (*obedience*), he asked them to increase the level, and so on. Subjects tended to rationalize their behavior; for some, their attitudes became consistent with their behavior over the course of the experiment.

*Page 501:* Contrary to our images of *devilish villains*, evil doesn't require *monstrous characters*; it's enough to have ordinary people corrupted by an evil situation. We tend to think that pain and suffering (*evil*) are always caused by inhumane and cruel people (*devilish villains* or *monstrous characters*), but the research in social psychology shows that almost anyone can be led to behave badly given the right (or wrong) circumstances.

*Page 503:* In a team *tug-of-war*, for example, do you suppose the effort that a person puts forth would be more than, less than, or the same as the effort he or she would exert in a *one-on-one tug-of-war*? In a game in which opponents pull on each end of a rope (*tug-of-war*), when two individuals compete (*one-on-one*), they work much harder (*exert more effort*) than if they were members of a group competing on the same task. This lowering of individual effort when part of a team is called **social loafing**. (Note: The term *to loaf* means *to work less hard, to slack off, to take it easy,* or *to free ride*.)

*Page 505:* Wrongly assuming that support was unanimous, he launched the *Challenger* on its *one-way flight to annihilation*. Irving Janis investigated the variables that led to bad decisions and their consequent fiascoes and tragedies. The space shuttle *Challenger* disaster was the result of **groupthink**: People were overly optimistic of success, there was a desire by some to be nonobstructionist team players, group pressure to go ahead was very strong, and important information was withheld from the ultimate decision maker. Believing that everyone was in agreement, the NASA executive gave permission to dispatch the shuttle, which exploded within minutes (*one-way flight to annihilation*).

*Page 506:* They have repeatedly found that a minority that unswervingly holds to its position is far more successful in swaying the majority than is a minority that *waffles*. Committed individuals and small groups of individuals can convince (*sway*) the majority to their point of view if they adhere strictly to their agenda and do not appear to be uncertain or unsure (*to waffle*).

*Page 507:* However, *norms* also *grease the social machinery*. Every society has its own rules and regulations about accepted and appropriate modes of conduct (*social norms*), and these standards differ from culture to culture. Although these proscriptions may sometimes seem unjust or senseless, because they are known and practiced by most people, they serve the function of helping society run smoothly (*they grease the social machinery*).

*Page 507:* When cultures collide, their differing norms often *bemuse or befuddle*. When people from different cultures meet, the interaction can be funny (*bemusing*) or confusing (*befuddling*). **Personal space** (the distance we like to have between us and others) varies; someone who prefers more space may end up constantly retreating (*backpedaling*) from someone who needs to be close in order to have a comfortable conversation.

*Page 507:* Traditionally, *men initiate dates*, drive the car, and *pick up the check*; women cook the meals, buy and care for the children's clothes, and do the shopping. **Gender roles** are a culture's expectations for male and female behaviors, but these behaviors change over time and across cultures. Historically, males ask females to go out (*initiate dates*) and pay for the meal and entertainment (*pick up the check*), and women look after the domestic concerns.

*Page 508:* *In the flick of an apron,* the number of U.S. college women hoping to be *full-time homemakers plunged* during the late 1960s and early 1970s. Over time, gender roles have changed. Within a relatively brief period of time (*in the flick of an apron*), the number of women engaged in the traditional female role (*full-time homemaker*) declined rapidly (*plunged*) and the number of women in the work force increased substantially, especially in traditional male fields such as medicine, law, and engineering.

### Social Relations

*Pages 509–510:* In one study, most whites perceived a white man shoving a black as *"horsing around."* Prejudices involve beliefs, emotions, and tendencies to behave in certain ways. They are a form of pre-judgment that influences (*colors*) how we interpret what we see. Thus, in an experiment in which white people saw a white man pushing a black person, most interpreted the behavior as playful activity (*horsing around*); when the roles were reversed, the behavior was more likely to be described as aggressive or hostile (*violent*).

*Page 511:* Even an arbitrary us-them distinction—created by grouping people *with the toss of a coin*—leads people to show favoritism to their own group when dividing rewards (Tajfel, 1982; Wilder, 1981). One of the factors affecting prejudice is our propensity to define ourselves through identification with a particular group (**ingroup bias**); this in turn creates an outgroup consisting of those who do not belong to our group. Even if the groups are artificially created by random assignment (*with the toss of a coin*), we will tend to see our own group as more deserving, superior, and so on.

*Page 512:* In addition to providing a *handy* emotional outlet for anger, despised outgroups can also *boost ingroup members' self-esteem*. When we have a problem, we frequently look for someone, who is usually innocent, to blame (*scapegoating*); these target people or groups are then a convenient (*handy*) source for venting our anger and frustration. In addition, having someone else to disparage can increase our own status and sense of self-worth (*boost our self-esteem*).

*Page 514:* A raging bull will become a gentle *Ferdinand* when castration reduces its testosterone level. Biological explanations of aggression examine the influences of genes, clusters of neurons in the brain, and biochemical agents in the blood, such as hormones and alcohol. Levels of the male sex hormone can be reduced by castration; thus, an aggressive, ferocious bull can be reduced to a playful, friendly animal similar to the fictional character (*Ferdinand*) of children's stories.

*Page 517:* In Beijing, for example, the percentage of homes with television *skyrocketed* from 32 percent in 1980 to 95 percent by the end of the decade (Lull, 1988). Researchers have studied the correlation between watching violent acts on TV and crime and aggression in society and have concluded that there is a positive correlation. Thus, in countries where TV-watching has risen dramatically (*skyrocketed*) in the past 15 years, there is likely to be an increase in violence.

*Pages 518–519:* In less graphic form, the same unrealistic script—she resists, he persists, *she melts*—is commonplace in TV scenes and in romance novels. A common theme in certain types of films and books is the idea that if the main male character overcomes the lovely female's reluctance to be romantically or sexually involved, then she will be totally devoted to him (*she melts*). This depiction of male-female relationships, in both pornographic and non-pornographic media, has little to do with reality and may, in fact, promote sexual aggression.

*Page 519:* Contrary to much popular opinion, viewing such *depictions* does not provide *an outlet* for *bottled-up impulses*. Laboratory studies have demonstrated that watching media that show sexual violence against women does not decrease the acceptance and performance of aggression against females. In contrast to what many believe, such portrayals (*depictions*) do not allow vicarious expression (*an outlet*) for pent-up hostile urges (*bottled-up impulses*) and may have the opposite effect.

*Page 521:* Psychologists have noted a curious tendency for those in conflict to form *diabolical images* of each other. We have a propensity to perceive our enemies in a very distorted manner, often categorizing them as evil, cruel, untrustworthy, and devilish (*diabolical*). They, of course, view us in the same way; the biased pictures we form of each other are called **mirror-image perceptions**.

*Page 523:* Within certain limits . . . *familiarity breeds fondness.* Under some circumstances, the more often we see (*become familiar with*) someone, the more likely it is that we will grow to like (*become fond of*) that person. This is called the **mere exposure effect.**

*Page 524:* . . . *"beauty is only skin deep"* . . . This saying suggests that physical attractiveness (*beauty*) is only a superficial quality (*skin deep*). Research, however, has shown that how we look influences social interactions, how frequently we date, our popularity, how we are perceived by others, etc.

*Page 525:* Until you got to know him, *E.T. was as ugly as Darth Vader.* E.T. was a small, unattractive, extraterrestrial creature (and just as repulsive looking as Darth Vader, another movie character), but as we came to know and like his cute little personality, he no longer appeared so ugly. Studies have shown that with increased exposure to someone, we come to like them and are less likely to notice their physical blemishes (*imperfections*) and more likely to become aware of their endearing characteristics.

*Page 526:* In real life, *opposites retract.* The old saying *"opposites attract"* has not been supported by research in social psychology. In fact, we tend to dislike those we do not perceive as similar to ourselves (*opposites retract*). Rather than fostering *contempt*, Myers humorously suggests that similarity breeds *content.*

*Page 527:* To be *revved up* and to associate some of that arousal with a desirable person is to feel the pull of passion. Research has shown that one component of romantic or passionate love is physiological arousal; a second aspect is some cognitive interpretation and labeling of that feeling. So, if a person is in an aroused state (*revved up*) and this is easily linked to the presence of an attractive person, then attributions of romantic love may be made. As Myers cheerfully notes, rather than *absence, adrenaline makes the heart grow fonder* (intensifies love).

*Page 528:* At each step, the presence of other *bystanders turns people away from the path that leads to helping.* Darley and Latané displayed their findings in a flow diagram (see Figure 14.12, p. 529). At each decision point (i.e., noticing the event, interpreting it as an emergency, and assuming responsibility), the presence of others who appear to have observed the event (*bystanders*) causes people to be less likely to give assistance to someone in need (*they are turned away from the path that leads to helping*).

*Page 528:* . . . *blasé* . . . This means to be indifferent or uncaring. We arrive at the decision (especially in ambiguous situations) to help or not to help by watching the reactions of others. If they appear to be unconcerned (*blasé*), we may conclude that there is no emergency and thus may not intervene or help. This **bystander effect** means that the presence of others decreases the probability that any particular observer will provide help.

*Page 530:* Before long, each group became intensely proud of itself and hostile to the other group's *"sneaky," "smart-alecky stinkers."* In Sherif's experiment, competitive conditions were created in order to foster the formation of two antagonistic groups. Each group soon saw itself as superior to the other group's "dishonest and sly" (*sneaky*) "rotten know-it-alls" (*smart-alecky stinkers*). Sherif then used shared objectives and common problems (**superordinate goals**) to create reconciliation and cooperation.

*Page 532:* Conciliations allow both parties to begin edging *down the tension ladder to a safer rung* where communication and mutual understanding can begin. Social psychologist Charles Osgood has developed a tactic called **GRIT** (Graduated and Reciprocated Initiatives in Tension-Reduction) for increasing cooperation and trust between parties in conflict. When one side makes a small gesture or offer of goodwill (*a conciliatory act*), the other side has an opportunity to reciprocate and thus move the conflict toward some resolution (*down the tension ladder to a safer rung*) and start the process of mutual respect and understanding.

# Statistical Reasoning

## Chapter Overview

A basic understanding of statistical reasoning has become a necessity in everyday life. Statistics are tools that help the psychologist and layperson to interpret the vast quantities of information they are confronted with on a daily basis. Appendix A discusses how statistics are used to describe data and to generalize from instances.

In studying this chapter you must concentrate on learning a number of procedures and understanding some underlying principles in the science of statistics. The graphic and computational procedures in the section called "Describing Data" include how data are distributed in a sample; measures of central tendency such as the mean, median, and mode; variation measures such as the range and standard deviation; and correlation, or the degree to which two variables are related. Most of the conceptual material is then covered in the section entitled "Statistical Inference." You should be able to discuss three important principles concerning populations and samples, as well as the concept of significance in testing differences. The ultimate goal is to make yourself a better consumer of statistical research by improving your critical thinking skills.

NOTE: Answer guidelines for all questions in the Appendix begin on page 425.

## Guided Study

The text chapter should be studied one section at a time. Before you read, preview each section by skimming it, noting headings and boldface items. Then read the appropriate section objectives from the following outline. Keep these objectives in mind and, as you read the chapter section, search for the information that will enable you to meet each objective. Once you have finished a section, write out answers for its objectives.

### Describing Data (pp. 536–542)

> David Myers at times uses idioms that are unfamiliar to some readers. If you do not know the meaning of any of the following words, phrases, or expressions in the context in which they appear in the text, refer to page 431 for an explanation: *top-of-the head estimates often misread reality and mislead the public; swayed; national income cake; gauges; gut-level; naked eye.*

1. Explain how tables, bar graphs, and percentile ranks are used to describe data.

2. Define the three measures of central tendency and explain how they describe data differently.

3. Describe measures of variation and the normal curve.

4. Describe the correlation coefficient and explain its importance in assessing relationships between variables.

5. Identify factors that may contribute to illusory correlation and an illusion of control.

*Statistical Inference* (pp. 542–544)

> If you do not know the meaning of the following expression in the context in which it appears in the text, refer to page 431 for an explanation: *Data are "noisy."*

6. Discuss three important principles in making generalizations about populations on the basis of samples.

7. Describe how psychologists make statistical inferences about differences between groups.

## Chapter Review

When you have finished reading the chapter, work through the material that follows to review it. Complete the sentences and answer the questions. As you proceed, evaluate your performance for each section by consulting the answers on page 426. Do not continue with the next section until you understand each answer. If you need to, review or reread the appropriate section in the textbook before continuing.

*Describing Data* (pp. 536–542)

1. The percentage of scores in a distribution that fall below an individual score is that score's

_____ _____ .

2. The three measures of central tendency are the

_____ , the _____ ,

and the _____ .

3. The most frequently occurring score in a distribution is called the _____ .

4. The mean is computed as the

_____ of all the scores divided

by the _____ of scores.

5. The median is the score at the _____

percentile.

6. When a distribution is lopsided, or

_____ , the _____

(mean/median/mode) can be biased by a few

extreme scores.

7. Averages derived from scores with

_____ (high/low) variability

are more reliable than those with

_____ (high/low) variability.

8. The measures of variation include the

_____ and the

_____ .

9. The range is computed as the _____ .

10. The range provides a(n) _____ (crude/accurate) estimate of variation because it _____ (is/is not) influenced by extreme scores.

11. The standard deviation is a _____ (more accurate/less accurate) measure of variation than the range. Unlike the range, the standard deviation _____ (takes/does not take) into consideration information from each score in the distribution.

12. List the four steps in computing the standard deviation.

    a. _____

    b. _____

    c. _____

    d. _____

13. The bell-shaped distribution that often describes large amounts of data is called the _____ .

14. In this distribution, approximately _____ percent of the individual scores fall within 1 standard deviation on either side of the mean. Within 2 standard deviations on either side of the mean fall _____ percent of the individual scores.

Calculate what a score of 116 on the normally distributed Wechsler IQ test would mean with regard to percentile rank. (Recall that the mean is 100; the standard deviation is ±15 points. Hint: You might find it helpful to draw the normal curve first.)

15. A graph consisting of points that depict the relationship between two sets of scores is called a _____ .

16. A measure of the direction and extent of relationship between two sets of scores is called the _____ . Numerically, this measure can range from _____ to _____ .

17. When there is no relationship at all between two sets of scores, the correlation coefficient is _____ . The strongest possible correlation between two sets of scores is either _____ or _____ . When the correlation between two sets of scores is negative, as one increases, the other _____ .

Cite an example of a positive correlation and a negative correlation. Your examples can be drawn from previous chapters of the text or can be based on observations from daily life.
An example of positive correlation is

An example of negative correlation is

18. The correlation coefficient _____ (gives/does not give) information about cause-and-effect relationships.

19. A correlation that is perceived but doesn't really exist is called an _____ .

20. When we believe that a relationship exists between two things, we are most likely to recall instances that _____ (confirm/disconfirm) our belief.

21. This type of correlation feeds the illusion of _____ —that we can control events that actually are due to _____ . It is also fed by a statistical phenomenon called _____ , the idea that average results are more typical than extreme results.

*Statistical Inference* (pp. 542–544)

22. Small samples provide a _____ (more/less) reliable basis for generalizing than large samples.

23. Averages based on a large number of cases are _____ (more/less) reliable than those based on a few cases.

24. Averages are more reliable when they are based on scores with _____ (high/low) variability.

25. Tests of statistical _____ are used to estimate whether observed differences are real, that is, to make sure they are not simply the result of _____ variation. The differences are probably real if the sample averages are _____ and the difference between them is _____.

# Progress Test 1

## Multiple-Choice Questions

Circle your answers to the following questions and check them with the answers on page 427. If your answer is incorrect, read the explanation for why it is incorrect and then consult the appropriate pages of the text (in parentheses following the correct answer). Use the page margins if you need extra space for your computations.

1. Percentile rank is defined as:
   a. the difference between the highest and lowest scores in a distribution.
   b. a statistical statement of the likelihood that an obtained result occurred by chance.
   c. the square root of the average of the squared deviations in a distribution.
   d. the percentage of the scores in a distribution that a given score exceeds.

2. What is the mean of the following distribution of scores: 2, 3, 7, 6, 1, 4, 9, 5, 8, 2?
   a. 5            c. 4.7
   b. 4            d. 3.7

3. What is the median of the following distribution of scores: 1, 3, 7, 7, 2, 8, 4?
   a. 1            c. 3
   b. 2            d. 4

4. What is the mode of the following distribution: 8, 2, 1, 1, 3, 7, 6, 2, 0, 2?
   a. 1            c. 3
   b. 2            d. 7

5. Compute the range of the following distribution: 9, 14, 2, 8, 1, 6, 8, 9, 1, 3.
   a. 10           c. 8
   b. 9            d. 13

6. Squaring the difference between each score in a distribution and the mean is the first step in computing the:
   a. median.      c. range.
   b. mode.        d. standard deviation.

7. If two sets of scores are negatively correlated, it means that:
   a. as one set of scores increases, the other decreases.
   b. as one set of scores increases, the other increases.
   c. there is only a weak relationship between the sets of scores.
   d. there is no relationship at all between the sets of scores.

8. Regression toward the mean is the:
   a. tendency for unusual scores to fall back toward a distribution's average.
   b. basis for all tests of statistical significance.
   c. reason the range is a more accurate measure of variation than the standard deviation.
   d. reason the standard deviation is a more accurate measure of variation than the range.

9. In a normal distribution, what percentage of scores fall between +2 and –2 standard deviations of the mean?
   a. 50 percent      c. 95 percent
   b. 68 percent      d. 99.7 percent

10. Which of the following statistics must fall on or between –1.00 and +1.00?
    a. the mean
    b. the standard deviation
    c. the correlation coefficient
    d. none of the above

11. In generalizing from a sample to the population, it is important that:
    a. the sample is representative of the population.
    b. the sample is large.
    c. the scores in the sample have low variability.
    d. all of the above are observed.

12. When a difference between two groups is "statistically significant," this means that:
    a. the difference is statistically real but of little practical significance.
    b. the difference is probably the result of sampling variation.
    c. the difference is not likely to be due to chance variation.
    d. all of the above are true.

13. A lopsided set of scores that includes a number of extreme or unusual values is said to be:
    a. symmetrical.
    b. normal.
    c. skewed.
    d. dispersed.

14. Which of the following is *not* a measure of central tendency?
    a. mean
    b. range
    c. median
    d. mode

15. Which of the following is the measure of central tendency that would be most affected by a few extreme scores?
    a. mean
    b. range
    c. median
    d. mode

16. The symmetrical, bell-shaped distribution in which most scores are near the mean and fewer near the extremes forms a:
    a. skewed curve.
    b. bimodal curve.
    c. normal curve.
    d. bar graph.

17. A homogeneous sample with little variation in scores will have a(n) _____ standard deviation.
    a. small
    b. moderate
    c. large
    d. unknown (It is impossible to determine.)

18. If there is no relationship between two sets of scores, the coefficient of correlation equals:
    a. 0.00
    b. –1.00
    c. +1.00
    d. 0.50

19. Illusory correlation refers to:
    a. the perception that two negatively correlated variables are positively correlated.
    b. the perception of a relationship between two unrelated variables.
    c. an insignificant correlation coefficient.
    d. a correlation coefficient that equals –1.00.

20. Gamblers who blow on their dice "for luck" are victims of:
    a. regression toward the mean.
    b. the illusion of control.
    c. hindsight bias.
    d. the fundamental attribution error.

## Matching Items

Match each term with the appropriate definition or description.

*Terms*

_____ 1. bar graph
_____ 2. median
_____ 3. percentile rank
_____ 4. regression toward the mean
_____ 5. mode
_____ 6. range
_____ 7. standard deviation
_____ 8. scatterplot
_____ 9. mean
_____ 10. measures of central tendency
_____ 11. measures of variation

*Definitions or Descriptions*

a. the mean, median, and mode
b. the difference between the highest and lowest scores
c. the arithmetic average of a distribution
d. the range and standard deviation
e. the percentage of scores in a distribution that fall below a given score
f. the most frequently occurring score
g. the tendency for extremes of unusual scores to fall back toward the average
h. a graph depicting a table of data
i. the middle score in a distribution
j. a graphed cluster of dots depicting the values of two variables
k. the square root of the average squared deviation of scores from the mean

# Progress Test 2

Progress Test 2 should be completed during a final chapter review. Answer the following questions after you thoroughly understand the correct answers for the Chapter Review and Progress Test 1.

### Multiple-Choice Questions

1. What is the mode of the following distribution of scores: 2, 2, 4, 4, 4, 14?
   a. 2
   b. 4
   c. 5
   d. 6

2. What is the mean of the following distribution of scores: 2, 5, 8, 10, 11, 4, 6, 9, 1, 4?
   a. 2
   b. 10
   c. 6
   d. 15

3. What is the median of the following distribution: 10, 7, 5, 11, 8, 6, 9?
   a. 6
   b. 7
   c. 8
   d. 9

4. The highest percentile rank in a distribution:
   a. depends on the size of the distribution.
   b. will equal 100.
   c. will equal 99.
   d. will equal 50, since this is the midpoint.

5. Which statistic is the average amount by which the scores in a distribution vary from the average?
   a. standard deviation
   b. range
   c. median
   d. mode

6. The most frequently occurring score in a distribution is the:
   a. mean.
   b. median.
   c. mode.
   d. range.

7. In the following distribution, the mean is _____ the mode and _____ the median: 4, 6, 1, 4, 5.
   a. less than; less than
   b. less than; greater than
   c. equal to; equal to
   d. greater than; equal to

8. Which of the following is the measure of variation that is most affected by extreme scores?
   a. mean
   b. standard deviation
   c. mode
   d. range

9. What is the standard deviation of the following distribution: 3, 1, 4, 10, 12?
   a. 10
   b. 15
   c. $\sqrt{18}$
   d. 4

10. Which of the following sets of scores would likely be most representative of the population from which it was drawn?
    a. a sample with a relatively large standard deviation
    b. a sample with a relatively small standard deviation
    c. a sample with a relatively large range
    d. a sample with a relatively small range

11. The *value* of the correlation coefficient indicates the _____ of relationship between two variables, and the *sign* (positive or negative) indicates the _____ of the relationship.
    a. direction; strength
    b. strength; direction
    c. direction; reliability
    d. reliability; strength

12. If a difference between two samples is *not* statistically significant, which of the following can be concluded?
    a. The difference is probably not a true one.
    b. The difference is probably not reliable.
    c. The difference could be due to sampling variation.
    d. All of the above are true.

13. The first step in constructing a bar graph is to create a:
    a. standard deviation.
    b. data table.
    c. correlation coefficient.
    d. range.

14. Why is the median at times a better measure of central tendency than the mean?
    a. It is more sensitive to extreme scores.
    b. It is less sensitive to extreme scores.
    c. It is based on more of the scores in the distribution than the mean.
    d. Both a. and c. explain why.

15. Standard deviation is to mode as _____ is to _____ .
    a. mean; median
    b. variation; central tendency
    c. median; mean
    d. central tendency; variation

16. In a normal distribution, what percentage of scores fall between –1 and +1 standard deviation units of the mean?
    a. 50 percent
    b. 68 percent
    c. 95 percent
    d. 99.7 percent

17. The precision with which sample statistics reflect population parameters is greater when the sample is:
    a. large.
    b. characterized by high variability.
    c. small in number but consists of vivid cases.
    d. statistically significant.

18. The following scatterplot depicts a correlation coefficient that would be close to:

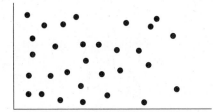

    a. +1.0.                        c. 0.00.
    b. −1.0.                        d. 0.50.

19. Which of the following correlation coefficients indicates the strongest relationship between two variables?
    a. −.73                         c. 0.00
    b. +.66                         d. −.50

20. A correlation coefficient:
    a. indicates the direction of relationship between two variables.
    b. indicates the strength of relationship between two variables.
    c. does *not* indicate whether there is a cause-and-effect relationship between two variables.
    d. does all of the above.

### True-False Items

Indicate whether each statement is true or false by placing a *T* or *F* in the blank next to the item.

    1. A percentile rank of 60 means that most of the scores in the distribution fall above it.
    2. In almost all distributions, the mean, the median, and the mode will be the same.
    3. When a distribution has a few extreme scores, the range is more misleading than the standard deviation.
    4. If increases in the value of variable *x* are accompanied by decreases in the value of variable *y*, the two variables are negatively correlated.
    5. Over time, extreme results tend to fall back toward the average.

    6. If a sample has low variability, it cannot be representative of the population from which it was drawn.
    7. The mean is always the most precise measure of central tendency.
    8. Averages that have been derived from scores with low variability are more reliable than those derived from scores that are more variable.
    9. If a difference between two groups is due to sampling variation, it cannot be statistically significant.
    10. Small samples are less reliable than large samples for generalizing to the population.

## Thinking Critically About Appendix A

Answer these questions the day before an exam as a final check on your understanding of the chapter's terms and concepts.

### Multiple-Choice Questions

1. Jack's score on the psychology exam was the highest in the class. What is his percentile rank for this score?
    a. 99
    b. 100
    c. 95
    d. It cannot be determined from the information given.

2. Compute the standard deviation of the following distribution: 3, 5, 6, 2, 4.
    a. 1                            c. $\sqrt{10}$
    b. $\sqrt{2}$                   d. 4

3. Jane usually averages 175 in bowling. One night her three-game average is 215. What will probably happen to her bowling average over the next several weeks of bowling?
    a. It will return to about the level of her average.
    b. It will continue to increase.
    c. It will dip down to about 155.
    d. There is no way to predict her average scores.

4. If height and body weight are positively correlated, which of the following is true?
    a. There is a cause-and-effect relationship between height and weight.
    b. As height increases, weight decreases.
    c. Knowing a person's height, one can predict his or her weight.
    d. All of the above are true.

5. The football team's punter wants to determine how consistent his punting distances have been during the past season. He should compute the:

   a. mean.                    c. mode.
   b. median.                  d. standard deviation.

6. If about two-thirds of the cases in a research study fall within 1 standard deviation from the mean, and 95 percent within 2 standard deviations, researchers know that their data form a:

   a. skewed distribution.   c. normal curve.
   b. scatterplot.           d. bar graph.

7. Which of the following exemplifies regression toward the mean?

   a. In his second season of varsity basketball, Edward averaged 5 points more per game than in his first season.
   b. A gambler rolls 5 consecutive "sevens" using her favorite dice.
   c. After earning an unusually low score on the first exam in a class, a "B student" scores much higher on the second exam.
   d. A student who usually gets Bs earns grades of A, C, C, and A on four exams, thus maintaining a B average overall for the class.

8. Which score falls at the 50th percentile of a distribution?

   a. mean                    c. mode
   b. median                  d. standard deviation

9. If scores on an exam have a mean of 50, a standard deviation of 10, and are normally distributed, approximately 95 percent of those taking the exam would be expected to score between:

   a. 45 and 55.              c. 35 and 65.
   b. 40 and 60.              d. 30 and 70.

10. Joe believes that his basketball game is always best when he wears his old gray athletic socks. Joe is a victim of the phenomenon called:

    a. regression toward the mean.
    b. the availability heuristic.
    c. illusory correlation.
    d. the gambler's fallacy.

11. Five members of Terry's sorority reported the following individual earnings from their sale of raffle tickets: $3, $6, $8, $6, and $12. In this distribution, the mean is _____ the mode and _____ the median.

    a. equal to; equal to
    b. greater than; equal to
    c. greater than; greater than
    d. equal to; less than

12. If a distribution has a standard deviation of 0:

    a. it must be very small in size.
    b. it cannot be representative of the population from which it is drawn.
    c. all of the scores in the distribution are equal.
    d. nothing can be determined from the information given.

13. Esteban refuses to be persuaded by an advertiser's claim that people using their brand of gasoline average 50 miles per gallon. His decision probably is based on:

    a. the possibility that the average is the mean, which could be artificially inflated by a few extreme scores.
    b. the absence of information about the size of the sample studied.
    c. the absence of information about the variation in sample scores.
    d. all of the above.

14. Which of the following sets of scores best fits the definition of a normal distribution?

    a. 1, 2, 4, 8, 16, 32
    b. 2, 2, 2, 2, 2, 2
    c. 1, 2, 3, 4, 4, 4, 5, 6, 7
    d. 2, 8, 10, 18, 35

15. Which of the following distributions has the largest standard deviation?

    a. 1, 2, 3                 c. 6, 10, 14
    b. 4, 4, 4                 d. 30, 31, 32

16. Bob scored 43 out of 70 on his psychology exam. He was worried until he discovered that most of the class earned the same score. Bob's score was equal to the:

    a. mean.                   c. mode.
    b. median.                 d. range.

17. The four families on your block all have annual household incomes of $25,000. If a new family with an annual income of $75,000 moved in, which measure of central tendency would be most affected?

    a. mean                    c. mode
    b. median                  d. standard deviation

18. How would you describe a scatterplot depicting a perfect correlation between two sets of scores?

    a. All the points fall on a straight line.
    b. The points are spread randomly about the graph.
    c. All the points fall on a curved line.
    d. It is impossible to determine from the information given.

**19.** Dr. Numbers passed back an exam and announced to the class that the mean, the median, and the mode of the scores were equal. This means that:

**a.** the scores formed a normal distribution.

**b.** the distribution had a large standard deviation.

**c.** the students did very well on the exam.

**d.** all of the above are true.

**20.** Dr. Salazar recently completed an experiment in which she compared reasoning ability in a sample of females and a sample of males. The means of the female and male samples equaled 21 and 19, respectively, on a 25-point scale. A statistical test revealed that her results were not statistically significant. What can Dr. Salazar conclude?

**a.** Females have superior reasoning ability.

**b.** The difference in the means of the two samples is probably due to chance variation.

**c.** The difference in the means of the two samples is reliable.

**d.** None of the above is true.

### Essay Question

Discuss several ways in which statistical reasoning can improve your own everyday thinking. (Use the space below to list the points you want to make and organize them. Then write the essay on a separate sheet of paper.)

## Key Terms

### Writing Definitions

Using your own words, on a separate piece of paper write a brief definition or explanation of each of the following terms.

1. percentile rank

2. mode

3. mean

4. median

5. range

6. standard deviation

7. normal curve

8. scatterplot

9. correlation coefficient

10. regression toward the mean

11. statistical significance

## ANSWERS

## Guided Study

The following guidelines provide the main points that your answers should have touched upon.

1. Constructing a table is the first step in organizing and describing a data set. Tables provide a clear picture of how scores are distributed according to the variables being measured. A bar graph, depicting the data in a table, makes the distribution even easier to see and interpret. To help interpret any single score in a distribution, a researcher can compute its percentile rank, which is simply the percentage of scores that fall below it in the distribution.

2. The mode is the most frequently occurring score in a distribution. The mean, or arithmetic average, is the sum of the scores divided by the number of scores. Although the mean is the most commonly reported measure of central tendency, it is extremely sensitive to unusual scores and therefore is potentially misleading as a representation of the average of a distribution that is skewed. The median is the score that falls at the 50th percentile.

3. The simplest measure of variation is the range, or the difference between the lowest and highest scores in a distribution. As a measure of variation, the range is rather crude because it is based

on only the two extreme scores in a distribution. A better gauge of variation is the standard deviation, which is computed as the square root of the average squared deviation of the scores from the mean of the distribution. A symmetrical, bell-shaped distribution forms a normal curve in which the three measures of central tendency are equal, most cases fall near the mean, and fewer scores fall near either extreme. Furthermore, in a normal distribution roughly 68 percent of the cases fall within 1 standard deviation on either side of the mean, and 95 percent of the cases fall within 2 standard deviations.

4. The correlation coefficient, which can range from +1.00 through 0.00 to –1.00, is a statistical measure of the extent to which two factors vary together and thus how well either predicts the other. It is represented graphically on a scatterplot. A positive correlation means that one set of scores increases in direct proportion to the other. A negative correlation means that one set of scores goes up as the other goes down. The strength of a relationship is indicated by the value of the correlation coefficient. A strong correlation is one that has a coefficient near +1.00 or –1.00. A correlation of 0.00 means that there is no predictive relationship between the sets of scores. While the correlation coefficient reveals whether changes in one variable can be predicted from changes in another variable, it does *not* indicate a cause-and-effect relationship between two variables.

5. Illusory correlation is a perceived correlation that does not actually exist. Believing there is a relationship between two things may make one more likely to notice and recall instances that confirm this belief and contribute to this misperception. Furthermore, because people are sensitive to unusual events, they are likely to notice the occurrence of two such events in close proximity and incorrectly perceive the existence of a correlation between them. Illusory correlations contribute to the illusion that chance events are subject to personal control. This illusion is also fostered by the tendency for unusual events to be followed by more ordinary happenings. Failing to recognize this statistical principle (regression toward the mean) can mislead people into believing that they can control the events in question.

6. Although it is tempting to overgeneralize from highly select samples, the most reliable inferences about a population are based on a representative sample. A second important principle is that averages derived from samples with low variability are more reliable than those based on samples with high variability. A third is that averages based on more cases are more reliable than averages based on only a few cases. Generalizing to the population from a small sample with high variability is therefore inadvisable and potentially misleading.

7. When psychologists compare two samples to determine if their difference is statistically significant, they want to know whether the difference is real and not due to chance variation between the samples. When sample averages are reliable, and the difference between the averages for two samples is large, researchers can say that the difference has statistical significance.

## Chapter Review

1. percentile rank
2. mean; median; mode
3. mode
4. sum; number
5. 50th
6. skewed; mean
7. low; high
8. range; standard deviation
9. difference between the lowest and highest scores in a distribution
10. crude; is
11. more accurate; takes
12. **a.** Calculate the deviation between each score and the mean.
    **b.** Square each deviation score.
    **c.** Determine the average of the squared deviation scores.
    **d.** Take the square root of this average.
13. normal curve
14. 68; 95

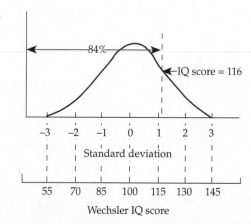

Since the mean equals 100 and the standard deviation is 15 points, a score of 116 is just over one standard deviation unit above the mean. Since 68 percent of the population's scores fall within one standard deviation on either side of the mean, 34 percent fall between 0 and +1 standard deviation unit. By definition, 50 percent of the scores fall below the mean. Therefore, a score at or above 115 is higher than that obtained by 84 percent of the population (50 percent + 34 percent = 84 percent).

15. scatterplot

16. correlation coefficient; +1.00; –1.00

17. 0.00; +1.00; –1.00; decreases

An example of a positive correlation is the relationship between air temperature and ice cream sales: As one increases so does the other.

An example of a negative correlation is the relationship between good health and the amount of stress a person is under: As stress increases, the odds of good health decrease.

18. does not give

19. illusory correlation

20. confirm

21. control; chance; regression toward the mean

22. less

23. more

24. low

25. significance; chance; reliable; large

## Progress Test 1

### Multiple-Choice Questions

1. **d.** is the answer. (p. 537)
   **a.** This is the range.
   **b.** This is a test of statistical significance.
   **c.** This is the standard deviation.

2. **c.** is the answer. The mean is the sum of scores divided by the number of scores. [(2 + 3 + 7 + 6 + 1 + 4 + 9 + 5 + 8 + 2)/10 = 4.7.] (p. 538)

3. **d.** is the answer. When the scores are put in order (1, 2, 3, 4, 7, 7, 8), 4 is at the 50th percentile, splitting the distribution in half. (p. 538)

4. **b.** is the answer. The mode is the most frequently occurring score. Since there are more "twos" than any other number in the distribution, 2 is the mode. (p. 538)

5. **d.** is the answer. The range is the gap between the highest and lowest scores in a distribution. (14 – 1 = 13.) (p. 539)

6. **d.** is the answer. (p. 539)

7. **a.** is the answer. (p. 540)
   **b.** This situation indicates that the two sets of scores are positively correlated.

**c.** Whether a correlation is positive or negative does not indicate the strength of the relationship, only its direction.
**d.** In negative correlations, there *is* a relationship; the correlation is negative because the relationship is an inverse one.

8. **a.** is the answer. (p. 541)
   **b.** Regression toward the mean has nothing to do with tests of statistical significance.
   **c.** In fact, just the opposite is true.
   **d.** This is true, but not because of regression toward the mean.

9. **c.** is the answer. (p. 539)
   **a.** 50 percent of the normal curve falls on either side of its mean.
   **b.** 68 percent of the scores fall between –1 and +1 standard deviation units.
   **d.** 99.7 percent fall between –3 and +3 standard deviations.

10. **c.** is the answer. (p. 540)

11. **d.** is the answer. (pp. 542–543)

12. **c.** is the answer. (p. 543)
    **a.** A statistically significant difference may or may not be of practical importance.
    **b.** This is often the case when a difference is *not* statistically significant.

13. **c.** is the answer. (p. 538)

14. **b.** is the answer. (p. 538)

15. **a.** is the answer. As an average, calculated by adding all scores and dividing by the number of scores, the mean could easily be affected by the inclusion of a few extreme scores. (p. 538)
    **b.** The range is not a measure of central tendency.
    **c. & d.** The median and mode give equal weight to all scores; each counts only once and its numerical value is unimportant.

16. **c.** is the answer. (p. 540)
    **a.** A skewed curve is formed from an asymmetrical distribution.
    **b.** A bimodal curve has two modes; a normal curve has only one.
    **d.** A bar graph depicts a distribution of scores.

17. **a.** is the answer. The standard deviation is the average deviation in a distribution; therefore, if variation (deviation) is small, the standard deviation will also be small. (p. 539)

18. **a.** is the answer. (p. 540)
    **b. & c.** These are "perfect" correlations of equal strength.
    **d.** This indicates a much stronger relationship between two sets of scores than does a coefficient of 0.00.

19. **b.** is the answer. (p. 541)

20. **b.** is the answer. (p. 541)

## Matching Items

1. h (p. 537)    5. f (p. 538)    9. c (p. 538)
2. i (p. 538)    6. b (p. 539)    10. a (p. 538)
3. e (p. 537)    7. k (p. 539)    11. d (p. 539)
4. g (p. 541)    8. j (p. 540)

## Progress Test 2

### Multiple-Choice Questions

1. **b.** is the answer. (p. 538)

2. **c.** is the answer. The mean is the sum of the scores divided by the number of scores. (60/10 = 6.) (p. 538)

3. **c.** is the answer. When the scores are put in order (5, 6, 7, 8, 9, 10, 11), 8 is at the 50th percentile, splitting the distribution in half. (p. 538)

4. **c.** is the answer. (p. 537)
   **a.** The highest score always has a percentile rank of 99, regardless of the size of the distribution.
   **b.** Since a score cannot exceed itself, the percentage of scores *below* the highest score cannot equal 100.
   **d.** The highest percentile rank exceeds *all* the others, not 50 percent of them.

5. **a.** is the answer. (p. 539)
   **b.** The range is the difference between the highest and lowest scores in a distribution.
   **c.** The median is the score that falls at the 50th percentile.
   **d.** The mode is the most frequently occurring score.

6. **c.** is the answer. (p. 538)
   **a.** The mean is the arithmetic average.
   **b.** The median is the score that splits the distribution in half.
   **d.** The range is the difference between the highest and lowest scores.

7. **c.** is the answer. The mean, median, and mode are equal to 4. (p. 538)

8. **d.** is the answer. Since the range is the difference between the highest and lowest scores, it is by definition affected by extreme scores. (p. 539)
   **a. & c.** The mean and mode are measures of central tendency, not of variation.
   **b.** The standard deviation is less affected than the range because, when it is calculated, the deviation of *every* score from the mean is computed.

9. **c.** is the answer, calculated as follows (p. 539)
   i. The mean = $(3 + 1 + 4 + 10 + 12)/5 = 6$.
   ii. The deviation scores are $3 - 6 = -3$; $1 - 6 = -5$; $4 - 6 = -2$; $10 - 6 = 4$; $12 - 6 = 6$.
   iii. The squared deviation scores are $-3^2 = 9$; $-5^2 = 25$; $-2^2 = 4$; $4^2 = 16$; $6^2 = 36$.

iv. The mean of the squared deviation scores is $(9 + 25 + 4 + 16 + 36)/5 = 18$.
v. The square root of this mean, and the standard deviation of the distribution, is $\sqrt{18}$.

10. **b.** is the answer. Averages derived from scores with low variability tend to be more reliable estimates of the populations from which they are drawn. Thus, a. and c. are incorrect. Because the standard deviation is a more accurate estimate of variability than the range, d. is incorrect. (p. 543)

11. **b.** is the answer. (pp. 540–541)

12. **d.** is the answer. A difference that is statistically significant is a true difference, rather than an apparent difference due to factors such as sampling variation, and it is reliable. (pp. 543–544)

13. **b.** is the answer. A bar graph is based on a data distribution. (p. 537)

14. **b.** is the answer. (p. 538)
   **a.** In fact, just the opposite is true.
   **c.** Both the mean and the median are based on all the scores in a distribution. The median is based on the number of scores, while the mean is based on the average of their sum.

15. **b.** is the answer. Just as the standard deviation is a measure of variation, so the mode is a measure of central tendency. (pp. 538–539)

16. **b.** is the answer. (p. 539)
   **a.** 50 percent of the scores in a normal distribution fall on one side of the mean.
   **c.** 95 percent fall between −2 and +2 standard deviations.
   **d.** 99.7 percent fall between −3 and +3 standard deviations.

17. **a.** is the answer. Figures based on larger samples are more reliable. (p. 543)
   **b. & c.** These sample characteristics would tend to lower precision.
   **d.** A test of significance is a determination of the likelihood that an obtained result is real.

18. **c.** is the answer. (p. 540)

19. **a.** is the answer. The closer the correlation coefficient is to either +1 or −1, the stronger the relationship between the variables. (p. 540)

20. **d.** is the answer. (p. 540)

### True-False Items

1. F (p. 537)    6. F (p. 543)
2. F (p. 538)    7. F (p. 538)
3. T (p. 539)    8. T (p. 543)
4. T (p. 540)    9. T (p. 543)
5. T (p. 541)    10. T (p. 543)

# Thinking Critically About Appendix A

## Multiple-Choice Questions

1. **a.** is the answer. The percentile rank of a score is the percentage of scores in a distribution that a given score exceeds. The highest score in the class exceeds 99 percent of the scores in the distribution—that is, all the scores except itself. (p. 537)

2. **b.** is the answer. The answer is calculated as follows (p. 539):
   i. The mean $= (3 + 5 + 6 + 2 + 4)/5 = 4$.
   ii. The deviation scores are $3 - 4 = -1$; $5 - 4 = 1$; $6 - 4 = 2$; $2 - 4 = -2$; $4 - 4 = 0$.
   iii. The squared deviation scores are $-1^2 = 1$; $1^2 = 1$; $2^2 = 4$; $-2^2 = 4$; $0^2 = 0$.
   iv. The mean of the squared deviation scores is $(1 + 1 + 4 + 4 + 0)/5 = 2$.
   v. The square root of this mean, and the standard deviation of the distribution, is $\sqrt{2}$.

3. **a.** is the answer. Although Jane's individual scores cannot be predicted, over time her scores will fall close to her average. This is the phenomenon of regression toward the mean. (p. 541)

4. **c.** is the answer. If height and weight are positively correlated, increased height is associated with increased weight. Thus, one can predict a person's weight from his or her height. (p. 540)
   **a.** Correlation does not imply causality.
   **b.** This situation depicts a negative correlation between height and weight.

5. **d.** is the answer. A small or large standard deviation indicates whether a distribution is homogeneous or variable. (p. 539)
   **a., b., & c.** These statistics would not give any information regarding the consistency of performance.

6. **c.** is the answer. (p. 540)
   **a.** In a skewed distribution, the scores are not evenly distributed.
   **b.** A scatterplot is a graph that depicts the nature and degree of relationship between two variables.
   **d.** A bar graph depicts a data distribution.

7. **c.** is the answer. Regression toward the mean is the phenomenon that average results are more typical than extreme results. Thus, after an unusual event (the low exam score in this example) things tend to return toward their average level (in this case, the higher score on the second exam). (p. 541)
   **a.** Edward's improved average indicates only that, perhaps as a result of an additional season's experience, he is a better player.
   **b.** Because the probability of rolling 5 consecutive

"sevens" is very low, the gambler's "luck" will probably prove on subsequent rolls to be atypical and things will return toward their average level. This answer is incorrect, however, because it states only that 5 consecutive "sevens" were rolled.
   **d.** In this example, although the average of the student's exam grades is her usual grade of B, they are all extreme grades and do not regress toward the mean.

8. **b.** is the answer. (p. 538)
   **a.** The mean is the arithmetic average of the scores in a distribution.
   **c.** The mode is the most frequently occurring score in a distribution.
   **d.** The standard deviation is the average deviation of scores from the mean.

9. **d.** is the answer. 95 percent of the scores in a normal distribution fall between 2 standard deviation units below the mean and 2 standard deviation units above the mean. In this example, the test score that corresponds to $-2$ standard deviation units is $50 - (2 \times 10) = 30$; the score that corresponds to $+2$ standard deviation units is $50 + (2 \times 10) = 70$. (p. 539)

10. **c.** is the answer. A correlation that is perceived but doesn't actually exist, as in the example, is known as an illusory correlation. (p. 541)
    **a.** Regression toward the mean is the tendency for extreme scores to fall back toward the average.
    **b.** The availability heuristic is the tendency of people to estimate the likelihood of something in terms of how readily it comes to mind.
    **d.** The gambler's fallacy is the false perception that the probability of a random event is determined by past events.

11. **c.** is the answer. In this case, the mean, or average (7), is greater than both the mode, or most frequently occurring score (6), and the median, or middle score (6). (p. 538)

12. **c.** is the answer. (p. 539)

13. **d.** is the answer. (pp. 542–543)

14. **c.** is the answer. This best approximates a normal distribution because most of the scores are near the mean, fewer scores are at the extremes, and the distribution is symmetrical. (p. 540)

15. **c.** is the answer. Even without actually computing its value, it is evident that the standard deviation of these three scores will be greater than that in a., b., or d., because the scores in this distribution are much more variable. (p. 539)

16. **c.** is the answer. (p. 538)
    **a.** The mean is computed as the sum of the scores divided by the number of scores.

**b.** The median is the midmost score in a distribution.

**d.** The range is the difference between the highest and lowest scores in a distribution.

17. **a.** is the answer. The mean is strongly influenced by extreme scores. In this example, the mean would change from $25,000 to (75,000 + 25,000 + 25,000 + 25,000 + 25,000)/5 = $35,000. (p. 538)

    **b. & c.** Both the median and the mode would remain $25,000, even with the addition of the fifth family's income.

    **d.** The standard deviation is a measure of variation, not central tendency.

18. **a.** is the answer. (p. 540)

    **b.** This will occur when the correlation coefficient is near 0.00.

    **c.** Correlations are linear, rather than curvilinear, relationships.

19. **a.** is the answer. (pp. 538, 540)

    **b. & c.** Neither of these can be determined from the information given.

20. **b.** is the answer. (p. 543)

    **a.** If the difference between the sample means is not significant, then the groups probably do not differ in the measured ability.

    **c.** When a result is not significant it means that the observed difference is unreliable.

## Essay Question

The use of tables, bar graphs, and percentile ranks is helpful in accurately organizing, describing, and interpreting events, especially when there is too much information to remember and one wishes to avoid conclusions based on general impressions. Computing an appropriate measure of central tendency provides an index of the overall average of a set of scores. Knowing that the mean is the most common measure of central tendency, but that it is very sensitive to unusually high or low scores, can help one avoid being misled by claims based on misleading averages. Being able to compute the range or standard deviation of a set of scores allows one to determine how homogeneous the scores in a distribution are and provides a basis for realistically generalizing from samples to populations. Understanding the correlation coefficient can help us to see the world more clearly by revealing the extent to which two things relate. Being aware that unusual results tend to return to more typical results (regression toward the mean) helps us to avoid the practical pitfalls associated with illusory correlation. Finally, understanding the basis for tests of statistical significance can make us more discerning consumers of research reported in the media.

## Key Terms

1. **Percentile rank** is the percentage of scores in a distribution that fall below a particular score. (p. 537)

   *Example*: A student whose **percentile rank** is 85 has outperformed 85 percent of all students.

2. The **mode** is the most frequently occurring score in a distribution; it is the simplest measure of central tendency to determine. (p. 538)

3. The **mean** is the arithmetic average, the measure of central tendency computed by adding together the scores in a distribution and dividing by the number of scores. (p. 538)

4. The **median**, another measure of central tendency, is the score that falls at the 50th percentile, cutting a distribution in half. (p. 538)

   *Example*: When the *mean* of a distribution is affected by a few extreme scores, the **median** is the more appropriate measure of central tendency.

5. The **range** is a measure of variation computed as the difference between the highest and lowest scores in a distribution. (p. 539)

6. The **standard deviation** is the average amount by which the scores in a distribution deviate from the mean. Because it is based on every score in the distribution, it is a more precise measure of variation than the range. (p. 539)

7. The **normal curve** is the symmetrical, bell-shaped curve that describes many types of data, with most scores centering around the mean and progressively fewer scores occurring toward the extremes. (p. 540)

8. A **scatterplot** is a depiction of the relationship between two sets of scores by means of a graphed cluster of dots. (p. 540)

9. The **correlation coefficient** is a statistical measure of how much two factors vary together, and thus how well either predicts the other. (p. 540)

   *Example*: When the **correlation coefficient** is positive, the two sets of scores increase together. When it is negative, increases in one set are accompanied by decreases in the other.

10. **Regression toward the mean** is the tendency for extreme scores to return back, or regress, toward the average. (p. 541)

11. **Statistical significance** means that an obtained result, such as the difference between the averages for two samples, very likely reflects a real difference rather than sampling variation or chance factors. Tests of statistical significance help researchers decide when they can justifiably generalize from an observed instance. (p. 543)

## FOCUS ON VOCABULARY AND LANGUAGE

*Page 536:* Unaided by statistics, *top-of-the head estimates often misread reality and mislead the public.* Without knowing actual data and numbers (statistics), people may guess at the figures (*top-of-the-head estimates*), which does not reflect the facts (*misreads reality*) and can deceive (*mislead*) the public. The figures generated in this manner are often easy to articulate, such as 10 percent or 50 percent (*big round numbers*) and, when repeated (*echoed*) by others, may eventually be believed to be true by most people (*they become public myths*).

### Describing Data

*Page 537:* Moreover, she knows that impressions are *swayed* by remembered information, often the vivid or extreme instances. Statistics are methods for helping us to summarize and interpret a large array of data or information. To avoid being influenced (*swayed*), we need to organize data in a statistical form such as a bar graph or **percentile ranking**.

*Page 538:* Because the bottom *half* of British income earners receive only a *quarter* of the *national income cake,* most British people, like most people everywhere, make less than the mean. Incomes are not normally distributed (they do not follow a bell-shaped curve when plotted as a data distribution), so a better measure of central tendency than the mean (arithmetic average) is either the median (the score in the middle) or the mode (the most frequently occurring score). In Myers's example, half the people account for 25 percent of all the money earned in the country (*national income cake*); in this uneven (*skewed*) distribution, therefore, most people earn below-average wages.

*Page 539:* It [**standard deviation**] better *gauges* whether scores are packed together or dispersed, because it uses information from each score. The most commonly used statistic for measuring (*gauging*) how much scores differ from one another (their variation) is the standard deviation (SD). Using this formula, each score is compared to the mean; the result is an index of how spread out (*dispersed*) the scores are. A relatively small SD indicates that most of the scores are close to the average; a relatively large SD indicates that they are much more variable.

*Page 539:* He does not trust his *gut-level* impression of how *consistent* his *punting* is. A football player kicks the ball (*punts*) various distances during a game. He does not rely on his intuitive (*gut-level*) feeling about how reliable (*consistent*) he is, so he calculates the standard deviation. Knowing that 68 percent of scores in a normal distribution fall within one SD of the mean and 95 percent within two SDs can help him determine how consistent he is.

*Page 541:* Statistics can help us see what the *naked eye* sometimes misses. When looking at an array of data consisting of different measures (e.g., height and temperament) for many subjects, it is very difficult to discern what, if any, relationships exist. Statistical tools, such as the correlation coefficient and the scatterplot, can help us see clearly what the unaided (*naked*) eye might not see. As Myers notes, we sometimes need statistical illumination to see what is in front of us.

### Statistical Inference

*Page 542:* Data are *"noisy."* Differences between groups may simply be due to random (*chance*) variations (*fluctuations*) in those particular samples. When data have a great deal of variability, they are said to be *"noisy,"* which may limit our ability to generalize them to the larger population. In order to determine if differences are reliable, we should be sure that (a) samples are random and representative, (b) scores in the sample are similar to each other (have low variability), and (c) a large number of subjects or observations are included. If these principles are followed, we can confidently make inferences about the differences between groups.